The International Series in

SECONDARY EDUCATION

Consulting Editor

JOHN E. SEARLES
Pennsylvania State University

The Junior High

and Middle School:

Issues and Practices

The Junior High and Middle School: Issues and Practices

ALVIN W. HOWARD

GEORGE C. STOUMBIS

The University of New Mexico

INTEXT EDUCATIONAL PUBLISHERS

Scranton Toronto London

ISBN 0-7002-2191-3

 Printed in the United States of America by The Haddon Craftsmen, Inc., Scranton, Pennsylvania. Library of Congress Catalog Card Number: 71-132902.

For Ruthie

Preface

In recent years the junior high school has increased markedly both in number and in student enrollment. There has also been a great deal of criticism, some merited, of junior high schools and their practices. Accompanying this scrutiny and examination have been suggestions for reorganization to different grade patterns; controversy concerning such problems as pupil conduct and dress, athletics, and activities; and experimentation and innovation in methods of instruction.

More is known now concerning the nature of adolescence and more is being done to implement an educational program designed specifically for the early adolescent in today's society. A reexamination of the educational and organizational requirements of a school for the middle years must take into account the controversies and problems, changing patterns of instruction, and the newer grade organizational patterns and curricula of the middle schools. Only by considering these factors in relation to the history and functions of the junior high school and the evolving curricular areas can one see the whole picture of the American junior high school.

ALVIN W. HOWARD
GEORGE C. STOUMBIS

Albuquerque, New Mexico
August, 1970

Contents

Illustrations and Graphs

part I

THE JUNIOR HIGH SCHOOL

The junior high school came into being as a result of several different factors and pressures, among which were concern by colleges about the increasingly older college freshmen; desire for more academics in grades 7 and 8; a feeling that these grades were repetitious and time-wasting; the high incidence of dropout in the elementary grades; and the need for some courses designed to provide prevocational training. These were reinforced by early work in studies of adolescence and a concern for developing an educational program specifically intended for the early adolescent age group.

Since the inception of the junior high school, changing social conditions, compulsory attendance, and child labor laws have altered its functions to such an extent that most of the original reasons no longer exist or are much different.

The worth of the junior high school has long been established, but there is still need for improvement in guidance practices, administration, and construction of facilities which will best implement the educational program for children of middle school years. Too often the junior high school has been adopted as a stopgap measure with little real concern for its functions, goals, or purposes.

chapter 1

History and Functions

The American junior high school is frequently described as a unique institution intended to provide an educational program best suited to the needs of that unique age, early adolescence. With a curriculum explicitly designed for this educational goal, physical facilities in accord with the same aim, and teachers specifically trained for the early adolescent age group, the junior high school should, and often does, attain this unique purpose. Even today it is easy to start a lively argument as to how much success is achieved in this worthy enterprise by the junior high school, and there may be even more disagreement regarding its functions, purpose and structure. This is at least partially due to the changing nature of the American society and to the modification of the several factors that brought the junior high school into being. A variety of reasons were behind its origin and growth, with no single cause really predominating, but most of these reasons no longer exist or are considerably altered.

HISTORICAL BACKGROUND

It is usually stated that the junior high school is a distinctly and peculiarly American institution, although this belief, widely accepted for many years, has sometimes been questioned. Cramer and Bossing[1]* point out that many ideas relating to the junior high concept may have originated with educational thinkers of Europe from such men as Comenius, Rousseau, Basedow, Pestalozzi, Herbart, and Herbert Spencer. In their concern with the application of educational ideas as they relate to the early adolescent, these men and others have had a direct influence upon American thinking for educating this age group as well as in the broader area of all education.

Popper[2] states, "The so-called junior high school of the 1910 period was in point of fact an American borrowing of a European idea." Denmark, he reports, established a middle school in 1903 to provide a broadening of the

*Numbers indicate references at end of Chapter.

foundation of educational opportunity. "The passage of a Higher Education Act in 1903 established a middle school in urban school systems to encourage larger numbers of elementary school pupils on to the secondary school."[3] The Danish middle school consisted of two branches: (1) the Examination Middle School, which had a distinct academic nature and a curriculum controlled externally by the high school, and (2) the Prevocational Middle School, which was vocational in character and possessed exclusive internal curricular control.

In the first days of the American colonies there was little resembling a system of education. In 1642, Massachusetts, early a leader in education, passed a law which required parents, guardians, and masters of apprentices to teach children and youth the basics of learning so that these future citizens might read and understand the Bible and the laws of the land. There were penalties provided for failure to comply. In 1647 the law now referred to as "the Old Deluder Satan Law" was passed providing for our first system of public elementary and secondary schools. (To prevent that Old Deluder Satan from leading the young people astray.) The key points of this law were those requiring every township of 50 families to hire and to pay someone to teach children to read and write, and every township of 100 families to set up a grammar school whose master could prepare older children for the university.

The first of the Latin Grammar Schools, secondary in nature and intended as college preparatory institutions, was established in Boston in 1635, and was approximately six or seven years in length. Students were probably accepted as early as ten years of age and entered college at sixteen or seventeen. The Latin Grammar School was strictly classical in nature with a curriculum consisting largely of Latin and, to a lesser extent, Greek. A classical education of this sort, almost wholly college preparatory in nature, was not suited to the practical needs and demands of the new and growing country. Here the conflict began to make itself felt between those who wanted a noncollege education beyond the basics of reading and writing and those who were college-oriented and wanted an earlier academic education to prepare the few.

As the United States grew, dissatisfaction increased with these limited offerings intended for a select clientele. The great mass of the people wanted an education more generally available and of more immediate use to their children. In response to this, a new kind of secondary school, the academy, appeared on the scene in the early 1700's. The academy offered a more practical curriculum directed primarily toward the noncollege-bound and stressed vocational and terminal education. New York City is said to have established an academy in the early 1720's that offered geometry, surveying, mariner's art, reading, writing, arithmetic, ethics, rhetoric, logic, natural philosophy, Latin, Greek, and Hebrew. The English Grammar School, established in New York in 1732, was intended for students approximately ten to fourteen years of age and offered geometry, algebra, arithmetic, trigonometry, navigation, bookkeeping, geography, and Latin. Course offerings in academies soon became extremely diversified, including writing, arithmetic, accounting, astronomy, logic, farming, mechanics, navigation, algebra, history, geometry, surveying, drawing, drafting, composition, spelling, natural science, Greek, Latin, French, Spanish, Italian, German, and Hebrew. That man of many talents, Benjamin Franklin, became interested in the potential of this kind of secondary education and, in 1751, helped establish an academy which was named for him. This school, intended for the early adolescent for whom it was terminal, offered a practical curriculum which included writing, arithmetic, mechanics, farming, navigation, algebra, accounting, surveying, astronomy, English, history, and geography. Franklin stressed the importance of English, although Greek, Latin, French and German were also taught. He advocated a school library, maps, globes, equipment for experiments, and even field trips to neighboring plantations to note their best farming methods. A part of his recommendation follows:

> That a House be provided for the ACADEMY . . . , not far from a River, having a Garden, Orchard, Meadow, and a Field or two. That the House be furnished with a Library . . . with maps of all countries, Globes, some Mathematical Instruments, an Apparatus for Experiments in Natural Philosophy, and for Mechanics . . . and now and then Excursions made to the neighboring Plantations of the best Farmers, their methods observ'd. . . .[4]

The popularity of the academy led to a decline of the Latin Grammar School which, in turn, heightened the conflict between the colleges, which needed college preparatory schools, and those who were primarily concerned with the needs for general education. Increasingly, therefore, the academies took over the college preparatory function formerly provided by the Latin Grammar schools. The result was a lessening emphasis upon the practical courses, a stress upon the precollege offerings, and increased dissatisfaction among the noncollege students.

In an effort to provide an education for those students who did not plan to go to college, there was established in Boston, in 1821, the English Classical School. This school had a three-year program which, except for excluding foreign language instruction, was much the same as that of the early academies and was intended for boys approximately twelve to fifteen years of age. The high school, being tax-supported, offering a practical curriculum, and open to rich and poor alike, had no real difficulty in making itself established. By the end of the Civil War it had virtually eliminated the fast disappearing Latin Grammar School, and a few years later it replaced the academy in American education.

The rapid growth of the American high school after the Civil War, a school attempting to serve both college-preparatory and terminal students, brought other problems into view. While the high school ultimately became predominantly a four-year pattern, so much variation originally existed in the years included that in 1888 at the National Meeting of the Department of Secondary Education, a resolution was passed urging national uniformity in establishing a four-year pattern.[5] In many Southern States it was common to find a school organization which had seven years of elementary school and four or five years of high school, while sections of New England operated under an 8-5 plan—eight years of elementary school and five years of high school. Scattered throughout the entire country could be found high schools of three years, four, five, and even six years; some including the equivalent of the first year of college, and a few of these even calling themselves colleges.

CRITICISMS AND PROPOSALS

In the late nineteenth century there was mounting criticism of the 8-4 plan, initially from college faculty and administrators. They were concerned because the average age of entering college students had increased until it was over eighteen years—in fact, nearly nineteen. One of the most influential of those speaking for the colleges was Charles W. Eliot, president of Harvard, who first expressed his concern in 1873.[6] In 1888, he again mentioned the problem and inquired if the public school program could be shortened and enriched so that students could enter college approximately one year earlier.[7]

Eliot's statements set off serious debate, chiefly among other college educators who, since they were far more prestigious than those in the public schools, soon took the lead in demanding some kind of reform.

In 1892, President Eliot addressed a National Education Association meeting and, noting the "keen interest which superintendents and teachers"[8] had taken in his suggested reform in education, made explicit recommendations:

1. Reduce the elementary school program to eight years to permit children to complete it by age thirteen or fourteen.
2. Permit more able students to move through school more rapidly—that is, complete two grades in one year.
3. Eliminate repetition and useless work.
4. Introduce certain academic subjects such as algebra and geometry to children of twelve or thirteen, and foreign languages even earlier.

5. Increased use of student choice of electives.
6. More flexibility in promotion and graduation.[9]

The immediate result of these proposals was the appointment in 1892 by the National Education Association of the Committee of Ten on Secondary School Studies. To no one's surprise, President Eliot was chairman of this committee which was composed of five college presidents, a college professor, one high school principal, two headmasters of private schools, and the U.S. Commissioner of Education. Thus the movement for reorganization of public education was underway, promoted and led by the colleges with the primary purpose of benefiting college programs. Nine conferences were set up with ten members for each, and one of the original Committee of Ten members designated as chairman of each conference. The disparity of representation was extended to the conference membership, approximately four-fifths of those participating representing higher education.

The influence of the colleges was reflected in the report of the Committee of Ten, presented in 1893, which stressed economy of time and earlier study of college subjects. This report, one of the most influential in the history of American education, proposed that several subjects regularly taught in the high school such as algebra, geometry, and foreign languages, be initiated in the last years of elementary school, or that elementary school be reduced to six years, which would provide a period of six years for secondary education.[10]

The Committee further recommended that all students study college preparatory subjects for their disciplinary value. Every subject in the secondary school, it was stated, should be taught in the same amount in the same way to every student, "no matter what the probable destination of the pupil may be or at what point his education is to cease."[11]

The feeling that public education beyond the elementary level was almost solely a college preparatory function had survived from the Latin Grammar schools, through the academies, and into the high schools.

So far as the college personnel were concerned, the problem was nearly solved. All that remained was for the public schools to put these proposals into practice and all would be right with the world—at least with the world of higher education. There were, in fact, some scattered efforts by public school systems to meet these recommendations by departmentalizing the upper elementary grades and by bringing some high school subjects down into the seventh and eighth grades. However, no massive changes took place.

The Department of Superintendence had, before the Committee made its report, appointed a Committee of Fifteen to investigate school system organization, the training of teachers, and the coordination of studies in primary and grammar schools.[12]

This committee, composed of thirteen school superintendents, one college president, and the United States Commissioner of Education, William T. Harris, in its report opposed the reduction of the elementary school from eight years to six. The report did, however, recommend a modified algebra in grade 7, and Latin, in place of English grammar, in grade 8. In approving the introduction of certain high school subjects into the upper elementary grades for "a proper transition to the studies of the secondary school,"[13] the point was made that there should be better coordination and articulation between elementary and high school. This has since become one of the basic arguments for the junior high.

Since many public school educators were somewhat disturbed by all this college interference, a committee was established by the National Education Association in 1895, the Committee on College Entrance Requirements, to investigate the problem of better relations between secondary education and higher education. The committee report in 1899 is of significance if only because this was the first major committee report which focused on the student first and the organization second. The committee recommended a six-year elementary program and a unified six-year high school course of study beginning with grade 7 because "the seventh grade, rather than the ninth, is the natural turning point in the pupil's life as the age of adolescence demands new methods and wiser direction."[14] The report also emphasized the need for a more gradual transition from elementary to high school, the addition of new subjects to grades 7 and 8, and the increased holding power possible with the reorganized secondary school. With its recommendation for a six-year high school, the committee became the first professional group to propose a specific plan for reorganization of the 8-4 system. This report stressed, as do today's junior high schools, the importance of the best program for children entering adolescence, rather than one to satisfy college requirements.

Economy of time and earlier study of college subjects were still being emphasized by college presidents. William Rainey Harper, president of the University of Chicago, in the first part of the twentieth century directed the attention of the annual educational conferences held at that institution toward public school reorganization, with the same aim as that first proposal by Eliot many years before: shortening and enriching. In 1903 Harper stated that the elementary grades should end at about the twelfth year of age, or at grade 6, and the high school should end at grade 12, or at the eighteenth year.[15]

The continuing concern for economy of time brought about the designation in 1903 by the National Education Association of the Committee on Economy of Time in Education. The Committee made several reports over a period of years which stressed that the total time spent in elementary and secondary education could be easily reduced by a total of two years without impairing the quality of that education. The 1913 report of the committee, coming as it did shortly after the first junior high schools were established, is of particular interest in that it recommended:[16]

1. Time can be saved in public education by
   (a) Providing a differentiation of methods for different courses.
   (b) Course work should be made more interesting and related to life.
   (c) Teaching and instruction should be adapted to the interests and ablities of the students.
   (d) Select for study the most important material and topics.
   (e) Simplify courses of instruction.
   (f) Eliminate repetition of subjects.
2. Include grades seven and eight in secondary education and begin foreign language, algebra, geometry, science, and history at this time.
3. Secondary education would have two divisions, a four-year and a two-year.

There was given at this same time a special report by Professor Suzzallo of Teachers College, Columbia, recommending a 6-3-3 division. Thus for the first time a major educational group considered the division of the six-year secondary section of public education which provided not two but three segments for grades 1–12.

Three other national committees presented reports in the early 1900's, all of which had material influence upon the reorganization both of the schools and of the curriculum.

The Committee on Equal Division of the Twelve Years in the Public Schools reported in 1907 that the six-year secondary plan was more expensive but the advantages were well worth it.[17] The educational advantages included: better retention, better instruction by subject specialist teachers, earlier lab science, better transition from elementary to high school, and more time for college preparation. Most if not all of these have also been claimed in later years for the junior high schools.

The Committee on the Six-Year Course of Study, which made reports in 1907, 1908, and 1909, remarked upon the successful operation of the 6-6 pattern in several areas, called attention to the recommendation of a New York City Board of Education member for a 6-3-3 plan, and suggested a curriculum for grades 7 and 8.[18] The committee recommended 70 percent required courses and 30 percent elective, a thorough examination of actual and possible vocational offerings, and promotion by units rather than by grade.

Perhaps the single most important national committee report for secondary schools was the oft-quoted *Cardinal Principles of Secondary Education*, which declared the freedom of secondary schools from college domination—a freedom that even today is not complete. This committee,

The Commission on the Reorganization of Secondary Education, noted that the relation of the high school to the college was secondary to that of providing an education to "be determined by the needs of the society to be served and the character of the individuals to be educated. . . ."[19] The Commission supported the six-year elementary program and the six-year secondary and recommended that the secondary years be divided into two three-year blocks—the 6-3-3 plan. The report further stated

> In the junior high school there should be a gradual introduction of departmental instruction, some choice of subjects under guidance, promotion by subjects, prevocational courses, and a social organization that calls forth initiative and develops the sense of personal responsibility for the welfare of the group.[20]

Reading the recommendations of this commission makes it apparent that thought concerning the reorganization of the public schools had changed substantially since the first proposals of Charles Eliot. There had been a shift from an emphasis on economy of time for the college-bound student to that of providing an educational program which would best suit the rapidly increasing elementary and secondary enrollments. In the process of reaching this shift in emphasis there was also a change in proposed organizational structure from 8-4 to 6-6 to 6-3-3. There were several other influences which helped to form the basis for the junior high school in the early years of the twentieth century.

FACTORS FOR CHANGE

While the reports of the various national committees and commissions from 1890 to 1920 were of great importance to school reorganization, a number of other factors and educational leaders also had pronounced effects upon public education during this same general period of time.

Kansas City, for example, had since 1867 been operating seven-year elementary schools and four-year high schools. In making this statement in an address before the Department of Superintendence in 1903, Superintendent Greenwood observed flatly that children of average intellectual ability could "learn all that was really valuable in a ward school course of seven years."[21]

Using supporting statistical data, Greenwood proceeded to prove that a higher percentage of Kansas City youth went on to high school than did young people in any other city of the same or larger size in the United States. Greenwood's documented address lent support to the move to shorten the elementary school.

John Dewey, philosopher-educator, and a figure whose influence is still felt in education, believed that truth is evolutionary and that human thought is an instrument for solving social and psychological problems. Dewey's instrumentalism held that, as problems change, so does human thought and activity; educational authoritarianism and rote are therefore unacceptable. With this central interest upon the pupil, John Dewey supported the six-year elementary and six-year secondary division, since these could do more for the individual. He believed that coordination and articulation were a major difficulty of the secondary school, since it was caught in the middle with the elementary school on one side and the college on the other. He predicted that the discussion of the past few years on the relation of the high school to the college would change its focus to the effect of what was taught upon the growth of the individual. That the effect was enormous was shown when a leader of the magnitude of John Dewey attacked wasted time in the upper elementary school and advocated a school and curriculum concerned with the individual, not with the precollege program.

This regard for the individual student did not always exist. Social conditions at the turn of the century were rapidly changing and the schools were, willy-nilly, forced to change too. An educational program aimed at the college-bound student did not fit the democratic structure of America. The schools were woefully deficient in providing an education for the great bulk of American youth.

A series of articles about American public schools appeared in *Forum* magazine in 1892. The writer, J. M. Rice, had visited schools in thirty-six cities in five months. He found the schools of different localities very unequal, "so much so that while those of some cities had already advanced considerably, those of others were still far behind the age"[22]—an inequality that often still exists.

The deficiencies noted by Rice contributed to the lack of holding power of the schools, a situation almost incredible by today's standards. One of the first dropout studies was in St. Louis which in 1900 indicated that for every 100 pupils in the second grade in St. Louis there were 44 in the fifth, 20 in the sixth, 8 in the eighth, and only 2 in the last year of high school.[23] These conditions were attributed to a "lack of interest because of a dull, dry, impractical curriculum and a lack of practical courses such as domestic science and manual training."

This situation was not limited to St. Louis. In the early 1900's in the larger cities the dropout rates for children in their early teens usually ran between 20 and 40 percent each year of total enrollment.

Dropout was not the only problem. The practice of retention was extremely common since teaching was pretty largely all of one kind: assigning lessons, giving examinations, and, "measuring their standards by the number of pupils they fail to pass; teachers who are giving much attention to their subjects and little attention to their pupils."[24]

In 1904, 39 percent of the children in elementary school in New York City were retarded in their grade one or more years. Between 1907 and 1911 several studies were made of the double problems of retention and dropout, and the findings of these studies were later used to support the rationale for the junior high school. Thorndike (1907) estimated that only onefifth of the white children in large cities stayed through the fifth grade, and that less than one in ten graduated from high school. Ayres (1909) found great variation in the holding power of different cities, one city keeping over 80 percent through the eighth grade and another city able to hold only 15–20 percent. The main reason for this, he believed, was the quality of the curriculum. Strayer (1911) surveyed 319 cities and found that most children completed grade 5 but from here to the first year of high school, grade 9, from 60 to 70 percent of those remaining in grade 5 were lost. Only eight to ten students out of every 100 completed high school. The academic curriculum and lack of practical education were generally accepted to be the major reasons for the high dropout and retention rate, although it must be remembered that the conditions of the times were far different from now. Irregular attendance, late entrance, child labor, and illness all played their part and were used as arguments supporting the junior high school when this was proposed. These studies reinforced the serious need for a reorganization of both the schools and the curriculum.

A major factor in shifting the central focus in school organization to the student was the child study movement, best exemplified by the work of G. Stanley Hall. The child study movement held its first formal meeting as the Department of Child Study, an affiliate of the NEA, in 1893. The major emphasis of this movement was, "the school for the child, not the child for the school," and the differences and importance of each individual were stressed by "child study."

A medical doctor, C. W. Crampton, director of the physical training program for theNew York City Public Schools, conducted an investigation in 1901 of the physical characteristics of nearly 5,000 New York City high school boys between the ages of 12.5 and 18.0. As a result of this investigation he developed a concept of "physiological age," prepubescent, pubescent, and postpubescent. Of significance was Crampton's discovery of pronounced physical changes that accompanied physical growth.[25]

G. Stanley Hall, in his classic two-volume study *Adolescence*, incorporated virtually all that was known about this age group. It emphasized "psychological age" and held that adolescence was virtually a new birth, a time of rapid and radical changes which occurred in all aspects of the adolescent's life, physical, emotional, mental, social, and moral. Obviously a new approach was needed for these children; a new school, new methods, and a new curriculum in order to work properly with the wide range of individual differences to be found most often in what later was the junior high age group.

The rapid growth of business and industry in the early 1900's added impetus to the movement for reform in education. "Business men and labor unions were insisting that the school assume the classical function of apprenticeship."[26] There was an increasing clamor for industrial and agricultural vocational education which resulted in urgings for experimentation with an "intermediate industrial school" for fourteen- to sixteen-year-olds.[27] A further effect was the steady pressure to include within the new junior high school curriculum provisions for vocational education, industrial arts, and fine and household arts.

The waves of immigrants increased school enrollments, and the great majority of these children were seeking a practical, not a precollege education. The vocational and practical pressures necessitated a revision of both the academic curriculum and the methods traditionally used in instruction. The accumulation of all these forces, business and vocational education, the child study movement, the influence of John Dewey, and the recommendations of national committees combined to force a reorganization of the schools, both in grade patterns and in curriculum.

THE JUNIOR HIGH EMERGES

One of the first efforts to reform the educational pattern was made in 1895 in Richmond, Indiana, where a 6-2-4 pattern was established. This was more than a name reorganization for curriculum changes were made as well. There were changes in seventh- and eighth-grade English, mathematics, and social studies; foreign language began in grade 7, algebra in grade 8, and an "exploratory program in the fine and practical arts and a homeroom advisor system was instituted."[28]

There were other efforts at reorganizing the schools in the last years of the nineteenth century and the first decade of the twentieth. Some of these show real imagination: Providence, Rhode Island, 1898, with a 6-2-4 plan; Baltimore, 1902, 6-3-2 plan; Kalamazoo, Michigan, a 7-3-2 pattern; Muskegan, Michigan, 1903, a 6-1-2-3 plan; and Concord, New Hampshire, at about the same time, with a 6-2-3 plan.

It was in Columbus, Ohio, in 1909 that a definite effort was made to revise the traditional 8-4 plan and a three-year intermediate school with grades 7-8-9 was introduced. Columbus was the first to use the term "junior high school." The recommendation was made that there be little if any curricular change for the ninth grade, "as that grade is practically standardized in all the high schools of the country."[29]

Four months later—January 1910—in Berkeley, California, the second junior high school in the United States was opened. The Berkeley superintendent had a broader goal in mind. He favored a 3-3-3-3 organizational plan because of the high dropout currently experienced at the end of the fifth grade. The new Berkeley "Introductory High School" had course offerings that would make many high schools today take a second look, including as it did the following: French, German, Spanish, Latin, music, chorus, printing arts, typewriting, stenography, freehand drawing, cooking, manual arts, bookkeeping, algebra, and science—in addition to the general education requirements. Most of these subjects were open to seventh- and eighth-graders, virtually all to the ninth grade.

By 1920 there were about 400 junior high schools and the number grew rapidly. In 1940 there were over 2,000 and by 1960 there were approximately 5,000 with an estimated three-quarters of these following the 7-8-9 pattern. By the early 1960's the number of junior high and middle schools had increased to approximately 7,000, and by 1969 the number had reached 8,000 or more.

As the years went by, the scope of the junior high school broadened. Attempts were made to meet the personal social needs of adolescence, and more stress was placed upon basic general education as well as delineation of the exploratory nature of the program. Compulsory school attendance, child labor laws, and changing social conditions had materially changed the picture.

In the middle 1950's a rising tide of criticism of public education found the junior high school a ready target. Charges were made of "playpen" education, lack of attention to intellectual development, practices which aped the high school, indecision as to purpose, and failure to provide such basics as reading, writing, and arithmetic. Undoubtedly there was, in some schools, a basic for truth although not enough to support such sweeping generalizations.

Experimentation, innovation, new technology, staff utilization studies, and a growing interest in the "middle school" have all added to the need for revisions to the junior high school program in light of present social and economic conditions. The junior high, as a reorganization of the 8-4 system, has proved its worth over the last sixty years as an intermediate institution which can and has successfully provided an educational program for the early adolescent. (See Figs. 1-1 and 1-2.) It has adjusted to altered demands and circumstances and continually improved that program. But change is becoming more rapid, and education, noted for its leisurely adoption of the new, cannot afford to wait. Criticism and innovation must be carefully examined, the total school program evaluated and revised where necessary, and whether it be changed instructional techniques, changed curricula, or a change in organization to some form of middle school, the steps must be taken—carefully, thoughtfully, and soon.

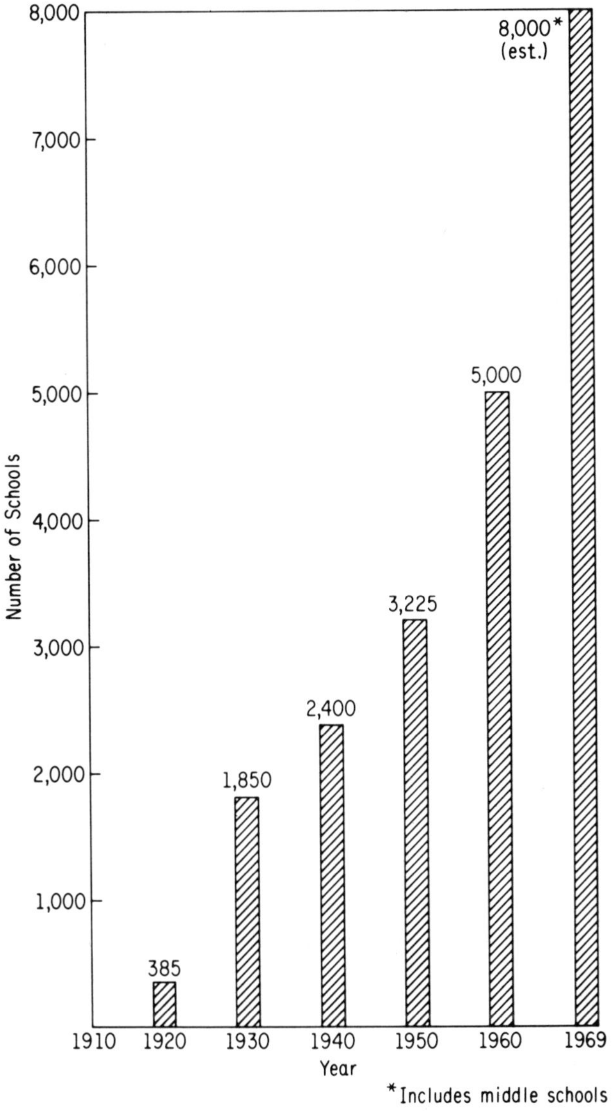

Fig. 1-1. Growth of the separate junior high school, 1910-1969.

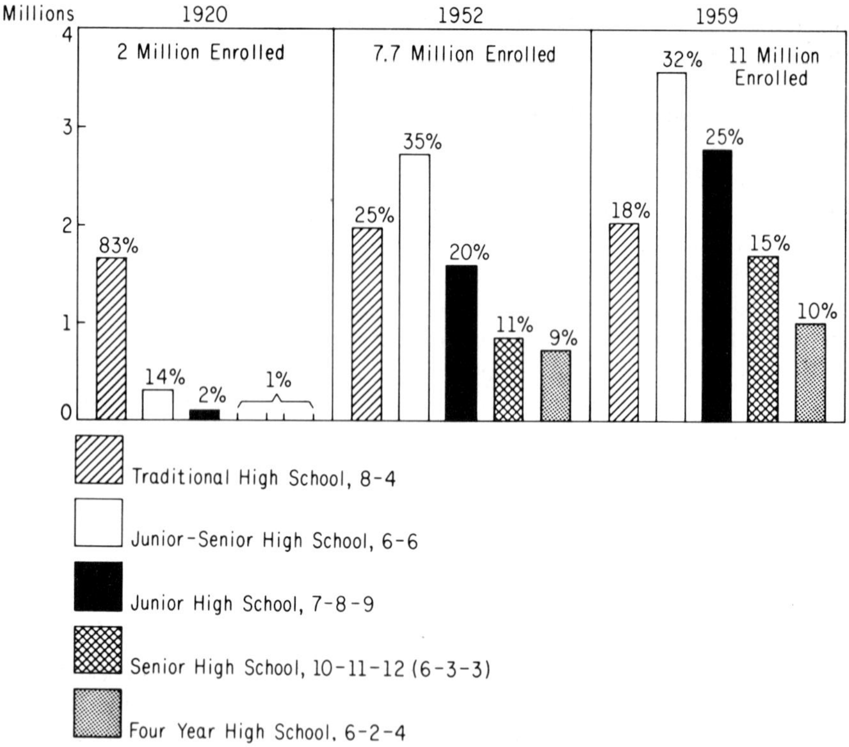

Fig. 1-2. Relative enrollments in various types of public secondary schools in the United States—1920, 1952, 1959 (From "Organizational Pattern of the Nation's Public Secondary Schools," *School Life,* May 1960, p. 3.)

FUNCTIONS OF THE JUNIOR HIGH SCHOOL

It has been indicated that the causal factors behind the establishing of the junior high school were diverse and many, with no single factor determining the purposes and functions of the new institution. Through the years the changing times and a changing society brought about shifts in emphasis upon what were considered to be the functions of the junior high school, as well as the deletion of some of these original functions and the addition of others. It has been said that the junior high school is an orphan organization with no real purpose, a school that attempts to justify its existence by claiming that it is a "unique institution for a unique individual." Factors contributing to the confusion regarding its functions include the diverse elements that influenced school reorganization in the early 1900's; the tendency of those interested in the junior high school to see the functions of this school as restricted almost completely to that level (which is a distinct error in thinking); the lack of recognition of the fact that changing times result in changing functions; the sometimes near-frenetic efforts to justify the junior high school (which results in claims for its value which could charitably be called hyperbolic); and the failure to concentrate upon the really basic need that the junior high and middle school meets—educating that truly unique individual served by this institution, the preadolescent and early adolescent. When it is recognized that this distinctly different age group needs a special kind of education that is best provided by a special kind of school, it may then easily be seen that the stated functions of the junior high and middle school pertain largely if not completely to this institution. As the world changes so do the functions, and, to an extent, the individual student of this age group. The junior high and middle school has no need to justify its existence, but there is a distinct necessity to modify and alter its curriculum and methods of instruction in accord with the needs of today's world and those of the early adolescent in that world.

EARLY STATEMENTS OF FUNCTIONS

In Berkeley in 1910 Superintendent Frank F. Bunker's report to the School Board stated that the two new junior high schools ("Introductory High Schools") would relieve the overload in the high schools, reduce the high pupil dropout that had been occurring at the end of the fifth grade, provide a natural grouping for those children who entered grade seven at the beginning of adolescence, and furnish these children ". . . with an opportunity to dip into a wide range of subjects and activities, which is Nature's way of insuring freedom of choice in determining occupation and of exercising somewhat of intelligence in the same."[30]

Koos reported that a study of statements and educational documents, most of which were published in the period 1910–16, indicated that the functions of the junior high school were seen at that time (in order of importance) as stressing pupil retention, economy of time, recognition of individual differences, providing conditions for better teaching, improving the disciplinary situation and socializing opportunities, exploration and guidance, the beginnings of vocational education, recognizing the nature of the child at adolescence, securing better scholarship, effecting financial economy, and relieving the building situation.[31]

In 1919 the influential North Central Association of Colleges and Secondary Schools, a major accrediting agency, defined the junior high school as a school in which grades 7, 8, and 9 were segregated in a building or a part of a building by themselves, had an administration and an organization distinctly their own, one that was apart from those grades below and above, and was a school that possessed its own teaching staff. Such schools were also to be characterized by:

1. A program of studies decidedly greater in scope and richness of content that that of the traditional elementary school.
2. Some pupil electives, selected under supervision.
3. Departmentalized instruction.
4. Promotion by subject.
5. A program for testing individual aptitudes in academic, prevocational, and vocational work.
6. Some recognition of the peculiar needs of the retarded pupil of adolescent age, as well as special consideration of the supernormal.
7. Some consideration of the plan of supervised study.[32]

A 1918 study of junior high schools conducted by Calvin Davis found that many of the earlier committee recommendations were being followed in that algebra, science, and foreign languages were commonly found in the seventh and eighth grades as were domestic science, manual training, music, and agriculture—subjects seldom offered these grades twenty years earlier.

Another early leader in junior high school education, G. Vernon Bennett, suggested in 1919 that the junior high school should function to reduce the rate of dropouts, to assist students in making vocational selections, and to adapt education to the needs of adolescent boys and girls.[33] A year later Thomas H. Briggs prepared one of the best known of the early statements on the purposes of the junior high school. Briggs' purposes were:

1. To continue, so far as is wise and possible, and in a gradually decreasing manner, common, integrating education.
2. To ascertain and attempt to satisfy pupils' immediate and assured future needs.
3. To explore, by means of material in itself worthwhile, the interests, aptitudes, and capacities of pupils.
4. To reveal to pupils the possibilities in the major fields of learning.
5. To investigate career choices from the pupil, which, as a result of the exploratory courses, he, his parents, and the school are convinced are most likely to be of profit to him and to the investing state.[34]

At about this same time, Calvin Davis summarized the educational thinking of the times concerning the junior high school from his examination of current practices and publications. He found the junior high school to have:

1. A separate organization of at least two of the three grades usually included, grades 7, 8, and 9, and preferably to include all three.
2. A separate building and a separate staff.
3. A program of studies that differed materially from that of the same numbered grades in a traditional school, and this program to be at least partially departmentalized.

4. Educational and vocational guidance, and certain student elective subject options.
5. Methods of instruction that were different from those of both elementary and senior high school.
6. A student activity program organized and administered for the needs of adolescent pupils, without regard for the kinds of activities in those schools above and below.
7. The admission of pupils to the school on the basis of what is best for each individual without undue concern for the conventional work he has completed satisfactorily.
8. The recognition of individual student differences in abilities, tastes, capacities, and purposes in the organization and conduct of classwork.[35]

Leonard V. Koos, a leader in the junior high school movement, in 1920 surveyed the literature relating to the junior high school and developed the following list of functions which are stated in order of frequency of mention:

1. Realizing a democratic school system through (a) retention of pupils; (b) economy of time; (c) recognition of individual differences; (d) exploration for guidance.
2. Recognizing the nature of the child.
3. Providing conditions for better teaching.
4. Improving the disciplinary and socializing opportunities.
5. Securing better scholarship.
6. Effecting financial economy.
7. Relieving the building situation.[36]

During the early 1920's several lists of functions for the junior high were circulated throughout the United States. The Department of the Superintendent of the National Education Association, in a list published in 1927, indicated the functions most frequently mentioned:

1. Meeting individual differences of pupils—permitting pupils to follow their interests and abilities.
2. Prevocational training and exploration which assists in wise choice of later school courses and life work.
3. Counseling or guidance—bringing pupils into touch with influences that give direction and purpose to their lives.
4. Meeting the needs of the early adolescents.
5. Articulation between elementary and secondary schools.
6. Development of qualities of good citizenship—educating pupils to play their part in the life of the community.
7. Supplying opportunities for early development of leadership, individuality, and initiative.

8. Retention of pupils in school beyond compulsory attendance age.
9. Continuation of common education and scholastic or academic training on all levels.
10. Providing a complete unit of training beyond the elementary grades for those who do not go on to high school.
11. Introduction of new subjects at an an earlier grade into the curriculum.
12. Effecting economy of time in education.
13. Beginning of definite prevocational and occupational training.
14. Assisting students to begin an earlier preparation for college.[37]

To summarize and clarify: in the early years of the junior high school and up to approximately 1930, this new school was viewed as an institution that should be separately housed, administered, and staffed; it was a school that attempted:

1. To reduce dropout and enhance the holding power of the schools.
2. To provide educational and vocational guidance for the early adolescent.
3. To effect an economy of time by eliminating repetition in grades seven and eight and by extending down into these grades much subject matter that had previously been offered only in high school. This subject matter included (a) academic areas such as algebra, geometry, and foreign languages, and (b) prevocational and exploratory areas, such as domestic science, manual arts, and music.
4. To develop and extend the exploratory opportunities and aspects of the program.
5. To pay more attention to individual differences in students in terms of course offerings, requirements, activities, and counseling.
6. To take into consideration the characteristics and needs of the early adolescent.
7. To improve articulation between the elementary school and the high school by increased use of the elective system and by departmentalized instruction.
8. To reduce discipline problems found in the 8-4 system.
9. To provide a complete unit of education beyond the elementary grades.

THE CHANGING ROLE

The passage of child labor laws and compulsory attendance laws did much to reduce the stress placed by the junior high school upon retention and the dropout problem. The function of vocational and prevocational training also became less important, and the increased recognition of unique characteristics of the early adolescent lent strength to the movement away from college preparation and toward developing a school and program designed specifically for this age group. Thomas Sears Montgomery, after conducting a study of junior high school literature for 1928–37, concluded that the junior high school was no longer responsible for definite vocational training; such vocational training should be a part of education beyond the junior high school. Aiding the pupil in making vocational choices, he said, was not a junior high function. Montgomery approved the emphasis in junior high upon the exploration of interests and the stress upon general education, and remarked that

> Because of the greatly increased tendency of pupils to stay in school beyond the junior high school grades, . . . no longer is the junior high school to be regarded as the educational terminus of a considerable portion of early adolescents.[38]

He noted a "strong tendency to relieve the junior high school of the responsibility for specialized educational training," with the exception of those subjects within the exploratory program designed to meet interests and needs of early adolescents." As a corollary to this he remarked upon the increasing interest in the general education program in the junior high school.

At the time of Montgomery's writing, A. A. Douglass asserted that

> . . . to a considerable degree the functions which distinguished the junior high school of twenty years ago have been transferred to the senior high school.[39]

An outstanding study conducted by William T. Gruhn in collaboration with Harl R. Douglass about 1940 resulted in the development of a widely accepted statement of junior high functions. This statement included six basic functions.

1. *Function I: Integration.* This is intended to provide learning situations in which pupils may use the skills, attitudes, interests, ideals, and understandings previously acquired, with the aim that these will become coordinated and integrated into effective and wholesome pupil behavior. To supply for all students common education in the basic knowledge and skills of a broad nature which results in integrated behavior, attitudes, interests, ideals, and understandings.
2. *Function II: Exploration.* To help students to discover and explore their particular interests, aptitudes, and abilities as a basis for decisions for further choices and actions, educationally and vocationally. To stimulate pupils and furnish opportunities for them to develop a constantly widening range of cultural, social, civic, avocational, and recreational interests.
3. *Function III: Guidance.* To help students to make intelligent decisions concerning present vocational and educational activities and

opportunities and to give them the training to make future decisions of these kinds. To help students to make satisfactory mental, emotional, and social adjustments in their growth toward mature personalities which are wholesome and well adjusted. To inspire students to participate as effectively as possible in learning activities so that they may develop to the maximum their personal powers and qualities.

4. *Function IV: Differentiation.* To provide differentiated educational facilities and opportunities in accord with the individual differences, the varying backgrounds, interests, aptitudes, abilities, personalities, and needs of all pupils in order that each pupil may achieve most economically and completely the ultimate aims of education.
5. *Function V: Socialization.* To supply more learning experiences intended to prepare pupils for effective and satisfying participation in the present complex social order, and for adjustment and contribution to future developments and changes in that social order.
6. *Function VI: Articulation.* To provide a gradual transition from preadolescent education to an educational program suited to the needs and interests of adolescent boys and girls.[40]

This summary of functions by Gruhn and Douglass reflected significant changes and emphasis regarding the functions of the junior high schools. These changes included (1) the elimination of economy of time as an important consideration; (2) no direct mention of the retention of pupils; (3) a reinterpretation of the concept of guidance; (4) still further increased emphasis on the individualization of instruction, provision for socializing experiences; and (5) addition of the concept of integration.[41]

This list of functions, while well stated and widely accepted, has been criticized in that the functions do not really delineate the purposes of the junior high school as compared with those of the elementary school or the senior high school. Actually, only function VI pertains almost exclusively to the junior high school, and the new middle schools with grades 6-7-8 or 5-6-7-8 may logically lay claim to this same function.

Lounsbury's study of the junior high school function during the 1950's showed that education specialists desired a program suited to the early adolescent. These specialists wanted the emphasis placed upon general education and integration of experience, shared responsibility and self-direction, socializing experience, individualization of program through adequate guidance and counseling, exploration of various interest areas and subjects, provision for electives, the establishment of special classes for advanced and/or retarded pupils, and the establishment of prevocational orientation and exploration.

In this same report, Lounsbury found some of the earlier functions being rejected, such as economy of time, vocational training for early school-leavers, promoting by subject rather than by grade level, elimination of duplication and repetition, and departmental teaching. Other purposes or functions considered invalid included providing for homogeneous or ability groupings, effecting financial economy, and segregating early adolescents.

After the junior high had been in existence for forty years, Gruhn summarized its purposes and observed that the basic purpose in 1952 was essentially the same as that stated at the beginning of the reorganization movement:

> To provide an educational program which is particularly designed to meet the needs, interests, and abilities of children during early adolescent years. With respect to the specific functions of the junior high school, there has been increased attention to the integration of learning outcomes, while our concepts of exploration and guidance have been greatly expanded.[42]

He went on to note the emphasis on the individualization of the educational program, provision for socializing experiences, and the articulation of educational activities among educational units in the school system. His conclusion was that the nature and interpretation of these functions had not changed; what has altered was our approach to implementing and accomplishing these functions.

Faunce and Clute in 1961 stated the following three major functions of the junior high school which they believe are unique to the institution because of the particular needs and interests of this age group:

1. To attack the common problems faced by young adolescents in our society, employing and improving command of basic skills and knowledge from many sources for this purpose.
2. To enrich and differentiate learning by exploration of vocational and other individual interests.
3. To assist the early adolescent to make a satisfactory personal-social adjustment.[43]

A somewhat more recent statement of the educational functions of the junior high school is that of Bossing and Cramer in 1965:[44]

1. Meeting unique needs and individual differences of early adolescents.
2. Developing basic learning skills.
3. Preparing to live in a democracy.
   (a) Principles of conduct of responsible citizenship.
   (b) Preparation for family living.
   (c) Appreciation of moral and ethical principles.
   (d) Conservation of natural resources.
   (e) Participation in our economic system.

4. Providing for personal interests and creative experiences.
5. Developing mental and physical fitness.
6. Providing for guidance-counseling.
7. Developing articulation between school units.
8. Providing integration in teaching and learning.

Van Til, Vars, and Lounsbury[45] remind us that the "final word on the functions of the junior high school has not been written and, hopefully, it never will be." They see the presently accepted broad purposes of the junior high school as primarily that of general education, continuing the common education needed by all citizens in a democracy; and, secondly, as education for diversity, providing "experiences especially suited to the diverse abilities, needs, and interests of widely varying individual young adolescents." To achieve these goals the junior high school must continue and extend the general education program; provide for transition between elementary and high school; bring in new subject areas as necessary; provide additional specialization in basic areas; supply opportunities for discovery and pursuit by students of special interests and abilities, and provide opportunities and experiences that will assist the early adolescent in developing values, leadership, self-management, social competence, and a philosophy of life.

THE EXPLORATORY FUNCTION

The exploratory function of the junior high school has been an important aspect of this institution for over half a century and has steadily increased in importance.

In 1929 Briggs designated exploration as one of the three more important conceptions of the junior high school. He linked exploration with the study of foreign languages, mathematics, science, social science, fine arts and music, industrial arts, and home economics. An interesting aspect of Briggs' plan of exploration involved the prescription of exploratory classes for all or nearly all pupils, regardless of their life ambitions. The purpose of this plan was to give young people a glimpse of many fields in the world and to integrate the whole social body.

As early as 1920 Leonard V. Koos, when preparing a list of junior high functions, had found exploration for guidance listed fourth in order of frequency of mention.

In 1927 William Smith defined the exploratory functions as (1) exploring the interests, abilities, and aptitudes of children of junior high school age and (2) exploring the major fields of human endeavor.[46] Further emphasis upon the provision for exploration of pupil abilities and interests appeared in the famous list of junior high school functions prepared by Gruhn and

Douglass about 1940. Exploration was further defined as the technique of leading students to discover and explore their particular interests, aptitudes, and abilities so that they would be able to make wise decisions regarding educational and vocational opportunities. Exploration, in addition, included opportunities for students to develop a continually widening range of cultural, social, civic, avocational, and recreational interests.

EXPANDING NATURE OF EXPLORATION

The expanding concept of exploration during the past two decades can best be understood by comparing the original and the contemporary views of the junior high school program.

Originally, exploratory activities were intended to help students choose their high school courses more wisely. Extracurricular activities, added at the end of the school day, included community exploration trips, introduction to new subject areas, and other experiences designed to help students learn more about their own potential abilities as well as interests. Exploratory courses such as shop, business, and the practical arts were used frequently to set students in curriculum tracks which they were to follow throughout the senior high school. For the majority of students, this procedure was a narrowing rather than a broadening experience.

Educators quite naturally associated the explorative function with guidance and vocational training, as high pupil dropout rate and limited educational opportunities gave encouragement to such a relationship.

A more recent interpretation of the exploratory function of the junior high, as outlined by Gruhn and Douglass, points out that increased retention of pupils in schools and extended educational opportunities for youth require a broader concept of exploration, one in which the schools provide opportunities for pupils to find themselves in cultural, social, recreational, and avocational pursuits. Such exploration "is concerned not only with vocational activities but also with every other area of human interest and endeavor."[47] Gruhn and Douglass went on to describe three new dimensions to the junior high school exploration function. First, exploration is not limited to a few courses but extends into every subject in the curriculum. Opportunities for exploration are found in social studies, physical education, art, music, foreign language, and every other course of study. Second, exploration is provided through a broad program of extraclass activities. Third, exploration is obtained through flexible methods of teaching in which students are given opportunities to plan and choose interesting learning activities.

Abraham Gelfond stated in 1960 that vocational exploration had been replaced by educational exploration.[48] Quite critically he reminded educators that the junior high schools (as with schools at all other levels) have a responsibility to help students explore all of their interests and aptitudes—vocational, educational, and social.

Contemporary writers have emphasized that exploration is as much method as it is content. Exploratory experiences can be achieved through required and elective subjects. However, self-exploration occurs also as a student participates in selecting activities, conducts self-evaluations, and engages in research activities. By wedding method and content, exploration is achieved through instruction, activity, social, and guidance programs.

The Southern Association of Colleges and Secondary Schools completed a significant junior high school study in 1958. The report included a section relating to broad exploratory experiences necessary to the educational development of early adolescents. The purposes were outlined as follows:

1. They should contribute to and be an integral part of the general education program.
2. They should help students develop present and future social and recreational skills and interests.
3. They should provide new experiences which broaden the horizons of boys and girls.
4. They should assist students in making present and future vocational plans and choices.
5. They should provide valuable assistance to students in making choices of future educational experiences.[49]

A group of secondary school principals identified several basic principles which should be followed in developing and carrying out the exploratory function. Several of the principles are similar to the purposes as listed by the Southern Association of Colleges and Secondary Schools. However, the following are significant and should be added to the list:

1. There should be sufficient opportunity for the teacher to get to know the student, note his reactions, and his degree of success in the experience.
2. Students should be assisted in the understandings of their strengths and weaknesses by a satisfactory record system.
3. Each student should have counseling available so that he may have the value of the observations and records in understanding himself and relating to a situation on the basis of an intelligent choice.
4. Exploration must be accepted by each teacher as a part of his teaching method and classroom procedure.
5. Each teacher should contribute to this function by providing the class with a variety of learning materials.[50]

KINDS OF ACTIVITIES

There are many kinds of exploratory experiences and courses available in junior high school programs. The types of courses provided should be determined after considering the needs, interests, and concerns of students, the desires of the community, and the competencies and special skills and interests of the faculty. A typical list[51] of experiences included:

Art	Vocational exploration	Typing
Choral music	General business	Folk dancing
Homemaking	Photography	Poetry writing
Manual arts	Science	Crafts
Creative dance	Creative writing	Hobbies
Public speaking	General language	Literature
Music appreciation	Choral speaking	Journalism

James Bryant Conant's study of the junior high school in 1959–60 has some bearing on the exploration function in these schools. Perhaps the most important suggestions he offers relating to this function are summarized as follows:

1. Required subjects for all pupils in grades 7 and 8 should include English, social studies, mathematics, and science.
2. Extraclass activities should be group activities which have particular relevance for early adolescents.
3. Block-time instruction should be provided in grade 7 for articulation and teacher counseling purposes.
4. Schedules should be flexible and include a seven-period day.
5. Adequate student guidance and testing services should be provided.[52]

A more recent view of the exploration function is expressed by Charles S. Partin, who contends that each student is attempting to obtain a view of himself. The student is constantly searching for answers to such questions as, "Who am I?" "What am I like?" "What things can I do well?" "How do people feel about me?" As these questions are answered, the student engages in self-exploration of feelings, values, and personal needs.[53]

CONCLUSION

It becomes apparent that the junior high and middle school serve a special purpose and are responsible for specific functions in the education of the preadolescent and early adolescent. While the functions may be in some instances similar to those of the elementary school and the high school, and much of the differences are only those of degree, the nature of the learner at this level, the characteristics of the early adolescent, require a kind of educational program that is neither elementary nor high school—that program provided by the school in the middle. The functions of the junior high school, taken in combination with the characteristics and needs of the early adolescent, have implications for the kind of curriculum offered, guidance policies and procedures, changing patterns of instruction, and the controversies and issues affecting these schools and their students.

SUMMARY

In view of the diverse factors that gave rise to the junior high school, it is not surprising that disputes still exist concerning its functions and responsibilities.

The late 1800's and early 1900's were a period of criticism and examination of the American secondary school. Descended from the Latin Grammar School and the academy, the emphasis was largely one of academics and preparation for college. A series of national commissions recommended shortening and enriching public education so that students could enter college earlier and with a better background in classical education. John Dewey, G. Stanley Hall, and the child study movement shifted the focus to a concern for an educational program intended for the early adolescent. Business and industry stressed the need for a practical and vocational education. The problem of massive dropouts and a serious retention rate underscored the need for a revised approach in the public schools.

While the first proposals were for a 6-6 plan, the 6-3-3 pattern was that which finally predominated, although a variety of others were instituted, and some, like the 6-2-4 organization, have persisted.

The purposes of the junior high school have changed as child labor laws, compulsory attendance, and a different social order affected the schools. The stress is no longer on vocational training and holding power but has shifted to providing an educational program for the early adolescent which includes a basic general education, guidance, and a strong exploratory aspect.

Since the beginning of the secondary school reorganization movement, the term "exploration" has been associated consistently with the junior high school. Exploration is one function that not only has prevailed over the years but has grown in importance and acceptance.

The first organized junior high schools in the early 1900's included exploration as one of the major functions. Initially, exploration was related to the guidance function. Through exploratory "tryout" classes, extraclass activities, and vocational experiences, students were prepared for the world of work and the termination of formal schooling.

Exploration has been receiving a broader interpretation since the late 1930's and early 1940's, when social, civic, cultural, and educational aspects were added to the vocational features of the exploration function.

In the past two decades all subjects and school activities have been associated with the junior high school's exploration function. According to one author, in the junior high school of today opportunities for exploration "seem to be provided through a broad curriculum, wide offering of activities, guidance services, extensive facilities, and through flexible methods of teaching."[54]

REFERENCES

1. Roscoe V. Cramer and Nelson L. Bossing, *The Junior High School.* Boston: Houghton Mifflin, 1965, p. 3.
2. Samuel H. Popper, *The American Middle School.* Waltham, Mass.: Blaisdell, 1967, pp. 9–10.
3. *Ibid.*
4. Cramer and Bossing, *op. cit.*, p. 8. From T. H. Montgomery, *A History of the University of Pennsylvania, 1749–1770.* George W. Jacobs, 1900, pp. 497–500.)
5. National Education Association, *Journal of Proceedings and Addresses,* 1888, pp. 403–404.
6. Frank F. Bunker, *The Junior High School Movement: Its Beginnings.* Washington, D.C.: Roberts, 1935.
7. Charles W. Eliot, *Educational Reform: Essays and Addresses.* New York: Century, 1901.
8. *Ibid.*, p. 269.
9. *Ibid.*, pp. 263–269.
10. National Education Association, *Report of the Committee of Ten on Secondary School Studies.* New York: American Book, 1894, p. 45.
11. *Ibid.*, p. 17.
12. National Education Association, *Journal of Proceedings and Addresses,* 1895, p. 232.
13. *Ibid.*, p. 339.
14. National Education Association, "Report of the Committee on College Entrance Requirements," *Journal of Proceedings and Addresses,* 1899, p. 659.
15. William R. Harper, "The High School of the Future," *School Review,* January 1903, pp. 1–3.
16. James H. Baker (chairman), *Report of the Committee of the National Council of Education on Economy of Time in Education,* Bulletin 1913, No. 38. Washington, D.C.: Government Printing Office, pp. 10–19.
17. National Education Association, "Report of the Committee on Equal Division of the Twelve Years in the Public Schools Between the District and High Schools," *Journal of Proceedings and Addresses,* 1907, pp. 705–710.
18. National Education Association, "Report of the Committee on Six Year Course of Study," *Journal of Proceedings and Addresses,* 1908, pp. 625–628.
19. Commission on the Reorganization of Secondary Education, *Cardinal Principles of Secondary Education,* Bulletin 1918, No., 35. Washington, D.C.: U. S. Bureau of Education,
20. *Ibid.*
21. James M. Greenwood, "Seven Year Course for Ward School Pupils," National

Education Association, *Journal of Proceedings and Addresses*, 1903, p. 258.
22. J. M. Rice, "Our Public School System: Schools of Buffalo and Cincinnati," *Forum*, Vol. 14 (November 1892), p. 293.
23. C. M. Woodward, "When and Why Pupils Leave School," *Report of the United States Commissioner of Education, 1899–1900*, pp. 1366–1367.
24. National Education Association, *Addresses and Proceedings*, 1908, *op. cit.*, p. 580.
25. Samuel Popper, *op. cit.*, p. 148.
26. Lawrence Cremin, *Transformation of the Schools.* New York: Knopf, 1962, p. 116.
27. National Society for the Promotion of Industrial Education, *Proceedings*, 1910, pp. 195–199.
28. Conrad F. Toepfer, "Evolving Curricular Patterns in Junior High Schools," unpublished doctoral dissertation, University of Buffalo, February 1962, p. 53.
29. Toepfer, *op. cit.*, p. 58.
30. Bunker, *op. cit.*, p. 3.
31. Leonard V. Koos, *The Junior High School.* Walthan, Mass.: Ginn, 1927, p. 506.
32. Calvin O. Davis, *Junior High School Education.* Yonkers-on-Hudson, N.Y.: World Book, 1924, p. 7.
33. G. Vernon Bennett, *The Junior High School.* Baltimore: Warwick and York, 1919, p. 2.
34. Thomas H. Briggs, *The Junior High School.* Boston: Houghton, 1920, pp. 162–174.
35. Calvin O. Davis, *op. cit.*, pp. 13–14.
36. Leonard V. Koos, *The Junior High School.* New York: Brace and Howe, 1920, p. 18.
37. National Education Association, *The Junior High School Curriculum*, 1927. Washington, D.C.: Department of Superintendence, p. 20.
38. Thomas Sears Montgomery, "A Study of the Philosophy and Changing Practices in the Junior High School," unpublished doctoral dissertation, University of Texas, 1940, pp. 56–57.
39. Aubrey A. Douglass, "Development in California High Schools," *Educational Record*, January 1939, p. 54.
40. William T. Gruhn and Harl R. Douglass, *The Modern Junior High School.* New York: Ronald, 1956, pp. 31–32.
41. William Van Til, Gordon F. Vars, and John H. Lounsbury, *Modern Education for the Junior High School Years.* 2nd ed. Indianapolis: Bobbs-Merrill, 1967.
42. William T. Gruhn, "The Purposes of the Junior High School—After Forty Years, in Arthur Foff and Jean D. Grambs, eds, *Readings in Education.* New York: Harper, 1956, p. 387.
43. Roland C. Faunce and Morrel J. Clute, *Teaching and Learning in the Junior High School.* Belmont, Calif. Wadsworth, 1961, p. 16.
44. Bossing and Cramer, *op. cit.*, pp. 53–64.
45. Van Til, Vars, and Lounsbury, *op. cit.*, p. 35.
46. William Smith, *The Junior High School.* New York: Macmillan, 1927, p. 195.
47. Gruhn and Douglass, *op. cit.*, p. 32.
48. Abraham Gelfond, "The Exploration Concept in the Junior High School", *NASSP Bulletin*, Vol. 44 (November 1960), p. 32.
49. Southern Association of Colleges and Secondary Schools, *The Junior High*

School Program. Atlanta: Southern Association of College and Secondary Schools, 1960, p. 58.
50. Delmar H. Battrick, "What Do We Believe About the Exploratory Function of the Junior High School?" *NASSP Bulletin,* Vol. 46 October 1962, p. 9.
51. Southern Association of Colleges and Secondary Schools, *op. cit.,* p. 59.
52. James B. Conant, *Education in the Junior High School Years.* Princeton, N.J.: Educational Testing Service, 1960.
53. Charles S. Partin, "To Sample—Or to Explore?", *Educational Leadership,* Vol. 42 (December 1965), pp. 194–199.
54. Nathan Krevalin, "A New Approach to Exploration in the Junior High School," *Journal of Secondary Education,* Vol. 42 (January 1967), p. 32.

chapter 2

Adolescence

Adolescence, that uneasy time between childhood and adulthood, is too often regarded as a temporary nuisance period which at best is tolerated or even ignored, joked about, and silently endured. Temporary and transitory (as are most things), and frequently of high nuisance value, it is much too serious and important a time of life to poke fun at or to ignore. As the elementary school is designed for the young child and the senior high school for late adolescent youth, so is the junior high or middle school intended to provide the best educational program for the preadolescent and early adolescent; roughly those children from eleven to fifteen years of age. On this point it is possible to find the least argument and the most agreement; this is the basic purpose of the junior high school.

There can be no question that the time of adolescence is one of great physical change, of uneven growth spurts, of wide variations among children in height, weight, and physical maturity—a period of stresses and strains. During this time the early adolescent often becomes openly rebellious at adult and parental controls yet, paradoxically, will complain bitterly that he is not given enough help. It frequently appears to bewildered parents that the early adolescent wants everything done for him—at his request—and with absolutely no restrictions nor controls to be imposed upon his actions. Not only does it *appear* this way; there is a great deal of evidence for this complaint. At the same time, the adolescent does not really want all rules discarded; he wants and needs direction and guidelines. Virtually all adolescents will at times exhibit insecurity, instability, indifference, sullenness, impudence, laziness, and resentment at being treated like children; yet they will also complain if the teacher cannot or does not maintain class control. They want to be treated like adults and to be able to get away with acting like kids.

Too many junior high school teachers either just give lip service or actually pay no attention to the really difficult problems children have in adolescence. It is, however, also possible to become so engrossed in the needs and characteristics of the adolescent that the primary purpose of the school—intellectual development—is pushed aside by an exaggerated concern with personal-social problems to the detriment of the intellectual program.

"What is the junior high school idea? . . . Asylum . . . a special environment . . . in which pubescence can be experienced without trauma or trepidation. . . . It gives disconcertingly little attention to intellectual development."[1]

There is some difference of opinion concerning the emphasis on the "storm and stress" theory of adolescence, the "psychological overacting."[2] It is held by some that this is an oversimplification in that there should be more attention paid to the "broad cultural influences on adolescents."[3] In this approach, it is held that strains and stresses are not inevitable but are brought about by the limitations and restrictions of the society in which the adolescent finds himself. If this is true, it becomes obvious that there is a definite responsibility for those who work with the early adolescent to have a real understanding of these children and to act accordingly.

CHARACTERISTICS OF ADOLESCENTS

Despite the really great range among and between individual adolescents, there are some characteristics which they possess in common:

1. A resentment of authority, especially if it appears to be arbitrary. This is very strong in the early adolescent and appears to be aggravated by the earlier drive for sophistication which increasingly manifests itself today. Parents complain that their children grow up too fast; teachers are accustomed to adolescents who dress, look, and behave like adults one day, and the next day look and behave like children who are years younger. Coleman warns that this sophistication is a two-edged sword in that adolescents are readier for new ideas and experiences, quicker to understand, but, ". . . . far less easy to teach, less willing to remain in the role of the learner, impatient with teachers, less likely to look at the teacher as a model of authority."[4]

Since he desperately wants independence, the early adolescent is quite ready—even eager—to accept responsibility. The mistake that adults make at this point is to expect complete acceptance of responsibility and performance on an adult level from an adolescent. It is right to set standards but it must be remembered that children will not miraculously and overnight perform as adults. Responsibility is earned, and developed by wise guidance and planned experiences.

2. A craving for acceptance and approval by their peers which was

formerly satisfied by adult approval. In his desire for independence, the early adolescent appears to become a rigid conformist to the mores, dress, speech, and attitudes of his fellows. Security is found in identifying with the group insofar as is at all possible. If group standards denigrate strong academic performance, then high grades are for "squares" and "goody-goodies." The seventh-grade pupil who was a strong student becomes only an average ninth-grade student, which confuses and shocks his parents and teachers. The early adolescent is almost certain to develop an air, a manner of sophistication or pseudosophistication, which he hopes will cover up the worries, doubts, and feelings of uncertainty which are usually with him. During this time the early adolescent is highly susceptible to undesirable influences and individuals—*if they are admired by his peer group.* To gain status and recognition he must conform to these new standards. The role of the school should be obvious in developing desirable values, attitudes, and standards, and in providing socially approved experiences and situations.

3. As a further illustration of the adolescent paradox, adolescents are likely to be extremely idealistic at the same time that they are easily influenced by undesirable elements. They have a keen sense of fair play and justice and are quick to join in projects that involve helping the less fortunate. Occupations related to service, doctors, nurses, and social workers, will probably be frequently mentioned as career choices. Common symptoms are daydreaming (in class and at home), extravagant plans (with little or no thought as to how they are to be implemented), near worship of celebrity teenage singers and actors, sad fantasies of selfless altruism, heroic deaths for noble causes—and a much increased rate of runaway children.

The emotional life of the adolescent is predominated by idealism, and his need to believe in something will never be stronger. If his parents were not decisive concerning values, the adolescent has had but little background to sustain him in determining his own values. This is the time for admiration and imitation of the hero figure, which makes it important that the proper figures for emulation are presented to the adolescent. While their parents and teachers are no longer likely to be the persons to be imitated and admired, partly because of their fallibility, familiarity, and authority symbols, the early adolescent will still seek an older model to emulate—preferably one who is competent and successful *by his adolescent standards.*

Wattenberg observes that, in dedicating themselves to high spiritual, ethical, and public service ideals, early adolescents may discomfort adults when ". . . they demand almost superhuman standards of conduct from themselves and from the adults they know."[5]

Lacking the superhuman, the merely successful becomes the object of admiration, because our society rejects failure (which has many interpretations) and rewards the competent and successful. We can now perceive why it is that idealism becomes diverted to imitating the undesirable and shoddy.

4. By adult standards, the early adolescent is extremely emotional. There really is no middle ground, no halfway mark. People, events, and things are superlatives—it is the *best* party or the *worst.* Terms are graphic and descriptive: "the most," "endsville" (nothing beyond this), "groovy," "Something else," "wild," "Where it's at," "stoned," and "freaked out." A thing is either superior beyond compare or so inferior as to be impossible to duplicate. Since emotions become so intense, many events and problems take on an importance out of proportion to their real value. Blighted romances, failures to make the team, or poor grades may result in depression so great as to lead to suicide. Friendships, in the main, are ephemeral. It is, however, a time for close attachments to one or two friends of the same sex. This same emotional variability is easily attracted to the ritualistic, the lure of mystic signs, symbols, and the claptrap of the secret society.

5. Although inclined toward idealism, the early adolescent will probably become quite self-centered and selfish. Parents wonder what happened to the sweet child that they used to know. Rules, particularly those concerning use of the telephone, watching television, or monopolizing the bathroom either do not apply to them, are unfair, or are to be ignored. Personal grooming goes beyond the needs of neatness and becomes a fetish, virtually a sacred ritual that can run on for hours. Among girls particularly, concern over body odor and attractiveness or general appearance results in extensive use of deodorants and lead to two or three baths a day. If cleanliness is next to godliness, then this time might be classified as "early religious."

6. The interests of early adolescents are rapidly broadening but change frequently, few being more than superficial. There is almost a mania for collecting, but the items collected change in nature almost from week to week, and the variety of collections identified in any given junior high school classroom is almost incredible. The early adolescent usually is interested in people, particularly those of similar age, and this may often be seen in their choice of reading material. Values change, and there is an increasing interest in an awareness of the opposite sex. The seventh-grade boy who frightened a girl with an angleworm out of pure mischief becomes the a ninth-grader who teases girls to attract their attention as sex objects. The ninth-grade girl is as pleased with the boy's teasing as the high school girl is at being taken to a movie or dance.

The instability of interests of young adolescents is augmented by the earlier sophistication previously mentioned. The enormous influence of television, magazines, newspapers, radio, and other mass media, coupled with the multimedia advertising aimed directly at the teenage market and geared to the swift tempo of modern life virtually drives the early adolescent from one interest to another. Here are the customers for the mail-order dancing lessons, the self-defense courses, the muscle builders, the boys who are not going to have bullies kick sand in their faces, the girls who send away for blackhead removers, beauty kits, Ouija boards, astrology pamphlets, fortune-telling cards, and the alluring secrets of the rock, TV, and screen stars. Here are the devotees of the rock sessions and the reckless experimenters with drugs.

7. This is a time of developing and changing values, so that long-anticipated experiences may not be all that they were hoped and expected to be. There is an increased awareness of self although it is a somewhat bewildered awareness most often characterized by a quest for identity; that is, "Who am I?" "Do people like me?" "What am I like?" "Can I do things well?" In finding the answers and developing self ideals, what was important a short time ago may not be of importance today. Seventh-grade boys will value skill in athletics, daring, and fearlessness, while the ninth grade boy will have added social ease, personableness, poise, and an easy way with the opposite sex to the list. According to Coleman, athletic prowess and popularity are valued by early adolescents, especially boys, while Tryon notes that the girls value sophistication and glamorous grooming.

8. Early adolescents share a common concern with physical growth. They are, in their own secret fears, growing too rapidly, too slowly, too unevenly, too tall, or developing too much in the wrong places. For many of these adolescents, there is a great deal of truth to this. It is not uncommon for a child to grow six inches in one year in height, yet the arms, legs, and trunk may grow disporportionately, which results in awkwardness and clumsiness. The smooth coordination developed during childhood may be seriously, if temporarily, impaired. Some girls are seriously concerned about the size of their hips and breasts—whether too big or too small—and boys and girls alike, who are slow to develop, feel out of place, fearful, and compensate by becoming either withdrawn or excessively boisterous. During this growth spurt, internal organs and functions change rapidly and unevenly—a fact that should be of particular interest and concern to physical education teachers and coaches. Appetites increase enormously. The average junior high school adolescent can easily outeat the rest of the family.

9. The physical growth of adolescence is accompanied by intellectual expansion. General intelligence for all pupils develops continuously as children grow older. It has been estimated[6] that the average seventh-grader has reached 50 percent of adult mental ability before going into grade 7, and the remainder is achieved during adolescence, probably to about age 18. There is obviously a wide range of inherent student ability to do schoolwork, and the performance of mental tasks will be affected by interests, abilities, and talents. The growth in mental ability continues for both bright

and slow pupils for about the same number of years, the difference being in extent or level reached.

These characteristics, held in common by early adolescents, serve to point up the really impressive variabilities and ranges of differences to be found in students, all of which should have an effect upon the junior high school program.

CONTEMPORARY VIEWS OF THE PREADOLESCENT AND EARLY ADOLESCENT

In the early 1900's G. Stanley Hall made monumental contributions to our knowledge of adolescence when he pointed out that the period of passing from childhood into adolescence was one of uncertainty, anxiety, and tumultuous emotions, characterized by a substantially quickened tempo of physical growth, followed by an equally swift deceleration of growth rate. In spite of Hall's work and that of others, such as the Child Study Movement, the schools in the first quarter of the twentieth century operated largely on the assumption that growth during childhood and adolescence was steady, gradual, and regular. More recent research, strongly flavored by anthropological and sociological views and findings, while accepting the "storm and stress" concept of adolescence, holds that this belief is oversimplified. In this new approach, strong emphasis is placed on the effect upon adolescence of broad cultural influences—that is, "the strains and stresses are not inevitable but are a result of the restrictions and limitations of the culture in which the adolescent finds himself."[7]

Recognition of the effects of the culture upon the adolescent, it is said by Van Til, Vars, and Lounsbury, ". . . places heavy responsibility upon those who work with adolescents for understanding adolescent development and for acting on that understanding."[8] Teachers, they note, should understand and be guided by the following principles to meet best the needs of students in preadolescence and early adolescence:

1. This is a time of seeking status as an individual.
2. This is a time when high importance is placed by the child upon group relationships.
3. Adolescence is a time of physical pattern and growth that is common to the race but peculiar to the individual.
4. This is a time of intellectual expansion and development.
5. This is a time of development and evaluation of personal values.[9]

THE SELF-CONCEPT

During childhood the individual develops a concept of himself, good, bad, or indifferent, which enables him to perceive himself with some surety in relation to the relatively limited world in which he functions. Whatever his concept may be of himself, he has become fairly certain of what he can and cannot do, what he may expect of himself both in mental and physical ambitions. As the child moves onto preadolescence, his environment changes and his experiences are altered and multiplied. His body, which he thought he knew so well, is growing and changing—often unevenly and disproportionately. His values are shaken or even destroyed as he finds contradictions between what he has been taught by his parents and other adults and what he sees in the world. A satisfactory self-concept permits the child a measure of the self-confidence essential to success and well-being. A poor self-concept may have many undesirable effects: The individual may become withdrawn; he may become an isolate; he may become sullen; he may become a behavior problem. He will certainly become unhappy—and an unhappy child does not learn as well as a happy child.

Accompanying this change in the self-concept is a movement away from parental dependency. "The child is in a sort of in-between world—a world between childhood and adulthood. He begins to view himself as separate from the family and the rest of the adult world."[10]

All that happens, and specifically all that occurs in school, affects the child's understanding and self-concept. Is he "good"? Is he "worthwhile"? Can he succeed in this independence? Is guidance and help available or is it like going to school, ". . . an adult cultural decision over which the child had no control"?[11]

In developing this self-concept the adolescent seems to adults to be paradoxical in several ways. He is at once more self-centered—concerned with what is happening to him, his body, and his environment—and more concerned with the world around him. What kind of society will he be a part of? An insightful response was made by one youngster in reply to the question, "What do you want to be when you grow up?" "Alive."

PHYSICAL CHANGE

Not all human beings mature at the same time in their lives, nor do they enter pubescence at the same stage in their development. Variations in rate and time of maturation occur because of inherited tendencies and because of the effect of environmental factors such as diet and general health. Nor do boys and girls develop physically at the same stage nor the same rate. Generally girls develop physically one to two years earlier than do boys.

Beginning in the early stages of puberty there is a sequence of changes in acceleration of height increase, body breadth and depth, lung capacity, heart size, muscular strength, glandular secretions, and the development of male and female sexual characteristics.

Breckinridge and Vincent report that:

> Girls at approximately 9 years begin their adolescent growth spurt which reaches a peak in the 12th or 13th year; boys begin their growth spurt around 11 years and reach their maximum gains, which are greater than those of the girls, in the 14th or 15th year.[12]

That period of time between ages 14–18 for girls and 16–20 of age for boys is described as the postpubescent period of late adolescence—the time of completion of the pubertal growth spurt. Alexander and Williams[13] point out that children's variations in age of entering pubescence and of rate in developing show that there is a range in organic maturity in the fifth grade of 7–15 years—an eight-year span, and that in the eighth grade there is a spread of nine years. However, the important factor, they believe is that a majority of children go through the transition period of entering pubescence sometime between grades 5 through 8, and that "all children will be in some stage of transition during this time."

As a part of this physical growth there is a changing attitude toward the opposite sex, an awareness of the difference in their roles. There is an obvious double standard in the identification of sex roles. An example of this is the boy who may be regarded as "feminine" if he plays with dolls, while the girl who plays baseball and other male sports is merely a "tomboy." Within our society the male role is one of toughness, aggression, and a role that is expected to be played by the male from childhood. Girls are expected to be sweet, gentle, and even docile. When a girl or woman displays attitudes of aggression and toughness, one is apt to hear, "She should have been a man," and the tone is more likely to be reproachful than admiring. Yet the fact exists that in the past few years our women have entered increasingly upon what were previously considered to be largely or exclusively male pursuits. When this changing role is observed by the adolescent, the problem of boys and girls identifying with their respective roles becomes aggravated.

Changing styles and fads have their effects upon role identification. It is common now to see boys with long hair—often shoulder length—and equally common to see girls wearing slacks, shorts, trousers, and even "pants-suits" both formally and informally. Activities in student dissent and even riots are characterized by substantial numbers of teenage girls who appear to be anything but docile, ladylike, or quiet. In this climate it becomes increasingly difficult for the junior high school teacher to help the growing girl to "understand the central place of marriage and motherhood in the life of the American woman and also help to understand the place of short-term employment and life-work careers."[14] It is also important that adolescent boys be helped to see that masculinity and toughness must be tempered with the gentle and honest respect for the rights of others that truly characterizes the "gentle" man.

INTELLECTUAL GROWTH

Intelligence and intellectual functioning are areas in which considerable research has been done in recent years, enough to provide some generalizations and assumptions. In 1951 J. W. French concluded that intelligence was more than a single quality; at least 15 to 20 factors of mental activity could be categorized as intelligence.[15] J. P. Guilford in 1956 noted that there are probably many factors of intelligence still to be identified, but of approximately 40 of these factors, "seven are memory factors and the remaining ones have to do with thinking."[16] In 1959 Guilford concluded that the structure of intellect ". . . is a theoretical model that predicts as many as 120 distinct abilities, if every cell of the model contains a factor. . . ."[17] He added that there were at least fifty ways of being intelligent, since there were about fifty intellectual factors presently known.

Wattenberg states that the factors affecting intelligence have had their greatest effect before a child reaches his teens.[18] Other authorities have estimated that the average child has reached about 50 percent of his adult status in mental ability before he reaches seventh grade and achieves the remaining 50 percent during adolescence.

The contributions of developmental psychologist Jean Piaget have had a large and growing effect in recent years. He holds that what we inherit is a method of intellectual functioning that remains basically constant through life and that through this functioning cognitive structures are generated, and only through this functioning. In Piaget's view cognitive development occurs as a progression through unvarying and sequential periods, although movement from one stage to another varies from one person to another in chronological age, and different individuals vary in the ultimate degree of the level finally reached. There are, says Piaget, three phases of intellectual development:

1. The time of sensorimotor intelligence, from birth to about two years old.
2. Preparation for and organization of concrete operations, from about two years to approximately eleven years of age. This span of time includes two subperiods:
   (a) Preoperational representations, from age 2 to 7, during which the child tends to operate within his own field of perceptions in somewhat fumbling efforts to cope with reality.
   (b) Concrete operations, age 7 to 11, during which time the child is moving from reality to potential reality. He is able to anticipate items in sequence and to recognize that a ball of wax or clay may be made into a square and still contain an equal amount of the original substance. He is developing the ability to "conserve" and is, in fact, toward the end of this phase evolving a conceptual

basis for dealing with his immediate environment. He can cope with and understand simple abstractions and concepts so long as such ideas are developed by direct experience. However, he cannot yet comprehend and operate with ideas about ideas until he moves into the third stage, the transition from childhood to adulthood.

3. The phase of formal operations begins approximately at age 11, during which time the child finds that the concrete operational process by which he had previously organized and structured a problem is not sufficient to provide a complete and logical solution. He begins to hypothesize, to consider all possible relations, to experiment, to analyze, to go beyond reality—in short, to work with abstractions, concepts, ideas about ideas on a high level. "Ten and eleven years olds approach problems in a much different manner than do children in lower elementary grades. They operate in much the same manner as do students in the present junior high school years."[19]

This ability to reason that develops to a greater extent in late childhood and early pubescence causes the child to look for cause-and-effect relationships. The implications for junior high and middle schools should be clear: it is necessary to provide facts and content as a basis from which to work, but adolescents prefer, need, and should have learning activities that challenge their powers of reasoning. As the child becomes a maturing adolescent he is able to understand and to see through situations and conditions with the inevitable result that he questions tradition, adult rules, and reasoning, and is no longer so likely nor so willing to accept something merely because the teacher says it is so.

Inhelder and Piaget observe

> . . . children of upper elementary school age show rapid progress in ability to generalize and to make deductions. They become increasingly able to draw conclusions from fewer and less concrete situations than are necessary in teaching . . . lower elementary school children. They learn fairly rapidly how to apply rules to specific situations and they become more skillful in solving problems in the mind. . . .[20]

All evidence available supports the belief that intellectual growth and the increase in the power to reason continues until the end of the teen years and perhaps longer. Passive acceptance of the ideas of others and memorization of facts—too often the way that teaching occurs in the junior high school—are not the kinds of activities highly conducive to creative and critical thinking.

> Pupils have to find a challenge and enjoyment in intellectual tasks, see a purpose in what they are asked to learn, discover relationships between the facts, and extend these relationships to larger generalizations and concepts.

> . . . Pupils must also have the opportunity to engage in learning experiences appropriate to their level of ability, and differentiated in complexity, not merely amount.[21]

SOCIAL NEEDS AND VALUES

One of the strongest needs of the preadolescent and early adolescent is to be one of the group, to be accepted, to be, if at all possible, "popular." The peer-group gang of the ten-year-old gives way to the clique of the adolescent. Popularity is a goal sought after and yearned for, and is the immediate reason for a number of early adolescent behaviors that bewilder both parents and teachers. It is essential to the child of this age group that he be accepted by his peers, and to the average early adolescent this means that social pressures and relationships take priority over and conflict with parental and academic pressures. He must feel that he "belongs" to his group, and conformity to the group is more important in terms of group approval and support than adult approval. This conformity to the group encourages the fads and styles characteristic to this group. Adult efforts to prohibit unusual hair styles and clothing is proof positive of authoritarian efforts to squelch independence even though parents and teachers are attempting to develop in these children the ability to think critically, to analyze, and to reason for themselves. The early adolescent is quick to recognize the contradiction.

This is the age in which a valid enough reason for doing something is that "everybody is doing it." At the same time, a rule that the child feels is reasonable is likely to be accepted because the early adolescent has a strong sense of what is fair, equitable, and just. These children are developing both the ability to reason and a sense of values. It must make sense and be fair; it is not enough for an adult to say, "Do it because I said so." It is further necessary in the development of values for parents and teachers to practice what they preach. "A given youngster's values are the product of the setting in which he grows up and the example set by those with whom he comes into contact."[22]

Consider the effect upon the development of student values when the homeroom becomes an administrative device; when the curriculum allows little if any choice of subject matter; when student activities base entry and acceptance upon payment of dues or an affirmative vote by the popular clique; when teaching method and content remain unchanged day after drab day and year after dull year; when four-letter words sprinkle the coach's locker-room language; when the principal vetoes the junior high student council proposals and restricts this body to decisions such as the date for the school picnic (which he has already determined); and when tardy students are sent to the office, but teachers are late because they took time out for a cigarette.

IMPLICATIONS FOR THE SCHOOLS

Today's adolescent is truly an unusual individual. He is confronted with serious problems of virtually every category at a really difficult time in his life. He is changing, his security is threatened, and those things which have always been important have lost their standing to different standards and interests. The various adjustments and achievements which adolescents encounter have sometimes been categorized as "developmental tasks." Havighurst, an early leader in developing the concept, holds that these are the things that people must learn if they are to be happy and successful. He defines a developmental task as one which arises at a certain period in the life of an individual and which, if achieved successfully, leads to happiness and to success with later tasks, while failure results in unhappiness and difficulty. Havighurst listed ten such tasks as needs of youth:

1. To achieve new and more mature relationships with boys and girls of the same age.
2. Attaining a feminine or masculine role socially.
3. Accepting one's physique and using the body effectively.
4. Attaining emotional independence of adults.
5. Reaching an assurance of economic independence.
6. Choosing and preparing for an occupation.
7. Preparing for marriage and family life.
8. Developing intellectual skills and concepts necessary for civic competence.
9. Wanting and attaining socially responsible behavior.
10. Acquiring a set of values and an ethical system as a guide to behavior.[23]

It may be that another task should be added to this list. Number 11 could well be, "To recognize and cope with failure."

Developmental tasks for adolescence are, in general, very much the same for everyone although they are sometimes stated differently. Erik Erikson recognizes four such tasks: industry, fidelity, identity, and intimacy. A document produced by a number of California junior high school administrators is similar to the Educational Policies Commission's Ten Imperative Needs of Youth for junior high school adolescents. Each statement begins with, "All high school youth need:"

1. To explore their own aptitudes and to develop occupational proficiency.
2. To develop and maintain physical and mental health.
3. To be participating citizens of their school and community with increasing attention to adult citizenship.
4. Experiences and understandings, in accord with their age and maturity, which are basic to successful home and family life.

5. To learn about their environment and to use the scientific approach.
6. Thc enriched living available through appreciation of the arts and expression in the arts and from experiencing the beauty and wonder of our world.
7. To develop a sense of values and an understanding of the rights of ownership.
8. A variety of experiences, socially acceptable and personally satisfying, which help in their personal growth and their development in wholesome group relations.
9. Experiences in group living which assist in developing character and personality; experiences which contribute to developing respect for the rights of others and in growth of ethical insights.
10. To grow in ability to observe, listen, read, think, speak, and write with purpose and appreciation.[24]

These are the tasks and needs as pereceived by adults. Surveys designed to elicit the feelings of adolescents indicate that they have many related worries and fears. They are concerned with lack of size, overweight, skin conditions, lack of muscular strength, boy-girl relations, vocational future, feelings about religion, the state of the world, money, independence, underdeveloped physical characteristics (i.e., breasts or genitalia too small or too large), clothes, appearance, popularity, attractiveness, school, social relationships, and posture. After examining this list one could be justified in concluding that it might be easier to list items which do *not* cause adolescent concerns and fears.

Obviously teachers of adolescents must have a thorough understanding of adolescents and the extremes of their emotional peaks and depths. This is not the time to aggravate feelings of insecurity. The curricula and total program must be such as to permit everyone some success in some area and there must be a wide range of curricular offerings. It should be equally clear that the range of curricular offerings must put a considerable stress upon the nonacademics; upon such content as sex education and consumer economics. It is of great importance that teachers understand what terrific differences exist in adolescents, not only from ages 11 to15 but within each age group. We cannot teach and treat adolescents as if they are identical units. As Friedenberg points out, "... the members of the dominant group (adults) must like and respect the subordinate group a good deal in the first place,"[25] or feelings on both sides become more frightened and hostile. Friedenberg reminds us frequently that "adolescence is conflict," conflict within the adolescent himself and conflict with society—primarily adults. While the adolescent virtues are courage and loyalty, even a moderate degree of compromise is humiliating to an extreme, and they will be pugnacious and quarrelsome about what they believe to be their rights but "naive and reckless in defending them." It is no wonder that the junior high school is afflicted with so many problems of student discipline! With children who feel like this and adults who are defensive and do not understand them, eruptions cannot fail to occur.

It is of interest to note that the role of the teacher is also recognized as important by the adolescent. Schmuck[26] found that at least 40 percent of adolescent youth remarked that they had major problems with teachers, primarily in three categories:

1. Teachers not getting to know the students. "Teachers don't care if they know you well or not." "Our teachers are like machines." It should be easy to see that adolescents are seeking consideration and respect as individuals. It is necessary to build up the adolescent's concept of himself as a competent and effective person.
2. Teachers lacking interest in teaching and in youth. "He doesn't seem to care if we learn." "He isn't even interested in what he is teaching." Here, indeed, is an indictment—and it is all too true. It occurs, unfortunately, at all levels of school, but it is literally a crime wherever it is found.
3. Teachers showing partiality for other students. This is a fairly common complaint and has much basis in truth. Teachers *do* have pets —sometimes unconsciously—and tend to favor girls, students who are conforming, and better students academically.

In view of these characteristics and feelings, there is valid reason for supporting a special school, the middle or junior high school, for a special case: the early adolescent. The young adolescents become "psychologically disoriented, not psychopathically disoriented, but disoriented enough to set them apart as a psychologically vulnerable group in society."[27] There is need for a school organization which keeps the young adolescent apart from the social systems of the older adolescents. Popper[28] says it very well when he comments that the protective intervention of a middle school is not for a special category of psychotics but for the entire population of early adolescents.

We have failed in the junior high school to the extent that we have not provided for differentiated instruction and content; we have failed when we lecture to all students every class all day and every day; when student elective options are minimal or nonexistent; when democracy is talked but not really taught nor practiced; when activity and athletic programs are for the gifted or popular or economically able; when creativity and nonconformity are struck out swiftly and effectively; and when the junior high school is an institution that has lost sight of the fact that its only reason for existence is the preadolescent and early adolescent.

The junior high and middle schools are successful to the extent that full cognizance is taken of what is known of the characteristics of the preadolescent and early adolescent *in every facet* of the school's operation: administration, guidance and counseling, required curricula, elective curricula, activity curricula, building facilities, teacher training, and actual teaching.

EARLIER MATURITY AND THE PLACE OF GRADE NINE

It is curious how our viewpoints change as we grow older—possibly people and things actually are that much different from the way they were when we were young. It is common to hear that kids aren't what they used to be and, judging from the fads and styles of the past few years, this statement as it relates to appearance is undoubtedly true. For several years many school personnel have been saying that kids are different now from what they were a few decades back in that today's children seem to mature earlier, grow taller and heavier, and become more sophisticated sooner. While this has been largely opinion there is increasing evidence that the onset of puberty and social maturity is occurring at an earlier age in the young people of today than was formerly the case. If this is true, then support is given to the position of those who believe that the grades in the middle school should be 6-7-8 or 5-6-7-8 but should not include grade nine.

Much of course depends upon *whose* opinion this is. What is this person's background of experience? His opinion may still be valuable but these influencing factors should be known and recognized. This is particularly true in dealing with a subject such as removing grade 9 from the junior high school, a topic which appears capable of arousing excited and impassioned arguments from both sides.

EARLIER MATURITY

The suspected earlier maturity of adolescents is not something that mushroomed in the past year or two. It has been building up and observers have been making comments on it for some time now. One of the more critical statements was made in 1957: "An integreated society of 7th, 8th, and 9th grade pupils is an unrealistic dream. The heels and hose of the 9th grade simply do not mix with the pigtails of the younger students."[29]

The author, at the time a junior high principal, went on to say that the 7-8-9 plan was too sophisticated for seventh- and eight-graders, that there was little mental and social affinity between grade 9 and those grades below, and that ninth-graders were capable of higher achievement and more advanced work than junior high offered.

In a speech to the NASSP Convention, Chicago, 1964, the principal of the Scarsdale School (grades 6-7-8), Scarsdale, New York, stressed the social maturity and sophistication of the ninth grade which "place them more logically with higher grades rather than lower."[30]

A Texas study raises some interesting questions concerning early maturity and sophistication.[31] Referring to a survey of Texas junior high schools which showed that 46 percent of the junior high principals were not pleased with their present grade level (6-3-3), the study contends that presently preferred grade combinations are largely an assemblage of opinions of leading educators and popular practices and do not coincide with student development. The conclusions of this study, "Grade Organizational Structure of the Junior High School As Measured by Social Maturity, Emotional Maturity, Physical Maturity, and Opposite Sex Choices," bring up some points of significance:

1. The study involved pupils in grades five through ten and found the least difference between pupils in grades six and seven and between students in grades nine and ten.
2. The most noteworthy aspect of the male sample was the pronounced differences in social and emotional maturity between grades eight and nine, while there were no observed differences between nine and ten.

Grades 6 and 7 were recommended as the best combination in the lower division, and grades 9 and 10 in the upper division since these pairings showed the least differences in maturity factors. Grade 8 should not be with grade 9. It is worth noting that the 6-3-3 plan with a junior high school of 7-8-9 violates all of these findings; it pairs grades 8 and 9, and it divides the grades between 6 and 7 and 9 and 10 where there is presumably the most affinity.

A 1967 statement[32] from the Committee on Junior High School Education, National Association of Secondary School Principals, noted that there is some indication that pubescence now begins somewhat earlier than previously. In addition, even before entering pubescence, children today adopt interests of an adolescent nature. Mass communication has raised their general level of information; thus "The current sixth grader or eleven year old may be as ready for junior high or middle school as the seventh grader was in former years."

It appears that there is a definite trend toward earlier physical development. Tanner[33] reports that there has been during the past 100 years a marked tendency for the time of adolescence, as typified by the growth spurt or menarche, to occur earlier. He goes on to say that this is more than guesswork; information on heights and weights of children of school age and before indicate that the whole process of growth has been stepped up progressively. Evidence shows that all age children born in the 1930's or 1950's, for example, were considerably larger than those born in the 1900's.

Mills[34] says that this growth change has resulted in a four-inch increase in height in America and a steady increase in height and weight for entering college freshmen.

This increase in height and weight is not restricted to young people who are of college age; nine-year-olds of today are as large as ten-year-olds thirty years ago. This trend toward earlier physical maturity is associated with earlier sexual maturity.[35] On the average, a girl today is likely to begin to menstruate some ten months earlier than did her mother. Kindred observes that "this downward trend of age at menarche must of necessity come to a stop in the foreseeable future although there is no evidence at present that it has stopped or slowed down."[36]

A comparative study of children in the same school from 1934–35 to 1958–59 reported that girls in the most recent sample were an average one inch taller and six pounds heavier than the first sample, and the boys in the latest sample were over two inches taller and ten pounds heavier.[37]

Bauer[38] compares today's adolescent with those of the 1920's and 1930's and finds the present example is somewhat taller, physically healthier, perhaps more intelligent, more sophisticated, enjoying more mobility and freedom, spending more money, and enjoying better nutrition than his predecessors.

Margaret Mead[39] mentions that children of today mature earlier and grow taller than their parents, and Havighurst[40] notes that sexual maturity comes perhaps a year earlier now than it did 100 years ago.

Eichorn[41] observes that human growth patterns are changing in the direction of earlier maturation; that our favorable socioeconomic situation augments this earlier maturation pattern; and that the trend shows every sign of continuing. He adds that this situation is at least partly due to better nutrition. Such earlier maturation, he believes, frequently causes emotional anxieties and tensions in children. It would seem, then, that the school which is intended to serve children at this stage in their lives should be organized to include the ages where this growth most often occurs today: ages 10 and 11 to 14, grades 6-7-8 or 5-6-7-8.

Today's culture, which has been a direct influence on earlier physical maturity, has also produced an earlier social maturity and has probably influenced an earlier mental maturity. Inhelder and Piaget[42] hold that the experiences provided by a particular social environment cause the environment to act as a variable in the stage development of mental operations. As noted earlier, children pass through a stage of concrete operations before reaching, sometime before entering puberty, the stage of formal mental operations. The development of the ability to perform formal thinking, conceptualize, and deal with abstractions, which was formerly reached by children somewhere between ages 12 and 14, is now being achieved by children at an earlier age. Educational and cultural factors are such as may be slowed down or speeded up, and therefore, it follows that earlier development of mental maturity in our cultural is not only possible, it is probable. Johnson[43] says that the sequential reaching of stages in growth does not change but the specific age is affected genetically, experientially, and culturally. Thus the stage of formal operations is reached nowadays before junior high school years.

If this is true, and Johnson believes with Piaget that it is so, then there are implications for the present beliefs about readiness. The problem may not be one of refraining from pushing children too soon and too hard but one of failure to provide such intellectual experiences as would develop readiness at an earlier age.

Bayley[44] emphasizes the importance of the effect of environmental variables upon the rate of intellectual growth. Environmental factors include cluture, experience, and emotional climate, and will vary in their effects for different individuals and for different growth stages.

Havighurst [45] points out that few mentally superior children of immigrant groups appeared until the second or third generation, when they contributed substantial numbers of the mentally superior.

If an earlier growth of today's children may be observed in physical and mental characteristics, the earlier sophistication and social growth of today's preadolescent and early adolescent is so apparent as to cause a considerable amount of concern, apprehension, and even adult resistance. Young people today have more experiences by the time they reach adolescence than did their parents. They have these experiences earlier, have more of them, and are exposed to a wider range and wider variety of environmental factors (such as television violence) then were their parents. Many—perhaps most—of these experiences may be desirable, although there will unquestionably be some of no value or doubtful value; but, good or bad, they have occurred.

Mead[46] describes as the most striking features of the last twenty years the steady movement downward in dating-age level, pairing off, "going steady"; the emphasis upon vocational choice, criminal behavior, competitive athletics, and permission to spend money at an increasingly rapid rate.

Coleman[47] also notes the big increase in "going steady" among adolescents and attributes it to the psychological security it provides since the family no longer provides the closeness it once did.

Havighurst[48] observes that today's adolescent is much more sophisticated—he may not understand a considerable part of what he sees but he is much more aware of the reality of human nature and society. There exists today, says Mead[49], an early reaching for adulthood which is accentuated by older siblings and encouraged by parents who let children do things too early. This in turn is compounded by schools which permit, induce, and encourage precocity. The end result, naturally, is an adolescent who is socially mature at an earlier age.

He starts going to parties earlier. He is permitted to read at an early age books or magazines in which sex and villainy are exploited to a degree that would have apalled his grandparents, who read nothing stronger than

Tom Swift, Sue Barton, or the Bobbsey Twins. Mass media with almost instantaneous national coverage permits the adolescent to become a witness to violence, accidents, and war scenes that are stark, brutal, and sensational. So-called "restricted" movies and picture magazines portray sex in most explicit form. Marriages are occurring earlier[50] and high school marriages or out-of-wedlock pregnancies are not at all uncommon—even in the ninth grade.

This picture of earlier participation in adult activities is especially hard to accept at the junior high level when it is recalled that for many years the transitional function of junior high school has been stressed as a protection for the young adolescent.

As a part of the cultural changes and the factors related thereto may be found the pressures—and they are great—which American society employs to force the individual to conform to the peer group[51]; the greater geographic mobility of Americans since World War II; the decline of the family; and the development of the teenage market and the teenage customer. The "teenager" is treated as comprising a distinct entity, a separate market that spends billions of dollars a year on cosmetics, recordings, movies, electronic equipment, clothing, and fads. The early adolescent is the target for millions of dollars of advertising written and produced specifically for this group. With the muscle of money behind it and the diffusion of mass media, the adolescent is a willing prey to fads in clothing, music, activities, and hair styling: a conforming nonconformist who is in conflict with the adults of his life—teachers, and parents. Riesman[52] comments that too many parents aggravate the problem of socialization and adjustment, and force the pace in the child's social life, with the result that parents today are the stage managers, chauffeurs, and booking agents, cultivating all the currently necessary talents, "especially the gregarious ones."

In today's America, then, the adolescent is pushed into early sophistication and social participation on the one hand, is held back on the other ("You're too young to do this"), and experiences conflict in virtually every aspect of his life. In fact, Friedenberg[53] points out that adolescence *is* conflict. Coleman[54] warns that sophistication and the desire for sophistication on the part of adolescents is a two-edge sword. Adolescents, it is true, are quicker to grasp things and readier for new ideas and new experiences, but in the flush of their new sophistication and suspicion of conflict they are harder to teach and less willing to remain in the role of learners. They are also ". . . impatient with teachers, less likely to look at the teacher as a model or an authority. . . . Of all the recent changes in adolescents, this early desire for sophistication poses perhaps the greatest problem."[55]

An early interest in more grown-up activities, early dating, a desire to get this part over with, a dislike for the old, a distaste for the past (the future is new and close)—all of these characterize today's adolescent. This same dynamic attitude is found in our culture, which is changing rapidly and cannot help but be reflected in our young people. Eichorn[56] notes that in the period since World War II the interests and attitudes of young people have shown a definite earlier trend. This is largely attributable to the earlier maturation of youth and to the cultural changes in the United States in the past two dozen years.

This social maturity and early sophistication is accompanied by an earlier physical maturity and an earlier mental maturity, and the transition in intellectual processes that now takes place before or about the sixth grade.

In 1964–65 the Committee on Junior High School Education of the National Association of Secondary School Principles asked a representative group of people, "Is today's junior high school student a different person than his counterpart of 25 or even 10 years ago?" Members of the Committee concluded that the answer may be "Yes."[57] Those writers whose thoughts were presented were in agreement that the junior high school student of today is more sophisticated, more precocious, more mature, and more complex.

The earlier maturity of today's children lends strength to the arguments of those who support the middle school with grades 6-7-8 or 5-6-7-8 and who argue that grade 9 should be returned to the high school or become part of some other upper secondary organization.

SUMMARY

The early adolescent is a complex creature, unsure, afflicted with fears, worries, concerns, and temporarily disoriented psychologically. The list of fears and concerns is virtually endless and the intensity of each varies with each adolescent. Nowhere are individual differences in physical, mental, and social development, interests, abilities, and growth spurts more pronounced than in adolescence. There is no difficulty in building a case for a special school for this age group. The implications for curriculum and teaching for the adolescent should also be clear. Unfortunately we still have too many schools in which the subject is more important than the individual, and too many teachers who neither understand nor respect adolescents.

While individual differences are pronounced, adolescents do have some characteristics in common. They have various needs, drives, and reactions, such as the striving for independence, which are much the same for all adolescents.

There is quite a bit of opinion and some evidence that children enter adolescence earlier and become mature physically, socially, and mentally at an earlier age than was the case some decades ago. Earlier maturity and sophistication reinforces the position of middle school proponents who see this as reason for moving grade 9 back to senior high school and picking up grade 6, or grades 5 and 6, from elementary school.

If the reason for the junior high school or middle school is to provide the best education possible for the preadolescent and early adolescent in a separate institution, and if the ninth-grader is in fact more mature than formerly, then the move should be considered.

REFERENCES

1. Mauritz Johnson, Jr., "The School in the Middle," *Saturday Review,* Vol. 45 (July 21, 1962), p. 40.
2. Samuel H. Popper, *The American Middle School.* Waltham, Mass.: Balaisdell, 1967, p. 275.
3. William Van Til, Gordon F. Vars, and John Lounsbury, *Modern Education for the Junior High School Years.* Indianapolis: Bobbs-Merrill, 1967, p. 133.
4. James S. Coleman, "Social Change, Impact on the Adolescent," *NASSP Bulletin,* Vol. 49 (April 1965), p. 14.
5. William W. Wattenberg, *The Adolescent Years.* New York: Harcourt, 1955, p. 80.
6. Harold E. James and Herbert S. Conrad, "Mental Development in Adolescence," NSSE Yearbook *Adolescence.* Chicago: U. of Chicago Press, 1944, pp. 154–155.
7. John E. Horricks, *The Psychology of Adolescence.* 2d ed. Boston: Houghton, 1962, p. 6.
8. Van Til, Vars, and Lounsbury, *op. cit.*, p. 134.
9. *Loc. cit.*
10. William M. Alexander, Emmett L. Williams, and associates, *The Emergent Middle School.* New York: Holt, 1968, p. 36.
11. Ira J. Gordon, *Human Development: From Birth Through Adolescence.* New York: Harper, 1962, p. 214.
12. Marian E. Breckinridge and E. Lee Vincent, *Child Development.* 5th ed. Philadelphia: Saunders, 1965, p. 188.
13. Alexander, Williams, and associates, *op. cit.*, p. 28.
14. Van Til, Vars, and Lousbury, *op. cit.*, p. 128.
15. J. W. French, "The Description of Aptitude and Achievement Tests in Terms of Rotated Factors," *Psychometric Monograph,* No. 5, 1951.
16. J. P. Guilford, "The Structure of Intellect," *Psychological Bulletin,* Vol. 53 (July 1956), p. 292.
17. J. P. Guilford, "Three Faces of Intellect," *American Psychologist,* Vol. 14 (August 1959), p. 477.
18. Wattenberg, *op. cit.*, p. 43.
19. Alexander, Williams, associates, *op. cit.*, p. 35.
20. Barbara Inhelder and Jean Piaget, *The Growth of Logical Thinking from Childhood to Adolescence.* New York: Basic Books, 1958, p. 332.
21. Leslie W. Kindred, *The Intermediate Schools.* Englewood Cliffs, N.J.: Prentice-Hall, 1968, p. 56.
22. Kindred, *op. cit.*, p. 54.

23. Robert J. Havighurst, *Human Development and Education.* New York: McKay, 1953, pp. 111–147.
24. California State Department of Education, Handbook for Junior High Schools, Bulletin No. 18, 1949, pp. 6–11.
25. Edgar L. Friedenberg, *The Vanishing Adolescent.* Boston: Beacon, 1959, p. 25.
26. Richard Schmuck, "Concerns of Contemporary Adolescents," *NASSP Bulletin,* Vol. 49 (April 1965), pp. 19–28.
27. Popper, *op. cit.,* p. 275.
28. *Ibid.,* p. 283.
29. Morris A. Shirts, "Ninth Grade—Curriculum Misfits?," *NASSP Bulletin,* Vol. 41 (November 1957), p. 136.
30. Walter F. Fogg, "Advantages of the 6-7-8 Junior High," Speech delivered to the NASSP Convention, Chicago, 1964.
31. Wildred P. Dacus, "A Study of the Grade Organizational Structure of the Junior High School," unpublished doctoral dissertation, University of Houston, 1963.
32. "Recommended Grades or Years in Junior High or Middle schools," *NASSP Bulletin,* Vol. 51 (February 1967), p. 69.
33. J. M. Tanner, *Growth at Adolescence.* Oxford: Blackwell, 1962, pp. 143–144.
34. C. A. Mills, "Temperature Influence Over Human Growth and Development," *Human Biology,* Vol. 22 (February 1950), p. 71.
35. Tanner, *loc. cit.*
36. Kindred, *op. cit.,* p. 41.
37. Anna Espenschade and Helen E. Meleney, "Motor Performance of Boys and Girls," *Research Quarterly of the AAHPER,* Vol. 32 (May 1961), p.187.
38. Francis C. Bauer, "Causes of Conflict," *NASSP Bulletin,* 49 (April 1965), p. 15.
39. Margaret Mead, "Early Adolescence in the United States," *NASSP Bulletin,* Vol. 49 (April 1965), p. 9.
40. Robert J. Havighurst, "Lost Innocence, Modern Junior High School Youth," *NASSP Bulletin,* Vol. 49 (April 1965), p. 1.
41. Donald H. Eichorn, *Middle School.* New York: Center for Applied Research in Education, 1966, p. 23.
42. Inhelder and Piaget, *op. cit.,* p. 337.
43. Mauritz Johnson, Jr., "The Adolescent Intellect," *Educational Leadership,* Vol. 23 (December 1965), p. 201.
44. Nancy Bayley, "On the Growth of Intelligence," *American Psychologist,* Vol. 10 (1955), pp. 813–814.
45. Robert J. Havighurst, "Conditions Productive of Superior Children," *Teachers College Record,* Vol. 62 (1961).
46. Mead, "Early Adolescence," p. 5.
47. Coleman, *op. cit.,* p. 12.
48. Havighurst, "Lost Innocence," pp. 3–4.
49. Mead, "Early Adolescence," p. 5.
50. J. T. Landis, "Attitudes and Policies Concerning Marriages Among High School Students," *Marriage and Family Living,* Vol. 18 (1956), p. 128.
51. Jackson Toby, *Contemporary Society,* New York: Wiley, 1964, p. 337.

52. David Riesman, *The Lonely Crowd: A Study of the Changing American Character* (New Haven; Yale U. P., 1950), p. 70.
53. Friedenberg, *op. cit.*, p. 32.
54. Coleman, *op. cit.*, p. 14.
55. *Ibid.*
56. Eichorn, *op. cit.*, p. 53.
57. "Foreword," *NASSP Bulletin*, April 1965.

chapter 3

Guidance and Counseling

The program of pupil personnel services, of which guidance and counseling is a major part, has in recent years experienced rapid growth to meet the increasing needs of the preadolescent and early adolescent in the junior high and middle schools. Pupil personnel services for this age group include, in addition to guidance and counseling, such school-provided professional activities as a school nurse, dental technician, psychologist, psychiatrist, school social worker, speech correctionist, remedial reading teacher, hearing specialist, and home tutor. On the nonprofessional level, services provided by the school may include transportation, recreation, food and cafeteria services, and making available low-cost pupil insurance. The number and extent of the services that will be provided by an individual junior high school and a school district will obviously vary with the degree of need of the student clientele, the amount of money available, and the attitude of the community and the school administration toward supplying these kinds of services.

Society is discovering that it is more practical from a human point of view, and less expensive in actual dollars and cents, to provide as much as possible to children. Because of the extensive changes in the structure of our society, our way of living, the family unit, and our mores, it is no longer a question of "Should the schools provide such a range of pupil personnel services?" Rather the question is now, "To what extent shall the schools supply necessary services not provided by other institutions in the community?" The problem has become one of priority and immediacy, the greatest good for the greatest number of children. In addition to competent, trained, and qualified school counselors, what services are most necessary in any specific school? A school nurse? Dental help? A psychologist? Cafeteria services? It is no longer an issue of "if" but "which"—which service and how much.

The function of guidance is one that appeared early in the junior high school movement and one that has become stronger and more important through the years. With our increasing knowledge of how children learn and our growing understanding of the characteristics of this age group, there is a distinct necessity to develop guidance programs in terms of the contemporary needs of the emerging and adolescent group served by the junior high and middle school. Certainly the guidance program and the counselors, when other services are not available, can direct some attention to individual student problems that would otherwise be ignored or have nothing done about them for lack of a specialist within the building or the school district. This is not to suggest that the junior high counselors should themselves engage in these varying kinds of services, but they should take such actions as are necessary and possible to secure necessary services for those identified as in need of specialized help.

As currently viewed, the guidance functions and services in the junior high and middle school are keyed first of all to the student served—his characteristics, his needs, his concerns, and his desires. Guidance becomes more than counseling, although the two terms are sometimes used synonymously (try "guidance counselor" for an exercise in confusion). "The guidance function includes more than decision making, course selection, and vocational planning."[1] In this concept, the school program includes the teaching function, the organizing and administrative function, and the guidance function, the last being performed by counselors and other specialists. A part of the problem involved in discussing guidance is the lack of complete agreement as to terms and definitions. Counseling, for example, is but a part of guidance, and counseling services are but a part of the complete program of guidance.

> Although guidance has been defined, is still being defined, and will continue to be defined, three points of commonality seem likely to appear and survive: . . . guidance is a point of view; guidance is available to all students; guidance is a program of services within the school structure.[2]

BACKGROUND

In the early 1900's those children who finished high school were largely college-oriented either in their own plans or by virtue of the secondary school curriculum then existing. Changing social and economic conditions, child labor laws, and compulsory school-attendance laws multiplied secondary school enrollments and required more diversified educational programs. The first guidance programs which made their appearance between 1900 and 1915 were largely concerned with vocational counseling and job placement for high school youth. Increasing high school enrollments brought out a wider range of student interests, abilities, and vocational plans, and a rapidly growing ratio of noncollege-bound students. Many students had no real idea what they wanted from school other than a high school diploma —they had neither vocational plans nor college aspirations. To provide something for everyone, high schools began to multiply their course offerings to such an extent that it was not unusual to find well over a hundred different courses offered in one high school. Vocational choices, college plans, general education—which was the best choice for any given student, and who was to advise the students?

Because teachers knew little about courses outside their own fields of interest and specialization, they were of little help in advising students. In 1908 Frank Parsons, a Boston high school teacher, was the first to begin counseling youth in vocational placement. He was interested in helping young people locate positions for which they had the necessary skills, abilities, and interest. As a result of Parson's efforts, the Boston Vocational Bureau was opened in 1908, and this new idea rapidly caught hold. In 1910, Boston hosted the first national conference on vocational guidance, and in 1913 the National Vocational Guidance Association was organized.

Another early leader in school counseling was Jesse B. Davis who, as principal of the Grand Rapids High School, Michigan, taught vocational and educational guidance through courses in English composition. In these classes his students were given encouragement in exploring their own abilities and interests and learning the basic knowledges and skills required by the natures of various occupations, as well as discovering the opportunities for advancement in these several vocations.

In 1918 John M. Brewer's book, *Vocational and Educational Guidance*, was published, which was influential in making educational guidance an accepted and integral part of the school's program. In these early years of the junior high school the guidance function was viewed as a high school responsibility with its primary purpose that of vocational guidance, and the educational aspect limited to advising students as to which courses were necessary for college entrance and which were most useful for various specific vocations. There were, it is true, class advisors for the various grades in high school—i.e., "senior class advisor," "junior class advisor"—but these positions were concerned almost exclusively with the social life and financial affairs of a class rather than with any instructional activity. As the high school guidance program grew, the junior high schools began adopting virtually the same guidance patterns as the high schools, including class advisors and vocational counseling. It is an unfortunate historical circumstance that practically all junior high school guidance functions and practices were taken piecemeal from the high school.

G. Stanley Hall and others, in their work with individual differences and studies of adolescence, helped to shift the focus of guidance from vocational planning to the needs of the individual. This shift was given increased emphasis by the historical Cardinal Principles of Education, 1918, which further stressed the needs of the individual.

In the years since these first approaches the concept of guidance has been broadened from vocational counseling to include virtually every phase of education and all stages in the development of the child.

> As now interpreted, guidance touches every aspect of the individual's personality—physical, mental, emotional, and social. It is concerned with all of an individual's attitudes and behavior patterns. It seeks to help the individual integrate all his activities, using his basic potentialities and environmental opportunities.[3]

Guidance services are now considered to be such an important part of the educational program that millions of dollars of federal funds were made available for the improvement of school guidance services by the National Defense Act of 1958, and the 1964 extension of this same act. Recognition that each person is an individual and is unique underlines the need for counseling, curricula, and an education which will develop the distinctive potentials of every human being. Concern in the mid-1960's with poverty, segregation, vocational training programs, early childhood education, dropouts, and equal educational opportunity brought forth a number of federal programs, much federal money, and a massive increase in counseling and guidance services and personnel in secondary schools, both junior and senior high.

Because of the critical age and nature of the junior high school student —the early adolescent—and because of the transitional nature of the school, the junior high school has very nearly from its inception recognized the importance of guidance. Early writers on the junior high school, such as William A. Smith (1926), Thomas H. Briggs (1920), and Calvin O. Davis (1920), referred to the adolescent as one who needs guidance, and the guidance program as "the very keystone of the junior high school."[4]

The guidance function has consistently been considered an important part of the junior high school: Briggs (1920) made guidance his third objective; Davis (1924) said that it was the "most important of all the functions of the junior high school":[5] Gruhn and Douglass (1949) listed guidance[6] as one of the six functions of the junior high school; James B. Conant in 1960 stressed the need for guidance services in Junior high school, but warned that "it is by no means easy to find competent guidance personnel":[7] and Mauritz Johnson (1961) stated that, "Guidance is a primary concern of the junior high school, which initial stage of secondary education is a crucial one in the guidance of youth."[8]

There is no lack of agreement concerning the need for guidance services in the junior high school, but there is a marked difference in the kind and quality of guidance services provided from one junior high school to another. Partly this is due to the cost of such services, partly because of lack of trained personnel, and partly because of a lack of understanding by all concerned, teachers, students, counselors, and administrators, of the roles and functions of guidance personnel.

JUNIOR HIGH SCHOOL GUIDANCE

We have discussed in Chapter 2 the characteristics and needs of the preadolescent and the early adolescent. The child of this age finds that his outlook and perceptions are drastically changed; this is also true of his self-concept. He is beginning to find and assert himself as an individual and to define his own set of values. He is inclined to be rebellious at adult authority, to be sure that he knows what is right and best; yet at the same time he is anxious for direction so long as it is not imposed upon him. He wants and needs someone who will listen to him, someone who can also point out educational options and prevocational choices. "It is the *individual* pupil's concerns that should determine our program, not our preconceived notions about what his concerns are likely to be."[9]

The overall guidance program in the junior high school, then, is concerned with the personal and social adjustment of the student, his educational plans, and to a much lesser extent at this level, his vocational plans. Guidance and guidance services are related to the entire educational program and are rendered to help children in making sound plans, wise choices, and satisfactory adjustments. Ideally, guidance personnel will include a nurse, a doctor, an attendance officer, a psychologist, one or more school counselors, and the school social worker.

Counseling, as a part of guidance services, is a person-to-person process involving individual and group sessions. A good counselor is regarded by the students as an understanding friend who will listen, ask questions, and occasionally offer suggestions but will refrain from expressing his personal opinions on various aspects of life. Individual counseling should be available to every student, and students should be provided with exploratory experiences and information so that they may reach their own conclusions without manipulation by anyone. A good counselor is concerned with all students, the potential and actual dropout, the vocationally inclined student, the discipline problems, the noncollege bound and the college bound. In performing his function, the counselor must work in close cooperation with school, staff, parents, and community referral sources.

> Counseling is just one of the services of the guidance program, but in regard to the individual student, it may well be considered the heart . . . [since] school counseling is concerned with the problem-solving issues common to all students.[10]

The guidance program as a whole has as its aims:

1. Helping the individual students, insofar as is possible through his own efforts, to achieve up to his maximum; to attain personal satisfactions in as many areas of his life as is possible; and to make his greatest contribution to society.
2. To assist the student to solve his own problems, to make an accurate analysis of the facts, and to make wise choices and adjustments.
3. To help each individual to establish a permanent basis for sound, mature adjustments.
4. To help each student to achieve a well-balanced life in every respect, physical, mental, emotional, and social.[11]

It would be safe to say that all teachers and educators are indirectly and directly involved daily in tasks which are identified as counseling or guidance functions. This involvement is inevitable, but a coordination of efforts in the development of a child is highly desirable. Therefore it can be easily argued that we need a department within each school, K–12, where coordinated guidance and counseling efforts can focus on the child's growth.

Piaget has identified stages of development in young people, and it is of significance that the beginning of the child's ability to think abstractly usually occurs just prior to or within the junior high school years. The difference between concrete and abstract thinking is important, but equally important is the socialization process attached to this vastly broadening world of thought in which the teenager finds himself. While this is not a sudden process, it is very real and important. Obviously this fact has implications for guidance and counseling at this level of instruction; we need all the help we can get to smooth the child's transition into the abstract world.

Coupled with this view of development, Broudy has suggested that "What an individual learns depends, among other things, upon the situations he is placed in, the operations he is required to perform in dealing with them, and the information available."[12] While Broudy is somewhat critical of Bruner, both agree that the development of the child and the curriculum should be continuous. Bruner's famous hypothesis, "Any subject can be taught effectively in some intellectually honest form to any child at any stage of development," emphasizes the need for coordination of the cirruculum and guidance services. The child's preparation for adult living should begin where he can understand it.

Conant's reports have suggested that one "full-time counselor [or guidance specialist] for every two hundred and fifty to three hundred pupils is a worthy goal, but hardly an ideal." His findings indicate that most junior high schools do not approach the realization of this goal, although some are trying. Presently the Pittsburgh school system, for example, is engaged in a plant design that will allow a counselor-teacher to have intimate contact with as few as forty students.

The homeroom plan practiced by some educators is one way of allowing greater student-teacher-counselor contact. Great things were prophesied for the homeroom when it first became well established in the 1920's and 1930's. It was believed that this period of time which scheduled the same group of students with the same teacher for the same amount of time daily would permit the kind of teacher-student acquaintanceship, friendship, mutual understanding, and rapport that would otherwise be impossible in a departmentalized schedule. As with nearly any aspect of teaching, it soon became apparent that the homeroom period, even when continued with the same students and the same teacher for two or three consecutive years, was only as successful as the teacher permitted and encouraged it to be. If the teacher believed in the concept and worked to make it function well, then it was successful. If the teacher used the time to correct papers and put her students to work on assignments, then it was not successful. A further complication comes to pass when the homeroom period is used as an administrative device for selling lunch tickets, collecting Red Cross money, and making announcements.

In addition, most teachers are not trained counselors and do not feel comfortable in attempting to serve in that area. The homeroom plan must have individual teacher guidance—this is critical for its success—and this plan was devised as a partial effort to secure more widespread guidance and counseling services. For these and other reasons, the homeroom, as a counseling tool, never achieved great success. As an administrative device with the euphemistic label of "homeroom," it is found in the great majority of junior and senior high schools of the United States even yet.

The core-homeroom arrangement was devised as a partial answer to the limited success of the homeroom period. Recognizing that it is desirable for the preadolescent and early adolescent to have someplace where they belong, to have a teacher who is more "their teacher" than anyone else, some junior administrators assigned homeroom functions and duties to the core teachers. This worked quite well with those teachers who were qualified teachers of core and in those classes that were truly core classes, but there have been many of each, so labeled, that in practice are something quite different. Teachers who understand core, who can teach it, and who want to teach it are few. In the rush to adopt the new, many school districts established a block of time, called it core, and felt quite self-righteous. Within such "core" classes, the homeroom situation was usually much the same as that in departmentalized schools where it is also an administrative tool, not a counseling technique.

There has not yet been found a method of counseling suitable for junior high and middle schools that is superior to the use of trained specialists with an assigned pupil load permitting sufficient time for all pupils who wish to take advantage of the services available. It is clear that there is an accepted need for counseling, but there is also a failure to meet the need, at least partly on the grounds of simple economics. The situation could be somewhat alleviated if every classroom teacher had some understanding of guidance functions and procedures. It is also very useful to school counselors to conduct training sessions for the faculty in the junior high school.

THE COUNSELOR IN THE JUNIOR HIGH AND MIDDLE SCHOOL

Much of the criticism of junior high school counseling, and there has been considerable, exists because the counselor is expected to be all things to all people, with the natural result that dissatisfactions are bound to arise. The principal often sees the counselor as a quasi-administrator who is assigned a list of duties of a mechanical nature, primarily attendance and scheduling. The counselor who is efficient in scheduling and attendance unburdens the grateful principal of a substantial part of his administrative duties and is warmly regarded as a useful staff member—by the administrator. These duties can be performed by good clerical workers at much less cost and with a real gain in time available for student counseling.

Some counselors find security in statistics, record-keeping, and the testing program. These items all have their places and contribute to the overall knowledge of the student which is useful to guidance services. They are not, however, the main function of a counselor. Again, much of this can be done by competent clerical assistance and questions can be legitimately raised as to the need or even desirability of the quality of paperwork of this nature frequently indulged in by counselors.

In recent years there has been a strong surge of interest in testing of children on an impressive range and variety of tests. Test instruments have increased greatly in number and kind, and it has appeared to some in education that a test was either available for every need or was in the process of construction. Because tests are useless until they are administered, large numbers of more or less compliant children at all levels have been busily responding to tests in subject fields, opinion surveys, attitude inventories, social-interest studies, and countless others. The kinds of information that these instruments are intended to elicit not only has been coming under attack as an invasion of children's privacy, but there has been questioning of belief that we must "understand" the child in order to help him. A major purpose of testing has been to collect information about individuals so that we will know more about them and then perhaps understand them better. If this is found to be unnecessary or of limited value, test-happy counselors throughout the land may have some difficulty in knowing what to do with themselves.

One of the biggest problems a counselor can have is lack of communication with the teaching staff. Certainly what a student says to a counselor should be regarded as confidential, yet teachers can be of real assistance if they are apprised generally and specifically of student difficulties. The counselor who hugs his information close to his vest and does not enlist the help of the teachers may regard himself as a pedagogical operator 007, but to the uninformed and often bewildered teachers he is merely an employee who sits around drinking coffee and complains about overwork. At the other extreme, it should go without saying (but unfortunately does not) that confidential information remains confidential with both counselors and teachers.

A counselor may become involved with disciplinary problems to the extent that he endeavors to discover causes and possible cures, but the counselor should never be the administrator's club or whip. If a disciplinary action is required, this should be taken by the principal. The counselor must be a friend, an understanding listener, the "good guy in the white hat."

The effective junior high school counselor will

1. Have plenty of time available for individual counseling sessions—yet he will make use of group counseling wherever practicable.
2. Work closely with teachers, keeping them well informed of student situations and problems.
3. Be a good listener and refrain from the easier path of supplying unnecessary information, answers, and advice.
4. Be honestly interested in children and accept that it is normal for junior high school students to have problems.
5. Remember that it is more important to know a student as a person than it is to know about him. Stress the positive with every child.
6. Be available to the students as they need and seek him; students should have a free choice as to whether or not they choose to participate. If we really believe in individual differences, freedom of choice, and democracy in action, then we have difficulty in justifying a requirement that all students see the counselor a fixed number of times every school year. When the student initiates the relationship, the situation is on firmer ground than if it is compulsory. If the counseling program is well operated, the number of voluntary referrals will reflect this. If there are few or no voluntary referrals, then there is also certainly something wrong with the guidance program—or with the personality and attitude of the counselor.
7. Devote time to determining pupil needs and how well the school's services and programs meet these needs. Follow-up studies and dropout studies are very useful and important.
8. Keep parents and the community informed as to the services available and necessary.
9. Work to develop a planned school guidance program which has

well-defined goals and procedures, rather than operating on a day-to-day, firefighting manner as emergencies arise.

10. Remember always that he is working with people. Too many schools seem to be operated for the convenience of teachers and administrators—not for the benefit of the students.

The American School Counselor Association defines the role of the secondary school counselor in part as follows:[13] A secondary school counselor is

1. A professional educator who has had specialized graduate-level training in counseling and guidance services. His main concern is for the normal needs and problems of his pupils.
2. An important and integral part of the staff of the school.
3. A person who realizes that each student will have a better opportunity to develop and fulfill himself within the structure of a nonevaluative and positive relationship in which he is accepted and assisted in understanding himself and his world.
4. A person who sees each pupil as an individual, unique in himself, with a right to be accepted, helped in his self-development, self-direction, and self-fulfillment and who has the right and responsibility to make decisions and to accept the results of his decisions.
5. A person who perceives the school as a democratic institution, society as continually changing, and himself as a meditator with the students in helping them to resolve conflicts and to find their place.

While this document was developed for the broader area of all secondary education, by directing the procedures to the specific kind of student involved, middle school and junior high, the statements are quite relevant.

THE JUNIOR HIGH SCHOOL GUIDANCE PROGRAM

The guidance function of a junior high school can be better understood by looking at its duties and accepting a middle ground between the stated ideal and the pessimistic pronouncement that guidance people are identifiable because of a need for support from their own profession. The following list indicates the expansion of the guidance program:

Admission and School Placement
Orientation in Successive Educational Levels
Assisting in Self-Understanding
Understanding Environmental Opportunities and Demands
Making Life Plans and Adjustments
  Vocational Guidance
  Educational Guidance
  Planning Educational Programs
  Extracurricular Programs

Students as Junior Citizens
Housing
Achieving Physical and Mental Fitness
Guidance in Learning to Learn
Self-Direction of a Life Plan
Fostering a Value System and Self-Discipline
Identification and Treatment of the Exceptional
Placement and Follow-up[14]

The modern guidance program encompasses five guidance services: (1) the individual inventory service, (2) the information service, (3) the counseling service, (4) the placement service, and (5) the follow-up or evaluation service.

This breakdown of the broad areas of guidance simplifies delineation. The first area is the analysis of the individual where all pertinent data are collected and filed by the counseling department. This would include any biographical or autobiographical information that could be used to help the pupil to have a better awareness of himself. A comprehensive account of personal information can be used effectively by a skilled counselor. A simple thing like attendance might provide some significant clues; an example would be a student who has missed as much as one-third of his school time and finds himself behind grade level in all subjects. If he has a record of absence of extreme nature and yet performs on a par level with fellow classmates, perhaps he has undiscovered ability. This is to say that home and school information should be carefully collected and analyzed for what it may contribute—not just stored.

The second area of the guidance services is the information service, which includes the testing program. The simple mention of a testing program sparks many arguments. Unquestionably there have been many abuses of testing information resulting in students and parents distrusting the basic premises underlying a testing program. A few points should be considered about such a program.

1. The major purpose for the testing program should be for guidance, although it may be effectively used for other purposes such as diagnosis and evaluation.
2. While tests are limited in their assessment of the total individual, honest use can be valuable. Even when combined with other data, test scores will not tell a pupil beyond all doubt whether he will succeed or fail in some choice, although they are too often so interpreted.
3. Standardized test scores provide data that can aid the pupil in his self-understanding and decision making. A teacher who understands only a little about testing should not be allowed to explain or inter-

pret information to the child or to a parent who has even less sophistication. The question as to how much information about test results should be revealed to students and parents is extremely delicate and passionately debated. There is no doubt that parents have a right to know something about their child's abilities, performance, and problems. The question is, "How much should be told?" It is important that the school establish good parental relations and that it communicate such information to the parents as is useful and readily understood.

Central to any guidance program is the counseling service. This area of emphasis depends upon administrative philosophy for support if it is to achieve its goals. It may be argued that a part-time counselor who is also a teacher or an administrator has closer contact with the pupil than the full-time counselor. Too often the basis of this philosophy is economics. The teacher-counselor may have his place, but it is not an alternative for the full-time counselor. The important thing to remember is that an effective counselor is a person who has analytical tools coupled with a knack for gaining the confidence of the student.

The placement service's function is to help pupils make personal decisions that are vocational, educational, and socio-personal. This function, when properly performed, will help pupils make their own decisions. Although the vocational emphasis in the junior high has lost the importance it once had, some kind of vocational orientation and planning should begin at this level.

The final function of the guidance program is the research or follow-up service. The junior high school must constantly evaluate the curriculum in terms of pupil success in the post junior high school life. Some sort of follow-up activities should be a continuous part of the guidance program of the junior high school. Any school that is successful in the placement and follow-up functions would be closely approaching the guidance program the junior high school would view as ideal.

THE TEACHER'S ROLE IN GUIDANCE

The teacher's influence is not limited in scope to the learnings which take place in the classroom. The teacher's actions, whether planned or unplanned, influence the pupil in many ways. Whenever the teacher counsels a pupil or groups of pupils, she is performing a guidance function. Guidance opportunities are found often in the classroom, in study periods, and in extracurricular activities.

In some junior high schools, the homeroom teacher is considered to play a major role in the guidance program. According to a program in one junior high school, the homeroom teacher has four major guidance duties:

1. To counsel with individual students.
2. To conduct group guidance sessions for the homeroom.
3. To serve as a contact between the student and the special subject teacher.
4. To serve as a liaison between the school and home.[15]

ORIENTATION

There is no question about the student need for orientation procedures in the transition period from elementary to the secondary school. One of the originally stated purposes in instituting the junior high school was to provide a transitional phase between the elementary and secondary educational programs. Whether this purpose has been accomplished is frequently debated within the professional literature. Most of these articles report trial-and-error procedures which have been evaluated by the administrative staff of the schools that practice them. Unfortunately there have been relatively few attempts to conduct formal studies of the extent or value of junior high school orientation programs.

While most orientation activities are directed toward immediate adjustment problems, there is also some recognition of the developing maturity of students. The junior high school age is not only an age of adjusting to external conditions, but a period in the life of the child when internal changes result in adjustment problems. The adolescent is confronted with many situations as a result of his natural growth and development. However, too much emphasis may have been placed upon the extreme emotional stress and strain features of the adolescent period. It is necessary to seek and find a balance between ignoring these characteristics and devoting all one's time to these emotional crises, with the result that one moves from one upheaval to the next.

Some characteristics of children at this age that suggest a need for emphasis on the major adjustments of youth include the desire for more independence and a more equal relationship with adults, especially at home. Increasingly important is the desire to attain recognition by and a standing with teenage peers, including boy-girl relationships. Of considerable concern is physical growth and development, and the wish to be big and strong or attractive. This period brings intellectual questions as well—and a reexamination of values. The adolescent no longer completely accepts authority, but must find his convictions of right and wrong through his associations with peers, adults, mass media, and reading materials. Moral, social, and religious values all undergo scrutiny, and changes of attitudes take place. Parents and teachers both must be aware of these patterns of growth and development if children are to be helped in making a satisfactory adjustment.

The changes a child must make in his daily routine when he enters junior high school may be characterized as follows:

> Imagine yourself in a similar situation. You have never been away from your own home, and suddenly you are placed in a huge city with instructions to find six or seven houses during the day and remember everything that happens. You will have a confusing time finding your way about the city, hesitant to ask questions of unsmiling strangers and worried lest you be late and have to face the stares of more strangers as you walk to the front of a great hall.[16]

It is not difficult to understand why so many children entering junior high develop a strong dislike for school at this point in their school careers. It should be obvious that the elementary school, junior high school, and the secondary school need to interrelate their programs of orientation so that these problems are minimized, and the transition of the child from one school to the other is made possible with the least disruption of the learning experiences of the student.

Too often schools do not have an effective, continuous orientation program. It is easy to concentrate on a one-shot orientation assembly, and the real problem here is that this type of program does not instruct the incoming students at the time of greatest learning readiness. New students are able to understand some of the differences in routine prior to entering the junior high building. However, understanding industrial arts, home economics, gym, cafeteria, class changes, and the student council—to name a few—all come more easily after school actually begins and after there is a planned program for orientation. There is little learning when all of this information is crowded into a single program.

SOME EXAMPLES OF ORIENTATION PROCEDURES

Parents and teachers can be effectively involved in orientation programs through PTA groups. Bonomi and Laritz[17] reported organized meetings with parents which were designed to aid in the orientation of children through helping parents understand the difficult age at which these children have arrived. The unique feature of this program was that it dealt with parents rather than with students. The PTA group discussed such problems as teenage behavior, parental attitudes toward education, and understandings of the various subjects, extracurricular activities, grading systems, discipline, and general organization of the junior high school.

Some efforts have been made experimentally to utilize the summer vacation to promote effective transition to junior high school. The Milne School, a junior-senior high school which serves the State University of New York at Albany, designed an experimental four-week summer orientation program for sixth-grade pupils who were to enter the seventh grade in the fall. Both social and academic activities were included in this program. It was reported that this experiment revealed that the classes involved in the summer program were significantly advanced over the groups which did not attend the summer sessions.[18]

The Cherry Creek School District, Arapahoe County, Colorado, designed and implemented a program of orientation with some unique guidance features. Their sixth-to-seventh-grade transition has been achieved smoothly for the students through the extensive activity of counselors. They implemented a summer program conducted by two counselors which include a visit to the home of each prospective seventh-grade student. The interviews were planned by geographical areas, with half-hour visits stressing informal friendly atmosphere. The advantage of this contact was that it tended to overcome the reticence students frequently feel about asking "simple" questions in the presence of a group.[19] Other orientation activities include (1) contact with elementary schools in meetings with students to provide information about the junior high school; (2) a "Buddy Day" during which sixth-grade students are assigned to seventh-graders, and attend junior high school for an entire day; and (3) a meeting with the parents of sixth-grade students at the junior high school to describe the curriculum, meeting teachers, and tour the building.

STEPS TO A GOOD JUNIOR HIGH SCHOOL ORIENTATION PROGRAM

Some of the essential characteristics of effective orientation programs include:

1. *Elementary teacher visitation.* It is extremely helpful for the junior high school to invite elementary teachers to visit the junior high school each year to attend an informal social event. During this time explanation could be given to the teachers concerning such things as groups, practices, use of pupil records provided by the elementary school, clubs and other student activities, grading policies, etc. This type of visitation would contribute to better understanding between elementary and junior high school teachers.
2. *Junior high school principal and/or counselor visitation.* This would provide an ideal opportunity for the counselor and principal to explain some of the similarities and differences of the two schools. In an informal meeting with sixth-grade pupils, an opportunity for questions from the students would let them get to know two important people in their seventh-grade world.
3. *Invitation to parents to attend junior high PTA orientation.* The purpose of this activity would be to provide:
   (a) Information on expected teenage behavior.

(b) Information given to provide understanding of subjects, extracurricular activities, grading systems, discipline, and general organization of the school.

(c) Discussion of appropriate parental attitudes toward education.

4. *Orientation day program.* Some of the more successful orientation assemblies of this nature are put on entirely by the student council. Sixth graders then receive much of their orientation from students of the junior high. Often such things as the reporting system, cafeteria, lost and found, passing between classes, etc., are reviewed by the president of the student council. This is also an ideal time for the student handbook to be passed to the sixth-graders and discussed.
5. *Fall assembly for seventh grade.* An assembly for seventh-graders only should be held during the first week of school. At this assembly the various school personnel (e.g., office, cafeteria, custodial) are introduced, rules are reviewed, and information requested can be provided.
6. *Continuing orientation and reevaluation.* Homeroom classes or block-time classes should continue the orientation process. A planned orientation program should be developed which included: explanation of clubs and membership, homeroom officers elected, and reevaluation of the student handbook.

Other orientation procedures which are recommended to be tried experimentally and evaluated include:

1. Combination faculty meetings with teachers from elementary and junior high schools to plan orientation activities.
2. Junior high teachers exchanging places with elementary teachers for a short time. (This is an eye-opener for both groups.)
3. Teachers or counselors visiting new or prospective students' homes.
4. Elementary school children presenting an assembly program at their future junior high school.
5. Teaching a unit on orientation to both sixth- and seventh-grade students.
6. Holding meetings with parents in small groups to familiarize them with regulations, the school plant, and the procedures in the junior high school.

SUMMARY

The need for guidance services in the junior high school is and has been recognized virtually from the beginning of this institution. Guidance services, which were largely vocational and precollege counseling, have been greatly expanded to become a basic part of the total educational program.

Because the junior high school student is in particular need of skilled counseling and guidance, it is essential that the roles and functions of guidance personnel in junior high schools be clarified.

Many counselors become administrative assistants; others become record keepers, testing specialists, and statisticians. There is a need for more counselors who work at being just that: junior high school counselors who are concerned with helping adolescents.

A good junior high school guidance program is designed specifically for the junior high school student and for the school and community which is served. Such a program includes the individual inventory service, the information service, the counseling service, the placement service, and the follow-up or evaluation service.

Guidance frequently becomes what the counselor makes of it—which may be very good or very bad.

REFERENCES

1. Leslie Kindred (ed.), *The Intermediate Schools.* Englewood Cliffs, N.J.: Prentice-Hall, 1968, p. 334.
2. LaVerne Carmichael, "School Guidance: Perspective, Purpose, and Performance," *Clearing House,* Vol. 43 December 1968, p. 223.
3. Lester D. Crow and Alice Crow, *An Introduction to Guidance: Basic Principles and Practices.* 2d ed. New York: American Book, 1960, p. 16.
4. William A. Smith, *The Junior High School.* New York: Macmillan, 1926, p. 377.
5. Ralph W. Pringle, *The Junior High School.* New York: McGraw-Hill, 1937, p. 80.
6. William T. Gruhn and Harl R. Douglass, *The Modern Junior High School.* 2d ed. New York: Ronald, pp. 31–32.
7. James B. Conant, *Education in the Junior High School Years.* Princeton, N.J.: Educational Testing Service, 1960, p. 27.
8. Mauritz Johnson, Jr., et al., *Junior High School Guidance.* New York: Harper, 1961, p. 1.
9. Kindred et al., *op. cit.,* pp. 336–337.
10. Wayman R. F. Grant, Sr., "A Functional Junior High School Guidance Program," *Journal of Secondary Education,* Vol. 41 (October 1966), p. 257.
11. J. Anthony Humpheys and others, *Guidance Services.* Chicago, Ill.: Science Research Associates, 1960, p. 79.
12. Harry S. Broudy, *Democracy and Excellence in American Secondary Education.* Chicago: Rand, McNally, 1964, p. 6.
13. American School Counselor Association, *The Role of the Secondary School Counselor.* Washington, D.C.: American Personnel and Guidance Association, 1966.
14. Leonard H. Clark, Raymond L. Klein, and John B. Burks, *The American Secondary School Curriculum.* New York: Macmillan, 1965.
15. Francis X. Vogel, "Guidance in the Junior High School," *NASSP Bulletin,* Vol. 46 (October 1962), p. 93–97.

16. William Plutte, "Going Into Junior High School—Bugaboo or Big Adventure?" *Instructor*, Vol. 68 (May 1954), p. 11.
17. Camillo A. Bonomi and Samuel J. Laritz, "Dynamic Study Group on Junior High School Orientation," *NASSP BULLETIN*, Vol. 45 (November 1961), pp. 82–83.
18. Edward Fagan and Anita Dunn, "Summer Is For Learning," *NASSP BULLETIN*, Vol. 48 (February 1963), pp. 109–112.
19. James W. Brinkoph. "Transition from Sixth to Seventh Made Easy at Cherry Creek," *NASSP BULLETIN*, Vol. 46 (February 1962), pp. 70–73.

chapter 4

Administration

Some aspects of administration are much the same regardless of the profession or business. Good administrators, wherever they are, find it necessary to gather all information and facts available, consider possible alternatives, and make decisions. As a part of this, administrators are expected to plan, control, direct, and evaluate the activities of the organization. The administrative duties and functions of the principal of a middle school or junior high school have much in common with those of elementary and high school principals. Differences exist in the matter of degree at the various levels, and there are definite differences in the student populations. Just as there should be different curricula at different school levels, differences in teacher preparation and varying facilities, so are there differences in administrative needs, problems, policies, and procedures at elementary, middle, and senior high school.

Specifically, the junior high school principal is expected to plan, direct, control, evaluate, and make decisions concerning educational programs for early adolescents. It is his job "to improve the school, to help those involved to plan goals, evaluate achievements, and redirect their efforts. . . . The curriculum is his basic concern. Its improvement is his most important single task."[1] In his efforts to improve the curriculum, he must always keep clearly in mind the characteristics of the students who attend the junior high and middle schools—the preadolescent and the early adolescent. Both the curriculum development and the administrative policies and procedures should reflect this same awareness, this thorough knowledge of the student population. Here we find clearly outlined a basic problem in the selection of junior high school principals. Far too often they are ex-high school coaches, or elementary principals who are being rewarded by moving them "up," or ex-high school principals who didn't make it to the satisfaction of all concerned at the high school level. If we need specially trained teachers for junior high schools—and we do——then the need is even more critical for junior high principals who are knowledgeable about junior high schools and early adolescents.

While the responsibility is that of the junior high principal, the actual administration of the school should involve a close relationship and cooperation with everyone concerned. Perceptions of teachers and principals of what a job entails and of what actions are necessary frequently differ widely. The principal must know what the staff expects of him, and obviously the staff must know precisely what is expected by the principal if there is to be harmony and maximum efficiency. In short, there must be complete two-way communication.

A basic tenet for principals is to learn to make use of the talents, techniques, and abilities of personnel. A good principal learns to delegate responsibility, authority, and work. There are several very good reasons for such delegation:

1. It is too easy for a principal to become engrossed in administrative detail, paperwork, and trivia, (i.e., the principal who guards jealously the key to the supply room and personally dispenses each box of paper clips).
2. Delegation permits a distribution of the load, giving everyone a feeling of being involved.
3. If the maximum number of students and staff participate in administration, planning, and decision making, morale is enhanced.
4. Potential leadership is discovered and encouraged.
5. The main task of the principal should be the improvement of instruction. Improvement of instruction and curriculum actually means working with people more than dealing with content. Delegation of some tasks and involvement of more people is conducive to such improvement. This can get the principal out from behind his desk.

There are some cautions and suggestions to keep in mind when delegating:

1. Be *sure* that everyone involved understands exactly *what* is to be done and when. Leave the *how* up to the person assigned the task.
2. Make suggestions, if asked, but avoid too many specific directions. The principal might as well do it himself as to repress all initiative.
3. Be sure each person involved knows precisely who is responsible for what.
4. Hold responsible the person given the job but *leave him alone* to perform the task. An occasional question relating to the work is legitimate as are progress reports, but there should never be a continued checking up nor constant supervision. This kills initiative. Give a man a job, set a final date, and leave him alone to do what

is necessary. Be available for suggestions and help, if asked.

5. Remember, if it succeeds, the individual or the staff did it. The principal may take what reflected glory there is. Should it fail, recriminations are valueless and the principal soaks up the blame by himself, for his is the ultimate responsibility.

QUALIFICATIONS AND ATTITUDES

Some characteristics, attitudes, and abilities are requisite for all good administrators. The effective junior high school principal must possess these, in some areas in more depth and concentration than would an administrator at other levels, besides having some special qualifications:

1. He must have a thorough knowledge of child growth and development. Highly desirable for this is elementary teaching experience and administration.
2. It is essential that the junior high school principal have a background of successful teaching experience in the junior high school, preferably for all grades included.
3. Experience in the junior high activity program will add materially to his competencies as will some time spent as a junior high school counselor.
4. The effective junior high school principal knows the development and functions of both elementary and junior high schools and how best to articulate their programs.
5. He reads widely in both educational and noneducational areas and is well up on current trends and practices, particularly as they relate to the junior high school.
6. He knows the background and development of the high school, is aware of their needs and problems, and endeavors to articulate the high school program with that of the junior high.
7. He has a thorough understanding of the early adolescent and a good background in adolescent psychology.
8. He knows what is involved in curriculum construction for junior high school and is concerned with the need for achievement of students of all levels of ability in both the subject and activity curricula.

Since the principal's primary task is improvement of curriculum and instruction, which requires much in developing effective human relations, there are several other factors involved which contribute to success:

1. Keep the staff informed. Teachers, and all personnel for that matter, find it difficult to be supportive if they don't know what it is that they are supporting. When everyone knows what the goals are

and has a part in determining them as well as deciding procedures for reaching these objectives, criticism and complaint may still exist but it is far less likely.

2. Stimulate teacher enterprise and enthusiasm. A healthy dissatisfaction with the shortcomings of the program encourages experimentation and efforts to do the job better. Avoid nit-picking and indiscriminate censure. Never say, "You're all wrong." Instead, ask, "Is there some other way in which we could do this?" A principal who consistently emphasizes, "*I* think," may produce change, perhaps not what he expected, and not so effectively as would be achieved by, "Could we . . . ?" Treat everyone impartially and avoid favoritism.
3. Get out and see what is going on in every aspect of the school: in classes, in the lunchroom, in activities, before school, and after school. Observe teachers and students wherever possible. When something commendable occurs, compliment the person responsible, but avoid false praise which fools no one. Be available to everyone who has an honest need—parents, staff, and students. When a teacher needs help, see to it that the help is forthcoming; preferably such assistance comes from someone other than the principal, such as a counselor, helping teacher, or the librarian.
4. Be supportive of the school staff. Compliment in public and rebuke in private. If someone wishes to try something different, never say, "It can't be done." Rather, let others examine and analyze the proposal. A great many good ideas come from teachers—they are not restricted to administrators—and virtually all administrators were originally classroom teachers. Furthermore, perhaps it *can* be done and should be done, and, if the idea has merit, the principal should do all possible to implement the suggestion.
5. Standards set for scholarship and behavior in which students and staff have had a voice will not only be easier to maintain, they will probably be more realistic.
6. Involving all parties concerned does not relieve the principal of responsibility for saying what he believes in a straightforward and honest way—and for basing his statements upon the most complete information available. The principal accepts what committees and individuals recommend without attempting to control such people and force statements to coincide with his beliefs. If possible, he endeavors to implement their decisions and recommendations.
7. The principal sets a climate in which teachers feel a sense of freedom in their work without feeling that there is a lack of leadership and direction. Remember, the final responsibility rests with the principal for all decisions.

8. Know the faculty, their ambitions, and hopes. Talk with them about matters outside of school as well as those relating to school. Try to do substantially more listening than talking, and avoid telling.
9. Be fair in division of duties and then see to it that those assigned are there and doing their share.
10. Teacher abilities, talents, interests, and wishes should always be considered when making schedules, whether the schedules deal with subject-matter assignments, activities, or duties. A great deal of dissatisfaction can be avoided and much more cooperation ensured when the principal discusses the scheduling needs and problems with the teachers, collectively and singly. When this is done teachers will frequently volunteer to help or to take some particular class, or a talent may be uncovered which was hitherto unknown.

A DESCRIPTION OF THE JUNIOR HIGH PRINCIPALSHIP

In 1966 the National Association of Secondary School Principal's Committee on the Study of the Secondary School Principalship published the results of a survey designed to derive information concerning problem areas as well as attitudes and opinions of junior high school administrators on issues and policies in education.[2] Questionnaires were sent to approximately 6,800 principals of junior high and middle schools throughout the nation, and responses were obtained from 66 percent of these, or 4,496. The information thus secured is revealing and of interest.

1. Ninety-six percent of the principals were male and their median age was 44 years.
2. There was a distinct lack of geographical mobility—over 95 percent of the principals had remained in the area where they themselves had grown up—but there was a strong pattern of social mobility, i.e., 70 percent of the fathers of the principals did not complete high school and were most likely to have worked at unskilled or semiskilled occupations.
3. Ninety-five percent of the principals had earned a master's degree or had further study beyond the master's—some to an educational specialist level or a doctoral degree.
4. About 70 percent had taught for seven or more years before becoming principals, although the more common road to the junior high school principalship was that of a previous elementary or senior high school principalship (60 percent). Only 30 percent had moved directly from teaching to the junior high school principalship. An item of interest was indicated here: The principal of a 5-3-4 school or a 6-2-4 school was more likely to have moved from teacher to principal

than was the principal of a 7-8-9 junior high school—he was more likely to have moved to this principalship from another administrative position. (This finding may partially account for the frequent complaint that the junior high school tends to lack an identity of its own, that it does not develop enough of its own programs but follows too often the patterns of other school levels.)

5. The median number of years as a junior high school principal was 4–5 years while the median number of years as a principal was 8–9 years.
6. Eighty percent of the junior high schools were reported as having separate and distinct buildings and facilities.
7. The great majority of the schools reported having a gymnasium, library, industrial arts and homemaking lab, science lab, amd music room.
8. The ideal grade organization was said to be
   (a) 6-7-8 structure: most principals in this pattern felt it was the ideal organization.
   (b) 7-8 plan: half of these principals believed a 7-8-9 pattern to be more desirable; one-fourth believed the 7-8 plan was the best. "There was pronounced dissatisfaction. Many would like to annex the sixth or ninth grade depending upon their educational background and orientation."[3]
   (c) 7-8-9 structure: three-fourths of the principals in these schools believed this pattern was the best.

There is a distinct need to develop administrative potential and leadership among those teachers who are experienced in the junior high school and who are knowledgeable concerning the preadolescent and early adolescent. It is true that a good administrator can adapt to a different school situation but success at the elementary or high school level is no guarantee of outstanding achievement as a junior high school principal. It is not common practice to reward success in one area with an assignment in another. Rare indeed is the first-grade teacher who is appointed superintendent of schools. When competent junior high school teachers could, with training and assistance, be appointed to the junior high principalship, it is difficult to support the designation of a high school administrator (who may never have taught in junior high school) as a junior high school principal.

TEN TENETS OF JUNIOR HIGH SCHOOL ADMINISTRATION

A group of about 100 junior high school principals began meeting once a year in New York City to exchange ideas and to stimulate and sponsor research on the junior high school program and administration. In 1964 they published a statement of their fundamental beliefs on junior high school administration.[4] This statement of belief, "Ten Tenets of Junior High School Administration," makes the following points:

1. The organization of the school must be such as to benefit all pupils who can profit from this type of education. As a part of this, "The academic record made in junior high school should not be a part of the requirement for senior high school graduation or a part of the requirement for college admission."[5] This would provide needed curricular flexibility.
2. Pupils of junior high age should have a broad program of general education. Such a program would serve individual differences through breadth and depth of learning in required language arts, social studies, mathematics, science, health and physical education, the fine and practical arts, and foreign language as a part of the broad language arts program. The content of the various subject areas must be constantly redefined.
3. A wide range and variety of methods and materials should be provided to deal with the extent of individual differences which are known to exist in children of this age. It is necessary to appreciate and provide for the learner's potential for growth and his degree of readiness.
4. Standards of achievement must be based upon a recognition of variations in student competency. All students cannot be judged on the same criteria.
5. The costs of inadequate administrative staffing for the junior high school far exceed the costs of adequate staffing. A minimum administrative unit of 300–450 pupils is suggested, and in large schools it is wiser to develop subunits, each with its own administrative personnel. Each pupil should be in at least one homogeneous class daily and overall scheduling must be in accord with the pupils' goals of learning. Different subject areas and activities may require different allotments of time and should be scheduled accordingly.
6. The junior high school age is particularly well suited to exploratory programs, and provisions should be made to permit a pupil to explore various subject areas as well as learning to understand his personal strengths and weaknesses. Inherent in the concept of exploration is the understanding that the individual student will experience more success in some experiences than in others.
7. Essential is a strong guidance program, one that will assist each student to attain his highest potential. A full-time load for a counselor is 250–350 pupils, and counselees should be assigned to the same counselor for their entire time in junior high school. All

teachers working with the same group of students should be scheduled to permit time for joint conferences.

8. The need for pupil personnel services is urgent at the junior high level, and to achieve the maximum in mental and physical health for each student there should be available to each junior high school the services of
   (a) A health team—doctor, nurse, and dental hygienist.
   (b) A psychological team—psychologist, social worker, and psychiatrist.
   (c) Attendance services on a social casework concept. The basic purpose of these services should be prevention, diagnosis, and referral.
9. The staff of the junior high school needs the kind of preparation that ensures knowledge of subject matter, understanding of the age group, and the necessary attitudes toward the junior high school. This implies developing a program of certification for junior high school staff members.
10. There must be continual and careful evaluation of all that is attempted in the junior high school. This requires the development of a sound philosophy, clearly defined objectives, a variety of techniques of evaluation, and the development, by the principal and the staff, of the criteria applicable to their own school.

DUTIES OF THE PRINCIPAL

It must never be forgotten that the primary task of the principal is the improvement of curriculum and instruction in an educational program designed for the early adolescent. That is the whole purpose of the school; nonetheless, it is not uncommon to hear comments such as, "Not in *my* school," or, "*My* school will not attempt this." *The school belongs to no one person.*

The principal, in working toward the major goals, may easily become involved in a multiplicity of duties which are time consuming, are but little related to the basic purpose, and should be delegated to others. In general, the duties of the principal are concerned with the educational program, providing students and faculty with direction and leadership, business management, and public relations. Within these broad patterns are many items that may easily be the task of someone else, depending upon the size of the junior high school. When the principal must spend a considerable part of his time on administrative trivia that could be handled by someone else, organization is not efficient. Certainly the principal should be involved minimally with student attendance, discipline, guidance, testing, counseling, clerical work, and routine tasks. He should be much more concerned with teacher recruitment, in-service training, best use of staff, scheduling, curriculum improvement, innovation, experimentation, the overall activity program, supervision, and public relations. Policies concerning grading, grouping, instructional methods such as team teaching and independent study, special programs such as reading, scheduling, homework, departmentalization, block-time, or core, should be determined by overall staff cooperation, involvement, and consultation.

The extent to which tasks may be delegated will depend upon the size of the student enrollment and what staff assistance is available. One recommendation[6] is that the ideal size for a junior high school is 700–800 pupils. Such a school should have:

1. A full-time principal.
2. Administrative assistant (assistant principal).
3. A full-time learning materials person with a full-time clerk.
4. A full-time counselor.
5. A secretary and a stenographer.
6. A full-time school nurse.
7. Sufficient custodial personnel.
8. A cafeteria manager.

Conant[7] recommended a minimum of 375 students in a three-year junior high, 125 per grade, and an ideal size of 750.

Actually, if techniques such as ungrading and large group/small group instruction are in use, a very efficient three-year junior high school may be operated with an enrollment of 500 or somewhat less. A school of this size would have a full-time principal, an assistant principal at least half-time, a boys' counselor, a girls' counselor, a secretary, an attendance clerk, librarian, and the learning-materials consultant, and a half-time nurse. With this much available assistance the junior high school principal may devote the bulk of his time to the tasks of real importance.

Public relations can be a touchy issue. There is a question as to what extent a principal should engage in salesmanship. Certainly he should keep the community informed as to what the school is attempting to do and what is being accomplished. He should not, however, be the glib caricature of the Madison Avenue type. Too often the only information the general public has about a school is what appears on the sports page supplemented by an occasional notice of a musical or dramatic production. The principal needs to report the school's achievements, share the hopes and efforts, and explain the school's needs. A regular newsletter to the parents can be very effective in this respect. Particularly when there is a change in the standard program should explanations be clear and concise. Ideas must be presented convincingly, their merits demonstrated, and every effort made to secure community understanding and support. Be sure when presenting an idea that recommendations are clear, that it is not oversold, that alternatives are considered, and that both sides are honestly presented. The public relations program must be continuous and represent all phases of the school program.

The ideal junior high principal is an experienced teacher at that level, seasoned in many roles, and in his position as educational leader should be

1. A student of the total curriculum, able to provide perspective, balance, and breadth of purpose.
2. Aware of good teaching practices and general learning needs.
3. Knowledgeable concerning this particular community.
4. A specialist in the process of planning and change.
5. Able to locate the best educational ideas, practices, and research, and adept at presenting them to the staff.[8]

A survey conducted by the Illinois Junior High School Principals Association in 1959 was designed to provide information concerning (1) "staff members who participated in the performance of certain services, (2) which staff members have major responsibilities for the various services, and (3) percent of total time devoted by various staff members to administrative and specialized services."[9] Approximately 50 percent (129) of the principals responded, 30 principals in schools of 199 enrollment and under; 41 schools of 200–499; 45 schools of 500–999; 11 schools of 1000 or more students—a total of 127 usable responses.

The services or functions performed by the junior high principals included:

Attendance
Discipline
Selection of Staff
Supervision
Student Activities
Public Relations
Guidance and Testing
Counseling
Curriculum Improvement
In-Service Education
Clerical
Transportation.

1. Principals of the smallest junior high schools had major responsibilities for all items listed except "Selection of Staff." The responsibility for this item was sometimes taken by the superintendent. These principals reported receiving considerable help from teachers in attendance, discipline, and student activities. One-half of the reports from the small schools indicated that teachers also participated in guidance and testing activities.

2. In schools of 200–499 enrollment, clerks usually performed most of the clerical duties. In nearly all of these schools the principal was actively involved in supervision, student activities, public relations, curriculum improvement, and in-service education. While the principal had a part in selection of staff in three-fourths of the junior high schools of this size, he

carried the major responsibility for this function in less than one-third of the schools. Principal, clerk, and teachers shared the task of record keeping and related duties, as well as sharing discipline procedures. Guidance, testing, and counseling were often delegated to the guidance director, teachers, or counselors.

3. In schools of 500–999 enrollment, the principal, assistant principal, and teachers shared responsibility for attendance problems. The major part of responsibility for discipline was assumed by principals with some assistance from assistant principals and teachers. The junior high principals in schools of this size were found to be largely responsible for supervision, public relations, curriculum improvement, and in-service education. Few principals did much clerical work and they were more likely to delegate responsibilities in student activities, guidance and testing, counseling, and transportation.

4. Because of the small number of returns from the large junior high schools (1,000 or more students) there are no firm conclusions drawn—only indicated tendencies. It appears that junior high principals, in schools of this size, are involved but little in attendance and discipline problems. They do, however, exercise major leadership in curriculum improvement, in-service education, public relations, and selection of staff.

As this study indicates, the junior high school principal is involved in a wide range of duties and activities, although the amount for which he is responsible in the various categories appears to vary somewhat according to school size. It almost certainly varies, too, in accordance with the various school district policies and with the kind of person the principal is. If he is one who counts paper towels, he will be reluctant to delegate even clerical tasks.

A study reported by Faunce and Clute[10] in 1961 described the responses from 135 Michigan junior high school principals to a questionnaire relating the functions and duties of the junior high school principal. The principals were asked to estimate the percentage of working time devoted to

1. Faculty affairs—staff committees and meetings, department meetings, hiring interviews, and similar items.
2. Student contacts—counseling with students, disciplinary action, planning student activities, and similar items.
3. Supervision of instruction—such things as conferences about instruction, classroom visiting, and preparing materials.
4. Community contacts—including PTA, other parent groups, conferences with parents, and advising committees.
5. Office routines—items such as scheduling, correspondence, telephone, athletic management, budget, and reports.

The study indicated that there was considerable similarity in how principals spent their time regardless of school size. As the schools get bigger the principal seems to spend more time on faculty affairs, supervision, and office routines, less time on student contacts, and about the same time on community contacts. The greatest differences seemed to be exhibited in the areas of student contacts and office routines. Principals of large junior high schools spent significantly less time with students.

The median distribution of the principal's time by school size is shown in the accompanying table.

MEDIAN SCORES AND ENROLLMENT

Category	Small Schools (under 300) Percent	Medium Schools (301–800) Percent	Large Schools (Over 800) Percent
Faculty affairs	12	14	20
Student Contacts	20	25	15
Supervision	11	12.5	20
Community contacts	7	10	10
Office routines	30	25	25

When asked how they would rearrange the way they spent their time, 97 of the 135 junior high principals reported that they would like to spend more time in supervision and curriculum planning. Forty-three of the principals wanted "less office routine," 17 wanted more faculty affairs contact, and 14 wished for more student contact.

In delegating duties to teachers, 63 of the principals reported that they delegated counseling, 33 delegated athletic management, 29 delegated community and parent contacts, and 16 delegated discipline. It is reasonable to ask why there was not more delegation of some of these duties. Only nine of the responding principals in the large junior high schools, for example, reported delegation of office routines.

In describing the chief blocks or needs in improving the junior high school, the principals listed:[11]

1. Lack of trained and dedicated teachers.......................... 52
2. Poor building facilities or space.............................. 23
3. Lack of funds.. 23
4. Senior high pressure or control.............................. 22
5. Lack of understanding of function and importance............. 16
6. Lack of status compared with senior high..................... 13
7. Heavy teaching loads.. 12

It is worth noting that these complaints stated by the junior high school principals are invariably included in the list of problems the junior high school has. They do not present new difficulties, they merely emphasize the old.

The National Association of Secondary School Principals previously mentioned study of the junior high school principalship[12] asked questions concerning the duties and activities of this administrator. Responses indicated that the junior high school principal had a 50–54 hour work week; that some kinds of activities made greater demands upon the principal's time such as administrative planning, meetings, and working with teachers regarding curriculum. These principals believed that the major impediments in their way toward accomplishing school objectives were

1. Variations in the ability and dedication of teachers.
2. Insufficient space and physical facilities.
3. Time consumed by administrative detail.
4. Teacher turnover.
5. Pressure from outside groups: local senior high schools, local newspapers, and PTA groups.

It is of interest that the first two of these four items are virtually the same as the first two in the Michigan study, the third item is a common complaint at all levels, and item four—teacher turnover—is a serious problem in staffing the junior high schools. Item five, outside pressures, is also often heard, particularly in regard to high school attempts to control curricula. Pressures from local newspapers very often are those concerned with sports, drama, and musical productions, although it is not unusual for the junior high school to be blamed for every high school slow reader and for all of those who have difficulty in spelling or counting. Many of these problems are either of our own making in that we fail to speak up for what we believe, or they are compounded by junior high school teachers and administrators who encourage the high school type activities and sports.

LEADERSHIP AND MORALE

It is often said that the principal sets the tone for the entire school. If he invites, encourages, and accepts faculty and student participation and involvement, the school will reflect this atmosphere in its operation and programs. If we are, in truth, attempting to teach and exemplify democracy to the early adolescent, here is the priority place to start. This is not to say that the principal takes no stands or positions. Leadership requires beliefs and integrity, *good* leadership is just that: leadership, not dictatorship. Johnson notes that

> . . . The principal must allocate resources equitably, establish and enforce rules and procedures to keep the school operating efficiently, and demand of his staff whatever performance is necessary to insure that institutional goals are met. . . . Finally he must motivate teachers and other staff personnel to innovate and go beyond the minimal demands of their assignments to higher levels.[13]

"Demand," is rather strong; "expect" might not, however, achieve the same degree of success. Certainly the principal must motivate the teachers to go beyond their minimal levels, and this is best achieved by encouragement, honest praise, sincere support, supplying the teachers with necessary materials, helping when asked and staying out of the way at other times, and remembering that teachers are people—human beings entitled to be treated as such. Morale can be a very touchy item. High faculty morale makes for good student morale, and good student morale creates a happy successful school. This is especially critical as it involves and affects the junior high school age student.

Faculty morale is strengthened by practices such as these:

1. Keep faculty meetings as short as is reasonable; work down from an agenda; have them *only* when necessary but as often as necessary. It is a literal crime to have a meeting merely because, "We always have a meeting every Tuesday at 4:00 p.m."
2. Involve everyone in the meetings. If they are worth having, then the athletic coaches must attend as well as the teachers of English. Requiring most teachers to attend but excusing some of them depresses morale. This brings up another point: no single subject, area, or department should receive special treatment above the others. Athletics is the most common offender in junior high school. It is not unusual to find a junior high school that spends $2,500–$5,000 annually on athletics but refuses to spend $15 to buy chess sets for the chess club.
3. Discipline procedures must be clearly explained and understood by all, and the administration *must* support the teachers.
4. There must be free and open communication at all times from all personnel to the principal. The staff must believe that they are being treated fairly, that loads, duties, and assignments are equitable.
5. Faculty members must be involved in curricular development, activity programs, and establishment of policies and procedures. They should be encouraged to innovate and experiment.
6. Administrative and clerical procedures need to be carefully thought out, clearly stated, and thoroughly understood by all.
7. Good work should be recognized, publicly if possible. Problems should be considered, both individual and schoolwide, as soon as they are defined. A junior high school is not the place to ignore a problem in the hope that it will disappear.
8. Keep the staff supplied to the limits of the district's ability with materials and equipment. (Also, salaries are *very* important.)
9. Keep the faculty informed as to district and school policies and

problems, matters of general concern, opportunities for advancement, and all items pertinent to teachers and their work.

10. Encourage professional growth and in-service training.

A good principal builds self-confidence and self-esteem in his teachers; supports them in experimentation, provides them with materials, maintains open lines of communication; and involves the teachers in making decisions.

COMMON ADMINISTRATIVE PROBLEMS

It has been said that the difference between a good school and a poor school is frequently the difference between a good principal and a poor principal. No school nor any principal is completely without problems, and a strong measure of the quality of administration provided by a principal is his effectiveness in dealing with problems. Many difficulties are general in nature and may be found in schools at any level; some problems are peculiar to junior high schools.

1. It is not as common today as it was a few years back, but junior high schools all too often have inherited the old buildings when a new high school was constructed. Less frequently, the junior high school has become the second tenant of an outgrown elementary school. Either way, it is an undesirable situation. Junior high students need buildings designed specifically for the junior high school program, not an outmoded or decrepit facility left by some other group.
2. A shortage of teachers trained specifically for junior high who intend to make a career of junior high school work. This can result in a staff which is "marking time" until a move can be made or a staff of teachers who really do not understand nor care to teach this age group.
3. Senior high school pressures or even attempts at domination in curricular requirements. Sometimes there are efforts by coaches to establish certain training patterns or skills in the junior high schools to "save time" at the senior high level.
4. Attempts by personnel, parents, or students to copy senior high school practices and activities. Occasionally this is demonstrated in subject matter areas by teachers who picture themselves as crusaders who are "establishing standards" and follow some undesirable senior high teaching patterns.
5. Lack of status of the junior high school which is reflected in disproportionate allocations of funds, materials, equipment, and personnel.
6. Heavy teaching loads. It is customary for high school teachers to have daily planning periods but, unfortunately, less common in jun-

ior high school. In a departmentalized junior high school on a seven period day one teacher may meet with over 200 students. This is too many.

7. Unwillingness by school districts to provide proportionate numbers of counselors, clerical help, librarians, and assistant principals to junior high schools as compared with senior high schools. It is not uncommon to find junior high schools of 800–1,000 students without an assistant principal, where most high schools of this size would, as a matter of course, have administrative help for the principal.
8. The problem of Carnegie Unit requirements for grade 9 which causes scheduling difficulties for all grades.
9. A lack of a clear understanding of the nature and functions of the junior high school. When teachers, central office personnel, and sometimes even the junior high school principal are not certain of the precise nature of the junior high school direction an goals, the situation can become truly chaotic.

Problems of a more general nature which can afflict any school principal include lack of funds, lack of central office leadership, too much central office control, traditionalism, parental interference, lack of programs for students of different abilities, a shortage of time, shortage of administrative help, and too much detail work.

Faculty meetings are sometimes a major problem even though they may not be recognized as such by the principal. Teachers often resent faculty meetings because they come before or after school in time the teacher regards as her own. The situation is aggravated when the principal has no agenda or did not put it out before the meeting. It is even worse when the principal reads his notices word for word, harangues the teachers, and runs beyond the normal dismissal time. Faculty meetings can and should be productive. This is probably the only time the entire faculty is assembled together. Here is the time for open discussion by the group of proposals and problems, not for reading bulletins aloud that are better distributed to the teachers to read for themselves.

This brings up one more problem which is seldom regarded as such by principals but is considered a real trial by teachers: the school intercommunication system. Schools which have an "intercom" should restrict bulletins to the regular announcement time. Nothing short of a major emergency should permit breaking into classes, yet it is all too common to hear principals cut into every classroom in the building with some earth-shaking announcement such as, "Special bulletin: the wrestling team will report to the gym at 2:40 today instead of 2:30." And all through the building attention is diverted and the entire point of the lessons blunted. Teachers need administrative support, not administrative interference.

EDUCATIONAL ISSUES

The study by the Secondary School Principals'[14] Association of attitudes and opinions of junior high school principals included a section concerning educational issues. Respondents indicated that they considered acquisition of basic skills, immediately succeeded by acquisition of basic knowledge to be the most important target of education. Training in technical skills was rated as the least important skill in today's junior high schools.

Ability grouping of some kind was supported by approximately 90 percent of the junior high principals, almost all of whom reported using two or more criteria for such grouping—usually IQ scores, teacher judgments, and grades.

In curriculum, about 75 percent of the principals said that they had one of the "new" modern math programs, and another 13 percent said that they wanted to establish such a course. About one-half of the respondents believe that there should be an elective modern foreign language program available for all grades, although about 20 percent of the principals were of the opinion that foreign language should be an elective for only grades eight and nine.

Concerning reorganization of instruction in accord with such recommendations as those of Lloyd J. Trump ("The School of the Future"), about 50 percent approved and less than 10 percent disapproved. Team teaching was considered by 62 percent of the principals to have as its most important contribution provision for the students to capitalize on the teachers' specific skills and knowledges. Scheduling changes, flexibility, and consideration for individual differences of students was stressed as the second most important contribution.

While the responses of the principals displayed an appreciation for the block-time and a desire to use such a pattern, over one-half of the principals reported complete subject matter departmentalization and 34 percent said that they preferred this system with no block-time.

Interscholastic athletic competition in junior high school, a source of rich and continuing controversy, was reported as an existing practice in about 86 percent of the schools. Most principals believed it to be generally appropriate in sports, with some question concerning ninth-grade football. Slightly over one-half of the junior high principals believed that a properly organized and operated after-school recreation and intramural program would not only be beneficial, it might lead to a hoped-for reduction and perhaps even replacement of the existing interscholastic athletic program.

The activity program has long been considered desirable and an asset to the junior high school. Approximately 70 percent of the 7-8-9 junior highs had service clubs, while a little less than half of the 6-2-4 and 5-3-4 schools had service clubs. Those schools that had such clubs believed them to be desirable. The vast majority of the responding principals reported that they had no social clubs and considered such clubs to be undesirable, although many reporting schools had athletic clubs and believed that they were suitable.

In the preparation of junior high school teachers, the junior high principals emphasized the desirability of practice teaching at the junior high level, course work in reading instruction, and adolescent development courses. Approximately 75 percent of the respondents believed that the degree program should be expanded to five years and should include more liberal arts courses. Along with this there was an indicated feeling that course work should be more concerned with content and less with method.

Thirty-six percent of the principals preferred junior high school accreditation, recognition, and evaluation at the state level, about one-third preferred such evaluation at the local level, and approximately 20 percent favored regional accreditation.

Approximately 80 percent of the principals concurred with the Supreme Court decision relating to racial segregation in the public schools, although almost the same percentage disapproved of busing students to schools outside the district as a means of implementing integration. Less than one-half agreed with the Supreme Court decision concerning compulsory prayer and Bible reading.

The study presents some interesting findings in attitudes and opinions as well as areas for speculation. One wonders if the expressed opinions regarding more content and less methods in preparation of junior high school teachers is a reflection of the content background and previous teaching and administrative experience of the principals surveyed. Certainly content is important, yet it is also true that a serious criticism of the junior high school has been that there have been far too many teachers who literally do not know how to teach at the junior high level. Mere content is not likely to be of much help to them.

The problem of interscholastic athletics in junior high school has been another issue characterized by intense feelings and hot debate. Again it is reasonable to be curious concerning the basic interests and backgrounds of those principals who favored an interscholastic athletic program in junior high school. If this approving majority is largely constituted of administrators who were junior-high trained, experienced, and oriented, then a somewhat paradoxical situation exists. Who are those who oppose such a program and why?

In yet another area, studies and the literature regarding ability grouping indicate a fairly even division of evidence and opinion—roughly as many favoring as oppose the practice. Yet approximately nine-tenths of the junior high principals advocate ability grouping. Why? Is it probable that such a large percentage has been reading only the material favoring ability grouping? Do they really believe that this is the best approach, or is this a further demonstration of the effects upon junior high school education of the critics of the late 1950's and early 1960's?

THE PLIGHT OF THE PRINCIPAL

Change is not only coming—it is already upon us. Educational change, so often characterized by a thirty-to-fifty-year lag, is occurring at such a rate and in such quantity that the principal who is unaware of developments or who hesitates to experiment and innovate is not just lost, he is like a pathetic traveler who wonders when the last jetliner left. Teacher militancy, student unrest (and this is happening in a very great number of junior high schools), erosion of the principal's powers, authority, duties, and functions, and outside pressure groups are all creating situations that were not conceivable by principals ten years ago. New concepts in education, and computers and machines that drastically alter teaching methods and techniques are contributing to the problems of today's school principal at every level—and the junior high school principal feels it as much as any. The situation was well put by one principal when he observed:[15]

> Pity the poor principal! He must be a manager, supervisor, psychologist, financial wizard, master of law, public relations specialist, public speaker, school and community leader, a first aid specialist; and throughout it all, he must be a good guy as well. . . . He must inspire, ameliorate, meditate, organize, sponsor, attend, and react properly to pressures. He must try to avoid controversial comments about civil rights, segregation, integration, busing, socialism, automation, strikes, boycotts, unions, protests, the draft . . . and even Custer's Last Stand. In between he is expected to administer a school fairly and squarely.

Virtually all of these problems are faced by and affect the junior high school principal, whose actions are further influenced (or should be) by the knowledge that he is working with young people who are at a critical stage in their development; with a staff that is frequently described as taking a junior high school position as second choice and who lack training in working with the preadolescent and early adolescent; and in a school that is criticized as being unsure of its functions and too ready to imitate high school practices. The junior high school principal must truly be an effective and competent man.

SUMMARY

Administration, regardless of the field, deals with similar situations and problems. School administration is largely concerned with people—students, teachers, parents, and the general community. The school administrator is expected to plan, direct, control, and evaluate the educational program and the overall operation of the school. Junior high school principals, concerned with the improvement of instruction and curriculum for early adolescents, face most of the same problems of administrators of any school. In addition, because of the nature of the school and the student, they have some problems peculiar to junior high schools and need special qualifications and training for their most effective work.

Human relations are extremely important, and an essential technique for the principal is to keep everyone informed as to current plans, suggested procedures, and possible alternatives. Best results will be achieved when administrative decisions are reached after involvement of all concerned.

Changing educational times and a multiplication of duties and problems are altering the responsibilities of the junior high school principal. More than ever he must be aware of what is occurring in education and be ready and able to apply his knowledge and leadership to developing the best possible program for the preadolescent and early adolescent.

REFERENCES

1. Roland C. Faunce and Morrel J. Clute, *Teaching and Learning in the Junior High School.* Belmont, Calif.: Wadsworth, 1961, p. 338.
2. H. Richard Conover, "The Junior High School Principalship," *NASSP Bulletin*, vol. 50 (April 1966), pp. 132–139.
3. *Ibid.*, p. 135.
4. "Ten Tenets of Junior High School Administration," Council on Junior High School Administration, *Clearing House*, Vol. 38 (February 1964), pp. 329–333.
5. *Ibid.*, p. 330.
6. M. Dale Baughman, "Administration of the Junior High School," *monograph, Interstate Printers and Publishers*, 1966 (quoting Southern Association of Colleges and Secondary Schools).
7. James B. Conant, *Education in the Junior High School Years.* Princeton, N. J.: Educational Testing Service, 1960.
8. Fred T. Wilhelms, "On the Use of Principals," *NASSP Spotlight*, Vol. 79 (September–October 1967), pp. 1–4.
9. Baughman, *op. cit.*, p. 24.
10. Faunce and Clute, *op. cit.*, pp. 341–347.
11. *Ibid.*, p. 345.
12. Conover, *op. cit.*
13. Mauritz Johnson, JR., *American Secondary Schools.* New York: Harcourt, 1965), p. 31.
14. Conover, *op. cit.*
15. Harold Moody, "The Plight of the Principal," *Clearing House*, Vol. 42 (May 1968), pp. 543–545.

chapter 5

Housing the Junior High Students

It has been mentioned that the junior high school has all too often been the unwilling beneficiary of facilities previously used to house some other form of school organization. Presumably this is better than nothing, but if the junior high school student is unique and requires a program which is developed especially for the needs of this age group, it follows that the best results will be attained in facilities specifically designed for such an educational program.

The best of teaching methods, materials, and instruction are handicapped by a poorly planned building. The situation is even worse when the building was originally planned for some other purpose. The American community provides strange and paradoxical contrasts. We spend billions of dollars to develop the finest of space-age technology to put a man on the moon, yet lurking somewhere in the backs of many minds is the conviction that the best kind of education is Mark Hopkins on one end of a log and the individual child on the other. We spend more each year on cigarettes and liquor in the United States than we do on education—is this a criterion of worth? We cannot provide the education we should when we must make do with inadequate facilities. A good diversified junior high school program must have better facilities than abandoned small classrooms with poor lighting and fixed seats; buildings with narrow hallways, and inflexible provisions for the necessary specialized classes.

Even in buildings that have been newly constructed for the purpose of housing junior high schools, there have been problems. It has been common to base architectural specifications upon construction factors rather than upon the educational program desired. The determinants of the curriculum then become the construction factors. Another problem has been that of constructing junior high schools that are smaller carbon copies of the high schools. It is also quite common for a school district to construct a building and then develop the curriculum to fit the building—exactly opposite to what the procedure should be. The school board and administration of a district should, with the help of the teachers and the community at large, determine the curriculum which best suits their needs and desires and then construct the facilities to fit the program. Time spent in careful and thorough planning will more than pay for itself. A school building's value lies in its provisions for carrying out clearly defined educational goals and purposes.

It must be kept in mind that a school building is expected to last for many years. Buildings constructed before the turn of the century are still in use, and any given school will eventually serve thousands of children. Consideration must be given to more than the presently planned program; trends must be carefully studied and taken into account. Other factors are: possible enrollment changes; city growth and development; the functions, present and projected, of the junior high school; potential organizational changes as to a 6-7-8 or 9-10 school; and other school construction contemplated by the district. What is necessary is a built-in flexibility that will permit a district to make maximum adaptation to changing educational thought, methods, and technology, as well as accommodating enrollment and population changes without major structural modifications (see Fig. 5-1).

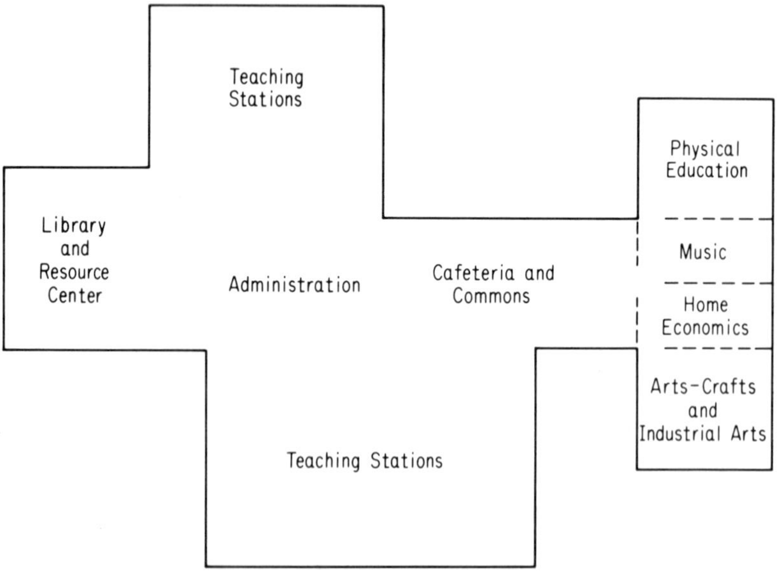

Fig. 5-1. A junior high school in one building with spaces large enough to permit present and future flexibility.

This is of particular relevance to schools for the preadolescent and early adolescent. As more is learned of the complexity of individual differences, as research provides us with increasing knowledge of readiness, maturity, and how people learn, the rigidity and conformity that characterized the junior and senior high schools are being reduced and eliminated. We are replacing the old straitjacketed procedures with flexibility in scheduling and time; with a range and variety of subject matter and course offerings; and with different teaching and learning approaches such as programed learning, independent study, team teaching, large-group–small-group learning, and television instruction. These changes require buildings designed and constructed to fit the new programs and methods—not the old.

SCHOOL FACILITIES AND EARLY ADOLESCENCE

The program designed and intended for the preadolescent and early adolescent must be distinctly different from that of elementary school and that of the high school. As one part of the program, there needs to be continuity and carryover from the elementary school in content, procedures, and organization, to ensure a smooth transition. At the other end of the junior high school program the student needs to be prepared for the transition to the high school, an institution with a more adult type of environment.

A brief review of the characteristics of the student in middle schools and junior high schools will help to define the kinds of facilities best suited to the needs of this age group.

1. The preadolescent and early adolescent is experiencing a maturation in mental ability. This developing ability to deal with abstractions and concepts coupled with his curiosity requires facilities far different from those provided by a small classroom and fixed seats where the teacher lectures to the class. There should be areas for large-group and small-group work, spaces for independent study, laboratories, learning material and resource centers, and spaces set aside for independent study.
2. One thing that we know for certain about people is that every one is different. If we really believe in the concept of individual differences, then our educational policies, procedures, content, methods, and facilities must reflect this belief. There must be multiple-learning aids and materials and provision for a real variety of curricular offerings and learning experiences, for at no time in their lives will the differences be more pronounced than is apparent with this age group.
3. Differences in rate and amount of physical maturation are also extreme. It is ridiculous to attempt to plan, construct, and furnish a junior high school as though all of the students were to be the same

size, mature at the same rate, and profit from the identical programs and facilities. (Anyone who has observed a seventh-grade classroom that has been equipped with identical desks will recall seeing some students whose feet scarcely touch the floor when they are seated, while in the same classroom gangling boys can barely get their knees under the desks.) There should also be activities suitable for the varying sizes and needs of this widely differing physical range, and facilities and equipment which provide the necessary variety.

4. This age group, because of the rapid changes in growth and maturity, must have a program that is highly flexible, one that can be easily adapted and adjusted to changing and differing interests. Obviously the buildings themselves must be flexible, not only to meet the current needs of these children but also to accommodate the potential and probable changes in attitudes, wants, needs, and interests of preadolescents and early adolescents of two and three decades from now. The quickening tempo of change in educational technology and methods and the creation of new knowledge make such flexibility imperative.
5. Children of this age group have a strong desire for independence yet need and want some adult guidance. In their inclination toward peer-group loyalties and withdrawal from adult direction, they are ready to spend more time in working and learning on their own and with others in their own social group. We do much talking about our efforts and wishes to develop critical thinking, analytic approaches, and democratic critical thinking, analytic approaches, and democratic processes, yet the average junior high school in the traditional buildings and classrooms does little but pay lip service to these shining goals.
6. One function of the junior high school is that of transition, to make the moves from elementary school and to the high school smoother for the adolescent. Implicit in this is an organization of both program and facilities that permits and encourages an easy transition. Provision for smaller units becomes quite important as the schools get larger, and it is necessary that students have a feeling of belonging to some group, to a teacher, and be a part of the school. As a corollary to this and to the changing interests of the students, the school should be so designed as to permit a variety of clubs, activities, and learning experiences, something for everyone, which may or may not be a part of the immediate curricular offerings.
7. We know that everyone needs to be successful and that this is critically important to the unsure and insecure child who is going into adolescence. It is therefore of prime importance that the junior high school have the facilities and teachers to provide a range of offerings

in "nonacademic" areas as well as academic. In this category the school should have available opportunities for children in such areas as industrial arts, home economics, music, arts, crafts, photography, drama, speech, and journalism.

In short, we say that we are attempting to develop creativity, that we seek to enrich the opportunities for the original and nonconforming thinker; we tell children not to follow the mob but to "be yourself." Yet much of our teaching, most of our content, and the vast majority of our buildings and facilities operate to restrict and even to prohibit deviations from conformity. Perhaps what we really mean is, "Be good, don't rock the boat, don't upset things and people, produce enthusiastically within the confines of what has been acceptable, and you can do more of what *you* really want when you are a little older. Then you will be ready for something different." (But not *too* different and, anyway, you'll be someone else's problem then.) If we really want to do more than talk about developing each student to the ultimate of his own individual potential, we *must* change drastically our overall approach, and changed facilities are an important step. It is almost a truism that it is much easier to change behavior once you have changed the environment.

GENERAL CONSIDERATIONS—THE SITE

Selection of the best site is extremely important and this problem is assuming more and more significance as our cities grow, as industries expand and multiply, and as land values skyrocket. Fortunate and farsighted is the school district that anticipated its needs and purchased potential school sites years before construction is actually necessary. Should these sites fall in the path of subsequent industrial development, the school district generally finds that it can sell at a profit or arrange a trade for some more desirable location. School districts in metropolitan areas have real problems in this respect and often find that it is necessary for them to abandon all thoughts of a campus style school and construct a multistoried building.

The site selected for a junior high school should not be more than two miles from the homes of those students who live furthest from the proposed school if it is intended that the students shall walk to and from school. Beyond this distance (and often less than this, depending upon community pressures, administrative beliefs, and the overall situation) it is necessary to operate school bus routes. In addition to the costs involved in busing children, it is necessary to consider the effects upon various out-of-class activities, both academic and nonacademic, and of the necessity of children catching the bus home at a given time. Accessibility is becoming more of a factor, too, in view of the increasing use of the schools, especially the facilities of junior and senior high schools, as community centers and for night classes. Since a junior high school serves children who are able to cross streets and find their way home by themselves, the site location may be such as to involve children crossing several streets to get to school. Even so, for any school the number of street crossings should be kept to a minimum and crossing arterial highways should be avoided if at all possible. The site of the school should permit the most direct student routes with a minimum of street hazards.

Industrial, community, and residential development may present the school district with a choice between a somewhat undesirable site in terms of its size, location in relation to other structures, and physical characteristics, and a more desirable site which is not so well located. It is better to take the site which provides more room, is away from undesirable areas such as a stockyard or a growing business district, rather than to put first priority upon centrality of location. Aesthetic qualities and factors should also be given considerable weight.

The ideal junior high school site would have the following characteristics:

1. Twenty acres, minimum, plus one acre per hundred students enrolled. An 800-student junior high school would then have twenty-eight acres.
2. Situated a considerable distance from airports, railroad lines, freeways, and industry.
3. Accessible by paved streets and sidewalks and in an area presently serviced by water lines, sewer lines, and power lines that are adequate to handle the increased load put upon them by the new school. It is most discouraging to a school board to find that they must expend a substantial sum of money to install original services or to enlarge those that currently exist.
4. The location should be as near the center of the community to be served as is possible. This means that there should be some prognosis as to the future development of this community.
5. The surroundings should be as pleasant as it is possible to obtain. It is often possible and desirable to locate a school adjacent to a good park or playground and take advantage of the additional areas thus provided. Whenever possible the school should be situated on high ground. This is aesthetically more pleasing, and practically it reduces dangers of flooding from heavy rains or increased drainage as the area becomes more heavily settled.
6. The school site should be in an attractive residential community. Do not consider an area in which there are existing businesses such as taverns, bars, dance halls, and similar operations. Particularly for junior and senior high school students such areas should be avoided. Too soon will entrepreneurs open as near the school as possible such

nuisance-value and litter-creating businesses as hot dog stands, drive-ins, walk-up hamburger places, and ice-cream shops.
7. Availability of fire protection. This is self-evident.
8. Physical characteristics and features that permit and encourage outdoor activities that are both educational and recreational in nature—in fact, properly developed, there may be but little, if any, difference.

PLANNING

There has been, in recent years, an effort by some state departments of education to develop a standard set of six or more school plans for each school level: elementary, junior high school, and senior high school. The reasoning here is that uniform plans will reduce costs. This is not true. In the first place, uniform plans, designed for five or six varying types of sites, cannot and do not include *all* types of potential sites. Second, while there are obvious similarities among and between school districts, no two districts are identical either in their needs, the kind of community to be served, or in student population. A school for 800 junior high school students in a rural area will need different facilities from that of an 800-student junior high school which is one of four or five in an industrial town of 50,000 to 60,000 population. Third, the determinants of the curriculum should begin with the community and student needs, not with a fixed construction plan. It should be obvious that a junior high school on the edge of a Navajo community in northern Arizona must have a curriculum different from that of a junior high school in a Phoenix suburb. Yet standard building plans direct identical or strongly similar curricula.

When planning a new junior high school it is of real value to do whatever is reasonable to permit inclusion of local ideas, support, and initiative. It is true that the increasing number of people involved also increases the number of opinions, convictions, and even difficulties in reaching conclusions. However, wider participation that invites local citizens to voice opinions and to become a part of the planning group also develops wider support and encouragement. Properly organized and planned, such inclusion of interested citizens becomes a strong positive factor. It is also quite important to include in the planning group a number of teachers, especially those who will probably be teaching in the new school. Teachers, since they are familiar with classroom facilities and the good and bad features of teaching stations and equipment, are a highly useful source of information. As a word of warning here, it is valuable to bring in consultants to talk with teachers for the purpose of presenting new and innovative practices, especially those that are actually operating in various junior high schools in different parts of the country.

Involvement of concerned groups, lay citizens and teachers, has a pronounced effect upon the interest and pride of the community, particularly since there has been a shared responsibility. The school plant is not only important to the administration, it is of vital concern to those who will teach there, to those whose children will be in attendance, and to the taxpayers in the community.

FLEXIBLE CONSTRUCTION

A little more stress upon the importance of flexible construction may be of value. The lag in ideas and classroom practice has been much reduced in recent years. Methods of instruction and curricular practices, ideas, and needs are changing at an ever-increasing rate. School districts, although they may be reluctant at times to initiate and adopt change, are usually compelled by circumstance to move in this direction, the rate of movement depending upon the particular school district. At the same time many school districts are actively and extensively engaged in attempts to modify and improve practices in their efforts to satisfy the changing needs of the students who attend their schools. Examples of this may be found in the increased importance placed upon college entrance, upon prevocational and vocational training, and upon education for satisfying hobbies and making profitable use of the increasing leisure time available.

Obviously what is needed is a different concept of short- and long-range school-plant planning and design, since a building must be able to house a range and variety of current educational programs. To go a step further, the new junior high school must be capable of housing a variety of programs not yet in operation, some of which are not yet even in the dreaming stage. To accomplish this there must be possible multiuse of space. A real danger here is that of expecting too many different instructional uses to be operating within these facilities over the years. Flexibility, both real and potential, is needed, without total abandon. One way of accomplishing this is by reduction and elimination of interior walls. See Figs. 5-2 and 5-3. This permits rearrangement of furniture, equipment, and dividers as changing needs require. At the very least, interior walls should not be load-bearing, so that they may be removed or penetrated as future plans render this desirable.

If the planning group keeps in mind that neither the population nor educational practices are likely to remain stable, flexibility in construction is more likely.

It is common to hear from various members of the community that school buildings should be multistoried, not single-storied, because this permits cheaper construction. This is true in metropolitan areas where land costs are extremely high. However, safety regulations, fire codes, and requirements relating to physical construction are now much stricter and

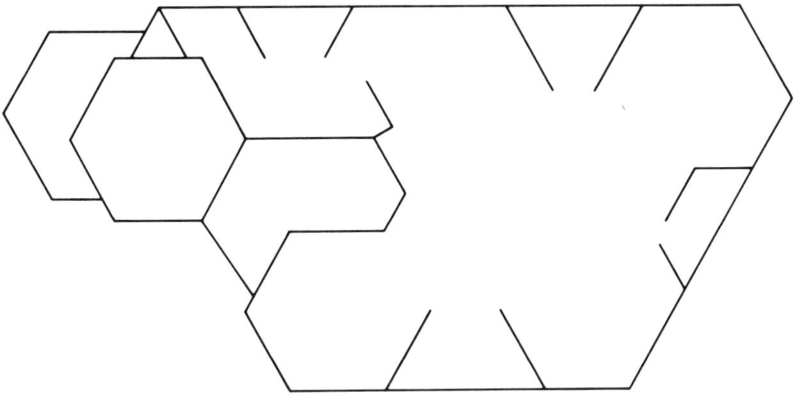

Fig. 5-2. Schools do not have to be compartmented boxes. The spaces in this wing of a junior high school are so designed as to permit a high degree of flexibility of use.

more rigid—and rightly so—than was the case fifty years ago. Because of these factors, it is usually less expensive and certainly more practical and esthetically desirable in most cases to construct single-story buildings. No space is lost to stair wells; evacuation of the building in case of emergency is more rapid; and passage of students from one area to another is expedited. There is no problem in restricting movement upstairs and down; "Up the Down Staircase" is not a factor.

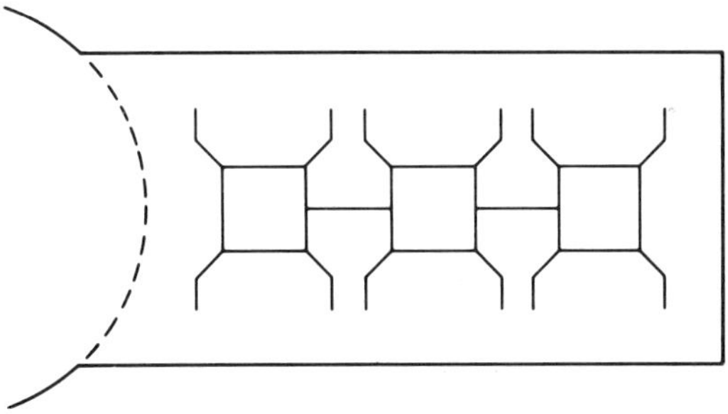

Fig. 5-3. Another arrangement for one wing of a junior high school.

ENVIRONMENTAL CONTROL

Schoolrooms and school buildings for years were characterized by their drab sameness, their ugliness, and their lack of planning for attractiveness and for the comfort of the students. There is no difficulty in spotting an old school building when driving around a strange town. Newer buildings, in addition to more attractive and esthetically pleasing design, are being designed with more consideration for the needs of the students. Research has also provided evidence to substantiate what many have long believed; learning is enhanced when the environment is more comfortable and attractive.

LIGHTING AND COLOR

The vast majority of the older school buildings have classrooms equipped with a number of overhead lighting fixtures that provide direct lighting. Such fixtures are not as efficient as indirect, semidirect, or diffused lighting, especially since the ceilings and walls are usually painted a uniform dingy white, cream, ivory, or beige—uniform from room to room for reasons of economy. Adequate lighting with balanced brightness lessens fatigue, creates a more pleasant and cheerful environment, and, by making seeing easier and better, improves the learning situation. Indirect lighting has the additional advantage of avoiding the considerable amount of heat gain which is a corollary of direct lighting. Indirect lighting is also more likely to reduce problems of glare, brightness, intensity, and distribution.

The question of color has some interesting aspects. Research indicates that the more subdued colors—those that are cooler and less stimulating—are green, blue, and violet. The least tranquil colors—those that are warmer and more exciting—are yellow, orange, and red. Tints of these various colors have, to a lesser degree, the same effect upon those students in the respective rooms. The cooler colors are more likely, therefore, to create an atmosphere free of distractions. The implications of this, especially for junior high schools, should be clear. In view of what is known of the characteristics of students of this age group, colors should be selected that will provide the best possible environment for learning; stimulating where this is necessary, and free of distraction and calming elsewhere. Small rooms, for example, should usually be painted in cool and light colors which will make the room seem larger; dark colors and warm colors are not only more exciting, they make a room appear to be smaller. Certainly every effort should be made to capitalize upon what is known of color engineering for the enhancement of the teaching-learning situation rather than using the same deadly ivory or gray throughout the building.

HEATING AND AIR CONDITIONING

It is indeed strange that a citizen who insists upon air conditioning in the office in which he works will complain vociferously about the cost of air-conditioning a school. To many people, there is no reason that the school should not adjust the temperature and ventilation by opening and closing classroom windows. Not only is this practice inefficient in that it provides little real control, but the outside noises contribute more toward class distraction than virtually any other factor. A classroom facing a busy street is so noisy that teachers and students are frequently drowned out by cars, heavy trucks, and buses. Too, there is scarcely anything more likely to pull student attention to the window than the sound of a fire engine, police, or ambulance siren. The fitful whine of the power mowers as the grounds keeper goes about his work is guaranteed to lessen the impact of the most critical moment in any lesson. Those classrooms on the sunny side of the building have an added disadvantage when the teacher attempts to lower the window shades to keep out the sun yet keep the windows open to permit ventilation.

Air-conditioned classrooms that are maintained at temperatures around 72°F at all times of the year reduce physical fatigue for teachers and students alike and provide the best learning environment. For classes involved in higher activity situations the temperature should be reduced to around 68°F. Students simply cannot work when the classroom temperature ranges up to 85° and 90°, and many schools have this problem in the spring and fall. It is essential that a competent heating engineer be a part of the school plant planning.

ACOUSTICS

Here we encounter another of the serious detriments to the learning process. School after school has been constructed without regard for soundproofing classrooms and learning spaces. The situation is aggravated when ventilation and cooling are so poorly planned that teachers find it necessary to open both windows and doors to provide crossdrafts—a practice that results in the distraction of a flood of outside noises and hall noises. Music rooms, industrial arts classrooms, and auditoriums, for example, are particular problems in this respect. In many schools these classes, even with all windows and doors shut, emit such a volume of noise that students in nearby classrooms have difficulty in hearing what is being said in their own classes. Within the individual classrooms, inadequate soundproofing results in every class in that area hearing the action and narration of an educational film being shown in any given room, and the voice of an enthusiastic teacher or student can penetrate for at least three rooms in any direction. A high noise factor contributes strongly to student and teacher uneasiness, discomfort, dissatisfaction, and actual physical fatigue. High noise levels are detrimental to intellectual work and endanger the learning possibilities of the school. A problem that should be considered here is that of the increasing use of accordion or sliding room dividers. Few of these really shut off completely the noise of activities from the adjoining classrooms. Those students who sit near the dividers find that the hum from the other side varies from a low but relatively continuous sound to a situation where they are actually able to hear with equal ease what is occurring both in their own classroom and that of the adjoining area. Probably the best divider is the lead-impregnated type, although it is fairly costly. A good case can be made for the extensive use of heavy-duty carpeting in the school building. Noise levels are drastically reduced and it appears that student deportment is improved in a quieter atmosphere.

SIZE AND ARRANGEMENT OF LEARNING AREAS

The term "egg-crate classrooms" has virtually become a cliché. In some instances educators have been so anxious to avoid standard classrooms that they have almost or completely eliminated them. The kind of curricular program desired and planned for the junior high school may indeed require their elimination. It is probable, however, that most junior high schools will have need for some classrooms of the traditional size and shape at the present time. Yet it is necessary to provide areas for large-group instruction, spaces that will hold at least 150 students, as well as spaces for 30–40 students, seminar rooms for 10–15 students, resource centers, learning-material centers, and laboratories. Certainly there should be far fewer interior walls and dividers than has previously been the case. How extensive should be the elimination of interior walls will depend upon the curricular program, the attention paid to heating and ventilation, the acoustical situation, and the lighting.

These factors have real importance for planning any new school, but considering the characteristics of the preadolescent and early adolescent who is a student in the middle school and junior high school, the importance of providing a learning environment suitable for developing a program intended to meet the needs of these students becomes critical. Loss of interest in school, dropout rates, and dulling of intellectual curiosity are aggravated by buildings and facilities that prohibit opportunities for diversified activities in the necessary environment provided by a variety of learning areas in a situation that should be cheerful, attractive, well lighted, properly heated and air-conditioned, and acoustically satisfactory.

RECENT TRENDS AND DEVELOPMENTS

It is characteristic of new junior high school construction that obvious efforts have been made to get away from the traditionally rigid compartmental construction with standard rooms side-by-side on each side of a long hall. Fire regulations, esthetics, and practical factors of use have gone far toward eliminating the two-story building. The junior high school today is more likely to fit the site, be constructed of a variety of materials, feature wide halls, classrooms, lobbies, and instruction areas, and be so built that modifications and additions may be made with a minimum of effort and cost. Sites are large (at least 30 acres for an 800-student school), play areas are large and graded, and the grounds are landscaped attractively. Inner walls of the school are often nonbearing to permit removal, and extensive use is made of accordion dividers. Furniture is movable, lighting is improved, libraries are larger, learning-materials centers are provided, and rooms may be readily darkened for audiovisual use.

Special programs require special facilities, but some general recommendations appropriate to the times and the trends are these:

1. There is still a need for subject or general purpose classrooms, with plenty of electrical outlets, TV jack, chalkboards, bulletin boards, movable furniture, a sink, storage, and provision for darkening the room. Size should be not less than 30 ft. X 30 ft., preferably 35 ft X 35 ft. Adjacent to each of these rooms, between each two, should be two small conference rooms suitable for individual or small group work.
2. Science rooms, at least one for each 225 students, somewhat larger than the general classrooms, with sinks, running water, gas connections, sufficient electrical outlets, dark out provisions, storage within the room, work counters around the walls of the room, demonstration table, and a storeroom and small conference room along one wall.
3. One teaching room for art for each 300–350 students, 1,200–1,500 square feet, with sinks, counters and work space, storage and display space, movable tables, kiln, sufficient electrical outlets, dark out facilities.
4. Industrial arts, one shop for each 250 students enrolled in school, at least 2,000 square feet. If there are two shops, one should be a general shop, heavy, and the other a general shop, light. Electrical outlets, gas connections, work tables, exhaust system, materials storage room, project storage room, and paint room should be included. There should also be a drafting room adjacent capable of seating 24 students.
5. Homemaking rooms, one for each 250 students enrolled in school, 1,500 square feet each. Each lab should include four kitchen units with both gas and electric stoves where feasible, electrical outlets, laundry area, clothing area, fitting room, teaching area, dining room for each two labs, and dark out facilities.
6. Two rooms suitable for teaching music for an enrollment of 250 to 600. One room for general and choral music, one for instrumental, 1,200–1,500 square feet each; the instrumental room should be constructed with permanent risers. The two rooms should have an instrument storage room and two small practice rooms between them.
7. A gymnasium capable of division by folding partition, or two gyms, one for boys and one for girls up to an enrollment of 750–900.

Beyond this it will be necessary to add additional physical education teaching stations such as a wrestling room, tumbling room, or handball courts. Locker rooms large enough to accommodate 35–45 students should be provided as should storage rooms, offices, showers, and toilets.

8. Typing instruction is becoming common in junior high school and there should be one typing room, approximately 1,000 square feet, for each 600–800 students. Because of the increased use of electric typewriters, this room should be extremely well-supplied with electric outlets. There should also be a sink and storage cabinets.
9. Use of large group/small group and independent study is increasing steadily. There should, therefore, be one large group area for every 250–300 students enrolled. This room should seat at least 150 students. The large room should be capable of being partitioned into three or more smaller rooms. Most new junior high schools include small group areas that will hold from 6–15 students. The number of these small rooms necessary will, of course, vary with the enrollment and with the curricular design. Independent work stations are equipped with study carrels, usually of the type in which one carrel seats four students.
10. One up-to-date language lab is recommended for each 800–1,000 students.
11. There should be a large learning-materials-center library, centrally located, open and spacious, for an enrollment of 600–900. There should be a workroom, audio rooms, preview rooms, and storage space equal to at least 10 percent of overall floor space. There should also be offices, conference rooms, and study carrels.
12. Some of the newer junior high schools are building dining rooms instead of cafeterias and equipping them with booths, round tables, and chairs. In any case, the eating area should seat not less than one-third and preferably one-half the enrollment at a time.
13. Many schools have built a student activity room, approximately 2,500 square feet, and other schools have constructed a lobby adjacent to the main office of about this same size for a student lounge. The lobby-lounge adjacent to the office is easy to supervise.
14. There should be a reading laboratory, two if enrollment exceeds 800 students. The reading lab may be standard classroom size but should seat only 20–25 students, for purposes of better instruction.
15. An auditorium to seat at least one-half of the enrollment would be ideal but few schools can afford them.
16. There should be an adequate administrative suite. It is a real mistake to skimp on office space. Sooner or later money will be forthcoming to add classrooms but it is extremely difficult to add office areas.

At the very least, each school should have an office for the principal and one for the assistant principal, one for each counselor, workroom, reception, conference room, and walk-in vault.

17. Health and nurse's room needs will vary with school size. Minimal is a nurse's office, a room for two cots, reception area, toilets, and storage.
18. False economy is also a mistake in planning the teachers' lounge. As enrollment increases, teachers will be unable to stay in their rooms during planning periods. This, plus the increased staff size, will, in a few years, overcrowd the lounge. Too, a teachers' lounge is not as easy to finance for remodeling or enlargement as are classrooms. There should be a separate teachers' workroom equipped with duplicating equipment, typewriters, paper cutter, and supplies. It sometimes happens, and is a mistake, that the work area for teachers is included within the lounge. This is noisy, distracting, and most unsatisfactory both to those who are trying to work and those who are relaxing. There must be adequate teacher work and office space.
19. There is increasing addition of special facilities in junior high schools. For example, Pierre Moran Junior High School in Elkhart, Indiana, has two greenhouses as a part of the facilities for science. It is considered standard for Los Angeles' junior high schools to be equipped with a classroom with a toolroom, storage, lath house, potting room, compost bins, and an acre of ground for agricultural classes. All students in Los Angeles are required to take agriculture. Swimming pools are also beginning to appear in new junior high schools. The John Muir Junior High School in Wausau, Wisconsin, has an Olympic sized pool.
20. Some new junior high schools are including one teaching station that is a space laboratory center that contains a planetarium, telescope, and photographic darkroom.

In an effort to economize, school districts often cut corridor size as well as room sizes. This is a very poor practice. Once built, it is hard to change, and while walls may be knocked out, the corridors are still long, narrow, and depressing. A wider corridor permit more socializing, whereas narrow corridors cause traffic problems, pushing, and accidents.

Student locker rooms need wide corridors and should be open at each end. It is most discouraging and a contributing factor to trouble to have narrow corridors in locker areas that end in a blank wall. Students who have the last lockers in must push their way in and out, and if the passage is narrow, there is a constant danger of injury from open locker doors.

The school should be a pleasant place, spacious, airy, well lighted, and painted in cheerful colors. Too many older schools are painted in a gloomy dark brown or gray. The use of color is important.

It is less expensive to plan and construct a school in which children and teachers are happy and comfortable than it is to cope with problem buildings, dissatisfied teachers, and unhappy children.

THE HOUSE PLAN OR THE SCHOOL-WITHIN-A-SCHOOL

The increasing population, the growth of cities, the consolidation of school districts, and the rapidly increasing school enrollments have sharply increased the number of large schools and brought about a proportionate decrease in the number of small schools. Economically it is more practical to bus children a considerable distance to a larger school than to build, equip, maintain, supply, and staff several small schools. Too, it is usually easier to build a good educational program in a school which is large enough to employ teachers who may teach all or most of the time in their specialized areas. A small junior high school, for example, may find it difficult to provide enough classes for a full-time teacher in a foreign language.

While size permits many benefits, it is not without fault. Children in a junior high school designed for 800, 1,000, 1,500, 2,000, or more complain that they feel like workers in a factory, that they know very few of their fellow students, and that they often have no one with whom to discuss their problems. In a departmentalized school they see each teacher one period daily and, unless they are in trouble, may never see the counselor. This loss of security and identity is not limited to a large junior high school. Reflections of the same problem may be found in large high schools and to an even greater extent in our colleges and universities.

In an attempt to overcome the more undesirable characteristics of bigness, many school districts have been examining the concept of the school within a school or the house plan. See Figs. 5-4, 5-5 and 5-6. In this arrangement the school's enrollment is subdivided into groups, each containing a fraction of the total enrollment, one fifth, one fourth, or one third, depending upon the total number of students in the school. Each group or house contains seventh-, eighth-, and ninth-graders in approximately equal numbers. A few schools assign students to the houses by grade level, i.e., one house contains nothing but seventh-graders, the next house is eighth-graders, and the third house is all ninth-graders. Each house has its own teaching staff, counseling personnel, and usually an administrative head—an assistant principal or dean. Usually the students will remain in the house for the full three years, receiving the bulk of their education there but sharing with the other houses such special facilities as cafeteria, library, learning materials center, central administrative offices, music rooms, gymnasiums, and, depending upon the size of the school, facilities for industrial arts, homemaking, and arts and crafts.

While the house plan is frequently associated with team-teaching techniques and in fact is an organizational pattern which encourages innovative approaches, there is no compulsion to adopt team teaching. The house plan can provide more security for the student, permit teachers to become more aware of individual student problems and needs, enhance student morale and conduct, allow scheduling by houses instead of compelling all students in the school to fit into a master schedule, and encourage teachers to cross departmental and subject-matter lines.

A New York junior high school[1] operates three houses of approximately 400 pupils each with each cluster having its own administrative head and staff. Each unit is assigned a block of rooms and contains students from all three grades. The three houses share gymnasiums, shops, and the cafeteria.

A Texas junior high school[2] has separate buildings for each unit but students in each house are restricted to one grade, i.e., the seventh-grade unit in one location, eighth in another, and ninth in a third.

A California junior high school[3] with an enrollment of 720 students, has organized in three clusters of 240 pupils each. A seven-teacher team is assigned to each cluster to plan and develop the educational program. This team is assisted by specialists, who work with all three houses, in P.E., home economics, practical arts, and foreign language, and facilities for these areas are shared by all houses.

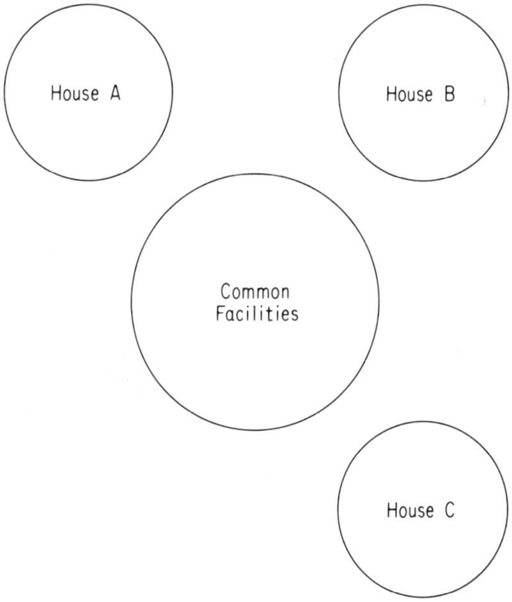

Fig. 5-4. House plan.

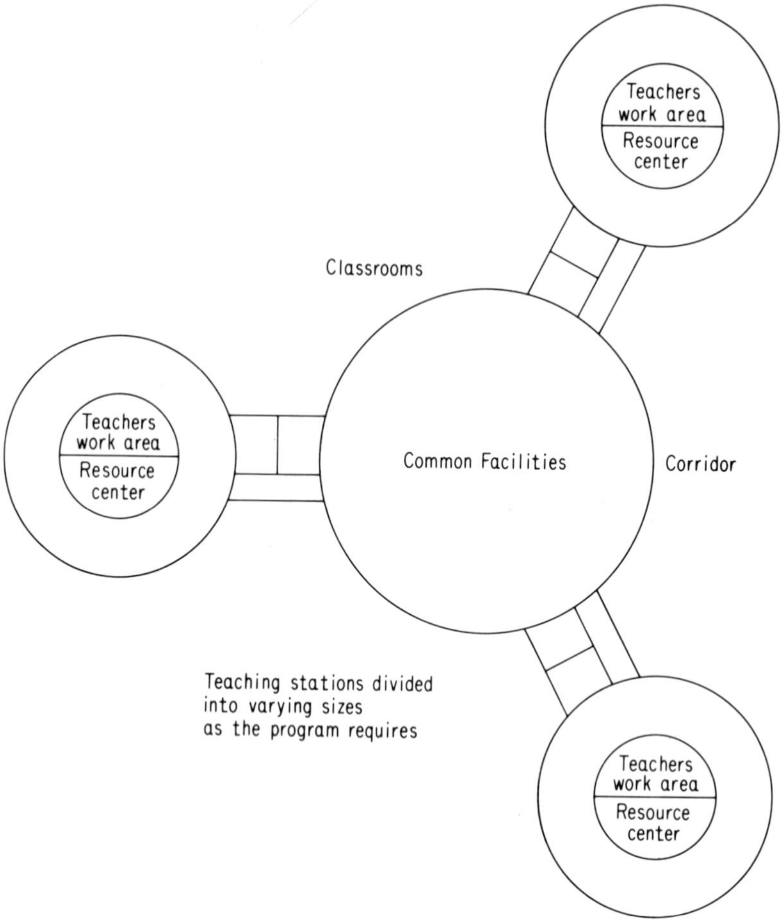

Fig. 5-5. One kind of house-plan construction.

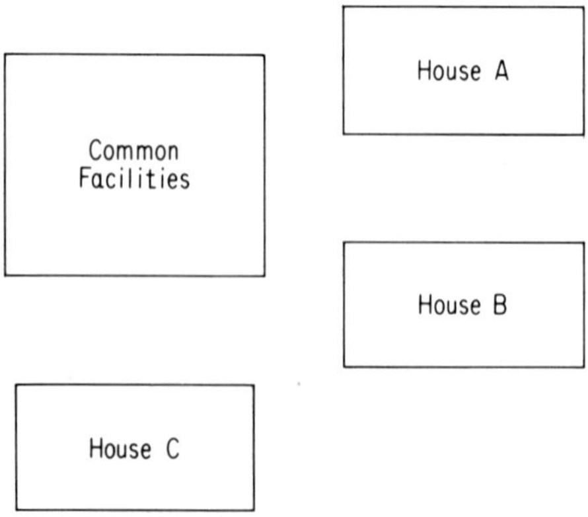

Fig. 5-6. Another house-plan design.

Newton South High School,[4] Newton, Massachusetts, was designed specifically for the house plan. The enrollment, roughly 1,500 students, was divided into three houses, each containing all three grades. Each house has its own administration, faculty, and counseling services. Team teaching is used extensively.

Topeka, Kansas, has gone to the houseplan for its junior and senior high schools as has Flint, Michigan, and a recently built junior high in Cincinnati.

Berwyn, Pennsylvania, recently constructed a junior high school based on the "little school" organization. There is a central or common building with three pods. The common facilities include home economics, remedial reading, a language laboratory, large group area, auditorium, main offices, instructional materials center, student activity room, dining facilities, health and P.E. facilities, and instructional areas for industrial arts and music. Each pod has instructional areas for English, mathematics, science, social studies, small group areas, a workroom, and its own administration and guidance.

It is important when planning instructional areas around a central common-use building that room be left for expansion both of the central facilities and of the wings. The library, for example, is usually a part of the "hub." If there is no room nor direction planned for enlargement of the library as enrollment increases, then the school is in this respect virtually obsolete before it opens.

There has been, on the part of those teachers, administrators, and students involved in house plans, substantial support, enthusiasm, and approval of the school within a school. Seldom has any criticism been mentioned.

SUMMARY

Junior high schools, frequently required to occupy buildings previously occupied by some other form of school organization, need facilities designed expressly for the educational program for early adolescents. The building should be planned and constructed after the junior high educational program has been determined; it is a mistake to construct the building and then attempt to devise a program to fit the facilities.

The house plan is one of the newer efforts made in recent years to improve the educational programs of the schools. As school districts have increased in size and schools in enrollments, students have complained of lost identity, unfriendliness, and feelings of not belonging. The house plan combats this by dividing enrollments into three or four "schools within a school." This may be done by grade or across grade lines. In either case, the "house," of 200–400 pupils, is assigned a group of teachers and its own area in the building although specialized facilities are usually shared.

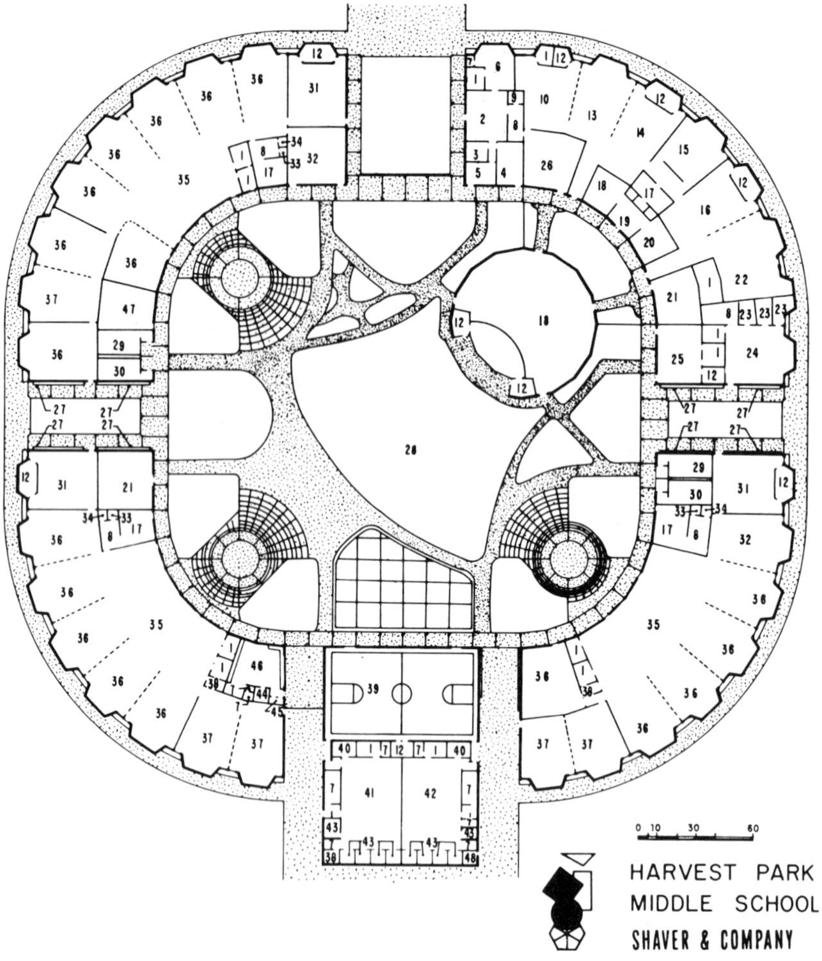

LEGEND

1. OFFICE
2. RECEPTION
3. VICE-PRINCIPAL
4. CONFERENCE
5. PRINCIPAL
6. HEALTH
7. TOILET
8. WORK AREA
9. VAULT
10. GRAPHICS CR.
11. DARK ROOM
12. STORAGE
13. ELECTRIC & POWER CR.
14. WOODS & METAL CR.
15. DRAFTING CR.
16. ARTS & CRAFTS CR.
17. TEACHERS PLANNING
18. LIBRARY
19. I.M.C.
20. AUDIO–VISUAL
21. MENTALLY RETARDED CR.
22. HOMEMAKING CR.
23. PRACTICE
24. MUSIC CR.
25. SPECIAL EDUCATION
26. BUSINESS CR.
27. STUDENT LOCKERS
28. AMPHITHEATER
29. BOYS' TOILET
30. GIRLS' TOILET
31. SCIENCE CR.
32. LANGUAGE CR.
33. MEN
34. WOMEN
35. MULTI-USE
36. CLASSROOM
37. MATH CR.
38. JANITOR STORAGE
39. MULTI-PURPOSE
40. MECHANICAL EQUIPMENT
41. BOYS
42. GIRLS
43. SHOWERS
44. FREEZER
45. MECHANICAL RM.
46. KITCHEN
47. JANITOR
48. UTILITY RM.

Fig. 5-7. The Harvest Park floor plan. The general facility relationships include (starting with upper right-hand corner, clockwise): unified arts unit, eighth-grade house, physical education, seventh-grade house, and sixth-grade house. Note the large interior court, amphitheater, and circular library/little theater. (Reprinted by permission of the SPL Reports, School Planning Laboratory, Stanford University, Stanford, Calif., Shaver and Company, Architects, Menlo Park, Calif.)

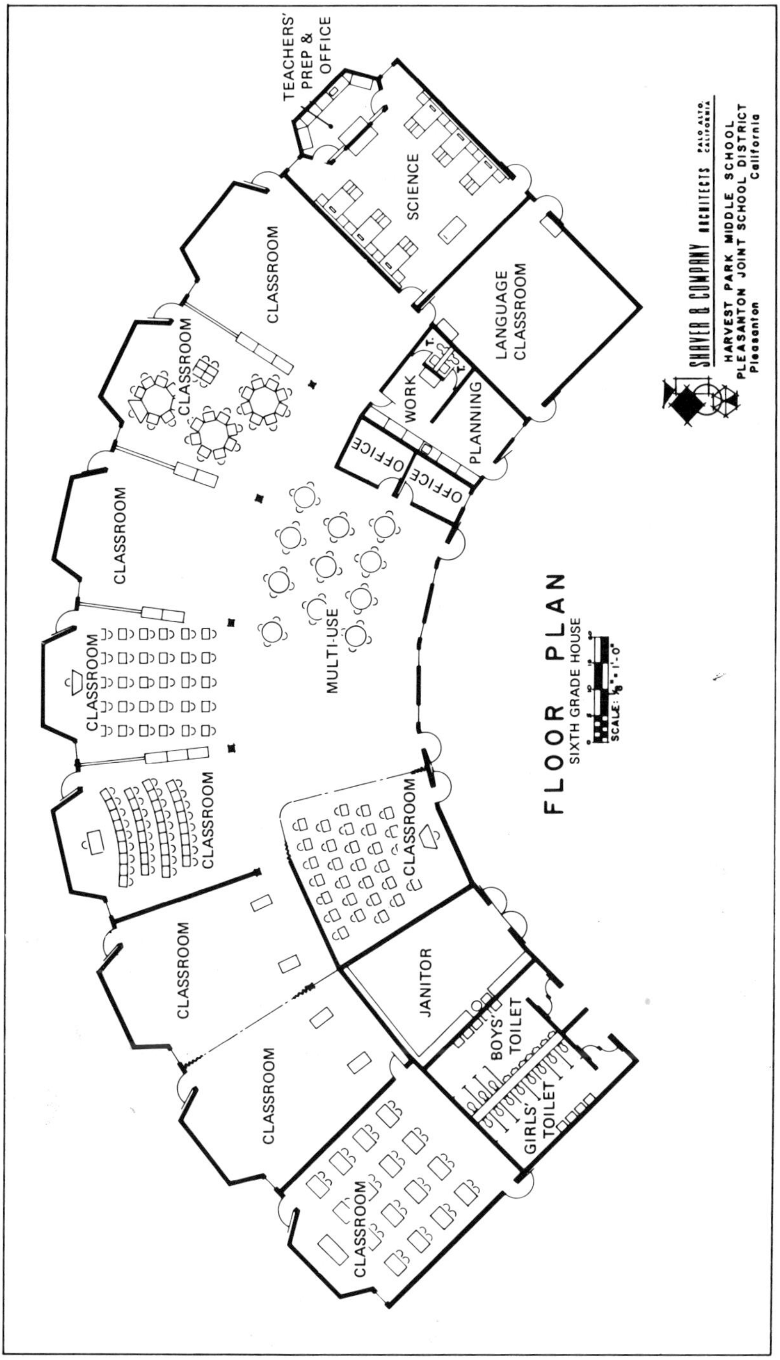

Fig. 5-8. (Reprinted by permission of the SPL Reports, School Planning Laboratory, Stanford University, Stanford, Calif.)

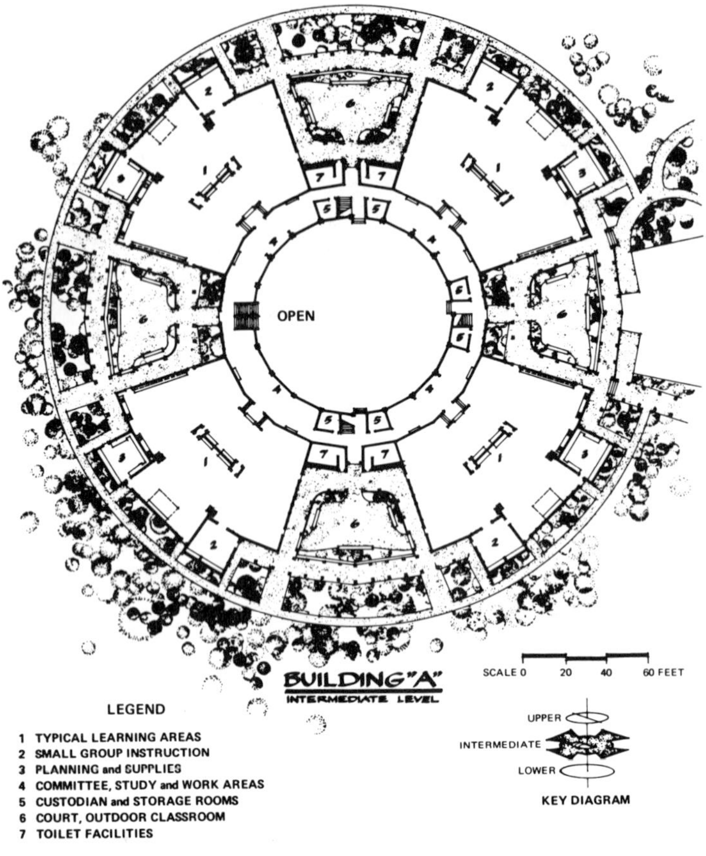

BUILDING A, the main instructional center at Reedland Woods.

Fig. 5-9. Reedland Woods Middle School is composed of four buildings—the main instructional center, an adjoining administration/counseling unit, the unified arts center, and a music/physical education building. Building A, the main instructional center is circular and trilevel. (Reprinted by permission of the SPL Reports, School Planning Laboratory, Stanford University, Stanford, Calif. Ron Young and Associates, Architects, Santa Clara, Calif.)

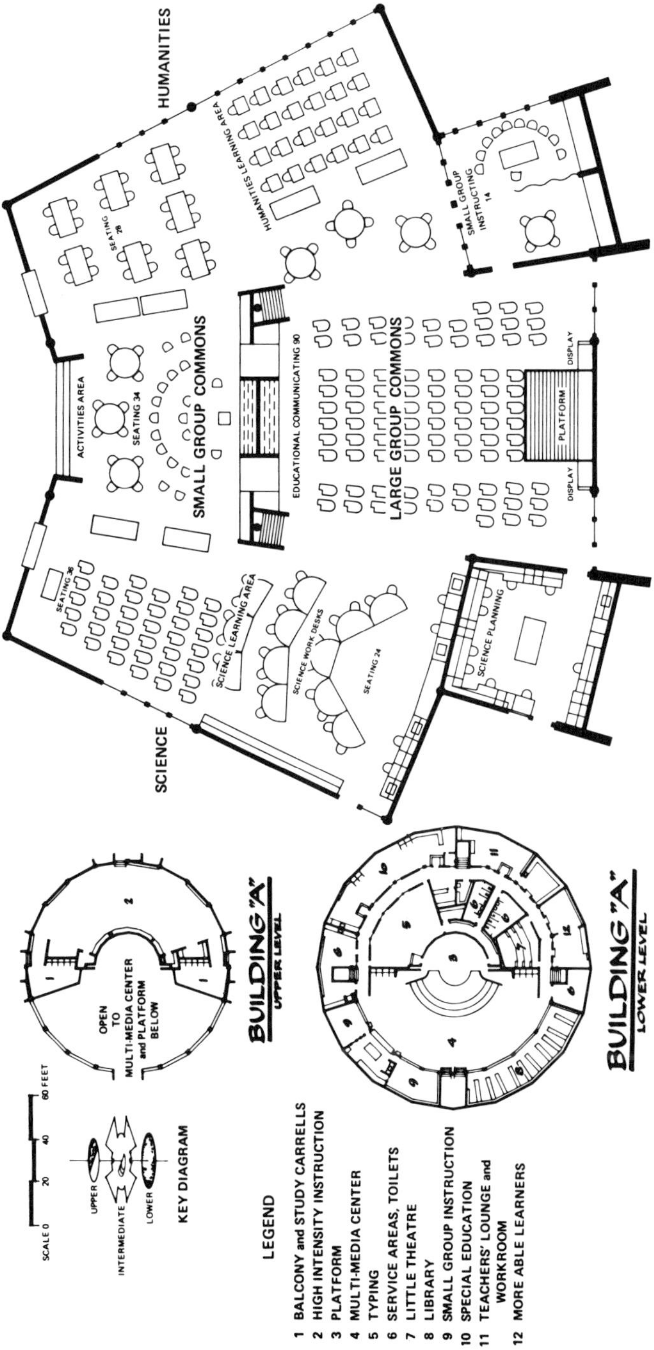

Fig. 5-10. A typical house unit at Reedland Woods. The large and small group commons can function as mixing areas for integrated science/humanities programs. The opening at the top of the picture leads directly into the walk ring that is used for small group and independent study/work activities. (Reprinted by permission of the SPL Report, School Planning Laboratory, Stanford University, Stanford, Calif. Ron Young and Associates, Architects, Santa Clara, Calif.)

REFERENCES

1. M. Dale Baughman, *Administration of the Junior High School,* monograph. Danville, Ill.: Interstate Printers and Publishers, 1966, p. 9.
2. *Ibid.*
3. H. A Taylor and R. F. Cook, "Schools Within A School: A Teaching Team Organized for Junior High School," *High School Journal,* Vol. 48 (January 1965), pp. 289–295.
4. J. Lloyd Trump and Dorsey Baynham, *Focus on Change, Guide to Better Schools.* Chicago: Rand McNally, 1961, p. 84.

part II

INSTRUCTIONAL PROGRAMS

Much has changed in curricular offerings, both in content and emphasis, in the past two decades. There is a "new" English, social studies, mathematics, and science. World War II and the events since then have brought to the United States the realization that we are permanently involved in international affairs, and as a partial result of this there has been a marked increase in foreign language instruction. Our culture, technology, and society are providing more leisure time for our citizens than they have ever known and a higher standard of living to enjoy it. The role of the family has changed and more is required of the schools. There is a real need for instruction in fine arts, practical arts, some form of consumer education, and a program of health and physical education which provides carryover values for adult life. The curriculum becomes more crowded, yet the junior high school finds little that may be reduced or eliminated and much that should be included. Certainly the junior high school must have a range and variety of offerings to provide a strong exploratory program. Newer scheduling practices alleviate problems to some extent, but it may be both necessary and desirable to investigate the possibility of the extended school day or an extended school year.

chapter 6

Common Learnings

The ideal junior high school and middle school will reflect consistency with the basic values of American life, and will be flexible enough to adapt to shifting conditions and to accept the swiftly changing ways of living in the world of today. The program of studies for children of this age will take into consideration the characteristics of the adolescent—the curiosity, idealism, desire for independence, searching for values, earlier sophistication and maturation, concern with physical growth, need for approval, and intellectual expansion. The curricular offerings will also be developed in accord with the accepted functions of the junior high school, with particular reference to providing common experiences for everyone and to provide exploratory experiences of a wide range and variety. Such opportunities will help to discover and develop special abilities and interests of every adolescent.

There are at least two major approaches to establishing the junior high school program of studies:

1. There is a general education curriculum which usually includes English (or language arts), social studies, science, mathematics, and health and physical education. All other courses are considered to be exploratory. All students are required to take the general education program and are usually required to take specified courses in the exploratory fields, such as one semester of art, one semester of music, and one semester of industrial arts or home economics. Opportunities for electives are restricted.

2. In the second approach the core of the junior high school curriculum is language arts, social studies, science, and mathematics, taken by all students—but with ***strong exploratory aspects in all these areas*** and crossing ***any*** subject-matter line. In the other course offerings there is a minimum of requirements but a maximum of elective and exploratory opportunities to help each individual to achieve the maximum possible of his own potential.

The exploratory offerings will not be limited to the fine and practical arts, but will include diversified work in science, English, social studies, and any field in which there are enough students interested.

In this second concept, general education includes an exploratory approach that fosters the education so desirable and necessary in junior high school—critical thinking, inquiry, analysis, and in-depth investigation.

SCIENCE*

> . . . We have already worked out programs in science for the senior high school level and, lest the "monster" created die of malnutrition, it is time to turn our attention to the design and implementation of functional, applicable science programs for the junior high school."[1]

The development of science, as a course of study, has been influenced by both sociological and technological events with the roots of science and scientific thought easily being traced back to Plato and the ancient Greeks. Plato's concept of science was quite different from the modern view. He believed that true knowledge could be derived only from philosophical speculation, not experimentation. This philosophy, of which science was a part, extended its influence down through the Middle Ages. The Renaissance triggered an intellectual awakening, yet science remained anonymous to the scholars. Leonardo da Vinci's name brings to mind great artistic works, but because of his development of scientific methodology he deserves an important place among the first true scientists.

Roger Bacon fostered the real beginnings of science in education by initiating the use of inductive reasoning, and he explained this technique in his publication of *Advancement of Learning* and *Novum Organum.*

Comenius was the first to make a place for teaching science in the schools with a methodology consisting of objective reality and inductive reasoning. Through the centruies men such as Rousseau and Pestalozzi used nature and natural objects for teaching. In the eighteenth and nineteenth centuries science became important in the curriculum because man relied more upon experiment to explore nature and add to his knowledge of nature. The teaching of science acquired its modern place in the curriculum when Herbert Spencer published his essay, *What Knowledge Is of Most Worth.*

The early history of education in the United States indicates that the curriculum of the elementary school was devoted primarily to the development of literacy, since to be able to read, write, and cipher was considered to be enough for most pupils. Science or science related materials were

*This section on science was written in collaboration with Joan G. Brown, Chairman, Science Department, Kennedy Middle School, Albuquerque, New Mexico.

incidental and dependent upon the interest and background of the teacher. When science was taught it was usually the natural history of the immediate environment or consisted of information from the materials that were part of the reading activity.

In the latter part of the eighteenth century the advent of the academies brought about a curriculum that was broadened to include more practical subjects for noncollege-bound students. The early public high schools grew out of the academy movement and adopted a similar curriculum. The science curriculum consisted largely of natural philosophy, natural history, and chemistry, and was taught largely for its informational and practical value, with emphasis on the memorization of factual material. The method of instruction was dominated by lecture and recitation with only a limited amount of demonstration.

The nineteenth century brought about many science discoveries and excitement about science. More and more teachers were receiving college training and degrees; a few of them had some contact with the sciences as taught in college. Science gradually grew to become an organized course in the senior high school curriculum, although it was usually a natural history course which dealt with limited aspects of science. This kind of course gradually became similar to the specialized courses of the colleges —botany, zoology, physiology, and the like.

In 1872 Harvard announced that high school science was acceptable for entrance to most colleges. This decision tended to cause the high school science curriculum to come under the domination of the colleges, with the result that there was increasing standardization of content, length, and sequence. The recommended and almost universally accepted sequence of the time was physical geography, biology, physics, and chemistry.

Through the reports and recommendations of the Committee of Ten on Standards and the Committee on College Entrance, the National Education Association began to influence the teaching of high school science. The ultimate result was the establishing of a sequence of science courses for the secondary schools.

At the close of the nineteenth century the college-dominated curriculum was criticized because it did not contain any vocational subjects. During the time when industry was beginning to serve as a model for getting things produced faster, more efficiently and economically, Eliot in 1888 and again in 1892 proposed that the elementary schools be both shortened and enriched. The Committee of Ten evidenced acceptance of Eliot's thesis by suggesting the maintenance of a four-year high school and making the seventh and eighth grades an intermediate organizational unit to bridge the gap between the six-year elementary and the high school. It was on this framework that the junior high school movement occurred. The combination of these forces was important in bringing about a change in the science sequence. A general science course was introduced to replace physical geography for the ninth grade. The purpose was to provide an exploratory course for the more specialized science courses, which would follow in the sequence for those who were college preparatory and at the same time provide a terminal course for those not going to college.

The only real innovation in science education during the first half of this century was the inclusion of a general science course in the ninth grade of the junior high school during the 1920's and 1930's. This general science course, which was very broad, consolidated the many areas taught in the senior high school and has until recently been the traditional approach to science in the junior high school.

During the period from 1930 to 1950, educators witnessed the emergence of many societies, committees, and commissions which published reports that greatly influenced the content, philosophy, and methods of science teaching as well as the entire curriculum.

World War II brought to light a critical shortage of scientists and engineers. This need accelerated the development of science and technology in the United States. The shadow of the German V-2 rocket and the technological advances of the Soviet Union caused a unique government agency to be established to support scientific research and science education. Congress gave birth to this agency in 1950 and named it the National Science Foundation. The movement to improve science education was slow but continuous until 1957 when Sputnik I was launched. This Russian feat bruised the scientific prestige of the United States and created an urgency from which programs in math and science were instituted. Through the auspices of the National Science Foundation, opportunities were offered to science and mathematics teachers to upgrade their subject matter by attending institutes. Improved teaching facilities and equipment were provided by the National Defense Education Act, which was later extended to a program of instructional materials of all types and teacher preparation.

Within the past decade the amount of class time devoted to science and the numbers of students enrolled in science have increased, especially in grades 7 and 8. One reason for this trend is that the exploratory function formerly fulfilled by ninth-grade general science is now being included in grades 7 and 8. During the past ten years all science related subjects have been undergoing continual revision and evaluation, that undoubtedly can be traced to our government's show of interest in the public school science curriculum as a result of the vastly increased concern with science in today's world.

It has been said that by the year 2000 the amount of scientific knowledge possessed by man will be 100 times as great as it was in 1900, that the most recent textbooks in science available today will be out of date in five years, and that teachers of science must "completely overhaul their knowledge every five to eight years just to keep ahead of obsolescence."[2] It has been further estimated that 95 percent of all the scientists who have ever lived are yet alive today.

Our concept of science has changed materially in recent years from that which defined science as a body of classified knowledge to that which considers science as an inseparable combination of process and content. The student is involved in inquiry and the teacher is guide and director, an approach which requires a great deal of student laboratory work, equipment, and resource. Content, too, is much changed, since the bulk of what was taught in science classes in the past twenty to thirty years has been considerably modified or discarded. There have been great changes in scientific hypotheses and theories and the knowledge explosion in science is more than a handy phrase—it is an almost frightening reality.

There are several forces influencing science teaching today, including:

1. An increasing awareness on the part of the public of the importance and role of science in our daily lives.
2. A national concern about science at all levels as evidenced by federal and foundation grants. In the late 1950's, private groups and national legislation combined to spur the improvement of science teaching on a scale which had most of the appearances of a crash program.
3. Participation of scientists in development of curriculum.
4. Appreciation by science teachers of the necessity for improving their teaching by in-service and continuing education.
5. A distinct and planned organization for curriculum development by public school districts, by state agencies, and by national organizations.
6. A realization, such as has occurred in other fields, that we have been underestimating pupil ability.

OBJECTIVES

Junior high school science is an area of considerable concern to scientists and educators alike. Instruction varies enormously, from very good to extremely poor. This is partly attributable to a crippling lack of facilities in many schools, partly due to the difference in preparation of science teachers, many of whom have not had a science course in years, and partially because of a lack of understanding of the purposes of science education and a failure to establish objectives. These objectives may be stated as:

1. To acquire a knowledge and understanding of the world of science with strong emphasis upon learning basic concepts and principles.
2. To develop in students the ability to think and work in the systematic methods of scientific investigation. This kind of performance, which results in scientific generalizations, must develop from hypotheses, data-gathering, and testing of conclusions.

3. To develop in students critical thinking and experimentation. This requires objectivity, an open and inquiring mind, and the ability to suspend judgment until it is reasonable to attempt to reach a conclusion.
4. Students who possess a special interest in or an aptitude for science should be identified, encouraged, and given opportunities to develop their talents.
5. Every effort should be made to make science interesting and exciting to all students.

To reach these objectives, junior high science should provide a great deal of laboratory work and opportunities for pupil experimentation with a corresponding decrease in teacher lecture. This will require "open" labs, a big increase in library materials in science, and science resource centers. Since science classes may easily take longer than a standard class period, varied schedules will probably be required.

Junior high school science teachers have often been unable to meet the demands in curriculum revision, although to assist the teacher, the National Science Foundation has done much in the past few years to retrain science teachers. As a result, school districts are moving away from the task of developing their own curriculum guides and are turning to the Foundation-sponsored curriculum. These new curricula include texts, films, tests, teacher training, lab equipment, and newsletters. District science supervisors often state that the federally sponsored curricula are so far superior to what can be produced locally that the trend is to adopt them as soon as possible.

NEWER DEVELOPMENTS FOR THE JUNIOR HIGH SCHOOL

The junior high school science curriculum attempts to articulate the science of the elementary school with the sciences of the senior high school. Often this has been done by offering one or more years of general science, and sometimes by including general science in a block of time course.

Science instruction in the junior high school has been a sometime thing. Some schools have offered virtually no science while others have had required science courses in every grade. The trend appears to be toward required science at each grade level, 7-8-9, although the science classes may not meet daily and may meet for only one semester in each grade.

Traditionally, the junior high school science course was general science, although the emphasis depended largely upon the teacher and was developed in those areas in which he felt most secure. In the new approaches the main difference between science in the junior high school and in elementary and senior high school is one of depth. It has been proposed that the junior high school science program should be adapted to various ability levels so that more able students could take high school science in the ninth grade. Conversely, slower students may need four years to complete the standard three-year program. The course of study suggested is:

Grade 7: Science and Man (includes life processes, body functions, and health and disease).

Grade 8: The Interaction of Science and Matter
- (a) Atoms
- (b) Behavior of matter
- (c) Matter is electrical
- (d) Power and energy
- (e) The many frontiers of discovery and invention

Grade 9: The Earth and Space
- (a) Nature and origin of the universe
- (b) The earth, gravity, magnetic fields, relationships with other bodies
- (c) The changing earth
- (d) Oceanography
- (e) Meteorology
- (f) Space travel

The Florida State Junior High Curriculum Project has proposed a rather different approach to the junior high science program.[3] There is planned a continuing course for all three grades, 7-8-9. (A common criticism of junior high school science programs is that they lack continuity; that they are isolated subjects.) "Another important feature of the project is the laboratory nature of the classroom. Each student works at his own rate in progressing through the investigative activities."[4] There are but few class discussions since there is a pronounced stress upon increased lab work. The theme for the seventh-grade program is "Energy"; for the eighth grade it is "Structure of Matter"; and in the ninth grade the program is almost nonstructured, but is directed toward individual research study where the more complex sciences of earth and life are studied. Throughout there is an emphasis upon the scientific approach and an attempt to show the interrelatedness of all science, so that the student may be able to develop basic scientific principles into major generalizations.

A science program developed for one large school district for use in junior high school takes the thematic approach:

Grade 8:
- (a) What is science? Fields, methods, and tools
- (b) Matter
- (c) Living things
- (d) Man and space
- (e) The changing earth
- (f) The interrelationship of living things

Grade 9:
- (a) Energy
- (b) Meteorology
- (c) Frontiers of science—space, oceanography, new biology

While the major emphasis in revising the science curriculum has been upon high school programs, there has recently been substantial interest displayed in extending these revisions to the junior high curriculum; as a result, there has been an expansion of biology, earth science, and physical science at this level.

BIOLOGY

The Biological Sciences Curriculum Study (BSCS) was not intended for the junior high school. The first course was developed for tenth-graders (ages 15 and 16). However, many junior high schools throughout the country have utilized this program, particularly for advanced students at the ninth grade level.

The purposes and objectives of BSCS are to contribute to the improvement of biological education through preparation of curriculum materials related to the study of biology. There are three versions of the BSCS: yellow, blue, and green. This is not a classification for slow, regular, and fast students since about three-fourths of the content of the three courses is the same. The difference is to be found in the approaches taken. The green version approaches biology from the point of view of ecology, the blue version approaches biology as a molecular study, and the yellow treats biology in cellular terms. Teachers' handbooks and teaching materials are provided, and the student is taught science as a way of thinking—drawing his own generalizations, searching for relationships, and finding his own answers. It is interesting to note that BSCS through its support from the National Science Foundation has developed a proposal for establishing guidelines for the development of a modern instructional program in the life sciences as a one-year course for intermediate grades (7 or 8). The BSCS project began at Boulder, Colorado, in 1959, and it is estimated that there are over 30,000 teachers now using the various versions of BSCS biology.

EARTH SCIENCE

Earth Science Curriculum Project (ESCP) includes all of the earth sciences: astronomy, geology, geography, meteorology, and oceanography. The program was designed for ninth-graders; however, many junior high schools are offering earth science in grades 7 and 8. The unique feature of this program is its interdisciplinary approach to earth science which weaves the various disciplines together to provide a comprehensive view of the planet earth and its environment. The student is led through a series of investigations which provide him with experiences to help him to understand the content; the concept of science as inquiry is continually stressed; and the text material is designed to lead the student into his own researches of the earth. This project first began at Boulder, Colorado, in 1963.

PHYSICAL SCIENCE

Better known as IPS (Introductory Physical Science), the major emphasis in the course is on the study of matter. This course is being used in grades 8 and 9 with students who have a wide range of abilities, although many schools have adopted the course for use in grades 11 and 12 for students who do not plan to take physics or chemistry.

In IPS the student laboratory work is of primary importance. Laboratory instructions in IPS are incorporated in the body of the text, but the results are not described. In addition, the equipment is designed in such a way that the students can perform the experiments in ordinary classrooms. The IPS project was begun in 1963 by Educational Services Incorporated.

All of the new programs have some characteristics as a common thread, although the emphasis varies:

1. There is less stress on facts and more on comprehension.
2. Basic principles, concepts, and generalizations are more important than technology.
3. There is more emphasis upon mathematics.
4. The program is laboratory centered.
5. There is considerable emphasis upon individual experimentation and lab work.
6. There is less lecture and more stress upon critical and creative thinking.

ISSUES AND PROBLEMS

In spite of the activity and massive curricular change in science, some of the old problems still remain and, as might be expected, new issues have arisen.

1. Textbooks. In these times textbooks soon become obsolete, and perhaps that's a good thing, since many are full of errors and inconsistencies.
2. Teachers are still too often inadequately prepared. Even worse, it is not uncommon in junior high school to find a teacher saddled with a science class he didn't want and can't really teach, but has it because of "scheduling problems."
3. There is still too much teaching from the text and not enough pupil lab work.
4. Many schools attempt to teach too much content. It is impossible to teach or learn everything.
5. We still tend to underestimate the ability of interested students.
6. There is still too much repetition of content.

7. Too many junior high schools are still plagued by a lack of facilities, lack of materials, and a shortage of time to teach.
8. Science changes so rapidly that there is a need for a continuing in-service teacher training program.
9. There is a conflict of opinion between those who believe that all science should be integrated and those who think that each subject should be distinct. General science is often criticized for just that —it is too general.
10. There is some feeling that there is a gap in the new programs, since there has been an omission of any real attention to applied science, engineering, and technology.
11. Unquestionably, the substantial majority of the new programs are aimed at the college-bound student.
12. There is a need for a correlation of instruction in mathematics and science.

TRENDS

The new developments in science exhibit specific directions that are worth noting:

1. A trend away from an emphasis upon proving what is already known, as well as a movement away from formal demonstrations and individual laboratory exercises. There is an emphasis upon the development of understandings of principles by means of problem solving carried on by the pupils themselves.
2. A trend away from the use of applied technology.
3. A stress upon the importance and necessity of pupil experimentation.
4. A trend toward laboratory experiences which take longer than a standard class period and require equipment setups for the entire time.
5. A trend toward recognition of science instruction as a part of the education for all.
6. A trend toward diversified science instruction in which different students seek solutions to different problems.
7. A movement from rigid and static facilities and scheduling toward flexibility in design and organization.
8. A trend toward increased use of audio-visual aids by individuals or small groups of pupils.
9. A trend toward the introduction of new units and topics, such as wave mechanics and nuclear energy.

Additional probabilities are that there will be a movement away from the one subject taught each year, increased in-service and continuing education for teachers and increased flexibility in content, organization, and instruction of the junior high school science program.

MATHEMATICS

The major uses of mathematics have traditionally been in the physical sciences and in practical application to the utilitarian needs of society, with the largest part of the mathematics program composed of arithmetic that was taught as a mechanical technique. In the colonial and frontier days there was good reason for this, since there existed a real need for people who could use arithmetic to survey, navigate, and keep books. Indeed, the mark of literacy was some knowledge of the "3 R's," "reading, writing, and 'rithmetic." As time passed, mathematics achieved respect not only for its vocational aspect but also as a superior medium for mental discipline, and in the nineteenth century algebra, geometry, trigonometry, solid and analytic geometry, and some theory of conic sections were added to many school programs. By World War I calculus was commonly the ultimate goal of the high school mathematics program, although it was a course that enjoyed but small enrollment, usually limited to the mathematically inclined or to those aiming at a technical college career. Since World War II there has been an unparalleled advance in the use, emphasis, and development of mathematics, a varied use which may be found in such diverse fields as industry, biology, social sciences, and game theory. Mathematics has moved from a position in which it was a dreary subject to be endured by most and assiduously avoided by many to become an exciting prestige subject, adorned with a variety of new approaches, terms, concepts, and content.

THE NEW MATHEMATICS

In the traditional programs of mathematics methods changed but little, students memorized tables and algorithms with minimal understanding of meaning or concepts and usually with minimal interest. Elementary arithmetic was intended to teach what was necessary for everyday living, usually with business applications. Junior high arithmetic was particularly criticized, especially in grade 8, as being largely review, watered down, and time-wasting. Algebra has usually been offered in grade 9 for the college-bound, while the noncollege-bound student took prealgebra, business arithmetic, general mathematics, or even more stigmatizing, "refresher math." Interest in revising the mathematics curriculum on a serious level preceded the furor attendant upon Sputnik by several years when a group at the University of Illinois, under the direction of Max Beberman began in 1951 to develop a new curriculum—the University of Illinois Committee on Mathematics Study (the UICMS program). Since then there have been many groups that have become interested in revision of the mathematics curriculum and several programs have been developed.

It has become obvious that the traditional mathematics curriculum is no longer satisfactory to train students for the many new uses of mathematics. The phenomenal increase in the use of computers has made training in computer use essential. New areas such as game theory, mathematical logic, and topology have become relatively common. Probability and statistics, although used and studied for many years, have made giant strides with the increased use of computers. The mathematics curriculum now requires more understanding of the structure of mathematical systems and less mechanical manipulation of formulas and equations; more stress upon the development of mathematical models and symbolic representation of ideas and relationships.

There is increased stress upon functions and functional analysis, more emphasis upon the foundations of mathematics, and much importance attached to student discovery of mathematical relations rather than teacher explication.

Criticisms of the traditional mathematics programs include:

1. The mathematics curriculum for the college-bound, in spite of changes and advancements, remained virtually unchanged since it first became a part of the secondary school program.
2. The noncollege student finds open to him mathematics courses which are largely rehashes of the mathematics he took in elementary school, with some additional material on income tax, installment buying, consumer education, and stock markets—which have little interest and less relevance to junior high school students. There is also a lack of status for students in these courses; students are slow to take them and teachers are reluctant to teach them.
3. The cultural and esthetic aspects of mathematics are almost completely neglected. Little is taught concerning the history of mathematics or of the contributions of famous mathematicians. Junior high school mathematics has become a mechanically applied collection of unrelated rules and techniques.
4. The mathematics curriculum is not only narrow in scope for both elementary and junior high school, it is repetitious, boring, and virtually saturated with useless material.

There is some difference of opinion as to how much is "new" in the "new mathematics." It has been said that there is really nothing in this that is mathematically new, that all within the new mathematics has been known for many years. What is new is said to be the reduced emphasis upon some topics, the increased emphasis upon other topics previously ignored, and the major reorganization of the mathematics curriculum.

In contrast it is held that "Mathematicians are constantly creating new mathematics . . . and that more than half the mathematics in existence today has been created during the twentieth century."[5]

In examining some of the new mathematics curricula, it would be well to keep in mind what the objectives should be for the junior high school mathematics programs.

1. There needs to be a balance between the theoretical and the practical. Not all children will become mathematicians or go on to college, but all will become consumers.
2. Junior high school mathematics content and instruction should be adapted to the interests, abilities, and needs of this age group.
3. The mathematics curriculum should avoid the mechanical and attempt to arouse the student to inductive and creative thought. It is becoming a truism that children are capable of learning and understanding far more complex ideas at an earlier level than has traditionally been presented to them.
4. The junior high school mathematics program should create an interest in further study of mathematics, develop an understanding of structure, and provide an exposure to the cultural and esthetic aspects of mathematics.
5. Students should develop the ability to discover, analyze, and generalize as well as to acquire the manipulative skills.
6. There should be developed in students an appreciation of the importance of mathematics and the mathematician in today's society.
7. Students should develop an understanding of the deductive methods of modern mathematics.

There are also answers which must be provided by any program of mathematics which is adopted:

1. For what purpose are we teaching mathematics? Vocational use? Use in daily living? For college? To change society?
2. Children can learn more and sooner than has previously been realized. At what grade level can we most effectively develop mathematical ideas, skills, habits, and attitudes?
3. What programs should be established and required for different ability levels?
4. How much stress is necessary upon computational skill?
5. It is necessary to teach for transfer of skills and learning in mathematics. What ideas, facts, and concepts are desirable—in short, what should the content be and how do we select it?
6. How may we evaluate the effectiveness of a new program?

NEW MATHEMATICS PROGRAMS

The revolution which is taking place in the field of mathematics teaching has placed great emphasis on junior as well as senior high school levels. Examples of experimental programs which are attempting to improve the teaching of mathematics on the junior high school level include that the University of Maryland, the University of Illinois, School Mathematics Study Group (Yale University), and Greater Cleveland Mathematics Program. Each program is seeking better content and a better approach and is experimenting with the placement of topics. The following examples illustrate some of the recent developments.

1. *University of Illinois Committee on School Mathematics.* This is the oldest of the experimental projects, having started in 1951. The discovery approach is utilized in varying degrees in most of the new programs, and in UICSM it is the central theme. So far in this project, materials for grades 9–12 have been developed. The textbooks emphasize consistency, precision of language, structure of mathematics, and understanding of basic principles through pupil discovery. Discovery of generalizations by the student is a basic technique used throughout the course, and there is stress upon interest, challenge, and adventure in mathematics. A thorough curriculum revision is not attempted by UICSM, rather the main concern is upon developing selected topics.

Test results so far compare the development of the manipulative skills between the experimental programs and the courses in the standard curriculum. The results of tests given and work done in courses after the completion of the UICSM project materials show performances equal to or better than the traditional program.

The bonus in the program, and one that does not show up in the traditional test results, was that the student in these classes learned substantial amounts of mathematics not included in conventional courses. Concerning the ability to think and understand, which is a basis upon which the UICSM materials have been developed, the Commission of Mathematics reports:

> Earlier mathematicians often looked upon algebra from a manipulative point of view. Skill in performing the operations within the system frequently was the goal of instruction, rather than an understanding of the properties of the system. The contemporary point of view, while not discounting the manipulative thought, puts chief emphasis on the structure or pattern of the system and on deductive thinking.[6]

2. *School Mathematics Study Group.* The school Mathematics Study Group (SMSG or the Yale Project) was founded in 1958 and financed by the National Science Foundation. This was one of the largest projects in terms of materials prepared and in terms of the individuals who worked preparing and testing the materials.

The major concern of SMSG has been the preparation of sample textbooks to direct the way into the curriculum of modern mathematics. Originally efforts were concentrated in secondary programs, but SMSG has increased its efforts to include elementary, as well as texts for teacher training. SMSG feels that mathematics in junior high school should be moving from real applications to abstractions. There is a program for junior high school low achievers and a study of a desirable program for gifted pupils.

The Minnesota National Laboratory's evaluation of SMSG, grades 7–12, found:

> In grades 6 and 9 the SMSG courses gave especially good results for the students in the bottom quartile. Thus, in 9th grade in 1959 we started with about 16.5 percent in the bottom quartile according to national norms for 9th grades. The following September less than 105 were in the bottom quartile for 10th graders; and, in fact, less than 17 percent were in the bottom quartile according to national norms for 11th-graders.
>
> In all grades the high-ability students also did well. For example, we started in 1959 with 68.6 percent of the 10th graders in the top quartile according to national norms, and a year later 66.9 percent of these students scored in the top quartile according to 12th-grade norms.[7]

3. *University of Maryland Mathematics Project.* The University of Maryland Mathematics Project for the junior high school was initiated in the fall of 1957, being financed by a grant from the Carnegie Corporation. The purpose was to prepare materials for seventh- and eighth-grade students that would lead to a more formal study of basic structures or basic principles of properties common to all systems of mathematics.

Here, as in the SMSG, emphasis was on concepts, understanding, and introduction to induction and deduction rather than the standard problem-solving techniques. "Language and structure of mathematics are stressed, distinction is made between mathematical symbols and the mathematical concepts the symbols represent. There is an emphasis upon number systems."[8]

As a result of their work, program developers have concluded that junior high school students are more capable of learning mathematical concepts than was formerly thought.

4. *Commission on Mathematics.* This Commission, which was primarily concerned with secondary mathematics for college-bound students, was sponsored by the College Entrance Examination Board and the Carnegie Corporation. Its purpose was to consider the college preparatory programs of the secondary schools and to make recommendations toward their improvement. The Commission expressed need for revision and proposed the following general program for the junior high school.

(a) *Seventh and eighth grade:* Extension of arithmetic, introduction to ideas of algebra, less stress upon business applications, introduction to intuitive geometry, and use of ratio, measurements, relationships among geometric elements, plus graphs and formulas.

(b) *Ninth grade:* Continuation of algebra much as it was then but with more emphasis upon concepts, terminology and symbolism, inequalities, deductive reasoning, some proof, concept and language of set theory, and absolute value. Much less emphasis on mechanics was recommended.

5. *Secondary School Curriculum Committee.* This committee, sponsored by the National Council of Teachers of Mathematics, was developed in 1958 to study the mathematics curriculum in grades seven through twelve.

The committee issued a report which singled out five topics currently in the curriculum of the secondary schools that could be eliminated completely.[9] These were (1) extensive and tricky factoring, (2) simultaneous quadratics, (3) involved and spurious fractions, (4) most of business mathematics, and (5) extensive computational problems in algebra and geometry.

At the seventh- and eighth-grade levels, the committee indicated that the new programs in mathematics sought to emphasize basic instruction for all in the fundamental skills, concepts, and principles of arithmetic, supplemented by significant topics from algebra and geometry. Regarding the placement of Algebra I in the eighth grade, they indicated that, for the time being, it seemed unwise to make a blanket recommendation, but that it was desirable to follow such a program. They preferred enrichment to acceleration. Among some of the topics they believed could be taught in the junior high school were elementary notions of statistics, many aspects of geometry including inductive and deductive conjectures, and especially set theory which they believed to be the most universally applicable part of mathematics.

6. *Greater Cleveland Mathematics Program.* This program, begun in 1959, concentrates upon a sequential mathematics program and is published by Science Research Associates.

SUMMARY OF PROJECT CONCLUSIONS

Perhaps the most important conclusion to be drawn from the several projects is that junior high school students are now believed capable of much more sophisticated reasoning than was previously thought. All of the studies stressed informal mathematical concepts through all levels of junior high school. Certain aspects of proof, induction, and deduction have been found to be successful. Emphasis on number systems of various bases have given greater meaning to the number system of base ten. All of the studies included some elements of set theory in their experimental programs. Much of informal algebra and geometry in conceptual form was recommended to be introduced throughout the usual arithmetic.

Certain elements of the junior high school program have been criticized as not contributing much to general mathematical instruction.

For the teacher, each of these studies provided reference materials as well as texts and complete study guides. It was noted that teachers would have to make a conscious effort to update themselves to teach many of the new ideas in mathematics. This updating process could be done either through group study or through individual work. Materials for various methods were provided by these groups.

Characteristics common to all programs include:

1. An emphasis upon making the language of mathematics more precise.
2. Old ideas are given new usages.
3. There *are* "new mathematics" included.
4. Interest is stimulated in understanding why and how.
5. Deletion of obsolete topics and introduction of new material.
6. Teaching more mathematics in a shorter time.
7. More student participation.
8. The student is expected to discover mathematical relations.
9. More stress upon recognition of the structure of mathematics.
10. There is widespread involvement of concerned people in mathematics curriculum revision, including college and public school personnel, mathematicians, and psychologists.

The new mathematics has been criticized for eliminating most of the scientific and social applications from the curriculum; for concentrating upon the noncollege group, for thinking in terms of future mathematicians instead of future citizens in every field, and for giving too light weight to applications.

JUNIOR HIGH SCHOOL MATHEMATICS PROGRAMS

The American Association of School Administrators has suggested a program for junior high school mathematics which would be designed for three ability levels:[10]

1. Accelerated: students' seventh-grade work will include much of the usual eighth-grade program; by the end of grade 8, they will have completed first year algebra, and by the end of grade 9 they will have completed plane and solid geometry.
2. Regular level:
   Grade 7: Arithmetic
   Grade 8: Introduction to algebra and geometry
   Grade 9: Elementary algebra
3. Slow: In grades 7 and 8 these students will complete a modern, slow-paced version of some of the content for these grades. In grade 9 some of these students will be ready for prealgebra, and will move into algebra in grade 10.

As part of a master's study, a letter inquiring about the mathematics program offered at the junior high school level was sent to fourteen Western school districts, of which eleven replied.[11]

Of those districts responding, ten indicated that they had ability grouping in the seventh, eighth, and ninth grades. All eleven districts reported teaching Algebra I to eighth-grade students. Of the six districts that gave information, three indicated they taught geometry to the accelerated ninth-graders; three taught Algebra II. Five of the districts were working with materials from the SMSG and two with UICSM; San Diego used both.

Portland, Seattle, and San Diego all reported they were conducting in-service training programs for their teachers.

In order to provide a junior high school mathematics curriculum varied enough for students to be placed according to their individual needs, interest, and abilities, rather than by age or grade level, the Granite School District, Salt Lake City, Utah, now offers eleven different courses.[13] Students are required to take mathematics in grades 7 and 8. In grade 9, mathematics is optional. However, it is strongly recommended, particularly for all of those who may be going to college.

Course	Description	Grade
Math 1R	Very low achievers.	7
Math 2R	Students below "regular seventh grade" level but not "rock bottom."	7 or 8
Math 3R	Remedial type work for students who can benefit from more "basic" work.	8 or 9
Math 1	Regular seventh-grade level.	7 or 8
Math 1X	Include grade material from seventh- and eighth-levels for students who are very capable in mathematics and plan on a full math program in high school.	7
Math 2	Regular eighth-grade level for students who are above low achiever level but who probably are generally below average.	8
Math 2X	For eighth-grade students who will take algebra in ninth grade.	8
Math 3	Ninth-grade general math for the noncollege-bound student who is above the level of Math 3R.	9
Prealgebra	For all ninth-grade students who plan on taking algebra in high school	9
Algebra	Regular first-year algebra course.	8 or 9
Geometry	Regular high school geometry for all students who took algebra in eighth grade.	9

TABLE 6–1
Junior High School Mathematics Offerings
of Eleven Western Districts, 1954–1960[12]

School District	Program		
	7th Grade	8th Grade	9th Grade
Boise, Idaho	Arithmetic Slow Remedial Average Accelerated Special Algebra	Arithmetic Slow Remedial Average Accelerated Algebra	Atithmetic Gen. Math Remedial Algebra Accel. Alg.
Coos Bay, Oregon	Arithmetic Slow Average Fast	Arithmetic Slow Average Algebra	Gen. Math Algebra Geometry
Denver, Colorado	Arithmetic	Arithmetic Gen. Math. (1 semester) Algebra (1 semester)	Gen. Math Algebra
Pocatello, Idaho	Arithmetic Slow Remedial Average Advanced Math	Arithmetic Slow Remedial Advanced Math Algebra	Arith. Review Gen. Math Algebra
Portland, Oregon	Arithmetic	Arithmetic Algebra	Gen. Math Algebra
Sacramento, California	Arithmetic Accel. Arith.	Arithmetic Algebra	Gen. Math Algebra Geometry
San Diego, California	Arithmetic	Arithmetic I Arithmetic II Advanced Math	Math 3–4 Gen. Math 1–2 Algebra 1–2 Math A–B
San Francisco California	Arithmetic Slow Average Fast	Arithmetic Slow Average Algebra	Gen. Math Algebra
San Jose, California	Arithmetic Accell. Arith.	Arithmetic Algebra	Gen. Math Algebra Geometry
Seattle, Washington	Arithmetic	Arithmetic Algebra	Gen. Math Algebra I Algebra II
Weber County, Utah	Arithmetic Remedial Average Fast	Arithmetic Remedial Average Algebra	Gen. Math Algebra I Algebra II

In the face of the ever-changing demands of modern living, mathematics education cannot stand still. Life's pattern is woven around a complex computation and mathematical system. The function of mathematics education is to teach the mathematics that will prepare people to adapt to our present system.

The mathematics needed, however, is not the same for all students. The student who plans a highly technical career or a college education of any kind needs a different type of mathematical training than the student who will terminate his education at the end of high school.

For the poorer students, the last formal mathematics instruction many will receive is in the junior high school. For these students, many of whom will drop out before graduation, a sound arithmetic preparation is of great importance to help them face the responsibility that being on their own incurs. These students should be familiar with such things as home management, long-term buying, interest and commission.

Junior high school mathematics have been afflicted with a number of problems and difficulties. Certainly, mathematics is a basic need and all students should be able to use computational skills. Some of the more common problems have been:

1. Excessive and boring wearisome drill. Mathematics can be and should be interesting, fun, and excite the student's curiosity, but too many adolescents literally hate the subject.
2. Repetition. Students complain that they are compelled to do the same kind of work that they have performed in previous grades.
3. Lack of relevance to the daily lives of the students.
4. The feeling on the part of many teachers of mathematics that all students can and should do the same kind of work. Programmed instruction and independent study could do and does much to alleviate this situation.
5. An obsolete curriculum taught by teachers who hold all students, able and slow, to a rigid course of study.

ENGLISH LANGUAGE ARTS

In recent years there has been much discussion and interest concerning the "new English," although the whole subject of English and its content appear to be marked by controversy and a lack of agreement and understanding. There is even disagreement regarding the name, one group titling the subject the "English Language Arts," and another group referring to the "English" curriculum. The name favored depends upon one's point of view—traditional or "practical."

When this point is reached, it is apparent that the argument becomes one which is even more basic, i.e., what is English for the junior high school? There are two widely separated positions which, in somewhat oversimplified terms, may be outlined as follows.

1. The group which believes that English has no content of its own but is a tool subject, a skill. Since the teaching of reading, writing, speaking, and listening skills is reasonably and acceptably the goal of general education, everything serving this goal may properly be regarded as "English," and every teacher, therefore, is a teacher of "English." Within this purview, learning English is regarded as "language arts," a skill of communication, a means of sharing attitudes, feelings, information, and ideas. This approach stresses the utilitarian, and it is in this approach to junior high school English that we will find instruction in the proper method of telephoning, writing friendly letters, listening to the radio, or watching television. In a somewhat broader appraisal, this definition includes specific content in reading, writing, speaking, and listening, and will probably include spelling, punctuation, and penmanship, plus literature and the study of the English language.

2. In the second and less inclusive concept, English (and this is not to be confused with Language Arts) is a content subject, an end in itself, and is concerned with language, composition, and literature.

There can be no question but that the English courses of study in many junior high schools have been titled language arts classes and have become catchalls for a great deal of extraneous matter and rubbish. Topics such as, "How to Write Letters of Invitation," "Making and Receiving Telephone Calls," "The Friendly Letter," "Facing Teenage Problems," "Temperance," "What to Watch on Television," and similar items, while supported as useful and directly related to student life on one hand, are sharply criticized by the opposition as having no part in the English curriculum.

Probably the most reasonable position and that which is most likely to give adolescents what they need (although it may not satisfy either contending group) is that which includes both a body of content and a body of skills. Certainly there are skills to be acquired—writing, speaking, listening, and reading—and there is a content that should be learned in language and literature.

BACKGROUND

Someone once observed that the problem was not that students enter college without knowing anything about English, but that they don't know much, and what they do know is different kinds of "not muches." This is easily perceived in English, where a great deal depends upon the point of view, interest, and likes of the individual teacher. Critics exaggerate the lack of emphasis upon "academics" in today's schools and enjoy pointing out what things were like in "the good old days." As Will Rogers remarked,

"Things ain't what they used to be and probably never was."

The formal study of English as a part of the curriculum, although occasionally tolerated in the past, received its first real impetus when Harvard College in 1873 included English composition as a part of its entrance examinations. The effect upon public education was immediate and pronounced. The National Conference on Uniform Entrance Requirements in Literature was formed in 1893 to design uniform literature requirements upon the public schools.

A 1917 committee recommended that the study of English stress activities, not information, and suggested that the outcomes of English could be classified as cultural, vocational, social, and ethical values. In 1936 another committee reinforced the earlier report by recommending that grammar be functional; writing be utilitarian, not artistic; that reading should not stress required books but emphasize free reading; and that English should be regarded and taught as it related to life situations.

The National Council of Teachers of English published about 1950 a three-volume study of the K–12 English curriculum and recommended that such a program include a wide range of content and instructional methods instead of a single prescribed curriculum; individualized reading and study of mass media; and a recognition of the value of the functional approach in teaching grammar.

Two more recent curriculum projects are: (1) the NEA Dean Longmuir Project on Improving English Composition, and, (2) Project English of the U.S. Office of Education, which has set up several curriculum study centers in several universities, sponsored research, and established demonstration centers. One aspect of these newer efforts is the attempt to develop specific tests, materials, and curriculum guides instead of broad outlines and general statements.

OBJECTIVES IN JUNIOR HIGH SCHOOL ENGLISH

Somewhat broadly put, the goal of the junior high school English curriculum is to help pupils to communicate more effectively and to develop more understanding and perception of literature and language opportunities. Specifically, we deal with what may be characterized as an embarrassment of riches. Curriculum guides include "Thinking Critically," "Choosing Magazines Wisely," "Debate," "Speech," "Judging Television and Radio Programs," and so many other topics that what may be needed is to establish primary and secondary objectives in English. Primary objectives are that the courses should (1) be sequentially teachable, and (2) appear to be a priority responsibility of the English curriculum. Secondary skills are those that do not meet either criterion. Critical thinking, it has been said, is not solely the responsibility of the junior high school English teacher, since it is hoped that some critical thinking takes place in other classes. Thus critical thinking becomes a secondary objective.

Primary objectives will include:

1. The ability to read with comprehension, understanding, and critical insight.
2. Knowing, appreciating, and understanding the literature of the past and the present. Literature differs from reading in that literature implies deeper analysis; the study of writing of lasting significance; and the acquisition of knowledge of material within the literature concerning such things as the author's life, the country of its origin, and the time during which the work was produced.
4. Acquiring a knowledge and understanding of the structure of the English language. This suggests that a decision must be made as to which grammar will be studied.

Secondary objectives will include:

1. The ability to speak clearly and effectively.
2. Learning to listen attentively and with critical understanding.
3. Developing a careful attention to critical and logical thinking.
4. To learn from, to enjoy, to appreciate, and to evaluate the mass media.

Textbooks used in junior high school English are more likely to be of the inclusive type, basing their proposals to teachers of English on factors such as social, philosophical, and psychological. Loban, Ryan, and Squire[14] are so convinced of the importance of values that they note, "The art of living depends finally upon the values by which decisions are made. . . . The English program rests, ultimately. upon a program for examining and judging values."

THE ENGLISH CURRICULUM

Gleason predicted a "reforming of the internal structure of English around three headings: the understanding of the language, the manipulation of the language, and the appreciation of the language."[15] In this view, understanding the language is much more than the study of grammar, and teaching of literature also includes the appreciation of language as a structure.

There is in this approach an interrelationship that maintains unity. Language includes necessary structures and kinds of English. Composition is concerned with a disciplined creation of thought in language; and literature stresses the most valuable forms of composition.

WRITTEN COMPOSITION IN JUNIOR HIGH SCHOOL

There has been so much interest in developing student ability to write that composition is now stressed at nearly every grade level. This would appear to indicate that this is an important part of the curriculum and that everyone favors it. However, there is substantial disagreement as to what kind of writing should be emphasized, the quantity of writing to be done, and the manner in which composition is to be taught. There is little argument with the idea that the adolescent's ideas in writing should be respected nor with the encouragement of creativity and improved communication. Yet there is a lack of agreement concerning the role in composition of the study of language, grammar, spelling, punctuation, and word usage.

Although it is largely the teacher's perception that determines content and method, grades 6 and 7 should see the development of the two-paragraph theme indicating an elementary type of coherence. Ninth-graders should be able to organize, write, and develop longer themes. It seems reasonable that writing should not be limited to one or two types; several kinds of writing should be used—narrative, argumentative, expository, and descriptive. Common pitfalls encountered in composition include:

1. Emphasis upon workbook exercises or thorough checking through papers for misspelling and poor punctuation does little to improve student writing, and may even harm it.
2. Writing requires continual practice. Two weeks at the beginning of the year and two weeks at the end will not help much.
3. The composition assignment must be carefully developed to avoid the hurried pencil-to-paper technique which results in poorly thought-out themes.
4. Too much time is spent by most teachers on book reports, business letters, and research reports. Probably one period spent on a business letter is enough, and may even be too much. Book reports tend to be a summary of the story, usually lifted from the blurb on the jacket. If book reports are used, then the style should be one of analysis and evaluation. Research reports probably have no place in junior high school for the average student. Some teachers have reported success with a research paper of four or five pages. This paper includes a bibliography and requires use of the school library.

In any case, the basis for student writing on the junior high school level should be student experience. We write best about that which we know. Such assignments should have some depth, character, and meaning and should surely avoid such insipid topics as, "My Most Embarrassing Moment," "Life As a Doorknob Sees It," or, "My Summer Vacation."

Writing on topics from sciences and social studies and reporting personal experiences have been believed to give students opportunities to develop clarity, organization, and self-expression. There are those who argue, however, that the program in composition should be solidly based in the unity of discipline—that is, the combination of language, literature, and composition which displays the many resources of the language such as imagery, vocabulary, and syntax.

LITERATURE IN THE JUNIOR HIGH SCHOOL

Reading, as distinguished from the study of literature, includes:

1. Remedial, for those students who are markedly below age and grade level in reading skills.
2. Developmental, which, as the term suggests, is designed to help improve reading skills for normal and better readers.
3. Recreational, reading selected by students, usually without adult direction or guidance, for pleasure reading or nonassigned reading.

The paperback-book explosion has had a marked effect upon reading and the study of literature.

In the approach to literature it is common to find the chronological organization—European or World Literature in grade 7, and American Literature in grade 8 on the theory that they would be correlated. Actually, there appears to be much more hope than fact in this.

Another approach to teaching literature is the "Great Books" theory. In this method a list of books or writings is developed without regard to theme or chronology. The selected books are determined by their "merit" and are considered important for their inherent worth. The problems that arise here are chiefly of two types: (1) Who selects the books? Whose judgment is supreme?, and (2) What flexibility is there in terms of the specific class and school situation as well as the interests and qualifications of the teacher?

If the list of books is drawn up within the school, then a few considerations must be kept in mind:

1. There should never be rigid teaching based on a fixed list of books.
2. The works selected should have inherent worth—not a value attached by the passage of time. How much literary merit is there really in *Silas Marner?*
3. Books selected should not be chosen solely because they are controversial, although controversy has its worth.
4. Selections should be increased in length as children grow older.
5. Selections should be neither all current nor all from the past, but should be balanced.
6. Books selected should be teachable and be appropriate to the classes using them.

A method of teaching literature which has been increasing in popularity in the junior high school is the Thematic Approach. A theme is assigned, such as "Animals," "Humor," "Decisions," or "Courage," to a specific grade level, and materials are found to fit these themes. Those who oppose this method complain that there is no real logic in assigning themes to grade levels, that minor works are included merely because they fit the theme, and that some fine literature will be omitted because it does not fit the theme.

Whichever method of teaching literature for junior high school is chosen, there are specific principles to be considered in developing the curriculum:

1. Literature is basically concerned with man and his relationship to his environment.
2. Literature deals with a subject, expressed as a theme, written from the writer's perspective, and flavored by the author's attitude and tone.
3. Style is the distinctive writing characteristic of the author, and the story is structured into forms and patterns.
4. Enjoyment and understanding are much enhanced by comprehension of literary terms and their use, such as *satire, irony, conflict, climax, antagonist, protagonist, complications, setting, scene, image, metaphor,* and *simile.*

More important than which method of teaching is used is the care given to the individual selections. Better to have a wide range of reading matter and literature that fits the class and school needs than to restrict the students to a rigid list.

GRAMMAR IN THE JUNIOR HIGH SCHOOL

Much confusion exists concerning what grammar is and its place in the curriculum. Actually, there are several grammars, and some definitions at this point might be helpful.

1. Formal or traditional grammar is based upon Latin, in turn derived from the Greek, and attempts to prescribe a correctness of form and usage for an evolving language from a rigid structure. This grammar, as taught, has had but little effect upon improving speech or writing, since the grammatical rules fail to relate closely to English—or any language.

2. Historical-comparative grammar is a study of the language as it actually developed. Little used even in the late nineteenth and early twentieth centuries when Jespersen published his eight volumes on this topic, it is still rich in inventory of grammatical features, forms, and uses.

3. Structural grammar attempts to describe the spoken word as it exists. Here is provided a clear concept of the phoneme, identification of the morpheme and its classes, classification of parts of speech in terms of shape and position, "identification of the five structures which can interlock to form the most complex English sentence, and the theory of immediate constituents."[16] The objective is to classify the types of structures actually

used by speakers of the language, and users of this system insist that grammar pay attention to such things as stress, pitch, and pause. Structural grammar stresses induction and provides a description of relationships among words and patterns of word groups (syntax); word forms (morphology); and language sounds such as stress and an intonation (phonology).

4. Tagmemic grammar states that language must be regarded as a structured collection of pieces, as a hierarchical sequence of waves, and as a field organization of relationships. It is an attempt to identify the basic linguistic units for all languages.

5. Transformational or generative grammar presents a set of rules by which all English sentences are produced or generated.

What is actually found in the textbooks for junior high school is still largely the traditional grammar, at least partially because so few teachers are yet trained in the newer forms of English. Transformational linguistics and tagmemics are enthusiastically supported by a small group but, confronted with the realities of materials and teachers, the best course of action is probably eclectic—taking the best from each and staying largely with traditional terminology.

The program of English grammar should be taught inductively. The language is systematic and we should use its systematic patterns to teach not only grammar but spelling, writing, and reading.

It should go without saying that the junior high school English curriculum will also include work in spelling, handwriting, and punctuation, *where needed.* This is one easy place to eliminate a general requirement and permit individualization of instruction.

SOCIAL STUDIES

The social studies, in describing the organization and development of society and the place of man as a member of social groups, include a content that is almost infinite in scope. Indeed, a part of the difficulty encountered by curriculum groups in the social studies is the delimitation and selection of area, content, and material. The social studies are usually defined to include history, geography, political science, anthropology, sociology, economics, and psychology or social psychology. "Thus man is placed in time [history] and space [geography], and his way of living is considered from a variety of references"[17] (represented by the others named).

The social science disciplines, in addition to these, are usually stated to include philosophy, religion, education, criminology, and law, although philosophy and religion are often listed as humanities. As a fine distinction, social studies are generally considered to be those taught in the public schools in describing man in society, while the social sciences, taught in colleges and universities, are concerned with discovering the truth about human relations.

The present social studies curriculum, which is not adequate for the needs of today's society, was firmly established in the public schools by 1900. Geography was a subject of prime importance in the elementary schools, and United States history, world history, and civics were found in the grades that were later to become the junior high school.

Although in 1900 a very small percentage of secondary students took economics, it was offered in about half of the high schools, and history, civics, and problems of American democracy were much more common.

In the first quarter of this century many students dropped out of school somewhere between the sixth and ninth school year. This was a major factor in the stress placed by educators upon the social studies as part of the junior high school curriculum, because of the emphasis placed upon democratic values and preparation for citizenship.

Thus the pattern most frequently followed was to require American history in grades 7 and 8 along with some combination of world history and geography. Emphasis was definitely upon Western cultures and problems; American government and/or civics was incorporated in the American history course, which was deemed adequate in view of the almost universal requirement that students would have a more comprehensive government and civics course in the senior high schools.

SOCIAL STUDIES IN THE JUNIOR HIGH SCHOOL

The social studies curriculum in the junior high schools presently consists of varying courses commonly offered in grades seven through nine. Looking at a typical junior high school student handbook one finds the following information about the social studies requirements:

> SOCIAL STUDIES
>
> The purpose for the social studies is to acquaint the student with his responsibilities in a democratic society and to prepare him for effective citizenship. Courses are designed to help students develop understandings in history, government, economics, social patterns, and to become aware of the influences of geography upon man's activities.
>
> To achieve these goals the following courses are required of all junior high school students:
>
> Grade 7: State History and Community Problems
> (one semester)
> Citizenship in our Community
> (one semester) (elective)
> Grade 8: United States History
> Grade 9: Geography and World Affairs
> (including a unit on vocations)

This pattern has many variations. In grades 7 and 8 one finds great similarity in most junior high schools throughout the United States. Many states no longer require a state history. When this is true the usual pattern is to provide a world geography course instead.

In an effort to avoid fragmentation, some version of the core curriculum or block-time scheduling in the social studies has been tried in many junior high schools. The core curriculum movement, however, has never reached the magnitude its proponents hoped it would. A study by the United States Office of Education of junior high schools and junior-senior high schools in 1958 reported fewer than 12 percent of the schools which reported core type programs had a true core program.[18]

Among the most influential reports concerning the junior high school has been Conant's report on the junior high school. In it Conant recommended that social studies be required in both the seventh and eighth grade, in an English-social studies block of time.[19] He was very specific in ruling out a unified studies or core approach, primarily because it was too controversial.

While viewing the social studies subjects in the junior high school, an examination of the social studies offerings commonly found in the elementary schools may help the teacher better to understand the typical early adolescent's attitude toward the social studies.

In Grades 4 through 6 the pupil is usually provided with his first contact with the subjects in the social studies. This is where the more formal study of geography and history begins. In the fourth grade the children usually study the ways of life in other lands, an approach which is based upon geography.

United States history is most commonly taught in the fifth grade. This is usually biographical and narrative in nature, and earlier periods of our history are generally stressed. Whether by design or by chance, the student seldom has an opportunity to become exposed to anything more recent than the Civil War or Reconstruction.

Geography usually provides the unifying structure in the sixth grade. Students study European backgrounds or the "Old World."

It is not difficult to understand why the junior high school student becomes bored with the offerings in the social studies. Often the junior high social studies curriculum is so nearly identical to the elementary social studies that the student feels it is just more repetition.

It is unfortunate that the junior high social studies curriculum lacks the challenge for students at such a critical age. Only recently has it been widely recognized that elementary and junior high school years are vital in the socialization of the students and that the foundations for the political, economic, and social behavior of adults are formulated during these early years. Much of this research is summed up by Cammorata in the following:

1. Children begin to learn about government and politics even before they enter school. The formative years in politics appear to be those years between the ages of 3 and 13.
2. Children's political attitudes and values are firmly established by the time they leave the eighth grade.
3. During the high school years, youth obtains much knowledge about government and politics, but this knowledge has little effect upon values and attitudes previously formed.[10]

OBJECTIVES OF THE SOCIAL STUDIES

The social studies occupy a firm position in the junior high school curriculum and the significance of this area is most apparent in the contemporary curriculum. Although there have been many statements of purposes and goals for the social studies, and many groups have prepared long lists of objectives, there appear to be three general goals directing this area:

1. The social studies should help the child comprehend his experiences and find meaning in life. This should be interpreted to include opportunities for the student to analyze some aspects of his environment and his reactions to it and the forces operating in society that tend to make people what they are.
2. Each child must be prepared to participate effectively in the dynamic life of his society. Correspondingly, his society needs active, aware, and loyal citizens who will work devotedly for its improvement.
3. Each person needs to acquire an understanding of analytical processes and other problem-solving tools that are developed by scholars in the social sciences. With increasing maturity, the students should learn to ask fruitful questions and examine critical data in social situations.

To achieve these goals, it is necessary that junior high students become acquainted with the world and society of today, become educated for citizenship, and learn and maintain the values of democracy. Specifically, then, there must be a balance in social studies which will prohibit a concentration upon the past, encourage active *living* citizenship immediately, and develop an understanding of the meaning and responsibilities of democracy.

Social studies should be centered on the student's examination of his social world, and he should be helped to examine topics in such a way that he progressively learns to apply, not merely memorize, the intellectual tools of the social sciences.

Most educators would agree that the social studies have a key role to play in the development of the early adolescent who must become able to live in a world characterized by pervasive and tumultuous change. They would also agree that the social studies should play a key role in the development of the knowledge and skills necessary to help the early adolescent comprehend his society and to participate effectively in it. The social studies, then, have value not merely for their own sake, but for the sake of understanding the pertinent wisdom available for dealing with contemporary issues.

> It must be recognized at the onset the social studies are part of a hierarchy of educational goals; they derive their focus from broader institutional aims and give point to instructional objectives. It must also be realized that their essence lies in human relationships—to other men, to the physical and social environment, and to the self. . . . To be effective, social studies objectives must be explicit, balanced, weighted in accordance with the priorities established by local needs, known by the participants in a particular program, and used skillfully.[21]

CRITICISMS AND FERMENT

Many educational leaders throughout the country are urging a new look at the social studies curriculum, both for the junior high school years, and for a new social studies curriculum for grades K–12. The National Council for the Social Studies reported:[22]

> It is an astonishing fact that for more than a generation there have been no effective recommendations at the national level concerning the total social studies curriculum. The general pattern of the social studies now taught in grades 4 through 12 evolved during the years from 1893 to 1916, when national committees of scholars and educators considered the problem of what social studies content should be utilized in the school program.

There can be no doubt that the social studies are under fire from many sources. The junior high school is considered to be a mistake by some critics because it apes the high school, and the social studies at this level are pointed out as among the worst offenders. These courses in the junior high school are customarily text-oriented, fact-centered, and most of the learning process is a routine of lecture, read, and memorize. It is probably no understatement to say that most students dislike and avoid the social studies as much as possible.

Throughout the United States one becomes particularly aware of the ferment and the increasing interest in upgrading the social studies program. Many of the more outstanding reasons for the need to upgrade the social studies in the junior high schools can be best understood by reviewing some criticisms and problems of the social studies programs as they now exist:

1. An articulated and coordinated program is claimed, yet we continue with a scope and sequence that is sketchy, repetitive, and that fails to provide ample consideration for the new and valid areas of study that are pertinent to our times. A disproportionate portion of the curriculum is

concentrated in local and Western culture areas, yet the United States is exercising a role of world leadership and our children as citizens must function in this arena; there must be increased attention to the non-Western world. The treatment of American history is frequently repeated at several grade levels, with very little differentiation of content or difficulty. History is the heart of most existing social studies programs and this, with geography, and often civics, usually constitutes the entire junior high school social studies curriculum. We have reached this position in most instances by following what has been traditionally done rather than by careful planning.

2. We claim to produce an enlightened and inquiring citizenry, yet we avoid many critical issues, conflicting ideologies, and social problems. Social studies must be concerned with controversial issues and this requires teachers who understand these problems, have enough background to provide student direction, yet can remain objective and see that all points of view are presented. This is difficult and is aggravated by communities whose feelings, attitudes, and biases cause teachers to walk a delicate line between what they believe should be taught and what they feel may put them in a vulnerable position.

3. Educators claim to develop skills related to the disciplines in the social studies, yet we have authoritarian texts and authoritarian teachers from whom students expect to receive answers, and teachers who expect students to commit these answers to memory.

4. The interrelatedness of knowledge is discussed, yet it is segmented and not interrelated. History is taught for history's sake. Each discipline is treated separately with little effort to structure the social studies into a conceptual framework that demonstrates relationships and has utility for life. This is partially because the various social sciences are divided among themselves as to whether there should be a fusion or whether each discipline should be taught separately. Another reason for this is that few teachers feel qualified to teach a variety of subjects and find security in the separate-subject approach.

5. With the exception of classroom time that is delegated to social studies education, social studies is placed in an inferior position when compared to other content areas of the curriculum. Witness, for example, the expenditure of funds at the national level for the development of science and mathematics programs since 1958 as compared to that for social studies. Social studies need comparable funds for curriculum development and teacher training to those of the other major content areas.

6. The claim is made that a social studies program is designed around sound educational policies and practices, yet social studies courses that act as obstacles to education are frequently developed. The social studies are more susceptible to influence by vested interest groups than any other content areas. All students are required to jump the same hurdles in the

same fashion. The curriculum is often so designed that it supports the idea that man lives in a static sterile world.

7. It is said material must be relevant—that is, current, and have applicability for present time. Yet a great proportion of irrelevant and unapplicable materials is used. Teachers should more and more ask themselves the question, "why" certain things are taught or certain materials are used in social studies, and if educators cannot come up with a reasonable or practical answer, it may then be that there are better things that could be done with the time.

8. Programs are often accused of being superficial and unchallenging without adequate consideration for new media, changing conditions, and the maturity level of the students. On the other hand, at times some rather sophisticated materials are thrust upon students who are not yet intellectually ready for them.

9. Sequence and grade placement of topics are handicapped by lack of agreement among the social studies as to what order is necessary for presenting concepts and content.

10. There is too much effort and emphasis upon "covering" material. Complete coverage is impossible. Selected topics probed in depth and the development of concepts and understandings will yield more learning. It should be apparent that every discipline cannot be taught, every part of the world cannot be studied, nor is it possible to present what scholars in each field consider the minimum for their subject.

Selakovich summarizes the most serious flaws in the secondary social studies curriculum as follows:[23]

1. It is repetitious and boring for the students.
2. It is poorly articulated.
3. It is not based on the needs of children.
4. It does not reflect the needs of society.
5. Its organization ignores principles of learning.
6. It does not provide for the integration of knowledge in the social sciences.

DIRECTIONS

The present social studies curriculum, developed in the early 1900's is not adequate for the needs of today's society. Although it is out of date, it has not remained completely static, since the forces of change which began largely with science, mathematics, and foreign languages in the 1950's are more widespread than ever before. In the social studies a number of shifts of location of subject matter, introduction of new subjects and topics, changing emphasis, and reorganization of content have taken place since World War II.

Scattered efforts, spurred by the American Council of Learned Societies, were reinforced in 1962 by the appropriation of federal money and the organization of Project Social Studies. This project is a recognition of the importance of social studies in the school curriculum and is intended to encourage:[24]

1. Basic and applied research.
2. Curriculum improvement.
3. Experimental designs, evaluative instruments, and models.
4. Demonstration of new procedures.
5. Research and development centers.

At a quick glance, Project Social Studies appears to make recommendations which are contradictory and confusing relative to content, emphasis, and placement of subject matter. This is easily understood when one considers the several disciplines included in social studies. Project Social Studies is attempting to replace "coverage" with concept understanding and ability to solve problems as well as considering citizenship, sequence, and subject matter.

Under Project Social Studies, curriculum study centers at the University of Minnesota, Harvard University, and Carnegie Institute of Technology have been established. It is interesting to note that the Harvard program deals especially with critical thinking skills for junior high school students. Others are working on programs for the academically talented and an examination of the total social studies curriculum, kindergarten through grade 12.

Since Project Social Studies began in 1962, the interest and reform movement has grown to where there are more than fifty major projects for the social studies. They range from kindergarten through college, and are financed by government, local school districts, and private foundations.

Several of these projects are emphasizing improvements in the teaching of a particular subject, i.e., history. It is agreed that the knowledge explosion has created a mountain of new documentation and encyclopedic coverage of a wide range of topics and issues. This can overwhelm the curriculum worker, the teachers, and the students. As a result many are now urging that the emphasis be placed upon developing a "feeling" for history and the historical methods. Therefore, history is increasingly viewed as a tool, and not as a master. It is felt that if students understand how the facts and conclusions that they are studying were determined by scholars, they will be better prepared for new information, new interpretations, and to recognize the need to revise their own concepts in the future. Thus junior high school students can be helped to become more intelligent consumers of social data. If the early adolescent has gained some comprehension of the gathering and treatment of social data, he is more likely to use it discriminately as a basis for rational choices.

Other projects are attempting to identify basic ideas or concepts from the social sciences which might serve as a unifying structure of the social studies. This concept approach recognizes that, in spite of the enormous growth in the social sciences, educators have not kept pace conceptually with the changes in the nature of our social order. A curriculum built around concepts would be concerned with concept formation as well as concept attainment. Students and teachers should be given opportunities to revise and develop concepts as well as to learn what the expert means by the concept he uses. Thus the concept-development approach recognizes that knowledge must not merely be expanded but must also be constantly reorganized.

The most promising of the social studies curriculum development projects are attempting to provide some structure for the social studies based upon such a conceptual framework, one that draws from all the social sciences and not primarily from history and geography. When considering the scope and sequence development in the public schools, educators must think in these terms. They must also provide for the insertion of changes, substitutions, and increases in the body of knowledge without necessarily recasting the entire social studies curriculum. There is considerable evidence that this has already begun, especially at the junior high school level.

Findings by Bruner, Senesh, and others clearly indicate that more complex ideas can be taught to a much younger child than had formerly been believed possible, so long as we adapt the approach to the maturity level of the child.

Once progress of this nature begins at the primary level, the door is open to provide for a sequence of the development of concepts and generalizations with greater consideration for the maturity of the child throughout his entire educational career. By beginning at the primary grades and developing a well-coordinated and articulated program, the fundamental idea relationships of the knowledge of the disciplines can be related to the child's experiences on all grade levels, increasing in depth and complexity with the increasing maturity of the child. Thus the expanding environment theory, with its concentric circles representing a wider horizon for each succeeding grade level, appears to be yielding to the conceptual spiral approach to learnings in which various areas, from local to worldwide, are a part of each year's program, with the focus upon unifying ideas that are returned to, refined, and elaborated.

One of the most stimulating aspects for the junior high school is the trend toward improving teaching methods in the social studies by incorporating a discovery approach and an inductive process. Educational psychologists have long proposed that it is through these methods that what has been learned is really understood and put to use. However, most advocates of the use of inquiry and discovery recognize that, because of the limits of the pupils' ability to handle research tools and the limits of time, only selected parts of the total social studies program can be taught in this way. Yet the benefits of the discovery approach, along with the use of more conventional methods, can be made to carry over to portions of study that proceed through methods considered more traditional. As a part of this, there needs to be a use with children of the scientific method, problem solving, which involves use of raw data rather than secondary sources. More attention is being given to the modes of inquiry, skills, and treatment of data that are utilized by the scholars representing those disciplines involved in the social studies.

Many teachers are dissuaded from a more extensive use of induction and/or a reflective thinking process by being made to feel that it is highly esoteric or that they must understand all the work of educators before they are competent to utilize it in any form in their classroom procedures. Rather, a relatively simple change of emphasis on the types of questions teachers utilize might produce progress in this direction much more rapidly. Questions such as: "Why should this be?" or "Can you prove it?" "Is there additional information available?" might do more toward arriving at these desired goals of our social studies program than questions that merely require students to commit masses of data to memory. While it is desirable and even necessary for a teacher to understand the goals and objectives while using a specific teaching strategy, theoriests must avoid the pitfalls of stifling teacher initiative by overritualizing the teaching process.

For many years a multimedia approach to classroom instruction in social studies has been advocated. This may be interpreted to include multiple texts, paperbacks, original documents, programmed materials, readings from the period, field trips, artifacts, and audiovisual aids. The availability of funds through various educational legislation should add impetus to this movement.

Much attention is being devoted by curriculum planners and social studies teachers to a greater emphasis upon the nonhistoric aspects of social studies. This emphasis includes non-Western cultures, international relations, and, particularly, the behavioral sciences.

Other new approaches are stemming from the increased emphasis upon the study of human behavior by quantitative and experimental methods. Some of these approaches use simulation and some are using gaming. This is a relatively new innovation in teaching in the public schools but has been used extensively by the military. College students in business have claimed to have learned more about economic principles and practices from playing Monopoly than by attending economics classes. This is why political and behavioral scientists are devoting increasing attention to various uses of games and simultation.

PROGRAMS OF SOCIAL STUDIES FOR JUNIOR HIGH SCHOOL

The current interest in changing the social studies curriculum for the junior high school has brought about a number of proposals for revisions, three of which follow.

The American Council of Learned Societies has proposed that there be a sequence in elementary school which "explores man's origins and the history of Western man up through Minoan Crete and Mycenean Greece, combining the insights of anthropology, history, music, art, and classics, and drawing upon other disciplines where appropriate."[25]

The junior high sequence which was recommended to follow has as its core an eighth-grade course dealing with the seventeenth and eighteenth century origins of American culture which stresses transition from "subject of the Crown to citizen of the United States." Also proposed was an optional six-year classics sequence beginning with the seventh grade. This is to be concerned with developing an understanding of the roots of our civilization and the part played by Greece and Rome.

Alpren and Cammarota[26] have suggested an immediate social studies revision, Plan A, and a long-range revision, Plan B:

Plan A—Grades 7-8-9

1 year, study of various areas throughout the world in light of their geography, history, government, economic conditions, how people live, and education.

1 semester each of geography and political science.

1 year of U.S. History to 1900.

Plan B—Grades 7-8-9

1-year continuation of area studies.

2 years of geography, political science, social psychology, and education.

Trump and Miller[27] report three approaches suggested by an ad hoc curriculum committee for social studies from the National Association of Secondary School Principals.

1. Grades 7 and 8: American History to 1870; government, and U. S. geography.
   (a) Grades 9 and 10: World history and world geography, presented by culture areas.
2. Grades 7 and semester one of grade 8: Broad field, geographic-centered, socioeconomic units on key and representative nations and regions of the world.
   (a) Grade 8, semester 2: The citizen and his government.
   (b) Grade 9, semester 2: Introduction to understanding of peoples and their institutions.

(c) Grade 9, semester 2, and grade 10: World history and problems.
3. Grade 7: History of the peoples of Africa and Eurasia.
   (a) Grade 8: United States history to 1876.
   (b) Grade 9: State history and American government.

In these and other proposals it may be seen that there is some shift in both emphasis and content from what has been traditional. There is more interest in non-Western culture and history and in increased inclusion of social study disciplines other than history, geography, and civics. It is worth noting that the proposed courses of study suggested by various groups are more alike than different, and that an important fact is that many groups and individuals are interested in improving what has been a static situation.

SUMMARY

There are two major approaches to establishing the junior high school program of studies.

1. A general education curriculum that usually includes English (or language arts), social studies, science, math, and health and physical education. These are required and all other subjects are considered to be exploratory.
2. In the second approach the core of the junior high school curriculum is language arts, social studies, science, and math, with strong exploratory aspects in all these areas that permit and encourage crossing subject-matter lines with each other as well as into the fine and practical arts.

The junior high school curriculum is experiencing substantial examination and change.

Revision of the science curriculum on a national scale was begun in the 1950's. It was stimulated by the National Defense Education Act, and many groups have been working on and developing new programs, most of which are intended for use in the senior high schools. There are new programs in physics, chemistry, biology, physical science, and earth science. Recently there have been several efforts to develop new junior high school science programs. Science education is necessary for all students, not just for the few who intend to enter a specific field of science. Our knowledge in that various science disciplines is expanding so rapidly that texts and materials become out-of-date in only a few years.

Revision on a large scale of the mathematics curriculum began in the early 1950's—before any of the other curricular areas had made any pronounced efforts to change. Several groups have developed or are working to develop newer mathematics programs. Common threads run through these programs, including a strong emphasis upon discovery, deletion of some topics and introduction of others, and a change in stress upon what is taught.

The program of English language arts in the junior high school is pulled in two directions. Some teachers believe that anything involving communication should be a part of the curriculum, while another group is even firmer in its conviction that English involves only the study of composition, literature, and grammar. The best approach appears to be one that is eclectic and combines the best features of both.

Composition is accepted and encouraged by all, although there are differences of opinion as to how much, when, and upon what topics.

Literature, too, has stresses and strains. According to one group it matters little what is read so long as there is virtually constant reading. Another group wants a selected and rigid book list. Still others want to work around a preselected theme.

The same kinds of difficulties are found in grammar, since not one but several English grammars exist.

The social studies, which deal with man in society, include several distinct areas and disciplines. Among these are history, geography, political science, anthropology, sociology, economics, and psychology. The social studies curriculum, established 50 years ago or more, has been one of the last to become involved in the wave of curriculum revision of the past decade. Project Social Studies, established in 1962, by the U.S. Office of Health, Education, and Welfare, and the efforts of such groups as the National Council of Learned Societies, indicate increasing interest and concern in improving the social studies curriculum. The social studies curriculum has suffered from several difficulties. There is a lack of agreement among the various disciplines as to what should be taught, what should be stressed, and how much time is needed. There is and has been a disproportionate concentration upon Western culture—and most of this upon Western history. We dodge controversial issues, which may be good sense but is not good teaching. The interrelatedness of knowledge becomes a label with little done to implement it—partially because the disciplines are divided among themselves, and, to some extent, because teachers feel safer in a single-subject field; there is far too much concern with "covering" material when it should be obvious that is is impossible to "cover" all aspects of every discipline.

Newer developments indicate that there are attempts to break the chains, to teach by induction, and to move content and concepts to different grade levels.

REFERENCES

1. L. M. Bennett, "Present Plight of the Junior High School," *Science Education*, Vol. 49 (December 1965), pp. 468–476.
2. *Curriculum Handbook for School Administrators.* Washington, D.C.: American Association of School Administrators, 1967, p. 111.

3. Robert E. Yager, "Innovations in Junior High Science," *Midland Schools*, Vol. 81 (March–April 1967), pp. 28–32.
4. *Ibid.*, p. 29.
5. Stephen S. Willoughby, "What Is the New Mathematics?" *NASSP Bulletin*, Vol. 52 (April 1968), p. 5.
6. *Commission on Mathematics*, Program for College Preparatory Mathematics. New York: College Entrance Examination Board, 1959, p. 2.
7. School Mathematics Study Group, "Reports on Student Achievement in SMSG Courses," *SMSG Newsletter No. 10*, Stanford U. P., November 1961, p. 13.
8. Eugene D. Nichols, "The Many Forms of Revolution," *NASSP Bulletin*, Vol. 52 (April 1968), p. 21.
9. Secondary School Curriculum Committee Report, *Mathematics Teacher*, May 1959, p. 389.
10. *Curriculum Handbook for School Administrators*, *op. cit.*, pp. 166–167.
11. Lee Ruthven Haueter, *A Comparative Study of the Salt Lake City Junior High School Mathematics Program, 1959–60*, unpublished master's thesis, University of Utah, pp. 31–33.
12. *Ibid.*, pp. 31–32.
13. *Mathematics Education.* Salt Lake City, Utah: Granite School District, January 19, 1968, mimeo.
14. Walter Loban, Margaret Ryan, and James R. Squire, *Teaching Language and Literature.* New York: Harcourt, 1961, p. ix.
15. H. A. Gleason, Jr., "What Is English?" *College Composition and Communication*, Vol. 13 (October 1962), pp. 1–10.
16. Harold B. Allen, "The 'New English' Anew," *NASSP Bulletin*, Vol. 51 (April 1967), p. 21.
17. Morton Alpren and Gloria Cammarota, "Social Studies Curriculum," in Morton Alpren, *The Subject Curriculum: Grades K–12.* Columbus: Merrill, 1967, p. 121.
18. Grace S. Wright, *Block-Time Classes and the Core Program in the Junior High School*, Bulletin No. 6. Washington, D.C.: U.S. Department of Health, Education, and Welfare, 1958.
19. James B. Conant, *Education in the Junior High School Years.* Princeton, N. J.: Educational Testing Service, 1960, p. 22.
20. Gloria Cammarota, "Children, Politics, and Elementary Social Studies," *Social Education*, April 1963.
21. Frank J. Estvan, *Social Studies In a Changing World.* New York: Harcourt, 1968, p. 113.
22. *Curriculum Planning in American Schools: The Social Studies.* Draft REport from the Committee of the Social Studies of the National Council for the Social Studies, 1958.
23. Daniel Selakovich, *Problems in Secondary Social Studies.* Englewood Cliffs, N. J.: Prentice-Hall, 1965, p. 3.
24. Gordon B. Turner, "The American Council of Learned Societies and Curriculum Revision," in Robert W. Heath Ed., *The New Curricula.* New York: Harper, 1964, p. 138.

25. Turner, *op. cit.*, p. 153.
26. Alpren and Cammarota, *op. cit.*, pp. 118–120.
27. Lloyd J. Trump and Delmas Miller, *Secondary School Curriculum Improvement.* Boston: Allyn and Bacon, 1968. pp. 192–193.

chapter 7

Health, Physical Education, and Exploratory Areas

The pronounced and uneven physical growth of junior high children underscores the need for a carefully developed health and physical education program that is specifically designed for this age group. Health education may be the most neglected and poorly taught area in the junior high school—a situation that has long existed. Physical education, a curricular field that should literally be just that—physical education—often becomes a preliminary training ground and weeding-out area for the interscholastic sports program.

From its earliest days exploration has been an important part of the junior high school program and functions. The nature of the early adolescent is such as to call for a wide exploration of interests, aptitudes, and investigation of many fields of learning. A necessary part of the junior high school program is a rich variety of exploratory experiences that are available to students on an elective basis. All grades in junior high school should be permitted several elective choices, and with the expanded use of flexible scheduling, nongraded classes, and independent study, students are able to take an increased number of exploratory subjects.

HEALTH AND PHYSICAL EDUCATION

Within the curriculum for health and physical education it is possible to find confusion, paradox, misunderstanding, and disagreement which probably exceeds that of any other curricular area of the junior high school. Health education appears as the first of the famous Seven Cardinal Principles of Education of 1918 and is found as a major item in virtually every statement of like nature since then. Yet health education is frequently considered a fringe subject and is invariably taught as only part of the teaching load of a teacher who also teaches other subjects. Disagreement exists as to who should be responsible for various areas of the health program. Medical societies and public health associations alike are critical of the extent of the public school health curriculum, in some instances protesting that the schools go too far, and at other times complaining that not enough is done. While courses of study are available, what is actually taught in health varies greatly from school to school, depending upon the school schedule, community attitude, finances, beliefs of the school administration, and background, training, and attitudes of individual teachers.

Some schools have a well-developed program in health education with clearly defined courses of study required of all students in grades 7, 8, and 9. In other schools health is taught by teachers who happen to be unassigned that period, and the program is a one-semester or alternating-day course as it best may fit the junior high school schedule. The health course itself may actually be almost entirely focussed on physiology or anatomy, or be strongly oriented toward safety education, mental health, or sex education, at the whim of the individual instructor. Since health education is seldom the responsibility of any one department, it may be found within the province of science, home economics, physical education, or within the core of block-time. As is usually the case, lack of specific responsibility finds no one responsible and a great many curricular sins and deficiencies are committed in the name of health education. To an extent the same situation may be found in the confusion, disagreement, and even malpractice frequently existing in the physical education program.

HEALTH EDUCATION

Put briefly, health education is concerned with understandings and learnings intended to reduce disease and to better the individual's personal health practices as well as those of the community. Lacking any other place to put these subjects, safety education and driver education are sometimes included in the school health curriculum, especially that of the ninth grade. It is not unheard of, for example, to find a required health course in the first semester of the ninth grade and an elective driver-education program in the second semester for those students who are age 15½ or older.

Objectives for health education fall into two general categories: (1) those which are basic and which may be achieved by instruction, and (2) those which are individually achieved and indicate attitudes, personal behavior, and practices which are difficult to achieve and measure and which may not be accepted as the institutional function of the schools. Within these categories work is centered around the health needs of American youth in areas which include:

1. Family and home living.
2. Emotional adjustment.
3. Protection against disease and illness.
4. First aid.
5. Opportunities for maximum physical development.
6. Developing physical skills and competence.
7. Education and information to protect against dangers and injuries.
8. Sex education.
9. Oral and dental health education.
10. Mental health.

For purposes of instruction in these areas health education has been provided into three broad categories: school health service, school living, and school health instruction. Within these, the curriculum should include education in care and protection of foods, problems of water pollution, sanitation, reduction and elimination of fire hazards, necessity for adequate lighting, proper ventilation, and elimination of potential disease and vermin-breeding situations. To achieve this will require a minimum of one semester of health education in junior high school years, preferably on a daily basis within one grade level.

Within this program it should be expected that there would be work with and instruction in communicable disease control and sanitation, first aid and safety from injury and accident, health appraisal, and health counseling and follow-up. Provision should be made to supply hot lunches to those children who are in need.

Schools differ greatly in the quantity and quality of health services provided. Some schools are fortunate if they have a school nurse on duty one-half day each week, while other districts provide a long-range sequential program involving medical and dental examinations, immunization clinics, and even the services of a clinical psychologist or psychiatrist.

School health instruction, in addition to the regular course of study, can include such activities as assembly programs, clubs, and poster programs. It has been suggested that, in order for health instruction to receive the proper emphasis, all junior high school instruction in their classes whenever it is appropriate and may be related to a given curriculum area. Certainly proper health practices should be stressed, but a broad statement like this can produce a host of difficulties. One of the big problems of health education has been that "everyone taught health, so no one taught it." Too, if health has a body of content worth teaching, then someone whose fields of training include health education should be teaching health.

There are some perceptible trends in health education which include:

1. A developing curriculum for K–12 in "broad health content areas, including growth and development, accident prevention, consumer health, community health, environmental health, food and nutrition,

personal health practices, dental health, communicable and noncommunicable diseases, family life and sex education,"[1] and use and misuse of drugs.

2. Instructional emphasis is aimed toward what the individual should know, understand, feel, and do about health, rather than memorization of facts.
3. There is a movement away from correlated instruction and a trend toward establishing health as a separate subject.
4. There is also a movement toward separating health education and physical education. A continual problem when this is a combined course is that students get health instruction only on rainy days or when the gym cannot be used.
5. There is a definite move, whether desirable or not, to include safety education and even driver training in health education.
6. There are developments of mental health curricula and programs in sex education for early adolescents in the junior high schools.

Health education should be accepted in its own right. For too long it has been a catchall, tossed from one subject area to another—in science last year, in core this year, and in physical education next year.

PHYSICAL EDUCATION

Confusion frequently exists as to what is to be included in physical education. In the strictest sense, by physical education is meant the regular class instructional program which is usually required of all students for at least one year, generally more, in junior high school. Even in this definition we may not all be talking about the same thing, for "required physical education may mean daily classes, classes every other day, or classes that change at quarter or semester to alternate with other subjects. The term "athletics" is usually defined to mean competitive games involving physical activity with accepted rules of play, a system of scoring, and a winning team or player. The term "sports" is commonly accepted to include athletics and also all individual or team activity or a noncompetitive nature such as hiking, water skiing, and fishing. Some of the problems in the junior high school physical education program result from this lack of definition of terms and the need for common understanding. When one person, for example, is talking about "sports," he is referring to an interscholastic athletic event, while another person may mean only what is to be included in the school's regular physical education program.

KINDS OF PROGRAMS

A good sequential junior high school physical education program has several goals:

1. Obviously a physically educated person is physically fit, knows how to become physically fit, and remains in this condition.
2. The physically educated student has developed a wide range of basic skills such as running, walking, jumping, throwing, and controlling his body.
3. A physically educated student has learned team sports, the need for team action, the necessity for knowing the rules of the game and abiding by them, and the need for and desirability of sportsmanship.
4. A good physical education program teaches more than team sports. The student becomes competent in individual sports suitable for carryover and use in out-of-school and adult life. Here is where one of the big complaints concerning physical education centers. Too many programs and instructors devote little if any time to developing individual skills, instead concentrating on team games.
5. The physically educated student has a wide knowledge of games and sports. He knows the rules and background of many games which enables him to derive more pleasure from being a spectator.

A basic junior high school physical education program designed to achieve these objectives will include:

1. Games, sports, athletics, play, aquatics.
2. Self testing activities and gymnastics.
3. Rhythmical activities.
4. Physical fitness and developmental activities.

The physical education program for girls is usually better organized, better planned, and has more activities than does the boys' program. Too often the program for boys is considered to be football in the fall, basketball in the winter, and baseball and track in the spring. Body contact games for junior high boys are not approved. Physical education should be more than just athletics or sports. A good program will include dancing, tumbling, exercises, team games, and individual or dual games.

Physical education should be required for all three years of junior high school for a minimum of one full period every other day. A better program will require physical education of all children, grades 7-8-9, for one full period every day. The physical changes that the early adolescent experiences and the accelerating rate at which these changes occur make physical education a necessary part of the junior high school instructional program. Physical education not only improves physical development, it contributes to social growth, mental health, and emotional maturation. Adolescents need opportunities to work off tensions and pressures, and certainly athletic skill and ability provide a measure of peer status which, for some, is to be acquired in no other way.

INTRAMURALS

Intramural activities are competitive and noncompetitive sports and athletics which take place within the school situation. Participants do not engage in competition with students of other schools. Participation is voluntary and permits students to develop skills in sports and games which they have learned in the basic physical education program. A good junior high school intramural program includes a wide variety of activities, has carefully selected sponsors, coaches, and advisors, is well financed and equipped, and actually becomes a recreation program. Too often there is a weak intramural program limited to football, basketball, and baseball, or even no program of intramurals at all. The intramural program, which should have more activities and more participants than the interscholastic athletic program, is frequently neglected, underfinanced, understaffed, and forced to take second best in facilities and equipment. No junior high school should engage in an interscholastic athletic program until a comprehensive intramural program is in operation. Unfortunately, however, the reverse is usually true. Interscholastic athletics, which are of doubtful value in junior high school at best, usurp personnel, money, and facilities. The varsity basketball team has priority on the gymnasium—sometimes on the girls' gym as well as the boys'.

The intramural program for boys and girls should include such activities as Ping-Pong, volleyball, badminton, tennis, soccer, speedball, golf, dancing, swimming, bowling, shuffleboard, track and softball. All students should be eligible for intramural participation; there should never be any limitation by scholarship or by dues. Intramurals should be offered at least twice weekly, preferably more often than that. Intramurals can provide the competition and team loyalty which is important to children of this age without permitting excessive emphasis upon undesirable features which occur in interscholastic sports.

PHYSICAL EDUCATION PROBLEMS

1. The question of interscholastic sports for junior high school is discussed in a subsequent chapter. As a flat statement, a very good case can be made for eliminating interscholastic athletics from junior high school and strengthening the intramural program; conversely, no very strong arguments have been presented for retaining interscholastic athletics. The usual claim is that interscholastic athletics are necessary to provide opportunities for students who are quite able athletically and that interscholastics, as such, are not bad; what is bad is the undue emphasis. This may be the case, but the actual facts show that this program for the athletically gifted child takes a disproportionate share of money, personnel, time, and facilities.

A statement such as, "Varsity athletics should be a part of the whole physical education program,"[2] is not defensible for junior high school.

2. A constant problem is that of overloaded classes in physical education. Apparently some administrators feel that a gymnasium, being a large teaching station, requires a large class. It is not unusual to find as many as 90–120 students with two teachers in one physical education class. This is almost criminal. There is little that can be done in terms of individual differences and the quality of instruction cannot help but deteriorate.

3. It has already been mentioned that some instructors limit the program to three or four team sports. A related problem occurs when these classes become training periods for the high school. This situation exists when the junior high physical education instructor is told by the high school staff, by the director of athletics, or by someone in administration, that he must teach certain skills to his classes "to save time in high school." The junior high instructor may even decide to do this of his own volition. In any event, the result is the same: the junior high school physical education program is not designed to provide what these students need but becomes a "feeder" for the high school. This should never be permitted.

4. Much of the criticism which has fallen upon physical education programs, instructors, and coaches, has resulted from poor practices or even downright foolish activities. For example, it is probable that some knowledge of the history of sports is valuable and that the physical education program should include aspects of intellectual study. However, in an effort to prove its worth, many instructors of physical education stress the academic features to the detriment and virtual exclusion of physical activities. Grading policies are often unfair and even absurd in physical education—top grades being limited to those boys who are on varsity teams. Other instructors appear to place emphasis in grading upon everything except the physical education they teach. As an example of this, one parent was amazed to find that the grade of D which her daughter received in P.E. was based as follows: one-third for "dressing out," one-third for a "project," and one-third for written work. Nowhere was any consideration given to the actual physical activities.

Further earned criticism results from the strong language which is frequently reported as used in locker rooms, shower rooms, and gymnasiums by coaches and physical education instructors. There can be no question that this occurs but how extensively it happens is debatable.

5. Physical education is often cited as a source of moral and ethical values. It is true that the potential exists for this, but the problem is that P.E. is all too often an area where little ethical or moral work is done, or even where the contrary holds sway. Overcrowded P.E. classes and locker-room bullies are common, and overworked instructors with classes far in excess of what they should be cannot be expected to perform miracles.

6. Students should not be permitted to substitute marching band or

some such activity for physical education any more than they are permitted to substitute marching band for algebra. A required physical education program is easily defended, and short of physical handicaps or illness which prevent participation, substitution of some other course for physical education should not be permitted in junior high school.

A survey[3] of 387 male P.E. teachers found an overall belief that physical education had serious problems, including these:

1. Coaches don't have time to teach P.E., and the majority of coaches believed the coaching was more important to their career and advancement anyway.
2. Seventy percent said teachers of P.E. lack interest, skill, and knowledge in individual and dual sports.
3. There is a lack of dedication of teachers to the educational phase of the program.
4. There is not enough teaching of new skills.
5. Class sizes are too large.
6. Programs are too limited.
7. There are shortages of equipment and supplies.
8. There is a tendency to overemphasize physical fitness.

ART AND MUSIC

The fine arts have been affected, perhaps more than any other area, by two strongly opposed pressures. Since the middle 1950's several people, events, and influences have vigorously stressed the academic values. There has been much crying for "excellence," referring in this instance to an academic approach, as though both excellence and academics, by definition, are to be found only in mathematics, science, languages, history, or English. On the other hand we have the undeniable trend toward more leisure time available for the average citizen to use and a distinct lack of training, values, and education in how to use it for his own best purposes. Alarmists have painted a gloomy picture of the American citizen, with more free time than he has ever had and little knowledge of what to do with it, driving aimlessly around the countryside or anchored for unending hours at the television set watching old movies.

The fine arts have also been regarded as "frills" and "fringe" subjects by economy-minded members of the community who believe erroneously that elimination of these programs would result in massive tax reductions. In responding to the academicians and the "frill" seekers, teachers and educators in art and music occasionally overreacted, and in their efforts to justify their subjects made claims that verged on the ridiculous. It has been asserted, for example, that the study of art or music was conducive to better health. It is only necessary to observe the average musician and artist a short while to conclude that they show little evidence of being healthier adults because of their chosen occupations. The only justifications necessary for the fine arts are that music and art have a content and a value for everyone, and that they emphasize use of the intellect and assist in the development of sensitivity, creativity, and the capacity to make reasoned esthetic decisions.

The dual function of art and music in terms of general education on one hand and exploratory education on the other are of real importance at the junior high school level, both in terms of the functions of the junior high school and in terms of the nature of the early adolescent.

ART

An interesting paradox is to be found in statements such as these: "The arts are enjoying the most receptive public climate ever manifested in the United States. Art is fast becoming 'big business' . . . over 15 million Americans are 'Sunday Painters',"[4] and, ". . . a report by the NEA Research Division . . . indicates that fewer than half of U.S. schools offer courses in visual arts (and that approximately 50 percent of these schools show proportinate enrollment to that of 1956-57) . . . while 10 percent indicate a decrease."[5]

It appears that the public is interested in art, wants to know more about art, but the schools do not offer enough art or perhaps do not give it enough value. Part of the trouble may stem from the common feeling that a special talent or ability is a prerequisite for learning art. Too, there has long been an association of art with relaxation and play which has resulted in further suspicious regard.

Art is a personal thing, formed through emotional involvement, includes intellectual experiences within it, and is a form of creative expression. The study of art should be required of all students in junior high school for at least one year in order to provide

1. Experiences in developing creativity.
2. Expansion of the student's means of communication and expression by means other than the spoken or written word.
3. Identification and development of special individual abilities.
4. Development of a sense of esthetic values.
5. A satisfying and creative use of leisure time.
6. Opportunities for exploration and prevocational training.

To achieve these goals, expression is achieved through various media such as graphics, painting, and sculpture. The characteristic substance and form of art is its content; the direction and range is the scope; and the order in which it develops is its sequence. The junior high art curriculum in a three-year sequence should include:[6]

1. An understanding of the principles and elements of art which will

include use of design elements, decorative design, crafts, applied design principles, and an emphasis upon functional design.

2. A fulfillment of esthetic needs to be accomplished by cultivation of initiative, flexibility, and fluency; development of problem-solving techniques; use of graphic and plastic problems requiring creative solutions; and assorted problems which require creative and inventive solutions.
3. An understanding of cultural and historical contributions. This is developed through art history, a survey from cave paintings to present day; the study of major cultural contributions such as Greek, Roman, and Egyptian; a stress upon comparative functions and use of materials and decoration, followed by an expansion of study to other cultures and an emphasis upon changes of function and style.
4. Skills and techniques. This involves extensive experience in and exposure to a variety of materials, media, and method from silk screening to mechanical drawing and photography.
5. Development of critical comparison of art forms and an understanding of the necessity for variety.
6. Provision for the identification of special student talents, interests, and abilities. This can be encouraged through use of special projects and optional assignments.
7. Opportunities for personal communication and expression such as may be found in designing signs, posters, and displays.
8. Increasing abilities to become discerning creators and consumers through examination and analysis of consumer products, advertising, painting, sculpture, architecture, and other art forms.
9. Supplemental work to other learnings in the school and prevocational and exploratory work.

The junior high art program should include work in drawing, painting, carving, sculpture, graphics, lettering, and modeling. Some of the media used are plastics, paint, clay, wood, stone, concrete, glass, metal, yarns, and inks.

Two dangers that occasionally beset junior high art programs are: (1) too much teacher talk, lecture, history, and analysis, and (2) an exaggerated effort to tie art into all aspects of every subject field, as is often done in social studies. Doubtless art can become a part of every subject, but art has a content of its own. An honest question is: *Should* it become so involved and, if so, to what extent?

ART TRENDS

Instruction in art is not static, and various innovations and trends have become apparent:

1. Art education is required in most junior high schools, with 80 to 90

percent of all children in grades 7-8-9 receiving some art instruction for a part or all of these three years.[7]

2. Teachers of art are better qualified, often exhibiting their own work.
3. Some efforts are being made to integrate fine arts with other areas including industrial arts, language arts, social studies, and humanities.
4. There is a wider range of art offerings—more exploratory courses in art.
5. Courses in consumer art are being developed.
6. There is increased emphasis upon carryover activities for use of leisure time.

MUSIC

As is true of other fine and practical arts, music has had to compete, often desperately, for a place in the curriculum. Music has suffered such severe attacks as an educational frill that some of the justifications for its inclusion in the curriculum tend to sound somewhat frenzied. Actually, music needs to justify itself no further than esthetic enjoyment and appreciation, but many music educators, forgetting the aspects of individual differences, establish quite rigid goals. It is somewhat difficult, for example, to defend a statement such as

> Everyone ought to be familiar with the best operatic, orchestral, choral, and chamber music because he needs knowledge of music to operate as a thinking individual in a well-developed civilization.[8]

It is obvious that music is a part of today's culture and should be a part of every person's life. Music education makes an immediate contribution by providing an outlet for self-expression and opportunities for socialization, pleasure, and relaxation as well as providing a real sense of personal achievement. Music is certainly a part of everyone's environment. Music and its literature have been accumulating for hundreds of years; it is a universal means of communication. Esthetic experience contributes to one's satisfaction in living, and music can be enjoyed, participated in, and somehow produced by everyone.

MUSIC OBJECTIVES

The objectives of junior high school music instruction include

1. To teach all children to sing who can possibly be taught.
2. To teach all children, who can be taught, to play a musical instrument.
3. To supply enough knowledge and listening experience to permit all or nearly all children to enjoy listening to music.

4. To develop in all junior high students an appreciation and a love for music.
5. To identify the talented student in music.
6. To furnish students a satisfying use of leisure time.

KINDS OF JUNIOR HIGH MUSIC CLASSES

A variety of music classes may be found in today's junior high schools although some schools are more limited than others. The more common courses include the following.

1. *General Music.* Sometimes called music appreciation, this course, usually required in grade 7, has the advantage of not necessarily requiring a teacher with special talents. It *does* require a teacher with a thorough background of music knowledge. The class can study the background of music, its history, various composers, and its relationship to other apsects of culture. The danger here is one of overemphasis upon academics. It is easy for teachers of general music to overstress the academic aspects, since these are usually easier to teach. What is desirable in a general music course is maximum student participation in singing, rhythm, playing such simple musical instruments as the autoharp and the recorder, and listening to a wide variety of recordings. Music is a performing art, and the general music course should include much student participation in the exploratory and fundamental offerings.

A general music program will be much more successful and receive a great deal less student criticism if it is so organized as to work around and within music which is currently popular with teenagers. From this it is much easier to move to ballads, folk music, and classical than to attempt to force certain kinds of music down their throats which adolescents consider to be "dead" and of no value.

2. *Instrumental music.* Commonly, instrumental music is construed to mean orchestra or band. Actually there are several other instrumental groups to be found in many junior high schools, such as stage bands, novelty bands, and special ensembles. There are some real problems connected with performing groups, whether they are orchestras, bands, or special instrumental groups.

(a) In order to have good instrumental performing groups it is necessary to practice, practice, practice. Students on the whole are not highly talented or skilled performers and the question here is how much practice should be required before it becomes detrimental to the students, the music program, or the school program. If a program is being prepared for the parents or the community at large, an overzealous principal or music teacher may put so much stress on the performance that students are used rather than served.

(b) There has been much talk, mostly derogatory, about the junior high school marching band. The quantity and tone of the talk has apparently had little effect so far in reducing the emphasis upon or the number of junior high marching bands, since they are still found in increasing numbers in their natural habitat—football games and civic parades. Some arguments against these bands are that the practice is merely an imitation of the high school; the cost of putting 50 to 100 adolescents into band uniforms is $25 or more apiece (and they never fit next year's band members); that the band needs to practice playing and marching for long periods of time; and that a marching band is an excess emphasis upon entertainment which leads to exploitation of the students. A marching band can easily get to be a full-scale affair with all the extras—majorettes, Rockettes, flag twirlers, baton twirlers, flag bearers, acrobats, and drill teams. Those who favor junior high school marching bands claim that they present opportunities for students to be a "part of something," and to be in the public eye, as does athletics, and that a band helps build morale and spirit that benefits the entire student body. It is further held that the marching band, since it appeals to general public and students alike, satisfies a distinct community need, attracts more students to the music program, and permits more individual self expression.

(c) Conflict with other subjects, particularly in grade 9, has been a difficulty for many years. In grades 7 and 8 the student takes instrumental music as an elective or as a substitute for general music or as a substitute for some other fine or practical art. In grade 9 he has to make a decision between instrumental music and something else, usually an academic subject necessary for college entrance. Orchestra is usually harder hit than band by this, since many junior high ninth-graders are loath to give up the flashy uniforms of the band, and the orchestra seldom has such outfits.

Band is the most common instrumental group, being found in about 94 percent of all junior high schools, and orchestra in about 67 percent.[9] While the marching band is more popular, many junior high schools have a "concert" or "stage" band which does not march and is strictly limited to the performing area. Many junior high schools have pep bands whose function is to play at athletic events, pep rallies, and the like. Probably the case for pep bands would be quite similar to that for marching bands. In any event, this performing group is common, permits another kind of student participation, and is quite popular.

Orchestras, in both junior and senior high school, have suffered a decline in the past few years. Both the public and the school administration are more interested in bands than in orchestras. Too, orchestras seem to require more practice time and then have fewer opportunities to play. When compared to marching band with its flash, color, and brilliance, the orchestra has less appeal for adolescents.

In addition to these large instrumental groups, there are opportunities in junior high school for a variety of novelty groups and ensembles, such as a German band, a string quartet, a brass ensemble, or a "pop" band. Such specialty groups do provide more opportunities for student participation as well as seizing upon student interest and enthusiasm. Furthermore, because novelty groups and stage bands are more likely to play music which is current and popular with teenagers, they are well received in student assemblies.

3. *Chorus.* This program is especially important to junior high school, since virtually everyone can participate. There are no instruments to buy or haul around, other problems of equipment and storage are much reduced or eliminated, and the group is highly mobile. Because nearly all children can be successful in chorus and receive some recognition, this is a program that merits the full support of the staff and administration. Opportunities are countless for varieties of vocal groups and ensembles which range from such groups as barbershop quartets to a cappella choirs. Chorus need not meet daily, but should have from 120 to 180 minutes weekly. It should be pointed out that the chorus or vocal ensembles are more often exploited than any other performing group because of their mobility and lack of problem with instruments. This demand for public performance can also exert a strong influence upon the kind of music the chorus or ensemble practices, and this in turn can be a detrimental factor.

It should always be remembered that the purpose of the musical curriculum is to develop musical knowledge, musical skill, and musical taste. The purpose is not to be construed primarily as pleasing the crowd.

INDUSTRIAL ARTS AND HOME ECONOMICS

Today's junior high school industrial arts curriculum, an important part of the exploratory program, satisfies important needs for both boys and girls and should be available to both. The industrial arts curriculum, originally brought into the junior high school as "manual training" for prevocational preparation, has shifted its emphasis to the exploratory and general education role.

The first tax-supported manual training school opened in Baltimore in 1884. It was immediately successful, and several other schools of the same kind opened in the next few years. Coeducational training was first given in the manual training school in Toledo, where instruction was offered in cooking, sewing, typing, clay modeling, and woodworking.[10]

Industrial arts was first proposed as the description of these subjects by a Columbia University professor in 1904 to replace the terms "Manual Training" and "Manual Arts." Manual training emphasized hand skills, woodworking, and prevocational training, and served to reduce student dropout. Manual arts more closely resembled today's "crafts" courses and permitted some freedom in choosing projects, allowed students to make useful articles (although still stressing skills), and emphasized appreciation of good design. Industrial arts was characterized by the development of the technical high schools, of junior high school industrial arts programs, and the exploratory function of industrial arts. Design and problem solving were still stressed and there was increased freedom in choice of content. Industrial arts in these early days included drawing, woodworking, metalworking, electricity, and some work in crafts.

THE INDUSTRIAL ARTS CURRICULUM

Industrial arts is taught at both elementary and secondary levels, with elementary industrial arts emphasizing planning and instruction. The overall program is intended to provide a broad view of our industrial culture and to educate all students in the fundamentals of technology. Specifically, industrial arts, as with art and music, is becoming increasingly useful to all citizens because of increased leisure time. There are also opportunities to appreciate craftsmanship, to learn about future occupational choices, and different industries, to get acquainted with the use of different materials and methods, and to develop creativity and problem-solving techniques.

In junior high and middle schools industrial arts is often required for at least one year, and often two. Ninth-grade industrial arts is usually an elective offering. The junior high program is generally exploratory in several industrial arts areas, including "industrial" crafts, drafting, electricity, electronics, graphic arts, metalwork, and woodwork. The trend is toward the comprehensive general shop[11] for these grade levels, which may include work with wood, ceramics, radio, concrete, plastics, drafting, metal, textiles, leather, electronics, photography, welding, forging, small motors, lapidary work, and graphic arts. In large schools which have more than one shop there may be a division of instructional areas into something such as General Shop, Light, and General Shop, Heavy. The comprehensive shop may even be replaced by an industrial arts laboratory which abolishes "the traditional division of materials and processes among a number of individual industrial arts shops."[12]

Particularly for the junior high school student, the industrial arts program needs to stress the exploratory function and permit relating to other school curricular offerings. The development of the industrial arts subject-matter area as the beginning of a specialized education for some students is also an important aspect of the program. When industrial arts is a required course—part of the general education program—the comprehensive shop is most useful in the removal of arbitrary divisions of materials and procedures now in general use in industrial arts.

Where there are opportunities for eighth- and ninth-grade electives, provision should be made for specializing in areas including graphic arts, drafting, metal, wood, and plastics.

There is considerable variation from district to district and even from school to school within a district as to what constitutes the program in industrial arts. The amount of time allocated, the program, materials, tools, and equipment will vary with the amount of money available and the staff's attitude toward industrial arts.

For example, a somewhat unusual program was first instituted in the Los Angeles City schools in 1908—a required agriculture program. All seventh-grade boys take ten weeks of Exploratory Gardening. Eighth- and ninth-grade boys may elect the second course in Gardening, which is a semester course, and there is a ninth-grade elective for boys and girls—Floriculture. This last course includes "instruction in preparation of soil and flower planting, how to cut, preserve, and use flowers in arrangements and corsages, propagation of plants by seeds and cuttings, plant identification, and maintaining planters."[13] Junior high schools are equipped with a special classroom, toolroom, storage, lavatory facilities, potting room, lathroom, compost bins, and about an acre of ground.

There is a definite trend for more industrial arts, with a variety of subjects, taught in a single shop area in the junior high and middle schools of the United States. Common in newer schools are arts laboratories, facilities for woodworking, metalworking, drafting, ceramics, graphic arts, and textiles. The usual seventh-grade curriculum includes drafting, woodworking, metalworking, electricity, and crafts. The eighth-grade industrial arts program usually includes wood, metal, textiles, electricity, graphic arts, and crafts. The ninth-grader is usually given some choice among metal work, wood, crafts, drafting, and power mechanics.

Middle schools in Bedford, New York, were built with a unified arts area, and all students—grades 6, 7, and 8—take industrial arts and homemaking. The unified arts area is constructed circularly around the little theater and provides instruction in crafts, metalwork, ceramics, drawing, painting, cooking and laundry, sewing, cutting, and fitting of textiles, woodworking, electricity, and graphic arts.

A New York junior high school[14] reports considerable success with an industrial arts program which centers around automobile and electrical-appliance repairs. This program, designed particularly for the nonacademic student, provides for one semester in auto service and repairs, and one semester in servicing and repairing household appliances.

What is important in all of these programs is the realization that we must move away from the old manual-training concept, one so often exemplified in the junior high schools as one semester of woodwork, one of metalwork, and one or two of mechanical drawing. This is *not* an industrial arts program. Industrial arts needs the same imagination, creativity, and thought that is needed by other disciplines, both in curriculum planning, instruction, and student participation.

HOME ECONOMICS

Homemaking programs are in the peculiar position of being denigrated as a frill and occasionally patronized as a nonacademic at the same time that their status is strengthened by receiving substantial federal financial support. A good case can be made for requiring some home economics work for all students sometime in grades 7–12, yet there are many problems affecting home economics that need to be resolved.

1. Homemaking—home economics, domestic science, or whatever it is to be called—has always been portrayed as a subject that should be part of everyone's education because of its practicality and application. Still, when the cry of "frills" and "more academics" went up, there was a perceptible scramble by some in home economics to point up and increase the academic flavor, work, and requirements.

2. The very presence of federal funds causes problems in that vocational home economics teachers (ninth grade and up) get more pay and are expected to visit student homes. Some teachers make the visits and some do not, but all vocational teachers receive the extra pay—a fact that tends to irritate teachers in other fields. Again, because of federal funds, there is often a plethora of state supervisors in home economics who set standards (and they are really fine standards) for home economics teachers such as, "No home economics teacher shall have more than four classes daily, and class size shall not exceed 24 students." To the teacher of history or English who has five or six classes daily in junior high school (sometimes more) with an enrollment in each class in excess of thirty, this appears to be an admirable ruling when generally applied to all teachers but most unfair in its specific application.

3. Because a year of homemaking is often required of girls in senior high school, the high school frequently "encourages" the program in grade 9, thus satisfying the requirement and permitting more flexibility and latitude in the senior high. This encouragement sometimes goes so far as to become a pressure or a requirement in grade 9. When this happens, the junior high school loses its identity and becomes a vestibule for the senior high.

4. Lack of agreement as to what should be the curriculum; should it be

a specialized program in areas such as child development or home management, or should it be a broad general program? The broad program, it is said, leads to duplication and lacks depth, and it is better to develop each area in depth. Home economics teachers are striving more and more to change the emphasis of instruction from clothing construction and food preparation to include more work in family living and home management. Yet a survey[15] published in 1963 indicated that almost two-thirds of the time spent in courses in clothing and foods was devoted to actual clothing construction and food preparation. This would seem to demonstrate that either the teachers themselves are not sure what the emphasis should be, or that pressures of parents, students, or administrators compel such allotments of time.

When we see a statement such as, "Seventh- and eighth-grade pupils enjoy laboratory activity and are eager to engage in homemaking experiences"[16] contrasted with another statement, "The proportion of time spent on construction in foods and clothing surprised and disappointed many teachers who had assumed that course content had been adjusted to include more emphasis upon such areas as child development, housing and home management,"[17] there is an apparent lack of clarity of purpose.

5. There is the difficulty of determining how much home economics instruction is desirable. Should there be a required program for all seventh- and eighth-grade girls? Should it be required daily, every other day, or for one semester in junior high school? Should boys be required to take homemaking?

6. How much space and equipment is desirable for a good junior high school home economics program, and how much is essential?

CURRICULUM AND TRENDS

The most common areas taught in homemaking in junior high school are clothing, foods, management, consumer education, housing, family relations, child development, health, and home nursing. Because there is much overlap with other subject areas, it can easily happen that certain topics which should be taught are not because it is assumed that other teachers have covered this material. These include such topics as sex education, personal grooming, cleanliness, buying, color schemes, art in the home, and consumer education.

There should be a strong, well-balanced program of home economics available, particularly for those youngsters who are going on to college and for potential dropouts. It is reasonable to propose a year of required homemaking for girls and one semester for boys. It is readily possible in junior high school to correlate homemaking with other areas.

The usual seventh-grade course includes clothing selection and construction, foods, textiles, and personal finances. Eight-grade courses commonly include more clothing and foods, grooming, buying food and clothing, and home management. In the ninth grade, usual offerings include consumer education, clothing and foods, home management, child development, health and home nursing, and home decorating.

Right here is where a major problem exists. Some very good syllabi and course outlines have been prepared, and there is no lack of suggestion as to what could be taught. There is, however, a marked variation, often from school to school, on what *is* taught, depending upon the facilities, administration, individual students, and funds available. This reaches an extreme where seventh-grade girls in one school make very fine clothing while in another school they are limited to embroidering a tea towel.

Some trends are showing up in home economics:

1. Broad course offerings in grades seven and eight with specialization in grade nine.
2. More boys involved in homemaking, particularly in food preparation, family relations, and consumer education.
3. A year of home economics required for junior high girls, which may be divided into one semester each in grades 7 and 8.
4. More emphasis upon personal and social homemaking as opposed to technical and vocational.
5. More emphasis upon content such as consumer education and family relations.
6. Use of flexible scheduling to provide blocks of time.
7. Crossing subject-matter lines into areas of art, health, science, and social studies.
8. Operating home economics classes in grades 7 and 8 on a rotating or alternating basis with other subjects; for example, all students take nine weeks of industrial arts, home making, and arts and crafts.

BUSINESS AND CONSUMER EDUCATION

Business and consumer education contributes both to the general education of the early adolescent and to the prevocational, exploratory, and guidance functions of the junior high school. Because of the importance of consumer education to each individual in the community, there has been a marked increase of interest in the inclusion of this kind of education in the program for every student sometime during his junior high school years. Business education, like industrial arts, homemaking, and agriculture, has been stigmatized and has suffered from the emphasis placed upon the academics. If a bright student wishes to take business courses, especially in high school, he is likely to find a counselor questioning the wisdom of his choice. And yet the United States does have a business economy. In his lifetime the junior high school student will buy many items of expense; he will have to make many decisions and choices in buying and in money management. It is not difficult to make a case for required work in business and consumer education. In view of the number of dropouts (who perhaps need such education most) and the number of required courses in high school, it may be best to develop business and consumer education courses in the junior high schools.

Business education was originally brought into the junior high school to provide training for clerical occupations. It was common in early junior high schools to find that typing, shorthand, and bookkeeping had been shifted down from the high school. Compulsory attendance laws, child labor laws, and changing job requirements have virtually eliminated the need for vocational training in junior high school. The emphasis has changed to a modification of the traditional academic courses and to a more practical approach as reflected by course names such as Business Mathematics and Commercial Geography. Sometimes the *only* change made was in the name. In the next stage there were really two developments, often parallel, upon occasion sequential. One is the experimental approach where business subjects are made available on an elective basis, either limited in number or a wide choice; the other is, the fusion stage in which business subjects are either blended into one general course offering or fused with a core or block of time. These developments, too, have met with only limited success.

In determining what should be included in the junior high curriculum for business and consumer education it will be necessary to make decisions concerning several things. What will be elective and what, if any, will be required? Will the business and consumer courses be fused with other course offerings, taught as separate units within other course work, or taught as completely separate courses? What content is desirable for this age level? How much content should be offered, and what facilities will be required?

There are at least four general objectives which may be provided by business education—personal, consumer, social, and communication. Everyone needs to know how to manage his own personal business affairs, but it is surprising how many adults are inept in this respect. If they did not learn from their own parents (who may have been equally inept), they had to learn by trial and error—often a painful process.

All of us are consumers, and the adolescent is a spending consumer on an ever-increasing scale. In our society consumption of goods is of such magnitude that it has reached the point where it is essential that economic competencies be developed in our young people.

By social business objectives is meant economic literacy, the understanding of the economic institutions in the cultural perspective of today's world. It is unfortunate but true that there is a high degree of economic illiteracy that is not confined to the high school dropout. A substantial number of college graduates may also be found in this category because in most schools there is no place for business and consumer education to be fitted into the precollege course work. Once a student enters college he may elect a course in economics. Some do, but most students are never exposed to business or economics courses.

The ability to type is becoming a highly desirable if not essential skill for nearly everyone. When typing was considered to be solely for vocational training, it was offered almost exclusively in the high schools. Today typing for personal use is becoming accepted as a communication skill that should be provided to all who need or want it. As a result, typing instruction is common in junior high school and may even be required.

Business education performs several functions in the junior high school in meeting its general objectives and also in conforming with stated junior high school functions:

1. *Exploratory.* Not everyone can or should go to college, just as not everyone can or should be a barber or a physician. A good junior high or middle school program supplies a program that is diversified and exploratory for all students. As a part of such a varied program, business and consumer education have a definite place in offerings which include typing, personal bookkeeping, consumer economics, and economics.

2. *Prevocational.* The exploratory aspect permits the student to become acquainted with a variety of subjects and courses. A student may find an area of particular interest and concentrate somewhat upon it without an intense degree of specialization. In this manner a basic interest or amateur competency can be developed into a vocational interest or professional competency at a later time.

3. *Differentiation.* If we believe and mean even a part of what we say concerning individual differences, interests, talents, and abilities—about a diversified program intended to provide the best education for all young people—then we cannot exclude business and consumer education in some form and in varying amounts for different children. Students of all levels of ability can achieve and find something of interest in these subjects.

4. *Guidance.* Helping individuals to learn to make choices and to solve problems is important at all levels of education. The guidance function is closely related to the exploratory function in junior high school. Through guidance the student can learn more about his own interests and abilities and more about educational and vocational opportunities. Business education can provide both kinds of opportunities.

COURSE OFFERINGS

Business and consumer education have had many of the same problems as other courses offered in the schools. Among these are poorly trained teachers, or teachers who are given classes because "anyone can teach business"; the "vocational" label; the practice of many administrators of using business classes as dumping grounds; poor facilities and lack of materials. In addition, business and consumer education courses seem to have been afflicted with more than their share of aggravations, such as the course in consumer economics which becomes a highly theoretical course in economic theory; the hodge-podge and lack of organization of some material; the tendency of some teachers and many students to regard these courses as snap courses —a chance to "take it easy" and "play around."

There is a very real question as to what specific courses should be offered. Perhaps the best answer is to include with the block of time or core some aspects of business and establish special courses, elective or required, for courses such as typing. Regardless of whether content is fused or offered separately, in junior high school there should be instruction in several areas of business and consumer education.

1. *Typewriting or typing.* Business teachers generally prefer to refer to typewriting as that which is done on a typewriter. This is a skill subject, formerly taught as a vocational skill, now in demand as a necessary tool for both college- and noncollege-bound students. As a result of the increased recognition of the value of typing and the swelling enrollments in typing classes, the trend is now to offer typing in the junior highs and even the elementary schools. One survey[18] found that somewhat over one-half of the junior high schools questioned offered typing, and approximately 6 percent of the elementary schools had typing for grades 5 and 6. Students find use for typing in learning spelling and grammar, preparing better papers and reports, and producing more legible copy.

2. *Personal bookkeeping and record keeping.* Everyone should be familiar with bank accounts, checking accounts, taxes, budgeting, discounts, trade-ins, financial statements, and insurance. In many schools, instruction in bookkeeping has not kept up with the times. It has been estimated[19] that 95 percent of all bookkeeping entries today are made by card punch or electronic data processing, with less than 1 percent still made manually. This suggests that some of the more formal and technical parts of bookkeeping could be reduced or eliminated.

3. *General business.* When this course was first introduced into the curriculum over fifty years ago, it was called Junior Business and was designed to be an introductory course to business. It became something of a catchall course, overloaded with trivia, but recent trends indicate that the content of general business is becoming one of basic business and economic

principles including the roles of government and labor in business, economic security, price theory, individual and family finance, and money and banking.

4. *Business mathematics.* This is occasionally offered as a separate course, sometimes as a part of general business, and sometimes as a part of bookkeeping. The impact of automation and computer mathematics may bring about a complete revision of business mathematics or integration with other courses.

5. Some junior high schools, rather than providing separate courses for business math, bookkeeping, and general business, offer a course called Personal Business. Topics usually covered in personal business include satisfactory cash records, personal and family finances, money management, savings, taxes, investments, insurance, property ownership, social security, retirement and pension plans.

6. *Notehand.* This is an extremely useful tool which can be readily learned and used by junior high children. It is an abbreviated form of longhand based upon the phonetic alphabet so that the student is not compelled to learn the whole new language of shorthand.

7. There is some feeling by a few in the field of business education that the following areas should be included in junior high school, either as a composite package or integrated with the block of time or core: clerical practice, salesmanship, distributive education, advertising, and secretarial practice.

8. *Consumer education.* There is a desperate need here for instruction for today's youth. Adolescents are active consumers; they are saturated with advertising aimed especially at them, and they are painfully uninformed concerning different products, competing brands, and discount and installment buying. They need to know how to discriminate, whether to buy now or wait until later, what publications are available for help, such as *Consumer Reports* and U.S. Government Bulletins.

A carefully planned and well-taught course in consumer has much to offer everyone, particularly for those children who generally are the most trouble—the nonacademic and the disadvantaged. This kind of course makes sense, especially to those children who have difficulty seeing much purpose in studying academic courses. They can learn more economics than would be learned in an economics class and more money management than they would learn in a mathematics class. This can be a one-semester course or a year's course, or can be included within the block or core. However offered, the topics covered should include buying food and clothing; comparison of quality, banking services, credit, advertising, budgeting, income tax, insurance, buying or renting a home; buying major appliances, furniture, automobile, savings and investment, and interest.

Consumer education can be a part of the homemaking course and may be required for both girls and boys. They may plan, purchase ingredients, and cook meals, and they may shop and compare prices. A teacher in a school in a low-income area taught her girls how to buy quality clothing in a used-clothing store and remodel their purchases.

The key to success in consumer education is student participation. They must go out and shop, must compare prices and quality, read the advertisements, dig out the facts, spend money, and make choices.

FOREIGN LANGUAGES

It has been said that "foreign languages are strangers to the junior high curriculum and particularly below grade nine."[20] If we consider the junior high school curricula from the 1930's up to the latter 1950's, this comment contains considerable truth, but from the time of the inception of the junior high school to the 1930's foreign language was an accepted part of the junior high school program. It will be remembered that one of the forces leading to the establishment of the junior high school was the feeling, primarily by college personnel, that academic subjects should be started in grades 7 and 8. In the early junior high schools it was not uncommon to find foreign languages, both classical and modern, in all grades of the junior high school. Those who stressed the downward extension of academics had in mind precisely that: more solids, and preferably required for everyone. It had been suggested in 1896 that Latin be substituted for English for the eighth grade in Richmond, Indiana. The disciplinary values to the budding intellect were considered to be so great that all students could profit from study of a foreign language, even though adult opportunities to read, speak, and understand Latin were (and still are) distinctly limited. In 1908 the Committee on Six Year Courses of High School Study specifically recommended foreign languages be taught for five periods a week in each grade the languages were offered.

As the junior high school developed and child labor laws and compulsory attendance laws kept more children in school, economy of time and efforts for earlier college preparation became less and less important, with the result that there were fewer schools offering foreign languages below grade 9. Curricular experimentation of the 1930's and the social and economic conditions of the times caused less importance to be attached to instruction in foreign languages, and enrollments in these courses fell off even further. Foreign language became almost completely an elective beginning in grade 9—usually Latin, although the larger junior high schools might offer French, German, or Spanish in conjunction with Latin.

World War II and the developments since then have once more attached an importance to foreign language study which has not only had a major effect in junior high school but has led to a massive program of foreign languages in elementary schools. It has been brought home to the people of the United States that there are many other languages and cultures in the world, and that many people in the world do not speak English or have any real desire to do so. With United States military forces, businessmen, and ordinary tourists traveling all over the world, we need to know as much as possible of other languages and cultures. The day is past when the tourist could hope that the louder he talked the better he was understood by the natives.

Historically, foreign language offerings in the United States began in the colonial days, with Latin and Greek being taught in the Latin Grammar Schools. In 1749 Benjamin Franklin promoted the study of modern foreign languages when he added French and German to the course offerings of the Philadelphia Academy. The Boston Classical High School added French in 1832, but, ". . . progress was very slow because in 1870 a survey showed that French was taught in only twenty-nine high schools and German in only thirteen."[21] The addition of Spanish to public secondary school offerings was first noted, again in Boston, in 1852, and this language grew in popularity until it is today the foreign language most often found in the public secondary schools. There was for a short time in the 1930's a general language course offered which involved an introduction to several languages, usually four, in a year's time. This course, almost invariably a junior high school offering, was short-lived, requiring as it did some degree of teacher proficiency in several languages while developing student competency in none.

The interest in foreign languages over the past few years has been reflected in the increased offerings in junior high school and in the grade levels at which these are found. A recent survey[22] found that the number of junior high schools offering a foreign language in Grades 7 or 8 had increased from 17 percent in 1954 to 52 percent in 1964. Junior high school foreign languages are usually French, Spanish, and German, although some schools offer Latin, Russian, Italian, and even Chinese.

Junior high school students, as a part of the exploratory education function, should definitely be given opportunities to study one or more foreign languages, at least as elective offerings.

WHY STUDY A FOREIGN LANGUAGE?

Probably the principal reason for studying a foreign language today is to develop the ability to understand a native speaker and to make oneself understood in that language. In 1898 the Committee of Twelve stated that the four immediate objectives of teaching foreign languages should be the progressive development of the ability to read the foreign language; to understand the language when spoken; to speak the language; and to write the language. Today the objectives are the same, with only a change in order of importance: understanding, speaking, reading, and writing. Foreign languages are increasingly heard in the United States and millions of our citizens travel to foreign countries every year. The world is truly a smaller place and a good case can be made for requiring study of at least one foreign language for many students in our public schools.

While some of the arguments given for including foreign languages in the junior high school curriculum appear somewhat tenuous, the following statements have considerable validity for today's students:

1. The undeniably increased need for our citizens to communicate with foreign speakers both within and without the United States.
2. The increased understanding of the culture, problems, and thought processes of citizens of other countries.
3. The increased information available to those who can read foreign journals.
4. Widening of esthetic boundaries.
5. Occupational and professional opportunities are enhanced.
6. The very real sense of achievement and gratification provided.
7. The recognition that language is the verbal manifestation of a culture.[23]

To reach these objectives it is clear that more is required than a one- or two-year general or introductory course. The student must achieve a competency in the language, which will necessitate study for a period of at least three or four years.

WHO SHOULD STUDY A FOREIGN LANGUAGE?

John Dewey once observed that what is wanted by the best family in a community for its children is what the community should want for *all* its children. It is possible in these times to disagree on the definition of "best" family and "best" education. There are at least two distinct fields of thought concerning who should study a foreign language. (1) Not everyone can profit from foreign language study, either by reason of inherent ability or circumstance, and (2) "All children should have this opportunity for self-discovery,"[24] How do we decide what experiences will be had by only some children? The state of California requires the study of foreign language for all students for three years, beginning no later than grade 6, and similar bills have been introduced into the New York State legislature.

The Modern Language Association and the National Education Association issued the unequivocal joint statement, "Preferably not later than the third grade, all children should have the opportunity to listen to and speak a foreign language."[25] The National Association of Secondary School Principals, in 1959, recommended that all students should be given the opportunity to study a foreign language and to continue such study as long as their ability and interest allow.

Birkmaier[26] points out that since we attempt to give elementary school children experiences in all fields, "why not in the learning of a modern language?" If the language instruction has been begun in grade 3 or 4, selection of those to continue could be made, if this is considered desirable, at grade 5. Research evidence points out at least two factors of importance in connection with this: (1) the ability to learn foreign languages seems to decline from infancy to adolescence, and (2) foreign language classes should not be "considered an enrichment course for the gifted only . . . some below-average or average students seem to do better than some children with average intelligence."[27]

It is common to find that students in elementary and junior high schools are selected or permitted to elect foreign languages on criteria such as IQ test scores, achievement-test scores, reading level in English, grades earned in other school subjects, results of various prognostic tests, teacher or administrative judgment, or some combination of these. Many school people, including quite a number of teachers of foreign language, firmly believe that such standards are necessary since students of less than above-average ability cannot easily achieve in a foreign language. Research studies,[28] however, indicate that all of these supposedly valid prognosticators of success are of little value in predicting student success in foreign language study. Motivation, interest, and personality characteristics are strong factors in a student's ultimate success in learning languages. It appears that the best method of ascertaining if a student will succeed is to give him an opportunity to study a foreign language. Although supported by research, these conclusions are slow to find favor with a considerable number of teachers and administrators.

Two problems are related to who should take foreign languages and when: (1) the argument that says that capacity to learn does not necessarily mean that all students *should* study a subject, and (2) problems of scheduling and the possibility of restricting junior high school student exploratory experiences in other areas because of foreign language study. It is true that the junior high school curriculum is crowded. However, part of the problem arises because so many of those educators involved in junior high school instruction are difficult to sell on the idea that schedules do not have to be rigid. It is not necessary for all classes to meet daily for the same length of time, nor to alternate days or quarters on a "swing" or rotating schedule. Different subjects should have differing amounts of time. By making the schedule a flexible tool instead of a rigid master, there is no reason that all students cannot enjoy homemaking, industrial arts, music, art, foreign languages, and activities.

WHICH FOREIGN LANGUAGE?

Selection of which foreign language or languages to be taught in the junior high school will be at least partially determined by such noneducational factors as geographic location of the community, size of the school and the community, and availability of teachers, money, and materials. Particularly in smaller schools and communities, the question of which foreign language is to be offered may well be decided by the teacher available. In areas such as the Southwest, the language is more likely to be Spanish, sometimes in two tracks: one for non-Spanish speakers, the other for those students who speak Spanish at home—since these children, often from low economic areas, are sometimes characterized as being illiterate in two languages.

While French, German, and Spanish are the usual languages taught in the public secondary schools, there are schools that teach Russian, Italian, Portuguese, Hindi, Chinese, and Arabic. Greek has virtually disappeared from the curriculum, and Latin has lost much in popularity.

The classicists are fighting a strong holding action to reinforce the place of Latin in the curriculum of the secondary schools. Far from conceding that Latin is a dead language, one enthusiast inquires, "Who Buried Latin? It Has Never Died!" (*Clearing House*, February 1968). The author stresses that Latin is "no longer the vernacular of any country but is spoken in every country west of the Orient." The Endicott House Conference of 1962 recommended that Latin be started no later than grade 7 and "concentrate in the seventh and eighth grades on elementary linguistic skills and vocabulary, while accumulating the facts of geography and everyday life of the Romans."[29] Grade 9 students should study the structure and progression of the language as well as reading Latin authors. It was further suggested that a three-year sequence be established in Latin on the high school level with the first year featuring the history of Rome in prose; the second year, Latin poetry, and the third year to include the logic and philosophy of Latin authors. Obviously, the teachers of Latin expect to continue offering a program of scope and sequence.

According to some authorities, the specific language learned is not a matter of concern, since what is wanted is the insight into language structure and the process used in acquiring these insights. In any case, it appears that the choice of the language should be decided in terms of the individual community and school situation.

TEACHING THE FOREIGN LANGUAGE

Regardless of which language is selected for the junior high school, there are some essential considerations. There must be a sequential program, one that is articulated for the years in junior high school as well as with any existing programs prior to or following junior high. There must be sufficient materials provided for instruction—texts, tapes, supplies, and equipment—and a trained language teacher. Time must be provided so that the language instruction is not "squeezed in"—or even left out. Decisions must be made as to who will study the language. It has been pointed out that foreign language study is no longer intended for an elite group. Since World War II a Gallup Poll survey lent strength to this position by reporting that 86 percent of those sampled favored a second language requirement.

The audio-lingual approach is at present receiving considerable fanfare, but instruction in reading and writing the language is also an important part of the program. Foreign language instruction, however, perhaps varies more than any other in availability, purpose, and method. Conflict arises as to the best approach between two general categories:

1. Traditional: expository and deductional techniques which stress phonetics, grammar, reading, composition, and literature.
2. Audio-lingual: listening and speaking first; inductive grammar approach; serious attention to literature after student has achieved proficient communication.

What we often forget is that what is natural for some students is not necessarily so for others, and the older the student the more likely it is that certain audio-lingual approaches are psychologically not suited to adult learning processes. The main purpose of the audio-lingual approach is that of mastery—the ability to converse fluently with a native speaker and to read the literature in that language.

Assumptions of the audio-lingual approach include:

1. You learn by acquiring the speech habits of the native speakers.
2. This process requires more than two years of course work—longer sequences are needed.
3. You understand the speech before you read and write it.

As one might expect, the classicist views this as of doubtful wisdom when oral fluency is stressed at the expense of a richer reading program. Actually the audio-linguists hope to attain fluency without sacrificing accuracy in reading, a reasonable accuracy in writing, and the acquisition of some knowledge of the culture.

Nelson Brooks[30] sums up learning a modern foreign language for communication by describing it first in terms of what it is not, and then in terms of what it is. It is not, he says, a constant exercise in written translations, since this involves the use of the learner's native language. There is no preference for any single method, nor is there the matching of an isolated work in one language with a word in another. It is not the measure of "*x* number of words" in vocabulary nor learning lists of names of persons or places memorized out of context. It does not permit much use of English in the classroom by the student, nor is he permitted much recourse to a printed script, nor are there extensive explanations of rules of grammar.

In describing what such a program is, we find that

1. There is a minimum or no use of students reading aloud from a printed text.
2. There is a maximum of student talk and a minimum of solo teacher talk.
3. At the start of the program, students are given exact information about objectives and how they will be achieved.
4. Considerable importance is attached to the model (the teacher) and the reward (success).
5. Stress is placed upon the principle that language is something you are able to understand and speak before it is something you read and write.
6. There is emphasis upon learning of structure at early levels which coincides with norms of communicative language.
7. There are cultural and literary objectives studied for their own sakes.
8. There are five critical points in classroom procedure, and success or failure of the class depends upon what is done about: the use of English, translation, explanation of grammar, the use of the open book, and tests.

The audio-oral approach has been demonstrated to be a highly effective approach—up to a point. The weakness lies in prolonging the hearing-repeating phase; there must be a coordination of oral skills with challenging reading materials, adjusted to age groups and student interests.

A degree of disagreement exists even within the ranks of the audio-linguists. At least one[31] foreign language teacher believes that most texts available are too large, contain too many hard-to-understand idioms, too many chapters on culture, too much vocabulary. He goes on to stress drill, drill, drill, and recommends that hat dances, plays, clever songs, and geography lessons be reduced in number or eliminated from the course—nearly all class time must be utilized for drill.

The philosophy of teaching a foreign language needs to be eclectic, using methods that work best for each individual teacher and each class, and adapted to the school and community situation. Grammar and vocabulary should be taught where needed, for the more intelligent students are likely to be discontented with a program solely of "listen and say." Audio-lingual materials should be supplemented with any and all materials available to eliminate boredom.

SUMMARY

The junior high school student, as an early adolescent, is going through rapid and uneven physical growth. He is also experiencing anxieties because of what is happening to his body. A good health and physical education program is essential to his physical and mental well being.

There is a perceptible difference of opinion concerning the place, content, and responsibility for instruction in health education. There is also variance in amount of health education taught. Health education deals with three major areas: school health instruction, school health services, and healthful school living. There should be a minimum of one required semester of health in junior high school, and this course should be taught as a separate subject—not as a unit in science, homemaking, or core.

Physical education should be required for all junior high school students in all grades included, for not less than one full period every other day. A good physical education curriculum does not stress team sports at the expense of individual or dual activities but gives training to students that has carryover to out-of-school and adult life.

Art and music are and should be an integral part of junior high school. All junior high school students should be required to have at least one year of both art and music, preferably for at least three periods each week. While these fine arts are often regarded as frills, they have much to offer today's students. Certainly we are exposed to various forms of art and music every day, and the increased leisure time adds to the need for some form of training in how best to spend it. Few people have the talent or patience to become really great artists or musicians, but everyone can learn enough about art and music to become somewhat creative and derive considerable self-satisfaction from this, even if his activities are restricted to viewing or to listening. Music and art are experiencing a trend toward correlation with other subjects, primarily social studies, language arts, and humanities. Correlation is desirable, but both music and art have contents of their own and should not be regarded patronizingly as handmaidens of another discipline.

Industrial arts and home economics, practical arts which are sometimes scorned as nonacademics and wasteful in today's schools, have a merited place in the program of general education for the early adolescent. Changes in our society and technology, the increase in leisure time, and the vastly different way in which we now live make education in these fields necessary for everyone.

Industrial arts has long since departed from the manual-training concept, and the general-shop approach is becoming common in junior high school. This method involves exposure to a great variety of training and experiences which permits specialization in the higher grades.

Home economics education, as well as industrial arts, should be required of all students sometime during the junior high school years. There is a disagreement between theory and practice concerning the amount of emphasis to be placed upon actual clothing construction and food preparation and the desirable amount of work in family relations, consumer education, and home management.

Business and consumer education is being recognized as necessary knowledge for virtually everyone. While we do not all need to know shorthand, typing is a desirable skill for anyone, and there are other areas of business and consumer education which should be available to all students. Instruction and offerings are being found more frequently on the junior high level as it becomes evident that adolescents have a real need for this kind of learning.

Consumer education is a must for young people in the world of today. Ours is a business society and economy. It is necessary to have an understanding of our economic system as well as a knowledge of buying and money management. Certain goals and trends in instruction in business and consumer education are

1. Typing is available as an elective in about one-half of the junior high schools reporting in one survey. A few junior high schools require it.
2. There is a trend away from memorization of facts and an increase of students actually *doing.*
3. Notehand is being taught in many junior high schools.
4. There is real concern about our economically illiterate adult society and a desire to provide education in these subjects for today's adolescents.
5. Business and consumer education programs are increasing in junior high schools.
6. Efforts are being made to help every student to become a discriminating, rational, selective, and intelligent consumer. This has immediacy for the early adolescent, since the teenage market is presently in excess of $15 billion yearly.
7. It is not enough to select and buy wisely; one also needs to know how to *use* efficiently.

The junior high schools included foreign language study from their earliest days. Indeed, recommendations leading to the formation of the junior high school contained provisions for study of foreign languages in grades 7, 8, and 9. Changing conditions brought about a marked decrease in junior high school foreign language enrollments so that only a small minority of these schools had foreign language offerings below grade 9 by the end of World War II.

The recent interest in foreign language instruction and use, again caused by changing world conditions, has resulted in rejuvenation of foreign language curricula in the junior high schools. The old standby, Latin, has declined greatly in popularity, but over half the junior high schools now offer a modern foreign language to students, beginning in grade 7 or 8. While French, Spanish, and German are most commonly offered, some junior high schools offer Russian, Italian, Portuguese, and even Chinese. The "oral-aural" method of instruction, while presently receiving the most publicity, contains some weaknesses, chief among which is student boredom. The best method of instruction appears to be that which is achieved in terms of the teacher's abilities and interests, the nature of the class, and the school and community situation.

REFERENCES

1. F. E. Conner and William J. Ellena, *Curriculum Handbook for School Administrators.* Washington, D. C.: AASA, 1967, p. 105.
2. John K. Archer, "Physical Education: A Principal's View," *NASSP Bulletin,* Vol. 47 (November 1963), p. 107.
3. Elmo S. Roundy, "Are Our Physical Education Programs Meeting Today's Needs," *Journal of Secondary Education,* Vol. 41 (May 1966), pp. 221–224.
4. Charles M. Dorn, "Fine Arts, Issues, and Developments," *NASSP Bulletin,* Vol. 47 (November 1963), p. 42.
5. *Ibid.,* p. 43.
6. Edward H. Hergebroth, "Art Curriculum" in Morton Alpren, (ed.), *The Subject Curriculum: K-12.* Columbus: Merrill, 1967.
7. Charles M. Dorn, "Art Education," in Forrest Conner and William Ellena, *Curriculum Handbook for School Administrators,* p. 5.
8. Leonard H. Clark, Raymond L. Klein, and John B. Burks, *The American Secondary School Curriculum.* New York: Macmillan, 1965, p. 283.
9. "Music and Art In the Public Schools," *monograph.* Washington, D.C.: National Education Association, 1963, p. 34.
10. Harold Decker, "Industrial Arts Education," in *Curriculum Handbook for School Administrators.*
11. *Ibid.,* p. 144.
12. William G. Floyd, "Industrial Arts: A New Approach," *NASSP Bulletin,* Vol. 51 (March 1967), p. 25.
13. Lester O. Matthews, "All Pupils Take Agriculture in Los Angeles," *NASSP Bulletin,* Vol. 46 (February 1962), p. 79.
14. Edward J. Davey, "Provide the Tools," *The Clearing House,* Vol. 39 (February 1965), pp. 351–352.
15. "Home Economics in the Public Secondary Schools," Circular 661. Washington, D.C.: U.S. Office of Education, 1963.
16. Johnie Christian, "Home Economics: Issues," *NASSP Bulletin,* Vol. 47 (November 1963), p. 60.
17. Edna P. Amidon, "Home Economics: Developments," *NASSP Bulletin,* Vol. 47 (November 1963), p. 66.
18. John C. Roman, "The Business Curriculum," *Monograph.* Chicago: Southwestern, 1966, p. 17.
19. Conner and Ellena, *op. cit.,* p. 30.
20. Joseph M. Vocolo, "Foreign Language Program in the Junior High School," *Clearing House,* Vol. 42 (February 1968), p. 358.

21. Joseph La Bue, "Foreign Languages Curriculum," in Alpren, *The Subject Curriculum: K –12*, p. 145.
22. John H. Lounsbury and Harl Douglass, "Recent Trends in Junior High School Practices," *NASSP Bulletin*, Vol. 49 (September 1965), p. 92.
23. E. M. Birkmaier and C. L. Hallman, "Foreign Language Education," in Conner and Ellena, *Curriculum Handbook for school Administrators*, p. 77.
24. Vocolo, *op. cit.*, p. 358.
25. *Ibid.*, p. 359.
26. Emma M. Birkmaier, "Modern Foreign Languages: Issues," *NASSP Bulletin*, Vol. 47 (November 1963), p. 85.
27. *Ibid.*, p. 86.
28. Vocolo, *op. cit.*, p. 361.
29. Carolyn E. Bock, "Classical Languages: Developments," *NASSP Bulletin*, Vol. 47 (November 1963), pp. 23–25.
30. Nelson Brooks, "Learning A Modern Language for Communication," in Alfred de Grazia and David John (eds.), *Revolution in Teaching*. New York: Bantam Matrix Press, 1964, pp. 233–238.
31. Gene D. Matlock, "A Conversationalist's View," *NEA Journal*, Vol. 55 (October 1966), p. 49.

part III

MIDDLE SCHOOLS

A considerable interest has been generated in recent years in a reorganized junior high school which includes grades 6-7-8 or 5-6-7-8 instead of the traditional 7-8-9 or grades 7-8. These schools, sometimes called "intermediate schools" but more often "middle schools," are said to be a better organizational pattern because they are not hampered by ninth-grade (high school) course requirements, are not restricted by Carnegie Unit time restrictions, have a name and status of their own, are more likely to avoid the oversophistication caused by imitating high school practices, and have better potential for flexibility in curriculum and programming. There is increasing evidence that today's adolescent matures earlier than the adolescent of a few decades ago. This maturity, evidenced socially, physically, and mentally, strengthens the position of those who maintain that the middle school more nearly includes the early adolescent age range.

chapter 8

The What and Why of Middle Schools

The past few years have seen many changes and much that is new in education. Technological advances have been responsible for some of the newer developments, but there appears also to be an increased questioning of the customary way in which schools have been organized and taught and a growing interest in attempting something different which, it is hoped, will do a better job. The traditional junior high school, with its 7-8-9 grade organization, has been inspected critically and has perhaps received more than its share of unfavorable comment. As a result a substantial number of school districts have become interested in a grade organizational pattern different from the 7-8-9 junior high, usually including grades 6-7-8 or 5-6-7-8, and most commonly called a "middle school" or even an "intermediate school."[1] It has been said that the term "middle school" should properly be applied to the 7-8-9 grade structure,[2] but to most people this organizational plan describes the "junior high school," which as any middle school advocate will assure you, is something quite different from a true middle school.

If there is some confusion concerning the name, there may be even more regarding which grades are included in middle schools. Although the 5-8 and 6-8 are most common, some districts operate schools with grades 6–9, 5–9, 5–7, or 6–7, and call them middle schools.[3] The Minnesota State Department of Education, for example, stated that their legal definition of a middle school, proposed to the legislature in January of 1969, is ". . . any school giving a full course of study in grades over 3 but below 9 with building, equipment, courses of study, class schedules, enrollment, and staff meeting the standards established by the state board of Education."[4] It may be even more difficult to classify schools which include grades 7–8 only, for these are sometimes called two-year junior high schools, sometimes middle schools, and occasionally intermediate schools.

Proponents of middle schools say that this is more than a shuffling of grades, more than creating new terminology. Technically a middle school is designated as one between elementary and high school, includes grades 6-7-8 or 5-6-7-8, and involves different curricular and instructional approaches that are neither elementary nor secondary. The standard junior high school, it is claimed, is too often precisely that: a little high school which possesses most of the undesirable features of the high school and too few of those characteristics desirable for the education of the preadolescent and early adolescent.

WHAT IS A MIDDLE SCHOOL?

"A middle school is different things to different people. This has no doubt resulted from the fact that a good deal of information available on middle schools is theory rather than practice or is based on the experiences of a single school. The middle school should develop and is developing differently in individual schools."[5]

The middle school concept, to establish an educational program designed to meet the needs and interests of the preadolescent and early adolescent, has been described as having specific prerequisite features:[6]

1. Includes at least three grades to provide for the transition from elementary methods to high school instructional procedures. Grades 6 and 7 must be included with no grades below grade 5 nor above grade 8.
2. A movement toward departmentalization, more pronounced in each higher grade, to effect the change from the elementary self-contained classroom to the departmentalized structure of the high school.
3. Flexible approaches to instruction characterize the middle school—team teaching, flexible scheduling, individualized instruction, independent study, programmed learning, and such other procedures as will help children learn how to learn.
4. Special courses, required of all students, usually taught in a departmentalized structure in such fields as industrial arts, home economics, foreign languages, art, music, and typing. These may be taught in an interdisciplinary manner such as unified arts, humanities, or exploratory fields.
5. A guidance program that is a distinct entity, especially designed for the preadolescent and early adolescent, and one that is comprised of more than tests and record keeping.

6. A faculty that is specifically trained for this age group and this sort of school. If this kind of teacher is unavailable, then it is necessary to have teachers with both elementary and secondary certification or, at the very least, some teachers of each type.
7. A program of interscholastic sports and social activities that is substantially limited from that commonly found in the traditional junior high school.

   "That the middle school is more than a grouping of grades is evident from an examination of the degree to which each of the above mentioned seven essentials of a middle school is part of the programs. . . ."[7]

Williams notes that, ". . . The middle school is characterized by extreme variety. However, despite the fact that middle schools probably differ from one another more than they resemble one another, they do have some features in common:"[8]

1. An effort to combine the best features of the elementary school and its self-contained classrooms with the best aspects of the specialization of the secondary schools.
2. An instructional program that emphasizes self-understanding and includes units on the special concerns of young adolescents.
3. An observable, definite, and planned emphasis upon greater student self-direction and self-responsibility for learning. This requires extended use of independent study and student selection of activities of the individual's own choosing and design.
4. Expanded use of innovations such as team teaching, nongrading, the newest of educational media, flexible scheduling, programmed learning, and laboratory facilities. "The middle school movement is an exciting development and part of the excitement grows out of its newness—the excitement of creativity is felt in these schools."[9]

The Connecticut legislature defined the middle school in an act of 1965 as an extension of the definition of a secondary school to include

> ". . . any separate combination of grades five and six or grade six with grades seven and eight in a program approved by the State Board of Education when the use of special facilities generally associated with secondary schools is an essential part of the program for all grades included in such a school."[10]

Alexander and his associates[11] see the middle school as

> . . . bringing together in one facility and organization specific school years, commonly grades 5–8 or 6–8, that have previously been separated by elementary and junior high school organization patterns under the 6-3-3 plan.

The new structure should be considered, they believe, in a larger sense as an effort to "reorganize the total school ladder," not just one of its divisions. The middle school, in this concept, is defined as

> . . . a school providing a program planned for a range of older children, preadolescents, and early adolescents that builds upon the elementary school program for earlier childhood and in turn is built upon by the high school's program for adolescence. Specifically it focuses upon the educational needs of what we have termed the "in-between-ager." . . .[12]

The emergent middle school, then, should have these characteristics:[13]

1. Serving the educational needs of older children, preadolescents, and early adolescents in a framework that comes between the elementary school for children and the high school for adolescence.
2. There is a maximum of individualization of curriculum and instruction to provide for students who are characterized by great variability.
3. "To plan, implement, evaluate, and modify, in a continuing curriculum development, a curriculum which includes provision for: (a) a planned sequence of concepts in the general education areas, (b) major emphasis on the interests and skills for continued learning, (c) a balanced program of exploratory experiences and other activities and services for personal development, and (d) appropriate attention to the development of values."
4. There is emphasis upon the promotion of continuous movement through and a smooth articulation between the various phases and levels of the entire educational program.
5. To make the maximum use possible of personnel and facilities available for continuous improvement of education.

Atkins[14] mentions the following as dinstinguishing features of the middle school that promise to render it "uniquely appropriate for the children it serves:"

1. Attitudinal stance, a difference in the approach to the task at hand. "The uniqueness of the middle school is not so much a matter of organization, of grouping, of schedules, or of staffing, as it is a matter of attitude, of expectation, of sensitivity, and of perception. The mission of the school is viewed as neither remedial nor preparatory." In such a concept the transitional condition of these children is both recognized and valued.
2. The middle school is "characterized organizationally by flexibility, environmentally by sensitivity to changing needs, and instructionally by individualization." There is more awareness of the need for

reexamination of school practices in middle schools which, in turn, makes these schools more open to innovation.

3. There is an emphasis upon the shift from mastery of knowledge to utilization of knowledge. "The prominent features of the program include some form of these four ideas: diagnostic teaching, individualized instruction, self-directed learning, and learner-centered evaluation."

Compton describes the middle school as "a promising alternative to the inadequate 6-3-3 organization—it focuses attention on a portion of the school population too often treated as second-class citizens in the public schools."[15] In noting that the ". . . middle school varies from school district to school district, as well it should. . . ." Compton observes that it is just as impossible to describe *the* middle school specifically as it is to specify *the* elementary school or *the* junior high school. She did, however, point out some common elements found in middle schools:

1. Planned articulation with the elementary school that may require "a pseudo-self-contained classroom approach" for a part of the school day in the first year of the middle school program.
2. Use of subject matter specialists in a team teaching technique in closely related areas of general knowledge such as language arts, "literature, history, geography, economics, anthropology, science, art, and music."
3. Establishment of skills laboratories within the middle schools that are staffed by technologists who possess subject matter competencies to furnish "remedial, developmental, and advanced instruction in such skills as reading, listening, writing, mathematics, science, foreign language, art, music, and physical education."
4. An independent study program for all students in accord with the individual student's needs, interests, and abilities, and commensurate with the topics chosen for study.
5. Home base groups should be assigned to teachers who have special training in guidance and counseling and who also have the time and opportunity to help children both with personal and academic problems.
6. An activity program in which all students are encouraged and able to participate. Such a program is aimed at the individual student's development rather than building the school's prestige or providing public entertainment.
7. A vertical school organizational plan that permits continuous progress of students.
8. A system of evaluation and grading that is based upon individual

progress rather than some mythical average for a particular grade or chronological age group.

9. Individualized student programs designed to fit the needs of each student, and individualized student schedules.
10. A faculty and administration that is knowledgeable concerning this age group, competent in at least one subject field, and that indicate a sincere desire to provide the best program possible for the "in-between-ager."

Kopp[16] states that, "Much has been claimed by individuals who have created organizational patterns. Perhaps we need to probe a bit deeper and ask the question: Do the 'new' organizational patterns tend to meet the needs of children as identified in the accepted public school objectives?" To identify educational outcomes, he observed three "so-called basic organizational types—namely, the nongraded elementary school, the middle school, and the flexibly scheduled school." In his opinion these three patterns are not necessarily distinct and completely different patterns and may, in fact, impress one more with their similarities than with their differences. He noted the following common outcomes and trends:

1. One objective is a content achievement on an individualized basis.
2. Teachers are likely to become specialists in content areas, i.e., a teacher of English.
3. There is unscheduled time available to teachers for planning and independent work with children.
4. There is a distinct and apparent mobility of children, i.e., movement to different resource centers, laboratory facilities, and classrooms.
5. Principals are more likely to develop a feeling of involvement in and with the program.
6. There is a lack of comprehensive information about the total child. "There is a tendency to know him, for example, as a 'science' student."
7. There is a tendency for cumulative record data, which ought to be more complete and inclusive because of the kind of program, to be less comprehensive.

An informational brochure prepared by the Grosse Pointe, Michigan, Public School System is fairly specific in delineating the differences between a middle school and a junior high school:[17]

> A middle school program is designed to recognize the uniqueness of the growth stage spanning the transition from childhood to adolescence. The junior high has evolved into exactly what the name implies—*junior* high school.

Middle School Emphasizes	Junior High Emphasizes
A program that is child-centered	A program that is subject-centered
Learning how to learn	Acquiring a body of information
Creative exploration	Skill and concept mastery
A belief in oneself	Interstudent competition
Skilled guidance for student self-direction	Conformance to the teacher-made lesson plan
Students assuming responsibility for their own learning	Student learning is the responsibility of the teacher
Student independence	Control by the teacher
A flexible schedule	A six-period day
Scheduling involving student planning	A schedule administrative constructed
Variable group size	Standard classrooms
Use of team teaching	One teacher per class
Students learning at different rates—self-pacing	All students at the same place at the same time; textbook approach

Certain statements consistently appear in discussions of what the middle school is or ideally should be. Among these are dissatisfaction with the actual practices of the junior high school—although not with its stated goals and functions; the opportunities for innovation; the conviction that the middle school more nearly answers the question, "How can we best serve the educational needs of pupils who are no longer children and not quite adolescents?"[18]; and the claim that the middle school program should be a distinct entity in itself, not a carbon of the high school nor a fancy version of the elementary program. There appears to be a near-unanimous feeling that the middle school must avoid practices and curricula like those that now appear to characterize the traditional junior high school. It must establish itself as a truly middle unit in a three-segment system of American education, one comprised of elementary, middle, and high school.

WHY A MIDDLE SCHOOL

From its inception in the early 1900's there has been disagreement regarding the grades that should be included in the junior high school, although the 7-8-9 pattern has been most common. Most of those factors which originally brought the junior high school into being are much changed or no longer exist: The Committee of Ten Report in 1894 recommending that secondary education begin in grade 7 for economy of time—to begin academics such as Greek, Latin, and algebra earlier; the high pupil dropout rate of the times (as much as two-thirds by the ninth grade); and the desire to hold children in school longer and to offer prevocational and vocational courses before high school. These were supported by the influence of the new studies of adolescence, especially those of G. Stanley Hall, which lent strength to the movement toward grade reorganization.[19] It would appear, therefore, that the junior high school was instituted more as an expedient, an attempt to overcome presumed weaknesses of the 8-4 system rather than as a response to expressed and proven educational values. Indeed, it was strongly recommended by some educational authorities that the schools establish the 6-6 division as standard.

As the years passed, compulsory attendance laws and child labor laws have reduced the problem of early dropouts and the need for early vocational education, and more importance has been attached in the junior high school to guidance, exploration, and to providing a transition from elementary school to high school.

Such research as has been made provides little basis for supporting any one organizational pattern over another, whether it be the 7-8-9, 6-7-8, or 5-6-7-8. There is no lack of opinion concerning which is the best grade pattern, and the enthusiasm for personal persuasions displayed by various individuals and groups exhibits much of the militant flavor of a religious war.

Substantial agreement exists as to the advantages of having the preadolescent and early adolescent in a school situation in which they are not associating with older and more mature youth nor with younger children. There is increasing evidence of an earlier maturity of children. The majority of girls today enter puberty between the ages 10 and 12, the majority of boys between the ages 11 and 13, and these children share common developmental problems. (See Chapter 2, Adolescence.) It is also generally accepted that children of this age need an educational program that is different from the self-contained classroom of the elementary school yet is not that of the departmentalized high school. Th middle school can provide sixth-graders—and fifth-graders, if they are included—with more constructive challenges, more leadership opportunities, and more teaching specialists. Moreover, it slows down the more undesirable aspects of early sophistication and the rapid growth process.

American education has customarily been classified as elementary and secondary, with junior high school included as a part of secondary. Middle school advocates believe that it is time to recognize the third major division of education, the intermediate area, to take its place between elementary and secondary.

The middle school, it is contended, provides an educational program aimed at the 10–14 age group, one that stresses flexibility rather than the acquisition of specific skills as does the elementary school; further, it does not emphasize the specialization of the high school.[20] There is a shift to the student in responsibility for learning; students are encouraged to explore subjects on their own; assignments are designed to fit the individual student's needs, and student schedules depend upon individual student progress.[21] Too often the junior high school, it is claimed, grew too large, became too involved with high school type activities, and followed the lecture and textbook instructional techniques of the high school. The name itself, "junior high school," has been a handicap in that it carries the suggestion of "senior high school" and, by implication, relates the junior institution to senior high school practices and activities. The name also carries the connotation of immaturity.

> Looking back over the years of the movement, one can wish that the label *junior* high had never caught on. . . . As long as these schools continue to be called junior highs they may have a difficult time achieving the prestige and status owed them. . . .[22]

The name, "middle school" gives this structure a standing of its own. The middle school exists in its own right, separate from the image of the senior high school. The school is intended to depart drastically from the elements of the present junior high school which are conducive to an undesirable early sophistication. Specialization is introduced gradually in areas such as art, music, science, and industrial arts. Stress is placed upon learning in action rather than sitting, reading, and reciting.[23] Techniques, programming, and curriculum permit the greatest possible flexibility of scheduling to provide for the varying rates, abilities, and interests of the individual.[24]

The middle school may be ideally suited for nongraded classes wherein some students go through the school in two years, most in three, and a few may take four years. Basic general subjects should be offered, but there should be available an even wider range of exploratory subjects than most junior high schools provide.

Much of what has been proposed for middle schools has been attempted with differing degrees of success in a number of junior high schools. Supporters of the middle schools maintain that the junior high school, in addition to the implications of the name, suffers from a number of other disadvantages, difficulties, and problems which have not been well met. These should not afflict the middle school—at least, not to the same extent.

As an example, the Carnegie unit and the articulation of the junior high school with the high school has posed some difficulties. It is true that the Carnegie Unit is not the universally demanding restriction that it once was;

nonetheless many colleges and universities still use this system of accounting. Ninth grade is considered a part of high school, earning Units, and required to meet Unit standards in class organization. While there are ways of getting around the Unit, it is undeniably true that there are high school and junior high administrators who are fearful of tampering with the standards or who use them as an excuse for their failure to change methods, techniques, and curricula.

Many junior high schools have adopted (amid growing criticism) a wide pattern of high school type activities which contribute to a deplored early sophistication. Common in junior high are elaborate graduation exercises, night dances, night games, sophisticated dating patterns, excessive emphasis upon interscholastic athletics, marching bands, pep bands, drill teams, cheerleaders, yearbooks, and formal dinner dances.

Children of today are becoming physically mature at an earlier age, and even more evident is an earlier social sophistication.[25] Moreover, because of the increasing number of school districts which require entering first-graders to be six years old on or before October 1, children tend to be chronologically older in grade than those of thirty years ago. These factors indicate that some, perhaps most, ten- and eleven-year-olds may be better placed in a middle school than in elementary school, and also that the present ninth-grader may be better served in high school. It has been said that, developmentally, children in grades 6-7-8 are probably more alike than those in 7-8-9, and the middle school can help to slow down this aspect of sophistication in the "growing-up process."[26]

An in-service assessment of the social, physical, mental, and emotional characteristics of children from kindergarten through grade 12 was conducted by the Saginaw, Michigan, school district. It was concluded that the same traits were possessed by children from kindergarten through grade 4, that similar straits were found in children in grades 5 through 8, and that children in grades 9 through 12 had like characteristics.[27]

Jones made a comparison of the opinions, interests, and activities of ninth-graders in 1932 (using data from the Oakland Growth Study) with ninth-grades of 1953 and 1959 from the same junior high school. It was believed that the neighborhood and the socioeconomic situation of the residents had remained relatively stable during this time. Jones concluded that

> One fact is outstanding in our results. In the more recent tests, boys and girls in the ninth grade marked items in such a way as to indicate greater maturity and greater social sophistication. We now find that ninth-graders in the '50's are more comparable to the eleventh or twelfth grade students of 20 years earlier.[28]

In recent years there has been an increased stress upon academics which has frequently led to restriction of the exploratory function of the junior high schools and to more rigidity of departmentalization. District, state, and college requirements have in many instances forced the junior high school to give priority to scheduling ninth-grade classes, with the inevitable result that seventh- and eighth-grade classes are bound inextricably to the ninth-grade program.

Staffing the junior high schools has long been a problem. A study at Cornell[29] of 600 teachers found that those teaching grades 7 and 8 were markedly less satisfied with their assignments than were those teachers in both the grades above and those below. Other studies support these findings. (See Chapter 11, Staffing the Junior High.) Furthermore, there are but few teacher training programs for junior high school teachers and even fewer states with a special junior high school certification.

It has been suggested[30] that curriculum planning for the junior high school has not been successful in defining the scope and sequence of a satisfactory general education. The result of this may be that the junior high school has intensified the adolescent's disrespect for intellectual activity and heightened the ideals of athletic prowess and popularity.[31] There is but little quarrel with the stated goals of the junior high school: ". . . today's interest in a new middle school stems in part from dissatisfaction with what the junior high school has become, not with the original conception of function."[32]

There has also been a growing feeling of dissatisfaction with what are termed the inadequacies of the program and organization of the upper years of the elementary school.[33] The teaching patterns within grades 5 and 6 are too often very like those of the lower grades. The self-contained classroom predominates, and within this is frequently found the same segmentation of suject areas as that of a departmental program—without the instruction provided by specialists. A great number of elementary teachers are competent in many fields yet feel inadequate and insecure in teaching such areas as science, art, industrial arts, home economics, and physical education.

A reduction in the number of discipline problems reported by junior high school principals when the ninth grade is moved out is matched by comments from elementary principals relative to the improved disciplinary picture resulting from the placement of eleven-year-olds in middle schools. "Partly because of their . . . growth characteristics, many 11-year-olds tend to be noisy and boisterous and to create discipline problems. When they are removed from the scene, the steadier 10-year-olds do not seem to evidence the same behavior patterns."[34]

The feeling that neither the elementary schools nor the junior high schools are meeting the needs of their older students was summed up by one adminstrator, who remarked:

> I personally believe that the elementary schools are not able to satisfy the demands of fifth- and sixth-graders, and the ninth-graders seem to be intellectually apart from junior high school students. I further believe that

the K-6 and 7-8-9 arrangements are failing to meet the social, emotional, and curricular needs of children in the 11–15 age bracket.[35]

Small high schools can profit by including the ninth grade, since they are able, with a larger enrollment, to provide a wider range of offerings, both curricular and in their school activity programs.

Three principal kinds of justification for adoption of the middle school are postulated by Alexander:[36]

1. The middle school provides a program specifically designed for the wide range of individual differences and particular needs of the "in-between-ager."
2. The middle school establishes a school ladder concept that encourages continuity of instruction from school entrance to school completion.
3. The middle school, as a new organization, encourages the introduction of necessary innovations in curriculum and instruction.

There are many reasons given by school districts for changing from the 7-8-9 junior high to middle schools but the pressures of finances, building needs, enrollments, and desegregation should not be overlooked. New York City,[37] in discussing their proposed change to the 4-4-4 plan (middle schools with grades 5-6-7-8), issued a policy statement which said that there is apparent a need to move to a new intermediate program.

> The forces which produced the junior high school are not at all significant at this time. New priorities of educational need have emerged. . . . Shifts in the curriculum have radically changed the subject-matter emphasis of intermediate grades.

One educator[38] observed that what distinguishes a middle school from junior high schools or such near relatives as "upper grade centers or intermediate schools . . . [is] innovation. It seems that some districts have been primarily interested in breaking the old mold to establish a better climate for change." In this view, some districts have adopted middle schools because of a disappointment with the "worst of the junior aspects of the junior high school"—their inclination to copy the programs and activities of older children without much regard, imagination, or concern for children. The middle school provides a youthful atmosphere and a stress upon development. Other districts believe that the middle school affords better facilities for younger children, particularly in science and in fine and practical arts.

The schools of Geneva, Illinois, changed from a 6-3-3 plan to a 6-7-8 plan in 1968 for these principal reasons:[39]

1. Human growth is continuous. The middle school provides substantial advantages for a smoother transition into adolescence by maintaining continuity in educational development.
2. The middle school organization permits improvement possibilities

in "all major areas—classroom organization, special services to pupils, in-service stimulation to the professional staff."

3. The middle school provides emphasis upon intellectual development "with its opportunities for special staff, facilities, and program."
4. The middle school encourages an atmosphere free from many pressures that exist in the junior high school—social, academic, and athletic.

Moss[40] holds that ". . . a new organizational pattern has evolved." This, he says, is the natural development of the change from the 8-4 plan to that of the 6-3-3 which took place in the early 1900's.

> With the appearance of the so-called middle school, comprising grades 6 through 8, or 5 through 8, a second phase of the organization movement is already underway. . . . Perhaps it is still too early to expect clearly defined purposes for the middle school. However, there is a parallel between the early history of the middle school and the appearance of the first junior high school.[41]

The rationale for the middle school will include such factors as

1. Children now reach puberty at an earlier age; therefore, sixth-graders can be better served in a school with grades 6-7-8.
2. The middle school is not restricted by college entrance requirements nor Carnegie Units. Therefore, greater curriculum experimentation is possible and the school can concentrate upon the needs of 11–14 year olds.
3. "Ideally, middle school certification will be developed which will result in teachers trained especially to work with this age group."[42]
4. It will be easier to develop a nongraded structure that will make possible a smoother transition from elementary school to high school.
5. It will be possible to put more emphasis upon a program of educational guidance specifically designed for this grade level.
6. The problem of college orientation for the ninth grade is eliminated.

Pumerantz,[43] in noting that more than 1,100 middle schools were in operation in 1967–68, observed:

> The forces behind this movement are numerous. A good deal of the professional literature suggests that the junior high school has not fulfilled its original purposes and functions. Moreover, studies documenting earlier maturational trends of today's youngsters make impressive points which support the planning and implementation of middle school programs and organization as a more viable alternative to the junior high school.

A middle school principal, in discussing the advantages he perceived in this organizational pattern, emphasized that the middle school,

> . . . being unencumbered by the requirements of the high school, has the opportunity to develop an identity which is uniquely characteristic of the boys and girls it serves. No outside rules can be inflicted upon it for the only requirement placed against it is the demands of meeting the needs of boys and girls in early adolescence.[44]

In summary, the more commonly stated reasons for adopting the middle school organization are:

1. Earlier maturity of children.
2. Permit a program especially designed for this age group.
3. To provide better transition for elementary and high school.
4. To provide a better elementary program.
5. To overcome the weaknesses of the junior high school.
6. To initiate various innovations.
7. To move the ninth grade into the high school and the sixth (or fifth and sixth) grade into the middle school.
8. To alleviate problems of finances, enrollments, buildings, community pressures, and de facto segregation.

SURVEYS, ADVANTAGES, AND LIMITATIONS

The growing interest in middle schools has sparked several surveys which have endeavored to ascertain practices, curricula, advantages, disadvantages, and the number of such schools actually in operation. As early as 1949 the National Education Association, in a survey of city school organizations,[45] found that 12 percent of the secondary schools in the cities sampled were of the 6-2-4 organization and 2 percent were 5-3-4.

A 1964 follow-up[46] on a 1954 study indicated that junior high schools with grades 7-8-9 constituted 74.3 percent of the total junior high schools; 19.3 percent were those with grades 7-8; and all other grade combinations were 6.4 percent of the total.

A survey[47] which reported results from 40 percent of the nation's school systems found that 10 percent of these had middle schools with 5-6-7-8 or 6-7-8 or were changing to one of these patterns in the 1964–65 school year.

A nationwide survey of middle schools in the 1965–66 school year produced information concerning middle schools in 44 states and indicated that 446 public school districts in 29 states were operating 499 middle schools.[48] An Indiana survey[49] in 1967 found that only 82 of the 134 junior highs had a seventh grade, 131 an eighth grade, 16 a sixth grade, and one school had a tenth grade. Diversity appears to be common.

Some of these investigations reported what were believed to be advantages and disadvantages of the middle school organization. A survey of administrators of New York State Middle Schools[50] found that the chief advantage was the "synthesis of elementary and secondary teacher attitudes in such a school." They also felt that there was a movement in the middle schools away from the more traditional college preparatory practices of the junior high school.

As an observation it appeared to the respondents that grades 6-7-8 were more compatible than were 7-8-9. Fewer discipline problems were noted and sixth graders developed self-discipline earlier.

Other claimed advantages included: lessening of tension in the middle school because of no college preparatory requirements; earlier opportunities for sixth graders in some subjects and activities; more individual attention for sixth-graders; more opportunities to experiment with new programs; and fewer discipline problems with the ninth grade in the senior high school than had been the case when the ninth grade was in the junior high school.

Stated disadvantages included: problems in teacher certification; break in syllabi and teacher handbooks between grades 6 and 7; apparent inability of eighth-graders to assume leadership; need of ninth-graders for a year of leadership; and the fact that girls mature somewhat sooner than do boys.

Additional advantages claimed by respondents in the previously mentioned Educational Research Survey[51] were:

1. Uniqueness of 5-3-4 or 4-4-4 encourages creativity in both administration and teaching. This in turn improves teacher morale.
2. Special facilities, such as shop areas and laboratories for home economics are available to fifth- and sixth-graders.
3. Special services are available to fifth- and sixth-graders.
4. Improved facilities and services are available to ninth graders in the senior high schools.
5. No influence or limitation by the Carnegie Unit.
6. More homogeneous groupings.

Certain limitations were also noted by respondents to the 1965 Educational Research survey:

1. Requires more teacher time to plan and prepare.
2. Problems of scheduling may be complicated.
3. Reporting pupil progress may be more difficult.
4. Fifth-graders may be too immature.
5. More time and effort are required to keep teachers informed.

As a part of a 1965–66 study of middle schools in Oregon and Washington[52] there was considerable correspondence with districts operating middle schools throughout the United States. The study and the correspondence provided further stated advantages and disadvantages:

1. Losing grade 9 is losing activities and attitudes that are too mature; we also gain by eliminating varsity athletics, marching bands, sophisticated activities.
2. Creates more opportunities for staff utilization, flexible scheduling, independent study, team instruction.

3. Permits ungraded classes.
4. Easier to use ability grouping.

Named disadvantages included:

1. Sometimes the middle school, as the junior high school before it, is handicapped by inherited building facilities which are unsuitable.
2. It is easy to assume too much student maturity.
3. The grade organizational pattern of middle schools is weakened by its own flexibility; it is too easy for the administration to add or subtract a grade.

Of some interest is a questionnaire survey[53] of 186 school districts in the state of Washington, 1965, which requested information concerning changes contemplated in grade organization and the reasons therefore. Following are some of the typical reasons given:

1. We are convinced our ninth grade is better served in high school.
2. We will not longer be involved with the Carnegie Unit in 6-7-8.
3. Because of future housing requirements.
4. Better utilization of buildings and classrooms.
5. Building organization, finances, curriculum development.
6. Reduce overloading in elementary.
7. Believe grade 9 is too mature for 7 and 8.
8. Believe 5-3-4 is a better educational and social division.
9. Four-year senior high is easier to administer.
10. People seem to resent the earlier maturity fostered by junior high.
11. For a small district, 5-3-4 provides larger junior and senior high school student bodies. It also separates children better by age.
12. Present system (6-3-3) is too rigid.
13. Better use of teacher specialization.
14. Building program.
15. We have some concern and reservations about our junior high schools.

Zdanowicz,[54] in his investigation of changes in junior high schools in the Northeastern United States, found that approximately 16 percent had changed from the traditional 7-8-9 pattern to a middle school organization of 6-7-8 or 5-6-7-8. He concluded that the impressive increase in the number of intermediate schools in the Northeast was overshadowed by the proportionately greater increase in the number of middle schools. Most of the middle schools had been recently organized, and he found also that some junior high schools were in the process of investigating a change to the middle school pattern.

In 1966 Brod[55] stated that the data acquired from approximately 40 percent of the school systems of the nation indicated that 10 percent of these had moved or were moving to a middle school of 5-3-4 or 4-4-4 organization.

In 1967–68 Alexander[56] conducted a study designed to ascertain the growth of the middle school movement. He used a 10 percent sampling of the ten regions in the nation as described by the USOE and determined that there were, in the 1967–68 school year, 1,101 middle schools in the United States. This is twice the number that Cuff found (499) in his 1965–66 survey. Middle schools in both studies were defined as having grades 6 and 7 and not extending below grade 4 nor above grade 8. He found that 66 percent of the middle schools contained grades 6–8, 30 percent were 5–8 schools, and the remainder were schools with grades 4–8, 5–7, 6–9, and 4–7. Enrollment in the middle schools varied from below 100 students to over 1,300, with approximately 75 percent of the schools in the 300–1,000 student enrollment range. While only 10.4 percent of the schools were established before 1960, 42.9 percent were established during 1966–67.

Reasons given by the responding principals for adopting the middle school pattern included:

1. Elimination of crowded conditions in other schools.
2. To provide a program specifically designed for this age group.
3. To better bridge the elementary and the high school.
4. To provide more specialization in grades 5 and/or 6.
5. To shift grade 9 into the high school.
6. To remedy the weaknesses of the junior high school.
7. To try out various innovations.
8. To utilize a new school building.
9. To use plans that have been successful in other school systems.
10. To aid desegregation.

It was reported that 30 percent of the responding middle schools in this study were using variable and modular schedules that differed from the traditional uniform daily schedule of equal periods. Twenty percent of the schools provided independent study arrangements. Team teaching, although little used, was more often found in recently established schools, and many respondents indicated future plans for the development of such patterns. There was much variability in reporting and marking practices; a wide range of exploratory curriculum opportunities were available in the larger schools, and interest was expressed by several respondents in developing expanded programs.

The Educational Research Service of the American Association of School Administrators[57] reported in the spring of 1969 a survey of 51 school systems in 23 states. The survey identified 154 middle schools in school systems with enrollments of 12,000 or more. Ninety-seven of the schools had been middle schools less than three years and 43 of these opened in September 1968. Enrollment in the middle schools ranged from 227 students to 2,160, with the greatest number in the 500–1,000 student range. Forty-four of the 154 middle schools were housed in facilities especially constructed for this purpose; 46 were formerly 7-8-9 junior high schools; 18

were K–6 or K–8 elementary schools; 11 were previously senior high schools; 11 were 1–12 union schools; and 6 were 7-8 intermediate schools.

The responding principals in their statements ran the gamut from extreme dissatisfaction with the middle school plan to a sincere enthusiasm. The most commonly reported problem was the lack of adequate facilities, usually the need for special purpose rooms for large-group–small-group instruction, and rooms necessary for special subjects such as industrial arts. Difficulties encountered in recruiting properly prepared teachers were a principal problem as was orienting teachers and parents to the middle school philosophy and instructional patterns.

Other reported problems included:

1. Lack of precedent, necessary to develop the program as we go along.
2. Need for teachers to develop the proper attitude toward children of this age group.
3. Rigidity of district provided program and materials.
4. Slowness of accrediting agencies to adapt to the new patterns.
5. Difficulty in developing a flexible curriculum in terms of needs of specific students.
6. Teachers inadequately trained and oriented to the middle school philosophy.
7. Teacher resistance to change, to flexible scheduling, and to nonrigid lesson planning.
8. "Many school activities conflict with having the elementary and secondary grades together; there are many things these grades cannot do in common such as participation in interschool athletics and band."[58]

One wonders if the principals who made the last comment have missed a part of the rationale for the middle school, i.e., to avoid exactly that kind of activity for all grades included in the middle school. Such a comment is not, however, uncommon. Another principal responding in the same survey observed that, "We have had to curtail to some degree our extracurricular program in athletics, band and vocal music, and science, which has brought some unfavorable parent reaction."[59] Two points should be made here. (1) Any educational program should be designed for what is best for children and this should be stressed and explained to the public and (2) one of the most frequently encountered problems in the junior high school is that of high school type activities—and this poses a difficulty for the middle school—i.e., administrators, teachers, and parents who see the new middle school as a new kind of junior high school that ends with grade 8 instead of grade 9.[60]

The respondents states these favorable reactions to the middle school:

1. Permits the school to provide the continuity of program necessary

to help the individual students to develop their abilities to the fullest extent possible.
2. There is more time available for the student to identify with the school.
3. It is possible to retain the best features of the elementary school and still provide desirable specialization.
4. Offers an excellent transition from the elementary grades to the more departmentalized system.
5. "The most outstanding feature of our instructional program so far has been the enthusiasm of our faculty and the harmony that exists among the interdisciplinary teams.[61]
6. Team teachers have done a great deal toward providing student individualized instruction.
7. Emphasis placed upon intramurals has improved student self-concepts.
8. More time in the classroom, inasmuch as we have no longer the problems of pep rallies or popularity contests.
9. Problems engendered by the ninth grade are no longer with us.
10. We believe that the greatest advantage is that 6-7-8-graders are more compatible than 7-8-9.
11. Since we no longer have a "watered-down high school," we have an opportunity to function in a setting that provides better teaching for children in a more compatible grade situation.
12. There are great advantages in operating without the junior high and senior high pressures. Since the Carnegie Unit is no longer a factor, there are more opportunities to provide individualized instruction.
13. The middle school concept is an opportunity to start afresh. Teachers and parents must understand that the middle school is much more than a grade organization.
14. "In reality there are no disadvantages to a middle school." (!)

This last comment, if nationally true, should certainly end all argument and discussion relative to the merits, claims, advantages, and disadvantages of the middle school. The debate, however, still exists and as heatedly as before. It is still too early, except in some parts of the country, to accept unequivocally such as statement as "It is rather clear at this juncture that the junior high school-middle school-intermediate school debate is at an end. Middle schools and intermediate schools exist and will continue to exist."[62]

The author strikes to the center of the problem, however, when he goes on to say, "Our problems now do not consist of debating their relative merits but rather of answering some basic questions on curriculum, organization, function, and teacher effectiveness, among other topics."[63]

The middle school must be more than another grouping of grades. To be effective it must be a truly different approach to the education of the preadolescent and early adolescent. It *does* provide an opportunity for a new start. The situation was well put by Pumerantz:

> If there is to be change in the traditional public school organization, we are obliged to insure that it be an improvement and not just an innovation, that the change be substantive and not just a rearrangement of form."[64]

SUMMARY

Variations from the junior high school pattern of 7-8-9 have existed for many years. In the 1914–18 period, for example, Davis[65] reported that 7.5 percent of junior high schools were 6-7-8 schools, and Douglass[66] found, for the same period, that 6 percent of reported junior high schools were 6-7-8 schools. During this same period of time there were schools operating with grade combinations of 5–7, 5–8, 6–7, 6–7, 7–8, 7–9, 7–10, 8–9, and 8–10.

In the past few years, however, there has been increased interest, experimentation, and investigation of what are commonly called "middle schools" which contain grades 6-7-8 in a 5-3-4 plan or include grades 5-6-7-8 in a 4-4 plan. Several reasons have been offered for the change including earlier maturity of children, increased sophistication, the stigma of the "junior" name, college and high school requirements, the influence of the Carnegie Unit, tendency of the junior high school to mimic the high school, and the need for a third division in teacher training and public education: the middle school between elementary on one side and secondary on the other. Not so often given as reasons but sometimes the real causes are district finances, building problems, enrollment, and consolidation. Surveys indicate that the interest in middle schools as well as their number is increasing. Claimed advantages outnumber the disadvantages, which may be due to the halo effect, or the actual benefits of middle schools. Some educators go so far as to assert that the middle school concept may become the major educational development of our times. In discussing this, Vars summed it up neatly:

> Whether we regard the change from the junior high to the middle school as a revolution, a reformation, or a collossal mistake, let us seize this golden opportunity to make a fresh approach toward the goals we have always held for schools for young adolescents, however they are organized and whatever they are called.[67]

REFERENCES

1. Gordon F. Vars (ed.), "Guidelines for Junior High and Middle School Education," monograph. Washington, D.C.: NASSP, 1966, p. 1.
2. Samuel Popper, *The American Middle School.* Waltham, Mass.: Blaisdell, 1967.
3. "Middle Schools," *Educational Research Circular* No. 3, American Association of School Administrators and Research Division, May 1965.
4. Philip Pumerantz, "State Recognition of the Middle School," *NASSP Bulletin,* Vol. 53 (March 1969), p. 16.
5. "Middle Schools in Theory and in Fact," *NEA Research Bulletin,* vol. 47 (May 1969), p. 49.
6. *Ibid.*
7. *Ibid.,* p. 50.
8. Emmett L. Williams, "The Middle School Movement," *Today's Education,* Vol. 57 (December 1968), p. 41.
9. *Ibid.,* p. 42.
10. *School Building Project Procedures: A Guide for the School Building Committee,* The School Building Economy Series. Hartford, Connecticut: State Department of Education, May 1968, p. 1.
11. William M. Alexander, Emmett L. Williams, Mary Compton, Vynce A. Hynes, and Dan Precott, *The Emergent Middle School.* New York: Holt, 1968, pp. 4–5.
12. *Ibid.*
13. Joann Strickland and William Alexander, "Seeking Continuity in Early and Middle School Education," *Phi Delta* Kappan, Vo. 50 (March 1969), p. 398.
14. Neil P. Atkins, "Rethinking Education in the Middle," *Theory Into Practice.* Columbus: Ohio State University College of Education, June 1968, pp. 118–119.
15. Mary F. Compton, "The Middle School: Alternative to the Status Quo," *Theory Into Practice.* Columbus: Ohio State University College of Education, June 1968, p. 110.
16. O. W. Kopp, "The School Organization Syndrome vis-à-vis Improved Learning," *National Elementary Principal,* Vol. 48 (February 1969), pp. 42–45.
17. "Middle Schools in Action," *Educational Research Circular* No. 2, American Association of School Administrators and Research Division, March 1969, p. 17.
18. Emmett L. Williams, loc. cit.
19. Paul Woodring, "The New Intermediate School," *Saturday Review,* Vol. 48 (Oct. 16, 1965), p. 77.
20. M. Ann Grooms, *Perspectives on the Middle School.* Columbus: Merrill, 1967, p. 4.
21. "What's New At School," *Wall Street Journal,* Oct. 12, 1967.
22. William Van Til, Gordon F. Vars, and John H. Lounsbury, *Modern Education for the Junior High School Years.* 2d ed. Indianaoplis: Bobbs-Merrill, 1967, pp. 51–52.
23. W. D. Boutwell, "What Are Middle Schools?" *PTA Magazine,* Vol. 60 (December 1965) p. 14.
24. Judith Murphy, *Middle Schools,* monograph. New York: Educational Facilities Laboratories, Inc., 1965, p. 7.
25. Gordon F. Vars., *op. cit.,* p. 3.

26. Pearl Brod, "The Middle School: Trends Toward Its Adoption," *Clearing House*, Vol. 40 (February 1966), P. 331.
27. George E. Mills, "The How and Why of the Middle School," *Nation's Schools*, Vol. 68 (December 1961), pp. 43–53.
28. Mary C. Jones, "A Comparison of the Attitudes and Interests of Ninth Grade Students Over Two Decades," *Journal of Educational Psychology*, Vol. 51 (August 1960), pp. 178–179.
29. Mauritz Johnson, JR., "School in the Middle, Junior High: Education's Problem Child," *Saturday Review*, VOl. 45 (July 21, 1962), p. 41.
30. William M. Alexander, "The Junior High School: A Changing View," *NASSP Bulletin*, Vol. 48 (March 1964), p. 18.
31. *Ibid.*
32. Alexander and associates, *The Emergent Middle School*, p. 4.
33. Compton, *op. cit.*, p. 108.
34. Theodore C. Moss, "The Middle School Comes—And Takes Another Grade or Two," *National Elementary Principal*, Vol. 48 (February 1969) p. 40.
35. ERS Circular No. 2, 1969, p. 13.
36. Adapted from Alexander and associates, *The Emergent Middle School*, p. 11.
37. "Farewell to Junior High," *Education USA* (April 1965), p. 143.
38. Roy C. Turnbaugh, "The Middle School, A Different Name or a New Concept?" *Clearing House*, Vol. 43 (October 1968), p. 87.
39. *Ibid.*, p. 88.
40. Theodore C. Moss, *Middle School.* Boston: Houghton, 1969, p. 18.
41. *Ibid.*, pp. 18–19.
42. *Ibid.*, p. 19.
43. Pumerantz, *ibid.*, p. 14.
44. Eugene E. Regan, "The Junior High School Is Dead," *Clearing House*, Vol. 41 (November 1967), p. 151.
45. "Trends in City School Organization 1938–1948," *NEA Research Bulletin*, Vol. 27 (February 1949), p. 11.
46. John H. Lounsbury and Harl Douglass, "Recent Trends in Junior High School Practices," *NASSP Bulletin*, Vol. 49 (September 1965), p. 90.
47. Pearl Brod, *op. cit.*, p. 332.
48. William A. Cuffı, "Middle Schools on the March," *NASSP Bulletin*, Vol. 51 (February 1967), pp. 82–86.
49. Max Bough, "Indian Junior High Schools—1967," *Indiana State University Teachers College Journal*, Vol. 39 (November 1967), pp. 72–73.
50. Thomas E. Curtis, "Administrators View the Middle School," *High Points*, Vol. 48 (March 1966), p. 31.
51. ERS Circular No. 3, 1965, *op. cit.*
52. Alvin W. Howard, *Middle Schools in Oregon and Washington 1965–66*, unpublished doctoral dissertation, University of Oregon, 1966.
53. "Grade Organizational Plans," *School Information and Research Service*, Seattle, Wash., March 9, 1965.
54. Paul J. Zdanowicz, "A Study of the Changes That Have Taken Place in the Junior High Schools of the Northeastern United States During the Last Decade

and the Reasons for Some of the Changes," unpublished doctoral dissertation, Temple University, June 1965.
55. Brod., *op. cit.*
56. William M. Alexander, "The Middle School Movement," *Theory Into Practice.* Columbus: Ohio State University College of Education, June 1968, pp. 114–117.
57. ERS Circular No. 2, 1969. *op. cit.*
58. *Ibid.*, p. 14.
59. *Ibid.*, p. 13.
60. A. W. Howard, unpublished doctoral dissertation.
61. ERS Circular No, 2, 1969, p. 12
62. Thomas E. Curtis, "The Middle School in Theory and Practice," *NASSP Bulletin*, Vol. 52 (May 1968), p. 140.
63. *Loc. cit.*
64. Philip Pumerantz, "Imperatives in the Junior High and Middle School Dialogue," *Clearing House*, Vol. 43 (December 1968), p. 211.
65. Calvin O. Davis, "Junior High Schools in the North Central Association Territory," *School Review*, Vol. 26 (May 1918), pp. 324–336.
66. Aubrey A. Douglass, *The Junior High School*, Fifteenth Yearbook of the National Society for the Study of Education, Part III. Bloomington, Ill.: Public School Publishing Company, 1917, p. 88.
67. Gordon F. Vars, "Junior High or Middle School? Which is Best for the Education of Young Adolescents?" *High School Journal*, Vol. 50 (December 1966), pp. 109–113.

chapter 9

Criticism and Conflict: Which Grades in the Middle?

While strong opinions and fervent oratory are not lacking in any discussion of which grades should be included in the junior high or middle schools, this is precisely where the conflict centers. Only a few support a return to the 8-4 system and the abolition of a separate institution between elementary and senior high school. It is certainly reasonable to wonder why it should make any difference if grade 9 is found in a 7-8-9 plan or grade 6 is in a 6-7-8 school. What value is there is grade shuffling? How can this improve the educational program?

The advocates of middle schools content that an instructional pattern is contemplated for middle schools which is neither elementary nor secondary but is the third division in American education—elementary, middle and secondary. They believe that a school for preadolescents should bracket the grades where most of these children are to be found: 6-7-8 or 5-6-7-8. Grade 9 has become older, more sophisticated, and more mature than was formerly the case, and does not belong with younger children. Ninth-graders have more in common with tenth-graders and will be provided with a better education in a senior high school situation.

Certainly the junior high school has been the target of a substantial amount of criticism, much of this since the middle 1950's, and unfortunately some of it justified. Grade reorganization is not always presented as the solution; sometimes the criticism warns that the curriculum needs revision, sometimes it is said that teaching and administration are weak at this level and need strengthening, and often the critics rap the sophisticated junior high practices which differ little from those of the senior high school.

CRITICISM AND CONFLICT

Research may be scanty but convictions are strong, and educators have no hesitation in pronouncing positive judgment. For example, one superintendent of schools said flatly,

> The junior high school, in my opinion, may be American's greatest educational blunder. . . . It initially was an administrative device for controlling children in large groups rather than an organized effort to improve instruction.[1]

According to one principal,[2] ninth-graders are "Curriculum Misfits" and the 6-3-3 plan is so traditional that it is taken for granted and actually "corsets out ninth-grade group. Let's not kid ourselves that our present organizational patterns are adequate."

Junior high school supporters reply that there have been for many years patterns other than 6-3-3. What evidence is there that these have accomplished any more or have been any more successful than the 6-3-3 plan?

One inquiry,[3] which reported evaluations of 245 elementary and secondary teachers in Michigan, posed the wistful question, "The Junior High School—Weakest Rung in the Educational Ladder?" The conclusions were that, so far as staffing and teaching were concerned, the junior high did find itself weaker than elementary or senior high school. The author went on to observe that it seemed evident that the poorest teaching was perceived at the junior high school level. Although elementary and high school teachers were also observed, junior high school teachers were judged to be significantly less effective than other levels.

A valid criticism of the junior high school is that few states have separate preparation and certification programs for prospective junior high school teachers. In describing his situation one educator observed

> After 60 years the junior high school remains a no-man's land in teacher certification. . . . While extensions of elementary certificates have no doubt provided many fine teachers, they are hybrids at best and are not trained junior high school teachers.[4]

As Alexander[5] points out, teachers possessing teaching certificates in elementary education were felt to be competent to teach grades K–8, and those teachers who held secondary certificates were believed trained for grades 7–12. Actually, because of the lack of junior high coursework and preparation, the poorest teacher training in any area has been that of junior high teachers.

Wattenberg commented acidly but accurately upon this weakness when he said,

> . . . At colleges and universities there is a tendency to make believe that there is no such institution [referring to the junior high school]; schools are considered either elementary or secondary, young people either are children or adolescents.[6]

Junior high school champions point out that staffing the middle school will be no easier than staffing the junior high has been. In fact, it may be even more difficult. There are few teacher training programs for prospective junior high school teachers and even fewer if any designed specifically for teachers in middle schools.

In complaining that the junior high school is heavily burdened with the practices and traditions of the senior high school, one educator found much to condemn when he asked, "What's Wrong With Junior High School? Nearly Everything."[7] The junior high school, he believes, needs a more appropriate name and a freedom and identity of its own. At present it is a prep school for senior high, and apes senior high athletics, social life, class scheduling, and departmentalization.

Activities such as interscholastic athletics and marching bands in junior high receive considerable unfavorable comment. Conant[8] denounced these activities roundly when he said that there were no sound educational reasons for interscholastic athletics and marching bands in junior high schools, that such activities were to be condemned.

Social activities which are too sophisticated and come too soon are often a part of seventh- and eighth-grade life in a 7-8-9 junior high school. The school can easily become a pale copy of the high school.[9] Many junior high schools have, in some opinions,[10] become much more than pale carbons of the high schools they imitate.

As one principal observed, ". . . while the theory of the junior high school is excellent, in practice it has resulted in junior high schools becoming miniature senior high schools."[11]

It should be remembered, however, that there are junior high schools that have a minimum of these activities while there are ". . . some kindergarten-to-eighth-grade elementary schools [that] have well-drilled marching bands."[12]

This unfortunate tendency of many junior high schools to adopt virtually the full activity curriculum of the high schools—interscholastic athletics, night games, formal dances, fanfare, and excitement—has brought about a great deal of the most biting criticism. There is some truth to the occasionally bitter rebuttal of the junior high educators when they complain that community pressures force them to provide such activities, that not all junior high schools are guilty of these excesses, and that much depends upon the positions taken by individual principals.

These arguments lose some of their force when surveys[13] indicate that the great majority of junior high schools have interscholastic athletics and that over three-fourths of the junior high principals support such a program. As one study reported,

> The question of interscholastic athletic competition versus a well-constructed intramural program brought some interesting results. Approximately 86 percent [of the junior high schools] have some interscholastic competition, and most principals consider it appropriate in most sports, the limitation being football for ninth-graders."[14]

Related to the question of early sophistication and advanced activities is the criticism that the junior high school, in stressing athletic prowess for boys and popularity for girls, has unintentionally increased the "disrespect for intellectual activity too common among adolescents."[15]

This complaint has been voiced before in connection with some rather strong statements concerning the transitional function of the junior high, and the need for curriculum revision.[16]

"What is the junior high school idea? In a word, asylum. Within this transition school . . . pubescence can be experienced without trauma or trepidation. The author, Mauritz Johnson, Jr., of Cornell, does not advocate elimination of the junior high school nor, necessarily, a move to a middle school, but he does complain of the "disconcertingly little attention to the primary responsibility of any educational institution, intellectual development."

He adds that the junior high schools have attempted to be all things to all people with the inevitable result that they do little very well. The junior high school promised too much: healthy individuals, sound moral character, job competency, wise use of leisure; and is then expected to produce "worthy parents and good citizens to boot. Indeed, some assurance was offered that . . . the pupil might enjoy popularity among his peers, a tranquil adolescence, and protection from a sense of failure and frustration."[17]

In a later statement[18] Johnson remarked that the current middle school movement was but a continuation of an earlier one and it involves a further downward extension of secondary education. He cautions that there has been no evidence presented that the same results postulated for middle schools could not be obtained by introducing certain feature of secondary education within the present elementary school structure.

Moss[19] agrees that transition and articulation have been made easier for ninth-graders by moving the ninth-grade curriculum to the junior high school, but he doubts that the transition for the seventh-grader has been effective in the junior high school. In too many junior high schools there has been little attention given to easing the transition from a self-contained elementary classroom to a fully departmentalized junior high school. "The gradual transition envisioned by junior high school prophets gave way to clanging bells, scurrying students, a strange large building and unfamiliar faces."[20] It has also been said[21] that the junior high subject matter curriculum is but a "boiled-down version of the more specialized high school courses," particularly as it is found in biological science, physical science, American history, and civics. One could then reasonably expect to find the same methods, materials, and possibly some of the same textbooks in both the junior and senior high schools.

The New York City School Board, in deciding to change to a 4-4-4 plan, thus converting all junior high schools to 5-6-7-8, received a strong reaction from the New York Junior High Principals Association. The change, proposed because of "the need for high-quality instruction and racial integration,"[22] was met by advertisements in the New York Times taken by the Junior High Principals Association, protesting the move:

> Parents: The Junior High Principals Association Believes Your Child Belongs in Junior High School. . . . Principals Do Have Principles. We Want What Is Best For Your Child.[23]

Several points were made in the advertisement, including

1. The importance of the individual child in a full time program in a 1,500-student junior high school (as opposed to an afternoon student in a senior high).
2. Junior High schools have programs and facilities for enrichment in art, music, science, and activities which are not available to split shift freshmen in a high school.
3. Teachers in junior high school know and are trained to work with early adolescents.
4. A program of quality and integrated education can be achieved within the present 7-8-9 junior high without wasting millions in moving grade 9.

The advertisement, though well intentioned, may have done more harm than good. Proponents of middle schools seized happily upon several of these statements, for example, "Quality education *can* be achieved within the present 7-8-9 framework," and, "Teachers in junior high school know and are trained to work with early adolescents." If quality education *can* be achieved, they ask, why, in more than fifty years, has it *not* been achieved? What have the junior high people been waiting for? The statement concerning teachers trained especially for junior high school brought an even sharper reaction. They point out that few teachers in the country have been specifically trained for junior high school, and furthermore it is common knowledge that New York City has an inordinately high percentage of daily substitute teachers in its secondary schools.

Many of the issues were clarified and more sharply delineated by a New York junior high school principal, Paul Gastwirth, who charged[24] that there is a real problem of definition of middle schools. So much diversity in grades and in organizing principles is permitted and included that it is impossible to know what is being discussed. Mr. Gastwirth believes that the heart of the issue is that the standard junior high school with grades 7-8-9 provides the best education for the early adolescent. He decries statements such as Conant's that the kind of grade organization for the early adolescent is not as important as the kind of program supplied. Grade organization, he feels, is a vital factor. (It is fair to remind all of us in junior high school education that 7-8-9 junior high school is not the only type. One may find schools that are 7-8, 8-9, 6–8, 5–9, and 6–9, all of which consider themselves to be and bear the label, "junior high school.")

Among "Questions Facing the Middle School" is a list of some two dozen items described to Mr. Gastwirth as characteristic of middle schools. The list included a new building, effective use of school plant, flexible schedules, home economics and industrial arts, foreign language instruction, large and small group activities, air conditioning, library carrels, team teaching, nongradedness, and use of television. The point is made that none of these differentiate a 5–8 middle school from a conventional junior high school. In opposition to this statement it is reasonable to point out (1) that the items listed are largely mechanical, procedural, and are to be found in some schools at any level, and (2) that it would be very nice to find these items in all conventional junior high schools but that not many junior high schools can claim even half the list, and very few can claim all.

The article mentions criticisms of the traditional junior high school such as strict departmentalization, sophisticated extracurricular activities, marching bands, too much stress on interscholastic athletics, and high school type social events such as the senior prom. Gastwirth concludes that, with the exception of departmentalization, the criticisms are "superficial and peripheral," since the "number of schools is small to which such criticisms apply," and these objectionable features "can be eliminated or mitigated without undue difficulty." That only a small number of junior high schools are guilty of these practices is most debatable,[25] and a legitimate question here is, if such practices are easily mitigated or eliminated, why haven't they been? Surely this is one of the most sensitive aspects of the present junior high school and if these practices are undesirable for children of this age it would appear reasonable for steps to be taken to correct the problem.

A point well taken is Gastwirth's question: What assurance is there that the same problems will not afflict the middle schools? The unhappy truth is that, at least in some cases, this very situation does exist in middle schools.[26]

Finally, Gastwirth is "appalled" that contradictory reasons are given in different places for adoption of the middle schools, other than a belief that this is educationally better, include increasing enrollments, integration, retirement of old buildings, city population shifts, pressures for the restoration of the four-year high school, and criticisms of the junior high school.[27] It is worth noting, however, that adoption of other patterns, including the 6-3-3, has also been subject to a variety of reasons other than educational value.[28] So long as school districts have pressures of enrollments, finances, politics, and people, there will be instances of adoption by necessity and expediency.

Some very good arguments in support of the junior high school and in opposition to the middle school were made by Richard L. Post, a junior high school principal who described the middle school as "A Questionable Innovation."[29] The article voices the fears that "educational gimmickry is being substituted for genuine innovation." Educational innovations offering promise for the stimulation of instruction are primarily independent study, continuous progress curricula, team teaching, and flexible scheduling. Post "fails to see how the transfer of the ninth grade to the senior high and the fifth and sixth grades to the middle school can help us to move in this direction." He emphasizes that movement of the ninth grade into a more subject-centered school and the increasing departmentalization of fifth- and sixth-grade curricula "may set education back 50 years." Priority consideration should be given to where the ninth-grader will be provided the most appropriate program.

The social problems likely to accrue from moving ninth-graders into a four-year high school are, Post feels, an even more serious consequence.

> I do not see what useful purpose can be served by having 14 year-old girls going to the junior prom and riding home in cars with 18-year-old boys. . . . We should not encourage earlier sophistication of their social activities since early marriage is still an economic mistake and dating activities should be deferred as long as possible.

So far as interscholastic athletics are concerned, Post believes such activities will still exist if the community wants them, and the community will have them regardless of what grades are grouped in any given school. If these activities are likely to be available in the form of Pee Wee Leagues, Little Leagues, or the like, the children might be better served by having such programs under the direction of educators rather than under whatever citizen of the community is ready and willing to take responsibility. "If practices aping the senior high are undesirable—stop them."

This last admonition is well put and is easily applicable to both junior high and middle school faculties and administrators. It is often true that it is not necessarily the type of school that is at fault. Community pressures, and the ability of the administration and teachers to withstand such pressures, then become the deciding factors.

Another point frequently made by the supporters of the 7-8-9 junior high school is that there will be a distinct loss and perhaps an elimination of opportunities for leadership for ninth-graders. As the bottom grade in a four-year high school provision for developing leadership will of necessity be much curtailed. In a 7-8-9 school, members of the ninth grade customarily hold the majority of student offices, develop and form committees to deal with various problems and activities, and constitute the major part of the membership of the interscholastic athletic teams. It is also possible that the absence of the ninth-graders will permit a situation in which there are three levels of immaturity in a 6-7-8 school.

Middle school advocates insist that these same leadership opportunities are available to eighth-graders in middle schools. They maintain that the only difference, aside from the reduction or elimination of interscholastic sports, is that children are provided with training and opportunities in leadership a year earlier than has previously been the case, a training that develops ninth-graders who are better able to take responsibility when they enter high school. So far as three levels of immaturity are concerned in a 6-7-8 school, quite the converse is true it is claimed. Without the ninth-graders seizing leadership opportunities, the middle school student, who is achieving an earlier maturity, may move into the kind of responsibility and self-direction which is desired and which is provided by a good middle school program.

Supporters of the 7-8-9 junior high school have, frequently with justification, accused those who favor reorganization of playing the numbers game. Their position is clear: if the junior high school exhibits symptoms of ills, why amputate? There is no indication, evidence, or proof that reorganization is a cure-all, nor, for that matter, of any real value as a treatment. Resolution of problems should be by their thorough and accurate diagnosis; get to the root of the difficulty, then prescribe treatment. What reason is there to believe, they ask, that reorganization will prove to be more effective than the present junior high school?

In regard to the need for diagnosis before attempting reorganization, the Community Middle School, Eagle Grove, Iowa, (described as a "hotbed of tranquillity")[30] reported a study of their junior high school (7-8-9) program; an investigation that resulted in a shift to a middle school with grades 6–9. The administration and staff spent a year in evaluating what was being done in the junior high school by means of a comparison of their practices with a list of objectives for the junior high school. Some of their conclusions were that their junior high was characterized by

1. Fact dissemination and lecture-oriented teaching techniques.
2. A compartmented curriculum.
3. An inappropriate age group.
4. A program dictated by facilities, schedule, and the high school.
5. Inadequacies in curriculum integration, faculty communication, provisions for individual needs, diversified teaching techniques, teacher motivation, program direction and purpose.

It was decided that it was necessary to try a different approach, to create a new image, and to eliminate the connotations of the word junior. "No one had defined the 'ideal' middle school, thus flexibility and identification were open to interpretation."

In deprecating those who call for change in organization, however, the junior high supporters certainly have a reasonable argument. There are always those who feel the need to agitate for change, too often without much real idea as to what the change will involve nor what the eventual results may be, proposing change merely for the sake of something different which may be better. The junior high school, supporters maintain, is best suited to cope with that mixed blessing, the adolescent, by virtue of experience, philosophy of education, buildings, facilities, activities, curricula, and attention to the unique characteristics of this age group. Certainly there are great variations in adolescent growth: physical, emotional, and social; differences which appear most obvious and pronounced in those children age 12–16.

Margaret Mead[31] has remarked that the junior high schools were predicated on age and not on size, strength, or stage of puberty. This, she points out, has unintentionally classified together boys and girls at an age when the most differences exist within each sex and between the sexes.

In suggesting that the ninth grade be returned to the senior high school, Harl Douglass[32] observed that it is not good organization for the seventh- and eighth-graders to be in constant association "with ninth-graders who are chomping at the bit to take on the social habits and vices of the older adolescents."

It is probable that most junior high principals do not agree that the ninth grade should be removed from junior high school. A 1964 survey[33] of over 400 junior high school principals found that the 7-8-9 plan was preferred and that the 7-8-9 school was believed to be the best place for the ninth grade. There was no mention of any possible advantages to the sixth grade in moving them out of the elementary school setting. This was an opinion survey and those in opposition to statements of this sort refer somewhat disparagingly to the "vested interests" in junior high school.

Further differences of opinion exist concerning the strictures of the Carnegie Unit, the importance of a four-year high school transcript, granting of credit for ninth-grade coursework, and problems of coordinating and articulating junior and senior high school curricula.

WHICH GRADES IN THE MIDDDLE?

Junior high and middle school educators are in agreement that there needs to be a distinctly separate school for early adolescents, between elementary and senior high school. The disagreement concerns which grades are "functionally appropriate for this (middle) unit of public school organization."[34]

Throughout the years various proposals and arguments have been advanced. One suggestion[35] was that grades 7 and 8 be completely eliminated on the grounds that they are largely repetitious and time wasting, and that the schools should adopt a six-year elementary and four-year secondary pattern as do some European schools.

Another proposal[36] was that the schools be organized 5-3-3-3, with the last year of high school to be included in a junior college. The author's reasons for this were that children mature earlier, time is of more importance, and that students could be sooner introduced to lab experiences in science, industrial arts, homemaking, fine arts, advanced mathematics, and modern foreign language.

A 1957 recommendation[37] was that the American schools be organized on a more flexible basis: an ungraded primary for slow children age 5–9, fast children age 5–7, the equivalent of grades K–2; an elementary or middle school, slow children age 9–14, fast children age 7–12, equivalent to grades 3–6; and a high school including grades 7–10.

Lloyd Trump[38] has suggested that the best arrangement might be 5-5-5 (K through 4, grades 5 through 9, and 10 through 14).

A rather different proposal[39] is to begin children in the first grade at age 5, departmentalize grades 5 and 6, and begin foreign languages, algebra, geometry, astronomy, biology, chemistry, and physics at this level; have a middle school grades 7–10; and a high school with three different tracks—a two-year for terminal education, four-year for community college, and four-year with only three years in the middle school for those going to a liberal arts college.

Other organizational plans actually in operation are the 8-1-3 plan; the 5-3-2-2; the 6-2-2-2; the 3-5-4; 4-4-4; 5-3-4; 6-2-4; 4-5-3; 5-4-3; 4-3-5; and 5-2-5. It is obvious that there is no lack of variety in school organization.

Statements made by different educational associations concerning the best grade patterns are occasionally at variance with each other, and sometimes an organization's position will be modified within a few years.

A 1961 statement of the Association for Supervision and Curriculum Development[40] commented that the conventional junior high school was basically a hybrid, with the elementary school flavoring the programs for grades 7 and 8, and the ninth grade being closely related to the forms and traditions of the high school. Since this results in splitting both the program and functions of the junior high school, it was suggested that it might in the future be better to return the ninth grade to the high school and begin junior high with the sixth grade.

Conant[41] noted a lack of agreement among educators concerning grade placement but concluded that this was not so important as the program offered.

In commenting that the primary function of the junior high school is to "bridge the gap," Smith[42] said that this was a unit with a definite purpose: "A middle block capable of strengthening both ends." Grades included, he stated, could be 6-7-8, 7-8, or 7-8-9, optional with the locality they are to serve.

The 1962 Position Papers for Junior High School drawn up by the National Association of Secondary School Principals[43] took a firm stand for the three-year junior high school with grades 7-8-9 and stated that grade 6 should remain in the elementary school.

The Position Papers for the Association[44] a year later, October, 1963, were silent concerning a three-year junior high school but did warn that the junior high school "should not exclude grade six." The earlier maturity of youth plus sociological factors, it was said, made it necessary to refrain from excluding the sixth grade from junior high school.

Increasing evidence of earlier pubescence caused the Association, in February 1967, to consider the possibility that the present eleven-year-old or sixth-grader may be as ready for junior high school or middle school as seventh-graders were in previous years.[45] It was recommended that the junior high or middle school include grades 6-7-8-9 or 7-8-9. The burden of proof, it was warned, is placed upon those who advocate change. Middle school supporters, however, believe that the burden of proof is upon those who are reluctant to make a change and charge that those who do not wish to relinquish the ninth grade are attempting to retain advanced sports and activities.

A 1966 publication of the Association,[46] "Guidelines for Junior High and Middle School Education," stressed that the junior high school is intended to serve the preadolescent and early adolescent, but noted that this group ranges in age from 11 to 15. Although the three-year junior high school was preferred by the committee, it was recommended that flexibility be employed in admission and promotion at each end. While the inclusion of all fifth- and sixth-graders as opposed to ninth-graders was considered debatable, the earlier maturity and sophistication of the adolescent of today would seem to indicate that some eleven-year-olds might be better situated in a junior high or middle school.

A survey[47] of all junior high school principals in the United States got a return of 66 percent from the 6,800-plus junior high schools. Grade patterns reported were 6-3-3, 68 percent; 6-2-4, 17 percent; and 5-3-4, 4 percent. It was noted, however, that 18 percent of the responding principals believed that 5-3-4 is the ideal combination (1964–65).

It may be seen that there is considerable uncertainty as to which grades should be included in the middle school, although there seems to be little doubt that some kind of middle school will continue. The important thing to remember, which has sometimes had only small recognition, is that a middle school is not an elementary school nor a senior high school: it is "functionally differentiated."[48] As Lloyd Trump emphasized, it is not *whether* the middle school, it is *whither!* "Pupils aged 10 and upward should not be limited by the competences of one teacher per grade."[49]

THE PLACE OF GRADE NINE

If the ninth grade is older, more mature, and has outgrown the junior high school, then where should it be put—back into a four-year high school, or into some other organizational structure?

There are still many four-year high schools in the country and it is proposed by some [50] that the ninth grade be restored to the three-year high school, changing this back to a four-year school.

It has been argued[51] that the four-year high school makes more sense for transcripts, credit for ninth-grade subjects, and possesses teachers trained specifically for this level—which is not usual at junior high.

The six-year secondary school has proven to be quite popular and is ever increasing in number. It is, however, generally found in smaller school districts where enrollment encourages this method of maximum use of facilities. In larger districts, senior high school enrollments become so large as to prohibit any inclusion of grades 7 or 8, and sometimes that of grade 9.

At least one school district[52] operates a school exclusively for ninth-graders—grades above or below are not included. The superintendent states that this plan has virtually eliminated any discipline problems, since the real ninth-grade problem is the youngster who may not be quite ready for high school but creates chaos with younger children. He also reports high student morale and student desire to continue this plan.

There has been a growing interest in a high school organization which puts grades 9-10 together in one building and also 11-12 in another. Grades 9-10 are referred to as "mid-high" or "lower high" or "lower secondary school." Regardless of the name, here are some of the advantages claimed for this pattern:[53]

1. Reduced duplication of facilities.
2. More effective grouping of students.
3. Individually tailored student schedules.
4. Fullest use of specialized teacher ability.
5. Advantages of class sizes for course offerings.
6. Better arrangement of activities.
7. Strengthens ninth-grade program.
8. Provides more leadership opportunities.
9. There is a beneficial effect on the 7-8 grades in junior high in that discipline problems are sharply reduced—no increase reported for the 9-10 school.
10. Administrators feel that the 11-12 school takes on many of the desirable characteristics of a junior college.

All is not without fault, however, and certain disadvantages are also cited:

1. Requires strong teachers for the 9-10 division since this is a "volatile and impulsive age."
2. Students make three changes, not two, in six years.
3. Requires very close articulation for grades 7–12.
4. Problems of record keeping, curriculum, discipline policies, and guidance may be aggravated.
5. Most problems center around the relationship of the two high school buildings—are they separate schools or a single high school?

An administrator[54] who was for three years principal of a 9-10 school and then became principal of an 11-12 school is in agreement with most of the advantages and disadvantages stated, and also believes that grade 9 is more closely related to grade 10 than to grade 8. He believes that ninth-grade students have much more in common with tenth-grade students than with eighth-graders; the 9-10 school provides more opportunities for leadership in every area. Varsity teams, he says are made up of 11-12-graders; junior varsity teams of tenth-graders; and junior high interscholastic teams of ninth-graders; while seventh- and eighth-graders are involved almost exclusively with intramural sports.

He concluded that the advantages of this pattern outweigh the disadvantages. For the most part, he believes, the factors associated with advantages have to do mainly with the educational program and its objectives whereas those associated with disadvantages are mainly administrative.

Harl Douglass[55] stated that in 1966 there were 100 or more school districts with their high schools in the 2-2 (9-10 and 11-12) pattern. He added that testimony from districts employing this form of grade organization is uniformly favorable. Many of the previously listed advantages were claimed, and emphasis was given to reduce discipline problems, benefits to be derived from separating younger students from older students, better educational program available, and increased opportunities for leadership. Douglass predicted that the 2-2 high school will gain ground in company with a middle school of some kind, 7-8, 6-7-8, or 5-6-7-8.

The grades generally included in the high school are usually the result of tradition, community pressures, buildings available, finances, or administration fiat. A study[56] concerned with what grades should be included when opening a new high school found that similar answers were often given by administrators who were asked, "How did you decide what grades should be included on opening your school?" Common responses made were these:

1. In this district we always open high schools with these grades.
2. Opening with these grades is accepted by parents in this community.

3. We had to include these grades in order to accommodate the students needing to be housed.

The author of the study observed, "It would seem that the decision as to what grades should be included . . . would be made only after careful consideration of all the alternatives based on the most reliable data. It might seem so, but it isn't."[57]

The absence of consideration of educational factors make these statements most disquieting.

Perhaps the best questions would be: where will the ninth-graders best achieve, and what can the high school do that the junior high cannot do, and vice versa? Unfortunately, there is virtually no research in this area. A study[58] reported in February 1967 of ninth-grade achievement compared ninth-graders in a 7-8-9 junior high school with ninth-graders in a 9-12 four-year high school. It was found that difference in academic success in grade 9 has little to do with its place in a junior or senior high. More depends upon the program of instruction and staff involved.

If the ninth-grader can achieve equally well at either level, then what can the high school do that the junior high cannot? Certainly the average high school should have better facilities and equipment that the average junior high school, as in auto shop and graphic arts, and will probably have more activities available than the average junior high school should provide. The answer to this question should be determined by assessment within each district of what the program and facilities may offer.

THE PROBLEM OF THE CARNEGIE UNIT

A distinct factor in the shaping of the junior high school program has been the influence of the Carnegie Unit. Since ninth-graders earn units for successful completion of their course work, there is a restricting effect upon the overall junior high school scheduling and curriculum.

The very existence of the Carnegie Unit has provided many in education with a built-in excuse for doing little or nothing toward innovation, improvement, and change. There are those who honestly believe that requirements, regulations, and policies connected with and attributed to the Unit prohibit any variation of time allotments, either in minutes, days, or weeks. It is also true than many in education complacently ignore the Carnegie Unit standards and develop the program they think best for their schools.

Since slightly more than half of the colleges and universities are estimated to be using the Unit method of evaluating high school work,[59] the Carnegie Unit is still an active force in American education, although there are ways of working around the Unit requirements. The Unit affects both the high schools and junior high schools, since one Unit is granted for each class that meets one class period daily, five days weekly, for one school year,[60] grades 9–12. (A class that meets only half as often or for only one semester would be given only one-half a Carnegie Unit.) While sixteen units are usually required for high school graduation, fifteen units usually constitute the minimal amount acceptable for college entrance and are interpreted as four years of high school preparation, thus including ninth-grade work.

Ninth-graders, therefore, are granted Carnegie Units for work successfully completed, in accord with these standards, whether the ninth grades are a part of a junior high school or a four-year high school. Herein lies the problem. In some junior high schools and in some districts, change and experimentation proceed with no concern for Unit requirements; in other junior high schools, change moves haltingly with fearful thoughts that Unit standards may not be met. Then what will be the position of the school as regards accreditation, and the students in regard to high school credits and college entrance? In some school districts high school and junior high school principals have refused flatly to permit any changes in scheduling, either through ignorance of what the Carnegie Unit really means or because it is easier to maintain the status quo and blame it on the Unit.

The Unit, by requiring students to attend classes in each subject for at least 120 clock hours each school year, obviously has wide implications for schedule construction, curriculum planning, selection of required and elective subjects, recording, marking, and measuring pupil progress, and ultimately for determining completion of high school and awarding diplomas.

The Unit equates bodies of subject matter as being roughly equal to each other, assumes that all students need the same amount of exposure to every class, and measures achievement largely in terms of the amount of time put in by the students.

What *is* the Carnegie Unit, and how did it become such a strong factor in secondary education?

ORIGIN OF THE CARNEGIE UNIT

It is a curious fact that the Carnegie Unit which virtually dominated the secondary schools for decades resulted from a beneficent proposal to found a pension plan for college professors.

Prior to 1900 college admission requirements tended to be highly specific, usually stating subjects required, often the books to be used and sometimes even editions of books. Requirements differed from college to college, as did those of the secondary schools. The growth of the academies brought about a vast increase of subjects, elective and required, which often ran into the hundreds, and to add to the confusion, time allocated to the different subjects varied from school to school. It was not uncommon to find that algebra as taught by one school might be quite different from that taught by another school only a few miles away, both in time spent and material covered.

The growth of the American comprehensive high school during the late 1800's and early 1900's found public opinion favoring an increase of course offerings of a practical nature.

The ever-increasing number of schools and subjects accompanied by a greater mobility of the American population developed a need for a common standard for the high school program. The Committee of Ten in 1893 attempted rather unsuccessfully to establish some curriculum organization standards, although it did not define the number of periods per week per subject. The College Entrance Examination Board, from its inception in 1900, recommended course outlines and suggested methods as well as time allocations. While this met with some success, the real standardization followed the establishing in 1905 of the Carnegie Foundation for the Advancement of Teaching.

Throughout the history of mankind there have been events and actions which have had effects, unexpected or only partially suspected, far in excess of what might reasonably have been anticipated. There is a certain amount of irony in that the provision of pensions to college professors in the United States, Canada, and Newfoundland, resulted in establishing requirements and standards for high schools which, however desirable they may have been at the time, resulted in rigidity which became virtually a straightjacket for over half a century.

The pension funds granted by the Foundation were to be paid directly to the college for the professors, but considerable confusion existed as to where a high school stopped and a college began. This was compounded by those colleges which contained one or more grades normally considered as belonging in a high school, and by those high schools, (and there were many) that called themselves colleges. For purposes of distributing funds the Foundation found it necessary to define a college. They stated that a college must require four years of academic or high school preparation or its equivalent. It defined in 1909 the four years of high school work in terms of the Unit. In a very short time nearly all high schools measured their offerings in Unit terms: one class period daily, thirty-six weeks for a school year, and a period 40–60 minutes long. In this manner the Carnegie Foundation, whose stated function was that of providing pensions for college professors, determined and virtually compelled an acceptance of educational standards in secondary schools.

In 1911 the Committee of Nine recommended that the fifteen units for college entrance be apportioned as follows: three English, one social studies, and one natural science, the remaining units to be completed with two majors and two minors of electives. It was recommended that not more than two years of mathematics nor two years of foreign language be required. Physical education was required but not included for credit. The effect of this was to impart prestige and rigidity to segments of the secondary curriculum which still exist in many communities.

Critics point out that the Unit makes its basic criterion the amount of time spent on a subject, not the results obtained. It thus controls the pattern of time distribution in the secondary schools and requires padding in some courses and trimming in others.

It is doubtful that the Foundation intended to establish such restrictions on the secondary schools, although it was recognized that some sort of yardstick for comparison purposes was an inevitable result.[61] Ease of use, of standardizing, and of scheduling soon developed the practice of working for credits. The schools came to be regarded as akin to an educational savings bank with credits earned and on deposit. The Carnegie Unit very largely overcame the lack of a common denominator for college admissions, and its theory of equivalent units makes it a most convenient method of academic bookkeeping. It compares, superficially, the academic backgrounds of students from anywhere in the country and has the further advantage of nearly universal acceptance.

The advent of the Carnegie Unit coincided roughly with the introduction and growth of the junior high school with grades 7-8-9. Since ninth-grade students were granted Carnegie Units it was necessary to schedule and operate ninth-grade classes in accordance with Unit requirements. Inevitably then, ninth-grade subjects, scheduling, and programs were the first consideration of the school, and seventh- and eighth-grade courses of study and scheduling were compelled to fit into the ninth-grade pattern as best they could. In many if not most junior high schools the schedule and curriculum became just as rigid and inflexible as those of the high schools to which its students ultimately went.

RECENT DEVELOPMENTS

It has become increasingly apparent that the high school diploma tends to be a certificate awarded for so much attendance in so many classes for the required number of hours and the requisite number of years. Obviously the Units earned in one school compare only superficially with those earned at another. Instruction varies, facilities are different, the course content is not identical, scholastic achievement varies, and all subjects are not of the same importance to all students although equal credit is granted. It is a measure of time served, not of achievement.

Various alternatives to the Carnegie Unit have been proposed and attempted, but one of the major problems is that no satisfactory substitute has yet been agreed upon. When educators have difficulty agreeing upon what basic knowledges and skills are essential and should be required for all—and how much of each may be necessary—it is evidently even more of a problem to determine a means of measuring and evaluating what has been included in the curriculum. In short, when may a student be said to have completed his secondary education?

Innovations and experimentation of the past few years such as programmed learning, flexible scheduling, ungraded classes, and team teaching virtually require that the rigid requirements of the Carnegie Unit be abandoned. Some schools have eliminated the daily pattern of compliance but still meet the yearly total of 120 class hours per subject. Classes may not meet at all on some days, and meet for varying lengths of time on other days. In some cases students are given credit for coursework upon passing tests although they may have put in less time than the Unit requires. Since the junior high and high school transcripts are considered to be statements of satisfactory conformance to requirements, some principals operate the programs they consider most satisfactory and make such entries on transcripts as will permit their students to be credited with the necessary Units.

Other ways have been explored in an effort to avoid the rigidity of the Unit. The City Schools of Boston have instituted a point system,[62] as have Cleveland and several cities. Many school administrators consider that a point system is but a temporary expedient and an attempt to evade the issue rather than a solution.

A proposal similar to this is to break the unit into sections, that is to allow .4 Unit for one course, 1.5 for another, and .75 for yet another.[63]

Point systems or fractionalizing are only other bookkeeping methods and take little cognizance of the fact that children learn at different rates and possess different backgrounds, knowledges, and skills. It is more desirable to work toward a standard involving a quality of excellence rather than a quantitative measure.

It has been proposed that the Unit be abandoned in favor of the hour as a measure.[64] This, it is said, would provide an accurate count of the number of hours the student is in the class, i.e., algebra, 100 hours; literature, 75 hours; biology, 150 hours. It is somewhat difficult to see what might be gained by this other than permitting students to take classes for varying amounts of time. There is no way of knowing precisely what the students have learned nor of comparing this with students in other schools. It would appear to be only a more complicated variation of Unit accounting, although it is claimed that with this method schools could offer a greater variety of courses, and that there would be a statistical measure.

A suggestion that appeals to many is to adopt the system used in elementary education—that is, completion of a year's work at a satisfactory level. This involves a sizeable amount of written information, evaluations, conferences, and consideration of chronological age and other maturation factors. To those who say that this method will not work it may be pointed out that it has worked for a long time in most elementary schools, many junior high schools, and some high schools.

Colleges in several states accept the high school diploma as evidence of completion of the four-year course of study. Since many if not most of the high schools involved have based their courses of study and therefore their diplomas upon the Carnegie Unit, little change is noted here. Other college base their acceptance of entering freshmen upon various tests and examinations. In 1947 the Educational Testing Service was formed by a merger of the testing efforts of the American Council on Education, the Carnegie Foundation for the Advancement of Teaching, and the College Entrance Examination Board. ETS has worked toward more exact, more comprehensive means of evaluating student progress in learning. Efforts by organizations of this kind to develop better instruments for determining a student's school achievements and predicting his ability to succeed in college will do much to render the Carnegie Unit unnecessary.

Toward the end of World War II the American Council on Education formed a Commission on Accreditation of Service Experiences. From this Commission came the valuative instruments known as the General Educational Development Tests, one for use at the high school level and one at the college level. These tests have been used both for placement and for issuing equivalency certificates or diplomas for high school graduation, a procedure that has been well received by some educators and regarded by others with wariness, suspicion, and the feeling that standards are certainly not what they used to be. These tests have been quite successful. Variations and adaptations of the GED tests should not be difficult to develop to provide instruments for use with secondary school pupils. A problem that arises here is that of getting all colleges to accept results of such tests.

In some states secondary schools and colleges have worked out agreements in which the public schools are given more latitude in subject-matter requirements provided they comply with certain college specifics: recommend for college only their more able students; keep better records for all students; make constant appraisals of the school's curriculum, instruction, and goals; perform regular and continuous follow-up studies of all ex-pupils.[65]

Under the administration of Robert Maynard Hutchins, the University of Chicago made fairly extensive use of the concept of early admission to college and challenging of courses. Students take a comprehensive series of tests and are placed in college and in courses according to their success on the tests. As a part of Advanced Placement there has been an increase in the number of college courses taught at the high school level to those whose ability and interest permit enrollment, and college credit is given for successful completion.

One effort to develop a more comprehensive and descriptive system than the Carnegie Unit is that known as the "Deiderich Profile Index,"[66] which attempts to appraise several major values of "the good life." Each major element has several subheadings arranged on a scale from zero (weak) to 100 (strong). Students are to be rated for each of these objectives which the school accepts as having meaning in its community. For example, a student might be rated at 50 under "Necessities: knows how our own and other economic systems operate." In the same major category he might be rated at 75 in "Respects property rights."

Progress reports, inventories, assessments, profiles, and similar suggestions all require a great deal in judgments, qualitative measures, paperwork, clerical help, money, and time. Since there are many such subjective evaluations for each student, however, it is reasonable to hope that a more complete picture would be provided of the individual student's performance. Even so, such appraisals are probably no more subjective than the single-letter grade that characterizes the Carnegie Unit.

A recurring fear of many educators is that elimination of the Carnegie Unit might cause one of two evils: either a situation wherein there are no standards and few requirements, or a replacement of the Unit by something far worse such as a system of standardized tests, in which case the question would be, Who makes the judgments?

Examination of the controversy concerning the Carnegie Unit would seem to indicate that there are ways to circumvent and escape its rigidity. At the same time it must be conceded that the influence of the Unit is more than a paper dragon; its presence still hovers darkly from the past into the future.

Inasmuch as it still has a definite effect upon ninth-grade curricula and in a larger sense upon the entire junior high school program, there is some validity to the arguments of those who see moving the ninth grade into the high school as a means of avoiding the influences of the Unit. This would provide the graduating high school senior with a continuous four-year transcript, and would also make easier the development of an unrestricted middle school program.

SUMMARY

Criticisms of a number of junior high school practices have lent impetus to the interest in middle schools. Such criticisms have not gone unanswered by those who believe in the 7-8-9 junior high school and both factions have become, on occasion, somewhat impassioned. To some educators a change to a middle school pattern, as New York City is doing, is but "following a trend," while others consider such a change to be a sort of game of musical chairs with grade numbers. A good case may be made by either side and it is undoubtedly true so far as the quality of the school is concerned, that a great deal depends upon the individual staff and administration within the respective schools regardless of the grades included.

It is generally agreed that there should be a separate school placed between elementary school and high school to serve the adolescent, but not much agreement exists as to which grades should be included. A wide diversity of grade patterns are currently in use. So far as the ninth grade is concerned, it has been suggested that school districts could do one of several things: restore the ninth-grader to a four-year high school; establish six-year secondary schools; put all ninth-graders in one school by themselves with no other grades; or develop a four-year high school composed of two divisions (2-2), grades 9-10 in one division and building and grades 11-12 in a second.

The Carnegie Unit, often blamed for restriction of programs in both senior high and junior high schools, has probably outlived its usefulness. In the confused situation in which the high schools and colleges found themselves at the turn of the century, the adoption of the Carnegie Unit came as a stabilizing influence that was badly needed. Before many years had passed, however, inherent disadvantages of the Unit began to operate against the secondary schools. Chief among these are the inflexibility of the time required for subject credit, the lack of qualitative measure and emphasis upon quantitative, and the tendency of colleges and secondary schools to use the Unit as a requirement for progress from one level to the other.

The past few years have seen many changes on the educational scene, nearly all of which have found themselves impeded and obstructed by the Unit. The need for universal compulsory education and the attendant growth in diversity of course offerings, increased knowledge of child growth, development, and learning, the rapid increase in technological materials and equipment, and the explosion of knowledge have all caused schools to seek better ways of doing their work. There is an increasing reluctance on the part of colleges and secondary schools to be dogmatic in their positions concerning requirements.

It would appear that we are going to see an eroding, supplementing, and supplanting of the Carnegie Unit on a noticeable scale within the next few years. Probably the replacement for the Unit will not be one method but several, or a combination. Whatever emerges has every chance of being a measure of how well our students are prepared, instead of how much time they put in.

REFERENCES

1. J. H. Hull, "Are Junior High Schools the Answer?", *Educational Leadership*, Vol. 23 (December 1965), p. 213.

2. Morris A. Shirts, "Ninth Grade—Curriculum Misfits?", *NASSP Bulletin*, Vol. 41 (November 1957), p. 137.
3. Glenn R. Rasmussen, "The Junior High School—Weakest Rung in the Educational Ladder?", *NASSP Bulletin*, Vol. 46 (October 1962), pp. 63–69.
4. Theodore C. Moss, *Middle School.* Boston: Houghton, 1969, p. 14.
5. William M. Alexander and Associates, *The Emergent Middle School.* (New York: Holt, 1968, p. 55.
6. William W. Wattenberg, "The Junior High School—A Psychologist's View," *NASSP Bulletin*, Vol. 49 (April 1965), p. 34.
7. Arthur H. Rice, "What's Wrong With Junior High School? Nearly Everything," *Nation's Schools*, Vol. 74 (November 1964), pp. 30–31.
8. James B. Conant, *Education in the Junior High School Years.* Princeton, N.J.: Educational Testing Service, 1960.
9. Gordon F. Vars, "Change and the Junior High," *Educational Leadership*, Vol. 23 (December 1965), p. 187.
10. William D. Boutwell, "What Are Middle Schools," *PTA Magazine*, Vol. 60 (December 1965), p. 14.
11. Judith Murphy, *Middle Schools.* New York: Educational Facilities Laboratory, 1965, p. 47.
12. Leslie W. Kindred (ed.), *The Intermediate Schools.* Englewood Cliffs, N.J.: Prentice-Hall, 1968, p. 383.
13. Ellsworth Tompkins and Virginia Roe, "A Survey of Interscholastic Athletics in Separately Organized Junior High Schools," *NASSP Bulletin*, Vol. 42 (October 1958), pp. 14—18.
14. Richard H. Conover, "The Junior High School Principalship," *NASSP Bulletin*, Vol. 50 (April 1966), p. 138.
15. William M. Alexander, "The Junior High School: A Changing View," *NASSP Bulletin*, Vol. 48 (March 1964), p. 18.
16. Mauritz Johnson, Jr., "School in the Middle—Junior High: Education's Problem Child," *Saturday Review*, Vol. 45 (July 21, 1962), pp. 40–42.
17. Johnson, "The Dynamic Junior High School," *NASSP Bulletin*, Vol. 48 (March 1964), p. 122.
18. Johnson, "Research and Secondary Education," *Educational Forum* Vol. 31 (March 1967), pp. 292–301.
19. Moss, *op. cit.*, p. 15.
20. *Loc. cit.*
21. R. P. Brimm, "Middle School or Junior High? Background and Rationale," *NASSP Bulletin*, Vol. 53 (March 1969), p. 4.
22. Murphy, *op. cit.*, p. 9.
23. *Ibid.*
24. Paul Gastwirth, "Questions Facing the Middle School," *High Points*, Vol. 48 (June 1966), pp. 40–47.
25. A. W. Howard, *Middle Schools in Oregon and Washington, 1965–66*, unpublished doctoral dissertation, University of Oregon, 1966.
26. *Ibid.*
27. William A. Cuff, "Middle Schools on the March," *NASSP Bulletin*, Vol. 51 (February 1967), p. 85.

28. Howard, *op. cit.*
29. Richard L. Post, "Middle School: A Questionable Innovation," *The Clearing House,* Vol. 42 (April 1968), pp. 484–486.
30. Bruce Howell, "The Middle School—Is It Really Any Better?," *The North Central Association Quarterly,* Vol. 48 (Winter 1969), pp. 281–287.
31. Margaret Mead, "Early Adolescence in the United States," *NASSP Bulletin,* Vol. 49 (April 1965), p. 7.
32. Harl Douglass, "What Type of Organization of Schools?" *Journal of Secondary Education,* Vol. 41 (December 1966), p. 360.
33. William T. Gruhn, "What Do Principals Believe About Grade Organization?," *Journal of Secondary Education,* Vol. 42 (April 1967), pp. 169–174.
34. Samuel H. Popper, *The American Middle School.* Waltham, Mass.: Blaisdell, 1967.
35. Charles Schutter, "Should We Abolish the 7th and 8th Grades?," *School Executive,* Vol. 74 (May 1955), p. 53.
36. Lawrence E. Vredevoe, "Let's Reorganize Our School System," *NASSP Bulletin,* Vol. 42 (May 1958), p. 40.
37. Paul Woodring, *A Fourth of a Nation.* New York: McGraw-Hill, 1957.
38. Lloyd J. Trump, "The Junior High School—Curriculum Changes for the Sixties," *NASSP Bulletin,* Vol. 47 (February 1963), p. 16.
39. R. Baird Sherman, "Reorganization in Public Education," *Peabody Journal of Education,* Vol. 40 (May 1963), pp. 239–240.
40. *The Junior High School We Need,* Monograph ASCD. Washington, D.C.: National Education Association, 1961, p. 8.
41. Conant, *op. cit.,* p. 12.
42. William Smith, "Junior High School—A Launching Pad," *NASSP Bulletin,* Vol. 46 (April 1962), pp. 95–101.
43. Gene D. Maybee (summarizer), "What Do We Believe—Position Papers for Junior High," *NASSP Bulletin,* Vol. 46 (October 1962), pp. 5–7.
44. Ralph E. Chalender (summarizer), "What the Junior High School Should Not do," *NASSP Bulletin,* Vol. 47 (October 1963), pp. 23–25.
45. "Recommended Grades or Years in Junior High School," *NASSP Bulletin,* Vol. 51 (February 1967), pp. 68–70.
46. Gordon F. Vars (ed.), "Guidelines for Junior High and Middle School Education," *NASSP monograph,* Washington, D.C., 1966.
47. Donald A. Rock and J. K. Hemphill, "Profile of a Junior High School Principal," *Education Digest,* Vol. 32 (January 1967), pp. 8–11.
48. Popper, *op. cit.,* p. 8.
49. Lloyd J. Trump, "Whither the Middle School—Or Whether?," *NASSP Bulletin,* Vol. 51 (December 1967), p. 44.
50. *The Junior High School We Need,* p. 23.
51. Hull, *op. cit.,* p. 214.
52. Carl Burt, "High School Just for Freshmen," *Nation's Schools,* Vol. 76 (July 1965), pp. 27-28.
53. Carl J. Manome and Allan J. Glathorn, "The 9–10 School: A Novelty or a Battle Answer?," *Educational Leadership,* Vol. 23 (January 1966), pp. 185–189.
54. Unpublished correspondence with Council Rock School District, Newton, Pennsylvania, and with Pennsbury School District, Pennsbury, Pa.

55. Douglass, *op. cit.*
56. Grant Maculay, "What Grades Should Be Included When Opening a New High School?," *Journal of Secondary Education,* Vol. 43 (November 1968), pp. 326–331.
57. *Ibid.*, p. 326.
58. Virgil E. Strickland, "Where Does the Ninth Grade Belong?," *NASSP Bulletin,* Vol. 51 (February 1967), pp. 76.
59. Ellsworth Tompkins and Walter Gaumnitz, "The Carnegie Unit: Its Origin, Status, and Trends," *NASSP Bulletin,* Vol. 40 (January 1964), p. 19.
60. Sidney L. Bisvinick, "The Expendable Carnegie Unit," *Phi Delta Kappan,* Vol. 42 (May 1961), p. 365.
61. Tompkins and Gaumnitz, *op. cit.*, p. 16.
62. Grace S. Wright, "High School Curriculum Organizational Patterns and Graduation Requirements in Fifty Large Cities," Department of Health, Education, and Welfare Circular 587, June, 1959, p. 13.
63. Norman K. Hamilton, "What Can Be Done About the Carnegie Unit," *Educational Leadership,* Vol. 23 (January 1966), p. 272.
64. Bisvinick, *op. cit.*, p. 366.
65, Tompkins and Gaumnitz, *op. cit.*, pp. 63–64.
66. *Ibid.*, pp. 52–54.

chapter 10

Middle School Curricula and Programs

A real middle school is intended for children approximately ten to fourteen years of age and is designed to meet the needs of preadolescents and early adolescents. Middle schools should benefit from certain inherent advantages such as the elimination of rigid departmentalization and interscholastic competition, and "Free from the pressures of older adolescent social functions . . . the middle school organization should make a reality of the long-held idea of individual instruction."[1]

Among other things, such an ideal requires time and place for independent study, increased guidance facilities, individual projects, a wide range of course offerings, and physical facilities such as industrial arts areas and fine arts areas not customarily found in an elementary school. Earlier maturity of children is a definite factor. One superintendent stated that earlier maturity of sixth-graders was the basic reason for going to the 6-7-8 plan; the sixth-grader, he says, is ready for a more diversified program than is possible in a self-contained classroom.[2]

THE STUDENT

Since the middle school is intended to serve the preadolescent and early adolescent child, a brief review of the characteristics which they possess in common may be of value, keeping in mind that there is a great range among and between individual adolescents:

1. A resentment of authority, especially if it appears to be arbitrary; a resentment that is aggravated by their earlier drive for sophistication.
2. A readiness, even an eagerness, to accept responsibility. The im-

plications for guided approaches to student self-direction and self-study should be clear.

3. A craving for acceptance and approval by their peers which was formerly satisfied by adult approval. Security is found by identifying with the group, an attitude that emphasizes the importance of group standards. To gain status and recognition the child must conform to these criteria. The school must, therefore, develop desirable values, attitudes, and standards.
4. A strong tendency toward idealism and a keen sense of fair play and justice. If his parents were not decisive concerning values, the adolescent must have guidance in determining his own values. The successful becomes an object of admiration—that is, one who is competent and successful by the adolescent standards.
5. The adolescent is, by adult standards, extremely emotional. There really is no middle ground, no halfway mark. Since emotions become so intense, many events and problems take on an importance that is far out of proportion to their real value.
6. Paradoxically (at least to adults), although he is inclined toward idealism, the early adolescent is likely to become quite self-centered and selfish.
7. The interests of early adolescents are rapidly broadening but are likely to change swiftly and frequently. As these children learn to accept responsibility and as they mature, they need direction and expectations that are in accord with each individual student's ability.
8. An increasing although uncertain awareness of self compounds the problem of developing values. What was important yesterday may not be important tomorrow in terms of the child's own self-perception.
9. There is a common concern with physical growth and the individual's physical appearance, physical ability, and physical skills.
10. The physical growth of adolescence is accompanied by intellectual expansion. General intelligence for all pupils develops continuously as children grow older. There is obviously a wide range of inherent student ability to do school work, and the performance of mental tasks will be affected by individual interests, abilities, and talents, as well as peer group standards.
11. This is an age of conflict—conflict within the adolescent himself, and conflicts with society, primarily adult society. There is a need for a school organization that keeps the young adolescent apart from the social systems of the older adolescent.
12. There is a growing body of evidence that children today are maturing earlier physically, socially, emotionally, and mentally. They are

ready at an earlier age to work with concepts and abstractions and to assume responsibility.

The preadolescent and early adolescent, described by Eichorn as the "transescent,"[3] needs a school environment and school program that emphasizes development of student self-direction and self-responsibility, one that stresses what is relevant to him, and an instructional approach that avoids the traditional concentration upon lecture and note-taking. This is the time for a truly exploratory curriculum, for wise adult guidance, and a real concern for the individual student that is exemplified by individualization of student programs. Virgilio observes that

> We should not need to be reminded that children come to school with more than mental processes and academic diversity. They come differing physically, socially, emotionally, and morally. Consequently, those involved in middle school development must, of necessity, seek new ways in which to provide for the diverse needs of a diverse age group.[4]

Some areas of learning, Virgilio continues, lend themselves to common understandings and group processes. Other areas need sequential skill development and individualized attention. A good middle school, therefore, includes all types of grouping and instructional programs, "each flexible enough to take care of common group and separate individual concerns." Further, the curriculum must incorporate "immediate concerns of children who are in the sensitive transescent period of development and who are in the active process of reacting, counterreacting, or rebelling to grow up in today's world."[5] Such a curriculum will of necessity be innovative and include learnings and experiences that have meaning for the children as well as those required by society for the perpetuation of our culture. To achieve this, the middle school must further develop the nongraded and continuous progress approach for each individual student. Individualized instruction will result from individual diagnosis and individual prescription. This is a far cry from a traditional departmentalized six- or seven-period day comprised largely of lecture-oriented instruction.

The kind of activities and social life desirable for these students must be clearly resolved. Interscholastic athletics and sophisticated social activities should be replaced by a social program "that is multipurpose with a variety of activities operating at one time instead of the single purpose activity."[6] Such a program permits and encourages free selection and changing choices.

While this is the kind of activity program that is generally accepted and recommended for middle schools, the rejection of inappropriate activities tends to create a void for lack of accepted substitutes. "The elimination of interscholastic athletics, for example, has not yet been matched by the initiation of an appropriate preadolescent activity."[7]

IMPLICATIONS FOR THE MIDDLE SCHOOL PROGRAM

It has been said that "each middle school should have its own planned program of learning opportunities—that is, its own curriculum plan."[8] In this view, the program of the middle school must be especially designed to serve the educational needs of a school population that has a wide range of differences in many traits. This requires a high degree of flexibility in all aspects of the school's operation. In addition, the program of the middle school must be developed with regard for the elementary school which it follows and for the high school into which the middle school students ultimately go. There will also be opportunities and limitations occasioned by buildings, facilities, and staff competencies.

Such a middle school program, then, would be developed in three major areas:[9]

1. Personal Development: counseling and referral, development of values, health and physical development, individual interests (a pattern of special-interest activities that includes exploratory experiences, laboratory courses, and the activity program).
2. Skills for continued learning: in reading, listening, asking questions —interviewing, viewing visual aids, using library tools and resources, observing the natural and social environment, organizing information, generalizing from observations and readings, evaluating information and opinions, and problem solving. There must be opportunities for learning skills in every classroom, for specialized instruction in learning skills, and for independent study.
3. Organized knowledge: systematic instruction must be provided in all middle schools and at all levels in English, mathematics, science, and social studies. The actual content and emphasis will vary from school to school.

It cannot be too strongly stressed that the kind of curricular approach just described must be designed and developed *in terms of the characteristics and needs of the transescent student*—and herein are the differences from programs found in most current school organizational plans.

There may be no inherent philosophical differences between the middle school and other well-thought out school organizations and programs, since

> The middle school should be seen as a *concept*, an *idea*—a school recognizing that changes are continually needed in the educational process. Some of the "visible" differences frequently mentioned include: freedom from stresses of interschool athletics—more emphasis on intramural activities; more counseling services; more personal exploratory experiences than the typical "exploratory" course approach; freedom from Carnegie Unit pressures; better utilization of specialists; and more emphasis on independent study and self-reliant behavior.[10]

Brunetti reports that the implications that student developmental characteristics have for the middle school program result in " . . . a rejection of standardized curricula, grouping practices, and instructional methods. Most recent developments have emphasized a program of exploratory experiences centered in a flexible curriculum."[11] The middle school, he says, provides two kinds of experiences for its students: those common to all students, and those experiences that are highly individualized and diverse. In so doing, the middle school stresses the continual development of fundamental skills, and aids in the beginnings of specialization. It also reduces societal pressures commonly placed upon students of this age group, and helps them to develop fully as children without pushing them into adult roles too soon.

1. The middle school is adapted to a wide range of children who, although they are extreme individualists, have more in common with each other than with children in grades above or below.
2. The middle school, as one assumption, operates on the belief that its students have some mastery of the skills of learning but are not yet ready for the academic specialization of the senior high school.
3. The middle school concentrates upon provisions for individual differences without losing sight of the increased sophistication and knowledge of the 10–14-year-old over previous generations.
4. The middle school is designed to facilitate "a program that introduces fifth- or sixth-graders gradually to specialization, and provides all kinds of physical means to realize individual differences, on one hand, and to encourage group activities large and small on the other."[12]

The middle school curriculum and program, to be effective, necessitates a thorough analysis and diagnosis of what have been the practices in elementary and junior high schools, and a completely fresh approach to designing the program for this school. Robert B. Davis, Director of the Madison (new math) Project at Webster College, directed attention to the nature of the student in grades 5-8 and the implications for the curriculum when he said[13]

> We are finding . . . that fifth-graders are "natural intellectuals," and can enjoy choosing a set of algebraic axioms and proving a variety of algebraic theorems from them. (This topic was formerly encountered in the latter years of college or in graduate school.) By contrast, seventh- and eighth-graders are *not* "intellectuals": it might come closer to say they are "engineers" at heart. For seventh- and eighth-graders the usual school regime of sitting at desks, reading, writing, and reciting seems to ignore the basic nature of the child at this age; he wants to move around physically, to do things, to explore, to take chances, to build things, and so on . . . we are asking ourselves if mathematics, social studies, etc., *need* to be sedentary subjects at this grade level.

To implement what is said and implied in these statements is to change content, curricula, instructional method, and facilities, from what has been traditional in the junior high schools to something quite innovative in the middle schools.

"What is the middle school like across the nation?"[14] In addition to displaying a considerable variety, middle school programs throughout the country appear to have some common characteristics, Williams reports:

1. Distinct efforts to combine the best features of the elementary school's self-contained classroom concept with the best of the specialization of secondary schools. This implies a nearly full-time self-contained situation for fifth-graders, a block of time of approximately one-half day for sixth-graders, and shorter blocks of time for seventh- and eighth-graders. In each grade students are assigned to a "home-base" teacher.
2. Inclusion of units in the instructional program on special concerns of young adolescents to lend strength to the middle school's emphasis upon self-understanding.
3. There is increased stress upon student self-direction and student self-responsibility for learning. This emphasizes independent study, requires resources centers and materials, and necessitates a much-changed instructional approach.
4. A marked reduction in student activities, especially of those considered to be highly sophisticated, as well as elimination of interscholastic athletics. Of necessity, the middle school must develop suitable alternatives in activities.

> The Barrington Middle School in Barrington, Illinois, manages to provide for many student interest groups by devoting the last block of time in the school day to an interest activity period. During this time students read, play chess, bridge, checkers, participate in sports, go to the art room, work on Boy Scout merit badges, learn Morse Code, assemble radios. . . .[15]

5. The middle school capitalizes on innovations such as team teaching, nongrading, flexible scheduling, programmed instruction, laboratory facilities, and other new media. Such approaches are not, of course, limited to middle schools, but the very newness of the middle school, itself an innovation, encourages investigation and use of those techniques and materials that depart from the traditional. A distinct characteristic of middle school programs is flexibility, as indicated by its readiness to consider change.
6. A strong feature of the middle school is its more personal approach to learning, a concern with each student, a greater use of individualized student programs.

MIDDLE SCHOOL CURRICULAR DESIGN

An examination of proposed and actual curricula and programs for middle schools provides certain conclusions of interest:

1. Much of what is proposed is being attempted and to some measure accomplished in a few reported junior high school programs.
2. An even smaller number of elementary schools have reported curricula and programs which have many points of similarity to middle school programs.
3. In spite of this, there *is* something different, if only in degree, proposed for middle schools (and in many cases practiced in middle schools) from the conventional upper elementary and the junior high school, both in curricula and practices.
4. To an extent the middle school has borrowed what have been considered the better features of both elementary and junior high school, thus producing an eclectic institution which has characteristics of each but is a separate entity. Contributing to this distinction is the lack of influence of the Carnegie Unit, elimination of restrictions of ninth-grade programming, a reduction of excessive sophistication, and the earlier maturity of children.

It is this eclecticism, those points of similarity with program features of elementary and junior high, that produces some blurring of the sharply defined lines of difference between middle schools and junior high. This in turn causes many junior high school supporters to complain that middle school proposals are in operation already in the junior high schools. To an extent and in a limited number of schools they are, but not to the degree postulated for middle schools.

For example, one is more likely to find the core approach accepted in middle schools, although, in spite of the enthusiasm of its backers, it never has achieved acceptance in a majority of the junior high schools. A statement such as, "What is it about block-time and core that has made it so popular in the junior high school?",[16] loses something of its impact when surveys[17] indicate a core program is in effect in only 13 percent of the junior high schools surveyed.

The content of the curricula, according to Grooms,[18] differs from the "fragmented collection of content" typical of conventional elementary and junior high schools in that it is determined by students and professional staff members rather than by tradition, textbooks, and courses of study. It is intended to encourage student inquiry, problem analysis, and decision making. It stresses student investigation, questioning, conception of new approaches, evaluation of possible courses of action, and decisions as to which procedures to follow. The middle school tries to foster the growth of individualism. Actual curricular areas begin, according to Grooms, with the four disciplines—social science, science, mathematics, and language arts—

and include unified arts, foreign language, music, and physical education.

There is no grade-level breakdown within the courses, Grooms says, such as science grade 7 or 8, nor is any topic restricted by the student's age or his years in school. Disapproved are such practices as grades used for reward or punishment, "acceptance of fact regurgitation as evidence of learning," interscholastic athletics, and the "use of professionals to teach one or two subjects such as seventh-grade geography." This last statement appears to be in contradiction with those who recommend the use of teacher specialization in middle schools.

Alexander and Williams,[19] in their proposed middle school model, stress individualized instruction, nongrading, diagnostic services to permit divergence from standard programs by individuals, scheduling of pupils to special instructional centers, and use of individually paced materials such as programmed learning. By emphasizing that learning can be its own reward, the intellectual elements of the curriculum receive high priority; grades are not used for motivation. Emphasis is placed on skills of continued learning; speaking, listening, reading, writing, and considerable importance attached to use of library tools and techniques of independent study. There is a program of common learnings to include social studies, languages, mathematics, science, and fine arts. A strong exploratory program is encouraged by use of special interest centers operated on a flexible time basis with offerings in such areas as photography, typing, drama, and ceramics, which are tied in with such activities as club and youth programs. Health and physical education is designed specifically for children of this age group.

The organization for instruction described by the authors is one in which students would not be expected to be at the same grade level in all subjects, nor would all students be expected to move at the same speed. Homeroom units of approximately 25 pupils are established and four such units constitute a wing, the teachers of these composing a curriculum planning committee and teaching team. A distinctive feature of such middle schools is the Special Learning Center designed to serve the special needs, remedial needs, and exploratory interests of all students. These centers are well equipped and staffed with special personnel competent to direct group and individual study. Students are scheduled into the Centers individually and time allotments are flexible. The Centers should be open to students after school and on Saturdays. All aspects of the middle school program should provide an emphasis on values.

Leadership and vocational aptitudes could be explored[20] by involvement in such student-managed activities as school stores, school banks, school publications, student government, and assembly programs. An organized student activity program other than these is probably unnecessary except as each wing develops its own activities.

Eichorn[21] proposes two curricula for the middle school: the analytical, and the physical-cultural. The analytical includes four content areas: language, mathematics, social studies, and science. The bodies of knowledge within these fields are to be used as the vehicle for stimulating mental growth by developing thought processes. This means that students are involved in thought processes characteristic of moving from the stage of concrete operations to the formal mental operations stage. Curricula and learning experiences are constructed sequentially from the concrete to the abstract and include those elements necessary to stage-level progression. Essential to this is the element of actual pupil experience. In achieving this, common thought processes are stressed and narrow subject division eliminated, as are the practices of rigid time schedules, comprehensive examinations, and standard grading procedures. Student participation in planning is most important.

Within the physical-cultural curriculum are also four content areas: fine arts, physical education, practical arts, and cultural studies. An example stated is that of a physical-cultural unit on Japan which includes Oriental art and music, "projects involving Japanese clothing, foods, crafts, and hobbies; participation in sports, games and dances," and content concerning Japanese government, and social institutions, and customs.

Implementation of this program requires a nonrigid schedule, massive use of individual scheduling and instruction, flexible grouping practices, specialized training of instructional personnel, extensive faculty interaction and joint planning, teaching teams, and a strong guidance service.

The "Guidelines for Junior High and Middle School Education" makes several recommendations for curriculum and instruction for both middle schools and junior high, including:

1. In teaching every subject, consideration must be given to point out opportunities for further study, to assist pupils to learn to study, and to help them to evaluate their own interests and abilities.
2. Block time or core may be the best approach, or, as an alternative, use of an interdisciplinary teaching team.
3. Size of student group may vary from time to time, and stress is placed upon independent study.
4. Creativity in students is fostered by flexible assignments.
5. "Pupils need such skills as . . . use of reference materials, listening, observing . . . instruction in the use of the typewriter should be provided."[23]
6. There is a need to devote more attention to the individual differences among pupils.
7. Experimentation with nongrading should be judiciously attempted.
8. Pupils should be operating under programs individually designed with different course schedules and variations within each course.
9. Increased use should be made of newer methods and technology.

10. Wider participation in fine arts and activities is to be encouraged and an increased exploratory program.

Examination of these and other sources[24] indicate that further suggestions often include:

1. Grade 6 (and grade 5, if included) should have a block of time together, usually half a day.
2. Achievement groupings in academic areas and opportunities provided for acceleration and independent study.
3. Foreign language, ideally open to all, to begin at the lowest grade of the middle school.
4. Industrial arts, homemaking, music, arts and crafts, and typing, to be offered at each grade level.
5. A wide range of elective offerings, open to all.
6. Heterogeneous groupings in nonacademic classes.
7. Provision for extended day opportunities.
8. A basic club program, simplified student government, no cheer leaders, no marching band, no interscholastic athletics.

Moss[25] describes a four area approach to the middle school curriculum:

1. Area I Skills (individual): reading, spelling, writing, computation, typing, library, listening.
2. Area II (group): English, social studies, science, mathematics, foreign language.
3. Area III (group and individual)—The arts: art, music, drama, industrial arts.
4. Area IV (group and individual)—Health, recreation, and physical education: personal health, sex education, recreation, outdoor education, physical fitness.

Moss recommends, for Area I skills, an individualized and continuous progress approach in which students move from larger groups to smaller groups to individual work as they are ready. Rather than all students spending the same amount of time on the same skills, they devote such time as is necessary and desirable to each skill. Consequently there will be no need for each student to have, for example, nine weeks of a subject such as reading and then rotate to a nine-week block of writing. Extensive use is made of programmed materials, teaching machines, and teacher aides.

In Area II, students will be involved in a core program for English and social studies, tracking in mathematics and science, and a foreign language program based upon FLES. The core program is intended to have approximately 50 percent of its time unstructured to permit students to pursue topics in which they are interested—under teacher guidance. The balance of the core time is to be spent in studying in depth preplanned units in English and social studies. The core is heterogeneously grouped while mathematics and science classes are homogeneously grouped within a track system. All students should take a foreign language for their first year in the middle school. The regular classroom program should include activities, such as special interest clubs, that are related to Area II subjects.

Area III subjects should be required for all students for all years of the middle school. Creativity through experiences related to the developmental characteristics should be emphasized in the art program. Art appreciation is a part of the program, but more stress is placed upon students experimenting with various art media. There are special classes both in art and in music for those students who possess special talents in these fields. There are required general music classes as well as singing groups and instrumental groups. A special class in dramatics is available for those children who are dramatically talented. There are learning experiences in creative writing of plays as well as stage set design. Both boys and girls are required to take industrial arts classes. These classes include small tool work, home mechanics, project work and technology. An interesting approach here is a cross-disciplinary team of teachers in social studies, mathematics, science, and industrial arts to provide more scope and depth in planning and teaching technology. Public performances are held to a minimum and interscholastic competitions in music are not a part of the program.

In Area IV, outdoor education receives major emphasis as a part of the recreation program. A cross-disciplinary approach is used involving English, social studies, science, mathematics, music, and art. Included for all students is a week of overnight camping. Intramurals, physical fitness, and gymnastics are a valued part of the program and, for lasting recreational value, individual sports instruction. (This last is an important item. Our society is providing more leisure time and too many physical education programs concentrate upon team sports to the virtual exclusion of individual sports.) A health program, related to the physical growth changes of the middle school student, is an important part of the curriculum. There is an intramural program that is scheduled both within the school day and after school to permit maximum student participation.

The kinds of proposals made by middle school curriculum designers include emphasis upon approaches to instruction and content that are not commonly found in junior high schools nor elementary schools. While there are some things that are identical in middle schools, and many similarities are to be found, it is necessary to develop the program for each individual school with consideration for the needs of the community, the needs of these particular students, the planned educational environment, and the spatial requirements to meet these needs.

MIDDLE SCHOOLS IN OPERATION

Those schools which were specifically planned and designed to be middle schools have a distinct advantage over those which have been converted from another grade organizational pattern. Those which have been the product of reorganization and are occupying inherited facilities sometimes bear a perceptible likeness to the elementary school or junior high school which was their immediate predecessor.

The middle school at Barrington, Illinois, grades 6-7-8, which opened January 3, 1966, with 900 pupils, is an example of a carefully planned middle school. It is referred to by the superintendent as an institution which "is not a junior high school. It's a school with a curriculum built for specific groups of kids at a specific learning stage."[26]

Sixth grades are divided into three groups of about 100 students each with a teaching team of three to four teachers each.[27] Modular scheduling is used, and sixth-graders follow individually planned schedules within the modular patterns as use of facilities or special area teachers is necessary or desirable. Sixth-graders are housed in one wing although individual students or groups may move into other parts of the building or to specialized teachers.

Teaching teams for seventh and eighth grades are so constructed that each team works with one curriculum area: language arts, science, social studies, mathematics, and physical education. Groups in seventh and eighth grades also average about 100 each. Team leadership develops and may shift as needs occur, and it is the responsibility of the team to group and reassign students as it appears necessary and desirable. Instructional groups may vary in size as the situation requires. The week is divided into 70 one-half hour modules for seventh and eighth grades, with classes varying in length from one to three modules. Seventh-grade history, for example, has two modules on Monday, one on Tuesday, one on Wednesday, none on Thursday, and three on Friday. Seventh-grade science has two modules on Monday, none on Tuesday or Wednesday, three on Thursday, and one Friday.

The Director of Guidance works with the instructional staff for the individual programming of each student so that there are opportunities for student pursuit of activities which are of special interest only and do not necessarily fit into the regular framework of schedules and subjects. The school is working methodically toward a program of complete nongrading within five years.

The literal center of the school is the 7,000-square-foot Learning Center, the heart of self-initiated student learning activities. This is a library, research, and study facility containing a listening center, visual equipment areas, a meditation area, and individual study carrels. All students spend some time in the Learning Center each week and, because it is in the center of the school, everyone must pass through it to get to the dining area, the gym, or the arts and crafts wing. There is an open stage for theatrical and special projects and a planetarium.

The middle school in Easton, Connecticut, grades 5–8, was completed in 1965 and opened with 670 students.[28] It is intended to give the preadolescent and early adolescent "a fuller and more flexible experience than was previously available." Students attend regular classes for a block of time with a core program of language arts and social studies and move to special areas for music, art, homemaking, mathematics, science, and industrial arts. All rooms are carpeted except science; and the art, homemaking, and industrial arts spaces can form one large open suite for group sharing similar projects.

School personnel at Amory, Mississippi, feel that their middle school, grades 5–8, provides a strong middle unit which is far superior to junior high school. Grade 5, at Amory is almost completely self-contained, grade 6 has team teaching, grades 7 and 8 are largely departmentalized. There is a large materials resource center to expose children to arts and crafts, science, shop, and homemaking. There is a big library with facilities for independent study. Use is made of specialized teachers, facilities, and equipment.

In the middle school at Bridgewater, Massachusetts, grades 5–8, the program for fifth- and sixth-graders is in three major parts. Special subjects such as art, music, French, home economics, industrial arts, and physical education are taught to heterogeneously grouped classes by subject specialists. Classes in reading and arithmetic are ability grouped, and these constitute the second of the three major areas. The third portion of the fifth- and sixth-grade program is a core composed of all other subjects, heterogeneously grouped. The seventh- and eighth-grade program is departmentalized. Use is made of ability groupings, language labs, and large and small group instruction. As a part of the curriculum, French is available on a selective basis, while home economics, industrial arts, art, and physical education are open to all students. The intramural program is felt to be the outstanding cocurricular activity,[29] although others include band, orchestra, glee club, chess club, science club, chorus, press club, typing club, and student government.

Saginaw School District[30] built its classrooms for its 5–8 school three to a side, the rooms being three-sided and featuring openness, spaciousness, freedom, and much glass. There is a raised "mall" down the center of the six classrooms. The mall has sinks and storage and may be used for large group instruction since all six classrooms are open on the side facing the mall. The mall is a multipurpose common work area, and is used for homemaking, arts and crafts, and industrial arts. There are quiet spaces for individual study. The students have a dining room with booths, round tables, and chairs instead of a cafeteria. There is a social center, gymnasium, and library. Fifth and sixth grades are essentially self-contained, although teachers for these grades plan together for team teaching. Grades 7 and 8 are departmentalized for foreign language, mathematics, science, arts and crafts, homemaking, industrial arts, music, physical education, and health, and blocked for language arts and social studies. Special classrooms are used for teaching most departmentalized subjects. Students are grouped on a "performance level" basis.

Bedford Public Schools,[31] Mt. Kisco, New York, planned and build a middle school with grades 6-7-8 for 1,000 students. Considerations of importance in the planning were

1. Emphasis upon small group instruction, seminars, independent study, and project work with newer tools such as programmed learning and learning laboratories.
2. All instructional programs will become more and more individualized—"keyed to a new number, number one."
3. The school will become ungraded as soon as possible—no grade levels or labels.
4. There is to be a desk or study station for each child for independent study and space for laboratory and art projects.
5. "There will be a richly resourced and comfortable library, woodworking and metal machines, art and theatrical equipment."[32]

The program and scheduling is completely flexible. Procedures and standards of performance, especially in the Unified Arts area are aimed at different interest and ability levels. The growth in manual skills, technical knowledge, and attitude of work finds change provided as needed.[33] The unified Arts portion of the curriculum includes crafts and metalwork, ceramics, drawing, painting, cooking, sewing and textiles, woodworking, electricity, and graphic arts. The little theater seats 400. Teaching areas for the Unified Arts are all contiguous. There are offerings in general music, instrumental, choral, and practice.

The school is organized on the school within a school or House Plan with about 350 students to a house.

The school district of Scarsdale, New York, has built two middle schools with grades 6-7-8. These, too, are organized on the house plan with approximately 350 students to a house, each with fourteen classrooms, and three houses to a school. Pupils from all three grades are assigned to a house and usually remain there for three years. Art, general music, science, mathematics, language arts, and social studies are taught within each house. Each house contains a large visual-aids room for projection, informal dramatics, and house meetings. The houses share areas such as administration, library, auditorium, specialized music, gyms, dining rooms, shops, and homemaking rooms. There is a gifted program and remedial classes in each grade. Classes are heterogeneous for English, social studies, art, music, physical education, and French, and are ability grouped for science, reading, and mathematics. Foreign language, either French or Spanish, is required of all students. All three houses participate jointly in orchestra, band, chorus, student council, special interest clubs, and intramural sports. The principals of these schools believe that "the combination of 6-7-8 is here to stay."[34]

Ann Grooms[35] describes program aspects in three middle schools: Fox Lane, Valley Green, and Belle Vista, all with grades 5–8.

The Unified Arts program at Fox Lane includes homemaking, woodworking, ceramics, fine arts, and music, and student work makes use of all five areas as a project is developed. There are teaching teams, teacher-pupil planning, and opportunities for students to follow projects of special interest. Students progress at their own rate and no attempt is made to keep students in groups with similar abilities and interests.

In Valley Green Middle School there is a "unique mathematical program which features team teaching, ungrading, and individualized instruction for its 800 students . . . curricula evolve as the capabilities and skills of the students are determined."[36] The curriculum content makes substantial use of self-study materials and students work alone using worksheets, individual texts, programmed lessons, and taped lessons.

At Belle Vista Middle School foreign language instruction is intended to extend communicative skills; it is not considered an extra. Languages offered are not restricted to those considered to be the common classical languages.

In all three of these schools stress is put upon the individual in programming, scheduling, and progress. Flexibility in all aspects is a key feature.

A junior high school principal who developed a philosophy, program, and organization for a middle school, to implement a change from the 7-8-9 to the 6-7-8 plan in the Morestown (New Jersey) Township School District, proposed the following which was adopted the following year:[37]

1. Sixth grade: two teachers in the major subject areas are paired into teams for Language Arts-Social Studies-Reading, Mathematics-Science. Two classes of 25 students each are assigned to this team and each teacher is homeroom teacher for one group of 25 students, and as such is responsible for guidance, general supervision, and welfare of the homeroom student in all phases of his school life. Scheduling is flexible to permit large-group and small-group work.
2. Foreign language instruction is available for all students in French, Spanish, or German, five times weekly, 25 minutes per session.
3. There are four evaluation periods each year, at least one of these involving a conference between the parent and the homeroom teacher.
4. The special-interest program provides enrichment for students with strong interests in specific subjects; opportunities to investigate areas not a part of the sixth-grade student's regular program (i.e., typing); and time provided within the school day for students to be transported to participate in intramural, music, and club programs. Special-interest areas include: art, band, foreign languages, choral groups, clothing, debate, dramatics, food, typing, mathematics, mechanical drawing, newspaper, nursing, orchestra, photography, science, shop, sports, future homemakers.

As a means of time computation, the unit used is a 40-minute period, and the sixth-grade program shows the following blocks of time:

Sixth Grade	Periods per Week[18]
Language arts, social studies, reading	12
Mathematics, science	12
Physical education	3
Foreign language	5*
Music	5†
Art	5†
Industrial arts—home economics	5†
Health	5†
Special interest or homeroom	3

*Shortened periods, †rotates each quarter. This program permits a range of courses not commonly found in sixth grades when they are a part of an elementary school.

The seventh-grade program includes

1. Interdisciplinary teams of four teachers with approximately 100 students in the major subject areas.
2. Seventh-graders are assigned a homeroom teacher with whom they remain through grade 8.
3. Foreign language instruction continues daily for 25 minutes each day.
4. Special interest groups are the same as for grade 6.

In the eighth grade, foreign language instruction continues for a full period daily; students who do not choose to take a foreign language receive developmental or remedial reading; science has one double period weekly; special-interest groups continue as in grades 6 and 7.

The curriculum for the seventh and eighth grades is quite similar:

	Periods per week[19]	
	Seventh	Eighth
Language arts, reading	7‡	7
Mathematics	5	5
Social studies	5	5
Science	5	5
Foreign language (or reading for grade 8)	5*	5
Physical education	4	5
Music	5†	5†
Art	5†	5†
Industrial arts—home economics	5†	5†
Health	5†	5†
Special interest or homeroom	4	4

(*shortened periods; †rotates each quarter; ‡plus 5 shortened periods.

In planning the conversion from a 7-8-9 junior high school to a 6-7-8-9 middle school, accomplished in the fall of 1967, the Community Middle School of Eagle Grove, Iowa, included as part of the program:

1. *Quest period:* a daily period in which individual students pursued topics of interest under a contract plan.
2. *Independent study:* students, under the contract plan, worked toward ends which they had helped to define and determine.
3. *Continuous progress:* a nongraded approach in all basic skills that allowed students to move forward at their own speed.[40]

The Educational Research Service conducted a survey, published in 1969, of 154 middle schools in districts enrolling 12,000 or more students. The results of this study are of real interest.[41] See tables 1 and 2.

TABLE 1
INSTRUCTIONAL ORGANIZATION AND PRACTICE, 154 MIDDLE SCHOOLS*

Organization and Practices	Number (and percent) of Schools by Grade Level†			
	Grade 5 (20 schools)	Grade 6 (146 schools)	Grade 7 (154 schools)	Grade 8 (148 schools)
Organization				
Self-contained classrooms	10(50.0)	31(21.2)	3(1.9)	3(1.0)
Partial departmentalization	7(35.0)	74(50.7)	55(35.7)	36(24.4)
Total departmentalization	3(15.0)	35(24.0)	91(59.1)	105(70.9)
No reply	——	6(4.1)	5(3.3)	4(2.7)
Practices				
Subject-area teams	4(20.0)	45(30.8)	51(33.1)	52(35.1)
Interdisciplinary teams	2(10.0)	19(13.0)	29(18.8)	25(16.9)
Small-group instruction	7(35.0)	55(37.7)	63(40.9)	66(44.6)
Large-group instruction	4(20.0)	35(24.0)	45(29.2)	47(31.8)
Flexible scheduling	5(25.0)	39(26.7)	44(28.6)	43(29.1)
Closed-circuit TV	1(5.0)	22(15.1)	24(15.6)	25(16.9)
Independent study	3(15.0)	30(20.5)	39(25.3)	40(27.0)
Individualized instruction	4(20.0)	39(26.7)	47(30.5)	48(32.4)
Tutorial programs	3(15.0)	32(21.9)	33(21.4)	31(20.9)

*Reprinted by permission of the American Association of School Administrators and NEA Research Division. *Middle Schools in Action.* Educational Research Service Circular No. 2, 1969. Washington, D.C.: The Service, March 1969.

†Percentages are based on the total number of middle schools in the survey which include each of the grades. The number of schools with each grade is shown in the column heading.

Certain patterns become apparent from descriptions of these and other middle schools. Subject-matter areas of language arts, social studies, mathematics, and science are usually required. Efforts are made, with varying success, to provide an exploratory program which has a wide variety of offerings. Foreign language, typing, industrial arts, homemaking, drama, fine arts, and music are quite common—usually on an elective basis, although they may be required. Ability grouping is usually seen in academic subjects, although all others are likely to be heterogeneously grouped.

TABLE 2

SPECIAL SUBJECTS TAUGHT, 154 MIDDLE SCHOOLS*

Special subjects	Number (and percent) of Schools by Grade Level†							
	Grade 5 (20 schools)		Grade 6 (146 schools)		Grade 7 (154 schools)		Grade 8 (148 schools)	
	Elective	*Required*	*Elective*	*Required*	*Elective*	*Required*	*Elective*	*Required*
Typing	...	...	4(2.7)	11(7.5)	11(7.1)	13(8.4)	19(12.8)	11(7.4)
Art	...	17(85.0)	8(5.5)	123(84.2)	41(26.6)	103(66.9)	89(60.1)	48(32.4)
Music	2(10.0)	19(95.0)	12(8.2)	124(84.9)	54(35.1)	99(64.3)	84(63.5)	51(34.5)
Industrial arts	1(5.0)	4(20.0)	2(1.4)	46(31.5)	31(20.1)	86(55.8)	59(39.9)	76(51.4)
Home economics	1(5.0)	4(20.0)	2(1.4)	48(32.9)	30(19.5)	85(55.2)	56(37.8)	76(51.4)
Spanish	...	...	5(3.4)	30(20.5)	32(20.8)	13(8.4)	45(30.4)	11(7.4)
French	1(5.0)	1(5.0)	11(7.5)	2(1.4)	35(22.7)	7(4.5)	45(30.4)	1(0.7)
Spanish or French	1(5.0)	1(5.0)	1(0.7)	17(11.6)	9(5.8)	12(7.8)	15(10.1)	6(4.1)
Other language	...	...	3(2.1)	2(1.4)	13(8.4)	4(2.6)	29(19.6)	2(1.4)

* Reprinted by permission of the American Association of School Administrators and NEA Research Division. *Middle Schools in Action.* Educational Research Service Circular No. 2, 1969. Washington, D.C.: The Service, March 1969. 80 p. $2.00.

†See footnote on Table 1.

While fifth and sixth grades are usually self-contained for half or more of the day, seventh and eighth grades may be partially or completely departmentalized. Frequent use is made of specialized teachers, team teaching, large group/small group learnings, and stress is placed upon the individual in programming, independent study, scheduling, and pursuit of special interests. The activity program is more closely tied to the regular curriculum than is usually the case with junior high schools, and interscholastic athletics, marching bands, and other evidences of excessive sophistication are not common. There is increased interest in experimentation and innovation as demonstrated by statements concerning use of ungrading, programmed instruction, television teaching, and other curricular and instructional ideas of recent emphasis.

It would seem that the current interest in middle schools, combined with dissatisfaction with certain aspects of the conventional junior high school, is creating an atmosphere within which many districts are developing a school which has definite possibilities for improving educational opportunities for the preadolescent and early adolescent.

SUMMARY

Proposed curricula and programs for middle schools with grades 5–8 or 6–8 bear certain similarities. All include the standard academics: language arts, social studies, science, and mathematics. A wide exploratory and elective program, open to all, is stressed, with real emphasis placed upon the individual student in programming, scheduling, and independent study. Examination of actual middle school programs indicates that some schools come very close to recommended practices, some are in accord with a part of the recommendation, and some are very similar to elementary schools or junior high schools.

As a generalization, it appears that the interest and real desire to improve the education of preadolescents and early adolescents is sparking many programs which are materially different from the traditional junior high school. There is little or no evidence that these programs are any better, but there is reported a material increase in student, teacher, and administrative satisfaction with the newer approaches.

REFERENCES

1. William M. Alexander and Emmet L. Williams, "Schools for the Middle School Years," *Educational Leadership*, Vol. 23 (December 1965), p. 219.
2. Unpublished correspondence: Superintendent, Caroline County, Denton, Maryland, Jan. 27, 1965.
3. Donald H. Eichorn, *The Middle School.* New York: Center for Applied Research, 1966.

4. James D. Virgilio, "The Administrative Role in Developing a Middle School," *Clearing House,* Vol. 43 (October 1968), p. 103.
5. *Ibid.*, p. 104.
6. *Loc. cit.*
7. Emmett L. Williams, "The Middle School Movement," *Today's Education,* Vol. 57 (December 1968), p. 42.
8. William M. Alexander, Emmett L. Williams, Mary Compton, Vynce A. Hines, and Dan Prescott, *The Emergent Middle School.* (New York: Holt, 1968, p. 63.
9. *Ibid.*, pp. 65–73.
10. Emmett L. Williams, "This Issue," *Theory Into Practice.* Columbus: Ohio State University College of Education, Vol. 7 (June 1968), p. 106.
11. Frank Brunetti, "The School in the Middle—A Search for New Direction," *School Planning Laboratory Reports* (June 1969), p. 2.
12. Judith Murphy, *Middle Schools.* New York: Educational Facilities Laboratories, 1965, p. 15.
13. Robert B. Davis, "The Madison Project's Approach to a Theory of Instruction," *Journal of Research in Science Teaching,* Vol. 2 (1964), pp. 146–162.
14. Emmett L. Williams, "What About the Junior High and Middle School?" *NASSP Bulletin,* Vol. 52 (May 1968), p. 128.
15. *Ibid.*, p. 132.
16. Gordon F. Vars, "Core Program in the Middle School," *Ideas Educational,* Kent University School, Kent State University, Vol, 5 (Winter 1962), pp. 25 –29.
17. J. H. Lounsbury and Harl Douglass, "Recent Trends in Junior High School Practices," *NASSP Bulletin,* Vol. 49 (September 1965), pp. 87–98.
18. Ann F. Grooms, *Perspectives on the Middle School.* Columbus: Merrill, 1967, p. 74.
19. Alexander and Williams, "Schools for the Middle Years."
20. William M. Alexander, "What Educational Plan for the In-Between-Ager?" *NEA Journal,* Vol. 55 (March 1966), p. 32.
21. Eichorn, *op. cit.*
22. Gordon F. Vars (ed.), "Guidelines for Junior High and Middle School Education," monograph. NASSP, Washington, D.C., 1966.
23. *Ibid.*, p. 6.
24. A. W. Howard, *Middle Schools in Oregon and Washington, 1965–66.* Unpublished doctoral dissertation, University of Oregon, 1966.
25. Theodore C. Moss, *Middle School.* Boston: Houghton, 1969, p. 44.
26. "Nation's School of the Month, Barrington Middle School, Barrington, Illinois," *Nation's Schools,* Vol. 76 (November 1965), p. 62.
27. "Barrington Middle School: A Report," *Barrington School District,* Barrington, Ill., 1966.
28. "A Middle School Above Par," *American School and University,* Vol. 38 (April 1966), pp. 68†69.
29. Paul J. Zdanowicz, "The Meredith G. Williams Middle School," *Educational Horizons,* Vol. 41 (Winter 1962), PP. 45–52.
30. Howard, *op. cit.*, p. 42.
31. Murphy, *op. cit.*

32. "Planning and Operating the Middle School," *Overview*, 4 (March 1963), pp. 52–53.
33. Sheldon R. Wiltse, "Developing a Unified Arts Program In an Ungraded Middle School," *Industrial Arts and Vocational Education*, Vol. 54 (March 1965), pp. 45–46.
34. Walter F. Fogg and Hugh J. Diamond, "Two Versions of the House Plan," *Nation's Schools*, Vol. 67 (June 1961), p. 94.
35. Grooms, *op. cit.*
36. *Ibid.*, p. 78.
37. W. George Batezel, "The Middle School: Philosophy, Program, Organization," *Clearing House*, Vol. 42 (April 1968), 487–490.
38. *Ibid.*, p. 488, as adapted.
39. *Ibid.*, pp. 488–489, as adapted.
40. Bruce Howell, "The Middle School—Is It Really Any Better?" *North Central Association Quarterly*, Vol. 43 (Winter 1969), p. 284.
41. *Middle Schools in Action*, Educational Research Service Circular No. 2. Washington, D.C.: American Association of School Administrators and Research Division, NEA, 1969.

part IV

CONTROVERSY AND PROBLEMS

Criticism, ferment, and lack of agreement in education have not left the junior high school untouched. The junior high school teacher and administrator face problems and must make decisions concerning questions that reflect our changing times and values. The change in pupil dress and hair styling has resulted in much publicity, some precipitate actions, and considerable soul-searching by those involved in junior high school work. Should the junior high school foster interscholastic athletics for its pupils? What is a reasonable program of student activities? What does research tell us of the best organization of time for instructional purposes? There are problems in grading and reporting, and although it is a common practice, questions are raised regularly concerning the efficacy of student grouping. A constant difficulty is that of staffing the junior high school with teachers and administrators trained to work with the early adolescent. All of these problems and more influence the curricula, organization, administration, and instructional patterns of the junior high school.

chapter 11

Staffing the Junior High School

It has never been as easy to get qualified and trained personnel for junior high school teaching as it has for elementary or high school. Traditionally, teacher training programs in the United States have either been elementary, with a small part of the program intended for the upper grades in a K–8 plan; or secondary, with the major emphasis upon the high school level. It has too often been assumed that those similarities between junior and senior high were of considerably more weight than their differences and both have been described as "secondary education." In too many instances teachers have accepted a position in junior high school as a temporary and poor second choice while they awaited an opportunity to move up to the high school. In other cases, a school district, finding a prospective high school teacher who appears to be a good candidate, hires this teacher and then literally puts him into storage in the junior high school for a year or two until a high school opening appears. These practices increase the rate of turnover and tend to staff the junior high with a disproporionate number of inexperienced teachers. The preference of prospective teachers for either elementary or high school rather than junior high teaching has been aggravated by the shortage of training programs intended specifically for those planning to teach in junior high school. This has continued a situation in which good junior high school teachers are even harder to secure than good senior high or good elementary teachers. It has been said that the junior high school, because of the lack of teachers trained specifically for this level has become "a school without teachers," an "institution in search of teachers," and a "training ground for the high school teachers."

THE PROBLEMS IN SECURING TEACHERS FOR THE JUNIOR HIGH

The reasons for the shortage of teachers specifically trained to teach in the junior high school are varied, many of them being so interrelated as to make their solutions most difficult. Where do we need to start? Conant remarked that "Neither the elementary school teacher nor the senior high school teacher is usually well adapted to give instruction in grades 7 and 8. This is a problem for state certification agencies and teacher training institutions."[1]

As a pat answer, this is true, but the problem goes deeper than this. Some teacher training institutions have offered programs designed to train teachers for junior high school and many still have such training available. But they do not find enough prospective teachers who select the junior high school as their first teaching choice, and coursework and teacher training programs cannot operate without students. State certificate requirements have required specific kinds of coursework and training for prospective junior high teachers and, once more, have found a shortage of those who wish to teach in junior high schools. School administrators, desperate for junior high teachers, then request emergency or temporary certification for a candidate who has, they hope and believe, some qualifications for a junior high position, and has expressed a willingness to take the job for a year. As Popper points out, the junior high school principal finds himself in the unenviable position of being held responsible for the attainment of specific goals in a "functionally differentiated unit of a professional service organization whose technical personnel lack the special skills and institutional commitment for the performance of essential functions."[2]

It appears that a major difficulty is the lack of interest of prospective teachers in teaching in the junior high school. This lack of interest is partially attributable to a lack of prestige for the junior high teacher as opposed to high school teaching; partially to a desire to work with younger children on an elementary level; a wish to teach subject matter in depth to high school students; a lack of understanding of the early adolescent and of the background, history, philosophy, functions, and goals of the junior high school; and even a dislike verging on fear for the entire age group and junior high concept.

Some elementary teachers, particularly those who have taught upper elementary grades, will accept a transfer to junior high school and may even regard it as a step up. Rare indeed, however, is the high school teacher who will regard a junior high school teaching assignment as anything even resembling a promotion.

This is a problem for more than teacher training programs in colleges and universities; more than for state certification standards. This is a problem for all who are involved in the education of junior high and middle school children: public school districts, junior high school administrators, teacher organizations, state and federal agencies, teacher training institutions, administrative organizations, and parent groups. The growth of the middle schools, particularly those that include grades 6–9 or even 5–9, will require that the teachers for those schools have an understanding of fifth- and sixth-graders—something not commonly expected of those who have high school certification.

The junior high school, classified since its inception as a secondary school, has suffered in many ways from this unfortunate label. So far as its teachers are concerned, the preparation for junior and senior high school teaching is in most cases quite similar, and in some instances it is identical. There is, however, a growing realization that the junior high school has its own unique problems, is not a secondary school, is significantly different (or should be) from both elementary school and the high school, and should, therefore, have teachers who are trained specifically to teach in junior high school.

> If . . . it can be agreed that the student in the junior high school is significantly different from both the elementary and the senior high school student, these differences should be translatable into a program of education not only for junior high school students but for junior high school teachers.[3]

The teaching staff of the junior high school has unusual responsibilities in working with children who are leaving childhood and emerging into adolescence, for them a new and complex situation. There is obviously a need, in an institution with special purposes and functions, for an unusually well-qualified and specially trained staff. Bossing emphasizes this when he states:

> It may be that we are reaching a point at which we are ready to say a teacher not specifically prepared and qualified would appear as unfitted to teach in the junior high school as would a well-qualified teacher for the senior high school be unfitted to teach in the elementary school.[4]

If the junior high school student is indeed a unique individual in a school environment that is neither elementary nor secondary, then the teachers for the junior high school must be prepared in programs that are distinct and different from those for elementary teachers and secondary teachers. As one educator put it succinctly and somewhat wryly, "Who should teach in the junior high school? The answer is obvious: junior high school teachers!"[5]

ATTITUDES TOWARDS JUNIOR HIGH TEACHING

A number of investigations have been conducted in attempts to determine exactly what the problems were in finding teachers for junior high school, keeping them once they have been hired, and to ascertain what attitudes toward the junior high school are held by prospective teachers.

A study at Cornell of 600 teachers found that those teaching grades 7 and 8 were much less satisfied with the level of their assignment than were teachers in the grades both above and below.[6] An analysis of the stated reasons for dissatisfaction indicated that "the nature of the curriculum [the ideas], rather than the nature of the pupils at this level, seemed to be predominant. Teachers who enjoy teaching many subject areas cannot do so in the junior high school, nor can those who enjoy teaching advanced content do that."[7] The holding power, Bienenstok reported, of the junior high grades was found to be markedly weak among young teachers of both sexes.[8] Another study found that, compared with teachers at other grade levels, teachers of grades 7-8-9 were less permanent at their grade level, less likely to remain in teaching, younger, and had less teaching experience.[9] The reason most often given for disliking to teach at this level was that of discipline problems, while "professional and salary advancement" and the "desire to teach more challenging subject matter" were the reasons most frequently stated for seeking a change to another level of teachings.

The findings of this survey caused its author to agree with the characterization of the junior high school as that of "a school without teachers."

A subsequent survey[10] on a nationwide basis of superintendents and junior high principals found that the chief cause for failure of beginning junior high teachers was an inability to cope with junior high children. Discouraging as the results of studies and such as these are, they become more distressing in view of the increasing school enrollments and the growing need for teachers at this level.

Hood described the great differences between the staffing problems of the elementary school and the senior high school when he reported in 1965 that

> The ratio of new elementary teachers to the number of new high school teachers is 6:9. . . . The ratio of the elementary vacancies to high school vacancies is just the opposite, 9:6. In other words, there are six elementary teachers for nine vacancies and nine new high school teachers for each six vacancies.[11]

The ultimate placement of the surplus high school teachers is obvious. Because they hold a secondary teaching certificate, many of these high school teachers will take a junior high school postion which they don't want, and for which they are not trained, as a temporary situation until they can move into a senior high school teaching position. Everyone loses.

Prestige, the image of the high school, as compared with that of the elementary school or the junior high school, is definitely a factor.

Hood[12] reported that a survey made on a West Coast campus of the status image of the several major fields of study available indicated that education students ranked 19th out of 49 majors listed—a position well above the median. High school teaching, however, ranked 11th, while elementary teaching ranked only 34th. Junior high school teaching was not stated but the status image of the junior high school is not as favorable as that of the high school, although it may well be said that no one really knows exactly what the image of the junior high school is.

Bienenstok also noted the prestige factor in a study of 1349 New York junior high teachers:

> Relative low prestige, in the eyes of colleagues and in the community, was particularly frustrating to some teachers. . . . It appears that disenchantment is most prevalent among those who prefer an academically oriented instructional climate and those who set a high value on professional status and prestige.[13]

A 1968 survey of the attitudes of 172 prospective and experienced secondary school teachers toward the junior high school produced some results of interest.[14] The sample, 172 respondents, 86 men and 86 women, included 120 teachers with one or more years of experience, 17 who had just completed student teaching but who had not yet taught, and 35 who had not yet been involved in student teaching. As a part of the findings, Hubert reported that

1. Secondary education students, whether junior, senior, or graduate, whether at the prestudent teaching, student teaching, or experienced teacher level, all expressed a strong preference for older students and higher grade levels.
2. Secondary education students, regardless of their reasons for entering teaching, preferred older students and higher grade levels.
3. The level at which the secondary education student did his student teaching was a definite factor in his later preference for age and grade levels for teaching. Junior high student teachers were far more receptive to the junior high age and grade levels. Senior high student teachers, "a much greater number," overwhelmingly preferred senior high grades. *Those who had student taught at both the junior high and senior high levels were the only group which preferred the junior high ages and grades.*
4. Teachers who had experience at the junior high level were far more tolerant of that age and grade level than were teachers without such experience. They were also more critical of the training received by junior high teachers than were teachers who did not have junior high experience.
5. Junior high school teachers were strongly critical of the policy of identical preparation and certification for junior high and senior high teachers.

6. Those who had taught at the junior high level showed strong support for a middle school organization of grades 6-7-8. This feeling was not expressed by teachers who did not have junior high experience.
7. Completion of a course on the junior high school affected positively attitudes of respondents toward the junior high age and grade levels. Stated preferences of those who had not completed such a course were strongly for teaching in the senior high school.

If one could generalize from these findings, it would appear that knowledge of the junior high school and of the junior high school student, combined with experience at this level by prospective teachers can materially increase the number of candidates for junior high school teaching. It is desirable and necessary that the junior high school be recognized as a unique institution in its own right with a distinct program and curricula, and as a corollary to this, that the preparation of teachers for this institution must also be distinctly different. Certainly the image of the junior high school must be more clearly defined, and the opportunities available in teaching at this level must be made more obvious. There is a distinct need for better public relations and presentation of information relative to junior high school teaching. This is a responsibility of all of those concerned with the education of this age group.

PREPARATION AND CERTIFICATION

Through the years there has been no lack of recognition of the need for specially trained teachers for junior high school, but there has been little progress toward alleviating the problem. In the early junior high schools there were few teachers with any specific training for junior high school work and this situation still persists in most studies, surveys, and reports. Conant[15] in 1960 noted that teachers for junior high school should be mature teachers with the understanding of children characteristic of elementary teachers plus a concentration of knowledge in a subject field. He added that such specially qualified teachers are unfortunately hard to find, a statement that surprised no one in junior high school education.

Teachers who are transferred to the junior high school from the elementary school are accustomed to the normative standard of the self-contained classroom, while those transferred from high school are accustomed to departmentalization. Neither of these is the norm in junior high schools, and teachers who have not become adjusted to junior high procedures are likely to concentrate on lecturing, excessive homework, and an emphasis upon grades for the sake of grades. Still, in the absence of teachers who are junior high school trained, there is no alternative for the desperate superintendent who still has junior high school staff vacancies, but to transfer someone who is at least not violently resisting the move.

In the opinion of many educators, a separate and specific program which is developed for the purpose of training junior high school teachers is not only desirable, but has become essential, yet for several reasons such programs are but few in number. Some institutions have offered such programs and after a short time have been forced to discontinue them because of a lack of interest and low enrollment. Other colleges and universities have felt that a third division in teacher training would require specialization and course development out of proportion to the benefits to be derived. Few states require special certification to teach in junior high school with the result that, in some states, an elementary certificate will permit junior high teaching. In others the secondary certificate is sufficient, and in still others one may teach in junior high school with either an elementary or a secondary certificate.

DeVane,[16] in a survey of 213 junior high school teachers, found that there was no specifically designed program of teacher preparation followed by the teachers as a group; neither was there any evidence that any of the teachers had deliberately prepared to teach in junior high school. Ackerman,[17] in 1960, found only twenty-eight teacher training institutions in the United States with a four-year program for training junior high school teachers. He found also that most of the special junior high curricula were but modifications of the curricula for elementary or general secondary teachers. Hoost[18] reported in 1963 that more than a dozen states issued special certificates for junior high school teachers, but many states having this special certification do not require it, but permitted holders of elementary or secondary certificates to teach in junior high school.

Bossing[19], in checking state certification requirements for 1965–66, found that only nine states could be classified as issuing special certificates for teaching the junior high school years. It was somewhat difficult, he noted, in some instances to ascertain just what was regarded by a state as a special junior high school teaching certificate, since many states issued certificates for K–8 for elementary teachers, and certificates to teach in grades 7–12 for secondary, and carried these standards along with the special certification programs for junior high school teaching. In states with overlapping certificates that permit a wider range of job opportunities, it is difficult to see why a teacher would wish to limit himself to the special certificate, and thus disqualify himself from the more general certificate that could be his with the same amount of preparation.

The University of Indiana at Bloomington pioneered a special training program for junior high school teachers resulting in a special junior high school certificate restricted to grades 7, 8, and 9. This special certificate became effective in September 1963. By November 1964 there were only an estimated 50 students in the entire state who were working toward the special certificate, largely because Indiana teachers could still secure a secondary certificate permitting them to teach grades 7 through 12.[20] A junior high endorsement on the Indiana elementary certificate requires six semester hours of course work distributed among adolescent psychology, junior high school curriculum and organization, and developmental reading. In addition, Indiana requires 24 hours in a subject teaching field and two or three semester hours in supervised teaching at the junior high school level.

New York State, in revising certification standards, included a requirement that all permanent elementary certificates incorporate five years of study and a 30-semester hour minimum in a department or interdepartmental planned program of liberal arts studies.

> A special junior high endorsement on this K–9 certificate is awarded for 36 hours of work in English or social studies, 42 in science, or 24 in mathematics—at least 80 of the 300 (required) clock hours of supervised student teaching must be in the junior high grades. . . . Unfortunately, no specific work in junior high school education, not even adolescent psychology, is listed as part of the required semester hours in professional education.[21]

ALTERNATIVE PROPOSALS

There are several avenues that can be followed in the preparation and certification of teachers for junior high and middle schools.

1. Continue with the common practice of overlapping certificates for teachers who have experienced a teacher training program that is either elementary or secondary. Such programs seldom give much time to training junior high school teachers but concentrate on elementary, usually grades below 7, or secondary, with a senior high school emphasis. Overlapping elementary and secondary certificates have the additional problem of variation in the grades included since state standards vary. It is possible to receive an elementary certificate that qualifies one to teach as many as eight, nine, or even ten grades, i.e., 1–8, K–8, 1–9, K–9. Secondary certificates are usually limited to 7–12 but may include 6–12. In any case, but little consideration is given to specific needs of junior high school students or junior high school teachers.

2. Overlapping certificates for elementary and secondary may be issued with a junior high endorsement, and with the stipulation that the prospective junior high school teacher take a minimum of course work and some supervised student teaching at the junior high school level. Such course work and student teaching *must be a planned sequence* and a part of a planned program of junior high school teacher eductation at a teacher training institution.

3. Issue three types of certificates: elementary, middle or intermediate, and secondary, with some overlapping still permitted. The elementary

certificate could include K–5 or K–6, middle or intermediate to include grades 5–9 or 6–9, and secondary to qualify teachers for grades 9–12. The middle or intermediate certificate would be issued to teachers who had completed a planned course of study that included supervised junior high school student teaching, adolescent psychology, junior high school curriculum, and junior high school philosophy, history, goals, and functions.

4. A fourth possibility is even more restrictive—to wit, issue three types of certificates and permit no overlapping: elementary, K–4; middle or intermediate, 5–8; and secondary, 9–12. Each certificate again should be based upon satisfactory completion of a planned program of teacher education, including student teaching, or each level of certification for which one is qualified.

At the very least, it seems reasonable to insist that any type of overlapping certificate require student teaching for the levels covered by such a certificate, i.e., an elementary certificate, good for K–8 or K–9, would include as a requirement student teaching in both elementary and junior high school. In the same manner, a secondary certificate qualifying a teacher to hold a position in grades 7–12 or 6–12 would require student teaching in both junior and senior high school.

Any pronounced change in certification standards and in teacher training programs will have to be accomplished through careful planning and cooperation of all concerned: state offices of education, teacher training institutions, teacher and administrative organizations, and public school districts. It is certain, however, that the time is long past for adopting standards and programs of teacher training leading to the best possible preparation for junior high school teachers.

A 1964 study[22] included as a major recommendation that colleges and universities, by providing teachers especially trained for junior high school, as well as furnishing leadership in conferences, workshops, and in-service training, can perform their greatest service.

The 1966 monograph of the NASSP, Guidelines for Junior High and Middle School Education,[23] picked up the same refrain in recommending that colleges and universities provide teacher training specificially intended for the prospective teacher at this level. A 1967 article[24] repeated a complaint of years before: teacher education programs do not take cognizance of the middle years—they are either elementary or secondary. The words are still the same and so also is the tune, although there have, in the past few years, been some indications of attempts to improve the situation. The problem is complicated since analysis of group and individual studies has provided little in the way of specific information on the characteristics of effective junior high school teachers. Authorities are, however, in agreement concerning some aspects of preparation, concepts, understandings, and qualities.

THE TEACHER WE NEED

Certainly the effective junior high school teacher will possess many if not all of the characteristics of successful teachers at other levels. It is essential with children of this age that he be enthusiastic in his teaching, interested in both his work and in the children with whom he works. Teachers are needed who will make the junior high school their career, who do not regard a junior high teaching assignment as a promotion from elementary nor a temporary delay on their way to high school teaching. The successful junior high school teacher has a thorough understanding of the preadolescent and early adolescent; he appreciates their wide range of differences; he likes this age group; and he has a sincere belief in the idea of the best education for all children. We need teachers who care.[25]

These teachers must have a solid foundation in subject matter, preferably in more than one field, and must be well trained in techniques of teaching which permit maximum flexibility and provision for the development of individual interests and abilities so that they can teach students effectively at different levels of achievement. One survey characterized the effective junior high school teacher as one who "is willing to go the extra mile."[26]

What kind of teacher training program can be developed which might contribute toward achieving such a desirable goal? In a general way it has been proposed that the program for prospective junior high school teachers consist of approximately 40 percent general education, 40 percent work in the subject field or fields, and 20 percent professional education.[27]

A study reported by Johnson indicated that instructional skills appeared as a top strength in successful beginning junior high teachers.[28] In second place was discipline ("control of the situation, student respect"), while professional demeanor was third in importance, and subject knowledge fourth.

Principals and superintendents who were the respondents in Smith's study stated that the primary reasons for failure of junior high school teachers were: "inability to cope with junior high students" (61 percent); "poor human relations" (24 percent); "inability to handle subject matter" (2 percent); and, "other" (13 percent).[29] As a matter of interest, these principals and superintendents responded overwhelmingly that the junior high school teacher must be well prepared in his subject field, although they believed that today's graduates are well enough prepared in this respect that only a very few fail for this reason. The respondents emphasized two points: (1) we must prepare teachers who are junior high oriented, and (2) that the teacher training institutions have a responsibility of providing leadership to help junior high school teachers and administrators keep abreast of increased knowledge and change.

Rock and Hemphill,[30] in a 1965 study with 4,496 responding junior high school principals, found that over 60 percent of these consider courses stressing physical and emotional development of the adolescent to be most essential; 43 percent of the responding junior high school principals believe that junior high school student teaching is essential; over one-third believe courses concerned with the teaching of reading are essential; and there was a consensus among the principals relative to the need for a good background in psychology. Course work concerned with teaching methods in specific junior high school areas were listed as essential by 37 percent of those replying. More than 70 percent of the principals favored extending the degree program to five years and including more liberal arts courses.

Such evidence as is available is in agreement that junior high school teachers should have as much exposure as is possible to the junior high school in their teacher training programs. Especially should they do their student teaching at this level and include work in the psychology of the early adolescent. Yet the bitter truth is that the great majority of junior high school teachers have had neither, but are teaching in a situation for which they are poorly prepared—if, in fact, they have had any preparation at all for this level. As Southworth remarked,

> The relatively easy access to the American classroom by any traditionally trained bachelor's holder is further evidence that standards are dictated by expediency, not sound rationale or belief in a body of professional knowledge.[31]

RECAPITULATION

Although the junior high school teacher training program should be considered as a separate entity in the educational structure, the program should provide a balanced college education. Teachers should have a broad general education in humanities, social sciences, and sciencies, as well as a thorough professional education. They should be aware of the various learning theories and have a real understanding of the psychology and characteristics of the early adolescent. They should know the purposes, functions, and historic background of the junior high school and how this level is articulated with those grades above and below. Other aspects of the junior high school curriculum should be familiar to them, and they should understand the school activity program. Prospective junior high school teachers need a competency in the variety of teaching techniques and technology, particularly in those which are of relatively recent development.[32] They should be familiar with the purposes and techniques of evaluation and measurement, and—even more important—they must realize that tests are but tools for teaching and the best tests are those which help the student to progress with his own potential as the standard.

Perhaps the single most important component of the program for training teachers for junior high school is student teaching. This should positively be at the junior high school level. Unless there is no junior high school in which prospective teachers may do their practice teaching, there is no excuse for the embryo junior high school teacher to perform his practice teaching at any other level. When it is stated again and again that junior high teachers must know and understand this age group, it would appear obvious that here is where the practice teaching should take place. Yet repeatedly, in all sections of the country, teachers take positions in junior high school who have never taught a day at this level. Indeed, for one who attended a public school under some other kind of organizational plan, such as 8–4 or 6-6, the day he steps through the doors to teach may be the first time that the beginning teacher has ever been in a junior high school. Equally undesirable is the practice of assigning student teachers to a school for only one or at most two hours a day for a semester or in some cases a quarter. Such a fragmented and partial approach can only provide an illusory and disjointed picture of a school. If state certification standards permit overlapping, such as K–8 and 7–12 certification, then student teaching should be required for all levels for which certification is granted.

The practice must be eliminated of going into junior high school teacher training and teaching as the least desirable of three alternatives. Standards need to be set which are if anything more severe than those for teachers at any other grade level, and the selection of teacher trainees should include a screening interview in depth.

In the course of the professional preparation every opportunity should be taken to observe junior high school classes, activities, and students, both before and after the practice teaching. Observation may be done singly or in small groups, but there should be a substantial amount of it, and observation should be followed by group discussion and analysis. Observation needs to be more than a bland inspection—specific behaviors should be noted. Perhaps the most logical way to train teachers for junior high school is to work toward a continual involvement in the junior high schools.

Beyond the college and university teacher programs it is most desirable to provide an orientation program for new teachers and continuous in-service training throughout the year for all teachers.

We want and need good teachers at the junior high school level. We have been fortunate that there are some good teachers who have taught and are teaching at this level, but there is a need for people who are trained for and will stay at this level. Too often the junior high school is the training ground for high school teachers, counselors, and administrators. It will be necessary to extend the status and prestige of junior high school teaching so that it has a recognized and developed program of its own. Prospective teachers must be made aware of junior high school programs and guided into them. The mere existence of a teacher training program does not guarantee enrollment.

The only way that we will get the professional teachers we need for junior high school is to prepare them specifically for junior high, although special preparation may not require special certification.

SUMMARY

Junior high school teachers were originally drawn from elementary and secondary teacher training programs. Through the years efforts have been made to develop teacher training programs aimed specifically at training junior high school teachers but the results to date have been small, with the effect that the great majority of junior high school teachers are still trained for elementary or secondary. The junior high school suffers a rate of teacher turnover considerably in excess of that for either elementary or secondary, partially because many junior high school teachers take such an assignment as a temporary position, hoping to move to high school teaching, and partially because of the prestige factor. There are not enough teachers trained specifically for junior high school teaching. Successful junior high school teachers are enthusiastic, interested in their subject, enjoy their work, feel affection for this age group, and intend to make a career of teaching junior high school. A program of training teachers for junior high school should include a broad general education, subject material specialization, and professional preparation. It must include adolescent psychology and student teaching in a junior high school—preferably on something approaching an all-day basis. Orientation for new teachers and in-service training for all teachers should be provided.

REFERENCES

1. James B. Conant, "Some Problems of the Junior High School," *NASSP Bulletin*, Vol. 44 (April 1960), p. 314.
2. Samuel H. Popper, *Middle Schools.* Waltham Mass., Blaisdell, 1967, p. 218.
3. Conrad F. Toepfer, Jr., "Who Should Teach in Junior High?" *Clearing House*, Vol. 40 (October 1965), p. 75.
4. Nelson L. Bossing, "Preparing Teachers for Junior High School," *High School Journal*, Vol. 50 (December 1966), p. 150.
5. Toepfer, *op. cit.*, p. 74.
6. Mauritz Johnson, Jr., "School in the Middle, Junior High: Education's Problem Child," *Saturday Review*, Vol. 45 (July 21, 1962), p. 41.
7. *Ibid.*, p. 41.
8. Theodore Bienenstok, "Strains in Junior High Teaching," *Education Digest*, Vol. 29 (May 1964), p. 34–35.
9. Ray Budde, "A Study of the Permanence of Seventh, Eighth, and Ninth Grade Teachers in Michigan," *NASSP Bulletin*, Vol. 46 (February 1962), pp. 389–390.

10. Mark C. Smith, "The Case for Teachers Who Are Specifically Prepared to Teach in Junior High Schools," *Journal of Teacher Education*, Vol. 17 (Winter 1966), p. 440.
11. Charles E. Hood, "Teaching As A Career," *Clearing House*, Vol. 40 (December 1965), p. 228.
12. Hood, *loc. cit.*
13. Bienenstok, *op. cit.*, p. 35.
14. Jeanne B. Hubert, *A Survey of the Attitudes of Prospective and Experienced Secondary School Teachers Toward the Junior High School*, unpublished master's thesis, University of New Mexico, 1969.
15. James B. Conant, *Education in the Junior High School Years.* Princeton, N. J.: Educational Testing Service, 1960, p. 13.
16. Leroy M. DeVane, "Teachers," *NASSP Bulletin*, Vol. 46 (February 1962), pp. 379–80.
17. Ralph E. Ackerman, *A Critical Analysis of Programs for Junior High School Teachers in Teacher Education Institutions in the United States*, unpublished doctoral dissertation, University of Connecticut, 1960.
18. William R. Hoots, Jr., "Junior High School Certification," *NASSP Bulletin*, Vol. 47 (October 1963), p. 45.
19. Bossing, *op. cit.*, p. 150.
20. Arthur H. Rice, "What's Wrong With Junior High? Nearly Everything," *Nation's Schools*, Vol. 74 (November 1964), p. 31.
21. Gordon F. Vars, "Preparing Junior High Teachers," *Clearing House*, Vol. 40 (October 1965), p. 78.
22. Smith, *op. cit.*, p. 442.
23. Gordon F. Vars (ed.), "Guidelines for Junior High and Middle School Education," *NASSP Monograph*, 1966, p. 17.
24. William A. Cuff, "Middle Schools on the March," *NASSP Bulletin*, Vol. 51 (February 1967), p. 86.
25. Jack E. Blackburn, "The Junior High School Teacher We Need," *Educational Leadership*, Vol. 23 (December 1965), p. 206.
26. DeVane, *op. cit.*, p. 381.
27. Vars, "Guidelines," p. 16.
28. Mauritz Johnson, Jr., "Profiles of Beginning Junior High School Teachers," *Journal of Teacher Education*, Vol. 16 (September 1965), p. 303–306.
29. Smith, *op. cit.*, p. 443.
30. Donald A. Rock and John K. Hemphill, Report of the Junior High School Principalship, *NASSP*, 1966, p. 8.
31. Horton C. Southworth, "Teacher Education for the Middle School: A Framework," *Theory Into Practice*, Vol. 7 (June 1968), p. 124.
32. Edward B. Weisse, "Re-Structure: A Proposal for Junior High School Curriculum Design," *Indiana State University Teachers College Journal*, Vol. 39 (November 1967), p. 61.

chapter 12

Junior High School Student Activities and Athletics

Criticism of student activities in the junior high school has been extensive, sometimes being heard from those who disapprove of virtually any school activity, and sometimes coming from those who favor the concept but do not like part or all of a specific activity program. When the cry goes up to "rid the schools of fads and frills," the student activity is often one of the first areas to feel the pressure for excision, amputation, or elimination. There is a strong feeling by some that the business of the schools is rightfully only the three R's and anything other than the academic program is a waste of time, money, facilities, and effort. From this point of view one may go to the opposite extreme where the activity program takes on an excessive emphasis, and in its most radical forms it may work to the detriment of the regular courses of study.

Within the activity program itself are rich areas for criticism—which is usually forthcoming. There is dissatisfaction when there is too little student participation, yet schemes abound for limiting participation because some students are said to participate excessively. There are claims that one or more activities—usually athletics and music—dominate the entire activity program, get more than their fair share of funds, and are favored in sponsorship, in support, and in meeting times and places. There are complaints that students are being exploited, as may happen with the industrial arts club that becomes the unofficial school handyman's association. There are criticisms of the organization of activity programs, of their administration and financing, and of the poor quality of sponsorship, guidance, and leadership. Some activities have been criticized for their tendency to be cliquish, exclusive, excessively sophisticated, and for establishing unreasonable student fees, dues, and costs. Eligibility rules for students who wish to participate in activities are warmly supported by some and still more warmly condemned by others. There have even been complaints from some church groups that school activities take too much student time that could be spent on various church activities.

An examination of the stated functions of the junior high school, regardless of which list is perused, supports a strong and well-planned program of activities in the junior high school. Such a program can and should be an integral part of the overall program. It provides experiences in exploration, integration, and guidance, differentiated opportunities in accordance with individual interests, abilities, and talents; facilitates socialization, and aids articulation. A good junior high school activity program enriches and differentiates learning, employs and improves basic skills, assists the early adolescent in making personal-social adjustments, aids in learning to live in a democracy, and provides opportunities for creative experiences.

Certainly the characteristics of the preadolescent and early adolescent are such as to make a good junior high school program of activities a necessary part of the school. Ninth graders, whether in a junior high school or a high school, can especially profit from a carefully planned and developed student activity program. Graham makes the following generalizations in regard to adolescents and student activities:[1]

A. Generalizations about Adolescents

1. As basic needs, adolescents need to be recognized and praised; to belong; and to have peer companionship.
2. The adolescent peer group is a distinct factor in shaping the personality of its members.
3. Adolescents perform better in both academics and in social activities when they feel secure.
4. Higher morale results when adolescents form a cohesive group.
5. Through peer association, adolescents learn and develop many of the skills of cooperative endeavor.
6. Learning to be adults is easier for adolescents when they associate with adults.
7. Adolescents learn to accept responsibility by being given responsibility.
8. Learning to make sound decisions results from practice in decision making.

B. Generalizations about Student Activities

1. Student activities more nearly approximate the kinds of learnings to be found in peer groups than do regular class activities.
2. Counseling and guidance receive substantial contributions from student activities.
3. The "need to belong" can be met by student activities, especially for an adolescent who is not a member of a peer group.
4. The kinds of recognition and rewards for achievement provided by student activities are satisfying psychologically.

5. The teacher, changing his role from that of a director of instruction, becomes an advisor who assists adolescents to improve their personal relationships, develop democratic behavior, and helps them to increase achievement in a student activity.
6. A favorable school atmosphere is enhanced when faculty and administration work cooperatively with pupils in class and extraclass activities.
7. It is probable that adolescents will learn more about some kinds of human relationships and democratic behaviors in extraclass rather than class activities.
8. The activities program provides opportunities for students to learn to apply skills acquired in classes and to explore various knowledges in depth.

In stressing the values of group membership and group leadership for adolescents, Mathes[2] notes that

1. Leadership can be learned.
2. Leadership is both diagnosis and treatment.
3. Leadership recognizes both group goals and individual needs.
4. Leadership implies good human relations.

Man is a social animal, and since social behavior is learned, the junior high school has the responsibility of providing those social experiences accepted by society and necessary for the fullest development of the individual. The experiences of the growing-up years have lasting effects upon the adult years. "The student activities in the junior high take on unique characteristics because adolecents have special needs."[3]

NAMES, DEFINITIONS, AND BACKGROUND

It has been said[4] that a substantial part of the difficulties that affect the student activities program may be directly attributed to the connotations of the various names under which such programs have been established. One of the earliest and most common designations was "extracurricular," which was interpreted to mean those activities which were in addition to and outside of the usual and approved functions of the schools. The passage of time found that many activities, formerly classified as extracurricular, became accepted and accredited portions of the standard curriculum. Classes in journalism and photography are instances in point.

In an effort to avoid the implication that activities were extraeducational, other names were devised, developed, and usually found wanting. "Extraclass," "semicurricular," "nonclass," "school activities," and "cocurricular" have all been used with varying degrees of acceptance, although the term which currently seems to be most descriptive and popular is "student activities." Except for the last name, all such terms share a common weakness in that they attract attention to the connotation of activities being outside of the regular curricular program. Frederick[5] believes that the best term is the "Third Curriculum," the other two curricula being the required courses of study and the elective program.

Difficult as it has been to find a name that offends no one and may even please the majority, a definition of student activities and their scope and nature has been if anything even harder to achieve. A somewhat loose definition describes student activities as those experiences, events, and programs which are not granted academic credit, are teacher sponsored, partially or completely student organized and administered, voluntary in nature and open to all who wish to participate, subject to some degree of control by the school authorities, and carried on under the auspices of the school within or without the regular school day. Obviously this definition has weaknesses—for example, what is "some degree of control"? Furthermore, in many cases the "cocurriculum" has become a part of the curriculum; one may in many schools attend and receive credit for a regularly scheduled chorus or publications class, yet these are usually classified as student activities.

Too, students and teachers began to wonder why there should be "all the fun in the science club and all the drudgery in the science class," with the result that student activities have begun to "flow into the curriculum to enrich it."[6]

Newer approaches to teaching and learning have integrated more activities within the regular curriculum and have tended to blur even more the lines of separation between activities and traditional school work. The student store, for example, formerly operated by a service club, may now be an accepted part of the business curriculum. The growing use of individual study, individual projects, and large-group–small-group work finds many students involved as a part of their study in what were formerly classified as extracurricular activities. The use of block-time and core classes in the junior high school and the practice of developing a comprehensive activity program which is scheduled within the school day has lent strength to student activities, giving this aspect of the junior high school what often amounts to equal curricular status.

Acceptance of student activities has increased to the point where a large number of high schools and many junior high schools have a staff member designated as full-time Activities Director. The function of such a director is to work with teachers and students in organizing, scheduling, and advising student activities.

Certainly such acceptance is relatively new; it was not always thus in American schools. Roughly, there have been four periods in the growth and expansion of student activities in the United States:[7]

1. The period of suppression that began in Colonial times and in some

areas still exists, at least to a degree. Characterized by the Puritan tradition —school is grim and school is serious just as life is hard and earnest— anything which was enjoyable and involved some pleasure in doing was suspect and sinful. The ironic aspect of this attitude in our present society may be observed in those critics of school activities (and of anything in school which is a divergency from straight academics) when such judges deliver another blast from their position at the bridge tables, bowling alleys, or golf links. We talk a good fight concerning the value of hard work—and surely there is value—but we tend to condemn the schools for fads and frills while seeking more hobbies, recreation, and "a change of activity from the regular routine" ourselves.

2. The period of toleration developed as the driving pressure to exist from day to day and month to month began to relax. When there was time to form literary societies, debating groups, and music groups, the schools "relaxed the rules and penalties"[8] and tolerated such student efforts, so long as they did not interfere with academic studies. To a degree, this feeling still exists with some people in some schools." The belief that student activities could offer a great deal, perhaps even more to many students than an academic subject, and therefore should be encouraged, was slow to be accepted.

3. The period of capitalization finds student activities considered to be a fundamental part of a school's offerings. In this phase, activities are encouraged, publicized, made readily available, and are well supported. Indeed, they are in many cases so interwoven with curricular offerings and methods of instruction that it is difficult to distinguish between "activities" and course offerings. This incidentally did not mean the end of criticism; it only broadened the field. For every one who pointed out that various activities were an integral part of the Greek and Roman education, for example, there was some one to say triumphantly, "Yes, and look what happened to them!"

As a measure of the significance more recently attached to participation in student activities, however, one may note several items:

(a) The space for recording participation in activities on applications for college entrance, enlistment forms for the armed services, job application forms, and applications for scholarship, as well as the importance accorded such participation by all of these.

(b) The terrific increase in leisure time which finds so many people at loose ends, at a loss as to how to spend it, and the need therefore to develop educational programs that will enable us to make the best use of such leisure.

(c) The increase in adult evening classes, hobby and handicraft associations, and the growth in number of "how to" publications, "do-it-yourself" magazines, and specific activity journals.

(d) Facilities, materials, supplies, and equipment provided as a matter of course to elementary, junior high, and senior high schools for normal operation.

(e) Scheduled time within the daily schedule for activities and the absorption and inclusion of many activities, such as art and music, within the regular curriculum.

(f) Extended school programs such as Saturday classes and summer programs that generally include as a substantial part of their offerings courses which were once considered extracurricular activities, such as camping, woodcraft, dramatics, and dance.

4. In the period of exploitation, the main purpose of the activity or activities becomes one of some advantage to the institution or sponsor rather than the main benefit accruing to the participating students. It is not difficult to find instances where music programs, dramatics, and athletics have become so important in terms of financial return or for prestige purposes that teachers of other classes find their programs subordinated to the demands of the activity. Students miss classes for rehearsals, for practice, for turnout, or may even miss half a day or more of school on the day of "the game." Exploitation can also exist when a glee club or singing group becomes a steady performing group for service club luncheons and dinners. One junior high school "star" ensemble of fourteen girls put on thirty-two performances out of school in three months.

It would seem that such exploitation and commercialization of student activities, even on the junior high school level, is on the increase, but this does not have to be. In schools where it is remembered that activities are but a part of the whole junior high school program, where educators have the courage and professional integrity to resist these encroachments, there will not be what has been termed "the inexorable drift to exploitation."[9]

PROBLEMS AND CONTENTION

A continuing problem in the junior high school student activity program is that of participation. Various schemes have been proposed to control overparticipation and domination by a few, yet there has long been concern by school people because of a lack of participation by so many students. It has been said that many administrators are "intent upon a student activity program limited to those few students who have learned to conform and live with the educational hierarchy."[10] These students are accorded the privilege of student activities much as a child is rewarded with dessert after eating his spinach.

If student activities are in truth valuable for all students, how can an eligibility system be justified that results in forbidding participation to those who most need activities? Such evidence as exists shows little or no correlation between grades and activity participation.[11] "Conversely, lack of participation in student activities is a significant characteristic of school dropouts."[12]

One study[13] found that slightly more than two-thirds of those students who were dropouts participated in no activities at all. There were also significant differences reported in the number of dropouts who served in leadership roles (2 of 212 dropouts).

A good activities program can be the decisive factor in creating interest and holding children in school. Those who disapprove eligibility practices maintain that they discriminate against the poorer students who should, if at all possible, be involved. The student activity program should not be restricted to only a portion of the student body—an average of 50 percent participating of all students is high; a more realistic figure is 30 percent.[14] Those who are banned from activities will find other, more undesirable, outlets.

The junior high school activity program should be open to all with no stated prohibitions nor hidden costs to limit participation. The activity program needs to be so well organized, sponsored, directed, and administered that, ideally, all students will want to become and will become participants. As with many other dreams, this falls far short of fulfillment. Compelling all students to engage in activities is generally frowned upon although one administrator describes a practice wherein all students attend an assembly, chooose an activity, and go the designated room for the selected activity. Those who have failed to make a selection are "ordered to go to a particular activity." The author goes on to say that, "This method of starting an activity program may sound dictatorial, but it can be effective. . . ."[15]

Over participation in the activity program can be a problem, too. There have been many proposed methods such as majors and minors, point values for different activities, and award systems that are partially or completely designed to limit student participation. While such systems are often intended to promote interest and participation by awarding school letters, pins, certificates, and similar intrinsic rewards, they are also capable of restricting participation to a set number of major and minor activities, and are frequently so devised. Within one school the difficulty may be the need for the right number of students in each activity balanced against student enthusiasm for joining as many as possible, and in another school the problem is under participation and complete lack of involvement. Either way, dissatisfaction and criticism find fertile ground.

The activity program as a whole and specific activities within it need constant evaluation, revision, and even elimination, if such seems desirable. A club which has outlived the need that gave rise to its birth can be a real source of trouble. If it is continued by a teacher who doesn't want to give it up, there is resentment from other staff members. A club which becomes too firmly established can lose its original purpose and become a tradition. One example[16] was described as the "Diana Club," formed when there was no girls' P.E. program within this school. It became a snob club, restricted to 35 members, with new members elected by the present group, and having the sole function of putting on the annual "Sweetheart Prom." This would certainly appear to be an instance of a club that outlived its usefulness.

It is a common criticism that junior high school activities are too quick to take on or to attempt to take on the sophistication, flavor, and qualities of their high school counterparts. The cry of oversophistication, too much too soon is often heard of junior high school programs—and unfortunately is frequently justified. Copying high school activities is not restricted to any one junior high activity such as athletics or drama; it may permeate every area from school dances to the school newspaper. When this occurs, "the junior high school apes the senior high school instead of adapting to its own particular needs and setting. . . . The result is an amateurish cut-down pair of pants neither complimentary nor valuable."[17]

A program dominated by a few activities with but small attention given to the others is also common. It is far from unusual to find a junior high school activity budget which unhesitatingly allots as much as $3 to $5 per student enrolled to interscholastic athletics but balks at a total of $25 for an activity such as Chess Club or Debate Team. As always, there are at least two sides to this problem. It is held by some that public relations and parental demands require publicity if not flamboyance in student activities of public interest such as drama, music groups, and athletics. These, it is said, "continue to catch and hold the attention of the community," and "lesser-known activities can then be carried to the community."[18] The all too frequent result is overemphasis upon a few activities which is fostered by newspapers, radio, and television releases. Dad's Clubs and similar organizations on the junior high school level encourage practices such as night games (so "parents can see their children play," although few wish to see a night mathematics class), paid admissions, pep bands, drill teams, and cheerleaders, none of which is appropriate to junior high school.

Sports banquets for members of varsity football, basketball, and baseball teams were not long in finding their way from high school to junior high. Varsity letterman clubs are also frequently found now in junior high with the result that "the students most recognized are athletes . . . [and] cheerleaders."[19] In an effort to combat this stress upon a few selected activities, some junior high schools have established award systems that grant school letters and certificates for service, music, and scholarship as well as for athletics.

The following excerpt from "A Junior High Award System That

Works," from the *School Activities Magazine*, Vol. 40 (January, 1969), pp. 18–21 (reprinted by permission of the publisher) is an example of this kind of award system:

> The awards given are inexpensive and consist of certificates, school letters, and pins. If but a few awards are given, they will be more highly prized; however, the easier they are to earn, the more students there are who will achieve success. Students whose academic abilities are limited may succeed on an average or above average basis in activities and feel that this is the most profitable part of the school's educational program.
>
> The award system which follows has been used for several years in a medium sized junior high school. It is basically a point system with four categories: Athletics, Scholarship, Music, General activities. Each category has three steps in awards: certificates, school letter, and pin. In the three years they attend junior high school the great majority of the students earn at least one certificate—many earn all four—and a few students, by the end of the ninth grade, have earned four certificates, four letters, and four pins.
>
> An activity period is scheduled during the school day once weekly. Since there is one such activity period weekly, and few if any groups meet more than twice monthly, a student has an opportunity to participate in more than one activity. Some activities, such as athletics, occur after school, which extends a student's participation opportunities.
>
> System
>
> This finished product is the result of Student Council, student, and faculty proposals, work, and revision.
>
> Junior High Award System
>
> I. Scholarship
>
> 1. A certificiate is given each time a student makes the honor roll.
> 2. A special certificate is awarded straight-A students.
> 3. A letter is awarded when a student has earned 6 honor-roll certificates or 4 straight-A certificates.
> 4. A pin is earned when 8 honor-roll certificates or 6 straight-A certificates have been earned.
> 5. A special certificate may be issued by the department to any student who is deserving of special recognition because of unusual achievement in a subject area.
>
> II. Athletics
>
> All major sports, football, basketball, baseball, track, and wrestling are to be governed by these regulations. Variations from regulations will be permitted only by agreement with the principal, the coach involved, and the awards committee.
>
> Requirements are:
>
> Certificate
>
> 1. Be present at 80 percent of turnout periods in one sport.
> 2. Exhibit good citizenship and effort around school.
>
> Letter
>
> 1. Be present at 80 percent of turnout periods in one sport.
> 2. Good citizenship and effort around school.
> 3. Participate in interscholastic games.

(a) One-third the number of quarters in football and basketball.
(b) One-third the number of innings in baseball.
(c) Earn 10 points in track (dual meets, district meets, etc.)
(d) Participate in two or more wrestling meets.

Pin
1. Be present at 80 percent of turn out periods in sports in which the student participates.
2. Good citizenship and effort around school.
3. Earn two letters in any given sport.
4. Earn a letter in three sports in any given year.

Girls Athletics
1. Awards are based on a 500-point scale.

Certificate	200 points
Letter	350 points
Pin	500 points

2. Points are earned as follows:

80 percent attendance	50 points
Manager of sport	25 points
Member of winning team	10 points

3. There are five major team sports during the year and two individual sports for which any girl may turn out an earn points. It is possible for any girl to earn the certificate her first year.

III. General Activities

There is a sponsor in each area who will judge, by your participation, how many merit points you are to receive in some of the activities (those that do not have a definite number of points)

Student Body Officers
(points are for the year)

President	7–9
Vice-President	5–7
Secretary	5–7
Treasurer	5–7

Song and Yell	3–5

Class-Elected Officers, per semester

President	2 or 3
Secretary-Treasurer	2 or 3
Homeroom representative to student council	2 or 3

Library (student helpers) points per year.

Morn-noon-after school	1–2
Class	0–1

School Committees appointed by Student Body Officers. These committees are appointed by the student body president and the sponsor of each committee. The people of these committees serve for the semester, and points are for the semester.

A maximum of 2 points will be given to all standing school committee members, 3 points to chairmen.

(a) Building and Grounds
(b) School Improvement
(c) Merits and Awards
(d) Lockers
(e) Assembly
(f) Stage Crew
(g) Projection Squad

Other committees may be formed as found necessary.

Special-Occasion Committees. The special occasion committees such as clothing drive are appointed by the student body president with the help of the sponsor. The members serve only during the particular drive.

Maximum one point to be given for all special committees, 2 points maximum for chairmen.

Special interest and Service Clubs (per semester)

Member	0–1
Officer	1–2

Other clubs may be formed when interest warrants it, by application to and charter from Student Council.

Music

Points toward the various awards may be earned in the following ways:

Activity	*Points*
1. Concert performance outside of school time—band, orchestra, chorus	1–2
2. Concert performance assembly—band, orchestra, chorus	0–1
3. Participation in parade, band	0–1
4. Morning orchestra or ensemble rehearsals before or after with 90 percent attendance not including excused absences and with 100 percent attendance at all performances	
1 rehearsal/week/semester	0–1
2 rehearsals/week/semester	1–2
5. Librarian, 1 semester	0–1
6. Accompanist (chorus), 1 semester	0–1
7. Flag bearer, parades, only if in parade each	0–1
8. Any small group or ensemble—each outside of school time or assembly performance.	0–1

Dramatics

All parts	1–3

Intramural Sports

Team member (each sport)	0–1
Team captain (each sport)	1–2

This award system takes cognizance of certain specialized community interests in such things as interscholastic athletics and a marching band. It attempts to equate other student activities so that every student has a reasonable chance to achieve success in one or more areas.

For this or any other award system to function to best advantage and contribute most profitably to education and the welfare of the students certain things must be kept continually in mind:

1. This must be a cooperative process, democratically involving the students, the faculty, and the administration.
2. Evaluation must be regular.
3. Each activity must have a qualified sponsor.
4. Activities must be regularly scheduled, whenever possible during school time.
5. Activities must be based on needs and interests of the students.
6. All students must be made aware of the opportunities available. An assembly shortly after the opening of school provides the best orientation.
7. The administration must, as a matter of school policy, give full support to the program by words, action, personnel, financing, facilities, and space.
8. New clubs will be formed from time to time as interest arises.
9. As with virtually all other phases of education, the faculty must realize the values which will accrue from a well-run program.
10. There *must* be careful records kept of each student's earned points, awards, and current standing. This is done by the student members of the Awards Committee.

The problem of overemphasis is one that can lead to exploitation, particularly in areas such as athletics, drama, and music. Especially in music is this possible, since much of our music education is performance oriented. Teachers, administrators, and parents are likely to feel that students need opportunities to display their musical accomlishments through concerts, parades, and festivals. Dissatisfaction can arise here from parents and students who feel too much time is spent on rehearsals and performances, from teachers who may be losing class time for the same reasons, and from other activity sponsors who resent the importance given to the chosen activity. Sometimes the emphasis occurs because some activities are prolific fund raisers and, when the junior high must have a self-supporting activity program, the dollar takes on added significance. At times like these it is necessary to keep in mind that every activity should have as its basic rule the furtherance of the education of the students.

Assignment of sponsors and teacher activity load is another frequent cause of dissatisfaction. Some teachers really do not like activities, do not wish to become involved with them, and see no real reason for an activity program. There are some teachers who accept activity sponsorship as a part of the teaching position and honestly do their best. Fortunately, many teachers enjoy student activities and enter into sponsorship wholeheartedly. There are problems when teachers are arbitrarily assigned to an activity which they do not like; problems when the sponsor dominates the activity; resentment when the activity load is uneven and inequitable; and bitterness from all concerned when a sponsor does less than his job and does not fulfill the role.

Activities require as much in planning and enthusiasm from the teacher as does any regular class, and in some instances even more. There has been some discussion and investigation of the possibility of using noncertificated personnel in junior high school activity sponsorship[20] although this is not a common practice.

GUIDELINES FOR ACTIVITIES IN JUNIOR HIGH

The activity program must have educational value or it cannot be justified; it should promote the commonly accepted objectives of the junior high school. The program should provide exploratory opportunities and wholesome outlets for adolescent enthusiasms, interests, and drives. The activity program should work toward developing citizenship, responsibility, cooperation, and leadership. The junior high school activity program should help students to develop satisfying leisure time interests which can carry over to adult life. For the best results, certain principles should be kept in mind in operating the junior high school activity program:

1. The administration must give full support in words, scheduling, financing, organizing, selection of sponsors, time, evaluating, and facilities.
2. The sponsor must have an interest in the activity, some knowledge of it, and be responsible for it, guiding but not dominating.
3. In the junior high school time should be provided for activities within the school day.
4. Where possible, activities and classroom instruction should blend so that activities become extensions of classroom learning.
5. Cost should never be a factor for membership or participation. There should be no dues, no arbitrary methods of selecting membership, and no eligibility requirements other than attendance in school.
6. Student activities should be financed by the school district as a regular expense. They should not be required to be self-supporting. Each activity should have a regularly budgeted amount, and reserve funds should be available for new activities which may develop during the school year.
7. Participation should be guided, encouraged, but never compulsory.
8. Activities should be regularly evaluated and students should share the responsibility for evaluating as well as for selecting, organizing, and executing activities.[21]

9. Avoid overemphasis on one or a few activities; also avoid high school practices and sophistication. This is not the age for formal dinner dances or night athletic contests.
10. Keep away from well-meaning but interfering parent groups. Do not emphasize competition; emphasize participation. Historically, there is clearly a significant lack of participation in school activities on the part of school dropouts.[22]
11. Handling of money is extremely important. Confusion, unhappiness, and recriminations are rife when the money isn't as much as was thought, has been lost or stolen, or expended without authorization. Be sure to have dependable student treasurers and an accurate system of bookkeeping.
12. Be sure that each organization and activity keeps accurate minutes and records. Much uncertainty and misunderstanding can be avoided this way.

KINDS OF ACTIVITIES FOR JUNIOR HIGH

Literally hundreds of different activities exist in junior high schools throughout the country, but they all fall into one of the following categories:

1. Assemblies: student drama and talent; guest speakers; concerts; scientific and technical; and those growing out of classwork.
2. Homeroom: intended originally as a literal home base for security and guidance, the homeroom has taken on many other duties and responsibilities, not all of them reasonable. In too many cases the homeroom has become an administrative convenience where announcements are made, money collected, attendance taken, and tickets sold.
3. Interest clubs and subject matter clubs such as photography, dramatics, industrial arts, foreign language, and others for which there is an interest, a sponsor, and facilities.
4. School service clubs which perform a real service to the school such as office helpers, school improvement, and projectionists.
5. Student government, which includes student council, student assemblies, and student conduct committees.
6. Physical education activities including intramurals for boys and girls; folk and ballroom dancing, and, if established, interscholastic athletics.
7. Music activities such as novelty bands, stage bands, ensembles, and vocal groups.
8. School publications including the newspaper, school yearbook, student handbook, and literary magazines. In large schools there is no reason for not having two of some of these publications, such as two newspapers.

9. Scholarship or honor societies: there is a place for an organization of this sort, but such organizations must be closely guarded against developing into situations where grades are the only thing of any importance and value.
10. Some schools have a separate classification for "athletically connected clubs" which includes cheerleaders and pep clubs.

> Quiet social experiences can be provided by use of the library and other rooms for reading, chess, checkers, cards, record-listening, movies, arts and crafts and others. The list of games which provide opportunity for physical activity and social interaction is almost endless. Table tennis, volley ball, softball, shuffleboard, singing, and dancing are but a few of the activities that some schools . . . [have adopted].[23]

INTERSCHOLASTIC ATHLETICS IN JUNIOR HIGH

Opinions are strong, argument becomes heated, and words are frequently fiery when discussion centers on the desirability of interscholastic athletics in junior high school. There are three main positions: (1) eliminate interscholastic (varsity) athletics completely for junior high; (2) permit a junior high school varsity sports program which is but little different from the high school program so long as it is properly coached, well equiped, adequately financed, and thoroughly supervised; and (3) first provide a superior program for all students in physical education, recreation, and intramurals and then develop a limited interscholastic program for those few who are physically gifted and interested in such a program.

Certainly some of the activities that often appear in connection with the interscholastic sports program reinforce the argument that junior high children become too sophisticated too soon. Children of this age cannot be expected to cope with the many strains and tensions which are a part of varsity athletics. Pointed out as excesses and inappropriate for junior high students are such items as blaring pep bands, screaming uniformed cheer leaders, strutting majorettes, snappy drill teams and colorful marching bands at halftime, night games, paid admissions, stress upon athletic prowess, and the strong emotional reactions, undesirable at this age, which result from the excitement and pressures of THE GAME.

> The conflict seems to center on whether they (interscholastic athletics) have grown beyond manageable control as well as whether they develop proper educational values. At present we believe that interscholastic sports foster values that are anti-educational. Athletic activities . . . contribute no more to citizenship than do other . . . programs. And claims that players succeed later in life because of their sports background have never been substantiated.[24]

Those who believe in interscholastic athletics for junior high school say indignantly that it is a problem of emphasis: There will always be abuses of privilege regardless of what the topic or level may be, and it is unreasonable to condemn an entire program because of the poor judgment of a few or the holy fervor of the opposition.

THE CASE FOR INTERSCHOLASTIC ATHLETICS IN THE JUNIOR HIGH SCHOOL

The United States of America is a sports-minded nation. It is natural for the youth of the country to become enthusiastic and to wish to excel. Rather than less emphasis on interscholastic sports, what the country really needs is more emphasis. In recent years there has been too much "spectatoritis," a situation where people are content merely to sit and watch. There is too much soft living, watching of television, of being driven to school, and not enough exercise—too much leisure poorly spent. This increasing softness of youth is reflected regularly in results of physical fitness tests and physical examinations for military service.

Interscholastic athletics can provide something of value for everyone. The United States is a competitive nation and the adult world as it exists is one of competition. Rivalry on the athletic field is one of the best ways to learn to meet problems and triumph over difficulties. Developing the desire to succeed, the will to win, is essential in modern life and such self-confidence comes naturally in participation in varsity athletics.

> The modern educator understands that basic to the educational process is the need for young people to succeed. Failure by a student to achieve or fit in somewhere in the school program can lead to disappointment, frustration, and eventually dropping out of school. . . . Many young people do not relate to the academic program of the school. Yet they are able to find a degree of success in . . . sports, the band, and clubs of various interest . . . [there is] a legion of critics who have overreacted. . . ."[25]

Furthermore, interscholastic athletics also provides a healthy outlet for aggressions and a release for tensions.

Physical skills, adeptness and adroitness, are of course an integral part of varsity athletics. While size frequently is a factor in "making the team," every coach can tell of the undersized player who has such an intense desire to succeed that he develops his physical skills, coordination, and ability beyond the level of his bigger teammates.

Team competition and play require that the individual learn to sublimate his own feelings and wishes to the larger needs of the team—in fact the word "team" means just that, a group working together for a common purpose. Cooperation among team members is not just desirable, it is essential. There is no place for the "shiner" or individual scene stealer. In learning this lesson of cooperation, the team members become more able in developing the quality of leadership.

The individual, in learning that his decisions affect not only himself but also the larger group, the team, and even the school, becomes able to accept and appreciate constructive criticism. He learns respect for the rules and to respect the rights and abilities of others, both those on the same team and those on the opposing team. Interscholastic athletics, by the very nature of the training, competition, and emotional reactions, creates opportunities for more and stronger friendships of the long term kind.

The team member can scarcely start too soon (and junior high may be later than it should be) to learn the importance of winning, how to lose gracefully, and the principles and practices of good sportsmanship. Interscholastic sports do present a positive program, one that has real educational value, and this helps young people to become better human beings by improving their self-image. An attitude that appears to be in the ascendancy in our society is that of seeking the easy way, avoiding the challenge and looking for job security; a feeling that few things are important anyway. Interscholastic athletics can teach a boy that being down doesn't necessarily mean being out; the real winners are those who never stop trying.

The boy who "makes" the junior high school varsity team learns the proper care of the body, and to avoid smoking and drinking, and to get adequate rest. In fact, because of the stress upon doing things right, athletes are much less likely to become involved in delinquency.[26] By serving as a standard and requiring a satisfactory level of overall achievement, varsity athletics become a motivator in other areas of school.

Social growth of both players and spectators is increased by the broadening effects of interscholastic athletics. Team members meet other students of similar ages and interests and by traveling to other towns and schools in general, and their own in particular.

Few schools are financially able to supply the variety and extent of student activities they would like to have. Whether it should be done this way or not, the cold truth is that paid admissions to interscholastic athletics provide funds that keep many activities going besides athletics. It is probably quite satisfying for those who take a pious stand against the "dirty" money brought in by athletics, but in a practical acceptance of need it must be recognized that interscholastic athletics are the chief money providers for school activities.

Those who support varsity athletics argue that the schools belong to the public—why fight what the people want? When you oppose night games for junior high, for instance, you forget that people want to see their children play but cannot get away from work to see them play during the day. Furthermore, even the educators cannot agree. For example, a 1958 survey[27] of 2,329 junior high schools found 85 percent of the junior high schools had interscholastic athletics and such athletics were supported by 78 percent of the principals involved. Similar results were revealed in a 1966 study.[28]

There is no evidence which conclusively supports the statement that junior high boys suffer excessive injuries in a varsity athletic program. Boys being what they are, they will participate in some kind of sports program whether the school sponsors it or not, and without school sponsorship less qualified agencies will operate the sports program under more dangerous conditions.

If the interscholastic athletic program cuts into the academic schedule, neglects the program for the girls, provides minimal intramural activities, takes more than a fair share of activity funds, and is overemphasized, this is an administrative problem and is not the fault of the program itself nor of the coaches. The major problem is that ". . . [critics] have mistaken competition for violence, involvement for entertainment, winning for achievement."[29]

The interscholastic athletic program supplements the physical education program rather than substituting for it, and criticisms of varsity athletics are largely based upon the abuses and poor administration of the program. Inherently it has many values and in eliminating interscholastic athletics, we will eliminate the desire to win, to do one's best, and we will lose the immeasurable benefits these athletics have in their effect on school spirit and morale.

THE CASE AGAINST INTERSCHOLASTIC ATHLETICS

Junior high school students are in their early adolescent years and need a program of physical education different from either elementary or senior high school.[30] It must be a program specifically designed for children who are experiencing rapid physical growth, who have a special need to improve coordination, who are interested in participating in an increasing number of activities, who have a driving need for peer-group acceptance, and who are becoming interested in the opposite sex. The real questions here are: (1) Does an interscholastic athletic program in junior high school really meet the needs of adolescents? and (2) Are the functions of the junior high school in any way fulfilled by an interscholastic program of athletics that could not be better satisfied by a planned program of physical education, intramurals, and recreation?

This is not the age for the highly organized interscholastic sports program with its required intensive training, its accompanying pressures to win, its strong emotional reactions, and the attendant excitement and trappings such as yell leaders, song leaders, pep bands, night games and majorettes. Junior high children are in general ready and willing to participate in many activities but they are not physically ready for those sports which require considerable strength, endurance, and body contact.

Early adolescents are most susceptible to joint dislocation, bone injuries, and cartilage injuries, since the epiphyseal cartilages are not yet calcified. It is easy, in the excitement of the game, to slip past the point of healthful fatigue to harmful exhaustion. Because of the wide range of maturity of children in junior high school, the best measure of maturity is an X-ray of bone development, but few schools require this. The standard physical examination for boys who are turning out for varsity teams is generally a situation where fifty or sixty boys line up and a physician gives each one a quick check. The whole process of examining the entire squad may be completed in an hour or less.

There are also psychological and sociological implications for the boys who do not or cannot "make the team" in that they do not get recognition, are deprived of participation, and do not experience success. High-pressure competition for those who are on the varsity team creates strong emotional reactions which can easily affect the emotional and social development of these immature youngsters. Tensions are actually increased by varsity athletics rather than being released.

In varsity athletics there is too much stress on winning, an emphasis upon the student who is an athletically gifted child. There is a false value and false emphasis attached to the athletically successful, to the detriment of the remainder of the student body and to the educational program.

> It is ironic to see on the editorial pages of newspapers the charges that schools have become anti-intellectual in their practices, but to notice on the sports pages the great emphasis placed on school athletics.[31]

The interscholastic athletic program demands the lion's share of student activity funds (to suit up one ninth-grade football player can easily cost $150 or more), stresses the gifted player at the expense of the other boys, neglects the athletic program for the girls, is at odds with the educational objectives of the rest of the school, requires a disproportionate and unfair amount of use of school athletic facilities, and often causes the school schedule to be constructed with the turnout periods for varsity athletics the first consideration, the academic program being fitted in as it may be. In some schools the need for varsity practice causes the gymnasiums and other physical education facilities to be usurped for lengths of time far out of proportion to the 5 percent of the study body involved. In other schools the last period of the day finds the star athletes in the P.E. classes so that the practice can continue without interruption when school dismisses. This means that scheduling of other subjects such as band must be set for other periods or they become mutually exclusive: that is, no athlete can be in band.

Interscholastic athletics frequently disrupt a school schedule and educational program when players are excused early for a game or for practice sessions. Often the whole school is affected as when there is a pep rally, athletic assembly, or early dismissal for games.

It is an interesting commentary upon our educational beliefs when we realize that school people who are much concerned with curriculum and with what is the best educational program for adolescents in virtually all other areas of the school usually yield so readily to the pressure for interscholastic athletics. Here is where the controversy centers: the interscholastic, the varsity athletic program which becomes a slightly smaller edition of the senior high school and college programs. Few people oppose physical education, but there is certainly opposition to the varsity program, at least at some levels. By bowing to community pressures, school administrators permit the sports-minded citizens to determine the school's athletic program. More will be determined than this because the kind of athletic program adopted will certainly have a pronounced effect upon the rest of the curriculum, the raising and expending of student funds, and upon the importance to be attached to athletics.

Some administrators say that it is impossible to hold off the public. Parents want to bask in the limelight of their children's achievements. Sports are too big a part of modern life—note the effect of radio and television; and it is impossible to turn off the effects of the sportswriters. In view of the results of the surveys previously mentioned, one may be permitted to question the accuracy of statements such as these and wonder if they are not excuses for doing what at least 78 percent of the principals wanted to do anyway.

Educators are expected to determine content for areas such as English, science, art, and mathematics. Why can they not determine the physical education program? Why should the stress be upon a program of specialization in two or three team sports instead of developing skills in individual sports which may be continued in adult life?

Where should the cutoff be for interscholastic athletics? They started as a student activity before 1900 and have become perhaps the most important—certainly the most publicized—aspect of the modern secondary public school. To an extent, interscholastic athletics, which pushed from college down to high school and from there to junior high, are now pushing down into elementary. Are these same arguments for promoting interscholastic athletics in junior high school valid also for elementary? As the junior high schools become training grounds, "feeders," for the high schools, will elementary schools fill the same relationship with junior high?

There is a frequent complaint that high school coaches require junior high school coaches to teach the same plays and use the same training as the high school, so that players will have learned much of the high school playing pattern when they leave junior high school. Will this be true also for elementary schools? If one wishes to look for excesses and abuses, it is easy to find many practices for which interscholastic athletics may be condemned.

Some coaches post a "quitters' list" or even a "yellow" sheet which lists the names of those boys who drop from turnout, whether by necessity or from loss of interest. Those coaches who use a "quitters' list" assert that it teaches boys to complete what they have begun; it develops responsibility. In opposing the list, a reasonable contention might be that the sport itself should engender enough interest to keep the boys involved. If it is not capable of maintaining student interest and participation, or if another activity or part-time job causes the student to discontinue participation in turnout, a "quitters' list" only records the failure of the sport to do for the students what it is claimed to do.

In the heat of a game or even a practice session those coaches who lose their patience and tempers create a bad image for the whole profession. The stories are legion of coaches who swear and use improper language with and to the boys. Some coaches are so critical of failure and mistakes that they deliver blistering locker-room and half-time tirades to the boys which so affect immature emotions that the game ceases to be a sport. One sees adolescent emotions keyed to a high pitch: grim anger, more suitable to avenging a murder; vicious intensity, and even tears. The claim of teaching sportsmanship again is impugned by those coaches who teach the boys that the most important thing is winning, and that how the game is won is secondary. Again, many parents and principals can relate instances where coaches such as these have done anything but teach sportsmanship. It is true that coaches who do these things are not universal in junior high school, but it is also true and extremely regrettable that these practices exist to such an extent that they are not at all uncommon.

There have developed around interscholastic athletics elaborate ceremonies reminiscent of the worst of pagan rituals:

> The ceremony begins with colorful processions of musicians and semi-nude virgins who move in ritualized patterns. This excites the thousands of worshippers to rise from their seats, shout frenzied poetry in unison and chant ecstatic anthems. The actual rites (are) performed by twenty-two young priests. . . . Before the game and at it, the atmosphere is that of combat. "Fight" urge pep session speakers. "Fight" exhort the coaches. . . .[32]

It is not difficult to find junior high schools in which interscholastic athletics have top priority. The frequent claim that junior high interscholastic athletics provides the bulk of student activity funds is true for a very few schools. The great majority of junior high schools spend much more on athletics than is ever repaid by admissions. Actually, it is not unusual to spend more on athletics, which have a program for about 5 percent of the student body, than is spent on all other activities combined.

WHAT IS THE ANSWER?

Convictions and emotions being as strong as they are about this issue, the best approach to finding a solution may be to pose some questions:

1. Is there something that may be accomplished by a program of interscholastic athletics that cannot be achieved within the scope of a junior high school program of physical education, recreation, and intramurals? It is somewhat difficult to find anything that fits this description. For example, competition may be found in the regular physical education and the intramural programs. Self-confidence, leadership, fellowship, and success may easily be a part of physical education, recreation, and intramurals.

2. Has the educational value of interscholastic athletics ever been established? This is a matter of opinion. As with many other controversies, it depends to a large extent upon who runs the study and what kinds of questions are asked of whom.

3. What is the cost of varsity athletics in dollars, facilities, teacher time, equipment and supplies as contrasted with other areas of the school, both academic and in activities? As was pointed out earlier, a varsity athletics program is quite expensive and certainly uses much more than its share in all of these factors.

4. Does the time spent by the student in varsity athletics detract from his academic work? Probably not. In fact, it is more likely that participation in athletics keeps some children in school who would otherwise drop out.

5. Can most junior high schools provide the necessary facilities, teachers, money, medical supervision, and equipment without slighting the other physical education programs?[33] Most school districts are perpetually short of funds and in constant need of money to maintain a minimum level and to keep up with enrollment. However, because of the general community interest in sports, most junior high schools seem to provide for interscholastic athletics, although they may be deficient in other forms of student activities and subject-matter areas. For example, there are probably more junior high schools with interscholastic athletics than there are with completely equipped industrial arts facilities.

6. Can we eliminate the pressures, tensions, and excitement typical of interscholastic athletics? It is doubtful, and there is even a very real question as to whether or not we should. Without these tensions and excitement, interscholastic athletics would probably be very dull indeed. The question here is, at what level should this begin?

7. What positions on interscholastic athletics for junior high youth have been taken by professional organizations and educators?

(a) In 1954, the Educational Policies Commission of the National Education Association recommended that

> No junior high school should have a "school team" that competes with school teams of other junior high schools in organized leagues or tournaments. Varsity type interscholastics for junior high boys and girls should not be permitted.[34]

The Commission further recommended that there be an elimination of body contact sports in junior high school and that the core of the athletic program be the required physical education courses. The intramural program should offer wide choices and involve all pupils.

(b. James B. Conant shook a reprimanding finger when he stated in 1960: "Interscholastic athletics and marching bands are to be condemned in junior high school; there is no sound reason for them. . . ."[35]

(c) In 1963 a joint committee[36] suggested that there were four areas for agreement on interscholastic athletics for junior high school between those who favor and those who disapprove.

1. There is a need for physical fitness for today's youth. Our mechanized society encourages sedentary living and the schools should provide a physical fitness program in which all youth can participate.
2. All youth can profit physically and educationally from competitive athletic activities suitable for their age group.
3. Schools must provide participation for all in physical education, intramurals, and recreation.
4. Athletic competition must be carefully supervised and controlled.

(d) A 1965 study[37] recommended that there be no varsity competition until grade ten although extramural play may be permitted in junior high school. Extramurals are defined as athletic competition (other than interscholastic) involving participants from two or more schools in which all students participate regardless of skill. They usually come at the end of the intramural season, require only a day or two, and need no practice sessions. There are no leagues, championships, or season schedules.

There are other statements, but the flavor is very much the same: no varsity sports below grade 10 and no contact sports below grade 10. A strong program of intramurals with an increased variety of sports and a wide participation is recommended. This program should be based upon a well-planned and well-developed required program of physical education. The great majority of junior high schools do not, however, follow these recommendations. Will the developing middle schools do better?

SUMMARY

The activity programs in junior high schools have been thoroughly criticized both within and outside the schools. Criticism has certainly not been restricted since there have been complaints about overparticipation, underparticipation, too much sophistication, too many activities, too few activities, eligibility requirements, domination of the program by one or more activities and/or people, time-wasting, and financing. Some of this criticism is justified and valid. It takes constant evaluation and careful administration to run a good activity program. Activities should be of educational value; there should be a student need and desire for them; and they should be supported by the administration. Some questions being asked are:

1. Do the programs need reduction or expansion?
2. In which areas?
3. Should recreational aspects be eliminated?
4. Should highly competitive activities be dropped?
5. Should activities characteristic of the high school, such as cheerleaders, be discontinued?

The question of permitting interscholastic athletics in the junior high schools is somewhat academic since over 80 percent of the junior high schools have such a program and over 75 percent of junior high principals support it. There is, however, heavy fire from many parents and educators on the varsity athletic program for a number of reasons. It is said that the junior high interscholastic athletic program is too costly, creates an athletic elite and snobbism, is unfair, is riddled with excesses and abuses, is unsuited to this age group, and has no educational worth.

A number of organizations, committees, and individuals have recommended that varsity athletics be eliminated from junior high school, but this recommendation has met with only limited success. Many school administrators cite community pressures and interest in a strong sports program as factors which prohibit any decrease in emphasis by the schools.

REFERENCES

1. Grace Graham, *Improving Student Participation.* Washington, D.C.: NASSP, 1966, pp. 5–9.
2. George E. Mathes, *Group Dynamics for Student Activities.* Washington, D.C.: NASSP, 1968, pp. 14–15.
3. Morrel J. Clute, "Student Activities for Early Adolescents," *Indiana State University Teachers College Journal,* Vol. 34 (November 1962), p. 62.
4. Robert W. Frederick, *The Third Curriculum.* New York: Appleton, 1959, p. 4.
5. *Ibid.*
6. Franklin A. Miller, James H. Moyer, and Robert B. Patrick, *Planning Student Activities.* Englewood Cliffs, N.J.: Prentice Hall, 1956, p. 8.
7. Frederick, *op. cit.*, Chap. 3.
8. *Ibid.*, p. 23.
9. *Ibid.*, p. 30.

10. Donald I. Wood, "Are Activities Programs Really Activities Programs," *School Activities*, Vol. 39 (September 1967), p. 9.
11. Wood, "Student Activities—A Hope or a Delusion?", *NASSP Bulletin*, Vol. 46 (April 1962), pp. 201–205.
12. Graham, *op. cit.*, p. 2.
13. James W. Bell, "School Dropouts and School Activities," *School Activities*, Vol. 35 (September 1964), p. 58.
14. *Ibid.*
15. Erwin F. Karner, "Make Them Join An Activity," *School Activities*, Vol. 32 (November 1960), pp. 75–76.
16. Donald I. Wood, "Archaic Student Clubs," *Clearing House*, Vol. 39 (October 1964), pp. 91–93.
17. John D. Danielson, "Problems Involved in the Publication of a Junior High School Yearbook," *School Activities*, Vol. 32 (February 1961), pp. 173–176.
18. Margaret I. Augustine, "The Public Relations Value of Extra-Curricular Activities," *School Activities*, Vol. 32 (September 1960), pp. 19–20.
19. Marjorie Lazarus, "Our Varsity 'W' Club," *School Activities*, Vol. 32 (October 1960), pp. 37–38.
20. Thomas O. Lawson, "Assignment of Non-Teaching Tasks to Certificated and Non-Certificated Personnel in Junior High School," *Journal of Secondary Education*, Vol. 42 (May 1967), pp. 210–216.
21. "Non-Athletic Activities Program," Position Papers for Junior High, *NASSP Bulletin*, Vol. 47 (October 1963), pp. 20–22.
22. James W. Bell, "A Comparison of Dropouts and Non Dropouts on Participation in School Activities," *Journal of Educational Research*, Vol. 60 (February 1967), pp. 248–251.
23. Clute, *op. cit.*, p. 63.
24. John J. Pietrofesa and Al Rosen, "Interscholastic Sports: Misdirected? Misguided? Misnomer?", *Clearing House*, Vol. 43 (November 1968), pp. 165.
25. Joseph S. Kennedy, "Interscholastic Sports: A Balanced Viewpoint," *Clearing House*, Vol. 43 (April 1969), pp. 471–472.
26. Wallace L. Jones, Jr., "Competitive Athletics Yield Many Benefits to the Participants," *Clearing House*, Vol. 37 (March 1963), pp. 407–410.
27. Ellsworth Tompkins and Virginia Roe, "A Survey of Interscholastic Athletics in Separately Organized Junior High Schools," *NASSP Bulletin*, Vol. 42 (October 1958).
28. Richard H. Conover, "The Junior High School Principalship," *NASSP Bulletin*, Vol. 50 (April 1966), pp. 132–139.
29. Kennedy, *op. cit.*, p. 472.
30. *School Athletics*, Educational Policies Commission, Washington, D.C., 1954, p. 33.
31. Pietrofesa and Rosen, *op. cit.*, p. 169.
32. Thomas Ferril, "French, Football and the Marching Virgins," *Readers Digest*, Vol. 79 (November 1961), pp. 152.
33. Charles A. Bucher, "A New Athletic Program for Our Schools," *NASSP Bulletin*, Vol. 50 (April 1966), pp. 198–218.

34. *School Athletics, op. cit.*, p. 36.
35. James B. Conant, *Recommendations for Education in the Junior High School Years.* Princeton, N.J.: Educational Testing Service, 1960, p. 42.
36. *Standards for Junior High School* Athletics, ASHPER, NASSP, NFSHAA. Washington, D.C.: AAHPER, 1963, p. 15.
37. Charles A. Bucher, "Interscholastic Athletics at the Junior High School Level," *New York State Department of Education*, Albany, N.Y., 1965.

chapter 13

Which Curricular Design?

A continuing area of disagreement in the junior high school is that of patterns of curriculum organization. Should junior high schools be completely departmentalized? Should junior high school students stay with the same teachers for a two- or three-period block of time while they study more than one subject? Or perhaps the junior high school should adopt a "core" approach in which subject-matter lines are obliterated, in which there is minimal preestablished fixed content, where strong emphasis is placed upon the "experience" curriculum, a block of time of two or more periods is necessary, and instruction is based upon learning units derived from common problems, needs, and interests of adolescents as determined jointly by the core teacher and her students.

Emphasis in recent years upon academic excellence, stress upon the "Three R's," increased interest in and criticism of the schools, and the expansion of knowledge in the various disciplines have encouraged those who advocate the departmentalized junior high school.

On the other hand, the core enthusiasts prophesy a dismal future for public secondary education, "until and unless core becomes the dominant curricular pattern throughout the country."[1] Departmentalization, they aver, presents a fragmented, compartmental, factual approach which is a most ineffective way to teach.

Use of block-time is a fairly common compromise between the other positions. The teacher does get to know her students better, she may disregard subject-matter lines, or she may teach in a strictly departmentalized manner. Whichever course she chooses, however, will probably be criticized by someone.

An unfortunate fact is that the junior high school curriculum has usually been a remarkably accurate reproduction of that found in the senior high school. There has been much talk of meeting the needs of early adolescents and of providing an education that fulfills the functions of the junior high school. Yet far too many junior high schools have a curriculum and organization that is generally out of touch with the real nature and problems of today's adolescent.

Consider again the characteristics of this age group. Uneven physical growth patterns, both within the group and individually; a desire for independence and a resentment of authority; a craving for acceptance and approval by their peers; an increasing desire for and ability to accept responsibility; a pronounced idealism; extremes in emotional reactions; marked self-interest; growing ability to deal with concepts and abstractions; rapidly broadening though frequently changing interests; earlier and increased sophistication; a time for forming and changing values; and a need to develop a satisfactory self-concept. This is a period in life marked by change, conflict, and a need to be moving and doing. The curricular design that takes these considerations seriously is not a carefully compartmented six-period day, within which children move like sheep from one lecture-pen to the next.

The functions of the junior high school—integration, exploration, guidance, differentiation, socialization, and articulation—require a curricular design that will provide a general education as well as education for diversity. Such a design necessitates individualized student programs suited to the widely differing abilities, interests, and needs of the diverse individual early adolescents. In some junior high schools, honest, sincere, and fruitful efforts have been made to provide this kind of program. But there are far too many schools in which all students are required to do the same things at the same time in all classes. It may be administratively easier to operate a traditional program, but it does not provide the education necessary for the junior high school student.

FACTORS AFFECTING CURRICULUM DESIGN

Certainly the major factor influencing the selection and development of a curriculum design should be the nature of the learner to be served. If adolescents are indeed widely varying, then the curriculum should make provision for these individual differences. It must include opportunities for exploration, for study in depth, for independent study, for self-discipline, and for self-direction.

A second factor is that of stated goals and purposes. For example, if it is accepted that one function of the junion high school is guidance and another is differentiation, the curriculum design must be such as to provide a differentiated program and to assist the student with a guidance program that is developed especially for these children. It becomes clear that the curriculum design must be something different from either that of the elementary school or that of the senior high school.

A third factor is that or cultural change. Much of what was considered necessary or highly desirable in past years has been deleted and replaced because of our changing world. At the turn of the century, for example, Greek was still being taught in many high schools, whereas auto mechanics was not. Yet which of these is of more value to the average adolescent today? The problems involved in the movement from rural to urban areas, pollution of our air and streams, the growth of the cities, the troubles of slums and ghettos, civil unrest, the rapidly expanding national and world population—these and like problems require that the curriculum be carefully examined and designed if we are going to do everything possible to give each child full and equal opportunity to develop.

One factor that has a real bearing upon the design of the curriculum is that of the enormous expansion of knowledge in recent years. As an instance, compare an eighth-grade science text of 1969 with one of 1939. Whole new vocabularies and entirely different concepts and understandings have developed. The same is true in varying extents for other disciplines. It is no longer possible (if it ever really was) to teach the history of the United States in two more or less equal segments—from the Pilgrims to the Civil War in the first semester and from Reconstruction to the present in the second semester of the eighth grade. So very much has happened, so many new ideas have borne fruit in new inventions and different ways of doing things, that it is impossible to "cover the subject." General education is necessary for everyone but no one can posssibly "cover the subject" today —and it is doubtful that anyone ever really did. In today's world with its constant and quickening change it is not reasonable to expect the curriculum to remain static, although this is precisely the situation in too many of our junior high schools.

Another factor is that of changing methods of instruction. Few junior high school children in the 1930's ever saw an educational film in the classroom or heard a phonograph recording other than music. Today's educational technology is such as to permit wide use of educational media of many kinds. When we know that sitting and listening is a far less effective way of learning than is seeing, hearing, and doing, what rationale can we bring to excuse the ubiquitous lecture classes? New technology, new curricula, new approaches to knowledge all require a change from the traditional setting of junior high school learning.

The scope and sequence of the curriculum must be determined. Scope refers to the actual content coverage of the curriculum; for example, seventh-grade students may study world history. How much world history? Is there a concentration upon specific time periods and emphasis upon certain countries and peoples? Sequence is a term designating continuity. At what point in each child's education are skills, concepts. and specific subject matter content introduced?

It is sharply clear that the education for today's early adolescent should devote far less time to accumulating quantities of information that are likely to be useless and obsolete all too soon, and place more stress upon problem-solving skills. It is certain than an essential competency for youth in our changing world is the skill to cope with new situations, the ability to face complex and demanding problems.

A LOOK AT THE BACKGROUND

At the time of its inception, the junior high usually facilitated the downward extension of college preparatory subjects into grades 7 and 8, and these subjects were taught by subject-matter specialists as separate disciplines. This departmental teaching and emphasis upon the separate subjects in grades 7, 8, and 9 encouraged pupil promotion on the basis of individual subject rather than by grade.

These academic subjects as taught by the subject-matter specialists in the high school manner, in conjunction with the secondary education concept in which the junior high school was placed, established the fixed-period departmentalized approach to instruction that became characteristic of the majority of the junior high schools.

As the junior high school developed, its early imitation of the high school encouraged the further emphasis of subject-matter specialists and departmentalization. Throughout the years, especially in the period 1930–50, efforts have been made to change this, but an examination of current practices of junior high school scheduling indicates that a great many seventh-, eighth-, and ninth-grade programs are as highly departmentalized as are those of high school seniors.

The 1966 *Report of the Junior High School Principalship*[2] indicated that 51 percent of the 4, 496 responding principals operated junior high schools with complete departmentalization in grades 7, 8, and 9; 13 percent had complete subject departmentalization for grades 8 and 9, with grade 7 being partially departmentalized; and 15 percent had complete departmentalization in grade 9 only, with block time and partial departmentalization in grades 7 and 8. Block time and partial departmentalization at all grades (7-8-9) were reported by only 12 percent of the respondents.

When asked what they preferred, 34 percent of the principals chose complete subject departmentalization for all three grades; 17 percent preferred complete subject departmentalization for grades 8 and 9, and partial departmentalization for grade 7; 19 percent chose complete departmentalization for grade 9, with block time and partial departmentalization for grades 7 and 8; and 14 percent preferred block time and partial departmentalization at all grade levels.

This abrupt change from the self-contained classroom environment most sixth-graders enjoy to the highly departmentalized environment facing a substantial number of seventh-graders is in direct conflict with the stated philosophy and functions of the junior high. Herein lies the problem.

Many people hold the firm belief that a good intellectual education, which permits some fine and practical arts, should for best instruction be strictly departmentalized. It is difficult and often impossible to find teachers who can be effective in two or more subjects; furthermore, the increase in knowledge has reached such a point that subject specialists are essential—in all subjects. A block of time, they feel, is asking too much of most teachers, and the core approach is visionary and impractical.

On the other hand, the supporters of core maintain with fervor and zeal that theirs is the only method that makes sense and provides the kind of education necessary to the young people of today. In the middle, for several reasons, one finds those who endorse block time—perhaps as a compromise between core and departmentalization, perhaps because of a sincere belief that this is the best of both worlds. Changing circumstances and social conditions which have affected the purposes and functions of the junior high school have compounded the problem.

According to a study by Lounsbury[3] on the role and status of the junior high during the mid-1950's, many of the original purposes, functions, and characteristics of the junior high were no longer valid. Included among the several earlier purposes rejected as being invalid was departmental organization of subjects.

This rejection of departmentalization should not be interpreted to mean that there is no place in the junior high program for the teaching of separate subjects, or that the subject-matter specialist is no longer necessary. It should, however, raise a question as to the manner and extent of departmentalization found, particularly in the seventh and eighth grades. If the junior high school is truly to promote the smooth transition from elementary school to high school, some modification of departmentalization is necessary.

Throughout the United States there are many variations and adaptations of the core program, block-time scheduling, and separate subjects offerings. This is especially true in the junior high schools, although evidences of various modifications of each are found in elementary schools and high schools. It is necessary that teachers, administrators, and parents have a common understanding of terminology when talking about these terms.

There is probably more confusion concerning the meaning of core and the definition of the core curriculum than may be found in discussing any other curriculum design.

> Some of the fairly common definitions are: a group of required subjects, a combination of two or more subjects, a large block of time in which learning activities are taught cooperatively, any course taught by "progressive" methods. Added to this confusion is the fact that many terms such as the following are used synonymously with core: common learnings, general education, unified studies, self-contained classrooms, basic courses, fused courses, and English-social studies. As a consequence, when one is told that a certain school has a core, it is unsafe to draw any conclusions whatever concerning the nature of the program.[4]

School systems have used terms as *core, common learnings, social living,* and *unified studies* almost interchangeably. If one were to examine the content of these arrangements he would find that, as presently used, they more truly represent the block-time classification. A brief distinction between the core curriculum and the block-time scheduling would help at this point. Grace Wright offers the following descriptions[5] of the two:

> *Block of time:* All classes which meet for a block of time of two or more class periods and combine or replace two or more subjects that are required of all pupils and would ordinarily be taught separately.

> *Core classes:* Classes having the block of time organizational pattern and which also unify or fuse their content around units or problems which may be either subject-centered or experience-centered.

CURRICULUM PATTERNS IN THE JUNIOR HIGH SCHOOL

In its early days the junior high school curriculum pattern was most likely to be one of two types. (1) The seventh- and eighth-grade curriculum was virtually a replica of the seventh- and eighth-grade programs in the elementary school, while that of the ninth grade was moved, almost intact, into the junior high from the high school, thus retaining a curriculum gap between the eighth and ninth grades that was as wide as before. (2) Since the junior high school was considered to be an earlier beginning of secondary education, academic subjects and complete departmentalization was instituted for all grades, 7-8-9. The new school, in organization, content, and method, literally became a "junior" high school.

Recent years have seen vigorous efforts to modify and change the departmentalized approach so that the junior high curriculum design more accurately reflected attempts to provide the special kind of education necessary for the young adolescent.

THE SUBJECT-MATTER CURRICULUM

In the separate-subject curriculum each subject is treated as a single discipline and has its place in the junior high school schedule. History, for example, is precisely that, and pays but little attention to geography, economics, sociology, or any of the related fields. Spelling is taught separately from penmanship, and English grammar and composition taught separately from these and from each other. The several scholarly disciplines are organized in accord with the structure and internal logic of each. Instruction is directed toward presenting such organized knowledge to the students, by the teacher, frequently from a single textbook.

A look at a departmentalized junior high school schedule gives a fairly clear picture of what is being taught. All students study the same subjects, with the exception of electives, for the same length of time. Elective options are frequently minimal or even nonexistent for seventh- and eighth-grade students, although ninth-graders usually have one elective choice, sometimes two, and infrequently they may select three. Students receive a grade in each subject and can profit from the specialized skill of the subject-matter teacher.

There is little provision or time for individual differences, nor is there much opportunity or effort to modify procedures to adapt to individual student needs or interests. The major emphasis is upon presentation of teacher-selected content, fragmented learning, and factual regurgitation. Course content will often overlap, causing wasteful repetition. Yet, on the other extreme, questions may never be answered and some content never taught on the grounds that this intrudes upon the material of another teacher. Curriculum guides tend to specify precisely what is to be taught each semester, each year, and for each grade. Woe to the ninth-grade teacher of English who permits her class to read *Julius Caesar*, for *that* is in the tenth-grade book!

Teachers in such a departmentalized program do not know their students as well as do block teachers or core teachers and they will have many more students daily in their classes. Departmentalized subject teachers will, however, usually teach only in their fields of specialization, which means that they should be quite knowledgeable in the subjects which they teach.

Students, it is said, will profit from classes taught by specialists in those subjects rather than studying a wide range of subjects with a teacher who is likely to be poorly prepared in all but one or two of the variety which she teaches.

The current explosion of knowledge and the demand for academic specialists places increasing stress upon teachers having a thorough knowledge of the structure, background, and developments of every subject field. It is a great deal to ask of a teacher that she be able and prepared in a number of subject fields as well as conversant with teaching techniques, knowledgeable in adolescent psychology, and a junior guidance counselor as well.

Societal pressures for academic excellence only increase the emphasis upon specialization and departmentalization of subject matter. A great many administrators feel that it is better to have competent and satisfied teachers who teach but one field rather than attempting a core or block approach with the possible resultant dissatisfaction and loss in efficiency.

THE SUBJECT-AREA CURRICULUM

In an attempt to overcome the worst features of the subject-matter curriculum, most junior high schools have adopted an integration of subjects in what is known as the "broad-fields" approach. A broad-fields organization recognizes that relationships exist within a content area, and groups together the separate subjects within these areas. Common examples are:

1. *Language arts:* includes spelling, penmanship, composition, grammar, literature, reading, punctuation.
2. *Social studies:* includes civics, history, geography, sociology, anthropology, economics.
3. *Science:* includes material from botany, meteorology, astronomy, physics, chemistry, zoology. Common junior high school science offerings (usually designated as seventh-, eighth-, and ninth-grade science) are: life science, earth science, and general or physical science.
4. *Fine arts:* may include art, crafts, ceramics, sketching, choir, orchestra, band.

The broad-fields approach does reduce duplication of content, promotes integration of learning, and permits some stress upon relationships within the various fields. There is an additional advantage in that subject-prepared teachers generally feel comfortable in teaching in a broad-fields program.

Classes are still usually limited to one period daily. Teachers meet five, six, or even seven groups of children daily. There is little time to be concerned with individual differences or consideration for student problems. The content sequence is still almost completely based upon the logic and structure of the subject matter, and there is often but superficial attention to critical thinking and problem solving because of the stress upon memorization of facts.

CORRELATION

In correlation each subject retains its own identity but efforts are made to establish a mutual relationship between two or more subjects. A history teacher who is teaching the Westward Movement would plan with the teacher of English to have the same pupils study in her class stories, essays, and poetry appropriate to those times. In a more expanded instance, the art and music teachers would study art and music of the same period; science teachers could stress inventions and scientific discoveries that influenced the period, and home economics and industrial arts classes would focus upon food, clothing, home life, handwork, and crafts of the time. However the form, correlation still retains the separation of the subjects. An examination of a junior high school schedule with a correlated curriculum design would indicate little if any difference from the usual subject-area curriculum. (Incidentally, "correlation" and "core curriculum" are *not* the same thing at all, although sometimes confused for each other by name similarity.)

Correlation requires time for joint teacher planning and necessitates cooperation between and among teachers, a situation that can pose problems. What to do if one teacher falls far behind? Should a teacher believe that a particular conceptual development is unnecessary or undesirable? What if one teacher does not get along with another? If a teacher does not approve of this approach, then there are difficulties and the rest of those attempting to correlate may give up in disgust. Correlation, though difficult of accomplishment, can reduce much duplication and repetition and does help students to see relationships. It is possible to do somewhat more for individual students in terms of individual differences and independent projects. Correlation, however, often occurs more by accident than by design, and a great many of these classes are no different from the traditional subject matter class.

UNIFIED STUDIES AND FUSION

Although there is occasional confusion of these two terms because of the usage of the word "fused" in both types, fusion, technically, is a synthesis of several subfields within a broad discipline. Junior high school general science is a good example of fusion; "Current World Problems" is another. Unified studies, a form of integration, breaks down subject-matter lines and "fuses" or synthesizes material from different disciplines. Programs of unified studies are generally largely based on social studies or science contributions from the language arts and mathematics areas as is necessary or desirable.

Another approach to a unified studies program involves the selection of themes, problems, or centers of interest around which two or more subjects are organized in such way as to highlight the relationships of these subjects. Teachers in unified studies programs in junior high schools are still responsible for some subject-matter areas, but are expected to unite the content of these areas and to help the students to become aware of common relationships. Specialist teachers from other areas, such as art, music, industrial arts, and home economics, will assist as their contributions are useful and desirable.

Since a unified studies program cuts across subject-matter lines, it is no longer possible to follow a textbook. Course material must be planned and written in what becomes a major reorganization. Paradoxically, a unified studies approach may be easier and more difficult to teach. Easier because the material studied in the context presented demonstrates relationships that make sense to the junior high school students, and skills learned are used in these and other learning activities. More difficult because traditional subject matter areas have lost their distinctive separation and teachers become somewhat uneasy. Such a program can provide learning experiences of more interest and use to adolescents; it can give considerable attention to individual differences and interests; and it often furnishes excellent opportunities for critical thinking and problem solving.

THE CORE CURRICULUM

Early concerns about the nature of the learner and changes in our understanding of the nature of learning brought about a demand that teachers know their pupils better, and that better integration of subject matter be achieved. There was a concern with breaking away from the traditional pattern of separate-subject offerings and developing a vital and reorganized curriculum that recognized the social and economic changes of the times. These early programs attempted to apply the findings of learning psychology to the classroom teachings methods and to take cognizance of the changing needs of youth in America.

Core enthusiasts regarded the school as an instrument to reform society. Ways were sought to eliminate the barriers between disciplines so that knowledge and learning were germane to the individual, his recognition of the world and his adjustment to and understanding of society.

Highly departmentalized seventh and eighth grades, it was claimed, limited opportunities for guidance, for the integration of learning experiences, or for a curriculum that related to children's lives. According to Gruhn and Douglass,[6] the core curriculum was the first major step toward providing the basis for better integration in the program of the junior high school.

WHAT IS THE CORE CURRICULUM?

The term "core curriculum" has been so loosely used that it has been confusing to everyone. Harold Alberty,[7] in analyzing the various uses of the term, developed several basic categories:

1. The core consists of several logically organized subjects or fields of knowledge which are taught independently.
2. The core consists of a number of logically organized subjects or fields of knowledge, and there is correlation for some or all of these.
3. The core consists of broad problems, units of work, or unifying themes chosen since they provide means of teaching effectively the

basic content of specific subjects or fields of knowledge. These subjects or fields retain their identity, but the material is selected and taught with special reference to the unit, theme, or problem previously selected.

4. The core consists of several subjects or fields of knowledge which are fused. Usually one subject or field (e.g., history) becomes the unifying center.
5. Selected learning experiences are taken from broad preplanned problem areas, which constitute the core. Selection is made in terms of individual and social needs.
6. No basic curriculum is predetermined, but the core is made up of broad units of work or activities which are jointly teacher-pupil planned in terms of group perceived group needs.

Faunce and Bossing[8] defined the core curriculum as a pattern of the experience curriculum organized into a closely integrated and interrelated whole. This concept envisions the core curriculum as one in which there are no subject-matter lines, content is not preestablished, the curriculum is experienced rather than learned and evolves according to the needs of the group. The core, in this definition, is considered to be general education, necessary for all students, so that they might develop requisite competencies necessary for citizenship in our democratic society. There is no question that some authorities would disagree with this definition, but this lack of agreement as to definition has been one of the problems connected with core. Rather than attempting further to define and redefine the core curriculum, perhaps it would be helpful to look at some of the characteristics of the core curriculum.

In a recent study of the secondary school curriculum, Clark, Klein, and Burks[9] identified the following as characteristics of the "true core":

1. The core must be the same for and required of all pupils.
2. The core takes a large block of time, usually one-third to one-half of the school day.
3. The core is guidance-oriented.
4. The true core is problem-oriented.
5. The core recognizes no subject matter lines since it considers all knowledge to be its province.
6. Pupil-teacher planning is a basic part of core.
7. Subject matter and skills are taught as the need arises rather than in any predetermined sequence.
8. Considerable teacher preparation, more than in a traditional situation, is essential.
9. In the core individual differences are recognized by method rather than by curricular structure.

It should be remembered that differences exist within the ranks of those who advocate the core curriculum. For example, many who believe firmly in the core approach also believe that the core program should have a definitely defined content. Such content, however, is expected to be derived from a thorough examination of the problems of adolescents that result from their own basic drives, and from the environmental tensions and pressures that affect them, as well as from the democratic values necessary to our society. Within the core concept are three categories: structured core, unstructured core, and the experience curriculum.

STRUCTURED CORE

A structured core approach has no commitment to any specific subject or content areas. The emphasis is upon guiding students in working toward the solution of problems that have real meaning for them; therefore, content from any area may be used if it helps students in solving the problem, but no content must, of itself, be taught. Broad problem areas of a personal, social, or societal nature are selected and the teacher and the class jointly plan specific learning activities. Topics and units are broadly predetermined, thus defining the scope of the curriculum; sequence is determined by interests, needs, and abilities of the specific group of students. Typical core topics might include: "Prejudice," "Air and Water Pollution," "Government in a Democracy," and "Using Community Resources."

A core curriculum requires a block of time of two or three hours and it is essential that the teacher be nonautocratic, well versed in adolescent psychology, and able to provide direction without killing interest and initiative. Because students are involved with real problems, not with textbook statements of them, motivation for learning is enhanced. Opportunities for small group and individual work predominate, and there is substantial attention to individual differences and self-directed study. With a larger time period available, there is more flexibility in learning and more provision for student guidance—certainly a function of the junior high school. It is also a program that can devote more attention to the kind of general education necessary for adolescents.

UNSTRUCTURED CORE

Within the unstructured core there is no basic curriculum structure established; nothing is predetermined. The choice of topics or problems is completely at the discretion of the teacher and his class. Selection of a problem is determined by such questions as

> Is the topic worthwhile? Have we studied it before? Does it interest most of the class? Are there adequate instructional resources for study? Does it provide opportunities for a wide variety of learning activities, including practice in fundamental skills?[10]

It is obvious that an unstructured core is not likely to remain the same year after year if there is sincere attention to pupil interests and needs. The content studied is contemporary and changes in accordance with the changing adolescent and society. With wise direction and counseling from the teacher, students are quite likely to become deeply involved, to experience a resultant increase in motivation and interest. To a greater extent than in the structured core, teachers and students must secure necessary learning materials on new and different topics. This curriculum approach also requires a strong teacher and a block of time of two or three hours.

Since there is no established scope or sequence, it is possible that there will be gaps and omissions in learnings that may cause difficulties in later school grades. It is certain, however, that opportunities to provide for student interests, abilities, and individual differences are vastly multiplied. There is marked teacher insecurity and a concern expressed by the community over subject-matter coverage.

THE EXPERIENCE CURRICULUM

The experience curriculum is, in effect, an unstructured core program for the entire school day—every day. "Since there is no predetermined sequence, the only possible way to examine the actual content of an experience program is to look backward at any given point to ascertain what has been covered."[11]

What is studied by any specific group at any given time will be decided by that group as it works with the teacher. Obviously, there will be minimal preplanning, and equally certainly this curriculum approach necessitates a highly skilled teacher. Surprisingly, in view of the lack of preplanning and preliminary organization possible, Wright's survey[12] of 1956–57 reported that approximately 6 percent of the junior high schools responding indicated that they had an experience-type program. Presumably the experience curriculum would afford the maximum in learning experiences designed to meet the needs, problems, and interests of the students participating. At the same time, all of the difficulties, disadvantages, and problems plaguing the structured and unstructured core would exist to a greater extent.

WHY CORE?

The future of the core program, based as it is upon the needs concept of junior high school children, lies in the better learning opportunities provided for the student. There appears to be a growing trend toward a subject-centered curriculum rather than one that is focused upon the student. As one educator asks, "Must the program be adjusted to fit the student, or is it the other way around?"[13] He goes on to point out that there appears to be a companion trend toward intellectual segregation throughout the country, as demonstrated by increasing stress upon academics, tracking, and grouping. The core curriculum dissolves "barriers between people—economically, racially [and] intellectually."

There is research evidence available that indicates that pupils in block-time and core classes do no worse than pupils in separate-subject classes but achieve, in fact, as well or better than those in separate-subject classes.[14] Neither does there appear to be a loss of learning in subject-matter areas by core students. Those schools that have utilized the core approach believe that students benefit from improved criticial thinking ability, better adjustment socially and personally, and develop more democratic attitudes. The methods used by the teacher in a core program emphasize a problem-solving approach which involves the students in the planning, the activities, and the evaluation of learning, which is in harmony with the best learning theories.

In the core program, the teacher is not in the position of dispensing bits of knowledge which the students must memorize. Instead, the teacher's role becomes one of guiding learning activities; for, as Francis Keppel writes: "Knowledge takes a greater meaning if it is gained through struggle and self-questioning rather than through passive acceptance."[15]

A major advantage claimed for the core program is that of the integration of subject matter around problems of the learner. This approach results in learning that makes sense to students and effects genuine changes in behavior.

In the core program, provision for individual differences can become a reality more readily than in the traditional program. In providing for individual differences, the teacher has more opportunity to capitalize on varying methods which aid in working with these differences. Because the core teacher spends from one-third to one-half of the school day with the students, there is better opportunity to utilize methods which a highly departmentalized schdule does not permit.

Another advantage of the core program is that the guidance function of the junior high school can be greatly enhanced because of the better understanding the teacher has of each of the pupils. The longer blocks of time set aside for the core period enable the teachers to have ample opportunities for group and individual guidance, particularly as they delve into the problems of youth and society.

Students in the core program are more likely to develop better skills of research and to apply the principles of scientific method than those in noncore programs. It appears that the students in the core area are more likely to be exposed to the "how" as well as to the "what" of a subject. In evaluating the core programs in selected junior high schools, Ralph Tyler found that students in core programs demonstrated somewhat more progress, on the average, than matched students in standard classes, in content material, "in ability to interpret data, to apply principles in science and social studies, and to interpret literature; in breadth and maturity of reading interests; and in democratic attitudes."[16]

The famous Eight Year Study of the 1930's involved thirty high schools that were assured by over three hundred colleges and universities that graduates of the experimental high schools would be accepted without entrance examinations if the high schools wished to deviate from the traditional curriculum patterns.

Comparative evaluations were made of college success of students from the experimental schools and of students from traditional schools. Evaluations were made in terms of participation in activities, scholastic success, and evidences of broad cultural interests.

Students from the thirty schools excelled slightly in academic achievement, were perceptibly better in participation in student affairs, and had broader cultural interests.

The results were interpreted by one writer thus:

> The colleges got from these most experimental schools a higher proportion of sound, effective college material than . . . from the conventional schools. If colleges want students of sound scholarship, with vital interests, students who have developed effective and objective habits of thinking . . . they will encourage the trend away from restrictions.[17]

CRITICISMS OF THE CORE

Many of the advocates of the program insist that the claimed weaknesses are not inherent in the core idea, but are weaknesses in applying or implementing the program. Critics claim that because the core draws from several disciplines, it is almost certain that vital knowledge and information and fundamental skills will be omitted. Certainly there are cases where this is true, which in turn gives rise to many vocal and vehement complaints that the curriculum is being watered down.

The most serious problem for the core program is the lack of prepared teachers. Few teachers are available with the wide background of training in several disciplines which the core program demands, and few teacher training institutions include training in teaching of core. Real depth and breadth of background and a strong personality are essentials for skillful teachers in the core program. If a weak or mediocre teacher, or one with a narrow specialization, is placed in a core class the amount of damage to the students could be catastrophic. Yet this same teacher in a departmentalized curriculum is exposed to pupils for only a fraction of the school day—and that, presumably, in his area of strength. A very real problem has been the lack of definition. As has been noted, there are so many variations and interpretations of core as to leave school administrators, teachers, and the general public vastly confused as to exactly what a core program really is.

True, the core program is often more expensive to operate than a conventional program. Because it is problem or experience centered, it requires a wide variety of materials, flexible facilities, and many kinds of equipment. This is likely to be more expensive than a traditional departmentalized classroom where the only teaching tool may be the textbook.

Another problem is that pupil evaluation in a core program should take on a completely different nature, but often does not. Because of the different objectives and philosophy encountered in a core program, the purpose and nature of evaluation of pupils should be in line with the stated objectives and philosophy. Unfortunately, most core programs have not developed any unique evaluation and reporting practices and usually utilize traditional methods of testing and reporting.

To sum up, the core curriculum is a sincere effort to afford a better education to the adolescent. "The core curriculum arose out of a desire to make education more meaningful to students. This challenge continues to face our schools today, not only in the big cities but throughout the nation."[18]

The core curriculum is an attempt to give meaning to education for adolescents in the framework of today's world by means of reducing the sharp lines between disciplines, and

> . . . bring knowledge into some kind of humane relationship to the growth of the individual personality . . . to trip the balance of learning on the side of critical inquiry, discovery, and independence as opposed to repetition, regurgitation, and regimentation.[19]

BLOCK-TIME CLASSES

It is because of the failure of most schools to develop a program that has the content of procedural characteristics of core that the term "block time" has come into common usage.[20] As we have already seen, block time is nothing more than a scheduling procedure which places one teacher with the same group of pupils for two or more consecutive classes. Not including the core program, there are two basic types of block-time classes. The first is a block-time class in which the teacher teaches each subject separately. The teacher may or may not attempt to correlate the two subjects. Many teachers find it advantageous to correlate the two or more subjects at certain times but usually teach them separately.

In the second type of block time, classes are unified or fused around units or problems which stem from one of the subjects in the block-time class. In this type the subject-matter lines are eliminated. This type is much less common in the schools.

The subjects most commonly found in block-time classes are language arts and social studies. Less commonly found are science and mathematics. Wright's study[21] in 1958 found 78 percent of the block-time classes included language arts and social studies; 20 percent combined science and mathematics. There are other combinations, less often found, including social studies and mathematics, language arts block, and sometimes a combination of all three classes into a block of time. As might be expected, block-time classes are more prevalent in the seventh grade and gradually decrease through grade 9.

The purposes in providing block-time classes vary from school to school and from district to district. Frequently, the chief reason is to allow a gradual transition from elementary school to high school. With this purpose in mind a school could provide a three-period block in the seventh grade, a two-period block in the eighth grade, and complete departmentalization in the ninth grade.

A second common reason for using block-time classes is that the guidance function is improved since one teacher gets to know the students better as a result of longer periods of time with a single group of pupils. For example, if a teacher has three double-period block-time classes with 25 students in each, he would be in daily contact with 75 pupils. In a seven-period day this would still provide him with a preparation period. In a departmentalized program, a teacher meeting an equal number of students each period would be in daily contact with 150 pupils. In such a situation, there is little question that the block-time teacher could provide more effective guidance.

A block of time affords more flexibility in instruction by making more time available. Too, with a two- or three-period block, a teacher can more easily move from a departmentalized approach to one that cuts across subject-matter lines, such as a unified studies curriculum design. Within such a framework it is possible to come closer to developing an educational program better suited to the early adolescent and to make more provision for individual interests and abilities.

ADVANTAGES OF THE BLOCK OF TIME

Additional advantages of the block of time include

1. Block time encourages the utilization of more effective teaching practices, such as supervised study, field trips, guest speakers, utilization of community resources, cooperative planning, and cooperation with other staff members.
2. Block time encourages experimentation by the teacher.
3. Block time encourages the use of a variety of methods which are too time consuming in a departmentalized schedule such as: group

work, debate, research activities, utilization of community resources, and building displays and bulletin boards.

4. Block time encourages the teacher to correlate subjects and provide for the integration of learning experiences, especially when the subject-matter lines are reduced or eliminated.
5. Block time reduces the pressure to complete a lesson before the bell rings.

DISADVANTAGES OF BLOCK TIME

Any successful program requires the complete cooperation of all involved. This includes parents and students as well as the teachers and administrators. Orientation meetings for all involved certainly will help to assure success in implementing a block-time program. In addition, an ongoing program of workshops and seminars will greatly improve any such program in the schools.

The block-time program does have certain disadvantages which immediately become apparent. One serious problem is the lack of trained teachers for this type of teaching. The teacher must be equally well prepared in two subjects, usually language arts and social studies. Even then it is common for a teacher to favor one subject over another, and therefore to stress that area.

Scheduling of classes poses a problem. This is especially true when attempting to schedule the block-time classes back-to-back in order to facilitate cooperative planning, team teaching, interclass debates, and similar activities.

In addition, block-time classes require better and more flexible facilities, including large laboratory-type classrooms, work space, and flexible furniture. The use of a greater variety of audio-visual equipment in greater amounts is necessary also for this type of program.

STATUS OF BLOCK TIME

Although there is an increased stress upon the subject matter in the schools, particularly since Sputnik, block-time classes are becoming more common throughout the United States. Surveys have been periodically conducted by the U.S. Office of Education to determine the extent of block time class utilization in the junior high school. The following tabulation graphically points to a trend:[22]

Percentage Reporting Block-Time Classes

	1948–49	*1956–57*	*1959–60*
Junior high schools	15.8	31.4	40.0
Junior-senior high schools	6.4	12.1	16.4

Another investigation[23] indicated that, in a random sampling of junior high schools, by 1964 there were slightly more than 50 percent of these junior high schools which used a block of time in at least one grade, and 13 percent of these operated what appeared to be a true core program.

Obviously there are many junior high schools which are strongly departmentalized just as there are many using the block program and a perceptible minority utilizing the core curriculum.

In view of what is known of the nature of the adolescent and what has been accepted as the goals, purposes, and functions of the junior high school, the question that must be asked is: Which curriculum design provides the best education for the early adolescent? We can go on from there.

SUMMARY

Since the development of the junior high school there has been an attempt to provide better learning activities for the early adolescent. Early stress on subject matter and complete departmentalization have resulted in the development of both block-time and core classes. Each has certain features which are advantageous in assisting the junior high school to meet the needs and interests of the pupils.

There is much confusion existing as to what constitutes a core program. Many programs which bear the label "core" are actually block-time classes. Both arrangements may have similar advantages such as improving guidance opportunities, lowering the teacher-pupil ratio, encouraging innovative practices, improving learning, and providing a smoother transition from the elementary school to high school. Both have similar disadvantages which include lack of trained teachers, greater costs, and scheduling problems.

While the true core program is found in but a small percentage of schools, the block-time classes seem to be on an increase throughout the country in the junior high schools. Because of the trend toward academic excellence and the increasing amount of knowledge, combined with the demand for qualified teachers, departmentalization is, unfortunately, very common in junior high schools.

REFERENCES

1. Gordon F. Vars, "Core Curriculum in the Middle School," *Ideas Educational, Kent University School Journal,* Vol. 1 (Winter 1967), p. 29.
2. Donald A. Rock and John K. Hemphill, *Report of the Junior High School Principalship.* Washington, D. C.: NASSP, 1966.
3. William Van Til, Gordon F. Vars, and John Lounsbury, *Modern Education for the Junior High Years.* Indianapolis: Bobbs-Merrill, 1961, p. 39.
4. Harold Alberty, "A Sound Core Program—What It Is and What It Isn't," *NEA Journal,* Vol. 45 (January 1956), p. 20.

5. Grace S. Wright, *Block Time Classes and the Core Program,* Office of Education Bulletin No. 6. Washington, D.C.: Department of Health, Education, and Welfare, 1958, p. ix.
6. William T. Gruhn and Harl R. Douglass, *The Modern Junior High School.* New York: Ronald, 1956, p. 84.
7. Harold Alberty, "Designing Programs to Meet the Common Needs of Youth," *Adapting the Secondary School Program to the Needs of Youth,* Fifty-second Yearbook, Part I. Chicago: National Society of the Study of Education, U. of Chicago Press, 1953, pp. 119–120.
8. Roland C. Faunce and Nelson L. Bossing, *Developing the Core Curriculum.* Englewood Cliffs, N.J.: Prentice-Hall, 1958, p. 8.
9. Leonard H. Clark, Raymond L. Klein, and John B. Burks, *The American Secondary School Curriculum* New York: Macmillan 1966, pp. 144-147.
10. William Van Til, Gordon F. Vars, and John H. Lounsbury, *Modern Education for the Junior High School Years.* 2nd ed. Indianapolis: Bobbs-Merrill, 1967, p. 190.
11. Leslie W. Kindred (ed.) *The Intermediate Schools.* Englewood Cliffs, N.J.: Prentice-Hall, 1968, p. 129.
12. Wright, *op. cit.,* pp. 20-21.
13. Russell L. Hamm, "Core Curriculum At the Crossroads," *Teachers College Journal of Indiana State University,* Vol. 39 (November 1967), p. 63.
14. Van Til et al., *op. cit.,* 2d ed., p. 191.
15. Francis Keppel, *The Necessary Revolution in American Education.* New York: Harper, 1966, p. 116.
16. Ralph W. Tyler, "The Core Curriculum," *NEA Journal,* Vol. 42 (December 1953), p. 564.
17. Dean Chamberlain et al., *Did They Succeed in College?* New York: Harper, 1942, pp. 174-75.
18. Gordon F. Vars, "The Core Curriculum: Lively Corpse," *Clearing House,* Vol. 40 (May 1966), p. 536.
20. Grace S. Wright and Edith S. Greer, *The Junior High School: A Survey of Grades 7-8-9 in Junior and Senior High Schools,* Office of Education Bulletin No. 32. Washington, D.C.: Department of Health, Education, and Welfare, 1963, p. 22.
21. Wright, *Block Time Classes and the Core Program, op. cit.,* p. 21.
22. Wright and Greer, *The Junior High School,* p. 20.
23. Vars, "Core Curriculum in the Middle School."

chapter 14

The Question of Ability Grouping

Ability or achievement grouping is an effort to make teaching and learning easier and more effective by reducing the range of abilities within a class. Students are assigned to classes on the basis of a predetermined factor or factors, most commonly that of presumed academic ability. Ability may be assessed by intelligence tests, teacher judgments, students' past grades, standard achievement tests, reading ability, some combination of these, or all of these factors. Ability grouping, which in effect says that children are capable of performing at designated levels and should achieve to this extent, is often discarded in favor of "achievement" grouping in which children are assigned to levels and classes on the basis of past and present performance.

Disagreement as to the value of ability grouping becomes an argument between those who say that this is a far more efficient method of instruction and those who maintain that this procedure is undemocratic, creates and reinforces caste systems, and does not improve either learning or teaching. Ability grouping is usually recommended for academic areas, and students in nonacademic subjects are generally heterogeneously grouped. The United States Office of Education study[1] of 1959 reported that 74 percent of all junior high schools used homogenous groupings, with large majorities of seventh and eighth grades grouping in all four major subject areas: English, social studies, science, and mathematics.

The fact that ability grouping is a common practice does not mean that it is universally approved; indeed, a substantial number of parents, teachers, and administrators are in violent and vocal opposition. Ability grouping is said to be "unfair," "detrimental to democratic ideals," "an artificial stratification," "unreal," and "of no real value in improving learning."

In rebuttal, supporters of homogeneous ability grouping maintain that the democratic ideal requires that each individual shall have equal opportunity for the best education for him; that a flexible educational program implies, permits, and encourages student movement from group to group; and that students are relieved and learning enhanced when materials and texts are not markedly above nor below a student's level of ability.

In point of fact, we group children in many different ways continually and have done so for years. We group by age and grade in school, an athletic group is grouped by skill, physical education classes are grouped by sex, and we find self-grouping, interest grouping, or selective grouping in elective subjects.

In a larger sense, much stress is put upon grouping, the existence of groups and the necessity for having groups within our schools and our society. In grouping and categorizing so extensively are we destroying individuality? Simpson puts this very well by saying

> Is the role of education to provide the child with recognition, with group membership amd belonging—an unthreatened mass identity—which ignores the cost of conformity? The more thoroughly the child is socialized—that is, the more thoroughly the child accepts the standards of the group—the more he also accepts its perceptions and abandons his own.[2]

To provide a better understanding of the problem, it may help to get an historical perspective of grouping. This procedure is nothing new; it has been used throughout the country for many years, Yet it is obvious that there is considerable disagreement as to the value to the learner, an argument that shows no sign of abating even though surveys indicate that the majority of junior high schools use ability grouping in some form.

EARLY PLANS

At St. Louis, Missouri,[3] beginning in 1862, the school year was divided into four quarters of ten weeks each, for the purpose of making promotions possible at the end of each quarter, and encouraging the formation of ability groups.

Multiple-track plans of similar nature have been devised through the years by many schools to enable pupils of superior ability to complete their schoolwork in less than the usual time while requiring the slow pupils to spend more than the usually allotted to the average pupil.

In 1888 Pueblo, Colorado,[4] made provision for promotion to the next grade at any time during the school that the work of one grade was completed. It required the abandonment of the recitation as such and the substitution of individual or laboratory methods. There was some group work of pupils at the same point of development. Cambridge, Massachusetts,[5] in

1893, provided for three promotions yearly, with a six-year curriculum for the fast-moving group, the grouping based on ability. At Portland, Oregon,[6] beginning in 1897, the nine-grade course of study was divided into fifty-four units. The average child completed six units per year, while the brighter child was permitted to cover eight units yearly (except in the last year), completing the course in seven years, instead of nine.

North Denver, Colorado,[7] in 1898, established minimum sets of requirements for all pupils but made provision for the more able pupils to move at a more rapid rate into additional tasks. Santa Barbara, California,[8] instituted parallel courses of study designed for groups of varying mental ability in 1889. In 1910, Detroit, Michigan,[9] initiated the XYZ Plan which refers to three levels of assumed achievement and learning ability. A curriculum of minimum essentials was constructed for the slow group, while superior pupils received a greatly enriched learning program.

The Dalton Plan[10] was based on the principles of freedom, the intereaction of group life, and a time-budgeting contract plan to facilitate individual achievement. Community living was practiced daily by permitting pupils of three or more grades to pursue the same subject in the same room. Timetables were abolished and each child was allowed to apportion his own time, studying his subjects in any order he chose. Each grade's work in the academic subjects was divided into a series of related jobs or contracts, each divided into smaller units to be completed in a school month. Classroom gave way to subject room wherever possible or otherwise to "subject blocks" or "subject corners" on large tables.[11] Each subject was to be manned by a specialist. Formal recitations were replaced by weekly conferences to throw light on common difficulties encountered by individuals and to provide experience in social living,[12] an approach which was largely lacking in prevailing school practice. For all its virtues, the plan was deficient in socialized behavior outcomes. Its principal objective was the mastery of a preconceived body of subject matter. Individual differences were dealt with primarily in terms of time.

The Winnetka Plan[13] was an application of Burk's proposals for individual instruction. The curriculum was divided into two parts, "the common essentials" and "group and creative activities." Half of each forenoon and half of each afternoon was allowed for work in the essentials and the other half day was devoted to group activities. In work in essentials there were no recitations; the teacher's entire time was spent in teaching. There was no grade failure and no skipping of grades.

In general, children sat with others of approximately their own age and roughly the same degree of grade advancement, but could be freely transferred at any time of the year to an older or younger group. At least two and sometimes three grades of work in one or more subjects were to be found in practically every classroom. Great stress was placed upon self-government in the classroom and in assemblies presided over by the children themselves.[14] Pupil progress was influenced by self-instructional materials. The basic classroom unit was heterogeneous, but each student kept records or goal cards which personalized individual progress. Individual progress within the group was in effect a grouping process which retained many of the merits of ability grouping without some of the difficulties and problems of homogeneous grouping.

In spite of its emphasis on group activities, the Winnetka Plan has been criticized for its separation of the curriculum into discrete fields and the segmentation entailed in the units and tests pertaining to each field. It has often been referred to as an early attempt at programmed instruction.

As can be readily seen, many school systems have experimented with various methods of individualizing instruction—a process that still continues. Most of these plans call for the grouping of students according to their ability, usually into three groups.

OTHER APPROACHES

A variety of other grouping procedures have been attempted; those which were felt to hold more promise include:

1. *Variable grouping by subject.* In this method a student may be in a different ability level group for every subject instead of remaining in the same group for the full day.

2. *Platoon grouping.* First developed by William A. Wirt for use in Bluffton, Indiana, in 1900, this plan assigned children to two groups, one of which studied academic subjects in the classroom while the other group used special rooms for activities.

3. *Ungraded primary, ungraded intermediate, and ungraded secondary.* In this plan grade levels as such are abandoned and students may move through the curriculum at their own speed. This ungraded approach, sometimes titled "nongraded" classes, is growing in favor and incidence of use at the middle school and junior high school level. There are many arguments to support its use. Certainly it permits more attention to individual differences and provides more opportunities for individualizing instruction; classes are highly flexible and students may move from one to another whenever they are ready. Those junior high schools that have tried this method report a high degree of satisfaction from students, parents, and teachers alike, and virtually no criticism. Since each pupil moves at his own speed through a schedule based upon his own abilities, aptitudes, skills, and interests, this approach would appear to come closer to satisfying the demands for an educational program based upon the nature of the early adolescent and the functions of the junior high school than most other forms of grouping. Research relative to nongraded classes is scant, but such as there is indicates

that pupils in these classes do as well or better than those in standard classes. The reported high level of satisfaction, improved pupil attitude, and increased student effort make this method well worth considering.

4. *Intraclassroom grouping.* This may be found in virtually every elementary classroom in the country. The teacher has two or more groups, selected according to performance, for such subjects as she considers necessary, usually reading and arithmetic. The students in each group, generally five to ten, are a part of the regular class and separate from it only for these groups and subjects.

5. *Intergrade grouping* is becoming more common, in which several seventh-grade teachers, for example, might shuffle students around for a given subject, perhaps reading, and assign them to different teachers for different levels of work.

6. *Grouping by student interest* has to an extent existed for some time in the junior high schools. An exploratory program with students permitted to select electives such as art, music, indistrial arts, crafts, home economics, photography, drama, speech, journalism, electronics, and radio is not unusual. Unfortunately, elective options are nowhere near as common in grades 7 and 8 as they should be, and even in grade 9 it is not unusual to find students limited to but one elective. Some interest has been indicated by a few junior high schools in providing "interest" electives within required fields; for example, instead of offering only eighth-grade English, a student might choose among a variety of literature and composition courses. Social studies, too, permit a real range of opportunities in this respect.

7. A most unusual method of grouping was reported in a New York junior high school.[15] Using the Sheldon description of body types, *mesomorph*, *endomorph*, and *ectomorph*, students were classified and assigned to classes on the basis of their individual body types. This was done on the theory that physique plays a part in "the development of personality and is the basis for certain social judgments." The results reported indicated a possible conclusion that this type of grouping yields substantial gains in excess of those in heterogeneous groups.

8. Eichorn[16] suggests that certain variables exist that must be considered in grouping the preadolescent and early adolescent: physical characteristics, mental growth, and cultural impingement. Grouping children on this basis reflects a common educational base "centering on current level of cognitive growth rather than on intelligence scores." Such grouping of children by compatible characteristics would result in a procedure that could be described as grouping by maturational levels. Within the groups so formed, Eichorn further proposes that students be subgrouped into two levels, "one level characterized by concrete operational processes and the second level reflecting the processes of formal operations."[17]

CURRENT ARGUMENTS

At this time there is a major trend toward the increased use of ability grouping for the junior high years. Conant[18] gave this momentum in 1960 when he said that he personally recommended three ability groups in academic courses, with the majority of the pupils in a particular grade in a large middle group. It is preferred, he said, that the grouping should be accomplished subject by subject.

In view of the high proportion of schools that are using ability grouping, one might think that any debate concerning its value would be purely academic. This is most certainly not the case. Opinions are strong and positive both for and against the subject, and the charge is frequently made that grouping is an administrative device and decision in many schools. This it may be, but it often reflects pressures of teachers and parents upon administrators. In discussing this problem, one educator commented

> After reading extensively the professional opinion of educational authorities and after studying the results of educational research [it may be concluded] . . . that practically all of these people take a dim view of ability grouping. The "experts" say that it is extremely difficult to group students by ability, that even if you can, they don't stay grouped by ability, and that even if they would stay grouped by ability you would accomplish very little as far as efficient learning is concerned.[19]

He further remarks that one group takes sharp issue with these statements —the typical classroom teachers. "They say in no uncertain terms that—research or no research—a better job of teaching could be done if some of the poorer students were removed from their classes."[20]

There is much truth to these statements, and most teachers *do* favor ability grouping. At the same time it is of interest to note the last statement concerning the removal of the *poorer* students. Far more infrequently do teachers request transfer of the able students out of their classes, unless the strong student happens to be a discipline problem. On the contrary, if a teacher with an average class or a low class has one or two students in the group who are obviously above the group level, the teacher is likely to resist vigorously any attempts to reassign these students. "Often they openly say, 'Mary and Judy are discussion leaders and my only joy in the entire day. If I lose them the group will collapse.' "[21] The author adds that Mary and Judy are not on salary, probably don't like being intellectual misfits, and should, for their own good, be at least invited to transfer to a higher-level class, "but their teachers are too busy pounding at the counselor's door to switch little Johnny, 'who can't even write a sentence.' "[22]

A major factor in teacher preference for ability grouping is that few teachers want slow learners or poor students. Somehow a great many teachers are convinced that ability grouping will eliminate all of these students and leave teachers with only the average and above-average classes.

Undoubtedly, much of the disagreement concerning ability groupings for the junior high school years involves the nature and extent. Across the board ability groupings for every subject obviously have no place in the junior high school program. Especially has it been criticized in the core or block of time classes where one major objective is to help youngsters work effectively with others. However, in a mathematics class, it has been considered to be equally unfair to place a slow learner with a gifted pupil.

As a compromise and partial solution, Moss[23] recommends heterogeneous grouping for children in the core classes to establish groups that are academically and socially mixed. Students would be assigned to mathematics and science classes on the basis of a four-track ability grouping ". . . to provide for the varying academic abilities of middle school youth." It seems likely that this policy could offend both the advocates and opponents of ability grouping, with each side wanting more than part of the loaf. Furthermore, one might be prompted to ask, are the varying academic abilities not present in classes other than mathematics and science? Conversely, if a social mix is desirable in one field, why not in another?

Much of the demand for ability grouping stems from our concern with the extremes, the slow learner and the gifted student. Slow learners, with their limited intellectual ability, are able to learn if teachers supply them with materials, activities, and experiences suitable for their level. The identification and careful selection of slow-learner groups at the junior high school level is an extremely important function which cannot be left to the administrator or counselor or to the teacher; all must assume a shared responsibility. If homogenous grouping exists, the slow learners can develop and progress at their normal level of ability.

The teacher can do much to foster the growth and development of the slow learners. This teacher must have a sincere interest in helping to build confidence for these students. If members of their group are given the chance for achievement within their abilities, they can experience some success and considerable satisfaction.

A student who is superior in most academic subjects, or who promises to be, is called a gifted student. One who is superior in only one or more school subjects such as music, mathematics, foreign languages, or art, is usually referred to as being talented or academically talented. What these gifted or talented students learn in the junior high school depends not so much on the grouping arrangements, but on the teacher, the teacher's methods, and the types of materials and facilities available.

Materials for the fast learner or gifted must be more complex, and there should be more of them. Such students must have access to a variety of reference materials, and be provided the opportunity to utilize the school and community libraries as research centers. This type of student should have released time from class to do individual work.

The grouping of students according to their ability will do nothing unless the instructional program for the gifted and for the slow learner is changed. Special sections or classes do nothing in themselves to improve instruction, but within them varying content can be arranged and different methods of teaching can be utilized more readily. A teacher with a group of bright individuals is in a position to do a better job than several teachers with heterogeneous classes who must individualize instruction for three or four gifted or talented pupils in a class of 30 to 40 pupils.

It must be remembered that ability grouping is supposed to be established as an effort to make provisions for individual student differences in interest and learning ability—to improve the education of the student. It is not supposed to be a situation where the teacher provides more or less of the same to a class with a somewhat more restricted range of individual differences in academic ability and scholastic achievement.

Arguments for and against ability grouping are long on opinion and emotion and short on fact. This procedure may be described as a heaven-sent solution or as a Torquemada, depending upon whether the person speaking happens to be an opponent or a proponent.

Arguments against ability grouping include

1. It is undemocratic.
2. Pupils grouped by ability on any one kind of test will vary over a range of several grades in other abilities and traits.
3. Actual achievement does not always correlate with the capacity to comprehend.
4. Poor attitudes sometimes result; some students will develop inferiority or superiority complexes.
5. True homogeneity cannot be achieved since any specific factor used for such grouping may be the single point of simularity in the class.
6. Studies have not proven conclusively that ability grouping is worthwhile.
7. The majority of teachers do not like to work with the slow learner.
8. To date, very few differentiated materials are available for the teacher.
9. The teacher in the lower group gets the higher percentage of discipline problems.
10. Homogeneous ability grouping depends too much on the validity of test data that may vary from one situation to another.
11. Teachers with homogeneously ability-grouped classes have a tendency to assume that students are quite similar and neglect the differences.
12. Homogeneous classes do not provide the personal contacts of the kind the students will encounter as adults. Pupils of lower ability

profit from class situations in association with students of higher ability.

13. Problems of grading and marking are seriously aggravated.
14. While ability grouping may be satisfactory for some grade levels and some subjects, junior high and middle schools are *not* the proper grade levels, nor do they teach the appropriate subjects to attempt ability grouping. Children this age suffer more than they profit from ability grouping.

Arguments for ability grouping include

1. It is more democratic to have pupils competing with their own kinds of abilities.
2. Better methods of grouping are available because of improved testing procedures.
3. The range of traits can be reduced through grouping.
4. Better attitudes can be developed through grouping.
5. Methods of teaching can be utilized more effectively when pupils are grouped.
6. Acceleration of the gifted student is facilitated through grouping.
7. The most effective effort is put forth by pupils when they attempt tasks which fall into their range of challenge.
8. Some late bloomers may eventually surpass pupils who seem far ahead of them in schoolwork. Many of these pupils experience so much criticism and failure in a standard classroom that their self-confidence and levels of aspiration are damaged.
9. Studies have shown that teachers favor ability grouping.
10. There is a challenge to the student to do his best in his assigned group so that he may qualify for a move to the next higher group.
11. There is association with students of all ability levels by means of athletic programs, the school activity program, and other joint activities.
12. To provide for individual student differences in a heterogeneous classroom requires more in materials, time, and money.
13. Teaching in a heterogeneous class tends to cause the teacher to slant her efforts toward the average, thus giving but little to either the high- or the low-level achiever.
14. A good teacher establishes her own kinds of groups within the room in any event. Witness the reading groups in elementary grades.
15. Grouping is a fact of life throughout the country. Ungrouped classes are really the artificial situation.

Unfortunately, objective data that could help solve these differences are quite meager, inconclusive, and often contradictory. However, it is known that, in practice, ability grouping has generally not been accompanied by the changes in methodology and curricular reorganization upon which the theory behind grouping is predicated. There can be but little question that teachers of above-average students prefer ability grouping, but there is a very real doubt that those who teach lower groups are widely in favor of it. While ability grouping may solve some problems, there are others, some of a serious nature, which appear to result from grouping procedures, or at least are aggravated by them.

PROBLEMS

1. The caste system which is decried among students is often exhibited by teachers of various levels and groups, those who teach the high groups regarding other groups and teachers with amused tolerance and even some patronizing.

2. A strict classification of students and groups catalogs children in teachers' minds and produces an accompanying freezing of expectations, standards, and teaching methods. For example, "This is a remedial class—you can't really expect a great deal from them," the teacher remarks *sotto voce* while the "remedial" student becomes more convinced than ever that efforts are futile. Similarly, "I've had superior classes like this one for several years. If I have to take a low group, I'll quit." Meanwhile, the "superior" students take on a little more self-satisfaction.

3. Grouping which places junior high children into inflexible tracks and programs is rightfully criticized. Tests are far from infallible, and judgments of counselors, teachers, and administrators even more subject to error. There *must* be constant opportunity to move students into and out of groups.

4. Grouping implies screening and screening is usually achieved by IQ and achievement tests plus opinions of staff. There is little or no attempt made or consideration given to evaluating student motivation, desire, persistence, disposition to do hard work, interest, and willingness to extend oneself. As a result, students are often misassigned. If the groups are not flexible, they are trapped for the balance of the term, along with the teacher.

5. Ability grouping or homogenous grouping is not any easier method of arranging classes, but administratively, is, considerably more of a problem. Scheduling conflicts and problems are multiplied unless the enrollment is quite large. Even then, problems are posed.

6. Selection and assignment of teachers must be carefully accomplished. Not only is it necessary to be sure that teachers are well prepared in their subjects, but there is the problem of determining if a teacher can and will work with a specific group. Teaching methods must be revised and materials supplemented. It is sometimes hard to keep from going too fast or too slowly. A related problem is that of teachers who overwork a top group

because their idea of changed methods and better instruction is to pile the work on.

7. Grading, a never-ending problem in any school, becomes a many-sided difficulty in ability grouping. Is it, for example, impossible for a student in a low group ever to earn an A or a B? Commonly, this is the rule. Will a B in a high group be the same as an A at the next level? If so, then there will be parents insisting that their children be moved to the group where an A is assured.

8. Pupil turnover and insufficient data on some of the regular students make ability grouping more dependent upon second sight than on valid evidence.

9. A group that is relatively homogeneous in September will, because of student differences in growth patterns, interest in the subject, motivation, maturity, and a host of other factors, develop a surprising range by June. If groups are not flexible so that students may continually be moved in and out, the grouping factor loses a great part of its potential.

10. Groups must vary in composition from subject to subject. While the larger part of the group will probably be constant, it is certain to have variations from one class to another. Not all of those children who are strong in mathematics will be of equal strength in English, and this necessitates a shift of students from one group to another.

11. If either the teachers or the administration do not favor grouping and do not do all possible to implement it, the procedure will never be successful. As in every other aspect of teaching, when we get down to the ultimate point, the teacher can make or break a program.

12. The danger of formation of an intellectual elite is increased in those schools that group children into fixed sections which do not change at all during the day, week, or year. This can work in reverse for the lowest group which is never exposed to any other kind of association. It is probable that the low group will have a high proportion of children who are frustrated, feel inadequate, and are discipline problems.

STUDIES AND OPINIONS

It has been claimed[24] that ability-grouped classes tend to increase social and racial bias, are detrimental to the average group, and possibly harmful to the lowest group, although they do encourage content achievement. Statements such as this do not go unchallenged, however, since there are many who are convinced that, if any group profits from ability grouping, it is the lowest group, for the high group will doubtless learn in spite of the teacher.[25]

It is plain that there is nothing approaching complete agreement. Brimm notes in a solemn vein that "There is no evidence to show that ability grouping increases achievement as measured by standardized achievement tests."[26] He remarks further that there is little objective evidence to show that it is detrimental.

In contrast to this, it has been said that "There is a good deal of evidence that ability-grouped students may experience greater growth in achievement than students in heterogeneous classes."[27] In supporting this statement, its author refers to studies which indicated that, in those cases where materials and methods were adapted to the varying levels of ability, ability-grouped classes did show greater gains than those which were heterogeneously grouped. This survey[28] of 42 high schools indicated that teachers and principals believed that students achieved better; that there was no serious problem of snobbery or stigmatization; that a more appropriate pace for all students could be maintained; and that there was more student participation in the classroom. There were some disadvantages mentioned, including the loss of leadership of faster learners, the more difficult motivation required to keep students maintaining a standard in average and low classes, and misplaced students and inflexible scheduling.

A National Education Association Research Report[29] summarized the findings and conclusions from 50 research studies on ability grouping since 1960 as follows:

1. Although the research was extensive concerning effects upon pupil achievement of various organizational procedures for ability grouping, the results were inconclusive and indefinite.
2. Such evidence as is available indicates that factors other than ability grouping per se may be responsible for the differences found to occur in achievement-test results when ability-grouped children are compared with children who have been taught in heterogeneously grouped classes.
3. Standardized tests in some studies showed gains in achievement that favor ability-grouped classes, other studies and standardized tests favored heterogeneous groupings, and still others showed little or no statistical differences among grouping methods in pupil achievement.
4. There is a tendency for ability grouping to succeed when it is accompanied by a modification of teaching methods, materials, objectives, and curriculum.
5. Most studies of ability grouping are concerned with the effects on academic achievement as measured by standardized tests. There are but few studies that attempt to ascertain the effects of ability grouping on pupils' attitudes, self-concepts, and other factors in their development. It is quite possible that for some children ability grouping produces undesirable effects in certain areas of development.
6. There has been but little research that attempts to determine possi-

ble effects of different types of grouping on pupil growth in such areas as ability to think, on the development of creativity, or in the development of values.

7. Research studies note the difficulty in attempting to group children by ability. "Especially in the early years, it is likely that grouping by ability cannot be accomplished with assurance and accuracy."[30]
8. Empirical data are virtually nonexistent to support a positive or negative position concerning the merits of ability grouping.

The report concluded that there appear to be three major areas of agreement in spite of the diversity in evaluation, opinion, and practice concerning ability grouping:

1. Teachers tend to prefer ability grouping, although ability grouping per se has not proven itself as a means of meeting effectively and efficiently the individual needs of all students in most areas of educational concern.
2. There is a need for more and better research that will account for or control a larger number of the variables involved.
3. There must be a change in objectives, curriculum, and teaching methods to fit each of the homogeneous groups of students at each of the different levels of ability.

The 1966 *Report of the Junior High School Principalship*[31] found that 15 percent of the 4,496 responding principals utilized a form of ability grouping for all students in all grades in all subject areas; 53 percent grouped in all grade levels but only in some subjects; 15 percent grouped only some grade levels and some subjects; and 9 percent reported no ability grouping in any subject or any grade.

In answer to a question concerning what the ideal ability grouping might be, 7 percent of the principals said that there should be no ability grouping; 19 percent favored ability grouping in all grade levels in all subject areas; 52 percent preferred ability grouping in some subjects at all grade levels; and 14 percent believed that ability grouping should be limited to certain grade levels and restricted to only certain subjects.

Concerning the criteria to be used for ability grouping, 84 percent of the responding principals reported that some combination of two or more of the following were utilized: grades, IQ scores, teachers' judgment, and standard achievement tests.

Since it is so often reported that teachers tend to prefer ability grouping, there may be reason to wonder if such a high percentage of junior high schools have adopted ability grouping to satisfy the staff rather than through concern for the best educational program for the adolescent.

Other surveys and studies point out that ability grouping *does* make a difference, that ability grouping does *not* make any difference in achievement, that a wide IQ range in the classroom results in greater individual achievement than when IQ's are comparable, and that mental rather than chronological age is a better guide to grade grouping. It appears that one can take a position and then find documentation to support it.

Since one of the major criticisms of ability grouping is that it is undemocratic, a look at the rebuttal to this argument may be of interest. "Ability grouping is the practice of democracy,"[32] it is said, because in a competitive society people compete in all areas. Our democratic ideal holds that each individual shall have an equal opportunity for the best education for him. Lumping all students together, heterogeneously, ". . . is socialism, not democracy."[33] Discipline problems are aggravated by putting the turtles with the hares—slow students are relieved to have books that they can read, materials that they can understand, and competition that they can meet.

It appears that the success of ability grouping depends upon the belief and enthusiasm of the teachers and administrators, the revision of curricula, and the change in methods. The best grouping methods will probably vary from one school to another. In the proper situation, ability groupings may produce more learning than heterogeneous groupings, but such groupings should not be completely stratified. The best divisions involve some range of ability and contemplate three levels—high, middle, and low.

SUMMARY

Many plans have been devised to provide for the grouping of children at all grade levels. Historically, grouping is nothing new, having been used in this country for well over 100 years. Students have been grouped by age, subject, mental ability, interest, achievement scores, teacher grades, and a variety of different plans.

The controversy over ability grouping for the junior high school years rages more violently than it does for the elementary school or for the senior high school. Even though this controversy continues, there is a definite trend toward the increased use of ability grouping in the junior high school. Conant's recommendations undoubtedly have given some push in this direction.

The advantages and disadvantages for ability grouping are as numerous as the proponents and opponents. However, it must be remembered that the grouping of students according to their ability will do nothing unless it is accompanied by changes in methodology and materials.

REFERENCES

1. Grace S. Wright and Edith S. Greer, "The Junior High School," U.S. Office of Education Bulletin No. 32, 1963, p. 79.
2. Elizabeth L. Simpson, "The Individual in the Group," *Phi Delta Kappan*, Vol. 50 (February 1969), pp. 321–322.

3. James H. Dougherty, Frank H. Gorman, and Claude A. Phillips, *Elementary School Organization and Management.* New York: Macmillan, 1963, p. 23.
4. John Dale Russell and Charles H. Judd, *The American Educational System: An Introduction to Education.* Boston: Houghton, 1949, p. 256.
5. *Ibid.*, p. 257.
6. Henry J. Otto, *Organization and Administrative Practices in the Elementary School in the United States.* Austin, Texas: University of Texas Publication No. 4544, 1946, p. 236.
7. John Goodlad, *Fortieth Yearbook*, National Educational Association, p. 53.
8. R. Freeman Butts and Lawrence A. Cremin, *A History of Education in American Culture.* New York: Holt, 1953, p. 439.
9. J. Wayne Wrightstone, *Class Organization for Instruction*, Department of Classroom Teachers monograph, National Education Association, Washington, D.C., 1957, p. 6.
10. C. W. Kimmins and Belle Rennie, *The Triumph of the Dalton Plan.* London: Phillip and Son, 1926, p. 4.
11. *Loc cit.*
12. Adolph E. Meyer, *The Development of Education in the Twentieth Century.* 2d ed. Englewood Cliffs, N.J.: Prentice Hall, 1949, p. 490.
13. Otto, *op. cit.*, p. 144.
14. Charles W. Washburne, Mabel Voge, and William S. Gray, *Results of Practical Experiments in Fitting Schools to Individuals: A Survey of the Winnetka Public Schools.* Bloomington, Ill.: Public School Publishing Company, 1926, p. 20.
15. Raymond J. Yerkovich, "Somatotypes: A New Method in Grouping," *Clearing House*, Vol. 42 (January 1968), pp. 278–279.
16. Donald H. Eichorn, *The Middle School.* New York: Center for Applied Research in Education, Inc., 1966, pp. 78–79.
17. *Loc cit.*
18. James B. Conant, *Education in the Junior High School Years* (Princeton, N.J.: Educational Testing Service, 1960, p. 26.
19. Charles E. Hood, "Do We Expect Too Much from Ability Grouping?" *Clearing House*, Vol. 38 (April 1964), p. 467.
20. *Loc cit.*
21.Robert L. Kelly, "Ability Grouping in English,"Clearing House, Vol. 43(May 1969), P. 551.
22. *Loc. cit.*
23. Theodore C. Moss, *Middle School.* Boston: Houghton, 1969, p. 153.
24. M. J. Eash, "Grouping: What Have We learned," *Educational Leadership*, Vol. 18 (April 1961), pp. 429–435.
25. Fred T. Wilhelms and Dorothy Westby-Gibson, "Grouping Research Offers Leads," *Educational Leadership*, Vol. 18 (April 1961), pp. 410–414.
26. R. P. Brimm, *The Junior High School.* New York: Center for Applied Research, Inc., 1964, p. 91.
27. Gordon Cawelti, "Ability Grouping Programs in Selected Midwestern High Schools," *NASSP Bulletin*, Vol. 47 (March 1963), pp. 34–39.
28. *Ibid.*
29. "Ability Grouping," *NEA Research Bulletin*, Vol. 46 (October 1968), pp. 74–76.

30. *Ibid.*, p. 75.
31. Donald A. Rock and John K. Hemphill, *Report of the Junior High School Principalship.* Washington, D.C.: National Association of Secondary School Principals, 1966.
32. Alice Hall, "Ability Grouping Is Democratic," *Clearing House*, Vol. 40 (November 1965), pp. 159–160.
33. *Ibid.*, p. 159.

chapter 15

Evaluation, Testing, and Reporting

Debates concerning school policies and procedures in evaluation, testing, and reporting are not new but are becoming more heated among teachers, administrators, parents, and pupils alike. There are several reasons for these disagreements and dissensions, including a lack of understanding of terminology; failure to establish purposes and goals for evaluation and testing; lack of agreement as to values and standards; arbitrary adherence to what has traditionally been done; poor teaching and administrative practices; parental stress upon grades; inflated ideas as to the values and meanings of grades; teacher ignorance of methods of evaluation, testing, and reporting; community and social pressures; improper use of test results; drawing inferences and making authoritarian judgments from inadequate test scores; and teaching for tests.

The questions of evaluation, testing, and grading pose particular problems for junior high and middle schools both in regard to the characteristics of children of this age group and to the oft-stated intent to develop student self-direction and self-responsibility. If we really believe that these children are a unique group, if we honestly attempt to work toward development of each child to the ultimate of his own abilities, if we sincerely want individualized learning, then most of what we do in evaluation, testing, and grading is wrong and even conflicts with the accepted functions of the junior high school. We talk to our junior high school students of "self-evaluation," then turn around and force them into a comparison with a mythical "average" or the magic of a "curve."

An adolescent experiencing failure in school develops feelings of inadequacy, hopelessness, frustration, anxiety, and fear to the extent that he wishes to remove himself from the threatening situation—the school. His attitudes and feelings will almost certainly be expressed in his relations with the community and, should he remain in school, he is quite likely to become a discipline problem. The preadolescent and early adolescent *must* have success, they must succeed to some measure in some areas or the junior high school itself should be receiving failing marks.

The effect of marks upon adolescents is all out of porportion to their real importance. With poor marks (because marks become the standards), the adolescent sees himself as rejected, worthless, and inadequate—a perception based upon teacher-made tests and teacher evaluations, according to some mystic interpretations of such qualities as "effort," "citizenship," and "behavior." Test scores are assigned grades, such as 93–100 = A and below 70 = F, according to some caprice, wizardry, supernatural insight, or honest guesswork of some teacher or administrator. The difficulty is compounded in those junior high schools—and this includes most—that use the high school system of evaluation and reporting. Colleges want a four-year high school transcript; the high school wants consistency with their procedures from ninth-grade records, and the seventh- and eighth-grade teachers use the same procedures as do those teaching the ninth grade.

Thus we have a junior high school grading system, determined by teachers and administrators (though we prate of student self-evaluation and "self-direction") and the pressures from the high schools. It is true that this situation is not universal, but it does exist, as surveys indicate, in the great majority of junior high schools. A junior high school staff that has taken the time to formulate educational purposes; to select appropriate learning experiences for the students; to develop and state a philosophy, general objectives, and specific objectives, will find that traditional evaluation and marking practices are virtually worthless for students in general and particularly for junior high school students. These children, with their wide ranges in maturity, their diversity of interests and abilities, their rapidly developing and shifting curiosity, their unsureness—all of the characteristics that compose the preadolescent and early adolescent—generally receive a report card with one mark for each subject, occasionally a mark for some characteristic or behavior, on a card that purports to provide students and parents with a full assessment of learning progress.

THE PROBLEMS

Too often we really don't know what we mean or even what we are talking about when we discuss and establish junior high school "grading" standards and procedures. For example, what does an A mean? Is an A grade the same for every class? Is an A in English the same as an A in art? If not, why not? Is a B in a high-level class identical to a B in a remedial class? Is a B in this junior high school the same as a B in a junior high school twenty miles away or in any other junior high school? Or would this B equal an A in one school and a C in another? Here is a situation of such extreme variance that no one really knows what any given grade means—we know only what we *think* it means in terms of our own beliefs and experiences.

What factors are included in this single grade? Does this represent academic achievement solely, or has it been affected by student effort, citizenship, and a variety of other factors lumped in with the final grade to distort the picture of student learning? To avoid this problem, some junior high schools give separate marks for academic achievement, attendance, citizenship (however that may be defined), and work habits. One junior high school gives a numerical rating to each pupil in each subject as well as a 1 (high) to a 4 (low) in citizenship in these categories:

1. Does more than is expected of an average citizen.
2. Does what is expected of an average citizen.
3. Does not misbehave but contributes very little.
4. Disobeys rules, shows little respect, hinders progress of fellow students.

What is an "average citizen"? The amount of power wielded by a teacher's autocratic and subjective assignment of marks is truly frightening. One eighth-grade girl was kept off the "Academic Honor Roll" for her junior high school because she received two "Poors" in citizenship from the same teacher (a block-time class of English and social studies) although she received "A" grades in all six subjects and "Excellent" in citizenship from her other four teachers. There is something most peculiar in a situation of this sort.

"A fundamental question in marking is, 'What should be the primary basis for assignment of marks?' "[1] One study of marking practices in 129 secondary schools with varying grade organizational patterns found that 22 percent of the schools in the sample had no policy governing the basis used, 27 percent based grades on an absolute standard of achievement, 29 percent stated that grades reflect achievement with respect to ability, and 16 percent reported that grades represent achievement with respect to others in the class.[2]

Marks are further lacking in meaning when overzealous teachers adopt "tough" standards, have no clear idea what they are evaluating or how they are doing it, or attempt to grade all children in the same rigid manner. A common example of this is the teacher who grades "on the curve," whatever her conception of that may be. A normal curve is based upon normal distribution—that is, a small number of units on either end, high and low, with increasing scores or numbers of units until the midscore is reached. Note the term *midscore.* Yet the majority of grading scales set a passing score of 65, 70, or 75, anything below which is failing. Even if the passing marks were at 50 (the midscore), it still implies that one-half the students are failures. Since this is seldom the case, we can only conclude that the midscore on teacher tests and evaluation scales is at a point higher than 50 (perhaps 80 or 85), in which case the curve becomes meaningless. Yet we chatter happily of grading "on the curve," even though a normal curve is based upon thousands of scores or cases and teachers deal with but a few classes.

Grades and marks have even less meaning when teachers give lower grades than a student has actually earned because he isn't "working up to ability," or, "to shake him up," or, "to motivate him to work harder." It is no wonder that parents and students become unhappy and don't know what the grades mean. No one else knows either.

If ever there was a time when we need to ask "Why," it is when grading systems are constructed, and this is especially pertinent in junior high school where so often a high school marking system is adopted without real reason or justification.

The pressure to get into college—and often a *specific* college—has increased the emphasis upon grades, even in junior high school. Parents become more and more concerned that their children's grades will not be high enough to permit entrance to college, and these parents exert such influence as they can upon both children and teachers for higher marks. A junior high school that is having some difficulty in defining its grading practice finds that its position becomes peculiarly vulnerable.

"What we lack and need badly is a content or 'criterion-referenced' score based directly on proficiency in subject matter."[3] Such a score is easiest to use when there is an absolute unit of measurement, such as number of words typed per minute, but it is not impossible to develop a planned continuum in other fields—only more difficult. A criterion-referenced score is a "point along a continuum that indicates the degree of proficiency achieved by an individual without reference to anyone else . . . the student's score indicates *his* level of proficiency."[4] This approach necessitates clear and definite statements of objectives, a procedure that should be followed by all teachers at any level. General statements abound, but specifically what is to be taught and learned when the objective is stated as, "understanding democracy," or, "appreciating folk music"? A sequential statement of content objectives clarifies for the teacher the successive competencies that he may expect of the student, lets the student know what is expected of him, places the emphasis on learning and teaching where it belongs and not on marks, and gives each student an absolute measure of his own performance.

It is apparent that the school must determine what broad educational purposes are involved, what is supposed to be taught, what is being marked, and how this is to be done. Good marks do not necessarily equal success but are usually so interpreted, with the resultant fears, anxieties, and convictions of failure that are likely to develop in many adolescents.

Report cards and reporting practices also leave a great deal to be desired. Usually the student gets a single letter or mark for each subject although this may be accompanied by a brief teacher comment. Again, lack of understanding and confusion are more common than is clarity of communication. For example, there is usually an explanatory note which observes tersely that A is superior, B is excellent, C is satisfactory, D is below average, and F (or E or X or U) is failing. If C is satisfactory, isn't B satisfactory, too? And surely B is superior to C—or is it just less superior than A? If D is below average, what constitutes "average"? Average for what?

As an example of this, one junior high school dropped its letter system of grading (A-B-C-D-F) and substituted the following:

1—Above expectation
2—Up to expectation
3—Below expectation
4—Considerably below

This was reported as a distinct improvement over the letter system that the school had previously used. If this is an improvement, one can only speculate as to what chaos reigned before. What does "above expectation" mean? Above *whose* expectation? The principal's? The teacher's? The superintendent's? And what is the difference between "below expectation" and "considerably below"? If you have a ninth-grader who is "considerably below" in English, how do you explain to him that he isn't really "below expectation" but at some lower point on a fuzzy judgmental scale?

Misuses of tests, lack of understanding of standardized tests, and insufficient teacher training in test construction are also reliable and regular sources of difficulties for teachers, students, parents, and administrators. There are literally countless reported instances where teachers, knowing that a standardized test was to be used, have "taught for the test," that is, the content taught was determined by the questions in the test.

A test should be a teaching tool with feedback to the student to help further learning, yet it is common to find tests used as threats ("*Will* you be quiet or shall I give you a test?") as punishment, or as motivators—"You had better listen, this will be on the test." Test construction remains a mystery to many apprehensive teachers, and many more teachers, with the bland assurance of the uninformed, construct and administer tests which do not measure what was taught, test for the wrong reasons, or test only to collect grades. Much is said concerning the need to develop critical thinking in our junior high school students, and virtually all teachers espouse critical thinking as an important instructional objective, yet most tests do little but demand rote recall from the student. "Tests that place a premium upon rote memory may develop within the student a set for short-term retention. . . . He may be able to pass the quiz but fail to see the broader relationships."[5]

Properly devised and constructed, tests and examinations are useful tools in improving curricula and teaching. Objective tests, such as multiple-choice, can be constructed to stress critical thinking and understanding of the subject, perhaps even more than do some essay tests. But it requires thought and effort on the part of the teacher.

Common misuses of tests include:

1. Tests are overstressed and teaching is aimed at the test, not for the objectives of learning, or, so that the class will "look good," students are coached for the test.
2. Standardized tests are used by supervisors and administrators to determine the teacher's effectiveness and the quality of her teaching.
3. Scores on standardized tests are accepted as absolute truths—i.e., a single IQ score is used as a positive and final definition and limitation of a pupil's potential.
4. Test scores are used as definitive sources in counseling children as though there were no possibility for error or change.
5. The teacher concentrates her efforts upon creative and critical thinking and then constructs a test which has nothing in it but recall and recognition items. Only lip service is paid to self-evaluation, a practice regarded as highly desirable for junior high school students.
6. Teacher-made test questions are given arbitrary point values which have little relation to the importance of what was taught.
7. The test is used as a failing device. An example of this is the teacher who comes triumphantly into the lounge and gloats, "I certainly knocked those kids down that time. They've been thinking that they're so smart and over half of them failed this test." If over half of them failed, then the teacher should never announce it. Either they were not taught or the test did not test what was taught.
8. Pupil test scores are read aloud in class. This embarrasses good and poor pupils alike and multiplies discipline problems and resentment.
9. There is a distinct lack of pretesting and diagnostic testing to determine exactly where each student is and what deficiencies he may have.
10. The amount of importance attached to some tests, such as "the semester final," is often disproportionate and detracts from the value given to other student work and tests throughout the school term.

Standardized tests, which are those constructed, published, and sold to the schools by publishing firms, enjoy a variety of criticisms, too. Such tests are said to be undemocratic; too expensive and serve only to permit publisher exploitation of schools; unfair because pupils are labeled and categorized as a result of test scores; improperly used because those teachers and counselors who interpret them are too often untrained and inefficient in their use; and standardized tests tend to stabilize the curriculum. In this connection the proposed National Assessment Program, which will ultimately have some effect upon every junior high and middle school in the nation, has found itself the center of considerable controversy.

NATIONAL ASSESSMENT

An assessment of the progress of education, conducted on a national basis, to determine what progress is being made in raising educational levels, detecting which areas need more support and focus, and ascertaining differences in educational opportunities in economic and geographic sectors of the country is not a new concept. However, it is the first time that a proposal of this magnitude has received sufficient financial endorsement to make it appear possible of attainment.

In 1963 a conference of educational measurement people, in discussing a memorandum prepared by Ralph Tyler, concluded that development of a national assessment proposal was feasible at this time. Encouraged by the U.S. Department of Health, Education, and Welfare, the Carnegie Foundation granted funds for an exploratory project and appointed an Exploratory Committee on Assessing the Progress of Education. This committee held seven conferences with teachers, curriculum specialists, administrators, and school board members during the 1964–65 school year. It was recommended by participants in these conferences that, in cooperation with teachers, assessment instruments be developed and tried out in schools, modified as necessary and desirable, and then tried out nationally.

Contracts to construct the initial instruments were made with the American Institute of Research, Educational Testing Service, Psychological Corporation, and Science Research Associates. These assessment instruments were to be developed for reading, language arts, mathematics, science, writing, social studies, citizenship, music, art, literature, and vocational education. Included in the specifications for these instruments were the following:

1. Specifications for the instruments are to be developed with the assistance of teachers and specialists in the field.
2. The validity of each question, item, or exercise suggested for use is to be judged by two criteria:
   (a) It is an example of the behavior described in the criterion.
   (b) Intelligent laymen can recognize this behavior as worth learning.

3. Included are four groups of exercises, questions and items which are intended for use with four age levels of subjects to be tested: children approximately 9 years old, 13 years old, 17 years old, and adults.

The junior high and middle schools will obviously be affected, since most children who are 13 years old will be in these schools. Certainly there are implications, some as yet unguessed, for curricular and programs for junior high and middle schools as a result of such an assessment program. The groups to be tested are regional (Northeast, South, Midwest, and Southwest), from differing social environments (rural, suburban, and urban), and from different economic levels. Students will be tested from public, private, and parochial schools. It is contemplated that as many as six million students and adults will take sections of the tests, which will furnish the equivalent of 300,000 complete test batteries. This procedure should prohibit comparison of individuals, schools, and school systems since administration of sections of the tests will be to individuals within a classroom and school, rather than to complete classes. The assessments, it is proposed, should be repeated every three years.

Opposition to the National Assessment Proposal was immediate, fearful, indignant, and from a variety of sources. It was argued that:

1. A committee appointed by a private foundation is not the logical nor ethical group to determine what is to be included and what omitted in an assessment. Furthermore, such a committee should be composed of teachers, school administrators, curriculum specialists, and PTA leaders, instead of which the committee is actually composed of three public school people, a state superintendent, and a principal, who are outnumbered by a college president, a university president, two professors, the president of a life insurance company, and a publisher.
2. States and communities should appraise their own schools in regard to their self-established needs, goals, objectives, and programs without being forced into a national pattern which will inevitably become a national curriculum. Pressures will be immediate to teach for what is being tested, which will in turn stifle curriculum change, improvement, and innovation.
3. Pressures will also come to bear upon below-average schools to become average, a process doomed to failure since any average must have one-half below as well as one-half above. There will be pressures upon children to cheat, as well as upon teachers and administrators to become lax in proctoring examinations.
4. National assessment becomes an evaluation of national achievement which in turn will become national standards. In point of fact, the national standards created by the assessing instruments will place control of the curriculum and the schools in the hands of a few

committee members under the sponsorship of a private corporation. If this is doubted, one need only to observe the restricting effect for over fifty years of the Carnegie Unit which was developed by this same Carnegie Foundation.

5. Educators feel coerced by money and public pressures into programs for which they are but poorly prepared. In recent years similar influences have instituted such programs as language laboratories, programmed learning, team teaching, and educational television which have, too often, been fiascos.
6. A national testing program can only reduce equality of educational opportunity, since students who are academically poor performers will become a threat to teachers, administrators, and school systems. It follows, therefore, that such weak students will be extremely vulnerable to pressures to drop out of school so that the performance level of the school will be raised.

Supporters of the National Assessment Proposal become equally indiganant and fervent in their statements. They occasionally appear somewhat bewildered, and even a little flattered, by all of the excitement, and protest that much of the problem comes about from a lack of understanding. They take the following position:

1. Education is too big now to continue without a systematic appraisal. Federal participation in education and federal funds require that federal policies in education become coherent. For too long, policies have been determined on the basis of opinions and influence.
2. The dangers seen and disasters predicted by professional Cassandras are figments of disordered imaginations. There have been previous assessments of educational progress which appear to have done little harm and perhaps much good. For example, yearly rankings are produced by the National Education Association of amounts of money spent by each state for pupils. This is done also for salary figures for educational personnel. Literacy (often called illiteracy) rates are published which indicate the decline in illiteracy by state. Project TALENT, a Census of U.S. Youth's Abilities, was concerned with testing over 400,000 students in over 1,300 secondary aschools in 1960, and follow-up testing is scheduled through 1983. Further surveys and studies have been and continue to be conducted on such items as teacher-pupil ratio, percentage of dropouts, compulsory attendance laws, and a variety of other factors.
3. Unless we are euphoric, we must admit that there exist weaknesses both in our present educational system and in our methods of assessment. Standard achievement tests, for example, expect all students to run the same race without regard to their economic, social, racial, educational, or cultural backgrounds. National assessment, in point-

ing out weaknesses and differences in educational opportunity, only reveals inadequacies that exist. Do we blame the dentist when we need to have our teeth filled? We talk of the need for change, for improved instruction, but appallingly little is done to implement better approaches. National assessment can show that we still place a heavy emphasis upon academics and that educational experiences of children are little changed from what has been traditionally done. In short, if national assessment reveals deficiencies, that is scarcely the fault of the instrument.

4. National Assessment, far from being a monster, will be a helpful ally in bringing pressure to bear for more adequate financing, community support, better facilities, and improved special services. Instruction will be improved, since curricular deficiencies will stress the need for improved teacher training and improved teaching methods.
5. Assessment has long been needed. Rather than fight the opportunity, educators should step in and help in developing and using the tools which they have for so long ignored and used indifferently. The impetus has come and public education must take advantage of this and assume control of the situation. We as educators share with most other professionals accountability to the public we serve. "We should be able to produce demonstrable results which would show what we have been doing. . . . [But must] our results show up at a given time and place on a given set of objective test scores?"[6]

It is certain that

> [One of the] stickiest problems in education remains the problem of fixing responsibility. Among the causes of the stickiness is the very great difficulty in measuring student achievement, especially in schools that emphasize diversity to meet individual differences. In spite of the difficulties, a national Assessment of Educational Achievement is scheduled to begin in March or April [1969] in three areas—science, citizenship, and writing. . . . During the next two years it will continue in seven other fields—literature, art, mathematics, music, reading, social studies, and vocational education.[7]

Perhaps the greatest dangers lie in what use will be made of the test scores. Will schools with low scores receive strong adverse community reactions? Will such problems become political issues? Will teachers and administrators teach for the tests in an effort to survive? "If assessment is to work on a wide scale, then it must be preceded and accompanied by an intensive campaign to educate potential users on the meaning of the tests and their results."[8]

And so the debate continues. It is probable that there is some truth and reason on both sides. In either case, some implications for junior high school education are clear. We must reexamine our teaching methods. We must evaluate our present curricula. We must judge critically if we are doing the best we can for each student. We must be sure that we know our goals are and what it is, specifically, that we are attempting. And we must keep firmly in mind the kind of education best for preadolescents and early adolescents. If the results of National Assessment are used to remedy weaknesses, that is one thing. But if the norms established become standards, a host of problems can develop.

EVALUATION

In the school situation, evaluation is the process the teacher uses in judging or appraising pupil progress and achievement. Evaluation attempts to put a precise value upon pupil performance, an attempt that is more often characterized by subjectivity and even generalities. For example, we refer to a student as having "seventh-grade arithmetic ability," or "sixth-grade reading ability," and these terms presumably mean something. Yet what does it mean if we attempt to classify someone as having "fifth-grade typing ability," or ninth-grade piano ability," or "sixth-grade French"? The sins committed in the sacred name of Evaluation are countless.

It is worth mentioning that the teacher is also being continuously evaluated by the students, the parents, and by the administration, although the end result is reported not in terms of a letter grade but in terms of the teacher's characteristics, personality, attitude, and behavior.

Evaluation should be distinguished from measurement and testing. Although measurement and testing both are part of the overall evaluation process, it must be emphasized that they are only part of the process. Measurement is the act of determining the amount of progress or achievement. Testing is the employment of instruments which attempt to measure progress or achievement.

The junior high school teacher who is overly preoccupied with test scores and letter grades has a limited concept of evaluation. Such a teacher's objectives are invariably limited to subject-matter achievement and she is, therefore, satisfied with testing as the only means of evaluation.

PRINCIPLES OF EVALUATION

1. The objectives of each learning experience must be understood and accepted by all of the parties concerned—especially by the students. Preferably the students participate in determining objectives and, ideally, the objectives are completely student established.

2. Evaluation of students' work should be in terms of their progress toward the attainment of these objectives.

3. Since specific objectives will differ from class to class, the desirability of correspondingly different bases for evaluation from class to class should

be considered. In some schools, this has resulted in different report cards for different subjects.

4. Junior high school students are able to and should be encouraged to evaluate themselves on the basis of course or unit objectives. They should also at any time be able to determine their progress in any class. Teachers should compare these evaluations with their own, study critically any major discrepancies, and attempt to account for them with a view toward their elimination or reduction.

5. Evaluation should be conducted in a variety of ways, since it is important that the teacher not limit himself to the use of one or two specific techniques. Too often teachers fall into the rut of using the same kind of evaluative instrument and, even worse, may use the same instrument year after year. The types of procedure available for evaluating pupil progress are numerous: various types of tests, observations, rating scales, anecdotal records, questionnaires, check lists, diaries and logs, cumulative records, assigned written work, and conferences.

6. The major purpose of evaluation should be to assist the pupil by teacher utilization of various evaluative techniques to provide a diagnosis of pupil achievement so that pupils can work to overcome their weaknesses.

TESTING

Testing is an important part of evaluation. Usually the instruments teachers construct are of two kinds—those designed to measure factual knowledge, and those designed to secure information relative to attitudes, associations, relationships, and understandings. In constructing a test, the teacher must decide how the results are to be used. If, for example, the test is to diagnose weakness so that remedial work can be utilized effectively, the test should be different from one designed to determine student success in remembering or applying facts.

Carefully prepared tests can provide the teacher some indication of the effectiveness of instruction. For example, when the class as a whole performs poorly on a well-constructed test, it is a fair assumption that the instruction was ineffective.

There is no question that tests can serve as a form of motivation. They also frequently produce a great deal of undesirable anxiety in students. Undoubtedly, many students are encouraged to study when confronted with the threat of a test; however, such motivation as this all too often degenerates into a disciplinary crutch for the teacher. It must be stressed that tests should be only a part of the overall evaluative process in determining a grade, although a well-constructed test does provide the teacher with some tangible evidence of pupil achievement.

Tests are perhaps one of the commonest means in measuring pupil progress, yet they often fail to give the teacher the most important information needed to evaluate the pupil. The student who is deficient in reading, for example, will not be able to reveal his knowledge on tests which require him to read.

OBSERVATION

Observation of pupils' work in class is one of the most common techniques of evaluation. Like any other evaluative device, it has certain limitations—most importantly, the unreliability of observers. Too, pupils will behave differently when they know they are being observed.

To aid the teacher in being as objective as possible, a rating scale or check list can be prepared by her or by a group of students under her guidance. The preparation of such a device can be a learning experience in itself for the pupils since they are then more likely to understand the observer's analysis and also participate in establishing some of the criteria of evalution. A rating scale can help to prevent the teacher from being unduly influenced by a single aspect of what is being evaluated.

Rating scales and check lists can be effective in evaluating such activities as group work, bulletin boards, posters, map work, art work, and other creative activities. It must be emphasized that extreme care must be exercised when converting the results of a check list or rating scale to a numerical score or a letter grade. All too often such creative activities have a single aspect which may outweight all other items on the scale.

TEACHER PUPIL CONFERENCES

The conference with the pupil can vary from a highly formal interview to a friendly private chat lasting only a few moments. Usually, the conference gives the teacher greater insight into the student's interests, concerns, and aspirations than any other methods. The student has the opportunity to verbalize any difficulty he might be having, and the teacher and pupil have an opportunity to discuss conflicting expectations about such things as quality of work, class participation, fairness of grades, difficulties in completing assignments, or any number of pertinent matters, whether they are class or out-of-class activities. The individual pupil-teacher conference is a highly desirable and effective way of working with the junior high school student. He can, with teacher guidance, determine his own goals and objectives, select topics and areas for independent study, and develop self-direction and self-responsibility.

The teacher must be available and approachable by the students. They must feel comfortable in discussing problems. The teacher can guide, suggest, and clarify, but should never dictate. Not all interviews and conferences with the student can take place during class time; before school, after school, and during the noon hour are sometimes appropriate, especially for impromptu or unscheduled conferences which often are the most productive.

SELF-EVALUATION

Pupil self-evaluation enables each pupil to know continually what progress he is making and should be an important part of the junior high school program. The teacher should assist the pupils to develop skills in appraising their own progress and achievement by providing opportunities for their self-evaluation. The entire procedure must be carefully handled so that the student's confidence in himself is not damaged nor destroyed. In spite of their observable bumptious and brash manners, junior high children have a great many fears and are nowhere near as self confident as they may appear. A realistic self-appraisal should not become a crushing self-appraisal.

Pupils can participate in appraising their progress in several ways:

1. Through teacher-pupil planning they can assist in formulating the goals of a problem or unit. Individualization then becomes a reality rather than a lofty goal.
2. By assisting in checking or evaluating their own work, they can have information immediately about their own strengths and weaknesses.
3. By a continuous self-evaluation program, the student can see what progress he has made and which areas still need improvement.

MARKING SYSTEMS

1. In the percentage system, which is the oldest of our marking systems, marks are reported in numbers from 0 to 100. When all tests and assignments are graded on this system, the student receives his grades on the basis that 100 percent is "perfect," and all marks presumably have meaning in relation to an arbitrary passing percentage. Seventy percent is the most commonly agreed upon point of passing.

The percentage system by and large has been replaced by other marking systems for several reasons. First, teachers cannot distinguish with the precision this system requires. The margin of error is great in any evaluative system, and therefore a grade of 79 implies 79 percent of perfection. Secondly, human achievements do not lend themselves to such precise rating, especially something that is original or creative work.

2. The five-point marking system is an attempt to improve upon the percentage system. This five-point system, often with some modifications, is almost universally used in the junior high schools. Usually the letters A, B, C, D, and F are employed to designate the level of achievemement, with A being high and F failing. It is not likely that these grades mean the same thing to all teachers. Often it is difficult to say exactly how one arrives at

a grade. For example, averaging a C and an F yields a D, but if the C was for a score of 80 and the F was anything below 70, the numbers being averaged might be 80 and 20 which yield an average of 50—which in itself is failing. The five-point scale is often extended to several other gradations by teachers who pride themselves on their abilities to make fine distinctions, and they confuse the issue with a plus or a minus. Use of a plus or a minus is often considered to be a weak excuse for failing to give a straight grade.

Most school marking systems evidently combine elements of the percentage system and the five-point system. In this way the percentage system is used to help calculate the final grade, which is equated from the percentage marks. For example, A = 95–100; B = 89–94; C = 77–88; D = 70–76; F = below 70. In most cases, the letter grade becomes a disguise, since it is actually a percentage system based on one hundred gradations.

3. The Pass-Fail or Satisfactory-Unsatisfactory method of marking allows only two grades which are Pass (or Satisfactory) and Fail (Unsatisfactory). This system permits more flexibility and subjectivity than either of the others, but it is subject to criticism in that is sometimes said to reduce motivation, allow more able students to to do less than they should, and may not be acceptable to parents. Satisfactory may mean "satisfactory according to predetermined standards," or "satisfactory in terms of the teacher's opinion of student performance." Since these are not the same, confusion can easily arise. Ideally, with the S and U system, the stress is on the individual, his potential, and his progress toward achievement of individually selected goals. There is usually less pupil stress, pressure, and tension under this system and, with good teaching and motivation, there is no need to eliminate the competitive factor—just redirect it. When the S or U mark is accompanied by an evaluative and descriptive statement for each student in each subject, a far more accurate picture of student achievement is presented. This procedure, often used in elementary school, is followed in a minority of middle schools and junior high schools. Opposition to it generally stems from tradition, the extra time and effort involved, and demands from some parents and high schools for letter grades or a percentage system of marking.

There are several other marking systems in use, but in general they are a form of numerical or letter ranking which usually describes the student's performance in relation to other class members. The dual-marking system, sometimes found, gives two grades. The first is the pupil's standing in relation to other class members, and the second is a mark which is the teacher's evaluation of the pupil's performance in terms of his own (estimated) potential. For example, a seventh-grade student might receive a "D/1," indicating that, in relation to the rest of the class his work is at a D level, but so far as his own ability is concerned, the teacher believes that he is achieving at his highest level. As another instance, a student might receive an "A/3," indicating A work in comparison with the rest of the class, but the teacher feels that he is not producing up to his ability. Supporters of this system believe that it makes brighter students aware of unrealized goals without discouraging the less-able student who is doing his best. There is nothing within this system that could not be better achieved by a descriptive statement. It is doubtful that a student who receives a D/1 grade feels much in the way of success or has improved his self-concept.

REPORTING TO PARENTS

Reports to parents have been the major means of communicating between the teacher and parents. Although report cards have been criticized as being unsound, have created many misunderstandings, and have been altered repeatedly, they are still used extensively in the United States.

The junior high school, as well as other segments of the school, has been aware of the need for a revision in evaluating practices. This is especially true in the case of reporting to parents. In the modern junior high school with its heterogeneous pupil population, a reporting system that limits marks to a single grade representing achievement in each subject is certainly unjust and unimaginative.

> School marking practices have changed little during this century, probably less than any other single aspect of the educational enterprise. . . . Educators are resigned to the attitude that marks are a necessary evil and that marking practices are about as effective as they can be.[9]

Some junior high schools have, however, become dissatisfied with the more traditional methods of reporting to parents. Their goal is to develop and use the method which best communicates to the parents the information which they desire regarding the educational achievement and progress of their children.

Since 1946 the Stewart Junior High School staff, College of Education, University of Utah, has effectively eliminated the use of single grades on report cards sent to parents. The *Report to Parents* goes to the parents of each pupil four times a year and contains no scores or letter grades. This report has been modified numerous times since 1946, and perhaps this is one of its real values for the teachers, pupils, and parents. By actively involving all concerned, the Stewart staff has facilitated communication between the home and the school to a degree that may cause many schools great deal of soul-searching in regard to their own reporting practices.

In developing this program of evaluating pupil growth and learning, the Stewart Junior High School staff and parents agreed that it should be broad in its functions. The first consideration was to appraise the aims of the school and the home, and then decide what it is that they wish to evaluate and report. The parents wanted to know just what the school was trying to do, what kinds of records were being kept, the value of instruction, discipline and behavior, and their child's progress and achievement. With the development of this report to parents, communication became more of a reality rather than a goal. The report card then became a means to an end rather than an end in itself.

Questions often arise such as: "What about the student who goes to college and needs transcripts for four years of secondary school?", or "*My* child will need grades to get into one of the Service Academies." In the years that Stewart Junior High School has used this system, this has never been a problem. Many of their students have gone on to college and a number have been accepted into service academies on the basis of a letter from the principal of Stewart School.

THE CHALLENGE

Some of the most serious and challenging administrative problems in the junior high school are related to the problem of evaluation of students' work and reporting to parents. These problems are likely to be especially acute if evaluation and reporting policies differ considerably, as they frequently do, from policies to which students and parents have become accustomed in the elementary school. Whether or not such differences exist, a sound program of evaluation and reporting for the junior high school requirres that certain basic considerations be taken into account.

1. The objectives of each learning experience, in order to operate effectively, must be understood by and accepted by all of the parties concerned—and especially by the students.
2. Evaluation of students' work should be in terms of their progress toward the attainment of these objectives, each according to his own ability.
3. Since specific objectives will differ from class to class, the desirability of correspondingly different bases for evaluation from class to class should be considered. In some schools this has resulted in the development of different report cards for different subjects.
4. Students should at any time be able to ascertain the status of their progress in any class. They should be encouraged to evaluate themselves on the basis of course or unit objectives. Teachers should compare these evaluations with theirs, study critically any major discrepancies, and attempt to account for them with a view toward their elimination or reduction.
5. "Progress reports" should be used by the teacher between regular marking periods to communicate with the home relative to unsatisfactory work. This will ordinarily improve the chances of interested parents to assist in formulating solutions "before it is too late."

6. "Progress reports" should likewise be used to notify parents of praiseworthy work performed by their children, especially in cases in which marked improvement has been noted.
7. In order to reduce confusion in the interpretation of evaluative symbols, there should be separate evaluations for achievement, for citizenship, and for any other factor included in evaluation.
8. Since evaluative symbols, unless carefully defined by the users, are likely to be misunderstood, the school should develop clear definitions for each symbol and should include these definitions on every report card or other instrument on which such symbols are employed.
9. Since subjectivity in marking can at best be only reduced but never entirely eliminated, the use of some such phrase as "in the teacher's judgment" in defining evaluative symbols is strongly recommended.

These considerations are useful in that they allow for an inclusion in the ascertaining and reporting of pupil progress significant findings from research in the field of learning and psychology.

SUMMARY

Evaluation in the junior high school should be a continuous and cooperative process that takes into account the nature, characteristics, and needs of the junior high school students. It should be an integral part of the instructional program with both teachers and pupils actively involved. Teachers, parents, and pupils should all understand the underlying assumptions for evaluation and grading practices of the school. In determining grades, the teacher should employ a variety of devices to gather data about each student.

Numerous methods of reporting to parents are available to the teacher and school system. They range from the old percentage system to the newer parent conferences and check lists. Complete evaluation of the pupil and the perfect report card are certainly still goals of education. Efforts are being made to improve the marking and reporting of pupil progress.

Controversies continually arise concerning lack of clarity in marking, reporting, and testing. Much of this is because of deficiencies in teacher training, poor understanding, and failure to establish clear objectives. Test construction and testing procedures have been most susceptible to criticisms. An area of heated debate has been the must discussed National Assessment Program which will test four different age groups in various parts of the United States, from different socioeconomic levels. Opponents apparently have as a primary fear the possibility of a national curriculum and the loss of local control of schools.

REFERENCES

1. James S. Terwilliger, "Self-Reported Marking Practices and Policies in Public Secondary Schools," *NASSP Bulletin* Vol. 50 (March 1966), p. 33.
2. *Ibid.*
3. William Clark Trow, "On Marks, Norms, and Proficiency Scores," *Phi Delta Kappan*, Vol. 48 (December 1966), p. 172.
4. *Ibid.*
5. J. Stanley Ahmann and Marvin D. Glock, *Evaluating Pupil Growth.* Boston: Allyn and Bacon, 1963, p. 556.
6. Wayne P. Moellenberg, "National Assessment: Are We Ready?" *Clearing House*, Vol. 43 (April 1969), p. 452.
7. "Accountability," *NASSP Spotlight*, January–February 1969, p. 1.
8. Moellenberg, *op. cit.*, p. 453.
9. Richard Kindsvatter, "Guidelines for Better Grading," *Clearing House*, Vol. 43 (February 1969), pp. 332–333.

chapter 16

Student Unrest and Behavior

Within the past few years those who teach and administer the schools have experienced increasing difficulties and problems with student unrest, behavior, and control.

The focus of publicity concerning student unrest has been largely in the colleges of our country although the senior high schools have contributed numerous incidents, frequently with racial overtones. What is not so well known is the extent to which there have been protests and disturbances in the junior high schools of the nation.

Results of a survey of 1,026 secondary principals reported at the 53rd Annual Conference of the National Association of Secondary School Principals (San Francisco, March 1969), indicated that 67 percent of city and urban secondary schools experienced some form of active protest and 53 percent of those schools in rural areas.

> One of the surprises of the survey was the fact that protest is almost as likely to appear in junior high schools as in senior high schools. Among the junior high schools, 56 percent report protest activities, as compared to 59 percent of all senior high schools.[1]

The report stated that young people were speaking their minds on a range of topics from glue-sniffing to voting rights for eighteen-year olds. Dress and hair requirements headed the list, then complaints concerning smoking rules, cafeteria food, assemblies, censorship of student newspapers, and scheduling of sports events.

It is worth noting that 45 percent of the schools with protests reported that the activism was concerned with the way students are educated. There were complaints concerning poor teachers, curriculum content, scheduling, grades, and examinations.

In a later news release regarding this survey of the NASSP, it was reported that

> . . . . while dress and hair account for more protests than any other single topic, the principals enumerate many other regulations which students oppose. In fact, 82 percent of the schools have (had) protests against school regulations. . . . Underground newspapers which have spread from the colleges to the high schools and junior high schools are considered an important part of the protest movement.[2]

In the past it has been easy to label college protestors as draft dodgers, kooks, and hippies; high school students have been characterized as "too young to know better," "misled," and "attracted to the ways of the hippies." Where and when did these behaviors develop? Certainly the aspect of pupil conduct in terms of developing habits of pupils in the middle schools and junior high schools, at the dawn of adolescence, merits consideration here. What kinds of values have been taught when "complaints about hair styling and dress head up the list"?

The junior high schools say that they are teaching critical thinking, how to live in a democracy, and developing pupil self-direction and self-responsibility. Yet over half of the junior high schools have had activism and protests, with complaints about regulations concerning dress and hair styling at the top of the list, and a hefty 45 percent of the complaints were concerned with the way that students are educated. Obviously, too many schools and too many teachers are not really teaching what is believed to be valid or necessary, with resultant dissatisfaction and even open enmity. One educator reported that

> A short time ago I met one evening with a hundred junior high and senior high school students who were forming a city-wide (out-of-school) student organization. The questions addressed to me were searching, penetrating, exciting. But the evening was saturated with hostility toward "the establishment." And the establishment included me, the school system, all adults, even their peer group conformists who in their judgment were selling out to "the system."[3]

We are deeply caught up in a time of active, comprehensive, and bewildering social change; a change requiring substantial modifications in educational direction, curricula, and processes; a change apparently not yet realized by many in education. Because of the critical nature of the junior high school student, these dynamic forces have special implications for junior high school teachers and administrators.

> Attitudes toward morals are changing . . . some schools are even now building smoking rooms for their seventh- and eighth-graders. . . . It must be realized that secondary schools, even junior high schools . . . cannot long resist the penetration into their ranks.[4]

Unrest appears to permeate the teenage subculture. This should be of special concern to teachers of junior high school grades in view of the characteristics of the early adolescent— particularly regarding the adolescent need for values; his idealistically inclined nature; his striving, often in a brash and rebellious manner, for independence and identity; and because of the size, growth patterns, and apparent maturity of many children in the 11–15 age group, teachers are likely to assume more maturity of judgment than junior high students actually possess.

IMMEDIATE NEEDS

With the number of protests concerning the curriculum, teachers and teaching methods, grades and examinations in the junior high and senior high schools, it is obvious that a searching analysis of these items is immediately necessary. The heart of the problem now is to help our young people to find some creative expression for this intensity of feeling, to capitalize upon the characteristics of the early adolescents in finding a useful outlet for their rebellion. Such an outlet must be consistent with the needs of a changing society and aimed at helping them grow toward an understanding of the need for individual and social cooperation within the structure of laws and established procedures.

It has been suggested that there are four important things that need to be done:[5]

1. Policy making, usually restricted to school boards and administrators, must have participation by all those affected by policy. This will require involvement of students and all members of the junior high school to ensure that policy is relevant and viable.

2. There must be genuine communication involving both giving and receiving between all those concerned with the school business—staff, students, parents, taxpayers, legislators. This requires conscious and continued efforts and interaction.

3. It is necessary to develop a system of identification for individuals and situations containing the potential to become troublemakers so that maximum efforts may be made to help and alleviate concerns.

4. "The school program must grow with the expanding goals of education. These goals must encompass much more than mastery of the so-called 'basic tools' of learning."[6] It is necessary that sincere attention be given in the junior high schools to a number of things: the need for individual flexibility; developing critical thinking, inquiry, problem solving, and decision making; to develop a curriculum based upon relevance to present and future needs of youth; to continue and improve training in the basic skills of learning; to prepare young people for responsible and participating citizenship; to afford education for productive use of leisure time; to help young people to develop moral and ethical guidelines; and to supply opportunities

to investigate and understand urban life and standards.

Considering the growing edge of adolescent student dissent with the traditional social values and standards of institutional authority, it is apparent that a credibility gap exists between students and educators and between students and adults. The adolescent is told one thing but sees the converse in practice. "Personal learning to students is relatively more important than academic learning predicated upon future-time gratification goals. 'Now' must become a significant criterion to school officials. . . ."[7]

STUDENT CONDUCT

The item at the top of the list of protests reported by the junior high and senior high school principals[8] was concerned with school regulations relative to student hair styling and dress.

So far as student dress, hair styles, and behavior are concerned, what may school personnel do by way of control? Perhaps an even better question is, what should the school authorities do? It would appear that there are at least two well-defined and opposing positions: (1) young people behave in accord with their dress and appearance—that is, unorthodox clothing, hair styling, and jewelry are conducive to unorthodox and unacceptable behavior in school; and (2) adolescents have a right to a reasonable degree of freedom to do as they wish so far as their own appearance is concerned so long as their behavior is acceptable and they interfere with no one.

The real tragedy is that problems are created, relations become bitter, and feelings run high when the focus is shifted from the best education for the junior high school student to dress styles or, even more inanely, to hair styles. It is difficult to support judgmental statements relating to a correlation between length of hair or skirts and learning potential or even academic achievement. What valid reason is there for preventing a student from styling his hair any way he chooses or growing a beard, sideburns, or mustache (as many junior high schools boys have done), when we say that we are attempting to teach critical thinking and decision making? "Be creative" (but not *too* creative), and "think for yourself" (but be a conformist). When educators attach more significance to fashion than to the purposes of education and to human values, the creative, the nonconformists are almost certain to resist.

There are many junior high school officials who believe that extremes in appearance inevitably are accompanied by extremes in behavior. Their feeling is that it is really of little consequence if extremes in dress or appearance are merely a passing fad or a real change in fashion if, *at this time*, such extremes become a disruptive factor in the efficient operation and discipline of the school. Furthermore, education for life includes developing in the early adolescent a sense of what is appropriate. There is, however, considerable variance of opinion in the adult community as to what constitutes the appropriate. An observation of the mothers of adolescents as they shop in the stores and markets provides an almost unbelievable range of what is obviously considered appropriate garb for public wear. In the opposing view it is said that there is an undeniable change occurring, as it regularly does, in fashion, and the test of any new trend is acceptance. This test, it is asserted, has been passed by skirt and hair length, yet school regulations are directed toward compelling conformity solely for the sake of what has been traditionally accepted. While we may still look twice at males with shoulder length hair, there can be no question that the hirsute male is an accepted part of today's life. A full head of hair, sideburns, beards, and mustaches are now common on males from adolescence to old age.

It is not easy, therefore, for a junior high school principal to make a valid case with students or parents in supporting a regulation such as this:

> Hair must be away from the eyes and away from the collar line . . . neat (not bushy) around the ears and must not overlap the ears. Sideburns are not to extend beyond the midpoint of the ears. . . . [Ruled out are] hair fashions and styles which are excessive and detract from a healthy atmosphere conducive to good educational practices.[9]

It has been pointed out with a certain amount of satisfaction that standards vary not only from year to year but from one junior high school to another. A skirt that was too short or hair that was too long last year will be acceptable because skirts are shorter, hair longer, and hirsute faces more common this year than last. Lest one find satisfaction in the belief that the junior high school, because of the youth of its students, is exempt from problems of dress, appearance, and conduct, note these instances:

1. A 15-year old boy was banned from school because he grew a beard although, "It cannot be said to be notable."
2. A 12-year old California girl was suspended from school for wearing a miniskirt, the hem of which was four inches above her knees.
3. A junior high school boy in Baltimore was barred from attendance until his hair (which fell below his ears on either side) was cut.
4. A ninth-grade Michigan boy who grew a mustache was barred from school and, by court order, temporarily reinstated pending a court hearing.
5. A ninth-grade Cleveland boy, who had a full head of hair (somewhat over the ears but not to the collar) was ordered by his principal to get a haircut. The boy refused, and his father, a respectable middle-class businessman (who also had long hair and a short beard) supported his son. The results of their decision were almost incredible. The boy was suspended from school and, "although industrious, a

good pupil, and not a troublemaker," was charged with being "habitually truant and habitually disobedient"—by virtue of not attending the junior high school from which he was barred. As a next step, the boy was told by the judge to get a haircut, and upon his refusal, was put in jail for twenty-four hours with the threat of a six-month sentence if he didn't comply with the court ruling. The case was appealed.[10]

6. As a somewhat different problem but perhaps indicative of the times, a junior high school boy in Hobbs, New Mexico, was in difficulty with his principal for selling little red cinnamon candies (known as cinnamon drops) to girls as birth control pills and to boys as pep pills —at 37 cents apiece.

Throughout the country it appears that pupils and parents increasingly are testing and opposing school regulations. In Dallas, Texas, when school authorities sent three members of a professional music group home to trim their hair, the agent for a music company took the issue to court saying that the long hair was written into the boys' contract and they would not trim it. Ten teenage witnesses, all with hair as long or longer than the teenage musicians, took the stand to testify that they had been allowed to register in other schools with no difficulty. Another witness, a clothier, testified that "The long hair style is common among youth . . . a full head of hair balances the look . . . it's part of a new revolution in men's clothing."[11]

The principal who suspended the boys said the decision was made in the interest of orderly conduct in the school. The local school district has no written rule dealing with such matters but leaves it to each principal to determine what might be disturbing to the morale of the school. The court upheld the principal.

A fifteen-year-old Albuquerque girl was suspended from school because her skirt was three and one-half inches above her knees, while in places as far apart as Oregon and Maryland junior high school girls were sent home for wearing "granny gowns" with ankle-length skirts.

Another Oregon principal sent home nineteen boys at one time because of long hair, while the dean for discipline of a Bronx school met returning students at the door with scissors, which he used. In New York, the state education commission ruled that the school officials do not have the power to compel students to wear a uniform or particular kind of clothing in school, thus reinstating a girl who had been suspended for wearing slacks to school,[12] while another New Mexico high school girl was suspended for wearing a cowbell to school.

In some states legislation exists which charges school authorities to make and enforce reasonable rules for student dress, appearance, and conduct—the crucial word being reasonable. As one aspect of this problem of definition, the intervention of courts and legislatures may bring about mandates even to the extent of prescribing corrective actions for alleged disciplines. In the absence of specific statutes, however, the schools may find themselves challenged as oppressive, arbitrary, unreasonable, or illegal. At the very least, for the benefit of bewildered school personnel, written policies establishing guidelines should be adopted by local school boards. Usually actions relating to pupil control which reach the courts state some violation of constitutional rights, generally the Fourteenth Amendement to the United States Constitution, which has the widest application by virtue of this sentence:

> No state shall make or enforce any law which shall abridge the privileges or immunities of citizens of the United States; nor shall any state deprive any person of life, liberty, or property, without due process of law; nor deny to any person within its jurisdiction the equal protection of laws.

While the majority of court rulings have supported the actions of school administrators in establishing and enforcing regulations relative to dress and hair styles, there are instances in which the students's right to wear long hair or facial hair has been approved. In Madison, Wisconsin, a U.S. District judge ruled that "Freedom to wear one's hair at a certain length or to wear a beard is constitutionally protected, even though it expresses nothing but individual taste."[13] This decision struck down a local school board regulation prohibiting male students in the public schools from growing long hair or wearing sideburns, mustaches, or beards.

The U.S. Supreme Court's opinion on the Gault decision stated that children have rights too, "Neither the Fourteenth Amendment nor the Bill of Rights is for adults only." [*In re Gault*, 387 U.S. 1 (1967).] Thus, no minimum age may be held to be specified for citizenship. This is not to be construed as insulating children from the power of the state, but rather as protecting them from the improper application of that power. It is not so much that the scope of authority exercised over students has decreased but the manner in which such authority is used is modified.

Court rules such as these have caused some confusion among teachers and administrators and also incurred much bitterness. Many of those in education fear that the courts will succeed in restricting the school's ability to control student conduct, to establish standards, and to set educational goals.

In determining whether school authorities have the authority to enforce a specific regulation, the courts traditionally make use of the test of reasonableness, according to the facts in each particular case. To be considered not acceptable, nonconforming dress or behavior must generally be such as to be a distraction to other pupils and also such as to interfere with the orderly and efficient operation of the school. The court usually does not exchange its own discretion for that of the local school board. The enforcement of a rule is not prohibited because it is inexpedient or unwise; it must clearly be unreasonable. Rules must be related to the purposes of education, made in good faith, and equally applicable to all.

> The rules must be reasonable and proper . . . for the government, good order, and efficiency of the schools—such as will best advance the pupils in their studies, tend to their education and mental improvement, and promote their interest and welfare. But the rules and regulations must relate to these objects." (State *ex. re. Bowe v. Board of Education,* 63 Wis. 234, 23 N.W. 102.)

An essential point to be remembered is that constitutionally guaranteed freedoms have been limited if the limitation is reasonable and in the best interests of the public welfare. A Louisiana action testing a state ruling against Greek-letter fraternities in the public secondary schools brought the following comment from the court:

> It is not up to us to entertain conjectures in opposition to the views of the state, and annul its regulations upon disputable considerations of their wisdom or necessity." (*Hughes et al. v. Caddo Parish School* Board *et. al.,* 57 Supp 508 La 1944, aff'd per curiam 323 U. S. 685, 1945.)

In ruling upon a similar case a Florida court decision was eloquently stated:

> . . . It is pertinent to state that none of our liberties are absolutes; all of them may be limited when the common good or decency requires. . . . Freedom after all is not something turned footloose to run as it will like a thoroughbred in a blue-grass meadow. Freedom in a democracy is a matter of character and tolerance. The ideal recipient of it is one who voluntarily refuses to sacrifice the common good to personal possession. (*Satan Fraternity v. Board of Public Instruction for Dade County,* 156 Fla. 222, 22 S.2d, 892, 1945.)

One of the earliest cases involving student dress was the classic *Puggsley v. Sellmeyer* action (158 Ark. 247, 250 S.W. 538, 1923) which concerned a school board ruling prohibiting "the wearing of transparent hosiery, low-necked dresses, or any style of clothing tending toward immodesty of dress, or the use of face paint or cosmetics." In this 1923 case a high school girl was told to remove her face make-up. She returned to school with talcum powder on her face. In supporting her suspension by school authorities the court observed:

> Courts have other and more important functions than hearing the complaints of disaffected pupils of the public schools against the rules and regulations promulgated by school boards for the government of the schools. . . . The courts hesitate to substitute their will and judgment for that of the school boards which are delegated by law as the agencies to prescribe rules for the government of the public schools of the state. (*Puggsley v. Sellmeyer.*)

The court ruled that since local conditions might exist which would justify the adoption of a rule of this nature to aid in the discipline of the school, "We therefore decline to annul it, for we will not annul a rule of this kind unless a valid reason for doing so is made to appear; whereas, to uphold it, we are not required to find a valid reason for its promulgation."

While this specific regulation for student dress could scarcely be enforced today, the point worth noting is that the court upheld the school board's position.

In seeking legal precedents for their regulations school officials occasionally become confused by what appear to be two opposing decisions on an identical issue. A Mississippi school board prohibited the wearing of "freedom buttons" and expelled several students who wore them to school. The plaintiffs claimed that the buttons created only a mild curiosity and did not disrupt school operation. The court agreed and the students were reinstated. (*Burnside v. Byers*, 363 F. 2d, 744, Mississippi.)

In a similar case (*Blackwell v. Issaquene County Board of Education*, 363 F.2d, 749 Mississippi), the school board's ruling was upheld in court because

> Evidence indicated that wearing the buttons and attempting to have students remove them (was) . . . accompanied by commotion, boisterousness, collision with the rights of others, and undermining of the school's authority." (*Blackwell v. Issaquene County Board of Education.*)

Rules aimed at regulation of pupil dress must be in accord with school policies, and as such, dress, coupled with behavior, affects the satisfactory operation of the schools.

In *Tinker v. Des Moines Consolidated School District* (258 F. Supp. 971) school authorities were told that several students intended to wear black armbands as an antiwar protest. The school board passed a regulation prohibiting the wearing of the armbands and expelled three students who violated the rule. The court upheld the board ruling, saying that this was a reasonable action. Yet, the United States Supreme Court ruled that "School officials may not ban such a silent, passive expression of opinion unaccompanied by any disorder or disturbance . . . young people as well as adults . . . are persons . . . and have constitutional rights." A dissenting opinion argued that "[This decision] subjects all of the public schools in the country to the whims and caprices of their loudest mouth, but maybe not their brightest students."[14]

The courts have generally supported regulations which are reasonable and intended to maintain effective conduct, discipline, and operation of the schools. A 1964 Massachusetts action, brought by parents of a boy who had been suspended because he refused to cut his hair, found the school authorities supported by the court in the following statement:

> . . . Otherwise those in charge would be unable to cope on a day-to-day basis with the problems of management and discipline, to which the unpredictable activities of large groups of children may give rise. (*Leonard v. School Committee of Attleboro,* 212 N.E. 2d, 468 Mass. Sup. Ct. 1965.)

This position was echoed by the court in ruling against the long-haired Dallas musicians previously mentioned:

> It is inconceivable that a school administrator could operate his school successfully if required by the courts to follow the dictates of students as to what their appearnce will be, what they shall wear, and what hours they shall attend. (*Ferrell v. Dallas Independent School District,* 261 F. Supp. 545 N.D. Texas 1966.)

As a matter of interest, the Dallas case even reached the U.S. Supreme Court on the basis of plaintiffs' claim to a constitutional right to wear long hair. The court upheld the school district's ruling and the suspension (1968).

While it is unquestionably better for school authorities to solve dress and behavior problems by judicious counseling and public relations, the courts are inclined to feel that "There is a legal presumption in favor of the reasonableness of school rules." (*Bishop v. Houston Independent School District,* 119 Texas 403, 29 S.W. 2d., 312, 1930.)

It is well to remember that compulsory school attendance laws tend to credit school regulations with the force of law, and the quality and intent of those regulations with the force of law, and the quality and intent of those regulations become matters of real consequence to civil liberties. The question becomes one of stifling creativity and individual rights.

A ruling which appears to sum up the case for school board action was handed down in a North Carolina judgment:

> Schools to be effective and fulfill the purposes for which they are intended must be operated in an orderly manner. Machinery to that end must be provided. Reasonable rules and regulations must be adopted. The right to attend school and claim the benefits afforded by the public school system is the right to attend subject to all lawful rules and regulations prescribed for the government thereof. If the opinion of the court is to be substituted for the judgment and discretion of the board at the will of a disaffected pupil, the government of our schools will be seriously impaired, and the position of our school board in dealing with such cases will be most precarious. The court, therefore, will not consider whether such rules and regulations are wise and expedient. (*Coggin v. Board of Education* of the City of Durham, 223 N.C. 765, 28 S.E. 2d., 527, 1944).

Perhaps the real problem is not so much appearance as it is the changing times that have so shaken the security of a large number of teachers. Teachers and school administrators are, by nature, inclined toward conservatism and tend to resist change. It may be that the real problem is the conscious or unconscious wish of teachers—particularly of junior high school teachers, since this is where the first numerous evidences of nonconformity become so obvious, to have someone prepare a long list of precise rules and regulations. "Skirts cannot exceed so many inches above the knee; sideburns no more than to the mid-point of the ear," and so on ad nauseam. Administrators who draw up a list of specific and precise rules are going to find themselves in difficulty. If an eighth-grade girl's skirt is one-fourth inch too high or an eighth-grade boy's sideburns are one-fourth inch too long, will these children be suspended immediately? If not, of what value is the rule? If it can be broken for one-fourth inch, then what will be done about a three-eighths inch or one-half inch violation? If these children are suspended for hair or dress styling, are they not then second-class citizens if other members of the community (probably including their own parents) are able to wear what they wish in clothing and hair styling? What standards can reasonably be enforced other than health, decency (a definition with almost infinite variations), or the possibility of incurring violence—as might happen in the wearing of buttons and armbands? Junior high school and early adolescence is the time to develop honest and lasting values, to teach young people, by example, what is important and how to get along. Apparently we cannot agree among ourselves.

In a 1967 Louisiana suspension of a boy for the length of his hair, the court gave considerable weight to the evidence of the principal and superintendent in supporting the suspension.

The superintendent testified that

> . . . There is a distinct and direct relationship between student dress and conduct. . . . I know that a gross deviation from the norm does cause a disruption of the learning atmosphere . . . dress and appearance to have an effect upon conduct and decorum.

The principal testified that: ". . . these extreme hair styles have created distractions and disturbances in classrooms. . . . I am very concerned with preventive discipline." (*Davis v. Firment*, 269 F. Supp 524 (E.D. La., 1967.)

The court ruled that there was no fundamantal right of free grooming.

But in New Jersey, just the opposite decision was reached. The State Board of Education of New Jersey is authorized to hear and rule on school cases. The State Board reversed a commissioner's ruling and held that local boards of education could not interfere with hair and dress styles selected by students. The board's position was that these issues were not important enough to the conduct of the public schools.

One argument[15] that has not yet reached the opinions of the courts of record is that of denial of equal protection under the law. This occurs because standards vary from district to district and from school to school as principals. teachers, and superintendents attempt to determine what is "reasonable." Perhaps the only basis for regulation is that of a "direct measurable effect on safety, morals, or welfare of others, rather than reasonableness, necessity, or expedience."[16]

Courts are more frequently asking school authorities to prove that a clear and present danger is involved when there is a restriction of children's rights. It must be remembered that education, certainly for children through junior high school is a right (after which it is often termed a "privilege") and expulsion of students deprives them of a civil right.

Perhaps we in junior high school education should ask ourselves some questions:

1. How much nonconformist activity can be tolerated in the junior high school without actual harm to the learning environment?
2. Can responsibility be learned by early adolescents in the absence of freedom?
3. Are there valid reasons for limiting the requirements of due process of law to children of junior high and middle school age?
4. School officials have a lot of authority. Does this and should this include the authority to suspend and expel from the junior high school those who are nonconformists in hair and dress styling as well as those who constitute an actual physical threat?
5. If due process is not provided for junior high school children, although it is for adults, what have these children learned about law in our society?
6. If the junior high school child has not seen adult behavior that indicated concern for his civil and constitutional rights, will he be likely to show much concern for the rights and welfare of others?
7. If the early adolescent has had little experience with the use of freedom, will he be able to make judgments concerning civil liberties?

ENFORCING RULES

School personnel at all grade levels are empowered to use various methods to enforce rules, but these delegated powers are not identical in all states. For example, in one kind of decisions, teachers who administer corporal punishment will not be held liable for assault and battery nor for damages unless a permanent injury was caused or the punishment was administered in anger or malice.[17]

The classic case which set the pattern for this line of reasoning was decided in 1837 in North Carolina. A woman teacher chastised a pupil with a switch which left marks on his body for several days. In supporting the teacher's action the court observed:

> We hold, therefore, that it may be laid down as a general rule that teachers exceed the limits of their authority when they cause lasting mis-

chief but act within the limits of it when they inflict temporary pain. . . . The [school] master is the judge of when correction is required and of the degree of correction necessary. . . . If he use his authority as a cover for malice, and under pretense of administering correction, gratify his own bad passions, the mask of the judge shall be taken off. (*State v. Pendergrass*, 19 N.C. 365, 31 Am. Dec. 416.)

The determination of malice or anger in the punishment is a matter of fact for a jury to decide. Cruel or unusual punishment is of itself evidence of malice.[18] In the other line of decisions concerning corporal punishment (considered the better rule of law[19]) the teacher in administering discipline must demonstrate reasonable judgment and must scale the punishment to the size and age of the offender as well as to the nature of the offense. If, in the view of reasonable men, the punishment was excessive and unreasonable, the teacher is guilty of assault no matter how honestly he acted nor in what amount of good faith.

The line of reasoning supporting this second kind of decisions is well said in the oft-quoted "Old Jack Seaver" Case. In this action, a boy, after school, off the school grounds, in the presence of other pupils and in the hearing of the schoolmaster, referred to him as "Old Jack Seaver." The next day the schoolmaster thrashed him for his insolence. In upholding the teacher's action the court had this to say:

A schoolmaster has the right to inflict reasonable punishment. . . . Various considerations must be regarded—the nature of the offense, the apparent motive and disposition of the offender, the influence of his example and conduct upon others, and the age, sex, size, and strength of the pupil to be punished. . . . [A difference of opinion] exists in determining what is a reasonable punishment. . . . The advantage the master has by being on the spot to know all the circumstances—the manner, looks, tone, gestures, and language of the offender—which are not always easily described—and thus to form a correct opinion as to the necessity and extent of the punishment. . . . If the punishment be *clearly* excessive, then the master should be held liable for such excess. (*Lander v. Seaver*, 32 Vt. 114, 76 Am. Dec. 156.)

The use of corporal punishment in junior high school is undesirable and unnecessary in most instances; suspension or expulsion, if some action is essential, are likely to be more useful. Junior high personnel who administer coproral punishment may find themselves trying to convince a court that the punishment was reasonable, necessary, not excessive, did not cause permanent damage and was not administered in anger or malice. While physical punishment of high school students is not usual in these days, it is not at all uncommon to hear of a teacher or principal who paddles a junior high school student.

Generally, a teacher is permitted to disarm a child, to detain him after school hours, to remove a child from the room, to inflict such reasonable punishment as he deems necessary for the enforcement of school policies and the good discipline of the school, and even for misbehavior in respect to which no formal rules have been adopted. However, a teacher has no right to search children on mere suspicion or to inflict cruel and unusual punishment.[20]

A related problem in pupil control is that of pupil liability for damage to school property. The courts have been in agreement in ruling that pupils who accidentally destroy or damage property cannot be suspended nor expelled for nonpayment of damages. Court decisions in cases of deliberate damage by pupils have not been uniform. It is common, indeed, in junior high school to find desk and table tops carved with records of undying love, and rest room walls appear to evoke deep artistic impulses in many students. It is also common for administrators and teachers to attempt to compel payment for damages—even to the extent of withholding grades until payment is made. This cannot be done.

Examination of some court rulings may help to clarify these points concerning control of pupils and pupil liability. It must be kept always in mind that the actions of the teacher or principal must pass the test of reasonableness and that this depends upon the situation in each particular case.

For example, a Texas court in 1886 supported a teacher who used a big club on a pupil. Evidence disclosed that the pupil was taller and heavier than the teacher and that he came to school armed with a pistol and threatened to shoot the teacher. (*Metcalf v. State*, 21 Tex. App. 174, 17 S.W. 142.) In another action a court held a teacher liable for sitting on a pupil who was exhibiting a fit of anger. Evidence indicated that the teacher was over 200 pounds and the child was only ten years of age and weighed less than 90 pounds. (*Calway v. Williamson*, 130 Conn. 575, 36A. 2d., 377, 1944.)

The manner of enforcing the rule is a strong consideration. ". . . A school regulation must therefore be not only reasonable in itself but its enforcement must also be reasonable in the light of existing circumstances." (*Fertich v. Michener*, 111 Ind 472, 11 N.E. 605, 14 N.E., 68 Am. Rep. 709, 1887.)

An Ohio teacher who paddled a boy who threw a stone at a little girl on the way to school and "then fibbed about it," was charged with assault and battery. The court supported the teacher and stated:

> First the teacher stands in loco parentis (i.e., in the place of the parent). . . . Second, the teacher's responsibility attaches from home to home (i.e. while the pupil is on his way to and from school). . . . Third, there is a presumption of correctness in the teacher's actions. Fourth, there is a presumption that the teacher acts in good faith. . . . This record discloses no evidence that this teacher was actuated by any malice. (*State v. Lutz*, 113 N.E., 2d., 757, Ohio 1953.)

The courts have upheld the authority of school officials off the school grounds[21] and in out-of-school hours; also school regulations restricting students to the school grounds during school hours have been supported.[22] A Texas court declined to compel reinstatement of a fifteen-year-old girl who refused to remain on the school grounds at noon.[23]

With a growing problem of vandalism and rapidly rising costs, legislators have in many states passed statutes requiring that parents be made liable for deliberate damage caused by their children. Commonly accepted as the first case on record which was brought to the courts involving pupil responsibility for damage to school property was that of a twelve-year old boy who broke a window while playing ball. The boy was suspended from school because he could not pay the three-dollar replacement cost and his parents would not. The court ordered the boy's reinstatement, saying

> It would be very harsh and obviously unjust to deprive a child of education for the reason that through accident and without intention of doing wrong he destroyed property of the school district. Doubtless a child may be expelled from school as a punishment for breach of discipline, or for offense against good morals but not for innocent acts. (*Perkins v. Board of Directors of the Independent School District* of West Des Moines, 56 Iowa 476, 9 N.W. 356, 1880.)

A similar case was decided in Colorado in 1927 in the same way: "The plaintiff was expelled not because he broke the glass but because he did not pay for the damage sustained by the breaking." (*Speyer v. School District,* 82 Colo. 534, 261 Pac. 859, 57 ALR 203, 1927.)

When there is legislation requiring parental responsibility and where the damage is deliberate, the courts have rendered judgments in favor of the school districts which have sought to recover damages. In 1959 a New Jersey court awarded damages to a school district against the parents of a boy who set fire to a school and caused $344,000 damages.[24] In North Carolina an elementary school boy set fire to the drapes in a public school and caused $2,916.50 damages. The court held the parents liable.[25]

Without any question the junior high school should work with the early adolescent to develop standards of self-discipline, measures of self-conduct, and abilities in self-responsibility. This is the ideal and we must work toward this goal unremittingly. The great majority of junior high school dissent and protest centers upon items that may not be able to stand close examination: lack of any valid educational reasons for regulations pertaining to dress and hair styles; and weaknesses in junior high school curricula and teaching.

SUMMARY

Changing times bring changing fashions, and such changes, adopted to an extreme, are likely to produce conflict between adolescents and school authorities. The better solution is probably guidance, reason, and a well-developed public relations program. Unless they are clearly unreasonable, the courts may be expected to support school regulations.

Corporal punishment is supported by the courts in most states so long as it is not cruel, excessive, unusual, unreasonable, is not administered in anger nor malice, and does not produce any permanent injury.

Courts will not support suspension and expulsion of students who accidentally damage or destroy school property. They are, however, likely to hold the parents responsible for deliberate damage.

REFERENCES

1. "Protests? Old Story At Schools," *San Francisco Examiner*, Monday, March 3, 1969.
2. "Student Protests Worry Educators," *Albuquerque Tribune*, May 14, 1969.
3. Luvern L. Cunningham, "Crisis in School Organization," *Educational Leadership*, Vol. 26 (March 1969), p. 552.
4. Harold Moody, "Plight of the Principal," *Clearing House*, Vol. 42 (May 1968), pp. 544-545.
5. William N. McGowan, "About Student Unrest," *Journal of Secondary Education*, Vol. 43 (October 1968), p. 258.
6. *Loc. cit.*
7. Joseph Caliguri, "Adolescent Power and School Policy." *Journal of Secondary Education*, Vol. 43 (October 1968), p. 266.
8. "Protests? Old Story at Schools," *op. cit.*
9. "Boys In Long Hair," *Student Weekly*, Feb. 5, 1968.
10. "How Long Hair Uprooted A Family," *Parade Magazine*, July 14, 1968, pp. 10-12.
11. *Albuquerque Tribune*, Sept. 24, 1966.
12. *Eugene Register Guard*, Eugene, Oreg., Mar. 17, 1966.
13. "School Boards Barred From Banning Long Hair," *Albuquerque Journal*, Feb. 22, 1969, p. C-7.
14. "Young Students Win In High Court Ruling," *Albuquerque Tribune*, Feb. 25, 1969.
15. Elise M. Martin, "The Right to Dress and Go to School," *University of Colorado Law Review*, Vol. 37 (1965), p. 492.
16. Wallace E. Good, "Legal Aspects of Student Control," *North Central Association Quarterly*, Vol. 43 (Fall 1968), p. 245.
17. *State v. Thornton*, 136 N.C. 610, 48 S.E. 602.
18. *Boyd v. State*, 88 Ala. 169, 7 So. 268, 16 Am. St. Rep. 31.
19. Newton Edwards, *The Courts and the Public Schools.* Rev. ed. (Chicago: U. of Chicago Press, 1955, p. 612.
20. Robert L. Drury and Kenneth C. Ray, *Essentials of School Law.* New York: Appleton, 1967, p. 43.
21. *Deskins v. Gose*, 85 Mo. 485, 55 Am. Rep. 387, 1885.
22. *Flory v. Smith*, 145 Va. 164, 123 S.E. 360, 1926.

23. *Bishop v. Houston Independent School Dist.*, 119 Texas 403, 29 S.W. 2d., 312, 1930.
24. *Board of Education of Palmyra in County of Burlington v. Hansen*, 56 N.J. Super. 567, 153 A. 2d., 393, 1959.
25. *General Insurance Co. v. Faulkner*, 259 N.C. 317 (1963).

part V

CHANGING PATTERNS OF INSTRUCTION

Many changes have taken place in recent years in the organization and methods of instruction used in today's schools. Some of these innovations have passed beyond the experimental stage and are relatively common at all levels of instruction. Others have been watched carefully, tentatively tried, and slowly adopted. There has been resistance in varying degrees to much of what is new, but the hard truth is that, like it or not, change is a part of today's world and we must adjust to it. The traditional teacher and administrator who find it difficult to accept the newer concepts are finding that pressures of the community and the demands of the times compel them to alter, however reluctantly, the instructional practices so long in use. It is not possible to ignore such concepts as team teaching, independent study programs, ungraded classes, programmed learning, and continuous progress plans. Flexible scheduling, far from being a threat, is a mighty tool which, properly used, does much toward implementing a superior educational program.

chapter 17

Flexible Scheduling, Team Teaching, and Nongraded Schools

If there is one feature characterizing the traditional organization and routine of instruction in the junior high school, it is precisely that: routine sameness. Each class meets at the same time every day for every week of the school year, and the length of each class period is the same number of minutes as that of all other classes—or very close to it. Each teacher meets with the same number of classes as the other teachers and the classes are comparable in size. Each academic subject, particularly in the departmentalized junior high school, presumably needs and requires the students to spend the identical amount of time learning it as is allotted each of the other subjects. There are occasional exceptions. Science or health in the junior high school may sometimes be taught only for a semester on a rotating basis. Reading may be a part of a Language Arts block which means that it may be taught daily, or on regularly indicated days, or not at all. Fine and practical arts are frequently rotated on an every-other-day basis. But THE SCHEDULE is customarily a regular, compartmented, tightly constructed piece of administrative machinery with which one may not tamper.

When suggestions for change are made which involve a departure from the standard junior high school pattern, they are very often regarded suspiciously and the *coup de grâce* administered with the stock answer, "Your idea certainly has possibilities; too bad it can't be scheduled." This is gentler than the flat statement, "It won't work," however, anyone who doesn't want to leave the security of the set pattern will never run out of excuses—and it isn't always the principal who is dragging his feet.

WHY FLEXIBLE SCHEDULING?

The increasing amount of knowledge, the need to teach more and to do a better job of teaching, the growing use of technological aids, and the concern with differences in student interests and abilities necessitate a more efficient approach to the organization of instruction. Flexible scheduling is based on the premise that the order of each day does not have to be the same as that of the preceding day; that teachers will vary in the amount of time needed for daily lessons; that early adolescents vary in the amount of time they need to learn something; and that class size will vary in accord with the particular lesson being presented. All courses are not the same in the depth of understanding required nor in the time necessary to learn the subject. The size of the class, length of class time, and number and kind of weekly meetings necessary should vary according to the ability and interest of the pupils, the character of the instruction, the nature of the subject, and the intent of the teaching.

Flexible scheduling is a device that helps to change and improve traditional junior high school practices to provide an educational program more suited to the unique characteristics and needs of the early adolescent and to the functions of the junior high school.

The characteristics of the early adolescent (Chapter 2) require an educational program that affords opportunities to develop self-directed study and self-discipline; permits students to spend more or less time on a subject as their needs require; provides topics, subjects, and activities in a wide range for the rapidly changing interests of this age group; and affords time and opportunities to investigate areas of interest. The educational program of the junior high school must capitalize on the early adolescent's expanding intellectual abilities, and assist in the developing of values. Flexible scheduling, by making time a tool instead of the master, can be instrumental in helping the junior high school to perform its functions. A flexible schedule provides learning situations in which students may use previously acquired skills and develop new ones through large-group–small-group and independent study procedures; it permits a wide range of exploratory activities, affords more opportunities for guidance, permits more individualized and differentiated programs, and provides programs that are more in accord with varying student interests, needs, and abilities.

All this is what a flexible schedule can do, and schedules in some junior high schools come close to this ideal. As with any other innovation, this requires much preplanning and a high degree of cooperation among the faculty and with the administration, as well as extensive faculty involvement. A flexible schedule by itself will not cure many ills. There must be plans, cooperation, and constant evaluation. "The structure does not *cause* a good program, it *allows* a good program to succeed and encourages creative staff efforts."[1] This approach to scheduling identifies the individual in the junior high school, permits him to participate in developing his own educational program, and helps adolescents want to learn to think for themselves.

Manlove and Beggs,[2] in referring to the fallacy that there are "eternal laws about school organization," warn of the myths that impede progress toward individualizing instruction. A stated goal of the junior high school is individualized instruction, but most junior high schools arrange students in rigid groups that inhibit and prevent realization of this goal.The "myths" that block the way toward better education as permitted by a flexible schedule are:[3]

1. Equal time for unequal subjects—all classes must meet for equal lengths of time. Children learn at different rates and these rates of learning vary from subject to subject.
2. Accrediting agencies won't permit flexible schedules. Not true. Approval is given if a flexible schedule is adopted to improve instruction.
3. It won't work. This is patently false. Flexible schedules *are* working in junior high schools all over the country.
4. Change costs more money. This depends upon the school. It doesn't have to cost more.
5. Teachers don't want change. Some teachers don't—but a great many, perhaps most, are not satisfied with the results they are getting. If teachers have opportunities to see what a flexible schedule is, how it works, and what it will do for students and for them, they usually are eager to move in this direction.

It is essential that the junior high school principal understand flexible scheduling and be able to explain it to faculty, students, and parents. He is the key figure. It is he who must provide the leadership in questioning present practices and searching for better ways to educate the adolescent. "No teacher's full potential can be released unless an effective leader opens doors of understanding and provides the opportunity for teachers to teach in the grand manner."[4]

One approach to releasing both teacher and student potential is flexible scheduling. A fuller explanation of this procedure may help to clarify the possibilities.

FLEXIBLE SCHEDULING

The current interest on the part of teachers and administrators in flexible scheduling is often accompanied by much misunderstanding and confusion. Flexible scheduling, specifically, means only that there are variations in the daily instructional organization. In its simplest form, class periods may still all be the same length but there is opportunity for variation both in length and in the time of day in which they will be found. Flexible schedules are not necessarily modular schedules except that a junior high with 6 fifty-minute periods daily is actually operating with a fifty-minute module. A truly flexible modular schedule operates with a unit of time, ten minutes, fifteen minutes, twenty minutes, or any other amount that has been selected, but the number of modules allotted to each subject for any given day will probably not be the same as the time allotted that subject on the following day. An English class, for example, may have two twenty-minute modules or forty minutes on Monday, and have three modules or none on Tuesday, depending upon what has been determined as necessary for that class and that lesson that day.

Neither does flexible scheduling compel a staff to move into team teaching, large-group–small-group instruction, or any of the other practices currently riding the crest of the popularity wave. It does not compel but it does open the way to change by taking away the single most restrictive limitation. In itself the flexible schedule possesses no magic, but by permitting a rearrangement of the use of time, it becomes possible to offer more subjects, make better use of instructional time, plan for large-group–small-group work and independent study, and develop a better educational program.

Perhaps the easiest way to move into some form of flexibility is "back-to-back" scheduling.

Back-to-Back

Per.	Mr. White	Mr. Black	Mr. Green	Mr. Brown
1	Science Section 1	Math Section 2	Science Section 3	Math Section 4
2	Science Section 2	Math Section 1	Science Section 4	Math Section 3

These are traditional periods, fifty or sixty minutes each and may be operated in that manner, but they do not have to be. Mr. White and Mr. Black teach the same groups of children; White has Section 1 first period and Black has the same section, second period. White and black may agree that White will take both groups for part or all of periods 1 and 2, perhaps for a film or a demonstration, and the time lost may be made up by letting Black have the double class on another day. It is also possible to include Mr. Green and Mr. Brown with Sections 3 and 4, so that one of the four teachers can make a presentation to all four sections if this is desired. This piece of the schedule shows only four teachers and four class sections, but it is quite possible to extend the opportunities to include other teachers and classes for periods 1 and 2, and even to move down into periods 3 and 4. The teachers involved should be given the same planning period, since it is also possible to move into varying class sizes and large-group–small-group work with this system.

A schedule which permits a once weekly long period is the "period exchange." Again we are working with a standard schedule but all classes meet but four days a week, one day with a double period. This schedule does not vary; every Monday first period is double-length, and third period is omitted. Teachers can plan a film, field trip, or some other lesson which does not fit into a standard period length.

Six Subjects—Six Periods
Period Exchange

Period	Monday	Tuesday	Wednesday	Thursday	Friday
1	1	1	1	1	2
2	1	2	2	3	3
3	2	2	3	4	5
4	4	3	3	4	5
5	5	4	4	5	6
6	6	5	6	6	6

All classes have one double period weekly. All classes meet five periods weekly.

As a variation of the period exchange, some schools schedule double periods every other day, with a single period only one day a week. It is also possible with this schedule to have two or more teachers and two or more groups working together:

Alternating Blocks

Period	Monday	Tuesday	Wednesday	Thursday	Friday
1	1	1	2	1	2
2	2	1	2	1	2

A schedule similar to these first two involves a shared period between two regular periods:

Period	Monday	Tuesday	Wednesday	Thursday	Friday
1	Lang Arts	L.A.	L.A.	L.A.	L.A.
2	This period is shared by 1 and 3 as necessary				
3	Soc St	S.S.	SS.	SS.	S.S.

The first-period teacher may take all, part, or none of the shared period, and the third-period teacher has the same option, or either teacher may take part or all of the students during this time. This period may be used for large-group or small-group work, or for independent study. The open period is scheduled between each of the regular periods throughout the day and may be only half as long as the regular period.

There are several types of rotating schedules in use in junior high schools throughout the country. With a rotating schedule it is possible to have seven subjects in a six-period day or six subjects in a five-period day, and to have one free period for some activity such as assemblies. Most rotating schedules, in order to fit in an extra subject, have only four class meetings each week, and the classes never meet at the same time. This can cause some confusion, but it usually takes only a few days for the students to become familiar with such a schedule. If more time is wanted in each class and the comfort of a standard class length is considered desirable, one may set up a seven-period day which includes but six subjects. In this schedule five subjects have one double period each week and the sixth subject period is ten minutes longer than the other periods, which provides the same total time per week for all subjects.

Rotating Schedule—6 Subjects, 5 Periods

Period	Monday	Tuesday	Wednesday	Thursday	Friday
1	1	6	5	4	3
2	2	1	6	5	4
3	3	2	1	6	5
4	4	3	2	1	6
5	5	4	3	2	x

Rotating Schedule

Period	Monday	Tuesday	Wednesday	Thursday	Friday
1	1	1	1	1	1
2	1	2	2	2	2
3	2	2	3	3	3
4	3	3	3	4	4
5	4	4	4	4	5
6	5	5	5	5	5
7	6	6	6	6	6

Allows six subjects. Classes meet six times weekly except period six which is a longer period.

For real variety a rotating schedule may be adopted in which both time of meeting and length of class are different every day until the cycle is completed, at which time the whirl begins again.

Rotating with Varied Period Lengths

Period Length	Monday	Tuesday	Wednesday	Thursday	Friday	Monday
30 min	1	2	3	4	5	6
45 min	2	3	4	5	6	1
100 min	3	4	5	6	1	2
75 min	4	5	6	1	2	3
50 min	5	6	1	2	3	4
30 min	6	1	2	3	4	5

The foregoing schedule allows every teacher and every class to have lessons and activities which take more or less than the standard period length. Occasionally this schedule permits more time than teachers in some subjects can reasonably use. A teacher of seventh-grade general music, for example, may find herself at wits' end with a hundred minutes to fill, while the teacher of art is likely to be quite pleased with the long period but somewhat dissatisfied with the thirty-minute periods.

If the school staff wants to use a schedule which has the security of daily repetition yet permits variation in pupil class assignment and number of subjects taken, they may develop something such as an eight-period day within a six-period day. In this plan, classes which may be expected to need more time regularly, perhaps industrial arts or homemaking, may be allotted sixty minutes every day for every class while other classes have only forty-five minutes per class period every day. A student who takes only the shorter classes may carry five, six, seven, or eight classes, while the student who selects nothing but those subjects with long periods could never carry more than six. In actual practice virtually all students carry some of each type, and since there will then be some holes or open time in their schedules, they have opportunities for independent study. It is also possible with this plan to make use of team teaching and large-group–small-group instruction if this is desired.

45 minutes	45	45
Resource center	S.S.	Math
English	S.S.	Resource center
English	Plan	Math
English	S.S.	Math
Plan	S.S.	Plan
Lunch	Lunch	Lunch
English	S.S.	Math
English	Resource center	Math
English	S.S.	Math

60 min	60	60
Science	I.A.	Art
Science	I.A.	Plan
Science	Plan	Art
Lunch	Lunch	Lunch
Plan	I.A.	Art
Science	I.A.	Art
Science	I.A.	Art

This is a portion of a schedule for an eight-period day within a six-period day. A student could, for example, take I.A. first period, science second period, then have fifteen minutes for independent study, go to fourth-period mathematics, fifth-period social studies, lunch, sixth-period English, seventh-period music (not shown), and eighth-period P.E. (not shown). An alternative would be to go to independent study after sixth-period English, and then go to sixth-period art class. By use of independent study time, resource centers, and multiples of a time unit (in this case fifteen minutes), it is possible to run some thirty-minute periods or some ninety-minute periods within this schedule, thus reaching a simplified modular schedule.

Team teaching is not compulsory with modular scheduling nor is large-group–small-group instruction, but they are made possible by this system. A modular schedule assumes that individual students spend some time daily in self-directed study and varying amounts (or even no time at all) in daily classes. Students who cannot or will not direct their own studies find their schedules permit no free time; they are scheduled into a class or a controlled situation for the entire school day. In passing, it is worth noting that a modular schedule can become just as rigid as any other kind. It is essential that the master schedule and individual student schedules be examined, evaluated, and revised regularly to avoid letting the same old paralysis set in. It may be necessary to schedule a student into more class time, or more lab work, or more library research. The key point is that some rescheduling will become necessary and it must be done.

Student Schedule: 15-Minute Modules

Monday	Tuesday	Wednesday
Science	Math	Art
Typing	Science	French
French	I.A.	Social Studies
English	Social Studies	Independent Study
Lunch	Lunch	Lunch
Independent Study	French	Science
Social Studies	Independent Study	Math
Math	Typing	P.E.
P.E.	English	

The foregoing schedule shows only three days for only one pupil. Each pupil has his own individual schedule. The schedules for Thursday and Friday are probably not the same as those for Monday, Tuesday, or Wednesday. This schedule repeats every week. If the student needs more independent study time, the decision will be made as to whether he should drop a subject or merely reduce his attendance in one or more subjects. If a student is doing passing work or better there should be no need to require him to come to class just to sit and hear something he already knows. He can make better use of his time in a resource center in independent study.

A basic need in today's schools is to establish some criteria for students other than attendance and memorizing for a few tests. We need to determine what it is that we expect a student to learn, to establish performance criteria; and when a student demonstrates that he can meet these standards he should be passed on to the next level, regardless of how much time he has spent on the level just completed. A subject commonly used to illustrate this point, because of the ease of determining performance criteria, is typing. If the skill considered necessary for passing typing is 50 words per minute at the completion of the second semester, and if a student reaches this speed after two months, she is ready to go on to something else—either advanced typing or another subject. One thing that she should *not* do is to sit for the balance of the school year in typing class.

By use of a flexible schedule, modular or otherwise, it is possible to develop a better junior high program, and providing a broad exploratory program is one of the basic purposes of the junior high school. This will also permit but not compel teachers to move into team teaching and large-group–small-group work, and to develop independent study programs.

FACTORS IN SCHEDULING

Schedules take time to construct—sometimes hundreds of hours—but a good schedule is a tool that permits the school staff to provide a better educational program. Traditionally rigid schedules and most flexible schedules can be developed without the aid of computers, but a modular schedule, particularly for a large school, should be constructed by computer. The cost of computer scheduling for a year's operation will range from $.75 to something over $4 per student, depending upon rental charges for the computer, school size, program, staff, and facilities.

Scheduling can be made easier by giving consideration to a few important factors:

1. Classes for which there is only one section are mutually exclusive, they are conflicts, and cannot be scheduled at the same time. For example, if there is only one band and only one class in speech,

these cannot come at the same time or those students who wish to take both subjects will not be able to do so and will be excluded from one. The choice they make will please only one of the two teachers concerned, and the other will probably be righteously bitter about poor scheduling practices. Therefore, all single classes go on the schedule first.

2. Any other requirement which has to be given priority must go on the schedule immediately. An example of this is a traveling music teacher who splits her time between two or more schools.
3. Ninth-grade courses are probably counted for high school and are given Carnegie credit. Too, it is probable that the ninth-grade program will be more diversified than the lower grades. Therefore, the ninth grade will have to be put on the schedule before any other grades.
4. Try *always* to have alternative courses at every period of the day. Even with a schedule possessing some flexibility, it is poor practice, for example, to have only French, advanced math, or accelerated science as an alternative choice to home economics. If the school uses ability grouping, it is necessary to run courses *each period* suitable for different levels, although the courses may be in different subject areas—i.e., French, art, and speech.
5. Scheduling becomes simpler if the school forgets chronological grade lines and mixes students on an interest or ability basis. If the school is not ungraded, then schedule all of one grade before beginning another.
6. Never assign classes on the basis of which teacher is free that period. Make best use of teacher competencies. Talk to teachers and determine their interests and abilities. Involve teachers in schedule construction.
7. Keep firmly in mind what teaching stations are available or large-group instruction may suddenly become a fact in a small-group room.
8. Construct the schedule in such a way that experimentation and innovation are encouraged—i.e., back-to-back scheduling.
9. Quit worrying about how many classes of thirty each and start thinking about program. Devise the curriculum and then shape the schedule to it. This is not nearly so difficult as many people believe. It is easier to build a good simple schedule than to build a somewhat involved poor schedule—which makes one wonder why so many people work so hard to stay in a rut.
10. Get rid of the bell system and build flexibility in where possible. Remember, the schedule is an administrative device to provide an education for junior high school children.

BENEFITS AND PROBLEMS

If it did nothing more than break the monotony, flexible scheduling would be worth trying. Reports from schools using different forms of a flexible schedule indicate several claimed advantages over the traditional schedule. Students like the variety of a flexible schedule; each day provides something different.

Teachers find that the shift may cause a reappraisal and change of teaching method and content. More courses can be offered and students are able to explore more subject areas. Teachers and students become more involved in attempts to improve the curriculum. It is possible to use team teaching, large- and small-group work, and independent study. Opportunities are created to do many things previously considered impossible because "it couldn't be scheduled." Changes in teaching procedures stimulate enhanced use of libraries and learning materials centers. Parents and the community tend to react favorably and become more supportive when they know the junior high school is developing new approaches to teaching.

A junior high school[5] that adopted a schedule with thirty-minute modules reported that discipline was much improved because students changed classes at different times; this reduced congestion in halls, rest rooms, and student gathering spots. Moreover, teachers have fewer supervisory duties, and department chairmen are able to be of more assistance to teachers.

The Brookhurst Junior High School (Anaheim, California) has been operating under a sophisticated and advanced flexible schedule for several years, a system that could best be described as "demand scheduling." "This plan . . . is based on a schedule which changes daily according to requests for time and students submitted by teams of teachers."[6] Teachers, working in teams, submit job orders—requests for time, facilities, and students—daily to the program coordinator who makes up the master schedule. Job orders have priority categories. (These priorities should be determined by the individual school.) Students have some options in making up their own schedules. For example, "On days when academic subjects like English are taught in more than one section . . . the student, with the approval of his homeroom teacher, picks the one which is most appropriate."[7]

The staff at Brookhurst feels that there are significant advantages to their approach to the education of junior high school children. The greatest advantage is that each student may adjust his schedule constantly in accord with his progress and ability. Teachers also profit by benefiting from the special talents of other members of the team as well as feeling a strong sense of involvement, and students gain from the increased guidance available.

Others[8] have indicated that students evidence more responsibility; teacher recruitment and placement is enhanced; students study in more depth and learn as well or better than those in a traditional schedule;[9] and the traditional study hall can be eliminated.

Some of the problems encountered by different schools include

1. Far more difficult than anyone thought to teach small groups.
2. Students who don't participate in small groups.
3. When constructing and using a schedule, what should be done about lunch periods, activities, rallies, examinations, and testing programs?
4. What should be the policy concerning the number of classes a student may take?
5. Teachers and students who don't know how to use a large group session—i.e., try to have student interchange and discussion.
6. What kind of deference should be accorded the Carnegie Unit, if any?
7. Should attendance be taken and procedures set up and maintained for this purpose?
8. Distractions and nuisance value of other students in independent study.
9. How long should the school day be?
10. Flexible schedules may permit staff overload and inequities.
11. The problems of space, teaching stations, and meeting areas—where and when will teachers meet together; personalities; student meeting areas; material preparation; any necessary remodeling; supplementary furniture.
12. Additional equipment necessary of same or different type.
13. Additional text materials—i.e., if large-group instruction is used, the school can no longer get by with one set of literature books moved from class to class.
14. Detailed explanations to school board, parents, community, students, and teachers of what the school is attempting, the why, and how of the plans, and the anticipated results.
    - (a) What do you say to the parent who inquires, "What's wrong with your present scheduling system?"
    - (b) "How can my child learn when he has so little teacher direction?"
    - (c) "Don't the kids have too much freedom under this plan?"
    - (d) "Isn't this program just for the college bound?" (Certainly not! This program is basically designed to help the student who lacks initiative and responsibility.)[10]
15. Teachers are required to change their teaching patterns. (This may be an advantage.)

16. Students may not have enough identification with the teachers.
17. Flexible and modular scheduling require more in teacher planning and work.
18. Possibility of not giving enough time to a subject.

It is essential that teachers and principal alike get out of the straitjacket of thinking that classes *must* and teachers *must.* Whenever this phrase occurs, someone needs to ask, "why?" and keep asking, "Why?" Very few schools that have adopted a flexible or modular schedule have dropped it and returned to a traditional schedule. With today's increased knowledge and need for learning faster and better, flexible scheduling offers a great deal.

TEAM TEACHING

Among the many innovations and experimental enterprises to be found in the schools today, team teaching has become one of the most prominent. The concept emerged from the Staff Utilization Studies, sponsored by the National Association of Secondary School Principals, which began in 1956. For more than four years experiments were conducted in approximately one hundred junior and senior high schools throughout the United States. In an effort to develop better use of teacher time and talents, the studies were concerned with teacher aides, flexible scheduling, variability in class sizes, teacher specialization, use of technological equipment, different approaches to curriculum design and school construction, and changes in the assignment of nonteaching tasks, although the key factor has always been the use of teaching teams.

The various experimental programs in the late 1950's were watched with great interest by school people throughout the country. In a remarkably short time various forms of team-teaching and staff-utilization programs sprang up in hundreds of elementary and secondary schools. A 1960 six-state survey[11] found a total of 521 junior and senior high schools conducting some form of team-teaching program. A 1967 nationwide survey [12] of over 7,000 accredited high schools reported approximately 40 percent of these using team teaching.

Team teaching, with its related changed instructional procedures, is no longer in the talking stage. Schools of all sorts in every state—large, medium, small, elementary, junior high and senior high—are adopting or considering adoption of some part or all of the program. In spite of the clarity and specificity of Trump and Baynham's report,[13] a considerable variation exists in the organization and functioning of team teaching in different schools. One cannot speak of *the* Team-teaching Program; it is necessary to inquire, "What kind of program is in operation in this school?" Teams vary in number of teachers, in frequency of large-group–small-group instruction, in number of teaching and clerical aides, and in size of student groups as well as in subject matter—some teams being all of one discipline (as an instructional team in English) and others cutting across subject-matter lines and including members from several disciplines. There are very nearly as many kinds of teaching teams as there are school systems engaged in projects because of the varying circumstances, teacher backgrounds and personalities, and school situations.

TEAM TEACHING AND THE JUNIOR HIGH SCHOOL

Team teaching, as it grew out of the Staff Utilization Studies, is designed to make the best use of particular knowledges and competencies of a teaching staff. When more than one teacher is concerned with an instructional problem, the resultant teaching may be expected to be better than that of each teacher operating on his own. Team teaching, as used with large-group–small-group instruction and independent study, is most compatible with the accepted functions of the junior high school and the characteristics of the early adolescent. It is possible to do a great deal with exploratory work, to provide more guidance to develop more student responsibility and self-direction, to work toward interdisciplinary approaches in a broader and deeper body of knowledge than is usually available to students, and to provide more differentiation of instruction and individualization of student programs than is customarily the case in the traditional teaching situation.

> If the junior high school is to serve as a transitory step between the self-contained elementary classroom and the highly departmentalized arrangement of senior high school, then a junior high program which combines the strengths of both is a must! . . . As team teaching becomes a strong, vigorous element on the educational scene in junior high schools, we can expect to see significant curricular changes taking place. Schools will move in the direction of a non-graded curriculum with complete emphasis on continuous education for all students.[14]

The key factor is the potential available by virtue of the inherent flexibility of program, the better use of teacher and student time, and the improvement made possible by departing from the traditional.

The team-teaching program has two main objectives at the junior high school level:

1. To make maximum use of teacher time . . . [by means of] a flexible schedule . . . large-group lectures, small-group seminars and tutorial services to students when needed, and
2. To provide a program of student grouping which allows the subject matter to be geared as closely as possible to the abilities of the student.[15]

DEFINITIONS

Since no two teams are likely to function in an identical manner, an all-inclusive definition of a teaching team is not possible. There are, however, certain things that a teaching team is not and certain common characteristics to be found in teaching teams which together permit a general working definition.

Team teaching is an organizational arrangement of teaching personnel, intended to improve instruction, within which two or more certificated teachers, with or without the assistance of anyone else, have the responsibility, working together, for all or an important part of the instruction of the same group of students. Cooperation is the key, and stress is placed upon group planning, decisions, instruction, and evaluation. One may find a team of two teachers with a minimum of joint activity who work more as associates. At the other end of the scale may be found teams with high levels of organization and responsibility including aides, clerks, assistant teachers, master teachers, and team leaders.

Characteristic of teaching teams are the possibilities in scheduling, grouping, and meetings of the group of students assigned the team. The group may meet as one unit, be divided into smaller groups, meet as a large and a small group, or meet as one or more group with some students in independent study. It must be kept in mind that team teaching does not guarantee that learning is automatically improved; it only makes it possible to provide for independent study, small-group work, and flexibility in student assignment.

The same flexibility is possible in terms of subject matter and student grade levels. It is possible to include only students from one grade or to cut across grade lines. The team members may all work in the same subject area, or may include members representing several disciplines, as literature, history, music, and art. Ideally, the team membership includes the leader, team teachers, aides, and clerical help, regardless of the curriculum content with which the team works.

In achieving cooperative effort there may be an informal and unstructured agreement and division of labor among teachers of equal position, or there may be a structured hierarchy of position, authority, function, and monetary reward. There appears to be a trend toward this more structured system which is in accord with that recommended by the Staff Utilization Studies.

This hierarchy permits a pooling of staff knowledge and talents in the instruction of a larger group of pupils than can effectively be handled by one teacher alone. Different teacher interests, abilities, skills, and levels of competence are best utilized. With a larger structured team it is also easier to provide assistant teachers, teacher aides, clerical help, and equipment such as audio-visual and office equipment for each team.

Team planning is not only desirable but essential. There *must* be time available to select, determine, and develop curriculum content, schedules, instructional procedures, objectives, and methods of evaluation. The division of instructional tasks assumes that some team members will be responsible for large-group lectures, others for small-group work, others as resource persons and consultants to a few or individual students. A single team member may work in any or all of these areas. It is apparent that these procedures will require consideration in scheduling and in building facilities.

There is little research but much opinion concerning the most satisfactory class size in junior high school. Teachers tend to think in terms of 25–30 students to a class, yet for some situations it is probable that the class should be smaller or larger. Indeed, the experience of team teaching indicates that students that meet periodically in groups of several hundred achieve as well as or better than those students in a class of 25–30. Large-group instruction is a basic characteristic of team teaching, where the purpose is presentation and the large group meets only once or twice weekly.

Since group sizes vary and there is need for independent study areas, there should be at least one large meeting area, several small group areas, and several resource centers. There will not be a need for the same number of standard classrooms. Some junior high schools, built to operate under these concepts, actually have no traditional classrooms but do have areas capable of division by accordion doors or other measures. Many junior high schools which have changed over to the team-teaching approach have found it advisable to knock out walls, create study areas, and divide rooms for small-group work. Whatever facilities are developed should be soundproofed. An accordion divider which permits noise to travel from one side to the other represents poor planning and an even poorer investment.

A common misconception is that team teaching is all large-group instruction. This is not what was intended nor recommended. Roughly 20 percent of student time is expected to be spent in large groups, 40 percent in small groups, and 40 percent in independent study. Nor is team teaching intended to be complete departmentalization. Rather, full use of teacher competencies will provide broader instructional possibilities and may involve several disciplines.

It has been said that team teaching is but another approach to merit pay. To the extent that some teachers with more responsibilities may with team teaching receive more monetary return, this is true. However, a basic premise of team teaching is that different individuals perform different tasks —tasks for which they are individually best suited, and within this framework there may exist some pay differentiation. It is not the same thing as designating the teacher in Room A as deserving of merit pay and the teacher in Room B as not qualified for merit pay when both teachers function in the same setting with the same number of children, and presumably in the same general manner.

Team teaching can permit specialization in teaching, use of nonprofessional teaching aides, increased use of mechanical technology, and encourage independent study.

WHY TEAM TEACHING?

In education, the period following World War II has been one of trial, knowledge explosion, enrollment expansion, shortages of qualified teachers, and controversy. The shortage of teachers, intensified by the problems of new knowledge and social change, has further emphasized the need for quality in education. The question is increasingly asked, "Why must the talents of a really skilled teacher be limited to one classroom and one group of 25–35 children?" Efforts to devise solutions include increased interest in ability grouping, teacher specialization, and departmentalization—even on the elementary level; merit pay scales; use of parents and other community resource people as teacher aides and clerical assistants, and even the "traveling teacher"—one who teaches in two or more schools daily.

The situation was aggravated by the mounting criticism which began in the early 1950's concerning both the quality of American education as opposed to European, and the increased costs of schools. The attacks left no part of education untouched—public schools, colleges and universities involved in the education of teachers all felt the barbs of complaint. Potential teachers were often reluctant to enter a profession that featured overcrowded classes, mounting criticism, an increase in extra duties combined with low pay, and the snobbery of classmates for "education" majors. While circumstances were only made worse by these attacks, unfortunately they had some basis in fact.

Someone once said that the United States' public schools are the greatest twelve-year penal institution the world has known. At age 6 children begin the educational lockstep that moves most of them forward year after year, with little concern for individual interests, abilities, and talents, in uniform classrooms, in similar buildings, and often with the curriculum but little improved over that which their parents were offered.

School people are inclined to be a traditional group, conservative in outlook, secure in what they learn and how they teach, and slow to change. Limited to her classroom for the majority of the time, the teacher finds few opportunities to visit other schools and observe other teachers. The impact of professional change is frequently limited to yearly institutes and an occasional summer course taught by a college professor who the class feels is unaware of what occurs "in the field"—a resident of an ivory tower who doesn't get into the daily firing line of a public school classroom. Sometimes this, too, is true. Education can be fun, interesting, and stimulating, but all too often schools are not pleasant places to be in.

In recent years some real changes have been brought about which have led to significant improvements in education. Team teaching is one innovation that has shown considerable promise. But team teaching and its related approaches do not constitute a panacea or cure-all. Its success lies in the changed attitude of the school personnel involved and in the increased possibilities in educating children when traditional methods and restrictions are altered and removed.

Team teaching permits student groupings on one or more of several bases, groupings that can change from subject to subject and from time to time. It permits increased use of teacher talents and skills so that the education of a class does not depend upon the lucky assignment of a "good" teacher. It permits and encourages small-group discussion, independent study, and improved student self-direction. It permits use of varying time periods in terms of how much time is needed—not how much time is set by a rigid bell schedule. It allows an approach to teaching by specialists in various areas crossing subject-matter boundaries and fully relevant to the dynamics of the junior high school program.

However, little or none of this will occur simply because the organization exists. There must be planning and time for planning, and there must be teacher interest, enthusiasm, and a desire to improve the instructional program.

It will be necessary to examine and revise the curriculum. Teachers must be trained to perform new roles and accept new responsibilities. Teachers, team leaders, and principals all need training in leadership, in use of authority, morale, and counseling. Different methods of presentation and evaluation must be devised and new opportunities in instruction fully used.

TEAM OPERATION

While team teaching has been well accepted in senior high school and even in the elementary schools, its adoption in junior high schools has for various reasons been more gradual. Nonetheless, junior high school team-teaching programs do exist throughout the country in an increasing number and in a varicty of subject areas. An early program in New York City[16] combined three seventh-grade classes for team teaching in reading. Once weekly a lesson in basic reading skills was given to a group of 120 students in a large-group situation. The language arts teacher conducted a follow-up lesson in the regular classroom and small-group instruction was provided later for those who needed remedial help. The team included a remedial reading teacher and a teacher with experience in teaching reading at the elementary level, both of whom served as demonstrators in large-group presentations. The team also included participating teachers, observing teachers, and student teachers. Conferences were held after each demonstration, at which time evaluations and suggestions were made for improvement. The program was later expanded to mathematics and language arts.

A Florida junior high school[17] entered into a team-teaching program in 1961 which operated in English, American history, civics, algebra, and general science. Student groupings were sometimes made on an ability basis, sometimes not, depending upon the purposes and nature of instruction. Students met in large groups once or twice weekly and in regular classrooms the other days.

In a New York junior high school[18] the master schedule was arranged to permit two seventh-grade science classes to meet for team teaching and to permit three science teachers, two experienced and one new, to meet with this group. The team also included the librarian and the resource coordinator. Following the large-group presentation, the students were divided into three or four smaller groups for discussion, experiments, or independent library study and research. The units taught were developed by the entire team in weekly meeting. Specific lists of independent study assignments were given to the students, and team meetings were held before grading papers to reduce differences and reach agreement as to standards. Team members felt that the project required more planning and work, but that results were worth it.

The Claremont Project in California[19] has done considerable work in developing several junior high school team-teaching projects. These include programs in English, mathematics, social studies, reading, and geography. One program correlated not only English and social studies but English and mathematics, and social studies and mathematics.

In the Griffen Junior High School,[20] Los Angeles, the teachers who are involved in team teaching meet with their individual classes for a block of time of two consecutive periods. Once or more each week two teachers combine their classes in one room and present the material to a group of 65 to 70 students.

Teams in the Lakeview Junior High School,[21] Decatur, Illinois, are organized by content area on each grade level, 7-8-9. The school operates on a large-group–small-group schedule with 30 percent of time open for students' independent study.

Teaching teams for seventh and eighth grades at the University Junior High School,[22] Bloomington, Indiana, are so organized that each team includes a teacher from each of the areas of English, mathematics, social studies, and science.

A well-publicized team-teaching program is that of the Wayland High School[23] in Massachusetts. The faculty is divided into six teams. Each team includes all the teachers for a specific subject—all those in English on one team, for example. Instruction includes large-group lessons, small groups, and permits different-sized classes to meet at various times. Students are often grouped by ability and frequently have different teachers. Scheduling is conceived in terms of a week's instruction rather than daily. Instructional groups may (but do not necessarily) meet every day or at the same hour.

A California middle school,[24] grades 6-7-8, with 720 students is organized in three units of 240 students each. A seven-teacher team is assigned to each unit. Each team is assisted by a group of specialists representing P.E., home economics, practical arts, and foreign language. Scheduling is flexible and there are teacher aides for clerical work.

In Easton, Pennsylvania, the Easton Area High School has team teaching in English, history, and mathematics within a four-period block of time in an eight-period day.

Literally scores of middle schools reported using some form of team teaching in a recent survey,[25] including subject-area teams, interdisciplinary teams, large- and small-group instruction, teams-teaching classes comprised of students from all grades in the school, and teams by grade level.

It is clear that much variation exists from school to school in the team-teaching programs, and this is probably as it should be. Each program should be developed in keeping with the student population and needs, teacher abilities and personalities, physical facilities, and the curriculum desired.

ADVANTAGES, DISADVANTAGES, AND PROBLEMS

Surveys and reports indicate several advantages and disadvantages that are felt to accrue from team teaching in the junior high school. Unfortunately, these depend to a considerable extent upon perceptions and opinions. Nonetheless, they are worth noting and, depending upon degree, may all possess validity. Most often reported as advantages are

1. Permits more competent teachers to play a larger part in overall instruction.
2. Allows recognition of highly able teachers without losing them from instruction to administration.
3. Flexibility in class sizes; more individual help available; opportunities for student self-direction.
4. Reduction of routine clerical chores.
5. Ease of crossing subject-matter boundaries; use of resource people.
6. Permits extensive use of technological aids and equipment.
7. Involves counseling and administrative personnel so that they become better acquainted with students and curriculum.
8. Encourages use of new materials, examination, and improvement of curriculum

9. Improves professionalism by regular meetings, cooperative planning, and sharing of ideas.
10. Promotes a more reasonable division and better use of time rather than the same amount of time for every subject every day.
11. Provides in-service education for new teachers and teachers who may be in a rut.
12. Better scope and sequence in curriculum and student schedules.
13. Children report that they are more interested in school, learn more, and make more friends.[26]
14. Preferred by big majority of teachers involved.
15. Permits better scheduling of extracurricular activities.
16. Improved school discipline and student behavior.

Certain disadvantages and problems have been reported, many of which may be avoided if the teaching team takes these into consideration before implementing their program:

1. Strict equality has been emphasized in teacher pay and relationships for a long time. This attitude is sometimes hard to combat.
2. Some teachers are unable or unwilling to fit into team teaching. Teachers fail to perceive themselves as they are, personalities clash, perhaps one or more team members do not do their fair share.
3. Team leadership may be hard to identify. Occasionally the teacher who appears to be a master teacher when he functions in a room by himself does not perform well in a team situation and, even worse, provides little or no leadership.
4. Some schools have entered into team teaching without adequate planning, preparation, and teacher training, with the result that they rode but a short time on the bandwagon.
5. Lack of sufficient time for planning, for conferences, for evaluation, and for all phases of joint effort.
6. Lack of space and failure of administration to provide space by reassigning or remodeling.
7. Lack of administrative support in terms of morale, money, encouragment, equipment, scheduling, or clerical help.
8. Overuse or underuse of teacher aides and assistants.
9. Lack of continuity when several different teachers work with the same subject and the same group of students.
10. Excessive emphasis upon subject matter.
11. Insufficient curriculum supervision and development.
12. Insufficient attention to student differences.
13. Failure to develop community understanding and support.
14. Inadequate preparation of students for the new approach.
15. Failure to make changes in the team instructional procedures and in team membership.

It is probable that most of these problems and disadvantages can be foreseen, considered in planning, and reduced or eliminated. It is not likely, however, that any team program will be trouble-free. Any enterprise involving as it does so many people at so many levels and engaged in curriculum and instruction cannot escape some problems. What must be remembered is that some change is necessary in the traditional teaching approach if we are to do the best we can for the education of all children.

> Until we accept schools as places for the motivation of learning, and until we accept our students as idealistic youth in search of values to live by, there will be little success for the traditional, selective, and outdated mechanisms we currently use . . . to educate our socially sensitive youth.[27]

NONGRADED SCHOOLS

The graded school system, which is the most widely found and accepted plan of school organization in the United States, is a product of another time and another culture. The procedure of grouping students by chronological age was brought to this country from Prussia and instituted in the Quincy Grammar School in 1848. This is believed to be the first graded school in the United States, although

> Even as early as 1799, in Middlesex County, Connecticut, and 1800, Providence, Rhode Island, school districts were calling for some kind of pupil classification. The desire of educators to classify pupils into instructional groups is deep in the professional grain.[28]

The advent of the graded school was preceded in 1838 by the publication of the McGuffey Eclectic Reader, which was graded in six levels. The McGuffey Readers were so successful that textbook publishers were soon releasing graded materials for virtually all areas of the curriculum. By 1870 the graded concept of school organization—graded textbooks, graded schools, and teachers who were grade-oriented—had become almost universally adopted in the United States. The unit was now organizationally sound and each child was firmly cemented into his niche.

Almost from its adoption, however, there were expressions of dissatisfaction. Complaints were raised concerning the heavy pupil dropout, at least partially due to the high failure rate caused by rigid teaching methods and inflexible promotion policies. The graded system, said others, was nothing but an instrument for forcing mass conformity. The schools, unwilling to abandon such a neat system of pupil classification, attempted to work within the graded structure by varying the curriculum to meet some of the student differences. Ability grouping, for example, is not a new technique, nor is tracking. Midyear and even quarterly student promotions were established so that a child would not, through failure, be forced to repeat an entire year's work. Through the years a number of plans and variations of the curriculum have been attempted to deal with individual student needs, some with a measure of success. But the great majority of children still enter grade 1, move annually to the next numbered grade, and ultimately the majority will graduate from grade 12 after twelve years of schooling.

While virtually from the institution of the graded school organizational system there has been concern with the needs of the individual within the group, the child-centered movements of the past few decades have brought about a rising interest in ungraded or nongraded schools. A graded school operates on the premise that all children of a given age should be grouped together where they will all learn the same content in the same length of time. Increasing evidence of how people learn and the concern with the individual and his needs have demonstrated the weakness of the graded pattern.

> It is common practice in the graded school for the teacher to give a specific assignment to everyone in a class to be completed in a specified period of time. Examinations are invariably given to everyone at once. . . . Less able students fail to "keep up" with the group, and the most able students are held back.[29]

Once the examination is completed, the entire class is expected to move to the next unit or work even though some students may not yet be ready for advanced studies. The slower learner is doomed to failure and the more able student is condemned to boredom by the lockstep of grade organization.

DEFINITION

The concept of the nongraded school is not new, for this was what actually existed before the graded plan was established. Since then, in more remote school districts—particularly in one or two-room schools—it has been quite commonly accepted. Who has not heard (in nostalgic terms) of the joys of the "little red schoolhouse" with its quaint well and outdoor privies? What *is* relatively new is the mounting interest in what may be achieved in improving the educational program in the junior high schools and in increased student learning and self-confidence by ungrading classes.

Ungrading or nongrading, sometimes called the "Continuous Progress Plan," is an administrative arrangement in which grade levels and grade labels are eliminated in favor of multiphase classes in each subject, which include children of varying ages. Junior high school English, for example, is not designated seventh-, eighth-, or ninth-grade English, but may have as many as fifteen different steps or levels, flexibly organized, through which students move according to their abilities or readiness. Presumably a student progresses continuously at his own speed through sequential subject-matter levels with no concern for uniform academic requirements. The present chronological grouping that exists in most school systems says flatly that all six-year-olds are ready to enter grade 1 at the same time, are expected to meet the same standards, and are taught the same material in approximately the same manner. Much talk but little attention is given to what we know exists: individual differences in interests, abilities, and rate of maturation.

These differences are even more pronounced by the time children reach junior high school, where the pattern of requiring all children, regardless of ability and maturity, to take the same sequence of coursework is not only questionable but indefensible. Many children can gain more from two or three years of seventh-grade English than they can from dragging through the standard three-year sequence of English. At the same time, every junior high school has students who could reasonably and easily bypass certain basic courses and move on to those that offer more. Children would not necessarily finish junior high school in less than three years, but wider offerings and a richer program could be made available.

The ungraded school is organized to permit the student to achieve without regard to grade level or sequence, and is planned around an individual readiness for learning, allowing each student to progress at his best rate. The promotional or nonpromotional aspect traditionally met each June is eliminated; the ceilings are raised and floors lowered to adjust to the differing abilities of students.

THE NONGRADED JUNIOR HIGH

As with flexible scheduling, nongraded classes make it easier for the junior high school to perform its functions. Individualized and differentiated student programs, so necessary in the education of the early adolescent, are basic to the nongraded system. No predetermined barriers intrude, since the ungraded school establishes an unbroken learning continuum through which the pupils move in terms of their own needs and abilities. Thus the ungraded plan stimulates continuous individual progress.

> The prevalent secondary school organization is based on a premise—long ago proved false—that pupils develop at an equal pace in all academic areas. If we believe that pupils deserve the opportunity to progress as rapidly as they are able, and if we accept the notion that children differ in their abilities to learn, then we need to give careful consideration to the idea of the ungraded secondary school.[30]

There are several arguments for adopting an ungraded approach to instruction:

1. We know that there are wide differences in every group of children in ability, motivation, and interest. Yet we continue to group chil-

dren on the basis that every child of the same chronological age needs the same subject content for the same length of time. A student who might wish to study some topic more deeply is penalized by having to do the "regular" work as well as that in which he has become interested. "Students soon learn that school is not a good place to pursue their interests—such pursuits will interfere with their work."[31]

2. Practically any evidence available indicates that retention of a slow learner in grade serves no useful purpose. Undesirable growth characteristics, unrealistic school programs, and poor progress in school are commonly more closely associated with nonpromoted children rather than with slow learners who are promoted.
3. Instruction designed to meet the needs of all of the children in the school will judge each child by the best that he can do, not by progress through a graded school based on subject matter mastery.
4. "No child should be judged by the median performance of a nonselected group."[32] In any such standard it is obvious that one-half the group must fall below the median, and this will be true regardless of how any midpoint is selected.
5. Chronological age, it is true, has more importance attached to it than is reasonable. Certainly no child should be judged solely on this basis or on any basis that is not defensible in relation to what research tells us about child growth and development, intuition, cognition, and mental age.

The ungraded concept alters the traditional organization to create a continuous learning environment for each student who moves when he as an individual is ready, not when a graded system indicates that he is "statistically" ready.

ESTABLISHING A NONGRADED PROGRAM

Any change in education should be carefully planned, thoroughly discussed with and by all concerned, and completely explained and understood. Nongrading is no exception to this process. It is necessary that all involved are aware of the advantages and disadvantages, the potential problems, and what elements must be considered in establishing a nongraded junior high school. Some of the more obvious factors are:

1. Thorough preparation of teachers so that they understand the concepts and curriculum involved.
2. An accurate classification of students on an achievement and ability basis.
3. Provision for flexibility in grouping to permit student movement to another step when it is desirable.

4. Establishing curriculum and goals for each student.
5. Standards permitting all students to achieve and be successful.
6. Training of students in use and budgeting of their time.
7. A revised system of reporting to parents.
8. Constant teacher evaluation of pupil progress.
9. Parental understanding of the concepts involved, changes to be expected, and results anticipated. (Be sure that they understand that this method is not likely to be any cheaper.)
10. As much teacher involvement as possible from the planning stage to implementation to evaluation.

As is the case with so much that is innovative, research here is scant and contradictory. Reported advantages of ungraded schools by those involved in such programs include

1. Lower dropout rate.
2. Students recover quicker from extended absences.
3. When children and teachers are free to go beyond traditional limits, their potentials expand.
4. Student use of inquiry and discovery is extended and pupils are stimulated to greater effort.
5. Less pupil boredom and frustration.
6. Parental reaction is generally quite favorable.
7. Pupils' progress ranges one year or more ahead of those in graded classes.[33]
8. Ungraded schools provide an atmosphere in which individual differences are more readily seen and worked with.
9. Bright children are not held back, nor slower students frustrated.
10. This provides an unbroken learning continuum.
11. Many slow learners catch up.
12. Students are better adjusted generally and socially.
13. Fears concerning promotion or nonpromotion are eliminated. How can any child fail, regardless of ability, if he is working at his capacity?
14. There is no problem of encroachment upon material reserved for the next higher grade.
15. Nongraded schools attract the innovative and interested teacher.
16. Nongradedness fosters and stimulates further improvements.
17. The ungraded curriculum provides a more valid basis for individual learning.

Mere adoption of an ungraded structure is no guarantee of an elmination of trouble; problem areas can and do exist here, too:

1. It may be difficult to find teachers who are able and want to teach groups of pupils as though they were individuals. Teachers must be in agreement with the idea and understand what is involved in the

change from graded to ungraded classes and must change their teaching methods accordingly.

2. The curriculum must be completely reorganized on a sequential basis. The program will work but poorly or not at all if the old curriculum is retained.
3. Administrative personnel must provide real and honest leadership with strong ideas, convictions, and positive procedures for accomplishing the objectives.
4. Parents and community must be completely informed as to what is being attempted, why, and the anticipated results.
5. Students must also be prepared and understand. They must know what is expected of them, how, what progress they should make, the grading to be used, and methods of reporting to parents.
6. Record keeping is more involved.
7. Nongradedness requires more planning, work, and imagination of teachers.
8. Teachers must not expect every child to move at the same rate, any more than they expect every child to grow physically at the same rate.
9. No junior high school should move into the nongraded structure without careful preplanning. "There are enough problems in operating a nongraded program without foredooming it to failure through irresponsible decision making."[34]
10. Continued use of and reliance upon "phases" or "levels" indicates a lack of understanding of the ungraded concept.
11. If classroom practices remain unchanged, then nongrading becomes only an administrative device and a minor change.
12. Problems of articulation may arise for students who leave an ungraded school and enter a graded school.
13. There is the questionable validity of placement criteria.
14. There is possible an emphasis upon the capable students and some neglect of the less able.

RESEARCH AND PRACTICE

McLoughlin,[35] in summarizing the research relative to nongraded schools, concluded that ". . . the academic development of children probably does not suffer from attending a nongraded school; there is some evidence . . . to indicate it may be somewhat enhanced." Findings of the various studies indicate that children from nongraded schools generally do as well as children from graded schools and are more likely to excel those children from graded schools than they are likely to be excelled.

Nongraded schools are most frequently found in primary grades, although some junior and senior high schools have adopted this approach.

McLoughlin points out that many ungraded programs are not nongraded at all in that homogeneous grouping and semidepartmentalization in some subject areas are often passed off as nongraded programs. These, it is said, are but administrative expediencies put into practice to make a graded school operate more efficiently, not truly nongraded instructional programs.

To an extent the junior high schools already possess an ungraded program in many elective areas, yet this is not true in all schools. Those junior high schools who mix eighth- and ninth-grade students—and occasionally seventh-graders—in classes such as band, orchestra, and chorus are actually ungrading these subjects. Beyond this there are junior high schools which have completely ungraded or are planning to do so. One such school,[31] which includes children normally classified as grades 7-8-9, has fifteen sections or steps for each subject. There are no grade lines. Children are assigned a step on the basis of ability and performance and move from one section to another when ready. The staff believes that opportunities for student success are much improved that the teachers are better able to teach to the group and also to help those who need extra help, and that there is greater attention to individual needs.

An early program in ungraded classes was initiated in a New Jersey middle school,[37] with grades 6-7-8, in 1957. Each pupil pursued a schedule based upon his abilities, aptitudes, skills, and interest in each subject. Each pupil was therefore individually scheduled throughout. With the guidance of the teacher and the principal, each pupil selected any electives and areas of learning beyond required coursework. There were no grade levels as such. Each student moved at his own speed, and there was continuous evaluation of pupil progress which permitted students to move into other groups when desirable. Parents, students, and staff were well pleased by the entire program.

A small six-year high school in Kansas inaugurated nongraded classes for all seventh- and eighth-graders in 1963. The faculty at Roosevelt Junior-Senior High School[38] were concerned with developing a program to make the individual student's learning the center of the curriculum. The instructional program, emphasizing the needs and interests of each child, was designed to give each student opportunities for decision making and problem solving. Standards used for pupil placement included achievement scores, motivation, interest, teacher recommendation, student maturity level and social growth, student interests, student's self responsibility.

> Seventh- and eighth-grade students were placed in one of three levels in each area of learning on the basis of criteria established for each particular level. Each level reflected a different step or degree of achievement of certain content objectives that had been determined earlier.[39]

Students moved through the content of each area as they were ready rather than on a yearly grade -level basis. Each student was placed at a level that would, it was hoped, challenge him but would not require repetition of previously mastered material in an attempt to build a sequence of learning that would be continuously challenging.

Teaching teams evaluated each student each week for each subject area and reasssignments were made as were necessary. The school day was organized with a three-hour block in the morning for a coordinated program of language arts, social studies, and fine arts; a second division was a two-hour block of time for science and math, the rest of the day being used for exploratory work in practical arts, music, and physical education.

At the end of the year, analysis of test scores of the 62 students involved indicated that 61 made significant achievement gains for the year. "The class as a whole made about twenty percent more achievement gain than would have normally been expected as measured by national norms."[40]

In evaluating the project, the faculty concluded that there was much more flexibility; students felt more comfortable; more able students seemed to show a higher gain than did the less able; there is a definite need for a sound guidance program in this structure; and students with learning problems could be provided with more help.

The nongraded school shows promise of providing an opportunity for every child to develop his talents and skills to the fullest extent possible—something that the graded structure has never done. Such research as is available indicates that children in nongraded classes do as well as those in standard classes, and some reports indicate better achievement. What is of real importance is the improved attitude and effort ot students involved. The pressure is much reduced for both students and teachers. The key word is "relax," and in this setting teaching and learning will be enhanced.

RECAPITULATION

Flexible scheduling, team teaching, and nongraded schools are three approaches to improving instruction in the junior high schools that are currently receiving much attention. All of these hold much promise for improving the education of the early adolescent. The opportunities provided for individualizing student instruction, for affording more diversified student programs, and for meeting the unique needs of the early adolescent are virtually endless. Flexible schedules are of such variety that they can be easily tailored to the requirements of each school, and can be changed not only from year to year but almost daily if necessary.

Team teaching, by making the best use of teacher talents and competencies, may also be designed to fit the particular needs of each school, each staff, and each junior high school population.

Nongraded schools, by themselves or in combination with a flexible schedule and/or team teaching have the potential of being the most significant step forward in educating the adolescent since the impact of graded schools and subsequent departmentalization.

SUMMARY

The schedule in many schools determines the educational program. This is just the reverse of what should be. The educational program should be established and then a schedule devised to best implement it. In these days of experiment, innovation, and change the traditional bell schedule remains a useless anchor to which many schools are tied.

Flexible schedules do not have to be modular, but they may be. Flexible schedules do not necessarily involve team teaching, large- and small-group work, and independent study, but they permit these things and many others. The old excuse, "It can't be scheduled," is no longer permissible because virtually anything can be scheduled, and not necessarily by computer.

Team teaching and its related concepts constitute a major change in the way we teach children. Traditionally teachers have been assigned a classroom and one or more groups of children. Little attention has been given to differences in teaching ability, interest, and enthusiasm. It is equally true that not enough attention has been given to the individual differences in teaching ability, interest, and enthusiasm. It is equally true that not enough attention has been given to the individual differences of children. All too often the classroom group is treated as though it were composed of two or three dozen identical pupils each with the same abilities and interests. Dissatisfaction with the traditional system and mounting criticism of American education which followed World War II brought about in the middle 1950's the Staff Utilization Studies. These studies culminated in the Trump and Baynham report of 1961 which made recommendations for several sweeping changes, including variability of size in student grouping, increased use of technological aids, independent study for students, and teaching teams. These teams are so constituted as to include a team leader, master teachers, assistant teachers, teacher aides, and clerical assistants, with pay scales varying according to individual responsibilities. It is intended that the maximum use be made of teacher interest and specialization. The junior high schools did not at first move into team teaching as rapidly as the senior high schools or elementary schools, but in recent years there has been a pronounced effort in this direction.

The concept of ungrading, most popular in elementary school, but becoming more common in junior high school, eliminates grade levels and grade lavels. There is no such thing as seventh- or eighth- or ninth-grade mathematics, English, or other subject. Instead, the school offers a number of steps or phases in each subject and students are placed in whatever step they are ready to work. The classes are highly flexible, and students may move from one to another whenever they are ready. Virtually no criticism but instead a high degree of satisfaction has been expressed by all who have worked with ungraded schools.

REFERENCES

1. Gaynor Petrequin, *Individualizing Learning Through Modular Flexible Programming.* New York: McGraw-Hill, 1968. p. viii.
2. Donald C. Manlove and David W. Beggs, *Flexible Scheduling.* Bold New Venture Series. Bloomington, Ind.: Indiana U. P., 1965, pp. 29–36.
3. Manlove and Beggs, *loc. cit.*
4. Manlove and Beggs, *op. cit.*, p. 36.
5. M. H. Robb, "Modular Sheduling at Euclid Central," *NASSP Bulletin*, Vol. 46 (February 1962), pp. 66–69.
6. Elayne B. Hofmann, "The Brookhurst Plan," *NEA Journal*, Vol. 54 (September 1965), p. 50.
7. Hofmann, *op. cit.*, p. 51.
8. Thomas G. Leigh, "Big Opportunities in Small Schools Through Flexible-Modular Scheduling," *Journal of Secondary Education*, Vol. 42 (April 1967), pp. 175–187.
9. Gerald P. Speckhard, "Evaluating the Modular Schedule," *North Central Association Quarterly*, Vol. 41 (Spring 1967), pp. 300–308.
10. Richard A. Gorton, "Parental Resistance to Modular Scheduling," *Clearing House*, Vol. 43 (March 1969), p. 394.
11. Ira J. Singer, "Survey of Staff Utilization Practices in Six States," *NASSP Bulletin*, Vol. 46 (January 1962), pp. 1–14.
12. Gordon Cawelti, "Innovative Practices in High Schools: Who Does What—and Why—and How," *Nation's Schools*, Vol. 79 (April 1967).
13. J. Lloyd Trump and Dorsey Baynham, *Focus on Change, Guide to Better Schools.* Chicago: Rand McNally, 1961.
14. Edward G. Buffie, "Potentials for Team Teaching in the Junior High School," in David W. Beggs (ed.), *Team Teaching*, Bold New Venture Series. Bloomington, Ind.; Indiana Un. P., 1964, pp. 73–74.
15. Lorene K. Wills, "Team Teaching in the Content Fields," in Beggs, *Team Teaching, op. cit.*, p. 161.
16. D. H. Battrick, "How Do Team Teaching and Other Staff Utilization Practices Fit Into the Instructional Program of a Junior High School," *NASSP Bulletin*, Vol. 46 (October 1962), pp. 13–15.
17. Philip B. Glancy, "Brookside Junior High School, Sarasota, Florida, Strives for Quality Education," *NASSP Bulletin*, Vol. 46 (January 1962), pp. 157–160.
18. Edward R. Cuony, "Team Teaching in Junior High School," *NASSP Bulletin*, Vol. 47 (October 1963), pp. 67–72.

19. Nicholas C. Polos, *The Dynamics of Team Teaching.* (Dubuque: Wm. C. Brown, 1965, p. 37.
20. Wills, *op. cit.*, p. 162.
21. Buffie, *op. cit.*, p. 70.
22. *Ibid.*, p. 67.
23. William M. Griffen, "Some Ideas and Patterns at Wayland, Massachusetts, High School," *NASSP Bulletin*, Vol. 46 (January 1962), pp. 123–126.
24. H. A. Taylor and R. F. Cook, "Schools Within A School: A Teaching Team Organized for Junior High School," *High School Journal*, Vol. 48 (January 1965), pp. 289–295.
25. "Middle Schools in Action," *Educational Research Circular No. 2*, American Association of School Administrators and Research Division, National Education Association, 1969.
26. Andrew S. Adams, "Operation Co-Teaching, Dateline: Oceano, California," *Elementary School Journal*, Vol. 62 (January 1962), pp. 203–212.
27. James A. Meyer, "Teaming: A First Step for Interdisciplinary Teaching," *Clearing House*, Vol. 43 (March 1969), p. 406.
28. Edward G. Buffie, "A Historical Perspective," in David W. Beggs (ed.), *Non-Graded Schools in Action.* Bold New Venture Series. Bloomington, Ind.: Indiana U. P., 1967, p. 6.
29. Eugene R. Howard and Roger W. Bardwell, *How to Organize a Non-Graded School.* Englewood Cliffs, N.J.: Prentice-Hall, 1966, p. 11.
30. Sidney P. Rollins, "Ungraded High Schools: Why Those Who Like Them Love Them," *Nation's Schools*, Vol. 73 (April 1964), p. 110.
31. Howard and Bardwell, *op. cit.*, p. 12.
32. Maurie Hillson, "The Non-Graded School: A Dynamic Concept," in David Beggs and Edward G. Buffie (eds.), *Non-Graded Schools in Action, op. cit.*, p. 31.
33. Rollins, *op. cit.*, p. 130.
34. Stuart E. Dean, "The Future of Nongraded Schools," in *Nongraded Schools in Action, op. cit.*, p. 110.
35. William P. McLaughlin, "The Phantom Nongraded School," *Phi Delta Kappan*, Vol. 49 (January 1968), pp. 248–250.
36. Paul J. Gelinas and Aime Lacoste, "Setauket Junior High School," *NASSP Bulletin*, Vol. 47 (May 1963), pp. 68–69.
37. James C. Sandilos, "Gradeless Classes," *American School Board Journal*, Vol. 136 (February 1958), p. 55.
38. Charles Niess, "A Nongraded Program for a Small High School," *NASSP Bulletin*, Vol. 50 (February 1966), pp. 19–27.
39. *Ibid.*, p. 21.
40. *Ibid.*, p. 24.

chapter 18

Independent Study

Children learn in different ways, and each student develops his own learning style—an approach that may be similar to many others, but one that is uniquely his. We know that each individual is different and that nowhere are these differences more pronounced than in the early adolescent. Yet the vast majority of our junior high schools operate in a graded pattern, on a standard six- or seven-period schedule, using materials designed for group-paced learning in which the teacher bases her instruction upon the middle student.

Neither the functions of the junior high nor the characteristics of the adolescent learner are well satisfied by most of our present junior high school practices. Independent study is a procedure that puts a heavy emphasis upon necessary procedures in the junior high school: individualized programs, differentiated learnings, self-directed study, self-responsibility, critical thinking, and problem solving. The first priority in solution of the problems of the junior high school must be found in the awareness and the acceptance of the needs and characteristics of the junior high school age pupil. The next step must be to develop a program and systematically carry it out to eliminate the present evils of the system.[1] The "evils" to which reference is made include:

1. All subjects in the junior high school are assigned the same amount of time.
2. All students are assumed to need the same amount of time for instruction in every subject.
3. Growth of children must be constant and uniform, therefore, a new master schedule is unnecessary.
4. Because they know best, administrators should allocate time, number of students, facilities, and methodology to all teachers irrespective of their training and competency.

5. All teachers are effective and efficient to the same degree in a quality instructional program.
6. Children of junior high school age cannot be expected to be mature enough to make decisions respecting the use they will make of their time during the school day.

> Characteristically, the individual's learning in school has been largely other-directed, without a natural progression from teacher-direction to self-direction as the learner becomes more mature. . . . Indeed, the tendency has been to increase the amount of direction in the form of assignments of homework, typically uniform for all students, as the learner progresses.[2]

The adolescent, even as he is striving for more independence from adult authority, find that teachers usually require learning tasks of a group nature without regard for the individual student's interests, needs, and goals. The knowledge explosion and our rapidly changing world require that today's student be able to continue his learning by himself. He must learn to develop an interest in learning.

LEARNING RESEARCH AND INDEPENDENT STUDY

The long-held single-stage model of the learning process is that of a "connection" between a stimulus and a response. To bring about learning, the teacher presented a stimulus from the environment, reinforced it as immediately as possible, presented some sort of reward as reinforcement to the learner, and repeated the learning sequence—perhaps many times—to increase the strength of the connection.

More recent investigations indicate the existence of a multistage model of learning in which the learner recalls an internally stored process or cue —a representative or symbolic process—which is now generally called "mediation."[3] Hull noted that one could specify knowledge and purpose in observed behavior of animals finding their way through a maze. Such behavior, he felt, could not be sufficiently accounted for merely by the assumption of a chain of conditioned reflexes. The behavior of the animals indicated a kind of variability and adaptiveness that suggested that the animal was capable of representing to himself something about the goal he hoped to reach. This "fractional anticipatory goal response"[4] represents a mediational or multistage model as contrasted with the single-stage model.

> Something in the animal's learning system was reinstated as a representation of the external situation; something became a part of learning which did not come from the immediate stimulus situation in which the learner found himself.[5]

Further and more recent investigations indicate that

1. What has been previously learned has a pronounced effect upon what has been most recently learned.
2. The stimulus term in verbal learning is not what was responded to by the learner—he was responding not to the nominal stimulus but to a *functional* stimulus. He coded the verbal stimulus in terms of some predispositions or habits acquired earlier. The key point here is that there is some middle stage to the learning process if the learner is performing some operation (coding) on the stimulus.
3. Studies that deliberately intrude a coding process, (studies of mediation) find that a new association is markedly easier because the learner brings to the problem a previously acquired code. For example, . . . when the learner has acquired an association like BOP KING, it becomes very easy for him to learn the new association BOP QUEEN."[6]
4. Studies of short-and long-term memory suggest that learners do something to units of information before they are stored, i.e., engaging in a rehearsal, as well as coding. Something is done by the learner to the stimulus before he stores it.
5. In concept learning, situations have been used that seem to infer two or more stages in the learning process. To solve, in the first attempt, a reversed discrimination (as with two colors of cards) the learner must be able to bring to mind a concept such as "opposite" or "reverse."

An examination of this evidence indicates that the emphasis upon what must be explained changes to the middle of the learning process from the two ends. This middle process, what the learner himself does with the stimulus, is what is meant by "mediation," a coding by the learner's nervous system. Mediation is dependent upon what has been previously learned, since this is what has put the learner's nervous system into its present condition. There may also be effects produced by inherited factors.

The fact that mediation exists in learning introduces a strong element of unpredictability into the teaching and learning process, since *each* code is unique to each *individual learner.* The mediation is generated by the learner—some essential part of learning comes from inside the learner. It is often said that learning is an individual act, and evidence such as this supports the truth of this statement. Learning is a set of incidents that occur within the individual and depend a great deal upon the learner's nature and his previous learning. Gagne says that "The learner is, then, in a fundamental sense responsible for his own learning. . . . The student needs to learn that learning takes place within his own head as a result of his own 'thinking' activity."[7]

To refine, sharpen, and polish the mediational process there must be provided in the instructional program opportunities for discussion with other people, both adults and students, and there must also be provision for application of the acquired knowledge in practical situations.

What part does motivation play in independent study? The traditional junior high school curriculum and theory is more likely to stifle the early adolescent's spontaneous curiosity and interest, since he is expected to learn when taught and what is taught. He does not learn for himself, he learns for others even though this may be expected to come into conflict with goals held by each adolescent. What conditions decide these individual goals?

In reporting research in motivation theory and the implications for independent study, Sears[8] lists the following areas of investigation:

1. Under certain conditions (parents having so -called "right values" and administering reinforcement without creating anxiety) motivation for children by identification with the parent works well. The child must also be willing and have the ability to play the game according to his parent's values.
2. There is a competence or effectance motivation which recognizes that there is an urge to mastery of the environment within all children; a drive for each student to make an accomplishment on his own—and this *must* be on his own to satisfy him.
3. When a conflict situation is established (two incompatible or incongruous responses simultaneously), the curiosity so induced is a strong motivation factor.
4. Children who have a high anxiety need continuous success with a minimum of competition in order to do well. "When need achievement is high and anxiety low, we get persistence in work, remembering of tasks . . . wanting to take independent responsibility, a good grasp of principles, and a good reaction to failure . . . with a high need achievement and low anxiety, students can take the difficult material and so-called failure much better. This will only give them more motivation to do more."[9]

The implications for instruction for the early adolescent should be clear. Some children receive a measure of motivation because their parents have the "right values," but virtually all children are blessed with curiosity and a wish or need to succeed on their own. A situation with a minimum of anxiety is likely to produce more success and better learning. Instructional policies that diverge from the traditional junior high approach to permit individual student programs and projects, with a high degree of student responsibility and self-direction, are far more likely to succeed. Yet most of our instruction is group-oriented with mass assignments—"homework" which is to be completed in out-of-class time and usually in out-of-school time. In independent study the adolescent spends large amounts of his school time in such places as resource centers, libraries, and laboratories working on material which may be similar to that of other students but is not the same assignment.

Our instructional systems in the junior high schools have generally fostered dependence in learning by emphasizing marking systems, examinations, "covering the subject," and group assignments both for class and homework. Since homework seems to be so firmly cemented into the junior high school methods of instruction, an examination of this traditional procedure may be of help.

HOMEWORK—TRADITIONALLY AND HISTORICALLY

Virtually everyone who has attended school can regale an audience with tales of the quantity and quality of homework which was standard for children in his day. Some of the stories may even be true. Certainly, homework is one of the most common teaching techniques in junior high school as well as being one of the most controversial. Whether they approve homework with modifications or are against it as it now exists, the disputants enter into the argument with little research but strong enthusiasm and conviction. Most of the writing on the topic of homework reports opinions rather than experimental research. In reviewing 280 articles, Goldstein[10] found that 17 were experimental in nature and the rest were opinion articles, and that the opinions varied widely.

A statement such as "No one seriously questions the value of homework at a time when the amount of knowledge is increasing at an unbelievable rate,"[11] finds many who will seriously question both the comment and homework.

Discussions concerning the pros and cons of homework in general and specifically as it is found in junior high school usually include arguments and criticisms such as the following.

1. In junior high school the transition is being made from one elementary teacher who knows how much work has been assigned to four or five teachers who seldom know what other work a student has—and frequently don't seem to care. Often there is no district nor school policy and little or no coordination among teachers on homework. The result is that homework will vary from class to class in the same subject in the same building. No one really knows how much traditional homework is too much, or how much time is just right for maximum effectiveness. The reason is that the quantity of homework and time which is most desirable has varied from student to student, from day to day, and from subject to subject for the individual student.

Various maximum limits have been proposed such as 45 minutes per subject per day or 30 minutes per subject per day. The Junior High Position

Papers of 1963[12] approve one hour of homework a day in grade 7, progressing to two hours daily in grade 9, saying that this is in accord with Conant's study and, "is not excessive." It is reasonable, in passing, to point out that Conant's report is actually worded, "is not excessive *for many pupils.*"[13] Furthermore, Conant is not on record as ever having made any kind of study concerning homework in junior high school nor was he ever acclaimed as the authority in this field.

2. Junior high school teachers, when making assignments, are inclined to picture the home conditions under which pupils work (if they give it any thought at all) as pretty much the same for each student, i.e., a room of his own, desk, materials, reference books, good lighting, proper temperature control, and a quiet cultural atmosphere conducive to scholarly thought and production. Although it has been said that, "The home is an appropriate center for creative and expository writing,"[14] the unfortunate truth is that in many homes there is no place to study and it is impossible to do any school work. In a big-city one or two-room slum apartment with only a table and a ceiling light, a blaring radio or television, and the presence of other family members, how is a student to find time or place for schoolwork! The same problem exists wherever there is poverty, low income, and crowded housing—whether in the city or rural areas. To a substantial degree homework assumes a good income, socioeconomic level, and culture. To be something more than an exercise in frustration, homework requires that the assignment be clearly explained and begun in class and that all necessary texts and materials be readily available—in short, the kind of organization best provided at the school.

3. Undeniably there have been abuses in the assignment of homework and these abuses are bitterly resented by parents and children alike. An exasperated teacher who as a penalty gives several pages of homework has effectively related punishment and schoolwork for his students. Dull, drudgery, and drill are historically and presently accurate descriptions of a great deal of homework; work of dubious value, often excessive in amount ("Do problems 1 to 40"), and designed to increase student dislike of school. There is a very real question as to whether or not some teachers know how to use homework as a teaching technique. It seems likely that some teachers assign homework because they think they should, and others because they were given homeork when they were students. A practice that may easily be classified as a sin is to make homework assignments and fail to collect them. The evil here is compounded when the assignment is given a very short deadline—usually the next day—but is somehow forgotten by the teacher. Assigning new material without explaining it causes confusion and repetition of mistakes. It also causes poor parent-school relationships when father is called upon to help and has difficulty himself with the lesson. Assignments that are ambiguous, vague, or repetitious may cause parents

to wonder exactly why this assignment was given.

4. Most administrators, parents, and teachers favor homework.[15] Survey after survey finds overwhelming parental approval of the concept of homwork: one team found that only one family in 100 felt that homework should not be a part of family living;[16] only seven out of 205 parents rejected homework in another survey,[17] although about one-half of these respondents questioned the kind and quantity of homework assignments. Although the great majority of teachers favor homework ("How else can I cover all this? Education just can't be completed in a week of five short school days.") they are often somewhat at a loss as to how much weight or credit should be given to a homework assignment. There is also a frequent question as to who should get the credit. A parent? A schoolmate? An older brother or sister?

5. It is often said that homework is desirable for students because it develops self-discipline, strenghtens home-school relationships, stimulates independent research and study, permits extension and completion of work begun but not completed in class, reinforces classroom learnings, allows teachers to adapt assignments to individual differences, supplements classwork with projects that cannot be done in the classroom, encourages permanent leisure-time interests in learning, and develops initiative, independence, and responsibility. Teachers have, reportedly, also assigned homework to "keep children out of mischief," and because, "Keeping busy is a virtue—regardless of what one is doing."[18] All of these claimed advantages may exist but regretfully it is quite common to find that

(a) Many children, perhaps most, must be compelled to do their homework. Is this initiative, self-discipline, independence, and responsibility?

(b) Home-school relationships, instead of being strengthened, suffer when neither parents nor children understand the assignment, when necessary materials are not available, when parents feel that they must help the child, or when the assignments are too extensive.

(c) Independent research and study may exist for the length of time it takes to copy another paper or get to the phone to ask for help from other students.

(d) The extension and completion of classroom work receives the arguments that learning should take place in the classroom and would —if the teacher would do a little less talking; that study halls on the junior high level have been largely discontinued to permit supervised study in class; and that the "extension and completion" is too often valueless drudgery and drill.

(e) Classroom learnings may be reinforced by homework, but it is equally likely that a student will repeat and reinforce mistakes.

(f) The adaptation of assignments to individual differences, interests, and abilities is one of the very best arguments for out-of-school assignments. Critics will ask, "How many of these individual assignments did you ever have? Do your children get them now? Or is the assignment the same for all members of the class?"

(g) It is true that homework projects can supplement classroom work —in some homes and for some subjects. So far as a permanent interest in learning in leisure time is concerned, it is possible. But —as with most of the foregoing criticisms—it is far easier to develop such an interest in learning in surroundings designed for this purpose, and many homes are not.

(h) Assignments to "keep children out of mischief" are seldom justifiable. It is even more difficult to defend the statement that keeping busy is a virtue regardless of what one is doing. Presumably one is virtuous when devising plans to defraud the school lunch cashier.

RESEARCH AND HOMEWORK

The research which has been done on homework does not permit any positive conclusions; indeed, it is even difficult to make generalizations. For example, in Connecticut it was found[18] that homework did not necessarily increase student knowledge of a subject nor make for better work habits; but a year-long comparison[20] of two equated geometry classes indicated that the homework group consistently did better than the nonhomework group.

In another instance two equated groups were compared,[21] one of which had homework and the other supervised study in school. It was found that the supervised-study class showed a significantly greater gain in school achievement.

A limited experiment reported[22] with an American history class found that bright students did well whether they had homework or not, but a little better *with* homework. Average students did much better on written work in class with homework, and low-ability students also scored higher with homework. In contrast to these findings, a comparison of the work of 185 equated pairs of high school American history students found no differences in achievement between those who had homework and those who did not.[23] Results of a follow-up test really shake one's faith in the value of outside-of-school work, since the nonhomework students did better than those who had homework. Other studies have been just as confusing. A drop in high school grades was noted for those students who attended an elementary school which had eliminated homework. Students who had no assigned homework in elementary school achieved successfully in high school against those who had. Homework improved the grades of average students, and nonhomework and homework students scored about the same in high school tests.

As a variation on the above theme, a comparison was made of students in some junior high school social studies classes. One group was provided with enrichment study while the other was given traditional homework to see if an enriched kind of supplemental work would reveal more measured gain. To the surprise of many, no appreciable difference was found.[24]

Apparently one can choose a side and select a study to support one's stand. Within the concept of independent study, however, "homework" is regarded quite differently from what it has been in the past. Junior high school students participating in a program of independent study will spend less time in class and may have schoolwork which they will do out of school, but they will usually complete most or all of their studies in the libraries, resource centers, and laboratories available in the schools. The limited and so-called independent study that students have previously experienced with traditional after-school homework is replaced by an approach in which the pupil work is a part of, not apart from, the regular school activity. Teachers and the resources of the school are at hand to assist the student in work for which he has taken the responsibility.

THE USE OF INDEPENDENT STUDY

For a long time we have known that people are all different, that interests, abilities, and drives vary from student to student and even within the individual. Teacher training institutions have urged teachers to give consideration to individual differences, to plan their lessons accordingly, to do different things with different pupils. Yet in the great majority of junior high schools and senior high schools, class after class receives the same lesson, usually a teacher lecture, day after day. In recent years there has been an effort in many schools to develop educational programs for the individual, "keyed to each and every individual child—to the new number in education, the number one."[25] Independent study, which usually includes team teaching and large-group–small-group work, is an approach which offers promise of achieving individualization of studies. If educators really believe that individual differences exist, requiring all students to study courses for the same amount of time is paradoxical.

Independent study can provide a better education for the early adolescent in many ways. It can

1. Expand the curriculum content.
2. Allow a student to extend his knowledge of a subject by in-depth study.
3. Permit a student to move ahead of the rest of the class.
4. Challenge all students to do better—high, middle, and low achievers alike.
5. Help the student to learn how to learn.

6. Develop critical thinking.
7. Develop self-responsibility and self-direction.
8. Help the student learn research techniques and to value learning for its own sake.
9. Help the student become a producer of learning.
10. Make the best use of teacher and student time.
11. Stimulate creative thinking and creative work.
12. Encourage slow learner.

Independent study, as with many other departures from the traditional, is greeted with enthusiasm by some teachers and administrators, regarded with suspicion and doubt by others, and flatly rejected as impossible of attainment by still others. Common remarks are, "It will only work with a talented few of the students," or, "It's all right for *them* to try it—look at the quality of students they have. They ought to have *these* kids." or, "Junior high school children aren't responsible enough to be put on their own." Herein lies much of the difficulty. We have for so long operated in a prescriptive manner that children generally don't know how to function on their own to any extent, yet we say we are attempting to develop initiative, self-direction, and self-reliance in our students. Independent study in many cases has done just this.

An easy definition of independent study is, study that is self-directed by the student. Important differences from the conventional methods include an absence of supervised group-study halls, reduction and in some cases elimination of attendance in regular classes, and student work, self-directed, on a study or project which is partially or completely student-selected, student-planned, and student-outlined. The teacher doesn't ask the student *if* he is going to some independent study, but *when*. There are varying kinds of independent study including programmed learning, study as a supplement to organized instruction, as correspondence work, and study in honors programs, but the type referred to here is that of individualized, self-directed instruction as opposed to organized group instruction. Independent study students may be released from a portion of scheduled class time or may be required only to pass the subject tests, coming to class when they feel it necessary. When not in class the student may work any place in the school, either completely under his own direction or with the help of a teacher or teacher aide.

McDonald[26] describes three levels of conceptualizing independent study:

1. *Self-pacing.* The student is independent from restraints imposed by the abilities of his fellow student with group materials, and is free to move at his own speed.
2. *Individual instruction.* This is characterized by use of multimedia activities and multitexts.

3. *Self-selection.* The student not only chooses the activity but is independent to pursue his tasks.

The effective student in independent study is one who

1. Perceives worthwhile things to do such as comparing, summarizing, seeing relationships, and integrating information.
2. Personalizes learning by searching out projects and problems of interest and value to him, gives his own reasons for doing what is to be done, and presents his own plan for the study.
3. Exercises self-discipline.
4. Makes use of a variety of material and human resources.
5. Produces results acceptable in terms of his individual abilities and interests.
6. Strives for improvement.

INDEPENDENT STUDY FOR WHOM?

Usually those students who engage in independent study are carefully screened and selected. The "Quest Phase" at ungraded Melbourne High School in Florida[27] requires that the student have a B average in previous work in this subject or field, although this requirement can be waived. The student secures an application for independent study, gets approval from his parents and his faculty consultant, and turns in with the application an outline of the proposed semester's work. The faculty consultant is a specialist in the student's selected field of study. The third person involved is the faculty coordinator of the independent-study program. The coordinator considers the student's qualifications. Important are creativity, curiosity, intiative, interest, motivation, and responsibility. He also examines the student's study plans. With the guidance of the coordinator (who is available to the student at all times), and with the help of the faculty consultant, the student is embarked upon his study. The coordinator provides resource materials, guides the student in his writing, keeps all records, and maintains a file on the student's work. He also observes the student during study periods to note progress.

A New York school with grades 7–12 permits any interested student to apply, regardless of age or grade level.[28] The student applies for independent study in any subject, submits his plan to be reviewed by a selection committee, and, if accepted, is free to make up his own daily schedule. The selection committee is composed of the student's subject-matter teacher or teachers, his guidance counselor, the independent-study program director, and, if desirable, the principal. The student is excused from class attendance and daily assignments but is still responsible for the subject tests. Each student is assigned an advisor, usually the classroom teacher for the subject in which the independent study is taking place, and a guidance counselor.

This approach requires an understanding and supportive teacher for that class the student misses. Three essential elements are vital: Student projects, student planning, and close staff guidance, to which may be added the fourth—close cooperation by all teachers, since many find it difficult to believe that students are capable of learning without attending every class and having the teacher tell them all that they need to know.

Alexander and Hines[29] describe a 1,600-student junior high school with grades 7-8-9, in which approval of applicants is given by the teacher in charge of the independent-study program. Generally the particular independent-study plans are the result of teacher initiation, planning, and development, although with student participation, and carried out by students. Student participants may be recommended to the program by teachers and counselors, or students may elect to go into independent study. The student engages in this work in regularly scheduled periods, during study-hall time, or before and after school.

Another junior high school program[30] (enrollment 550) permits the upper-ability-level student to elect a "Quest" study. The student and his project must be approved by the directing teacher who makes his judgment on the basis of a personal evaluation of the student, plus test scores. Emphasis for independent study is placed upon enrichment and depth study of areas of the curriculum which are of special student interest. Evaluation is by means of written reports and oral examinations. Students spend about an hour daily in independent work in the library or conference rooms. A feature of the school is lack of attention to grade lines, and the goal is "continuous growth at the individual's best pace."

In contrast to these plans, all of which embody some type of selectivity, a Pennsylvania school[31] with grades 9–10 only has a program of independent study which involves 97 percent of the student body. Students are not scheduled into classes for about 25 percent of their time. During the independent-study phase the student may work anywhere in the building. He may work on his own or with a teacher aide, a teacher, or a student assistant. The school originally required passes and took attendance but the plan was so successful that, after the first year, passes were eliminated and no attendance check made. "Emphasis is on freedom of movement and freedom of choice; the goals are self-direction and self-discipline." There are but few rules: (1) if a student finds that there is no room in a specialized independent study area or that the help he wanted is not presently available, he must report to one of the general study areas; (2) the student must stay in the selected independent-study area for the full period, which is a 25-minute module; (3) one of the general study areas is a "talking commons" where conversation is permitted; no student may remain in this area for two or more consecutive periods.

About 3 percent of the total student body has proven unable to discipline themselves. They caused trouble, wasted time, and broke school rules. These children needed control and supervision which is provided in a study hall where attendance is taken and quiet maintained. When they indicate that they are ready to enter the independent-study program, they are given the opportunity. The principal and vice-principal are resigned to the need for 3 percent of the students to be under close supervision, but their observation is well said: "The frightening thing is that most schools still have 97 percent in a similar situation. So who has the problem?"[32]

All students at the Winnetka (Illinois) Junior High School are involved in independent study.[33] When the program was begun in 1964 it was believed that only those students of high intelligence and achievement would benefit, yet some of the most productive study programs have been carried out by children considered to be slow learners or low achievers. Students become participants in a program of independent study by teacher referral (for a program that may or may not be related to his classroom); by students who use the learning laboratory as an elective part of their program in mathematics, creative writing, reading, or foreign language study; or by student choice before and after school. Student programs are individually arranged to provide flexibility in each program, encourage self-discipline, and permit personal involvement in an interest area.

Theodore (Alabama) High School,[34] a six-year secondary school with an enrollment of 1,500 students, lets a student move through more than half of the course offerings as fast as his ability, initiative, and perseverance will permit. Courses are individualized in differing ways for continuous progress: by use of study guides; use of programmed materials, use of individual student assignments; and by use of levels of difficulty within the various instructional programs.

THE STUDENT IN INDEPENDENT STUDY

Students engaged in independent study do their work in many places throughout the school and cover a variety of projects. The student's work may necessitate use of the library, science labs, language labs, conference rooms, resource rooms, listening booths, industrial arts facilities, art rooms, typing rooms, homemaking rooms, guidance offices, photography lab, music rooms—and, in fact, any or all facilities of the school. One school[35] has two "commons areas," furnished with cafeteria tables and chairs, one of which is for quiet study and the other called "the talking commons." Study carrels may be assigned in libraries and study areas as the occasion requires. There is a need for a quantity and variety of equipment and materials such as tapes and tape recorders, filmstrip viewers, motion-picture projectors, overhead projectors, record players, typewriters, reference books, magazines, and paperback books.

The kinds of independent study in which students engage include doing independent research; conferring with a teacher, counselor, or resource person; doing special work on a project in art, industrial arts, or homemaking; writing a research report; conducting an experiment in science; listening to tapes or records; viewing a film or filmstrip; typing reports, and securing remedial help.

Mentioned as highly successful in one program[36] were intensive remedial work; special programs in dramatics and outside speakers; curriculum enrichment by means of noncredit, short-term courses; increased contacts and conferences with guidance and administrative personnel, and advanced research of an original nature.

Specific studies conducted by students in independent-study programs were of many kinds and covered a wide range. A sampling demonstrates the variety. One student worked on an advanced art project, filled a sketchbook with drawings, and produced a mural for the school research center; another student became interested in electronics and built a television receiver. A boy who was interested in dramatics wrote a history of the drama. Others have designed stage settings, written music, plays, and stories and made community surveys.

PROBLEMS

School personnel and students report generally a high level of satisfaction with independent-study programs. Difficulties do arise, however, and these appear to be the more common problems:

1. The student does not meet often enough with the consultant or advisor.
2. The student does not fully accept responsibility for his own work with the result that not enough effort is made nor enough accomplished.
3. Some teachers resist. Actually, it is of interest to note that many changes, modifications, and innovations are reported to have met this same resistance. Many administrators and teachers are disturbed when the customary ways are changed.
4. Some parents are dubious as to the dependability of student effort and as to the quality of learning that occurs.
5. In addition to those teachers who are reluctant to accept change, there are those who honestly do not believe that students will learn as well without attending every fascinating class and lecture.
6. Adequate guidance, counseling, and direction are lacking for the student. This is a developing process; few students in junior high can be thrown completely into a program of independent study without training and preliminary work.

7. There is a need for expanded resources for independent study, as well as increased demand for equipment, materials, and references. Instructional packages which are collections of information, designed and developed by teachers for student use, are most valuable. A package may include use of audio-tape, filmstrip, study guide, and similar materials.
8. There is need for careful allocation of instructional time and personnel—scheduling and teacher planning time.
9. There are problems of evaluation, both of overall goals and of student performance.

RESULTS OF INDEPENDENT STUDY

While some studies have been made in an effort to determine if there has been any measurable improvement in learning, much of what has been concluded is based upon individual perceptions supplemented by reports of use of facilities and reference materials.

It has been reported[37] that one independent-study program finds the library used by 70 percent of the student body every day with proportionate attendance and use of resource centers in art, English, business education, foreign languages, home economics, industrial arts, music, P.E., reading, science, social studies, speech-drama, and mathematics. Students in this program believe that they receive intensive remedial help, have more time free out of school, achieve more, and are developing responsibility.

A comparison[38] of equated groups, one of which followed the conventional program and the other engaged in independent study, found that the independent-study group did as well as or better than the control group in grades achieved, in regents' examinations, and in achievement. There was no measured adverse nor beneficial effect upon creativity. The independent-study group was likely to be more satisfied with school and to show gains in study habits and library skills. A follow-up of those students who went to college indicated that the independent-study group was likely to achieve somewhat higher college grades.

Alexander and Hines[39] note from their experiences that those school personnel who have established a program of independent study favor it overwhelmingly; that only a small number of schools are currently involved in such a program—probably only 1 or 2 percent; that it is probable that independent study should be in effect for all students although it usually reaches only the above average students; that independent study is probably just as practical for junior high as senior high school but the majority of students in such programs are in grades 11 or 12; and that independent-study programs designed for slower students have reduced drop-out rates.

Independent-study programs, although not numerous now, appear to have a promising future. The best learning takes place where there is pupil initiation, motivation, and interest. In the past a real problem has been that teachers' assignments have often left little room for the exercise of initiative. As teachers, pupils, and parents realize what students can achieve with guidance, encouragement, and direction, independent-study programs should multiply at an ever increasing rate.

PROGRAMMED INSTRUCTION

Many junior high schools make extensive use of programmed instruction in a variety of classes. Programmed instruction can be used within a traditional bell schedule, can be a part of team teaching, is most compatible with nongraded schools, and is distinctly a part of independent study. Students may progress at their own speed, and if the program is carefully constructed an enormous number of students can come into contact with one expert.[40] Certainly programmed instruction gives each student individual attention.

There is increased opportunity for independent study, and programmed instruction permits the student to learn more in depth while affording opportunities to investigate topics and materials not presented in class. All of these are desirable characteristics for the junior high school program and for the education of the early adolescent.

Programmed instruction and the various devices that are a part of it have been somewhat strongly acclaimed as innovations that will bring the most sweeping changes to education of any of the recent proposals and technology. In its more sophisticated forms the teaching machine has been accused of making teaching an impersonal process and threatening teacher jobs; it has been branded as another fad, soon to be replaced by something else. It has also been labeled a vogue whose meteoric rise and fall will be only an expensive mistake which has added to the problems of confused teachers.

While some programmed-instruction devices involve only printed material and texts, the common conception of programmed instruction is that of a teaching machine. Perhaps this is one reason for the intense interest in this approach and for its widespread initial acceptance. America is machine-minded and gadget-oriented. We tend to approve machines and appliances and are inclined to believe that machines can do most things better than human beings.

Many people regard programmed instruction as the most important advance in education since the printed textbook, while others have predicted that the teaching machine will eventually replace the teacher. Claims have been made which border on the extravagant. It has been flatly stated that teaching machines can teach more than twice as much in half the time a teacher would take—and do it better; that problems of teaching remedial and advance students are not only reduced but actually eliminated; and that the teaching machine and programmed instruction will administer the ***coup de grâce*** to teaching as we have known it. Specifically, what is meant by programmed instruction, and what is a teaching machine?

WHAT IS PROGRAMMED INSTRUCTION?

"Programmed instruction is a learning experience which is controlled for the most part by the learner and provides the learner with the specific paradigms that will lead him to a predesigned behavioral pattern."[41]

A program may be fed into a machine or it may look like an ordinary text or workbook. In either case the program is so designed that a question is asked at each step and the student must answer the question correctly before proceeding to the next step. The student may be required to fill in a word, to press a key, to solve a problem, or to select the correct answer from a multiple-choice item. The important thing is that the student must eventually select the correct answer and, by finding that this response is correct, his learning is reinforced by immediate knowledge of success before he can go on to the next item. The heart of this kind of instruction lies not in the device or machine but in the program. The program is the subject material to be learned by the student, and properly constructed, it is arranged in progressive levels of difficulty, carefully presented in such a sequence that it leads logically to the most efficient learning and retention.

A unit of programmed instruction is a series of questions arranged in a logically sequential pattern which will lead the learner to a specific desired outcome. It may be arranged in frames, a few or several hundred, and is limited to a specific subject area. A unit is begun by defining precisely what the desired final behavior of the student is to be, and the unit is designed in steps which will achieve this behavior.

Programmed instruction is different in that it permits teaching and learning without the continual presence of a teacher. Whether programmed instruction is more successful with a machine than with printed texts or workbooks has not been settled, although children appear to prefer the machines. This may be because of the gadgetry, the "toy appeal," because it is different and more fun, or simply because machines eliminate turning pages. From a practical point of view, printed materials are less expensive, easier to transport and store, and present fewer problems of use. Whichever is used, the student can check his learning and understanding at any time and correct his errors immediately without the embarrassment of making the wrong oral response in class. Each student, too, has the advantage of being able to move at his own speed. The teacher, instead of attempting to work with the extreme ranges of ability in a normal classroom, is free to move from student to student, helping where help is most needed—a prospect warmly greeted by many teachers and regarded suspiciously by others.

Yet in spite of fears, suspicions, mistakes, cost, and a number of poorly constructed programs, programmed instruction has been on the whole well received. It is probable that well over a million children are learning to some extent in this way at the present time.

CHARACTERISTICS OF PROGRAMS AND MACHINES

The basis for all programmed instruction is that of immediate reinforcement of the correct answer. The student, in receiving immediate knowledge of success, is enabled to learn more rapidly and to retain the knowledge longer. In programmed instruction students *must* succeed. Should an incorrect response be made, it is considered the fault of the program, not the student. There are, it is said, no incorrect answers, only wrong questions.

A properly constructed program will consider

1. Small sequential steps.
2. The necessity of learner response.
3. Student movement at his own rate.
4. Immediate feedback of results.
5. Reinforcement.
6. A record of student errors and successes.
7. Items presented individually.
8. The fact that the program is cheat-proof.

A good teaching machine will:

1. Record results.
2. Automatically advance from one step to the next.
3. Store entire program and responses.
4. Expose but one frame at a time and have a question for the student on each frame.
5. Include a place for student answer.
6. Inform the pupil as to the accuracy of his response.
7. Make the teacher's presence unnecessary.

A machine may be a very simple device smaller than a typewriter, manually operated, and low in cost (also of dubious value in this low price range) or it may be a highly sophisticated, sizable electric wonder with a panel or keyboard that is truly impressive.

KINDS OF PROGRAMS

Two types of programming have received the most attention—that of B. F. Skinner, the "linear" approach, and N. A. Crowder's "branching" programming. The Skinnerian program is characterized by

1. The presentation is in small sequential steps.

2. The unit is in ordered sequence of stimulus items.
3. The student gives his answer which is reinforced if it is correct.
4. The student should make but few mistakes.
5. The learner proceeds directly from what he is supposed to know to what he is supposed to learn from the program.

In the Crowder programming methods—the branching approach—the program frames are of varying length and customarily contain more exposition than does the Skinnerian, sometimes as much as a full page. Because of the length of some of these frames, the design of such teaching machines presents a problem in itself. In the branching technique there are multiple-choice items based upon the expository material which the student reads. He makes his choice, besides which there is a page number to which he refers. If he finds on this page that his answer was correct, he goes on to the next item. If he finds that his answer was erroneous, a number refers him to another page where he discovers what his error was and is told what to do about it. He is then told to go back to the original page and try again. Proponents of the branching method claim several advantages for their technique:

1. In the linear multiple-choice procedure the student is blocked by an incorrect answer and required to guess again. In the branching method the student is told why he is wrong, any misunderstandings are cleared up, and necessary information is provided.
2. The student has some opportunity to choose how deeply he wishes to go into the subject.
3. Branching methods are better for fine discriminations between known alternatives.
4. Branching techniques are superior for dealing with opinions and implications.[42]

Regardless of which method is selected, it is essential that the specific product, which is the end result of the program, be predetermined. The programmer must define the objectives of the program, ". . . including the responses the student should be able to make and the concepts or skills to be learned."[43] The program should be constantly tested and evaluated while it is being constructed. "The idea can be stated most simply: decided what is to be taught, determine the critical criteria, and systematically explore the most effective and efficient means of helping the student meet the criteria."[44]

A complete teaching machine, no matter which method is used, can be quite complicated and should include the following components:

1. The program itself.
2. Storage, the information and questions of the program and learner.
3. A method of display or presentation.
4. A method of student response.

5. A system of pacing, preferably by the student.
6. A method of comparing the response with the correct answer.
7. Feedback, knowledge of results or reinforcement.
8. Collator-recorder, collection and recording of student responses.
9. Selector: directions to the learner as to where to turn following his response.[45]

PROBLEMS AND ADVANTAGES OF PROGRAMMED INSTRUCTION

Although programmed instruction has enjoyed an enthusiastic reception, there are many people who remain unconvinced of its claimed advantages. They point out that most programs today follow the same behavioral approach that Skinner developed in his laboratory several years ago, and this rigid application of laboratory theory to classrooms disturbs them. The complaint is made that people are not white rats nor pigeons. It is further maintained that

1. Programmed instruction discourages critical thinking.
2. Programmed instruction fosters only *rote* learning and memorizing of facts but prevents the student from exploring on his own and discovering basic principles.
3. It is mechanical, monotonous, joyless, and an uninspiring way to learn.
4. Programs often create the impression that there is, for every question, only one correct answer.[46]

There are also fears that programmed instruction will lead to a lockstep curriculum with little concern for the individual; that the trend with this approach is toward mastering facts and concepts with little or no insight; that teachers who now depend heavily upon textbooks will find this an even better way to avoid creative teaching; that the move toward programmed textbooks will tend to solidify the form and concept of programming; that school systems and officials will force untrained, unready, and unwilling teachers to use something they cannot do well; and that too many programs are cranked out hurriedly and in an effort to capture a portion of the market without enough care and planning in their construction. Student interest, running high at first, tends to decrease, especially with those students of higher abilities.

> Even though they had been told that this new learning method gave instruction tailored to individuals, they were quick to see that the only tailoring was in the length of time required to work through the same material that everyone else had to work through. This should not really have surprised them, since textbooks have the same limitations.[47]

It appears that the majority of junior high school students and teachers who try programmed instruction are much in favor of it for the following reasons:

1. It makes learning fun—helps in motivation.
2. There is more teacher time available to work with individuals and small groups.
3. Learning is more rapid.
4. Retention is improved.
5. There is immediate success and achievement.
6. Learning is adapted to individual differences; students can progress at their own rate.
7. Learning is directed toward specific objectives.

Research indicates that children who are taught by programmed instruction do learn effectively although research results are sometimes contradictory. Some of the claims put forward for the success of this technique verge on the fantastic. However, evidence indicates that most students learn at least as well as those taught in the conventional manner, and there is some reason to believe that a good program, properly used, will produce better results than traditional teaching. It also appears that the best usage of programs and teaching machines is that which is in combination with regular teaching, rather than a full-time, all-day exposure to programs. The teaching machine has been said to be at its best in presenting factual material, although Trow observes that it is ". . . probably most effective in symbolic learning, the acquisition and use of appropriate verbal responses to verbal or pictorial stimuli . . . the correct use of words and numbers, the development of concepts, and discriminations in abstract meanings."[48]

IN THE SCHOOLS

Programmed instruction and teaching machines are in use in thousands of schools in every state in the union. A few schools have attempted this technique but for one reason or another have discontinued its use. Yet the great majority of those who have adopted some form of programmed instruction are continuing and expanding its use.

Manhasset Junior High School, Long Island, New York, was one of the first schools to try a programmed text—the English 2600 course. They found that those students who used this text made significantly higher gains than those who did not. The teachers believed that the program was a time-saver, that children needed a teacher available to help them, that less able children needed encouragement to continue, that poor readers were definitely handicapped in this kind of program, that students were inspired to work on the program on their own time, and that use of the program contributed to a more informal classroom atmosphere which was quite desirable.

The Denver schools developed some of their own programs in elementary school Spanish and French as well as using a commercial programmed text in English. There have not been any dramatic results reported, but the staff believes that there is improved teaching and increased learning and that it is worth continuing with programmed instruction.

The Brigham Young University Laboratory School in Provo, Utah, is intensively using various forms of programmed materials in grades K–12 as a part of a continuous progress curriculum. They have found, as did Manhasset Junior High School, that there is some student complaint about "boredom," "dullness," and taking too much time." They have also concluded that use of programmed materials is difficult in a conventional classroom; this requires a greatly changed approach by the teacher. Their conclusions are

1. Programmed instruction is effective and worth continuing.
2. This requires a comprehensive knowledge of the subject by the teacher, since in any given class children will exhibit an extreme range of performance.
3. Programmed instruction requires more, not less, work from the teacher—since he must be prepared to work with many pupils, few if any of whom are at the same place.
4. Children are so variable that it is difficult to write a single program that fits every child.
5. Discipline problems are reduced.
6. Effective learning cannot be expected from all students who use programmed materials.
7. Class participation and contributions of other students are reduced and may be eliminated.[49]

Some other districts reporting the use of programmed instruction include the following. Birmingham, Alabama, algebra in grade 9; Jefferson County, Alabama, foreign language, mathematics, and reading, junior and senior high school; Scottsdale School District, Arizona, research materials, grades 4–8; Berkeley, California, social studies, grades 8 and 9; Covina Valley School District, California, grammar, grade 7; Cupertino, California, all subjects, grades 2–8; Garden Grove, California, physical science, grade 7; Dade County, Florida, geometry, grade 9; Sarasota County, Florida, all subjects, grades 7–9; Chicago, electricity, grade 9; Gary, Indiana, home economics, grade 9; Independence, Missouri, machine shop, grades 10–12; Sewanhaka Central High School District, New York, home economics, grades 7–8; Tulsa, Oklahoma, study skills, grade 7; and Alexandria, Virginia, business mathematics, grades 9–10.

These are but a few of the many reported usages. It is obvious that programmed instruction, in many subjects and at virtually every grade level, has become an important part of American education and is becoming widely used in junior high school education.

LEARNING-MATERIALS CENTERS AND LIBRARIES

The junior high school library is an integral part of the school's educational program and is deeply involved in all approaches to independent study. Traditionally, the school library has served as a place for the housing and use of printed materials such as books, periodicals, pamphlets, government documents, and picture files. The new technology, the knowledge explosion, and the changed approaches to education and instruction require a vastly changed concept of the role and services of the school library—an idea not always well received or implemented by librarians, administrators, and teachers.

The adoption by many junior high schools of such practices as flexible scheduling, large-group–small-group instruction, continuous progress plans, and independent study necessitate a drastically changed concept of what the functions and physical arrangement of the library and learning materials center will be. There is need for such things as quiet study areas, conference rooms, seminar rooms, individual-student study carrels, and material production areas. Since independent study is intended to develop research skills, self-direction, and self-responsibility in the early adolescent, materials, facilities, and assistance must be available.

There is a pronounced shift in the schools from a "textbook-oriented" approach to one that may best be characterized as "materials-oriented." In this concept the library includes all of the school's resources for learning, all instructional materials, audio-visual and printed, as well as the facilities for using and constructing learning materials. It becomes a comprehensive learning and information center for students and faculty with space for audio-visual presentations, individual viewing of films and filmstrips, carrels or booths for listening to tapes, listening rooms for recordings, microfilm viewers and storage, space for use of reading machines and machines for programmed instruction, and space for construction and storage of a variety of curriculum materials.

> Today's libraries and librarians are too much on the fringe of education. Tomorrow they will be in the mainstream. It will be difficult to identify the library in the conventional sense because its services will permeate the totality of education.[50]

To many librarians and principals, broadening the scope of the functions of the libraries and the duties of the librarian is a chilling thought, and with good reason. Most librarians are so mired in paper and clerical work that they literally haven't the time for anything more. In order for this new approach to function, it is necessary for the librarian to be considered as the director of the center—whether it be called the "curriculum-materials center," "instructional-materials center," "learning-materials center," "education center," or the library—and to be given specialized help, which may be noncertificated, for assistance with audio-visual materials and for the construction of curriculum materials.

EVOLVING FUNCTIONS AND USE

All school libraries have and should fulfill certain common and continuing functions. Materials must be acquired, processed, and organized before they are merged into the files and collections of the library. The amount of effort and time devoted to the functions of acquisition, organization, and retrieval varies with the size of the library, but the important need, which is often slighted, is that of service to those who wish to use the facilities of the library. A school library today must be ". . . a centrally organized collection, readily accessible, of many kinds of materials that, used together, enrich and support the educational program of the school."[51]

In the past, the junior high school library has operated almost exclusively as a storage center for printed materials which appealed only to the sense of sight and depended upon the student's skill as a reader to secure the most benefit. The advent of electronic storage of information on magnetic tapes and the optical storage of images on film provide a combined appeal of sight and sound. We are rapidly reaching a point where a machine system which combines human intelligence and electronic and photocopying equipment will gather, classify, and store material and will retrieve and disseminate such information when requested. Indeed, as equipment becomes more sophisticated, the information-retrieval system will channel information to those who have need of certain information but have not yet asked for it. For example, the system would ". . . index the contents of a new document and mathematically select customers whose interest or information-need profiles indicate the content would be of some relevance to them."[52]

The shift of emphasis from group to individualized instruction has pointed up the need for expanded library services and a change in the role of the librarian, who is now expected to be well trained in traditional library practices, knowledgeable in audio-visual equipment and materials, and an instructional-materials expert as well.

The learning-materials center, curriculum center, or library gains its strength from the services offered to its patrons, and should become a source of ideas for curriculum improvement. The learning materials center should include:

1. *Materials collection.* The materials collection should incorporate the

traditional library materials—that is, printed materials in the form of books, magazines, newspapers, pamphlets, and similar materials. In addition there should be a growing collection of maps, charts, globes, films (both 16-mm and 8-mm single-concept films), filmstrips, disk and tape recordings, pictures, slides, prepared transparencies, realia which include three-dimensional objects, museum materials, dioramas, models, and videotapes. As newer media are developed and perfected, they should become a part of the materials collection.

2. *Local production facility.* In the production facility materials and equipment should be available so that charts can be prepared, pictures mounted, transparencies made, filmstrips and slides locally produced, tapes recorded, and models and dioramas constructed. In addition, equipment for the duplication and reproduction of printed material should be available.

3. *Equipment for the effective use of materials.* Equipment for student and teacher use should be available such as 16-mm movie projectors, 8-mm movie projectors and cameras, filmstrip and slide projectors, record players, tape recorders, opaque projectors, overhead projectors, and television sets.

4. *Adequate space to house materials, equipment, and patrons.* Standards for school libraries should be maintained so that sufficient space is provided for students to make use of the traditional materials as well as the newer materials. There should be

(a) A reading room large enough to house at least 10 percent of the students, and future school libraries should be planned with individual accommodations for as many as 75 percent of their readers.
(b) Conference rooms for group planning and discussion.
(c) Studios for listening to disk and tape recordings.
(d) Previewing room for both students and staff.
(e) Individual study areas.
(f) Work areas for processing and repair of library and audio-visual materials.
(g) Storage areas, large enough to house the books and other instructional materials and to allow for normal growth and expansion of materials, equipment and facilities.

5. *An effective cataloguing system and facility.* In order that maximum use may be made of instructional materials it is essential that they be readily available for use. All materials must be catalogued accurately and located for easy access. Sufficient funds should be available so that printed catalogue cards can be obtained for as much of the material as possible, particularly cards for books, films, filmstrips, and recordings. There must be sufficient help available to make instructional materials convenient to use when needed.

THE INSTRUCTIONAL MATERIALS SPECIALISTS

Personnel of instructional materials centers have been classified into three groups: the professionals, the paraprofessionals, and the clerical assistants. The librarian functions as the instructional-media coordinator, the audio-visual coordinator, and the instructional-materials coordinator. The para-professionals include technicians for operating the specialized equipment, artists for preparing the graphics, photographers for preparing local sets of filmstrips and slides, and any other personnel who might serve effectively. Clerical help is used in expediting the materials for the use of the teachers, typing catalogue cards, preparing bibliographies, and in other routine activities of the materials center.

Under this modern educational program for students at the junior high school level, the teacher and the librarian become a closely knit team as the exploratory nature of the junior high school curriculum lends itself to extensive library work. The very nature of the kind of instruction possible in the junior high school necessitates that the students utilize the vast array of materials to be found in an instructional materials center. This envisions a program that is ". . . correlated with all aspects of the curriculum and of each classroom, and is geared to the abilities, needs, and interests of every student and teacher."[53]

Even within a standard bell schedule and a traditional junior high school program, the general education and exploratory offering require increasingly more from the library and resource centers. With the changing concepts of education for early adolescents characterized by flexible schedules, nongraded classes, and the growing stress upon independent study, the junior high school libraries and resource centers find the demands upon them multiplied many fold. Students have more time available to them within the school day—time they can use in many places, the most common being libraries, resource centers, and laboratories. The increasing use of independent-study methods and nongraded classes in the junior high school means that adolescents will not only have more time for work on nongroup assignments, but they will need different facilities in which to work and a much increased quantity and variety of materials of many kinds. Books are only a part of what is needed.

It is often said that high school and college students are poorly prepared to use the library services, and the changing concept of the library and its facilities makes it probably that the difficulties will be magnified. Early adolescents are capable of using the newer approaches to learning, and the junior high school should plan, develop, and put into operation an educational program that trains students to make maximum use of the materials and technology available.

PROBLEMS

Increasing enrollments, shortages of buildings and space, the need for more funds, and the changing approaches to teaching and learning have caught many school libraries unprepared. The difficulties are compounded by those teachers, administrators, and librarians who are reluctant to accept the newer concepts or who guard jealously the materials that they have. Present-day teaching takes for granted that there is a substantial supply of books, magazines, and materials available to students, an assumption that is seldom supported by fact. School libraries too often do not have enough copies of specific titles or other reference materials, and the usual restrictions and rules on use only aggravate the situation.

In some cases the school librarian has so possessive an attitude that students find it easier to do without, or to use the public library. Rules for usage of school libraries occasionally verge on the ridiculous. For example, one junior high school student who had checked out a book, renewed it, and had reached the end of the time allowed was told that he could no longer retain the book. He could, however, check out the second copy of the same title, which was identical to the first, and retain it for both the check-out and renewal period. Thus the school librarian and the rules were satisfied. A ruling that proclaims that students may use only certain volumes or enter the library only if they have a pass signed by a specific teacher may preserve the sanctity of the library but it discourages student use. The library is frequently referred to as the "heart of the educational program," yet some librarians appear to consider it to be a distinct nuisance if books are taken from the orderly arrangement on the shelves, and they create the impression that they are doing the students a favor if they permit books and materials to be checked out.

Fortunately there are schools and librarians who regard their function as that of contributing the most to the education of the students. Highland Park High School, Topeka, Kansas, introduces its library services by saying, "If you can carry it out the door, you can check it out. We'll check out everything but the card catalog and the librarians."[54]

The library staff at Highland Park reports that students and teachers are using the library materials more and depending less upon textbooks. Reference books may be checked out overnight and quality films, books, recordings, periodicals, study and art prints, tape recorders, phonographs with headsets, microfilm readers, filmstrip viewers, and loop projectors are available for varying lengths of time.

Schools that have made materials accessible on a check-out basis report that vandalism, theft, and mutilation of materials are much reduced or even eliminated. Perhaps this misuse and abuse of materials and facilities is a major reason for the suspicion so often displayed by school officials and librarians and contribute heavily to the restrictive rules. Too, library staffs are notoriously short of help and funds and are also in need of a closer working relationship with teachers. It is probable that every junior high school librarian on the job has had difficulties with teachers who send one student or several or even the entire class to the library for the librarian to "help." Teachers are also notorious for making assignments without telling the students what it is that they are to use as references and, even worse, without prior investigation to see what materials are available.

It sometimes seems that libraries are operated for the convenience of the school staff rather than as a major adjunct to the teaching process. Rules that prohibit student use of the library until several days or weeks after the beginning of the school year and rules that require all library materials to be returned as much as two or three weeks before the closing of school are completely unjustified. There is a real need for all school personnel to understand the functions and potentials of the library, as witness the teacher who told a student, "You have already been to the library twice this week and that's enough for anyone."

Delays in reshelving of materials and failure to centralize location of related materials are common faults and are also unjustified. School libraries are further criticized because of the hours they keep. Many junior high schools open the libraries a few minutes before the first -class period of the day, restrict access during the lunch period, and close their doors shortly after school ends for the day. School libraries, presumably, acquire materials specifically intended to be used by students in their studies and may be expected to have a concentration of materials, printed and otherwise, unavailable to the same extent at the public library. Yet it often takes a very determined or extremely lucky student to locate and use the materials he needs.

A considerable part of this problem is attributable to the location of the library within the school. Since the library is said to be the "hub of the school," it is often so situated as to be difficult of access during out-of-school hours. This same policy of central location may be responsible for the inability of some schools to expand their library facilities to meet the needs of rising enrollments and the newer, more comprehensive concept of the learning materials center.

Not enough money is budgeted in many cases for materials or staff although it is also true that services suffer for lack of leadership, lack of foresight and vision, and a distinct shortage of trained professional librarians. This is a particular problem in the junior high school where so often there is no one available to serve as librarian or coordinator of a learning materials center, and the administration finds it necessary to assign a teacher to the task. If the school is fortunate, the assigned teacher is conscientious, interested, and may even take some courses in library techniques. If the school is not so lucky, the position is filled by a reluctant teacher who has little idea of what she is doing and is merely holding the line while she eagerly anticipates the end of the school year.

Research indicates that children in schools with centralized libraries that are staffed by professional librarians show evidence of improved achievement in reading and even a greater educational gain than do those students in schools without libraries. Until a substantial and perceptible effort is made to improve the junior high school libraries, train more librarians, budget more funds, revise the attitudes of a number of teachers and administrators, and adopt the changing concepts and approaches in library and learning-materials-center ideas, the junior high school libraries will not contribute more than a fraction of their potential to the education of our children.

SUMMARY

Independent-study programs appear to be proving their effectiveness. With current interest in flexible scheduling, staff utilization, and large-group–small-group work, the opportunities to develop independent-study programs will proliferate. Students who engage in such programs appear to be more highly motivated and develop a perceptible degree of self-reliance, self-direction, and improved study skills. While most independent-study programs have been instituted on the senior high school level, there have been successful efforts with junior high students. It seems likely that students are capable of more self-direction and that they have more potential for independent work than has been credited them. Most independent-study programs involve the more able students but there is reason to believe that the majority of junior high school students can participate in such a program with profit. The position of the teacher in independent-study programs is more likely to be that of a guide rather than one who tells.

The use of programmed materials and machines to assist in teaching is growing rapidly. The changing approaches to education and the new technology may be aiming for some such instructional devices as are afforded by the experimental "automated classroom."

The Systems Development Corporation has recently developed a complete educational facility that would have been regarded a few short years ago as a science-fiction fantasy. Designated CLASS (for Computer-based Laboratory for Automated School Systems), the system permits simultaneous automated instruction of 20 students, each of whom receives an individualized sequence of instructional materials adapted to his particular needs, or learns in a group mode of instruction mediated by the teacher or computer. Each student is provided with a manually operated film viewer that holds 2,000 frames of instructional material. He also has a response device connected to a computer which designates the sequence of slides to be viewed by the student, permits the student to respond to questions, and informs him immediately of the accuracy of his answers. The computer keeps performance records of each student, and these records are made available to the school staff. An added feature is the console that each teacher uses, which indicates the current progress of any student or group of students. There are even automatic alarm lights that call the teacher's attention to those students who are having difficulty. CLASS also permits instruction by television, films, and slides, as well as use of the traditional lecture and textbook methods. The computer will store and prepare student attendance, curriculum, and grade records, and provide simultaneous student scheduling and registration. Those who dread the dangers of mechanical instruction can imagine a galaxy of horrors with automation of this magnitude in the classroom, although they may take some comfort from the fact that a teacher is still necessary to work with the students.

Programmed instruction, whether by printed materials or by use of teaching machines, has in a matter of a very few years been enthusiastically adopted by a large number of teachers and school districts. In programmed instruction the student reads some expository material and then responds to a question before he goes on. He must give the correct response before he may proceed. There are two main ways of building a program: Skinnerian, which is linear, and that of N.A. Crowder, which is the branching approach. Each has its advocates.

Advantages claimed for programmed instruction include faster learning, more retention, more teacher time available for helping students, and a more enjoyable learning experience. Critics (and there are many) maintain that programmed instruction is dull, boring, stifles student independent thought and investigation, emphasizes factual information and recall, and that too many programs are sloppy, poorly constructed, and turned out in too much of a hurry.

Current trends in education suggest an expanded role for the junior high school library and the school librarian. New and better ways of recording and retrieving information have been proposed, researched, attempted, and developed, but a major problem is the delay by school personnel in adopting the newer practices and technology. In the changed concept, the library has a broader role and broader functions and may even have a changed name: curriculum center, learning-materials center, or instructional-materials center. Whatever the title, the library now finds itself responsible for more than printed materials. It includes a spectrum of audio-visual devices and materials in addition to facilities for the production of instructional materials.

REFERENCES

1. Gardner Swenson, "The Brookhurst Junior High School Program," in David W. Beggs III and Edward G. Buffie (eds.), *Independent Study.* Bold New Venture Series. Bloomington, Ind.: Indiana U. P., 1965.
2. William M. Alexander, Vynce A. Hines, and associates, *Independent Study in Secondary Schools.* New York: Holt, 1967, p. 3.
3. Robert M. Gagne, "Learning Research and Its Implications for Independent Learning," in Gerald T. Gleason (ed.), *The Theory and Nature of Independent Learning* Scranton, Pa.: International Textbook, 1967, p. 20.
4. *Loc. cit.*
5. *Ibid.*, pp. 20–21.
6. *Ibid.*, p. 22.
7. *Ibid.*, p. 31.
8. Pauline Sears, "Implications of Motivation Theory for Independent Learning," in Gleason, *The Theory and Nature of Independent Learning, op. cit.*
9. *Ibid.*, pp. 47–48.
10. Avram S. Goldstein, "Does Homework Help?" *Elementary School Journal,* Vol. 60 (January 1960), pp. 212–224.
11. Albert D. Waterman, "Homework—Curse or Blessing?" *NASSP Bulletin,* Vol. 49 (January 1965), pp. 42–46.
12. "Homework in the Junior High School—Position Papers," *NASSP Bulletin,* Vol. 47 (October 1963), p. 16.
13. James B. Conant, *Education in the Junior High School Years.* Princeton, N.J.: Educational Testing Service, 1960, 28.
14. "Position Papers," *op. cit.*, p. 17.
15. Margaret Epps, "Homework," *NEA Research Summary,* Washington, D.C., 1966.
16. Grace Langdon and Irving W. Stout, "What Parents Think of Homework," *NEA Journal,* Vol. 52 (December 1963), pp. 9–11.
17. John F. Check, "Homework—Is It Needed?" *The Clearing House,* Vol. 41 (November 1966), pp. 143–147.
18. Williard Abraham, *A Time for Teaching.* New York: Harper, 1964, p. 304.
19. *Ibid.*, p. 306.
20. V. A. Hines, "Homework and Achievement in Plane Geometry," *Mathematics Teacher,* Vol. 50 (January 1957), pp. 27–29.
21. Abraham, *loc. cit.*
22. R. L. Schain, "Another Homework Experiment in Social Studies," *High Points,* Vol. 36 (February 1954), pp. 5–12.
23. Check, *op. cit.*, p. 145.
24. M. Dale Baughman and Wesley Pruitt, "Supplemental Study for Enrichment vs. Supplemental Study for Reinforcement of Academic Achievement," *NASSP Bulletin,* Vol. 47 (March 1963), pp. 154–157.

25. Judith Murphy, *Middle Schools,* monograph. New York: Educational Facilities Laboratories, 1965.
26. James B. MacDonald, "Independent Learning," in *The Theory and Nature of Independent Learning, op. cit.,* p. 2.
27. Janet Whitmire, "The Independent Study Program at Melbourne High," *Phi Delta Kappan,* Vol. 47 (September 1965), pp. 43–46.
28. Don H. Richardson, "Independent Study: What Difference Does It Make?" *NASSP Bulletin,* Vol 51 (September 1967), pp. 53-62.
29. Alexander, Hines, et al., *op. cit.,* p. 26.
30. *Ibid.,* p. 46.
31. Allan J. Glatthorn and J. E. Ferderbar, "Independent Study—For *All* Students," *Phi Delta Kappan,* Vol. 47 (March 1966), pp. 379–382.
32. *Ibid.,* p. 382.
33. Joe A. Richardson and Donald G. Cawelti, "Junior High Program Lets Fast and Slow Students Take Time for Independent Study," *Nation's Schools,* Vol. 79 (February 1967), pp. 76–77.
34. John W. Jackson, "The Individualized School," *The Journal of Secondary Education,* Vol. 41 (May 1966), pp. 195–200.
35. Glatthorn and Ferderbar, *op. cit.,* p. 379.
36. *Ibid.,* p. 380.
37. *Ibid.,* p. 381.
38. Richardson, *op. cit.*
39. Alexander and Hines, *op. cit.*
40. Frances Olsen, "Programmed Learning in the Non-Graded School," in Allen D. Calvin (ed.), *Programmed Instruction,* Bold New Venture Series. Bloomington, Ind.: Indiana U. P., 1969.
41. Kent E. Myers, "What Do We know About Programmed Instruction," *Clearing House,* Vol. 39 (May 1965), p. 533.
42. William Clark Trow, *Teacher and Technology.* New York: Meredith, 1963, p. 101.
43. Myers, *op. cit.*
44. Gerald Gleason, "Will Programmed Instruction Serve People?" *Educational Leadership,* Vol. 23 (March 1966), p. 479.
45. Trow, *op. cit.,* pp. 104–105.
46. Richard Margolis, "Programmed Instruction: Miracle or Menace?" in Alfred deGrazia and David A. Sohn (eds.), *Revolution in Teaching.* New York: Bantam Books, 1964, p. 112.
47. W. Lee Garner, *Programmed Instruction.* New York: Center for Applied Research in Education, Inc., 1966, p. 41.
48. Trow, *op. cit.,* p. 109.
49. Jack V. Edling, "Programmed Instruction in a Continuous Progress School," in *Four Cases of Programmed Instruction.* New York: Fund for the Advancement of Education, 1964.
50. J. Lloyd Trump, "Changing Concepts of Instruction and the School Library as a Materials Center," *The School Library as a Materials Center.* Washington, D.C.: Government Printing Office, 1963, p. 6.
51. Eleanor E. Ahlers, "Library Service: A Changing Concept," *Educational Leadership,* Vol. 23 (March 1966), p. 452.

52. Don D. Bushnell, "Computers in Education," in Ronald Gross and Judith Murphy, *The Revolution in the Schools.* New York: Harcourt, 1964, p. 64.
53. Ahlers, *op. cit.*, p. 453.
54. Michael Printz, "High School Library Plus," *NEA Journal,* Vol. 57 (February 1968), p. 29.

part VI

THE MEASURE OF A SCHOOL

In one way or another all institutions undergo constant evaluation from virtually every member of the community. The junior high school is no exception to this rule. Like all public schools, it will find that it receives continual and often critical evaluation from the community, from parents, students, teachers, administration, the senior high schools, state departments of education, accrediting associations, and even colleges and universities.

This is good and serves a most useful purpose. Evaluation affords numerous incentives for instructional improvement, although it is better for a school to embark upon periodic formal evaluations rather than operating on a piecemeal basis inspired by the latest local editorial or phone call. Involving as many people as possible and making use of a well-constructed evaluation instrument provides many unexpected benefits. Although an evaluation points up strengths and weaknesses and makes recommendations, the greatest benefit afforded is the self-study by the staff over a period of months. This may well be the strongest encouragement for improvement of instruction within the school and the professional growth of the faculty.

chapter 19

Evaluation of the Junior High School

Evaluation, whether formal or informal, is a never-ending and continuous process, since evaluation of the schools by people in the community—administrators, teachers, students, and parents—occurs every day. All aspects of education have been receiving more general scrutiny and evaluation in the last two decades, and the junior high schools have received more than their share of the resulting criticism. Part of the blame for this criticism may be laid directly at the doors of those junior high schools that have had no planned and formal evaluation of their own programs and are therefore unable to state precisely their philosophy, purposes, and functions. Nor do they really know which of their practices and procedures need improvement, or how effective the successful aspects of their program are. A great many junior high school teachers and administrators see no need for formal evaluation procedures and do not want evaluations in their buildings.

These people have missed the point. They actually do not have a choice as to whether or not they will be evaluated, because this occurs every time any individual or group in the community takes any action regarding the junior high school, be it a vote on a school levy, attending a PTA meeting, or joining in a discussion over a cup of coffee. Every time a parent asks a child what he did in school that day, every news item that relates to the school or to the behavior of the students on the street and in public places —in all of these there is evaluation of the school. There is no choice as to being evaluated or not being evaluated, but there is a choice between an evaluation that is

> . . . a planned, organized and systematic one, effectively done by members of the professional staff, producing an accurate appraisal of the school program; or whether it be left to the incidental, unorganized, fragmented,

uniformed approach by citizens in a community drawing upon limited information and experience.[1]

Put simply, the staff of a junior high school needs to evaluate the program, the school, and themselves, so that they may know where they have been, at what point they have arrived, and thus have a planned idea of where they are going.

WHAT IS EVALUATION?

Evaluation is sometimes used as though it were synonymous with measurement. It is not. Measurement involves the collection and analysis of data, as with an achievement-test score, while evaluation goes a step further by placing a value upon the collected data and reaching a conclusion concerning its worth.

In past years educational measurement focused upon efforts to determine the degree of intelligence possessed by someone or upon development of tests of achievement. Since achievement of knowledge and skills taught in the classroom was most easily demonstrated and determined, measurement became concerned primarily with quantitative efforts to ascertain the extent of acquisition of subject matter—that is, the extent of factual memorization. As we have increased our knowledge of the learner and of the learning process, our concept of evaluation has grown to include appraisal of a much broader range of educational experiences and activities, including concern with school sites, buildings, facilities, staff, and curriculum.

Thus the current concept of evaluation in the junior high school is one that considers the contemporary goals of education, current knowledge of the characteristics of early adolescents and how they learn, and understanding of the influence of the environment and previous experiences upon the student, present educational programs, and an awareness of innovations in education. Evaluation therefore is concerned with all aspects of the junior high school program, curricular and extracurricular. Evaluation is a comprehensive, continuous, inclusive, and cooperative process of review, to be interpreted in terms of determining the extent to which stated purposes, goals, and standards have been or are being achieved. This process of inquiry attempts to measure a comprehensive range of objectives of the junior high school rather than being limited to subject-matter achievement. It endeavors to place a value upon a situation by selecting criteria—to present an inclusive portrait of the school.

PURPOSES OF EVALUATION

To be useful, evaluation must conform to the basic requirements of sound research and appraisal, and the purpose of a specific evaluation must be established before the process begins. Essentially, the purpose of an evaluation includes the following elements:

1. To ascertain if this particular junior high school program is acceptable in terms of the accepted functions of the junior high school, in accordance with what this specific school is trying to achieve (its philosophy and objectives), and in terms of the degree to which it meets the needs of its own student population. This requires that the evaluator must set aside his own predispositions and use for appraisal the explicit statements made by the school.

> It is obviously unfair to say that a school is of poor quality because it does not prepare students for further academic work when, in fact, it interprets its function as that of preparing youth to take the next step, whether that be in an academic, technical, or vocational field. . . . A school can hardly be considered a good school if it is responsible for the education of all the youth in the community and yet offers a program in which only a highly selected part . . . can make satisfactory progress.[2]

2. Since evaluation points up desirable practices, procedures, and objectives for the junior high school to follow, it fosters at least minimum standards of excellence and injects new spirit into the school's statement of philosophy and objectives.

3. Evaluation helps to ascertain the effectiveness of the junior high school program. There is, as one might expect, frequently a wide difference between expressed goals and actual achievement and performance. Self-study and self-evaluation are excellent and essential, but use of some outside personnel will help to attain more objectivity in determining causes for success and failure of various aspects of the program.

4. Self-evaluation, by interchange, cooperation, group involvement, and self-study, results in desirable interdisciplinary exchange among the faculty, and an increased awareness of what others are doing. Because of this staff participation, any changes and improvements made are more likely to have significance and to endure.

5. Evaluation looks more deeply into a program than figures that report averages. For example, a junior high school in a neighborhood that is well up the socioeconomic scale with a high percentage of above-average students may report a high average of achievement based upon standardized test scores. Yet the school may be providing inadequate programs for low achievers and remedial children.

6. Evaluation, particularly that which involves personnel from outside the school, does more than point out strengths and weaknesses. It also supplies indications for ways to overcome the weaknesses, extend the strengths, and improve the overall educational program.

7. The self-study phase of an evaluation, by its need for information not always kept available by a junior high school, develops increased understanding of the students and the community by the staff. For example, every junior high school should know how many actual dropouts there are each school year and the reasons for them. It is also desirable to know the number

of students from the junior high school who drop out during their senior high school years, and the reasons that they leave school early.

8. The emergence, recognition, and definition of various needs in the junior high school program encourage teachers to initiate innovations and change that they might otherwise be slow to attempt.

The successful junior high school evaluation requires a completely objective approach, full cooperation of all involved, and a thoroughly comprehensive examination of all parts of the school program. Since few aspects of education end with evaluation, the process must continue beyond the conclusion of the formal evaluation. Follow-up, to make recommended changes and improvement, is essential, for it is of little value to locate weak spots and undesirable procedures unless steps are taken to remedy them.

THE EVALUATORS

A number of individuals, groups, and agencies are available to assist in and conduct an evaluation of the junior high school, but regardless of which group is selected for this purpose, the staff of the particular school will profit most from the self-study that precedes the actual visit.

One approach to evaluation is that of using the entire staff of the school as a part of the evaluation team and drawing upon various people in the community to complete the group. It is often advantageous when using a local group as evaluators to include one or more of the central office personnel and some senior high school teachers. Parents and other members of the community may well be included, since they are continually evaluating the school in any event, usually without adequate data. Since personnel of the senior high school are often inclined to blame the junior high school for deficiencies they observe in their students, and to regard the junior high school as a preparatory institution for the senior high, serving as members of an evaluation team can easily expand their views. When the evaluators are all local people, however, their perceptions and understandings of what the junior high school can and should do may be limited and tend to lose objectivity.

State departments of education, by establishing criteria for approval of junior high school programs, set up minimal standards for state accreditation. Schools that meet such minimum standards presumably operate acceptable programs. Since this kind of accreditation generally depends upon written reports that are usually completed by the junior high school principal, there is little opportunity for self-study or in-depth evaluation. A better procedure involves the use of a number of state department specialists, personnel from other school districts in the state, and some members of college and university departments of education to make up the group. Such an evaluation team provides a wide spectrum of specialties and talents and has the added advantages of increased objectivity and a knowledge of worthwhile practices in other schools.

In recent years there has been some interest displayed in having the evaluation conducted by state associations of secondary school principals. California's State Association of Secondary School Administrators, for example, developed its own criteria for approval of junior high schools, called *Procedures for Appraising the Modern Junior High School.* In emphasizing the involvement of the total school staff and representatives of the community, the California procedure called for the establishment of four study committees—administration, instructional staff, classified staff, and students—all of which work independently of each other but are coordinated by a steering committee composed of the four subcommittee chairmen. Upon completion of the work by the subcommittees, the school is visited by a committee of five with representatives from a college or university, a county school office, the California State Department of Education, together with a secondary school administrator, and a curriculum specialist. The visiting committee spends not less than two days in the school studying the total school program. At the conclusion of the visit, the visiting committee, having examined the reports of the four local committees, meets with the four groups, makes a report to them, and discusses the evaluation. The primary purpose of the visiting team and their written report is to help the staff of the evaluated junior high school to perceive more clearly their own strengths and weaknesses, and to make suggestions for improvement.

The six regional accrediting associations, nonprofit, voluntary, and professional in nature, are unique to the United States. They do not attempt to accredit all schools and at this time only two of these agencies accredit junior high schools as well as senior high schools. The North Central Association of Colleges and Secondary Schools, the largest of the six associations, has developed its own document, *Policies, Principles, and Standards for the Approval of Junior High Schools.* Junior high schools seeking accreditation by the North Central Association must:

1. Examine carefully the Policies, Principles, and Standards with consideration for the implications of these for improvement of the junior high school's program.
2. Apply to the North Central's State Chairman for junior high schools for approval of the self-study instrument the school wishes to use and for any consultant service considered necessary for the self-study.
3. The staff of the junior high school conducts a self-study that should take several months and perhaps as much as a year.
4. Be visited by an evaluation team whose chairman has been trained in conducting such a visit.
5. "Satisfy the North Central conditions for continuing membership through an orderly and sustained plan for growth and development

of its educational program. These conditions will be reflected through a system of established reporting."[3]

EVALUATION INSTRUMENTS

Several self-evaluation instruments have been developed for use in junior high schools, the majority of them since the middle 1950's. Some of these are:

1. *Procedures for Appraising the Modern Junior High School* (Burlingame, Calif.: California Association of Secondary School Principals, 1960).
2. *A Manual of Evaluation for a Junior High School* (Oklahoma City: State Department of Public Instruction, 1959).
3. *Junior High School Evaluative Criteria* (Salt Lake City: Utah State Department of Public Instruction, 1959).
4. *Criteria for Evaluating Junior High Schools*, The Texas Study of Secondary Education, Research Study No. 37 (Austin: University of Texas, 1963).
5. *Descriptive Analysis for New Jersey Junior High Schools: A Device for Assisting in Evaluation Procedures* (Trenton: New Jersey Department of Education, 1958).
6. *An Assessment Guide for Use in Junior High Schools* (Hartford: Connecticut State Department of Education, June 1960).
7. *Evaluative Criteria for Junior High Schools* (Washington, D.C.: National Study of Secondary School Evaluation, 1963).
8. *Evaluating the Elementary School—A Guide for Cooperative Study* (Atlanta, Ga.: Southern Association of Colleges and Secondary Schools, 1951).
9. *Evaluative Criteria for Junior High and Middle Schools* (Washington, D. C.: National Study of Secondary School Evaluation, 1970).

All of these instruments stress self-study, self-appraisal, improvement of instruction, and as much involvement as is possible of all personnel concerned. Probably the best known of these is the *Evaluative Criteria for Junior High Schools*, developed by the National Study of Secondary School Evaluation. In its original form it was criticized as being unwieldy; slanted too much toward a senior high school program; not sufficiently raising significant questions concerning the staff's statements about philosophy, function, and needs; and being (sometimes) inadequate for the purpose intended.

Those schools that use *The Evaluative Criteria* usually order one or more sets of forms to be filled in by the staff in the self-study. The topics covered by the *Evaluative Criteria* (1963 ed.) are as follows.

1. *Philosophy, Objectives, and Functions.* The philosophy and objectives are to be determined and developed by each school although the six func-

tions developed by Gruhn and Douglass are accepted as the basis to which each school responds; i.e.,

> The junior high school will provide, for all students, constructive experiences in group activity. Programs will be planned to provide for both leadership and cooperation. An important goal will be that of assisting each student to increase his capacity to adjust to different types of people and to various situations.[4]

Following this statement is a space for the school to make comments relative to what they are doing to meet this function.

2. *School and Community.* This section asks for information concerning enrollment by grades over a period of five years, age-grade distribution, distribution of student IQ scores and uses of such tests as have been given, dropouts and transfers, educational intentions as stated by the students, and a number of questions relative to basic data regarding the community.

3. *The Educational Program.* The first section is concerned with the program of studies and is a somewhat general investigation of school organization, curriculum development procedures, extent of subject offerings, general characteristics of the program, comments about instructional activities, methods of evaluation, anticipated outcomes of the program of studies, special characteristics of the program of studies, and a general evaluation of the program of studies.

Each of these categories has a number of questions relating to the major heading, i.e., "Instructional Activities," "Community resources are used to enrich the instructional program," and those conducting the self study are expected to rate each question on a scale of 1 (poor) to 5 (excellent). The rating may also be M (missing) or N (does not apply). (In some parts of the Evaluative Criteria, there are check lists that require one of the following responses:

E Extensive provision or condition
S Some or moderate provision is made
L Limited provision made but is needed
M Provision or condition is missing but its need is questioned in this instance
N Not desirable or does apply.

As subcategories of the Program of Studies there are sections for

Art (including crafts)
Business Education
Core Program
English
Foreign Languages
Health Education
Home Economics
Industrial Arts
Mathematics
Music
Physical Education
Science
Social Studies

Each of these subcategories has several pages of questions that require respondents to come to value judgments and make ratings, i.e., "How extensive is the variety of experiences in speech?" or, "How adequate is the staff's preparation in English?"

(a) The student activity program. This section is concerned with the general nature of the program, organization, student government, service activities, publications, music activities, dramatics and speech, social life and activities, physical activities, clubs, finances, and special characteristics. There are questions relating to quality of offerings, variety, and student participation.

(b) *Instructional Materials Services—Library and Audio-Visual.* As the name suggests, this section is concerned with facilities, equipment, and use of audio-visual materials.

(c) Guidance Services

(d) Health Services

4. *School Plant.* This section asks for ratings and evaluations about the site, the buildings, lighting, heat control, water and sanitation, ventilation, classrooms, building services, special rooms, offices, buses, special characteristics of the school plant, and general evaluation of the school plant.

5. *School Staff and Administration.* This section is concerned with numerical adequacy, preparation, duties, functions, qualifications, leadership, selection of staff, experience and length of service, staff practices of self improvement, salaries and salary schedules, teaching load policy, tenure, leaves of absence, dismissal policies, pupil accounting, reports to parents, school finance, school schedule, community relations, and special characteristics of staff and administration.

6. Each individual staff member is to fill out a form that reports the individual's schedule, academic preparation, professional education courses, professional activities, teaching and student activity load, and teaching activities.

The summary section provides for a statistical summary and a graphic summary of much of the previous information presented.

As a comparison to *The Evaluative Criteria,* a committee of the Texas Association of Secondary School Principals developed a modified criteria that was felt to be more applicable to their schools and has the following sections, each section containing and "Overview" and "Criteria":

1. School Community and Pupil Population
2. Junior High School Administration
3. School Plant, Facilities, and Equipment
4. The Staff
5. The Junior High School Pupil
6. The Educational Program, (this starts with "The Core Program" and then lists all subjects considered likely to be offered in a junior high school)

7. Library Services
8. Pupil Activities
9. Guidance Services
10. Provision for Potential Dropouts
11. Staff Utilization Practices
12. Bibliography

The Connecticut State Department of Education *Assessment Guide* is made up of five major sections that are broken down into subgroups:

1. Who are our pupils?
2. What is our philosophy?
3. What program does this philosophy require? (The six functions of Gruhn and Douglass are listed here with several items for each.)
4. What staff does our program require?
5. What physical plant does this program require?

There is a list of criterion items utilized as standards for evaluations in each category with a place to check "5" (superior), "4" (excellent), "3" (adequate), "2" (inadequate), and "1" (not provided).

One rather unusual characteristic of the *Assessment Guide* is that it attempts to focus attention upon the functions of the junior high school and appraise each aspect of the curriculum as it is relevant to these functions, rather than evaluating each subject separately. This approach eliminates any restriction to a specific type of curriculum organization and encourages variation, innovation, and experimentation.

Some educators suggest that the junior high schools develop and use questionnaires with parents, students, and teachers. When these are carefully constructed and everyone understands precisely what is being attempted, this approach is quite valuable. Questionnaires should, however, be used as adjuncts to some evaluative instrument—not in place of it.

THE PROCESS

Regardless of what group is doing the evaluating or which instrument is used, the process of evaluation will be quite similar.

1. A steering committee is selected. (It is better to leave administrators off this committee and encourage teacher leadership and involvement.)
2. All members of the staff participate in writing the philosophy, objectives, and functions of the school.
3. Every member of the staff is involved with some aspect of the evaluation, plus such students and others as have been invited to participate.
4. All reports and forms are completed and returned to the steering committee.
5. If there is a visiting team, a two- or three-day evaluation visit is made.

6. The visiting team writes its report and this is sent to the school visited.
7. The staff follows up on recommendations made.

A common problem in evaluation is one of staff fears, uneasiness, and defensiveness. It is interesting to note that teachers apparently have no difficulty in marking students with fine precision on a 100-point scale, and can readily differentiate between an A (93), and a B (92). Yet many teachers become disturbed about being rated on a broad four- or five-point scale.

Another problem is that of underevaluation. Staff members, whether through apprehension or ignorance of other programs, are more inclined to underrate what they are doing than to overrate it. This has the advantage of permitting more positive statements by the visiting team, but it can make the staff feel that their teaching is not very good when they are conducting the self study.

Some staff members are reluctant to fill in and complete the self-study forms. This can pose a real problem since the evaluation, to be of the most value, must be as complete as is possible.

There is sometimes a problem when an autocratic principal fills in all forms himself or tells the staff how to complete them. This is not a self-study and provides but little benefit, if any, from the evaluation.

A different kind of difficulty arises when a number of a visiting team evalutes a school on the basis of his own feelings and beliefs rather than upon the school's self-developed statement of philosophy, objectives, and functions. This is not the time for a visitor to try to convert the unbelievers by critical comments. His task is to ascertain how well this particular junior high school is accomplishing what it has said it is trying to accomplish.

SUMMARY

Every junior high school can profit from evaluation. Such evaluation should be continuous, comprehensive, and involve cooperatively all members of the staff. There are several instruments available for the purpose of evaluating a junior high school, and a staff may, if it wishes, construct its own instrument, although this is time-consuming, difficult, and requires much effort.

A specific evaluation has as its greatest benefit the self-study conducted by a staff before a visiting team arrives. When a staff realizes that evaluation is for the purpose of instructional improvement and not intended as a destructive or negative device, much good can ensue. Follow-up of recommendations made must be a part of the valuation process, and evaluation must not end with the one specific effort.

REFERENCES

1. Donald C. Manlove, "Evaluation for Junior High Schools," *Indiana State University Teacher's College Journal*, Vol. 39 (November 1967), p. 70.
2. *Evaluative Criteria for Junior High Schools.* Washington, D.C.: National Study of Secondary School Evaluation, 1963, p. 4.
3. *Policies, Principles, and Standards for the Approval of Junior High Schools.* Chicago: North Central Association of Colleges and Secondary Schools, 1968, p. 5.
4. *Evaluative Criteria*, p. 33.

chapter 20

The School in the Middle

The junior high school came into being in the early 1900's for a number of reasons, many of which are now much changed or no longer exist. Emerging as a result of the problems and pressures of those times, the junior high school has seen its functions modified through the years; some, such as prevocational training, being virtually eliminated and others given more emphasis. This is as it should be. The purpose of the junior high school is to provide the best education possible for the preadolescent and the early adolescent. Conditions change, people change, and the junior high school must evolve and adapt to the changes. The school in the middle must truly be dynamic; it must be ready to attempt innovations, willing to experiment with new procedures and concepts, and be prepared to admit the possibility that differing grade organizational patterns may be more effective than the traditional 6-3-3 plan in the education of the early adolescent.

Among the many serious problems and issues affecting the junior high school, surely the most critical is the need for this institution to be honestly and actively reorganized as the middle division of a system of education that is composed of three segments: elementary, middle, and secondary. Recognition of the fact that this is a distinctly different and separate unit, neither elementary nor secondary, as unique in its way as they are in theirs, will result in alleviation of many of the problems of the junior high school, and even the solution of some.

When responsible educators make statements such as, "The junior high school concept is being seriously challenged," or, "The junior high school is an unfinished dream" or, "The junior high school is American education's biggest blunder," or, "The junior high school is a poor investment," then it is long past time to break with the past, improve what we have, or develop something better. It is curious that the junior high school, which has only been established for approximately sixty years, should be so conscious of tradition as to resist change to much of what is new. High schools change slowly—much more slowly than do the elementary schools. It is probable that the junior high school, again, is reflecting its high school preceptions and inclinations.

MIDDLE SCHOOLS

The rapidly increasing interest in middle schools is attributable to a number of factors. Certainly the speed of its growth, the number of districts adopting such a plan, and the numerous publications and surveys on this topic indicate a disenchantment with the traditional junior high school and a wish to develop something better. Most suggested remedies for the ailments of the 6-3-3 plan are intended to treat the ills of the present structure; middle school advocates propose an altered school organizational plan that will attack the roots of the problem by establishing a truly distinct middle unit.

Some frenetic and extravagant statements have been made relative to moving the ninth grade back to the high school and bringing grade 6 (or grades 5 and 6) up into the middle school. One educator, for instance, states flatly that the most important factor to be considered is "the institutional focus." Organizations that have no institutional focus, he says, can easily become revolutionary in nature. "Witness, for example, the loss of institutional integrity which is threatened by a 5–8 middle school organization that has emerged in response to the problem of de facto racial segregation."[1]

The middle school is emerging and gaining acceptance, not as a response to de facto segregation, but in response to the many concerns indicated by parents and educators alike relative to the claimed failure of the junior high school to provide the best education possible for early adolescents. Too many of those in junior high school education have not bothered to determine the nature, the functions, and the purposes of the junior high school, nor are they really aware of the nature and characteristics of the early adolescent. Too many junior high schools have accepted and instituted sophisticated and undesirable senior high school practices. The rationale for the middle school makes sense; children do mature at an earlier age, and they do require an educational plan different from elementary school or senior high school.

It *does* make a difference which grades are included when evidence indicates that grade 9 is more compatible with grade 10 than with grade 8; that both sixth-graders and ninth-graders are maturing earlier—as are all children within the adolescent age group; when we know that the ninth grade is hampered in junior high schools that pay rigid attention to Carnegie Unit requirements; and when surveys indicate that a majority of junior high school administrators favor such practices as interscholastic athletics. No, there is no loss of institutional integrity threatened by a middle school, but the institution of a real middle unit that is not a lower segment of the secondary division will establish an institutional integrity for the school for early adolescents that has never before fully existed. As an institution in its own right, free from the shadow of the senior high school, the school for educating early adolescents will have an institutional integrity that was previously only a hope and a dream.

It is true that pressures of enrollments, finances, buildings, and segregation have played a part in the expressed interest in middle schools. Some or all of these same factors affect the development of virtually any school, and it is certain that many junior high schools were established for these same reasons rather than because of a belief in the educational value of a 6-3-3 plan. What is of interest is the satisfaction evidenced by those who have adopted a middle school pattern regardless of the reasons.

JUNIOR HIGH SCHOOL AREAS OF CONCERN

Whether the organizational plan a district chooses is 6-3-3, 5-3-4, 4-4-4, or some other pattern, a critical problem that has received much discussion but not much improvement is the training of teachers and administrators for this age group. The lack of enough teacher training programs for training teachers specifically for junior high school is usually considered to be the fault of the colleges and universities. The real reasons go much deeper than this, although the teacher training institutions must surely share the blame.

State certification standards must require student teaching in junior high schools for certification to teach at that level, as well as some coursework in the history, philosophy, functions, and goals of the junior high school. School districts must insist that prospective junior high school teachers have satisfied these minimum requirements before they are placed in middle schools and junior high schools. The status of junior high school teaching must be put in a more prestigious position and more prospective teachers guided into this field. This is a job for all concerned with junior high school education. When the demand for coursework and specific training for junior high school teachers increases, the teacher training institutions will not only be compelled to develop programs for training teachers for this level, they will be eager to do so. It is of no use to develop junior high school teacher training programs unless prospective teachers will enter this field.

Problems of junior high school activities and athletics require that these programs be designed, developed, and operated specifically for children of this age group. The complaint that community pressures force the junior high schools to carry on activities and athletics of a sophisticated senior high school nature has several rebuttals. Surveys indicate that approximately three-fourths of the junior high school principals favor the more sophisticated programs: the junior high schools—and any school for that matter—are intended to provide the best possible program for a specific age group, in this case the preadolescent and early adolescent, and those in education must work toward a public relations program that informs parents as to what athletics and activities are desirable for junior high school children. A large part of the criticism of the junior high schools centers upon too sophisticated activities and athletics. When activities and athletics in the junior high school are distinctly for early adolescents and not pale copies of something else, much of this kind of criticism will be groundless and will disappear.

Concerning which curriculum design to be established in the junior high schools, this will depend to an extent upon the student population, the teaching staff available, facilities, and community and administrative attitudes. The curriculum design should *not*, however, be the same as that of the high school. Two major factors intrude here: (1) the best curriculum approach for the early adolescent is some type of core or block time and, again, a strong public relations and informational program is essential; (2) teacher training programs will then necessitate work and experiences that will prepare teachers to function in something other than a departmentalized and lecture approach.

Student evaluation, testing, and marking practices should not be those of either the elementary school nor the senior high school. The acceptance of the junior high school as a distinctly separate middle unit in education and the understanding of the characteristics of the early adolescent necessitate drastic revision and improvement of existing practices and require devising a system that is geared to the individual student.

With the movement toward flexible scheduling, nongraded classes, and independent study procedures in the junior high school, the question of ability grouping becomes almost academic, since each student moves at his own rate in a differentiated program geared to his own interests and abilities. Class situations, such as block time, core, and special-interest classes, become heterogeneous in nature. The junior high school sincerely interested in providing the best possible education for each adolescent will make extensive efforts to implement flexible scheduling, nongraded classes, and independent studies to achieve the goal of educating each individual to his fullest potential. The function of exploration in the junior high school is to be considered as more than a sampling, it is an endeavor to find meaning.

TRENDS

A number of trends are apparent in varying degrees in junior high school education.

1. Growing pressures on the student, including pressures for grades, social and economic pressures, emphasis upon going to college, and peer-

group pressures. Conflict, uncertainty, and dissatisfaction are increasingly manifested, even at the junior high school level, in protest, dissent, and student unrest. Both curricular and instructional procedures in the junior high schools must be modified and improved.

2. There is a rising tide of criticism of the junior high school as an institution unsure of its role and functions, many of whose practices are deserving of condemnation.

3. There is a shifting of interest by junior high school students themselves to place more emphasis upon education for leisure, family relationships, vocational preparation, consumer education, and cooperative living values. Again, the implications for reexamination and redesigning the junior high school curriculum to provide more relevant learnings should be clear.

4. Within the subject-matter offerings of the junior high school, there is more emphasis upon mathematics, science, foreign languages, and an academic approach that a few years ago was largely limited to the senior high schools.

5. The middle school movement has grown with amazing speed and shows every sign of continuing that growth. It is apparent that dissatisfaction with the traditional 6-3-3 system, in conjunction with such factors as rising enrollments, the desire for a distinctly middle segment in American education, finances, building facilities, increased knowledge of the adolescent and the nature of learning, is uniting in the development of a school that will challenge the conventional junior high school although it is not likely to replace it.

6. Innovations and improvements such as flexible scheduling, nongraded classes, and independent study are receiving serious investigation and use in the junior high school.

7. Junior high school building facilities are more often found to be breaking away from the traditional compartmented construction to provide wider and different learning opportunities, and to make use of developments in educational technology.

8. There is evident in the junior high school a growing attention to special education for slow and retarded students, remedial classes, and programs for the disadvantaged. Much of this is spurred by federal money and there is every reason to believe that these programs will continue and expand.

RECOMMENDATIONS

Whether the school in the middle is a conventional junior high school or some form of a reorganized middle school, several recommendations are applicable to schools for the preadolescent and early adolescent:

1. There must be a clear statement of the purposes and functions of

the school for the middle years—and this statement must be clearly understood by all involved in the education of the early adolescent.

2. The school for the middle years should include at least three grade levels, preferably grades 7 and 8, and either grade 6 or grade 9.
3. The school in the middle must have its own identity and status as an institution with its own curriculum, activity program, and physical facilities.
4. Teachers must be trained specifically to work with early adolescent children, and be knowledgeable concerning the characteristics of this age group.
5. The guidance program for these children must also be explicitly formulated for this age group.
6. Instructional and administrative procedures should be highly flexible to permit maximum student involvement, self-direction, self-responsibility, and continuous progress through the school.
7. A structured core-curriculum design that is concerned with problem areas relevant to junior high school students provides the best opportunities for learning for this age group.
8. The curriculum for the school in the middle must be designed with careful consideration of the growth characteristics of the early adolescent.
9. Such a curriculum must provide a broad general education and a rich variety of exploratory experiences available to all students.
10. Language arts learnings will include opportunities for reading, writing, speaking, and listening, and will be applied in all fields of study.
11. Social studies learnings will be designed to develop democratic values and attitudes and will be relevant to students' needs, interests, and lives.
12. Science learnings will provide opportunities for the adolescent to acquire an understanding of the basic principles of modern science and of the world in which we live.
13. Mathematics learnings will provide the adolescent with basic competencies and understandings necessary for life in our society.
14. Individualized student programs are essential to permit the more able student to go as far beyond the basic competencies as he is able to do in any field.
15. All students should have opportunities to participate in a wide exploratory program that includes as a minimum, industrial arts, art, music, foreign language, consumer and business education, and home economics. Elective course, available to all students, should be modified, deleted, or added to the curriculum as student interest and need indicate.
16. All students in the school in the middle should have a continuous

program in health, physical education, and recreation.

17. There should be a strong program of remedial education available.
18. Both learning materials and learning areas within the school must be modified and expanded in accord with newer approaches to learning and with what is known of the characteristics of the early adolescent.

The problems facing the school in the middle are many, but none is insurmountable. Indeed, in most instances we know better now what should be done and how to accomplish our aims than at any time previously. The consequences of failure to act will be most serious, even disastrous, but the advantages to be achieved by following the guidelines will enable us to provide a far better education for the preadolescent and early adolescent, the student in the school in the middle.

REFERENCE

1. Samuel H. Popper, *The American Middle School.* Waltham, Mass.: Blaisdell, 1967, pp. 313–314.

Bibliography for Middle Schools

BOOKS

1. Alexander, William M., and Associates, *The Emergent Middle School.* New York: Holt, 1968.
2. Eichorn, Donald, *The Middle School.* New York: Center for Applied Research in Education, 1966.
3. Grooms, M. A., *Perspectives on the Middle School.* Columbus: Merrill, 1967.
4. Howard, Alvin W., *Teaching in Middle Schools.* Scranton, Pa.: International Textbook, 1968.
5. ———, and George Stoumbis (eds.), *Schools for the Middle Years.* Scranton, Pa.: International Textbook, 1969.
6. Kindred, Leslie W. (ed.), *The Intermediate Schools.* Englewood Cliffs, N. J.: Prentice-Hall, 1968.
7. McCarthy, Robert J., *How to Organize and Operate an Ungraded Middle School.* Englewood Cliffs, N. J.: Prentice-Hall, 1967.

PERIODICALS

1. "A Middle School Above Par," *American School and University,* Vol. 38 (April 1966), pp. 68–69.
2. Alexander, William M., "The Middle School Movement," *Theory Into Practice.* Ohio State University: College of Education, Vol. 7 (June 1968), pp. 114–117.
3. ———, "The Junior High School: A Changing View," *Bulletin of the National Association of Secondary School Principals,* Vol. 48, (March 1964), pp. 15–24.

4. ———, "The Junior High School, A Positive View," *NASSP Bulletin,* Vol. 49)March 1965), pp. 276–285.
5. ———, "What Educational Plan for the In-Between-Ager?" *NEA Journal,* Vol. 55 (March 1966), pp. 30–32.
6. ———, "The New School in The Middle," *Phi Delta Kappan,* Vol. 50 (February 1969), pp. 355–357.
7. ———, and Joann H. Strickland, "Seeking Continuity in Early and Middle School Education," *Phi Delta Kappan,* Vol. 50 (March 1969), pp. 397–400.
8. ———, and Emmett L. Williams, "Schools for the Middle School Years," *Educational Leadership,* Vol. 23 (December 1965), pp. 217–223.
9. Atkins, Neil P., "Rethinking Education in the Middle," *Theory Into Practice,* Vol. 7 (June 1968), pp. 118–119.
10. Batezel, W. G., "The Middle School, Philosophy, Program, Organization," *Clearing House,* Vol. 42 (April 1968), pp. 487–491.
11. Berman, Sidney, "As a Psychiatrist Sees Pressure on Middle Class Teenagers," *NEA Journal,* Vol. 54 (May 1965), pp. 17–24.
12. Bough, Max, "Theoretical and Practical Aspects of the Middle School," *NASSP Bulletin,* Vol. 53 (March 1969), pp. 8–13.
13. Boutwell, William D., "What Are Middle Schools?" *PTA Magazine,* Vol. 60 (December 1965), p. 14.
14. Brandt, Ronald S., "The Middle School in a Nongraded System," *Journal of Secondary Education,* Vol. 43 (April 1968), pp. 165–169.
15. Brimm, R. P., "Middle School or Junior High? Background and Rationale," *NASSP Bulletin,* Vol. 53 (March 1969), pp. 1–7.
16. Brod, Pearl, "The Middle School: Trends Toward Its Adoption," *Clearing House,* Vol. 40 (February 1966), pp. 331–333.
17. Brunetti, Frank, "The School in the Middle—A Search for New Direction," *School Planning Laboratory Circular,* June 1969.
18. Buell, Clayton E., "An Educational Rationale for the Middle School," *Clearing House,* Vol. 42 (December 1967), pp. 242–244.
19. ———, "An Educational Rationale for the Middle School," *Clearing House,* Vol. 41 (December 1967), pp. 242–244.
20. Burt, Carl W., "High School Just for Freshmen Reduces Discipline Problems," *Nation's Schools,* Vol. 76 (July 1965), pp. 27–28.
21. Chalender, Ralph E., "What the Junior High Schools Should Not Do," *NASSP Bulletin,* Vol. 47 (October 1963), pp. 23–25.
22. Coleman, James S., "Social Change: Impact on the Adolescent," *NASSP Bulletin,* Vol. 49 (April 1965), pp. 11–14.
23. Compton, Mary, "The Middle School: Alternative to the Status Quo," *Theory Into Practice.* Ohio State University, College of Education, Vol. 7 (June 1968, pp. 108–110.

24. Cuff, William A., "Middle Schools on the March," *NASSP Bulletin*, Vol. 51 (February 1967), pp. 82–86.
25. Curtis, Thomas E., "Administrators View the Middle School," *High Points*, Vol. 48 (March 1966), pp. 30–35.
26. Curtis, Thomas E., "Middle School: The School of the Future," *Education*, Vol. 88 (February-March 1968), pp. 228–231.
27. Curtis, Thomas E., "The Middle School in Theory and Practice," *NASSP Bulletin*, Vol. 52 (May 1968), pp. 135–140.
28. DiVirgilio, James, "The Administrative Role in Developing a Middle School," *Clearing House*, Vol. 43 (October 1968), pp. 103–105.
29. Douglass, Harl R., "What Type of Organization of Schools," *Journal of Secondary Education*, Vol. 41 (December 1966), pp. 358–364.
30. Eichorn, Donald, "Middle School Organization: A New Dimension," *Theory Into Practice*, Vol. 7 (June 1968), pp. 111–113.
31. Fogg, Walter F., and Hugh J. Diamond, "Two Versions of the House Plan," *Nation's Schools*, Vol. 67 (June 1961), pp. 69–79.
32. Gastwirth, Paul, "Questions Facing the Middle School," *High Points*, Vol. 48 (June 1966), pp. 40–47.
33. Grambs, Jean D., C. G. Noyce, Franklin Patterson, and John Robertson, "The Junior High School We Need," *ASCD Bulletin*, 1961.
34. Gruhn, William T., "What Do Principals Believe About Grade Organization?" *Journal of Secondary Education*, Vol. 42 (April 1967), pp. 169–174.
35. Havighurst, Robert J., "Lost Innocence—Modern Junior High Youth," *NASSP Bulletin*, Vol. 49 (April 1965), pp. 1–4.
36. ———, "Unrealized Potential of the Adolescent," *NASSP Bulletin*, vol. 50 (May 1966), pp. 75–97.
37. ———, "The Middle School in Contemporary Society," *Theory Into Practice*, Vol. 7 (June 1968), pp. 120–122.
38. Howard, Alvin W., "Which Years in Junior High?" *Clearing House*, Vol. 33 (March 1959), pp. 405–408, (Reprinted, *Clearing House*, December 1966).
39. Howell, Bruce, "The Middle School—Is It Really Any Better?" *North Central Association Quarterly*, Vol. 43 (Winter 1969), pp. 281–287.
40. Hull, J. H., "Are Junior High Schools the Answer?" *Educational Leadership*, Vol. 23 (December 1965), pp. 213–216.
41. ———, "The Junior High School Is A Poor Investment," *Nation's Schools*, Vol. 65 (April 1960), pp. 78–81.
42. Hynes, Vince A., and William A. Alexander, "Evaluating The Middle School," *The National Elementary Principal*, Vol. 48 (February 1969), pp. 32–36.
43. Johnson, Mauritz, Jr., "Does the Junior High School Need New Direction?" *Bulletin NASSP*, Vol. 48 (April 1964), pp. 146–54.

44. ———, "The Dynamic Junior High School," *Bulletin NASSP*, Vol. 48 (March 1964), pp. 119–128.
45. ———, "School In The Middle—Junior High: Education's Problem Child," *Saturday Review*, Vol. 45 (July 21, 1962), pp. 40–42.
46. Kittel, J. E., "Changing Patterns of Education: The 'Middle School' Years," *College of Education Record*, Vol. 33 No. 3 (1967), pp. 62–68.
47. Kopp, O. W., "The School Organization Syndrome vis-à-vis Improved Learning," *National Elementary Principal*, Vol. 48 (February 1969), pp. 42–45.
48. Macaulay, Grant, "What Grades Should Be Included When Opening a New High School," *Journal of Secondary Education*, Vol. 43 (November 1968), pp. 326–331.
49. Madon, Constant A., "The Middle School: Its Philosophy and Purpose," *Clearing House*, Vol. 40 (February 1966), pp. 329–330.
50. McCormick, A. N., and A. G. Parkhan, "Junior Highs Should Be Eliminated," *The Instructor*, November 1965.
51. Mead, Margaret, "Early Adolescence in the United States," *Bulletin NASSP*, Vol. 49 (April 1965), pp. 5–10.
52. "Middle Schools in Action," *Educational Research Service Circular*, No. 2, AASA Research Division, Washington, D.C., 1969.
53. "Middle Schools in Theory and Fact," *NEA Research Bulletin*, Vol. 47 (May 1969), pp. 49–52.
54. Mills, George E., "The How and Why of the Middle Schools," *Nation's Schools*, Vol. 68 (December 1961), pp. 43–53, 72–74.
55. Mindness, David, "What to Do With Your Old High School," *American School Board Journal*, Vol. 156 (March 1968), pp. 21–22.
56. Moss, Theodore C., "The Middle School Comes—And Takes Another Grade or Two," *National Elementary Principal*, Vol. 48 (February 1968), pp. 37–41.
57. Nardelli, Walter, "Business Education in The Middle School," *Balance Sheet*, Vol. 48 (March 1967), pp. 307–309.
58. "The Nation's School of the Month: Hithergreen Middle School, Centerville, Ohio," *Nation's Schools*, Vol. 80 (August 1967), pp. 53–55.
59. "Nation's School of the Month, Barrington Middle School, Barrington, Illinois," *Nation's Schools*, Vol. 76 (November 1965), pp. 61–68.
60. Oestreich, Arthur H., "New Chrome or a New Bus," *American School Board Journal*, Vol. 149 (September 1964), pp. 19–20.
61. "Planning and Operating the Middle School," *Overview*, Vol. 4 (March 1963), pp. 52–55.
62. Popper, Samuel H., "Institutional Integrity and Middle School Organization," *Journal of Secondary Education*, Vol. 43 (April 1968), pp. 184–191.

63. Porter, S. R., "School in The Middle," *Journal of Industrial Arts Education,* Vol. 27 (November 1967), pp. 26–31.
64. Post, Richard L., "Middle School—A Questionable Innovation," *Clearing House,* Vol. 42 (April 1968), pp. 484–486.
65. Pumerantz, Philip, "Imperatives in the Junior High and Middle School Dialogue," *Clearing House,* Vol. 43 (December 1968), pp. 209–212.
66. Pumerantaz, Philip, "State Recognition of the Middle School," *NASSP Bulletin,* Vol. 53 (March 1969), pp. 14–19.
67. "Recommended Grades or Years in Junior High or Middle Schools," *Bulletin NASSP,* Vol. 51 (February 1967), pp. 68–70.
68. Regan, Eugene, "The Junior High School Is Dead," *Clearing House,* Vol. 41 (November 1967), pp. 150–151.
69. Rice, Arthur H., "What's Wrong With Junior Highs? Nearly Everything," *Nation's Schools,* Vol. 74 (November 1964), pp. 30, 32.
70. Rowe, Robert N., "Why We Abandoned Our Traditional Junior High?" *Nation's Schools,* Vol. 79 (January 1967), pp. 74, 82.
71. Shirts, Morris A., "Ninth Grade—Curriculum Misfits?" *Bulletin NASSP,* Vol. 41 (November 1957), pp. 135–137.
72. Shuman, R. Baird, "Reorganization in Public Education," *Peabody Journal of Education,* Vol. 40 (May 1963), pp. 339–344.
73. Skogsberg, Alfred H., and Mauritz Johnson, Jr., "The Magic Numbers 7-8-9," *NEA Journal,* Vol. 52 (March 1963), pp. 50–51.
74. Southwarth, Horton C., "Teacher Education for The Middle School: A Framework," *Theory Into Practice,* Vol. 7 (June 1968), pp. 123–128.
75. Strickland, Virgil E., "Where Does the Ninth Grade Belong?" *Bulletin NASSP,* Vol. 51 (February 1967), pp. 74–76.
76. Tree, Chris, "Middle Schools," *The Center* (for Urban Education) *Forum,* Vol. 2 (Nov. 4, 1967), pp. 1–2.
77. Trump, J. Lloyd, "Whither The Middle School—or Whether?" *NASSP Bulletin,* Vol. 51 (December 1967), pp. 40–44.
78. Trump, J. Lloyd, "Junior High Versus Middle School," *NASSP Bulletin,* Vol. (February 1967), pp. 71–73.
79. Turnbaugh, Roy C., "The Middle School—A Different Name or a New Concept?" *Clearing House,* Vol. 43 (October 1968), pp. 86–88.
80. Vars, Gordon F., "Change and the Junior High," *Educational Leadership,* Vol. 23 (December 1965), pp. 190–193.
81. ———, "Junior High or Middle School? Which Is Best For The Education of Young Adolescents?" *High School Journal,* Vol. 50 (December 1966), pp. 109–113.
82. Vredevoe, Lawrence E. "Let's Reorganize Our School System," *Bulletin NASSP,* Vol. 42 (May 1958), pp. 40–45.
83. Wattenburg, W. W., "The Junior High School—A Psychologist's View," *NASSP Bulletin,* Vol. 49 (April 1965), pp. 34–44.

84. "Why One District Is Building A Middle School," *School Management,* Vol. 7 (May 1963), pp. 86–88.
85. Williams, Emmett L., "The Middle School Movement," *Today's Education,* Vol. 57 (December 1968), pp. 41–42.
86. ———, Editorial, *Theory Into Practice,* Ohio State University, College of Education, Vol. 7, (June 1968).
87. ———, "What About the Junior High and Middle School?" *NASSP Bulletin,* Vol. 52 (May 1968), pp. 126–134.
88. Wiltse, Scheldon R., "Developing A Unified Arts Area in An Ungraded Middle School," *Industrial Arts and Vocational Education,* Vol. 54 (March 1965), pp. 45–46.
89. Woodring, Paul, "The New Intermediate School," *The Saturday Review, 48:77–78, October 16, 1965.*

BULLETINS, CIRCULARS, MONOGRAPHS, AND UNPUBLISHED MATERIALS

1. Dacus, Wilfred Pence, "A Study of the Grade Organizational Structure of the Junior High School As Measured by Social Maturity, Emotional Maturity, Physical Maturity, and Opposite Sex Choices," unpublished doctoral dissertation, University of Houston, 1963.
2. Howard, Alvin W., "The Middle School in Oregon and Washington, 1965–66," unpublished doctoral dissertation, University of Oregon, 1966.
3. "Middle Schools," *Circular,* Education Research Service of the American Association of School Administrators and Research Division, NEA, Washington, D.C., May 1965.
4. "Middle Schools In Action," *Educational Research Services Circular,* AASA, NEA, No. 2, 1969.
5. Murphy, Judith, "Middle Schools," a *Report of the Educational Facilities Laboratories,* New York, 1965, pp. 5–16.
6. Vars, Gordon F. (ed.), "Guidelines for Junior High and Middle School Education," NASSP Monograph, Washington, D.C., 1965.

General Bibliography

BOOKS

Alexander, Wm. M., *The Changing Secondary School Curriculum: Readings.* New York; Holt, 1967.

———, Vynce A. Hines, *Independent Study in Secondary Schools.* New York: Holt, 1967.

Alpren, Morton (ed.). *The Subject Curriculum; Grades K-12.* Columbus: Merrill, 1967.

Beggs, David W. (ed.), *Team Teaching.* Bloomington, Ind.: Indiana U. P., 1964.

Beggs, David W., and Edward G. Buffie (eds.). *Independent Study. Bloomington, Ind.: Indiana U. P., 1965.*

Bent, Rudyard K., and Adolph Unruh, Secondary School Curriculum. Boston: Health, 1969.

Brimm, R. P., *The Junior High School.* New York: Center for Applied Research, 1963.

Bush, Robert N., and Dwight W. Allen, *A New Design for High School Education.* New York: McGraw-Hill, 1964.

Butman, Alexander, Donald Reis, and David Sohn, *Paperbacks in the Schools.* New York: Bantam Press, 1963.

Clark, Leonard H. (ed.), *Strategies and Tactics in Secondary School Teaching.* New York: Macmillan, 1968.

Conant, James B., *The American High School Today.* New York: McGraw-Hill, 1959.

Conant, Theodore R., "Teaching By Television," in Ronald Gross, and Judith Murphy (eds.), *The Revolution in the Schools.* New York: Harcourt, 1964.

Conner, Forest E., and W. J. Ellena, *Curriculum Handbook for School Administrators.* Washington, D.C.: AASS, 1967.

Cramer, Roscoe V., and Nelson L. Bossing, *The Junior High School.* Boston: Houghton, 1965.

Deterline, William A., *An Introduction to Programmed Instruction.* Englewood Cliffs, N. J.: Prentice-Hall, 1962.

Dobester, Henry J., "Libraries and Information Retrieval," in Alfred de Grazia and David A. Sohn (eds.), *Revolution in Teaching.* New York: Bantam Books, 1964.

Downing, Lester N., *Guidance and Counseling Services: An Introduction.* New York: McGraw-Hill, 1968.

Drury, Robert L. and Ray, Kenneth C., *Essentials of School Law.* New York: Appleton, 1967.

Edwards, Newton, *The Courts and the Public Schools.* Rev. ed. Chicago: U. of Chicago Press, 1955.

Ely, Donald, "Facts and Fallacies About New Media in Education," in Alfred de Grazia and David A. Sohn (eds.), *Revolution in Teaching.* New York: Bantam Books, 1964.

Fader, Daniel, and Morton Shaevitz, *Hooked on Books.* New York: Berkley, 1966.

Faunce, Roland C., and Morrel J. Clute, *Teaching and Learning in the Junior High School.* Belmont, Calif.: Wadsworth, 1961.

Flowers, Anne and Edward C. Bolmeier, *Law and Pupil Control.* Cincinnati: W. H. Anderson, 1964.

Frederick, Robert W., *The Third Curriculum.* New York: Appleton, 1959.

Fund for the Advancement of Education, *Four Case Studies of Programed Instruction.* New York: The Association, 1964.

Gauerke, Warren E., *Legal and Ethical Responsibilities of School Personnel.* Englewood Cliffs, N.J.: Prentice-Hall, 1959.

Gleason, Gerald T. (ed.), *The Theory and Nature of Independent Learning.* Scranton, Pa.: International Textbook, 1967.

Gould, Samuel, "The Educational Promise of Television," in Alfred de Grazia and David A. Sohn (eds.), *Revolution in Teaching.* New York: Bantam Books, 1964.

Johnson, Mauritz Jr., Wm. E. Busacker, and Fred Qu. Bowman, Jr., *Junior High School Guidance.* New York: Harper, 1961.

Kindred, Leslie W. (ed.), *The Intermediate Schools.* Englewood Cliffs, N.J.: Prentice-Hall, 1968.

Lumsdaine, A. A., and Robert Glaser (eds.), *Teaching Machines and Programed Learning: A Source Book.* Washington, D.C.: National Education Association, 1960.

Manlove, Donald C., and David W. Beggs, *Flexible Scheduling.* Bloomington, Ind.: Indiana U. P. 1965.

Moss, Theodore C., *Middle School.* Boston: Houghton, 1969.

Petrequin, Gaynor, *Individualizing Learning Through Modular-Flexible Programming.* New York: Mc-Graw-Hill, 1968.

Polos, Nicholas C., *The Dynamics of Team Teaching.* Dubuque: W. C. Brown, 1965.

Popper, Samuel H., *The American Middle School.* Waltham, Mass.: Blaisdell, 1967.

Remmlein, M. K., *School Law.* 2d ed. Danville, Ill.: Interstate Printers and Publishers, 1962.

Scanlon, John, "Classroom TV Enters A New Era," in Paul Woodring and John Scanlon (eds.), *American Education Today.* New York: McGraw-Hill, 1963.

School Athletics. Educational Policies Commission. Washington, D.C.: NEA, 1954.

Schramm, Wilbur, *Programed Instruction Today and Tomorrow.* New York: Fund for the Advancement of Education, 1962.

Seitz, R. C. (ed.), *Law and the School Principal.* Cincinnati: W. H. Anderson, 1961.

Shaplin, Judson T., and Henry F. Olds, Jr. (eds.), *Team Teaching.* New York: Harper, 1964.

Sherman, John, "What the Secondary Student Should Know About the Library," in Leonard H. Clark (ed.), *Strategies and Tactics in Secondary School Teaching.* New York: Macmillan, 1968.

Stoumbis, George C., and Alvin W., Howard (eds.) *Schools for The Middle Years.* Scranton, Pa.: International Textbook, 1969.

Standards for Junior High School Athletics. Washington, D.C.: AAHPER, NASSP, NFSHSAAA, 1963.

Trow, William Clark, *Teacher and Technology.* New York: Meredith, 1963.

Trump, J. Lloyd, *Secondary School Curriculum Improvement Proposals and Procedures.* Boston: Allyn and Bacon, 1968.

———, and Dorsey Baynham, *Focus on Change.* Chicago: Rand McNally, 1961.

Van Til, W., Gordon F. Vars, and John H. Lounsbury, *Modern Education for the Junior High School Years.* Indianapolis: Bobbs-Merrill, 1967.

Wesley, Edgar B., and Wronski, Stanley P., *Teaching Social Studies in High Schools.* Boston: Heath, 1964.

PERIODICALS

"Accountability," *NASSP Spotlight,* January–February 1969.

Ahlers, Eleanor E., "Library Service: A Changing Concept," *Educational Leadership,* Vol. 23 (March 1966), pp. 451–454.

Allen, Dwight W., "Individualized Instruction: Resource Centers and Open Laboratories," *California Teachers Association Journal,* Vol. 61 (October 1965), pp. 27, 43–50.

Allen, Paul M., "The Student Evaluation Dilemma," *Today's Education,* Vol. 58 (February 1969), pp. 48–50.

Alley, L. E., "Junior High School Interscholastic Athletics?" *NEA Journal,* Vol. 50 (May 1961), pp. 10–13.

Anderson, Theodore, "From School to College in Foreign Languages," *NEA Journal*, Vol. 54 (April 1964), pp. 35–36.

Anderson, Vernon E., "Service Is the Center," *Educational Leadership*, Vol. 23 (March 1966), pp. 447–450.

Bauer, Esther, "The Fader Plan: Detroit Style," *School Library Journal*, Vol. 14 (September 1967), pp. 51–53.

Bauer, Francis C., "Causes of Conflict," *NASSP Bulletin*, Vol. 49 (April 1965), pp. 15–18.

Bell, James W., "A Comparison of Dropouts and Non-Dropouts in Participation in School Activities," *Journal of Educational Research*, Vol. 60 (February 1967), pp. 248–251.

Bennett, Lloyd M., "The Present Plight of Junior High School Science," *Science Education*, Vol. 49 (December 1965), pp. 201–204.

Beymer, Lawrence, "The Pros and Cons of the National Assessment Project," *Clearing House*, Vol. 40 (May 1966), pp. 540—543.

Birkmaier, Emma, M. C. Johnston, and R. G. Andru, "Modern Foreign Languages: Issues, Developments, A Principal's View," *NASSP Bulletin*, Vol. 47 (November 1963), pp. 84–98.

Bisvinick, Sidney L., "The Expendable Carnegie Unit," *Phi Delta Kappan*, Vol. 42 (May 1961), pp. 365–366.

Bloom, Samuel W., "Strengthening the Junior High School Science Program," *The Science Teacher*, Vol. 7 (November 1963), pp. 18–21.

Born, Sister M. Carla, O.S.F., "Who Buried Latin? It Has Never Died!" *Clearing House*, Vol. 42 (February 1968), pp. 365–368.

Bossing, N. L., "Preparing Teachers for Junior High," *High School Journal*, Vol. 50 (December 1966), pp. 147–52.

Bough, Max, "Theoretical and Practical Aspects of The Middle School," *NASSP Bulletin*, Vol. 53 (March 1969), pp. 8–13.

Boy, Angelo V., and Gerald J. Pine, "School Counseling," *Clearing House*, Vol. 40 (November 1965), pp. 170–173.

Bridges, E. M., "We Did Away With Study Halls," *Nation's Schools*, Vol. 66 (September 1960), pp. 67–68.

Brinkoph, James W., "Transition from Sixth to Seventh Made Easy at Cherry Creek," *NASSP Bulletin*, Vol. 46 (February 1962), pp. 70–73.

Brooks, Nelson, "Language Learning: The New Approach," *Phi Delta Kappan*, Vol. 47 (March 1966), pp. 357–358.

Bucher, Charles A., "A New Athletic Program for Our Schools," *NASSP Bulletin*, Vol. 50 (April 1966), pp. 198–218.

Budde, Ray, "A Study of the Permanence of Seventh, Eighth, and Ninth Grade Teachers in Michigan," *NASSP Bulletin*, Vol. 46 (February 1962), pp. 389–390.

Buethe, Chris, "Testing, Testing . . . 1 . . 2 . . 3," *Clearing House*, Vol. 43 (May 1969), pp. 536–538.

Carmichael, La Verne, "School Guidance: Perspective, Purpose, and Performance," *Clearing House*, Vol. 43 (December 1968), pp. 223–224.

Cartwright, William H., "The Future of the Social Studies," *Social Education*, Vol. 30 (February 1966).

Cawelti, Gordon, "The Counselor's Role, Real and Ideal," *NASSP Bulletin*, Vol. 51 (September 1967), pp. 63–71.

Check, John F., "Homework—Is It Needed?" *Clearing House* (November 1966), pp. 143–147.

Ciampa, B. J., "The American Testing Hypocrisy," *Educational Leadership*, Vol. 26 (April 1969), pp. 677–679.

Climo, James, "Pass/Fail At Longmeadow," *Clearing House*, Vol. 43 (February 1969), pp. 341–343.

Conafay, Katherine, "Begin With a Single Step," *NASSP Bulletin*, Vol. 51 (October 1967), pp. 55–63.

Congreve, W. J., "Independent Learning," *North Central Association Quarterly*, Vol. 40 (Fall 1965), pp. 222–228.

Conover, Richard H., "The Junior High School Principalship," *NASSP Bulletin*, Vol. 50 (April 1966), 132–139.

Crabtree, Charlotte A., "Inquiry Approaches: How New and How Valuable," *Social Education*, November 1966.

Cunningham, Luvern. L., "A Crisis in School Organization," *Educational Leadership*, Vol. 26 (March 1969), pp. 551–555.

De Vane, LeRoy, "Teachers," *NASSP Bulletin*, Vol. 46 (February 1962), pp. 378–380.

Emery, Donald G., "What Every Library Needs," *Saturday Review*, Vol. 48 (Apr. 17, 1965), pp. 74–75.

Eulie, Josephy, "Current Issues Enliven Social Studies," *Clearing House* (December 1967).

Fagan, Edward, and Anita Dunn, "Summer is for Learning," *NASSP Bulletin*, Vol. 48 (February 1963), pp. 109–112.

Fait, Hollis F., "Should the Junior High School Sponsor Interscholastic Athletic Competition," *JOHPER*, February 1961.

Farris, Ragene, "Independent Study for Less Academic Students in a Comprehensive High School?" *Journal of Secondary Education*, Vol. 42 (December 1967), pp. 344—357.

Fenton, Edwin, "History in the New Social Studies," *Social Education*, May 1966.

Fine, Thomas W., "Student Retention in the Junior High School," *NASSP Bulletin*, Vol. 45 (November 1961), pp. 84–85.

Fleming, Dan, and J. L. Stephens, "The Students Own and Operate Their Classroom Library," *Ohio Schools*, Vol. 40 (November 1962), pp. 30–31.

Fraenkel, Jack R., "Value Education in The Social Studies," *Phi Delta Kappan*, Vol. 50 (April 1969), pp. 457–461.

Franklin, Marian Pope, "Non-Graded Schools," *Educational Forum*, Vol. 30 (March 1966), pp. 331–334.

Friedenberg, Edgar Z., "Ceremonies of Humiliation in School," *Education Digest*, Vol. 32 (November 1966), pp. 35–37.

Gaston, Walter R., "Seventh-Grade Orientation on a Year-Round Schedule," *Clearing House*, Vol. 37 (March 1963), pp. 422–424.

Glatthorn, Allan A., and J. E. Ferderbar, "Independent Study—For *All* Students," *Phi Delta Kappan*, Vol. 47 (March 1966), pp. 379–382.

Gleason, Gerald, "Will Programed Instruction Serve People?" *Educational Leadership*, Vol. 23 (March 1966), pp. 471–479.

Goldsmith, Edward L., "Independent Study in the Junior High School," *Education Digest*, Vol. 30 (February 1965), pp. 40–42.

Goldstein, W., "Problems in Team Teaching," *Clearing House*, Vol. 42 (October 1967), pp. 83–86.

Gorman, Burton W., and W. H. Johnson, "Pupil Activity in Study Halls and Implications for Progress," *NASSP Bulletin*, Vol. 48 (September 1964), pp. 1–13.

Gorton, Richard A., "Parental Resistance to Modular Scheduling," *The Clearing House*, Vol. 43 (March 1969), pp. 392–395.

Graham, Grace, "Student Activities—An Overview and Rationale," *NASSP Bulletin*, Vol. 48 (October 1964), pp. 1–16.

Grass, W. A., "Directing Student Activities," *NASSP Bulletin*, Vol. 48 (October 1964), pp. 75–80.

Gronberg, A. F., "Is Audio Lingual What It's Gimcracked to Be?" *Phi Delta Kappan*, Vol. 47 (March 1966), pp. 361–364.

Gruhn, Wm. T., "Improvement of Instruction in the Junior High," *High School Journal*, Vol. 48 (January 1965), pp. 224–230.

Haefner, John H., "High School Social Studies: A Curmudgeon's View," *Epsilon Bulletin* (*Phi Delta Kappa*), Vol. 39 (1965), pp. 31–33.

Hamilton, Norman K., "What Can Be Done About the Carnegie Unit," *Educational Leadership*, Vol. 23 (January 1966), pp. 269–272.

Hand, Harold, "National Assessment Viewed as the Camel's Nose," *Phi Delta Kappan*, Vol. 47 (September 1965), pp. 8–12.

Hanes, Robert C., "The Challenge of Science Teaching in Junior High School," *High School Journal*, Vol. 44 (February 1961), pp. 177–180.

Hannan, Dennis, "Common Sense and the Direct Method in Language Teaching," *Phi Delta Kappan*, Vol. 47 (March 1966), pp. 359–360.

Hanson, Earl H., "What About Homework?" *NEA Journal*, Vol. 57 (January 1968), pp. 32–34.

Hartz, Frederic R., "Planning School Libraries for Independent Study," *Clearing House*, Vol. 40 (J:November 1965-, pp. 144–148.

Havighurst, Robert J., "Lost Innocence—Modern Junior High School Youth," *NASSP Bulletin*, Vol. 49 (April 1965), pp. 1–4.

———, "Do Junior High School Youth Grow Up Too Fast?" *NASSP Bulletin*, Vol. 47 (April 1963), pp. 151–162.

Heller, Melvin P., "School Activities Need an Open Door Policy," *Clearing House*, Vol. 40 (September 1965), pp. 41–42.

Hoffman, Orrin, "Flexible Schedule," *Journal of Secondary Education*, "Vol. 43 (October 1968), pp. 278–282.

"Homework in the Junior High School—Position Papers," *NASSP Bulletin*, Vol. 47 (October 1963), pp. 16–17.

Howard, A. W., "Letters from a Consultant," *Clearing House*, Vol. 41 (February 1967).

———, "Student Dress, School Policies, and the Law," *Clearing House*, Vol. 41 (February 1967), pp. 357–361.

———, "The Case Against Interscholastic Athletics in Junior High," in *Schools for the Middle Years.* A. W. Howard and G. C. Stoumbis, Scranton, Pa.: International Textbook, 1969.

———, "A Junior High Award System That Works," *School Activities*, Vol. 40 (January 1969), pp. 18–20.

———, "Problems in Junior High Activities," *School Activities*, Vol. 40 (January 1969), p. 2.

"How Award Winning Junior High Schools Compare," *Nation's Schools*, Vol. 75 (January 1965), pp. 58–65.

Johnson, Mauritz, Jr., "Profiles of Beginning Junior High School Teachers," *Journal of Teacher Education*, Vol. 16 (September 1965), pp. 303–306.

———, "Solving the Mess in Marks," *New York State Education*, Vol. 49 (November 1961), pp. 12–13, 40.

Johnson, R. Richard, "Better Ways of Measuring and Reporting Student Achievement," *NASSP Bulletin*, Vol. 46 (September 1962), pp. 94–97.

Jones, Douglas R., "Pressures and Adolescents," *Educational Leadership*, Vol. 23 (December 1965), pp. 209–212.

Jones, Wallace L., "Competitive Athletics Yield Many Benefits to the Participants," *Clearing House*, Vol. 37 (March 1963), pp. 407–410.

Kapfer, Philip C., and Gardner Swenson, "Individualizing Instruction for Self-Paced Learning," *Clearing House*, Vol. 42 (March 1968), pp. 405–410.

Kennedy, Joseph S., "Interscholastic Sports—A Balanced Viewpoint," *Clearing House*, Vol. 43 (April 1969), pp. 471–473.

Ketron, Sarah R., "Guidance—Junior High School Style," *Teachers College Journal*, Vol. 34 (November 1962), pp. 59–61.

Kindred, L. W., and C. C. Stanard, "How Have Schools Met the Problem of Eliminating Study Halls?" *NASSP Bulletin*, Vol. 49 (January 1965), pp. 42–46.

Klausmeier, H. J., and W. Wiersma, "Team Teaching and Achievement," *Education*, Vol. 86 (December 1965), pp. 238–242.

Komoski, P. Kenneth, "Programed Instruction—A Prologue to What?" *Phi Delta Kappan,* Vol. 44 (1963), pp. 292–295.

Kopp, O. W., "The School Organization Syndrome," *National Elementary Principal,* Vol. 48 (February 1969), pp. 42–45.

Lambert, Pierre D., "Junior High School, 1965," *Clearing House,* Vol. 39 (February 1965), pp. 323–328.

Lawson, Thomas O., "Assignment of Non-Teaching Tasks to Certificated and Non-Certificated Personnel in Junior High School," *Journal of Secondary Education,* Vol. 42 (May 1967), pp. 210–216.

Leigh, Thomas G., "Big Opportunities in Small Schools Through Flexible-Modular Scheduling," *Journal of Secondary Education,* Vol. 42 (April 1967), pp. 175–187.

Lerch, Harold E., "Academic Rigor," *Clearing House,* Vol. 34 (December 1959), pp. 242–244.

Levison, Melvin E., "A Path to Audiovisual Literacy," *NASSP Bulletin,* Vol. 51 (December 1967), pp. 80–92.

Litzinger, Wm. D., "Paperback Usage in Schools," *Clearing House,* Vol. 38 (April 1964), pp. 474–477.

Logan, (Ed.), "Pied Piper of Papterbacks," *Scholastic Teacher,* Vol. 89 (Jan. 20, 1967), p. 17.

Lorimer, Margaret F., "How Much Is a Credit Hour?" *Journal of Higher Education,* Vol. 33 (June 1962), pp. 302–306.

Marean, J., and E. Ledbetter, "New Approach to Ninth-Grade Science," *Science Teachers,* Vol. 33 (April 1966), pp. 18–20.

Marion, Marjorie A., "Independent Study: A First Attempt," *English Journal,* Vol. 56 (February 1967), pp. 235–237.

Marland, S. P., "The Education Park Concept in Pittsburgh," *Phi Delta Kappan,* Vol. 48 (March 1967), pp. 328–332.

Mayor, John R., "The Critical Role of Junior High School Science," *Journal of Secondary Education,* Vol. 39 (May 1964), pp. 201–204.

Maze, Clarence, "Business Education in the Junior High School," Monograph. Chicago, Ill.: Southwestern Publishing, 1965.

Maze, Clarence, "Philosophical Basis for Business Education in the Junior High School," *Balance Sheet,* Vol. 47 (October 1965), pp. 60–62.

McGuire, Brian Patrick, "The Grading Game," *Today's Education,* Vol. 58 (March 1969), pp. 32–34.

McLoughlin, Wm. P., "The Phantom Nongraded School," *Phi Delta Kappan,* Vol. 49 (January 1968), p. 250.

Mead, Margaret, "Early Adolescence in the United States," *NASSP Bulletin,* Vol. 49 (April 1965), pp. 5–10.

Mendenhall, James E., "Youth Needs and School Responsibilities," *Bulletin NASSP,* Vol. 51 (October 1967), pp. 14–20.

Meyer, Harvey Kessler, "Televised Learning," *Educational Leadership,* Vol. 23 (March 1966), pp. 463–469.

Meyer, James A., "Group Grope: Problems of Team Teaching," *Clearing House,* Vol. 42 (January 1968), pp. 362–364.
Moellenberg, Wayne P., "National Assessment: Are We Ready?" *Clearing House,* Vol. 43 (January 1968), pp. 451–454.
Moore, Joseph D., "The Junior High Designed for Learning," *American School Board Journal,* Vol. 152 (April 1966), pp. 16–23.
Myers, Kent E., "What Do We Know About Programed Instruction?" *Clearing House,* Vol. 39 (May 1965), pp. 533–538.
National Education Research Bulletin, "Nongraded Schools," Vol. 45 (December 1967), pp. 118–120.
Nichols, Eugene D., "The Many Forms of Revolution," *NASSP Bulletin,* Vol. 52 (April 1968), pp. 16–37.
Norton, M. Scott, "How to Initiate a Program in Individual Studies," *Clearing House,* Vol. 41 (January 1967), pp. 268–270.
Peltier, Gary L., and Charles Barth, "Using Classroom Tests To Promote Critical Thinking," *Clearing House,* Vol. 42 (April 1968), pp. 476–479.
Pietrofesa, John J., and Al Rosen, "What Is Wrong With Interscholastic Sports?" *Clearing House,* Vol. 43 (November 1968), pp. 165–169.
Pine, Gerald J., "The Existential School Counselor," *Clearing House,* Vol. 43 (February 1969), pp. 351–354.
Polos, Nicholas C., "Multimedia: A New Lamp for Learning," *Clearing House,* Vol. 41 (February 1967), pp. 350–352.
Printz, Michael, "High School Library Plus," *NEA Journal,* Vol. 57 (February 1968), pp. 29–30.
Richardson, Don H., "Independent Study: What Difference Does It Make?" *Bulletin NASSP,* Vol. 51 (September 1967), pp. 53–62.
Richardson, Joe A., and Donald G. Cawelt, "Junior High Program Lets Slow and Fast Students Take Time for Independent Study," *Nation's Schools,* Vol. 79 (February 1967), pp. 74–78.
Rollins, Sidney P., "Ungraded High Schools—Why Those Who Like Them LoveThem," *Nation's Schools,* Vol. 73 (April 1964), pp. 110, 130.
Roth, Robert H., "Student Reactions to Programed Learning," *Phi Delta Kappan,* Vol. 44 (1963), pp. 278–281.
Rowley, John V., and Justin B. Galford, "School Social Events," *Clearing House,* Vol. 43 (October 1968), pp. 110–112.
Rush, Joseph, "For Better Junior High Adjustment," *Instructor,* Vol. 72 (September 1962), pp. 97–98.
Schmuck, Richard, "Concerns of Contemporary Adolescents," *NASSP Bulletin,* Vol. 49 (April 1965), pp. 19–28.
Schoenfeld, David, "The Why and How of Consumer Education," *NASSP Bulletin,* Vol. 51 (October 1967), pp. 27–33.
Seymour, H. C., "The Principal as the Instructional Leader," *NASSP Bulletin,* Vol. 51 (November 1967), pp. 89–97.

Simpson, Elizabeth L., "The Individual in the Group," *Phi Delta Kappan*, Vol. 50 (February 1969), pp. 322–324.

Sister Mary Paul, "Admimistrative Problems of the Nongraded School," *National Catholic Educ. Assoc. Bulletin*, Vol. 64 (August 1967), pp. 144–147.

Sleight, Ralph H., "Administrative Problems as a Result of Flexible Scheduling," *Journal of Secondary Education*, Vol. 42 (December 1967), pp. 358–362.

Smith, Mark C., "The Case for Teachers Who Are Specifically Prepared to Teach in Junior High Schools," *Journal of Teacher Education*, Vol. 17 (Winter 1966), pp. 438–443.

Speckhard, Gerald P., "Evaluating the Modular Schedule," *North Central Quarterly*, Vol. 41 (Spring 1967), pp. 300–308.

Spray, Cecil O., "A Phase Level Program for Individualized Education," *Clearing House*, Vol. 41 (November 1966), pp. 136–139.

———, "Meaningful Grade Reporting," *Clearing House*, Vol. 43 (February 1969), pp. 338–341.

Stanavage, John A., "Educational Leader, An Authentic Role," *NASSP Bulletin*, Vol. 51 (November 1967), pp. 3–17.

Stephens, W. Richard, "The Junior High School, A Product of Reform Values, 1890–1920," *Indiana State University Teachers College Journal*, Vol. 39 (November 1967), pp. 52–60.

Streitmatter, Kenneth D., "Student Study Patterns—A Break from Tradition," *Clearing House*, Vol. 43 (January 1969), pp. 280–282.

Swinney, Vincent G., "Orienting New Students Through the Assembly," *School Activities*, Vol. 33 (January 1962), pp. 151–152.

Taylor, H. A., and Raymond F. Cook, "Schools Within a School: A Teaching Team Organized for Junior High," *High School Journal*, Vol. (January 1965), pp. 289–295.

Tewilliger, James S., "Self-Reported Marking Practices and Policies in Public Secondary Schools," *NASSP Bulletin*, Vol. 50 (March 1966), pp. 5–37.

Thomas, John I., "A Critique-The Appropriate Placement School," *Educational Leadership*, Vol. 26 (January 1969), pp. 355–362.

Thomason, Catherine D., "Junior High Learning Lab," *NEA Journal*, Vol. 52 (November 1963), pp. 15–16.

Thompson, Donovan A., "The New Mathematics In Our Schools," *NASSP Bulletin*, Vol. 52 (April 1968), pp. 1–3.

Tolonen, Paul O., "The Pedagogic Numbers Game," *Educational Leadership*, Vol. 26 (March 1969), pp. 556–562.

Tompkins, Ellsworth, and Gaumnitz, Walter, "The Carnegie Unit; Its Origin, Status, and Trends,? *Bulletin of the National Association of Secondary Principals*, Vol. 48 (January 1964), pp. 1–71.

Tripp, Robert L., "Self-Directed Study," *Clearing House,* Vol. 43 (February 1969), pp. 344–348.

Tyler, Ralph W., "Assessing the Progress of Education," *Phi Delta Kappan,* Vol. 47 (September 1965), pp. 13–16.

Vars, Gordon F., "Can Team Teaching Save the Core Curriculum?," *Phi Delta Kappan,* Vol. 47 (January 1966), pp. 258–262.

Vesely, Melvin N., "Mathematics: Issues," *NASSP Bulletin,* Vol. 47 (November 1963), pp. 73–76.

Vocolo, Joseph, "Foreign Language Program in the Junior High School," *Clearing House,* Vol. 42 (February 1968), pp. 358–361.

Vogel, Francis X., "Guidance in the Junior High School," *NASSP Bulletin,* Vol. 64 (Octover 1962), pp. 93–97.

Wagner, Robert W., "Machines, Media and Meaning," *Educational Leadership,* Vol. 23 (March 1966), pp. 481–497.

Wattenberg, W. W., "The Junior High School—A Psychologist's View," *NASSP Bulletin,* Vol. 49 (April 1965), pp. 34–44.

———, "Today's Junior High School Student," *Educational Leadership,* Vol. 23 (December 1965), pp. 190–193.

Waterman, Albert D., "Homework—Curse or Blessing?" *NASSP Bulletin,* Vol. 49 (January 1965), pp. 42–46.

Weisbruch, F. T., "Laboratory Oriented Course for Ninth Grade Students," *School Science, and Mathematics,* Vol. 63 (June 1963), pp. 493 –502.

Weisse, Edward B., "Re-Structure: A Proposal for Junior High School Curriculum Design," *Indiana State University Teacher's College Journal,* Vol. 39 (November 1967), pp. 60–62.

Weitz, Leo, "14 Years a Principal; A Self Appraisal," *NASSP Bulletin,* Vol. 51 (November 1967-, pp. 18–25.

"Who Should Do the Assessing?" *Phi Delta Kappan,* Vol. 48 (April 1967), editorial, p. 377.

Wilhelms, Fred T., "Key to Many Doors," *NASSP Bulletin,* Vol. 51 (October 1967), pp. 3–13.

Wilklow, Leighton B., and Samuel V. Cannelle, "Flexible Scheduling, Does It Affect the Pecking Order?" *Clearing House,* Vol. 41 (February 1967), pp. 362–364.

Willoughby, Stephen S., "What Is the New Mathematics?" *NASSP Bulletin,* Vol. 52 (April 1968), pp. 4–15.

Winthrop, Henry, "Contemporary Intellectual Ferment and the Curriculum of the Future," *Social Studies,* March 1965.

Wood, Donald H., "Are Activities Programs Really Activities Programs," *School Activities,* Vol. 39 (September 1967), pp. 8–10.

BULLETINS, MONOGRAPHS AND UNPUBLISHED MATERIALS

Baughman, M. Dale, "Administration of the Junior High School," Monograph. Danville, Ill.: Interstate Printers and Publishers, 1966.

Conant, James Bryant, *Education in the Junior High Years.* Princeton, N. J.: Educational Testing Service, 1960.

Epps, Margaret, "Homework," NEA Research Summary. Washington, D.C.: NEA, 1966.

Graham, Grace, *Improving Student Participation.* Washington, D.C.: National Association Secondary School Principals, 1966.

Howard, Eugene R., and Roger W. Bardwell, *How to Organize a Non-Graded School.* Englewood Cliffs, N.J.: Prentice-Hall, 1966.

Hubert, Jeanne B., "A Survey of the Attitudes of Prospective and Experienced Secondary School Teachers Toward The Junior High School," unpublished master's thesis, University of New Mexico, 1969.

Jensen, Marvin L., "Ninth Grade General Science Achievement of Students in Laboratory-Centered Instruction Compared to Lecture-Demonstration Centered Instruction," unpublished master's thesis, University of Utah, Salt Lake City, Utah, 1967.

Keim, E. B., and M. C. Jones, Jr., *A Guide to Social Activities.* Washington, D.C: National Association of Secondary School Principals, 1965.

Mathes, George E., *Group Dynamics for Student Activities.* Washington, D.C.: National Association Secondary School Principals, 1968.

Murphy, Judith, "Middle Schools." Monograph. New York: Educational Facilities Laboratories, 1965.

Roman, John C., "The Business Curriculum." Monograph. Chicago, Ill.: Southwestern Publishing Co., 1966.

Tyler, C. Edward, "Team Teaching," Oregon Curriculum Bulletin, No. 286, University of Oregon, January 1968.

Wright, Grace S., and Edith S. Greet, "The Junior High School, A Survey of Grades 7-8-9 in Junior and Junior-Senior High Schools, 1959–60," U.S. Office of Education Bulletin, No. 32, Washington, D.C., 1963.

Index